Generative Emergence

GENERATIVE EMERGENCE

A New Discipline of Organizational, Entrepreneurial, and Social Innovation

Benyamin Lichtenstein

OXFORD
UNIVERSITY PRESS

OXFORD
UNIVERSITY PRESS

Oxford University Press is a department of the University of
Oxford. It furthers the University's objective of excellence in research,
scholarship, and education by publishing worldwide.

Oxford   New York
Auckland   Cape Town   Dar es Salaam   Hong Kong   Karachi
Kuala Lumpur   Madrid   Melbourne   Mexico City   Nairobi
New Delhi   Shanghai   Taipei   Toronto

With offices in
Argentina   Austria   Brazil   Chile   Czech Republic   France   Greece
Guatemala   Hungary   Italy   Japan   Poland   Portugal   Singapore
South Korea   Switzerland   Thailand   Turkey   Ukraine   Vietnam

Oxford is a registered trademark of Oxford University Press
in the UK and certain other countries.

Published in the United States of America by
Oxford University Press
198 Madison Avenue, New York, NY 10016

© Oxford University Press 2014

All rights reserved. No part of this publication may be reproduced, stored in
a retrieval system, or transmitted, in any form or by any means, without the prior
permission in writing of Oxford University Press, or as expressly permitted by law,
by license, or under terms agreed with the appropriate reproduction rights organization.
Inquiries concerning reproduction outside the scope of the above should be sent to the
Rights Department, Oxford University Press, at the address above.

You must not circulate this work in any other form
and you must impose this same condition on any acquirer.

Library of Congress Cataloging-in-Publication Data
Lichtenstein, Benyamin
Generative emergence : a new discipline of organizational, entrepreneurial and
social innovation / Benyamin Lichtenstein.
   pages cm
Includes bibliographical references and index.
ISBN 978-0-19-993359-4
1. Technological innovations—Management.   2. Organizational behavior.
3. Emergence (Philosophy)   I. Title.
HD45.L474 2014
658.5'14—dc23

9780199933594

CONTENTS

Acknowledgments   *vii*

1. Why Emergence?   *1*
2. Prototypes of Emergence   *43*
3. Studying Emergence: 15 Fields of Complexity Science   *65*
4. Defining Emergence and Generative Emergence   *107*
5. Types of Emergence Studies in Management   *131*
6. Dissipative Structures—Theory and Experiments   *149*
7. Applying Dissipative Structures to Organizations   *169*
8. From Dissipative Structures to Dynamic States   *193*
9. Outcomes of Generative Emergence   *219*
10. Phase 1: Disequilibrium Organizing   *231*
11. Phase 2: Stress and Experiments   *259*
12. Phase 3: Amplification and a Critical Event   *279*
13. Phase 4: New Order through Recombinations   *297*
14. Phase 5: Stabilizing Feedback and Sustaining the System   *315*
15. A Cycle of Emergence   *325*
16. Re-Emergence: Cycles of Emergence over Time   *345*
17. Boundaries of Emergence and Re-Emergence   *373*
18. Enacting Emergence   *395*

Bibliography   *419*
Index   *455*

ACKNOWLEDGMENTS

This book began in 1982 in the redwood forests at the University of California Santa Cruz and in its libraries, where I first learned about evolution as a self-organizing phenomenon—an idea expressed by scholars like Ilya Prigogine, Erich Jantsch, Arthur Young, Irvin Laszlo, Gregory Bateson, Rupert Sheldrake, and Fritjof Capra, and by Kenneth Boulding, with whom I was so fortunate to take a class when he was a visiting scholar there in 1988. These were catalysts for a scholarly and spiritual journey that has continued for more than 30 years. In some ways, all the books and articles I've read and cited since then have contributed to my thinking and growth in this journey.

Another milestone for the theory was my dissertation research at Boston College. I am grateful to my committee who supported me in my rather risky and unconventional research project: Candy Jones (Chair), Jean Bartunek, Bill Torbert, and Candida Brush. During my training and since, I have gained so much from a host of academic colleagues whose engagement and friendship have been overwhelmingly helpful. These include especially Bill Gartner, Bill McKelvey, Jeff Goldstein, Kevin Dooley, Andy Van de Ven, Alan Meyer, Jane Dutton, Mary Uhl-Bien, Jim Hazy, Donde Plowman, Raghu Garud, Steve Maguire, Todd Chiles, Saras Sarasvathy, and Tom Lumpkin. So many others should be mentioned: my colleagues in the Entrepreneurship division of the Academy of Management, long-time academic friends in Boston and throughout the world, and more. Over the past 10 years I have been blessed to be in a uniquely wonderful academic environment; appreciations go to my colleagues in the College of Management and throughout UMass Boston, including David Levy, Maureen Scully, Pacey Foster, Nardia Haigh, Werner Kunz, Janice Goldman, Marc Levine, Ed Carberry, David McFarlane, and Stephan Manning, and everyone else in the department; also to Jeff Kiesler, Dan Shimshack, Robyn Hannigan, Alan Christian, Donna Haig Friedman, and many others. Then of course, the scholars whose work has contributed to much to the book—the list is as long as the bibliography—but I would especially like to mention Rod Swenson, Keith Sawyer, Alicia Juarraro, Peter Corning, Alex Osterwalder, Pierpalo Andriani, Ted Baker, Robert Baron, Bill Bygrave, Stephan Guastello, Violina Rindova, Stanley Salthe, Charles Smith, and Hari Tsoukas.

On a more personal level, blessings of appreciation go to my family: my beautiful children, Moriah and Simeon, and Sasha; my parents Diane and Stan, and my brothers and their families: Moshe and Rachelle and eight wonderful children in Israel; Gary and Kaye in Bluff, Utah; Scott and Sarah and Mia in England; to my other mom, Liz Bergmann, and her partner Carol; also Christopher, Kelly, Aden, and Makenzie; and to all my cousins in California and elsewhere.

My deep appreciation goes to my closest friends who have supported my vision unfailingly over the past 20+ years—Michael Shpak, Gwenyth Jackaway, David Jaffe and Janette Hillis, Marilyn Paul and David Stroh. Likewise, I'm grateful for all my friends and community: Dan and Lisa and Eliora, Seth and Hannah; Susan and Jordan and Lanie and Elise; David and Susan, Michael and Jessica and Nessa, Natan and Ilana, Joel and Laura, Dan and Lori, David and Ronit, Reena, and Peter. My community at Beth El Congregation in Sudbury—David and Marcy, Lorel and Arnie, Beth and Pam, Joel and Janet, Michael and Michelle, Carolyn and Dave, Jeff and Jocylyn, Paula and Carl and Rachel and Emma. How can I thank everyone?! Thanks go to Geoff, Andy and Albert, men in the MKP community, as well as the JCDS Men's Torah Study group—Mel, Alex, Bruce, Guy, Josh, Steve, Dan, Mike, Michael, Phil, everyone. And for my physician Glenn Rothfeld, a huge and abiding gratitude of health and vitality.

Oxford University Press has given me this unprecedented opportunity; many appreciations to my editor, Abby Gross, who helped me envision a book that would summarize all the scholarship in this area, and to Suzanne Walker and Emily Perry, for leading the book's production and marketing.

In sum, I am deeply appreciative for every person and all the communities that have supported me; all those I've named and the dozens and hundreds more I have not.

And most of all there is my relationship with G!d, the spiritual presence that gave me the initial vision and which has been at the core of my journey ever since. Your encouragement kept me on the path, even in uncharted territory and against the push of social belief. You—and all the guides and healers You helped me meet along the way—You are at the core of my appreciation, my commitment to this task.

May we all be blessed to find the task that we were put here to accomplish, and to gain the strength and support as I have to pursue it to completion.

Benyamin Lichtenstein
Watertown Massachusetts
April, 2014

CHAPTER 1
Why Emergence?

DESCRIBING EMERGENCE

Emergence is the creation of order, the formation of new properties and structures in complex systems. When emergence happens, something new and unexpected arises, with outcomes that cannot be predicted even from knowing everything about the parts of the system. Emergence is studied in every field; physicists study emergent properties of molecules and forces, biologists study emergent behaviors of cells and animal groups, sociologists study emergent structures in society, entrepreneurship scholars study the emergence of organizations. Emergence is one of the most ubiquitous processes in the world, and yet one of the least understood.

Three examples shed light on some of the key issues in emergence. The first example is seemingly simple: the V-shape that is made by a flock of flying Canadian Geese. The shape is emergent: it is not caused by any one bird's behavior, nor is there a leader in a flock. Instead, each bird individually is following simple rules that maximize its own efficiency in the group: (a) fly close together but avoid contact; (b) if you get too close, then separate; and (c) fly in the overall direction of the group. These rules, which guide the local actions of each individual bird, lead to an emergent structure—the V that we see in the sky—which increases the efficiency of all the birds in the group.[1] The V is emergent because it is not caused by any one bird but by all the birds interacting together; the V is composed by the birds but "transcends" them as well. The outcomes generate new aerodynamic capacity that could not have been created by the birds on their own.

As another example, consider a natural ecosystem, like a forested area. Each of the parts of the ecosystem—all the different species of trees, plants, animals, insects, and so on—are at one level competing for their own survival and growth. Yet from a systemwide perspective all of these apparently independent organisms are *inter*dependent—they each need the others in order to survive and thrive in the ecosystem. This is important to understand, because it means that each pair of (inter)dependencies had to co-evolve—the entire system developed these relationships across networks, all at once over time. Further, the dynamic interactions and relationships across the entire ecosystem have generated a *resilience*, an increased ability of the system as a whole to support the organisms within it. This systemic property of resilience is emergent, for it is not "in" any one element or species but arises through the interactions and relationships across all of them.

The same can be said for organizations as emergent systems. To the outside world, an organization *exists* as a distinct social entity: People perceive the organization as an agent in society—as a "person" in some sense. As an agent it "acts" in certain ways; it follows social rules, laws, and conventions, and contributes to the local community. But where "is" the organization? The business is not "in" the individual employees, for all of them could be replaced without necessarily destroying the company. Nor is the organization "in" its managers or the founders, even though they heavily influence the firm's emergence. The organization is not "in" the building (or website), nor is it "in" the individual exchanges that occur in person or online. Nor is the company to be found "in" its performance.

Thus, like the previous examples, *organization* is an emergent entity: it arises as a whole system, out of the combined interactions and relationships of elements, while not existing in any one of those elements. Likewise, this emergence process generates new opportunities and more energy than could be done by adding up all the activities of all of its parts—by a huge amount. Consider Adam Smith's calculations of the pin factory with an emergent division of labor, which was 1000% more efficient than the traditional model of making pins one by one.

Emergence is present at every level of reality. We encounter it, for example, in patterns of interaction that arise in our departments and workplaces, in the cultural norms that guide our behavior and expectations, and in the initiation of new projects and ventures. Emergence is also at the heart of complexity science—disciplines that use computation and nonlinear methodologies to explore the creation of order in the natural and social world.

Although more and more scholars are engaged in using complexity science and studying emergence, few people are aware of how many types of emergence have been being studied across the sciences, even the social sciences. To give some examples: Entrepreneurship researchers have been studying the emergence of new ventures,[2] the creation of new markets,[3] and the generation of regional clusters.[4] Organizational scientists are exploring emergence in group dynamics,[5] in the dynamics of innovation,[6] in the development and implementation of strategy,[7] in processes of change and transformation,[8] and in the creation of new institutions and industries.[9] Research in the psychological sciences has identified emergence processes in neurophysiology, cognition, and individual behavior.[10] Sociological studies have highlighted emergence dynamics in collective behavior.[11] Overall, the scholarship of emergence is dramatically expanding: the past 20 years has seen a 782% increase in research papers focusing on emergence within psychology, sociology, economics, education, and management.[12]

The same can be said for book-length treatises on emergence. In the social sciences, major contributions and compilations have been written by Stephen Guastello (1995) in psychology, Alicia Juarrero (1999) in philosophy, Harold Morowitz (2002) in evolutionary studies, Keith Sawyer (2005) in sociology, Clayton and Davies (2006) in physics and biology, Robert Reid (2007) in biological evolution, Bedau and Humphres (2008) in philosophy and the natural sciences, and Padgett and Powell (2011) in organization theory.

General introductions to emergence and complexity science have exploded as well, as evidenced in successful books by Michael Waldrop (1992), Roger Lewin (1992), Murray Gell-Mann (1994), Kevin Kelly (1994), Yaneer Bar-Yam (1997), Steven Johnson (2001), Steven Strogatz (2003), Neil Johnson (2009), and Melanie Mitchell (2009). These, of course, take their place among many precursors, including Erich Jantsch (1980), Depew and Weber (1985, 1994), James Gleick (1987), Richard Adams (1988), and Paul Cilliers (1998), among others.

Overall, we have seen a dramatic increase in the pace and scope of writing on dynamic complex systems and the emergences they describe. However, up to now, each contribution has been separate: Few books on emergence build on previous work, and few emergence scholars refer to others in different fields. Likewise, almost all of the scholarly books on complexity science have focused on one or a few disciplines. For example, Kauffman (1993) focuses on NK landscape models; Holland (1995, 1998), on genetic algorithms; Prigogine (Prigogine & Stengers, 1984; Nicolis & Prigogine, 1989), on dissipative structures; Bar-Yam (1997, 2004), on mathematical and computational approaches; and Bak (Bak & Chen, 1991; Bak, 1996), on self-organized criticality. Although each of these works is definitive in its field, they each introduce only one aspect or perspective within the multilayered context of emergence.

The time is ripe for an integration of this work into a discipline of emergence. Such a discipline would organize all of the writing and research on emergence and complexity science into a single framework, which could serve as the basis for synthesis of and further insights across many levels of analysis. This book makes an important step toward that goal, by drawing together the entire range of empirical literature on emergence into a single framework of prototypes, identifying the complexity sciences that can be used to study them, and presenting an integrative definition of emergence in social systems of all kinds.

The first part of the book takes the broadest perspective by drawing on emergence research from physics, chemistry, computational science, agent-based modeling, biology, ecology, evolutionary studies, philosophy, psychology, sociology, and organization science. After the first three chapters, the rest of the book focuses on one of the eight fields in the discipline, namely generative emergence, which explores the dynamics of creation and re-creation of and in organizations, ventures, projects, initiatives, and social endeavors of all kinds. The core of the book is the five-phase process model of generative emergence, an approach developed over 30+ years of my own research, in concert and collaboration with many others.[13]

Why Emergence? Problems and Potentialities

For those with some familiarity with emergence, the concept adds a positive and unique view to our understanding of social innovation. Equally, generative emergence solves some long-standing problems in management and the social sciences and unlocks new potential in the complexity sciences. In particular, by highlighting the underlying processes of generative emergence we can:

(a) Explain the dynamics of emergence and re-emergence and how they differ from the ontology of organizational change and transformation. These dynamics reveal a new causal driver of organizational creation and social organizing.
(b) Resolve debates in entrepreneurship and organization science by differentiating between the *process* of emergence and its *outcomes*—emergence vs. emergents.
(c) Expand the value and applicability of complexity science in management and other social sciences by showing how each of its 15 fields provides unique insights into emergence overall.
(d) Increase the rigor of applications in management by exposing the problems with using the term *self-organization*.
(e) Synthesize a host of research across entrepreneurship, strategy, organizational behavior, innovation, and institutional theory, through a model of emergence organizing.

Each of these five objectives is briefly described in the following sections.

Emergence and Re-Emergence vs. Change and Transformation

Among scholars who study how organizations grow and change, these processes are described in one of two ways: Organizational change occurs through incremental adaptations, whereas organizational transformation occurs through significant shifts in structures, systems, and processes (Bartunek & Moch, 1987; Gersick, 1991; Greenwood & Hinings, 1996; Weick & Quinn, 1999; Staudenmayer, Tyre, & Perlow, 2002). Thus, organizations can change by learning from their experience and incrementally improving their situation (March, 1981; Quinn, 1989; Levinthal, 1991; Huber & Glick, 1993), or, through transformation, organizations can call into question one or more guiding assumptions and values, leading to a major shift in several aspects of the organization at once (Bartunek, 1984; Romanelli & Tushman, 1994; Bacharach, Bamberger, & Sonnenstuhl, 1996; Street & Gallupe, 2009). Except for recent new thinking from scholars like Eisenhardt, Garud, Rindova, and O'Mahony, among others, the extant models for internal-to-the-organization change revolve around these two poles.

Although some consider emergence to be simply another way to describe transformation, it is not—emergence is a totally different category from transformation and change, a third distinct process. At the root of this difference is the fact that every case of organizational change and transformation involves the *modification* of existing elements, an alteration of design structures or internal processes or activity routines in the organization. Like all path-dependent processes, the outcome crucially depends on the history of the system as well as the trigger for change; the possible outcomes are conditioned by the existing state and by what initiates the process.

In a similar way, virtually all management theories argue that the trigger for organizational change or transformation is a *crisis*—a growing problem or a pending disaster—that is reflected in a decrease in performance. The theoretical logic is that the company is not performing well (enough) in its domain, as shown by declining revenues or profits, thus change or transformation is necessary. According to this logic only a crisis is strong enough to dislodge the inertia of current operations. The ensuing transformation should allow the organization to better match its environment, thus increasing its effectiveness and profits.

In contrast, emergence is significantly different from transformation. First, emergence is *creation*, not simply change. Emergence is the invention of something new, the origination of a distinct system and/or the structures within it. Consider again the V of a flock of birds. The emergent entity is not the result of a change; although the birds change, their changing is not what generates the emergent V. Nor can the V be explained as a transformation of the birds. Instead it represents a new creation, a "becoming" that was not there before its parts became interdependent.

A second difference lies in the trigger for organizational emergence, which is *aspiration*[14]—the vision and enactment of a new opportunity to be capitalized on. Whereas crisis leads to a reactive attempt to save the organization, aspiration is an entrepreneurial desire to create new value, to make a new contribution to a community or within a market. For this reason, emergence and re-emergence are often initiated when nothing is wrong per se in the organization; they are not triggered by problems or urgent issues. And if they are, they turn the reactivity into procreative action. Thus the origin of emergence is a potentiality, a spark of creativity, an open-ended possibility that can be enacted in a myriad of ways. One of the benefits of aspiration is that it can generate a projected future that may have fewer constraints and more creativity for the organization.

Third, this spark of creativity produces a whole different set of behaviors than is likely in crisis-driven change. According to creativity scholars, problems and frustrations like those caused by crisis lead to "reactive creativity," which is characterized by negativity and even a sense of desperation (Heinzen, 1994, 1999; Unsworth, 2001). In contrast, "proactive creativity"—the behavior from aspiration—is characterized by "intrinsic motivation, positive affect, and focused self-discipline" (Heinzen, 1994: 140). Research has shown that this prospective, problem-finding outlook is much more likely to spur useful ideas in organizations

(Axtell et al., 2000) and to improve innovation more generally (Unsworth, 2001). Thus, the potentialities for emergence are greater than for transformation.

Finally, these greater potentialities are easily seen in empirical studies of emergence. Research shows that emergent structures expand the capacity of the system by an unprecedented amount, vastly increasing the capability of the system to accomplish its work (Prigogine & Stengers, 1984; Swenson, 1988, 1989). Intuitively, this is evident in the three earlier examples of emergence, each of which improves the efficiency, adaptability, and performance of their systems in ways that would be impossible through common modes of change. Thus, in all these ways, emergence and re-emergence are distinct from transformation; they provide many more avenues for an emergent system to gain creative innovation and dramatic increases in capacity. Much more about these findings will be presented in the following chapters.

Emergence as a Process with Multiple Possible Outcomes

A second problem taken up by generative emergence revolves around the two distinct meanings of emergence. In organization science, emergence has mainly been used to describe an emergent *outcome*—as for example in the emergence of ethical issues (Sonenshein, 2009), or in the creation of a proto-institution (Lawrence, Hardy, & Phillips, 2002) or the generation of new practice areas (Anand, Gardner, & Morris, 2007). In contrast, complexity scholars have explored the *processes* that lead to emergence (see, e.g., Chiles, Meyer, & Hench, 2004; Plowman et al., 2007a; MacIntosh & MacLean, 1999). In fact, some of this research proposes a series of sequential phases that lead to emergence, as exemplified in the work by Smith and Gemmill (1991), Leifer (1989), and Purdy and Gray (2009) and in my own work (Lichtenstein, 2000b, 2000d; Lichtenstein & Plowman, 2009). These differences reflect an uneasy question: Is emergence more of an outcome, or a process?

This question has not yet been addressed, even with the growth of complexity science over the past 20 years. As one illustration, the long-standing focus of computational models is on the structure of the agents in the simulation (Levinthal & Warglien, 1999; Gavetti & Levinthal, 2000; Fleming & Sorenson, 2001; Gavetti, Levinthal, & Rivkin, 2005; Ganco & Agarwal, 2009). For example, NK landscape models (Kauffman, 1993) have identified stable patterns of interaction that emerge between interacting, interdependent heterogeneous agents. In contrast, there has been far less emphasis in the field on the underlying dynamics or processes that spark emergence.

Thus, this book presents numerous insights that can be gained by considering emergence as a process with a range of emergent outcomes. Specifically, most of the book is dedicated to exploring the processes and dynamics of emergence, especially the ways in which these dynamics are expressed in five distinct phases. Other aspects of the book focus on the range of emergents that can be generated—from no emergent to first-degree, second-degree, or third-degree emergents.

Another benefit of considering emergence as a process with outcomes is that the dual construct can potentially resolve two debates in organization science, which I will mention here briefly.

The first debate is based primarily in entrepreneurship, but it affects strategy and innovation as well. The question is whether business opportunities are primarily "objective," existing independent of an entrepreneur who may discover them, or "subjective" or "creative," coming into being through their enactment and organizing. This debate is quite current, as shown by the January 2013 Dialogue section in the *Academy of Management Review* (Vol. 38, #1). There, four sets of authors present alternative views regarding the existence and realization of opportunity. In particular, according to the "discovery" approach, opportunities are an outcome, the result of conditions and constraints in technology, markets, and entrepreneurs. According to the "creation" approach, opportunities are an emergent process; a viable opportunity is one that becomes increasingly visible through entrepreneurial organizing and enactment. An emergence perspective provides a unique integration by viewing opportunities as emergents (perceivable social entities) that are, and can be, enacted. As will be explained in depth in Chapters 8 and 10, the resolution is based on a different distinction, namely the degree to which an entrepreneur experiences "opportunity tension" (Lichtenstein, 2009). In this formulation, the focus is on an interaction between the opportunity—whether "objective" or "enacted"—and the "creative tension" of the entrepreneur (Fritz, 1989). Together, these drive the emergence of new organizations and ventures, the catalyst of social innovation and creation.

The second debate is the long-standing query into the resources, qualities, or conditions that lead to organizational emergence. This question has been asked by entrepreneurship scholars in terms of the activities that give rise to new ventures (Delmar & Shane, 2003, 2004; Brush, Manolova, & Edelman, 2008), the resource endowments that lead to a successful start-up (Cooper, Gimeno-Gascon, & Woo, 1994; Brush & Greene, 1996; Reuf, Aldrich, & Carter, 2003), and the environmental conditions that mediate business creation processes (Aldrich & Fiol, 1994; Schoonhoven & Romanelli, 2001; Almandoz, 2012). In the emergence perspective these questions are one-sided; they miss the fundamental contribution provided by the *process* of emergence. For example, our study (Lichtenstein, Carter, Dooley, & Gartner, 2007) showed that it did not matter *what* the entrepreneur did; the likelihood of emergence depended solely on the dynamics of the organizing process. Specifically, our findings, based on a nonlinear analysis of the Panel Study of Entrepreneurial Dynamics (PSED), showed that the content of entrepreneurial activity did not influence success. Instead, the likelihood of start-up was predicted solely by the temporal dynamics of entrepreneurial action—the rate, pace, and quantity of effort. In these ways emergence may allow researchers new ways to focus on the underlying processes of organizational creation. Adding these dynamics to our knowledge base may also spark new research into organizational growth and change.

Expanding the Potential for Complexity Science

A third issue taken up by the book refers to the assumption that research using complexity science refers to a type of computational study. That is, current perceptions in the academy are that the only way to explore order creation in complex systems is through computation and agent-based modeling. This bias is clear in the scholarly reviews of complexity in organization science, which treat the study of complex systems and emergence as a computational issue (e.g., Cowan, Pines, & Meltzer, 1994; Anderson, 1999; Axelrod & Cohen, 2000; Sorenson, 2002; Prietula, 2011). The same can be said of popular summaries (Johnson, 2001; Downey, 2009; Johnson, 2009; Mitchell, 2009).

Further, the predictive power of NK landscape research has made it into a premier methodology, as is easily seen by the increasing volume of top-tier publications using that method (Levinthal, 1997; Levinthal & Warglien, 1999; McKelvey, 1999a; Gavetti & Levinthal, 2000; Rivkin, 2000; Sorenson & Audia, 2000; Ararwal, Sarkar, & Echambadi, 2002; Rivkin & Siggelkow, 2003; McKelvey, 2004c; Gavetti et al., 2005; Siggelkow & Rivkin, 2005, 2006; Sorenson, Rivkin, & Fleming, 2006; Rivkin & Siggelkow, 2007; Porter & Siggelkow, 2008; Ganco & Agarwal, 2009; Sommer, Loch, & Dong, 2009). Clearly the methods are successful and provide knowledge that is consonant with mainstream management thinking.

However, these computational studies in complexity science were not present at the origin of the field, nor have they been the most common. Much of the early work on emergence in management was based on applications of Prigogine's work in thermodynamics (e.g., Odum & Pinkerton, 1955; Odum, 1969; Allen, 1982; Prigogine & Stengers, 1984; Wicken, 1985, 1986; Allen & McGlade, 1987; Adams, 1988; Dyke, 1988; Goldstein, 1988; Odum, 1988; Wicken, 1989; Depew & Weber, 1994; Juarrero, 1999; Morowitz 2002; Schneider & Sagan, 2005). These studies explored the underlying dynamics of order creation, but most of these researchers are virtually unknown to the current generation of complexity scholars.

Moreover, computational methods have limitations that are rarely expressed but are important to reveal. One broad problem with computational models is their reliance on effects that are programmed into the agents, rather than being truly emergent results of their interactions. Sawyer makes the strongest case for this issue (2004, pp. 164–165):

> First, the macrostructures or macroproperties do not themselves emerge from the simulation but are imposed by the designer. Yet in actual societies, macrophenomena are themselves emergent from microprocesses.... A second problem in applying these multilevel artificial societies to sociological theory is that agents do not have any perception

of the emergent collective entity (Castelfranchi, 1998; Conte et al., 1998; Servat et al., 1998). In the CORMAS simulation, agents do not know that they are being taxed, nor that a quota has been imposed. In the EOS simulation of group formation . . . no agent has awareness of its own group as an entity, and agents that are not in a group have no way of recognizing that the group exists or who its members are.

Another important limitation of computational models has focused on certain issues with the NK landscape methodology developed by Kauffman (1993) and extended by Levinthal, McKelvey, and others (e.g., Levinthal & Myatt, 1994; Levinthal, 1997; Levinthal & Warglien, 1999; McKelvey, 1999a, 1999b; Ganco & Agarwal, 2009; Sommer et al., 2009). Specifically, McKelvey and his collaborators (McKelvey, Li, Xu, & Vidgen, 2013) pursued an in-depth theoretical analysis of the NK model and found two important problems. First, the theoretical roots of the NK model in genetic biology and bioecology are based on the assumption that connections between agents will be *epistatic*, that is, agents are connected to each other through strong-tie effects. In contrast, most of the ties between members of an organization are weak ties. In the same way, often the most powerful connections in social networks are made through weak ties (Granovetter, 1973; Obstfeld, 2005). This leads to a challenge:

> As far as we know, then, genes cannot turn epistasis on or off. But employees in firms can—they can choose how and when to interact with other employees. . . . But if employees can turn their interactions on or off, then the Kauffman-designed NK model clearly offers unrealistic simulations of organizational phenomena. [Thus we] challenge the NK-design as *not* being broadly applicable to organizations, as current applications of the NK model generally presume. (McKelvey et al., 2013, p. 8)

Added to this theoretical challenge is a more complicated one based on their mathematical analysis of the underlying NK algorithms. McKelvey et al. conclude:

> NK-model results appear to be artifacts preordained by the code rather than by theory-based experiments. . . . Consequently, "moderate complexity"—i.e. when K is neither zero nor large—always wins.

Given that this is true in virtually all NK models, their critique of the method is intriguing and unsettling. While not questioning the importance of computational modeling, it does give pause to the applicability of these results for management, an issue explored further in Chapter 2.

Of course, computational modeling is not the only type of complexity science; many scholars have identified a wide range of complexity sciences. Goldstein (1999, 2000), for example, mentions nearly a dozen disciplines of complexity science in his introductions to its history and foundations. Maguire and his colleagues (Maguire, McKelvey, Mirabeau, & Oztas, 2006) identified 25 disciplinary origins of complexity science and framed a very wide spectrum of complexity contributions in four broad categories. These integrations are supported by the earlier work of McKelvey (2004c; Andriani & McKelvey, 2009) in his distinction between the American school of complexity, centered at the Santa Fe Institute and which emphasizes computational studies, and the European school of complexity, which is grounded more in the natural sciences' explorations of emergence and order creation.

Overall, my approach is to claim that dissipative structures theory is a very good alternative to computational modeling as a core metaphor for organizational emergence, a claim that is supported by my analysis in Chapters 7 and 8. As will be shown in Chapters 16, 17, and 18, the model provides many useful insights to organization science, findings and perceptions that complement and extend the computational work. Through this complementarity a new generation of effective and relevant complexity science research could be generated.

Problems with "Self-Organization"

A fourth problem that generative emergence aims to solve is related to the popular term for emergence, namely *self-organization*. Many of the original applications of complexity science in management were based on the idea of self-organization; for example, in the early 1980s two edited books (Schieve & Allen, 1982; Ulrich & Probst, 1984) applied self-organization to understanding population dynamics (Zurek & Schieve, 1982), urban systems (Allen, 1982), and economics (Davidson, 1982). Smith's work on self-organization (Gemmill & Smith, 1985; Smith, 1986; Smith & Gemmill, 1991; Smith & Comer, 1994) extended these ideas into organization behavior and management. Over the past 15 years, a host of management scholars have invoked the term *self-organization* in papers on the following topics:

- Leadership (Guastello, 1998; Lichtenstein, 2000c; Zaror & Guastello, 2000; Plowman et al., 2007b)
- Innovation and learning (De Vany, 1996; Saviotti & Mani, 1998; Lichtenstein, 2000c)
- Market economics (Lesourne, 1993; Lesourne & Orlean, 1998; Foster, 2000)
- Entrepreneurship (Zuijderhoudt, 1990; Buenstorf, 2000; Lichtenstein, 2000b; Biggiero, 2001; Lichtenstein & Jones, 2004)
- General management (Adams, 1988; Salthe, 1989; Zohar & Borkman, 1997; McKelvey, 1999b; Contractor et al., 2000; Gunz, Lichtenstein, & Long, 2001; Ferdig & Ludema, 2005)

Such applications remain common in even the most recent work (e.g., Butler & Allen, 2008; Saynisch, 2010; Tapsell & Woods, 2010; Stevenson, 2012; Wallner &

Menrad, 2012). Although *self-organization* is a popular term, there are two problems with its use, which I will summarize here briefly.

Lack of Rigor in Applications of Self-Organization and Complexity

First, self-organization is often used more as a metaphor than as a carefully specified scientific process. That is, with numerous exceptions mentioned later in this chapter, applications of self-organization are often developed with an eye to training and consulting advice, rather than being linked to rigorous science. This point was clearly made in an early analysis of the diffusion of complexity science, the first wave of business applications, by Maguire and McKelvey (1999) in a special issue *Complexity Applications in Management,* in the journal *Emergence* (Vol. 1, #2). They summarized the problems with many management consulting books in the 1990s, which ostensibly used complexity and self-organization to understand organizations, by concluding that most books suffered from

> loose, less than rigorous, oversimplified, and even sometimes incorrect use of concepts. And while metaphors are applauded, a number of reviewers feel that authors' over-reliance on metaphors contributes to these superficial treatments. The absence of at least some mathematics in many books is conspicuous and undesirable for a number of reviewers, as is also the insufficient harnessing of simulations and computer models. . . . Finally, although empirical examples are much appreciated, a number of reviewers feel that these are mere retellings of old tales using complexity terminology tacked on retrospectively, gratuitously and, in many cases, quite awkwardly. (Maguire and McKelvey, 1999, p. 23)

Fortunately, not all applications of complexity are loose and oversimplified; indeed, most complexity science research in organization science journals is tightly connected to its disciplinary foundation. Such studies are based on rigorous and often testable analogies to one of the underlying sciences of complexity. Likewise, many practitioner applications reveal very strong analogies. For example, the *MIT Sloan Management Review* special issue *In Search of Strategy* (1999) included two exemplars of rigorous complexity applications. Pascale (1999) reviewed "four bedrock principles" from the science of complexity, drawing on the work of Prigogine, Holland, and Kauffman. He then used those to identify four operational assumptions that underlie a more adaptive approach to strategy. Similarly, Beinhocker (1999) developed a careful analogy from adapting agents in an NK landscape theory to adapting organizations in a competitive landscape. Like many scholars who have made this link—but unlike most of his consulting colleagues who lack the necessary rigor—Beinhocker reviewed the underlying framework of NK landscape simulations and then made three strategic directives that are actionable applications of known experimental results.

Even so, this rigor is rarely found in articles that emphasize self-organization. This raises the first challenge to the term, namely the inherent difficulty of making rigorous analogies between self-organization (see Chapters 3 and 6) and organizational behavior. Still, beneath that challenge is a more fundamental issue—namely, the locus of agency in self-organization.

Is Self-Organization as Simple as It Seems?

Most studies of complexity examine the "bottom-up" emergence of agents into higher order entities. These studies of self-organization permeate the computational fields of complex adaptive systems theory (Holland, 1995, 1998), genetic algorithms (Axelrod, 1997; Axelrod & Cohen, 2000), and agent-based models (Epstein & Axtell, 1996; Sawyer, 2005). The problem is that all of these models present agents as relatively simple learning entities, which operate according to one or a few "simple rules." Likewise, these simulated humans only interact with local (proximate) others. These studies are able to find bottom-up emergence, that is, the creation of order solely through local interactions with no external influence or top-down control. As Clippinger (1999, p. 6) explains, "No one unit [agent] has any plan or even goal concerning how the overall system should act, and yet the system evolves into a complex structure adapted to its circumstances.... Because complex systems adapt from the bottom up, there is no way of planning for change."

Although this is a compelling description, does it reflect real and emergent behavior in social systems? Do emergent systems always act "of their own accord"?

Jeff Goldstein (2000) is especially clear about the problems with this perception that self-organizing can occur spontaneously. He notes that this interpretation of self-organization leads to a mistaken belief that

> novel structures would somehow emerge in organizations if only the "command and control" hierarchy would be dismantled in favor of individual action. This misinterpretation led to a spate of management books pushing for "self-organizing" as a form of laissez-faire leadership, [i.e.] that somehow relaxing managerial control would inevitably lead to "self-organization" to solve the organization's problems. (Goldstein, Hazy, & Lichtenstein, 2010, p. 80)

At least three issues are at play here. First, from a leadership perspective, Mary Uhl-Bien and her colleagues (Uhl-Bien, Marion, & McKelvey, 2007; Uhl-Bien & Marion, 2008) have shown that even if some organizing is motivated by purely bottom-up actions, this is always balanced in formal organizations by bureaucratic as well as adaptive leadership. Together these three factors provide the necessary strategies, resources, and decision-making context for so-called self-organizing activities. These additional layers of complexity highlight the limitations of computational agents, which can be programmed to follow only a specific number of rules and which interact only with proximate neighbors. In contrast, real managers would be very hard pressed to instill such constraints on their subordinates.

Second, from an empirical perspective, studies of order creation using computational models have revealed at most four "levels" of activity in an organization—individual agents, teams, sets of teams, and some executive functioning (Lichtenstein & McKelvey, 2011; see also Lichtenstein 2011b). Even the most sophisticated of these "self-organized" models leads to simple organizations with a CEO and two layers of management. However, our business world is filled with organizations that encompass five, six, seven, and more layers. Bottom-up organizing alone is unable to generate this complexity (Lichtenstein & McKelvey, 2011).

Equally important, it turns out that so-called self-organization is far from spontaneous and lacking in control structures. Instead, in all of the formal experiments that reveal self-organization, the outcomes are possible only because of constraints, containers, boundaries, and external structures, an insight developed by Goldstein:

> A careful reading of the experiments and instances of self-organization reveals they are replete with a legion of *non*-spontaneous *constraints* that far out-number and far exceed in significance any appearances of spontaneous processes. (Goldstein, 2011, p. 98, his emphasis).
>
> Open systems—like organizations—do have the capacity for self-organization, but only when they are constrained in specific ways and when there are the requisite flows of energy, resources, and information through the system and across its boundaries. (Goldstein et al., 2010, p. 80)

Recent innovations in complexity science have been exploring the issue of spontaneity by emphasizing the agency of individual agents within the social ecology. Further, researchers are investigating how agency can catalyze social innovations and emergents in ways that are both spontaneous and planned, emergent and constructive. Such applications, when developed through rigorous analogical maps, can tell us much more than was possible in the original work on self-organization.

Overall, my claim is that the term *self-organization* was useful at the beginning of complexity science, but now it is freighted with too many loose applications and theoretical confusion. As a result, I do not use that term at all in this book.[15] Instead, I turn back to its origins in dissipative structures theory, carefully distinguishing between the dynamics of the emergence process and the possible emergents that accrue.

Integrate Research Through a General Model of Emergence

A final benefit of generative emergence lies in its potential to offer a general model of emergence across multiple fields. This reflects the fact that there is already a very wide range of research on emergence in the social sciences, from applications in cognitive science to studies in leadership, organizational behavior, groups, entrepreneurship, organizational design, strategic change, collaboration, networks, economic geography, regional development, and sociology. See Table 1.1 for examples at each of these levels (unit of analysis).

Given this broad range, one might wonder what connections could be made between the emergence of, for example, group norms, the "self-organization" of

Table 1.1. "LEVELS" OF EMERGENCE IN THE SOCIAL SCIENCES

Emergence of: (from Title)	Topic Area or Field	Reference
Collective properties	Psychology; identity theory	Nowak, Tesser, Vallacher, & Borkowski, 2000
Leadership emergence	Leadership	Marinova, Moon, & Kamdar, 2013
Leadership emergence	Leadership	Zaror & Guastello, 2000
Group norms	Groups; organizational behavior	Arrow & Burns, 2004
Downward causation	Groups; organizational behavior	Sawyer, 2001
Emergence events	Entrepreneurship	Lichtenstein, Dooley, & Lumpkin, 2006
New ventures	Entrepreneurship	Lichtenstein & Kurjanowicz, 2010
Entrepreneurial networks	Entrepreneurship	Biggiero, 2001
Entrepreneurial regions	Economic geography; networks	Arikan, 2001
Entrepreneurial regions	Entrepreneurship; regional development	Chiles et al., 2004
Self-renewal in corporations	Innovation; organizational change	Nonaka, 1988
Organizational renewal	Organization transformation	Plowman et al., 2007a
Strategic renewal	Strategic change	MacIntosh & MacLean, 1999
New practice areas	Organization design	Anand et al., 2007
Ethical issues	Organization theory; organizational change	Sonenshein, 2009
Knowledge firms	Organization theory, organizational design	Oliver & Montgomery, 2000
Markets and organization	Organization theory, networks	Padgett & Powell, 2011
Phase transitions	Entrepreneurship; organizational theory	Tan, 2007
Alliance in semiconductor industry	Collaborations; networks	Browning et al., 1995
Institutional fields	Institutional theory	Purdy & Gray, 2009
Supply networks	Operations management	Choi et al., 2001
Stratification in complex systems	Sociology	Kimberly, 1971

entrepreneurial networks, the self-renewal of large corporations, the emergence of ethical issues, the emergence of new markets, and the emergence of institutional fields, to name a few. A general model of emergence reveals parallel dynamics across all of these studies.

In particular, connections across these fields are relatively easy to make with the use of the five-phase process model of emergence, presented in Chapter 7, and the continuum of emergent outcomes shown in Chapter 8. In particular, the process-based model allows researchers to make links across multiple units of analysis, such that insights from one level might be applied to others. Overall, this supports my claim for a discipline of emergence, with frameworks that cut across levels of analysis and even across supposedly separate fields of organization science, psychology, sociology, and so on. This approach has already been shown to integrate studies within organization science (Lichtenstein & Plowman, 2009) and to organize a myriad of studies in entrepreneurship as well (Lichtenstein, 2011a, 2011b).

Last, embedded in the emergence model is a general framework for organizing at all levels—that of dynamic states—developed by Levie and Lichtenstein (2010) and drawn out in Chapter 8. It is complementary and has important parallels to the approach taken by Padgett and Powell (2011). It also enables links to a host of other research in the areas of ecological resilience (e.g., Baldwin, Murray, Winder, & Ridgway, 2004; Folke et al., 2004; Liu et al., 2007), sustainability (Buenstorf, 2000), bioeconomics (McKelvey, 2004b; Foster, 2011), and perspectives on organizational evolution (Rosser, 1992; Foster & Metcalfe, 2012). Here again, emergence can become an integrative frame that connects previously divergent literatures.

In summary, a disciplinary approach to emergence leads to a number of important insights. First, emergence is distinct from organizational change and transformation, being initiated by aspiration and opportunity rather than by crisis, and generates new capacity in the system. Second, distinguishing the process of emergence from its outcomes solves some long-standing debates in entrepreneurship and organization science. Third, extending our understanding of emergence through complexity science reveals a much broader set of methods and approaches than are usually acknowledged in complexity-based applications, which increases the potentiality for a discipline. Fourth, with these shifts comes a much more rigorous explanation of self-organization, one which is true to the underlying science and integrates with a broader range of empirical findings. Finally, this integration is part of a general theory of emergence that incorporates a five-phase process model and a range of emergent outcomes; the general model allows for a synthesis of much previous work across multiple fields across the social sciences.

SUMMARY OF THE BOOK

These benefits are gained through a series of arguments that extend throughout the book. Understanding the entire scope up front will offer a valuable point of reference for each part, and provide some guidance for readers in where they may want to focus their attention.

The book begins with a proposal for a formal discipline of emergence that draws together insights from emergence scholars in the natural sciences, philosophy, and the social sciences. As a start, I suggest a set of prototypes of emergence (Chapter 2), survey the extant methods for studying emergence (Chapter 3), and offer an integrative definition for my main field of interest, generative emergence (Chapter 4). In addition, I review the types of emergence being studied in organization science (Chapter 5). Academics in all fields should find these chapters intriguing.

Ultimately, my goal is a highly rigorous, empirically driven map of generative emergence, an approach that is especially useful for social scientists. This starts with a careful examination of dissipative structures (Chapter 6), which reveals a specific process of emergence as well as experimental conditions for emergence. The process is then applied to organizations as a five-phase model (Chapter 7); separately, the distinct conditions of generative emergence lead to a general model of dynamic states (Chapter 8). Last, the four outcomes of generative emergence are presented (Chapter 9). These chapters are well suited to social scientists, including scholars and PhD students in entrepreneurship, management, organization theory, and policy studies.

At the core of the book is a full description of the five phases of generative emergence, through an in-depth presentation of re-emergence in entrepreneurial ventures (in Chapters 10, 11, 12, 13, and 14). Added to this is a theoretical claim for cycles of generative emergence and re-emergence (Chapters 15 and 16), a claim supported by several case studies. This segment of the book is well suited to entrepreneurs and professionals who seek tangible examples of emergence, as well as researchers and academics who want to pursue further study in these dynamics.

Finally, the last two chapters offer an aspiration for future work. While identifying the "boundaries" of generative emergence, I make some broad suggestions about studying emergents that are "beyond those boundaries" (Chapter 17). Then I make some exploratory claims about enacting emergence in organizations and society as a whole (Chapter 18).

Although I have designed the book such that readers can start with any of these four parts, their import is best understood with reference to the argument as a whole. Thus, what follows is a chapter-by-chapter summary, which will explicate the entire scope of generative emergence.

Chapter 2. Prototypes of Emergence

Making a claim for a discipline of emergence requires first that all of the different types of emergence can be identified. Although a complete list is nearly impossible to find in the literature, Chapter 2 begins by citing over 20 types of emergence that have been explored through physics, chemistry, computer science, biochemistry, biology, entomology, ecology, evolution, anthropology, sociology, linguistics, group dynamics, entrepreneurship, institutional theory, and economic geography.

All of these types can be organized into a single framework, one which is comprehensive yet parsimonious. My proposition is to present eight distinct prototypes of emergence, each being a basic form or archetype of order creation.[16] These prototypes incorporate the entire range of emergents in the physical, computational, biological, and social world. In the briefest summary, the prototypes are as follows:

I. **Relational properties,** such as temperature, pressure, and viscosity. These are systemwide properties that "emerge" out of the interactions of massive numbers of molecules in closed containers.

II. **Exo-organization.** When high energy is directed (pushed) into a contained system, the result can be creation of new degrees of order. Examples are laser light and dissipative structures; both are emergent structures that emerge in far-from-equilibrium systems.

III. **Computational order** refers to ordered patterns and stable structures that arise across computational agents. These structures are not directly programmed into the system but emerge solely due to "simple rules" for action and interaction that are programmed into each agent.

IV. **Autocatalysis** refers to self-generating networks of interaction within chemical or biological systems. Once initiated, the reactions across the network produce the catalysts that spark the set of reactions, producing a self-reinforcing emergent entity.

V. **Symbiogenesis** occurs when one organism envelopes another to create a new biological form. The classic example is the creation of the eukaryotic cell through the enveloping of mitochondria within it. Here, the emergent is over 1,000 times more effective at photosynthesis and other cellular functions than its prokaryotic precursor.

VI. **Collaborative emergence.** Dynamic structures arise through the interaction of many agents (organisms) that are guided by simple rules; examples include termite hills, traffic patterns, and the V-form in bird flocks. Another form of this is stable social emergents (Sawyer, 2004), which include slang words, global brands, and collective memory. As well, this prototype explains the emergence of institutions—material, social, and legal systems structured through shared cognitive frames. In each case, the higher-level emergent is an unplanned result of purely local interaction.

VII. **Generative emergence.** Social entities arise and remain stable through intentional creative agency and organizing. An entity (e.g., an organization) emerges through an aspiration—partly planned and partly evolving—to provide some kind of value, that is, a product, service, or offering that is valued by other agents. This offering is exchanged for money, which is then used to maintain the entity. Generative emergence is ubiquitous in society, being the basis for all businesses, companies, projects, initiatives, and innovations.

VIII. **Collective action,** a more macro form of generative emergence, refers to collaborative organizing processes that can lead to large-scale creation and change in society. Collective action has been explored by scholars of institutional entrepreneurship and by social movement theorists.

In sum, the prototypes provide a framework that allows us to view a much broader range of emergence than has been presented in most other complexity-science texts, a framework that allows for a discipline of emergence. At the center of this discipline is generative emergence, a form that until now has not been identified as a type of emergence. By understanding the nature of generative emergence, we can gain insight into the creation and sustaining of all kinds of social entities. Such an understanding requires a shared knowledge about complex systems and how to study them—the topics of the next chapter.

Chapter 3. Studying Emergence—15 Fields of Complexity Science

The origins of complexity science lie in 50+ years of research into nonlinear dynamics in the fields of mathematics, physics, biology, information science, and system dynamics, to name a few. Following numerous researchers who have argued for an inclusive definition of complexity, this chapter presents the entire range of complexity science in terms of 15 fields. Each of these fields has its own theoretical frame and analytic methodology, and a set of applications in organization science and other social science disciplines. All of them offer a unique and nonlinear perspective for understanding complex dynamic systems.

Some of these fields are more well-known than others. For example, NK landscape models are familiar from the work of Kauffman (1993), Levinthal (Levinthal & Warglien, 1999), and McKelvey (1999a). In contrast, few researchers have used autopoiesis (Maturana & Varela, 1980) or its related theory of autogenesis (Csanyi & Kampis, 1985; Drazin & Sandelands, 1992), although Padgett and Powell (2011) base their examination on these fields. No other text has presented this entire scope of complexity science.

The 15 fields of complexity science are presented in Table 1.2.

In full, Chapter 3 presents the theoretical and scientific origins of each field and suggests how the discipline has been used to contribute to our understanding of

Table 1.2. FIELDS OF COMPLEXITY SCIENCE

Complexity Science	Originating Discipline
1. Determinist chaos theory	Mathematics; atmospheric science
2. Catastrophe theory	Mathematics
3. Fractals	Mathematics
4. Positive feedback: cybernetics, increasing returns	Information theory; systems theory; economics
5. Self-organized criticality; power laws	Mathematics
6. System dynamics	Information theory
7. Complex adaptive systems	Computational science
8. Cellular automata	Computational science
9. Genetic algorithms	Computational science
10. NK landscapes	Computational science
11. Agent-based modeling	Computational science
12. Autocatalysis, autopoiesis	Biology; systems theory
13. Dissipative structures	Thermodynamics
14. Ecosystem resilience	Biology; ecology
15. Ascendency; evolutionary complexity	Ecology; evolutionary theory

emergence. As a whole, these descriptions offer a comprehensive toolbox for social scientists interested in studying emergence.

Chapter 4. Defining Emergence and Generative Emergence

To round out the idea of emergence as a discipline, I turn to a formal definition, which draws on the best work I have found in philosophy and philosophy of science, evolutionary studies, sociology, and organization science. The result is a definition that summarizes decades of discourse into five distinct qualities of emergence. Specifically, these qualities allow one to assess whether a particular phenomenon is strongly emergent (Bechtel & Richardson, 1992; Corning, 2002; Bar-Yam, 2004; Ryan, 2007), meaning that the emergent has properties or structures that are separate and essentially autonomous from the components that make it up.

Based on the analysis presented in the chapter, an entity or phenomenon is emergent (in the strong sense) if it expresses these five qualities:

1. **Qualitative novelty,** meaning that its properties *transcend* its components, producing outcomes that are unpredictable and surprising even with a full understanding of the components. The V-shape of flocking birds expresses this well.

2. **Nonreducibility,** meaning that the emergent properties cannot be reduced or explained solely by the system's components, nor to their interactions alone. An example from biology is a cell—a living entity that cannot be explained by examining all of its separate components on their own.
3. **Mutual causality,** such that the components influence the system as a whole (upward causation), and the emergent properties have causal impact on the components (downward causation). A social example is a small organization, which is impacted by the actions of each of its employees, but which has systemwide qualities that influence and affect the behavior of all of its members.
4. **Structioning,** which refers to a kind of co-creative interchange between *agency*, the drive and motivation within the system, and the *constraints* of the system, the boundaries and limitations of the container itself. An example is laser light, which is formed through an interchange between the electrical energy being forced into the system and the mirrored walls of the container which constrain that energy, allowing it to build to a threshold wherein a new, high-energy form of light is produced.
5. **Capacity is increased,** whereby the outcome confers greater efficiency, efficacy, and power to the components of the system and to the system as a whole. Many examples are presented in Chapter 6.

When all five qualities are present in an emergent, the outcome is defined as strong emergence; more broadly it reflects generative emergence. This definition provides a philosophical grounding for the discipline of emergence and sets the stage for a review of how emergence has been defined and explored in management and the social sciences.

Chapter 5. Types of Emergence Studies

A close look at the literature reveals that emergence studies tend to cluster around one of four types or styles, each of which corresponds to an aspect of emergence that is being studied. These types are complexity metaphors, complexity descriptions, complexity models, and generative complexity.

Complexity metaphors use figurative language to draw attention to certain patterns in social and organizational systems. *Complexity descriptions* go further by measuring or discovering an emergent, usually through post-hoc quantitative analysis. *Complexity models* are formal or computational systems that enact emergence through computer simulations or agent-based programs. *Generative complexity* refers to dynamic systems with emergents that actually generate greater capacity for the system as a whole.

All four of these types are needed for a complete understanding of emergence. At the same time, generative complexity provides explanations that are especially useful in the context of generative emergence. With this in mind, the book focuses more directly on generative emergence, starting with an examination of its underlying field, dissipative structures.

Chapter 6. Dissipative Structures

Of all the 15 fields of complexity science, dissipative structures is ideal for studying generative emergence because the "order-creation dynamics" at its heart are highly applicable to organizations, ecosystems, and all social entities. Perhaps for this reason, they have been used by so many researchers to explain transformation, innovation, and action in organizations[17] and across organizations,[18] as well as in psychology, economics, education, and history.[19] In formal terms, the order-creation dynamics of this field capture the tangible behavioral qualities of generative emergence.

The most well-known experiment in this discipline, the Bérnard experiment, was explored deeply by Prigogine and his collaborators (Prigogine, 1955; Prigogine & Glansdorff, 1971; Prigogine & Stengers, 1984; Nicolis, 1989; Nicolis & Prigogine, 1989). In the Bérnard experiment, a viscous fluid is heated from a source at the bottom of a round, low container; normal conduction currents dissipate the heat, which is drawn out of the container through a sink at its top. Increases in heat energy can be assimilated, up to a point. But if the amount of heat energy is increased beyond a critical threshold, the fluid will experience a change of state—what Prigogine described as the onset of "self-organization." At this point, the molecules across the entire container will organize themselves into stable structures which from above look like hexagons. These hexagonal structures dissipate far more heat energy than conduction currents can.

The second experimental paradigm of dissipative structures is a "chemical clock" known formally as the B-Z reaction. Here, with the right reactants, a far-from-equilibrium chemical system can generate its own autocatalytic reactions. At that point the system exhibits systemwide shifts—oscillations like a clock—whereby the entire system changes from one color to a different one and back again. An analysis of both experiments reveals numerous parallels in their processes:

1. Once initiated, the system can move into a far-from-equilibrium state.
2. Nearing a threshold, fluctuations (turbulence) arise throughout the system.
3. At the threshold, the system exhibits nonlinearity as well as bursts of amplification.
4. The emergent order that happens is a recombination of existing elements in the system.
5. Emergent order remains stable, even when perturbed.

In terms of outcomes, the two experiments reveal the following:

a. Emergent order increases the capacity of the system to a large degree.
b. Following the basic tenets of multilevel systems, the emergent order transcends but includes its components.

It turns out that these processes and outcomes can be applied to organizations; they describe the process of generative emergence.

Chapter 7. Applications to Organizations

Although many researchers have tried to make a direct (mathematical) parallel between thermodynamics and economics,[20] I take a more moderate approach by pursuing an analytical mapping of dissipative structures onto order creation in organizations. Following the science (in Chapter 6), this rigorous mapping approach reveals five sequential phases of generative emergence noted above: disequilibrium organizing; stress and experiments; amplification to a threshold; new order through recombination; and stabilizing feedbacks. These phases are described briefly in the chapter, and at length in Chapters 10 through 14. But to put those in context, I first introduce the notion of dynamic states and emergence outcomes.

Chapter 8. Introducing Dynamic States

The analysis in Chapter 7 provides a valuable map of the process; however, it leaves out the experimental conditions that lead to dissipative structures. A close examination of these conditions in thermodynamics shows that they are vastly different from the conditions that social entities face in their efforts toward new order emergence. Chapter 8 describes these differences in some detail, leading to a generalizable model of organizing in social entities, called a "dynamic state" (Levie & Lichtenstein, 2010; Lichtenstein, 2011b). My claim is that the outcome of generative emergence is a dynamic state, which is operationalized in terms of four components:

Its *substrate*—a social ecology that includes people, culture, technology, markets, sectors, and social networks
Opportunity tension—the driver of generative emergence, which is a compelling opportunity and the motivation to pursue it
An *organizing model*—the core activities and method for creating value
Value creation—the goal of the entity, expressed through its products, services, and activities. In economic terms, this value is exchanged for money, which (re)

generates the opportunity tension and the business model, thus creating a generative loop, that is, generative emergence.

In sum, the dynamic states model presents all aspects needed to understand generative emergence, distinguishing this prototype from the dissipative structures prototype of exo-organization.[21]

Chapter 9. Outcomes of Generative Emergence

What are the outcomes of generative emergence? Building on other complexity researchers, I identify four possible outcomes. The most likely outcome, although one rarely mentioned by emergence scholars, is a *lack* of emergence, due to the dissolution of the system. In the world of entrepreneurship, this occurs all the time as unsuccessful attempts to launch, leading to the disbanding of the project.

Achieving success in an organizing process can result in three increasingly strong degrees of emergence. *First-degree order emergence* refers to a pattern or structure within a system that arises and remains stable over time. Most computational emergence results in first-degree order, as in NK landscape models, or "gliders" in the Game of Life simulation (Bar Yam, 2004). Although such order creation is intriguing, it does not confer much additional capacity to the system.

Second-degree systemic emergence occurs in the creation of a coherent system that displays qualitative novelty and nonreducibility, but does not include downward causation. Examples include the innovation of new processes in companies and the creation (enactment) of new business opportunities. In both cases a system emerges but without the power to affect its components.

The strongest form of order creation is *third-degree radical emergence,* the only form that expresses all five qualities of strong emergence: qualitative novelty, nonreducibility, mutual causality, structioning, and higher capacity. The result is an autonomous, self-generating social entity that creates value, is fully integrated into its social ecology, and displays "downward causation." The prime example is the creation of new companies, which from their start-up have a causal impact on their employees. Likewise is the re-emergence of a venture, whereby the new organizing model and value proposition have a significant role in defining the future behaviors of the founders and employees.

In sum, the process of emergence can lead to no emergence, or to first-degree, second-degree, or third-degree emergence, with each subsequent degree reflecting greater systemwide impact and capacity created in the system. With this background, we can apply the insights from dissipative structures to real examples of organizational creation and re-creation.

Chapters 10–14. The Five-Phase Process Model of Generative Emergence

In the next five chapters, the five phases of generative emergence are carefully described; examples of each phase are drawn from my dissertation study of emergence in fast-growth companies. Although the cases have been summarized in previous papers (Lichtenstein, 2000a; 2000d; Lichtenstein & Brush, 2001), up until now the in-depth longitudinal data have never been published.

Phase 1: Disequilibrium Organizing (Chapter 10)

All generative emergence begins when a lead agent (a founder) experiences an opportunity tension, by envisioning a (business) opportunity that he or she is highly motivated to pursue. That motivation pushes the founder into action, organizing people and resources toward enacting or realizing the opportunity through a viable business, project, initiative, or endeavor. The process pushes the system out of its norm and into "disequilibrium organizing." This chapter gives numerous examples of the opportunity tension that drove the entrepreneurs and companies in my study.

Phase 2: Stress and Experiments (Chapter 11)

As anyone who has organized something new can attest, the process is never easy; two qualities are sparked as a result. *Stress* occurs because the system is pushed into an arena of high pressure and great uncertainty. These stressors are felt as personal strain and sometimes interpersonal conflict, as participants struggle to deal with the intensity of the organizing effort. In addition, many ventures experience *fiscal stress* and financial challenges, primarily because the efforts are being invested into making the leap to a new state, rather than into the maintenance of previous revenue streams.

The parallel aspect of phase 2 is *experiments*—new ideas, spontaneous actions, and unique behaviors that are designed to deal with the intensity, reduce the stress, solve the challenges, and capture the opportunity. Although most experiments are not fully pursued, one of them will become the seed of new order—the basic frame around which a new system can emerge.

Phase 3: Amplification and Critical Events (Chapter 12)

Up to a certain threshold of activity, the results of stress and experiments will be dampened by the system, which seeks to retain its current structure as much as possible. Beyond the threshold, however, these "fluctuations" are amplified, leading the entire system to a *critical event*. This critical event is usually clear after the fact;

retrospective sensemaking is used to explain the dramatic decisions that in some cases totally altered the system.

Phase 4: New Order Through Recombination (Chapter 13)

The result of this critical event is *new order*—something emerges, or the entire effort dissipates into failure. If successful, the emergent order accrues through a *recombination of elements* already in the system, along with the acquisition of new resources from across the social ecology. These shifts are usually rapid, expressing punctuated change.

Phase 5: Stabilizing Feedback (Chapter 14)

One of the insights from this research is the role that stabilizing feedback has in retaining the new order, whereas destabilizing feedback can push the system back into a critical mode. This stabilizing feedback occurs by strengthening new routines, developing formal ties with new stakeholders, or achieving certain goals. Such feedback processes are not described in dissipative structures theory; the fact that they can be seen in social situations offers an important example of how the transformative metaphor approach can double back to provide insight into the original science (Garud & Nayyar, 1994).

Chapter 15. Cycles of Emergence

My proposal is that these five phases are sequential, that is, they follow a causal logic, a specific succession in which each phase occurs in close relation to the one before. Once the entire process has occurred, the system settles down into its new dynamic state. Once a dynamic state emerges it may remain in place (even if growing incrementally) for many years. At the same time, it can become the preparation for another round of the process again. Thus, the entire five-phase process is really a cycle, what I call a "cycle of emergence."

This chapter presents four case studies that exemplify cycles of emergence: the initial emergence of Starbucks, Inc. (Lichtenstein & Jones, 2004); the emergence of the SEMATECH collaboration (based on the analysis in Browning, Beyer, and Shetler 1995); the emergence of HealthUSA (Lichtenstein, Dooley & Lumpkin, 2006); and the creation of The Republic of Tea (Lichtenstein & Kurjanowicz, 2010).

The cyclical nature of emergence provides a much more dynamic view of organizations as suggested by Tsoukas & Chia (2002) and Leifer (1989). Further, this frame is easily extended toward a new theory of organizational development in which companies grow through a series of dynamic states rather than through stages in a life cycle (Levie & Lichtenstein, 2010). These implications are explored in Chapter 16.

Chapter 16. Cycles of Re-Emergence

The final step is to introduce the idea of re-emergence—the re-creation of an organization into a completely new dynamic state. In a simple way, re-emergence specifies the continuing cycles of emergence within an organization: first emergence, then re-emergence, then re-emergence again, and so on.

Within this description it is important to note again the difference between a cycle of re-emergence and the process of organizational transformation. As mentioned earlier, transformation events are triggered by crisis, which leads to reactive behaviors that try to solve the problem. In contrast, emergence events are initiated by an aspiration to create or expand a company's potential; this leads to creative, proactive actions that draw on internal resources and values. Just as proactive creativity is more likely to spur innovation and more effective results (Heinzen, 1994; Axtell et al., 2000; Unsworth, 2001), so too similar positive effects are found for proactive entrepreneurial logic (Newey & Zahra, 2009), self-directed entrepreneurial behaviors (Baron, 1998; Baron & Markman, 2003), and proactive thinking by entrepreneurs (Yusuf, 2012). This chapter operationalizes these ideas using data from my dissertation.

Chapter 17. Boundaries of Emergence, and Beyond the Boundaries

The final two chapters offer a broader context for the work. Chapter 17 focuses on *boundaries*, in two specific ways. First, boundaries refer to the physical limitations of the container that holds a process. In the dissipative structures experiment the boundaries are the walls of the cylindrical vessel that holds the fluid and chemicals. It turns out that the dimensions of the boundary—literally the size of the experimental container—have an important influence on the outcome of the experiment (Swenson, 1997; Goldstein, 2011). In a similar way, the constraints of a creative situation play a constructive role in any emergence process. As Juarrero (1999, p. 133) suggests, "constraints can simultaneously open up as well as close off options." In this meaning, boundaries are "constructive constraints" that actually enable order to emerge. Thus, attending to the boundaries of an emergence process should have positive implications for our understanding and enactment of emergence.

Second, boundaries refers to the theoretical "boundary conditions" of the model I have presented (Whetten, 1989). These boundaries allow me to specify which phenomenon should be explainable by the five-phase process model, and which one is not. In brief, I will claim that the sequence of five phases is applicable to organizations as the unit of analysis. That is, I would expect the cycle of emergence or re-emergence to be valid for emergence *in* organizations or for the emergence *of* organizations.

This claim reveals two distinct dimensions that describe different contexts of emergence. The first dimension distinguishes emergence *within* organizations from emergence *of* organizations. The second dimension distinguishes emergence from re-emergence. Putting these together as a two-by-two typology suggests four avenues for continuing research in the field:

a. *Emergence of organizations* is best represented by the PSED research on new venture foundings (Gartner, Carter, & Reynolds, 2004; Gartner, Shaver, Carter, & Reynolds, 2004).
b. *Re-emergence of organizations* refers to entrepreneurial "re-invention" (Baker & Nelson, 2005; Mullins & Komisar, 2009), which may also reveal insights into the mutability of an company's identity (Gioia, Schultz, & Corley, 2000).
c. *Emergence within organizations* can explore the range of emergences in organizational settings, including emergence of systems, departments, products/platforms, and even governance systems, as has been done by O'Mahony and Ferraro (2007).
d. *Re-emergence within organizations* offers a unique lens to explore the re-creation of existing structures, systems, or routines. It can also draw forward strategy process research.

Related to this discussion of boundaries, I explore empirical contexts of emergence that lie "beyond these boundary conditions." For example, research in psychology and cognitive development suggests that several elements of a cycle of emergence are expressed during major shifts in cognitive learning and leadership development (Boyatzis & Kolb, 2000; Boyatzis, 2008) or in aspects of creative flow experience (Csikszentmihalyi, 1990; 1996).

In addition, the five-phase process model can be applied to more macro contexts, to see if and how it is validated in arenas such as the emergence of alliances and collaborations (Browning et al., 1995), self-organizing supply chains (Choi, Dooley, & Rungtusanatham, 2001; Pathak, Day, Nair, Sawaya, & Kristal, 2007), and network emergence (Biggiero, 2001). Broader contexts are also ripe for exploration, including industry creation (Garud, Jain, & Kumaraswamy, 2002; Garud & Karnøe, 2003; Tan, 2007; Dew, Reed, Sarasvathy, & Wiltbank, 2011), the emergence of institutional clusters (Chiles & Meyer, 2001; Ehrenfeld, 2007), and the dynamics of institutional entrepreneurship (Maguire, Hardy, & Lawrence, 2004; Maguire & Hardy, 2009; Purdy & Gray, 2009).

Chapter 18. Enacting Emergence

Can emergence be intentionally pursued or enacted? This last chapter explores an "emergence praxis"—three ways to instigate generative emergence. The first is to create the conditions for emergence in organizations (Marion & Uhl-Bien, 2001; McKelvey, 2004a; Hazy, Goldstein, & Lichtenstein, 2007; Osborn & Hunt, 2007; Uhl-Bien et al., 2007; Uhl-Bien & Marion, 2008; Goldstein et al., 2010). For example, we (Lichtenstein & Plowman, 2009) analyzed three studies on emergence to identify 10 actions that leaders can pursue to initiate emergence. Examples include generating disequilibrium by embracing uncertainty, encouraging rich interactions through "relational space," supporting collective action, accepting tags, and integrating local constraints. Together these behaviors of "generative leadership" increase the likelihood that innovations can surface in social ecologies and companies, leading to emergence.

A second way to instigate generative emergence would be to enact each of the five phases of emergence in sequence, with the aim of purposively generating an emergent entity. In brief, the process starts by assessing the social ecology for collaborators, resources, and synergies that can aid in the goal. The next step is to generate opportunity tension, pursuing actions that create disequilibrium while allowing for stress and producing experiments that may seed new order. If these continue, momentum will build to a critical event, a trigger point of system change. New order is created, encouraging a recombination of resources and elements, in an iterative process that increases the overall capacity of the system. Finally, if the new state is effective, the generative leader can apply stabilizing feedback, to retain the sustainability of the system. To be clear, this description is a proposal which will require a good deal of experimentation to test and clarify.

Third, the book concludes by making a proposal for the emergence of social change. The idea is to combine generative emergence with Gunderson and Holling's (2001) work on ecosystem resilience. Their research shows that natural and social ecosystems evolve through four phases of an "adaptive cycle." It turns out that these phases are extremely similar to the phases of generative emergence: An initial state moves through the stages of exploitation and conservation; these can lead to a rigidity state. In some cases the system is triggered to release the built-up resources; these get re-organized and recombined into a new initial state. Linking the two models suggests a way to extend emergence to economic and natural ecosystems. In addition, the resilience framework emphasizes sustainability, which is itself a core value of generative emergence—both focus on building a healthy and viable world.

Overall, my hope is that this book provides a foundation for rigorous and relevant studies of generative emergence, and for conversations that lead to a discipline of emergence. In one measure the book culminates 34 years of my own thinking and research, and it integrates the nearly 800 papers and books I've cited across over 100 years of study by others. At the same time, it should be read as a work in progress, a first step in an ongoing journey toward understanding the dynamics of emergent order in our organizations and our society as a whole.

NOTES

1. Research has identified these synergistic effects; see, e.g., Hainsworth (1986), Darley (1994), and Weimerskirch et al. (2001).
2. This work originated with the classic paper by Katz and Gartner (1988), which eventually led to the National Science Foundation (NSF)-funded Panel Study of Entrepreneurial Dynamics—the first randomized study of entrepreneurs in the world (see Gartner, Shaver, Carter, & Reynolds, 2004). This was followed quickly by parallel databases in Sweden. Studies showing the longitudinal process of organizational emergence are numerous; exemplars include Carter, Gartner, and Reynolds (1996); Delmar and Shane (2003, 2004), and Brush, Manolova, and Edelman (2008), who proved the accuracy of the original Katz and Gartner model. The first dynamic systems model of entrepreneurial emergence (Lichtenstein, Carter, Dooley, & Gartner, 2007) showed that for nascent ventures which successfully emerged, the *content* of organizing behaviors (e.g., doing financial projections, doing marketing; finding funding, hiring first employee, and 24 others) was insignificant compared to the *process* of those behaviors, i.e., their temporal pattern over time.
3. Key work in this area has been done by Sarasvathy and Dew (2005) and Chiles and his colleagues (Chiles, Bluedorn, & Gupta, 2007; Chiles, Tuggle, McMullen, Bierman, & Greening, 2010). Tan (2007) showed that developing economies like China emerge in "phases" or cycles.
4. An influential simulation study by Krugman (1996) used a single-chained genetic algorithm model to show why populations of businesses tend to aggregate. This dynamic explanation was expanded in Chiles's dissertation work, which showed that the emergence of the Branson, MO, music theater cluster occurred in four "cycles" of self-organization (Chiles, Meyer, & Hench, 2004).
5. Smith & Gemmill, 1991; Smith & Comer, 1994; Guastello, 1995; Arrow, & Burns, 2004.
6. Innovation has been explored by many, including De Vany (1996), Brown and Eisenhardt (1998), and Van de Ven et al. (1999).
7. Mintzberg & Waters, 1985; Bettis & Prahalad, 1995; Garud & Van de Ven, 1992; Stacey, 1995; also, Sonenshein, 2009.
8. Overviews of the change/transformation aspects of emergence can be found in Weick and Quinn (1999), as well as in Bigelow (1982), Levinthal (1991), Dooley (1997), Lichtenstein (2000a), Tsoukas and Chia (2002), and Plowman et al. (2007b).
9. The emergence of new social institutions has been empirically explored in studies of institutional entrepreneurship. For example, Maguire, Hardy, and Lawrence (2004) explained the dynamics of emergence for a new institutional field in medicine; Purdy and Gray (2009) showed the emergence of the new field of alternative dispute resolution; and O'Mahony and Ferraro (2007) studied the emergence of governance in open source software projects. For a summary of the emergence paradigm in sociology, see Sawyer's (2005) *Social Emergence: Societies as Complex Systems*.
10. Although my expertise is more limited for the field of psychology, several examples make this point clear. Some studies in neurophysiology have shown the unpredictably emergence of neural "subfields"—see Poirier, Amin, and Aggleton (2008). One

example of cognitive emergence is a recent study by McClelland and his students (McClelland et al., 2010) on connectionist and dynamical approaches to cognition. In terms of motivation, Guastello has been studying individual behavior using dynamic systems models for over two decades—these were summarized in his 2005 book, which shows how nonlinear dynamic models can improve the explained variance in certain longitudinal studies by over 400%, from r^2 of .15 to r^2 of .60 and more. See also parts of Strogatz's *Sync: How Order Emerges from Chaos in the Universe, Nature, and Daily Life*. Finally, for studies on the collective nature of individual behavior see Amabile, Conti, Coon, Lazenby, and Herron (1996) and Sawyer and DeZutter (2009).

11. For a summary of the emergence paradigm in sociology, see Sawyer's (2005) *Social Emergence: Societies as Complex Systems*. Padgett and Powell (2011) also provide a powerful reanalysis of socioeconomic change, using the complexity science of autogenesis. Some of the earliest applications of computational modeling were to understanding patterns of collective social behavior; see, for example, Schelling (1978), Macy (1991), and Epstein and Axtel (1996).

12. The search included EBSCO-Host's Academic Search Premier, EconLit, PsychArticles, SocIndex, ERIC, and Business Source Premier, on November 22, 2010. Title includes the word "emerge*" and (organization or group or management or industry or market or entrepreneur* or economic* or neuro* or cognit* or decision or individual or social or collective or behavior). Limiters = peer reviewed.

13. The five-phase process model has been shown to explain emergences in work groups (Goldstein, 1998, 1994; Smith, 1986); organizations (Leifer, 1989; Nonaka, 1988; MacIntosh & MacLean, 1999; Plowman et al., 2007b), start-up ventures (Lichtenstein, 2000d), alliances and collaborations (Browning, Beyer, & Shetler, 1995; Chiles, Meyer, & Hench, 2004).

14 Simon, 1955.

15. Except in reference to others' research.

16. Jeff Goldstein introduced me to the concept of a prototype of emergence; the following analysis owes a great deal to him.

17. Nonaka, 1988; Leifer, 1989; Goldstein, 1994; Smith & Comer, 1994; Bettis & Prahalad, 1995; MacIntosh & MacLean, 1999; Lichtenstein, 2000d; Plowman et al., 2007a.

18. Browning, Beyer, & Shelter, 1995; Buenstorf, 2000; Chiles, Meyer, & Hench, 2004; Tan, 2007; Foster, 2011; Padgett & Powell, 2011; Foster & Metcalfe, 2012.

19. Artigiani, 1987; Dyke, 1988; Lesourne, 1993; Juarrero, 1999; Gilstrap, 2007.

20. This was done by dozens or researchers. These applications started just a few years after Bérnard's initial work, in the research by Gibbs (1906) and Lotka (1922, 1945). Later, Schrödinger's classic book (1944) *What Is Life* inspired Odum and his collaborators (Odum & Pinkerton, 1955; Odum, 1988) to compute energy flows in ecosystems. Dissipative structures were applied to dynamic models of economics through efforts of Georgescu-Roegen (1971), as well as Odum and Odum (1976).

21. Note that a dynamic state is an exemplar of strong emergence, for it includes all five of the necessary qualities. Specifically, a dynamic state
    (a) expresses qualitative novelty—in the unique output (product, service, offering) that includes but transcends its components, the people who make it up.
    (b) is not reducible to its components—it cannot be explained as the simple combination of organizing behaviors, nor as the interactions across those behaviors (see Lichtenstein et al., 2007), and
    (c) reveals mutual causality—because the emergent organization alters the behavior of its members, just as its members create and influence the development of the venture.

The emergence of a dynamic state involves

(d) structioning—an ongoing interdependence of agency and constraint. In particular, the founder (entrepreneur) identifies the ideal way to create value for a targeted market, in the most parsimoneous way that she or he can. Organizing is thus a co-creative process of effectuation and bricolage.

Finally, if the dynamic state is to be sustained (sustainable), its emergence

(e) increases the capacity of the system in some way, either through efficiencies of scale, scope, or learning, or through new organizing models that save time and are more effective at producing real and reliable value to customers.

REFERENCES

Adams, R. N. 1988. *The Eighth Day: Social Evolution as the Self-Organization of Energy*. Austin, TX: University of Texas.

Aldrich, H., & Fiol, M. 1994. Fools rush in? The institutional context of industry creation. *Academy of Management Review*, 14(1): 645–70.

Allen, P. 1982. Self-organization in the urban system. In W. Scheive & P. Allen (Eds.), *Self-Organization and Dissipative Structures: Applications in Physical and Social Sciences* (132–58). Austin, TX: University of Texas Press.

Allen, P., & McGlade, J. 1987. Evolutionary drive: The effect of microscopic diversity, error making and noise. *Foundations of Physics*, 17: 723–28.

Almandoz, J. 2012. Arriving at the starting line: The impat of community and financial logics on new banking ventures. *Academy of Management Journal*, 55(6): 1381–406.

Amabile, T., Conti, R., Coon, H., Lazenby, J., & Herron, M. 1996. Assessing the work environment for creativity. *Academy of Management Journal*, 39: 1154–84.

Anand, N., Gardner, H., & Morris, T. 2007. Knowledge-based innovation: Emergence and embedding of new practice areas in management consulting firms. *Academy of Management Journal*, 50: 406–28.

Anderson, P. 1999. Complexity theory and organization science. *Organization Science*, 10: 216–32.

Andriani, P., & McKelvey, B. 2009. From Gaussian to Paretian thinking: Causes and implications of power laws in organizations. *Organization Science*, 20: 1053–71.

Ararwal, R., Sarkar, M., & Echambadi, R. 2002. The conditioning effect of time on firm survival: An industry life cycle approach. *Academy of Management Journal*, 45: 971–94.

Arikan, A. 2001. A complexity approach to entrepreneurial system emergence: The case of Silicon Alley: New York University.

Arrow, H., & Burns, K. L. 2004. Self-organizing culture: How norms emerge in small groups. In M. Schaller & C. Crandall (Eds.), *The Psychological Foundations of Culture* (171–99). Mahwah, NJ: Lawrence Erlbaum Associates.

Artigiani, R. 1987. Revolution and evolution: Applying Prigogine's dissipative structures model. *Journal of Social and Psychological Structures*, 10: 249–64.

Axelrod, R. 1997. *The Complexity of Cooperation: Agent-Based Models of Competition and Cooperation*. Princeton, NJ: Princeton University Press.

Axelrod, R., & Cohen, M. 2000. *Harnessing Complexity*. New York: Free Press.

Axtell, C., Holman, D., Unsworth, K., Wall, T., Waterson, P. E., & Harrington, E. 2000. Shopflor innovation: Facilitating the suggestin and implementation of ideas. *Journal of Occupational and Organizational Psychology*, 73(3): 265–85.

Bacharach, S., Bamberger, P., & Sonnenstuhl, W. 1996. The organizational transformation process: The micropolitics of dissonance reduction and the alignment of logics of action. *Administrative Science Quarterly*, 41: 477–506.

Bak, P. 1996. *How Nature Works: The Science of Self-Organized Criticality*. NewYork: Springer-Verlag.

Bak, P., & Chen, K. 1991. Self-organized criticality. *Scientific American*, January: 46–53.

Baker, T., & Nelson, R. 2005. Creating something from nothing: Resource construction through entrepreneurial bricolage. *Administrative Science Quarterly*, 50: 239–366.

Baldwin, J., Murray, R., Winder, B., & Ridgway, K. 2004. A non-equilibrium thermodynamic model of industrial development: Analogy or homology. *Journal of Cleaner Production*, 12: 841–53.

Baron, R. 1998. Cognitive mechanisms in entrepreneurship: Why and when entrepreneurs think differently than other people. *Journal of Business Venturing*, 13: 275–24.

Baron, R., & Markman, G. 2003. Beyond social capital: The role of entrepreneurs' social competence in their financial success. *Journal of Business Venturing*, 18: 41–60.

Bartunek, J. 1984. Changing interpretive schemes and organizationl restructuring: The example of a religious order. *Administrative Science Quarterly*, 224–41.

Bartunek, J., & Moch, M. 1987. First order, second order and third order change and organization development interventions: A cognitive approach. *Journal of Applied Behavioral Science*, 23: 483–500.

Bar-Yam, Y. 1997. *Dynamics of Complex Systems*. Reading, MA: Addison-Wesley—Advanced Book Program.

Bar-Yam, Y. 2004. A mathematical theory of strong emergence using mutliscale variety. *Complexity*, 9(6): 15–24.

Bechtel, W., & Richardson, R. 1992. Emergent phenomena and complex systems. In A. Beckermann, H. Flohr, & J. Kim (Eds.), *Emergence or Reduction? Essays on the Prospects of Nonreductive Physicalism* (257–88). Berlin: Walter de Gruyter.

Bedau, M., & Humphres, P. (Eds.). 2008. *Emergence: Contemporary Readings in Philosophy and Science*: Cambridge, MA: Bradford Books—MIT Press.

Beinhocker, E. 1999. Robust adaptive strategies. *Sloan Management Review*, Spring: 95–106.

Bettis, R., & Prahalad, C. K. 1995. The dominant logic: Retrospective and extention. *Strategic Management Journal*, 16: 5–14.

Bigelow, J. 1982. A catastrophe model of organizational change. *Behavioral Science*, 27: 26–42.

Biggiero, L. 2001. Self-organizing processes in building entrepreneurial networks: A theoretical and empirical investigation. *Human Systems Management*, 20: 209–22.

Boyatzis, R. 2008. Leadership development from a complexity perspective. *Consulting Psychology Journal: Practice and Research*, 60: 298–313.

Boyatzis, R., & Kolb, D. 2000. Performance, learning and development as modes of growth and adaptation throughout our lives and careers. In M. Peiperl, M. Arthur, R. Goffee, & T. Morris (Eds.), *Career Frontiers* (76–98). New York: Oxford University Press.

Brown, S., & Eisenhardt, K. 1998. *Competing on the Edge*. Boston: Harvard Business School Press.

Browning, L., Beyer, J., & Shetler, J. 1995. Building cooperation in a competitive industry: Sematech and the semiconductor industry. *Academy of Management Journal*, 38: 113–51.

Brush, C., & Greene, P. 1996. *Resources in the new venture creation process: Strategies for acquisition*. Paper presented at the National Academy of Management Meeting, Cincinnati, OH.

Brush, C., Manolova, T., & Edelman, L. 2008. Properties of emerging organizations: An empirical test. *Journal of Business Venturing*, 23: 547–66.

Buenstorf, G. 2000. Self-organization and sustainability: Energetics of evolution and implications for ecological economics. *Ecological Economics*, 33: 119–34.

Butler, M. J. R., & Allen, P. M. 2008. Understanding policy implementation processes as self-organizing systems. *Public Management Review*, 10(3): 421–40.

Carter, N., Gartner, B., & Reynolds, P. 1996. Exploring start-up event sequences. *Journal of Business Venturing*, 11: 151–66.

Castelfranchi, C. 1998. Simulating with cognitive agents: The importance of cognitive emergence. In J. Sichman, R. Conte, & N. Gilbert (Eds.), *Multi-Agent Systems and Agent-Based Simulation* (26–44). Berlin: Springer-Verlag.

Chiles, T., Bluedorn, A., & Gupta, V. 2007. Beyond creative destruction and entrepreneurial discovery: A radical Austrian approach to entrepreneurship. *Organization Studies*, 28: 467–93.

Chiles, T., & Meyer, A. 2001. Managing the emergence of clusters: An increasing returns approach to strategic change. *Emergence*, 3(3): 58–89.

Chiles, T., Meyer, A., & Hench, T. 2004. Organizational emergence: The origin and transformation of Branson, Missouri's musical theaters. *Organization Science*, 15(5): 499–520.

Chiles, T., Tuggle, C. S., McMullen, J., Bierman, L., & Greening, D. 2010. Dynamic creation: Elaborating a radical Austrian approach to entrepreneurship. *Organization Studies*, 31: 7–46.

Choi, T., Dooley, K., & Rungtusanatham, M. 2001. Supply networks and complex adaptive systems: Control vs. emergence. *Journal of Operations Management*, 19: 351–66.

Cilliers, P. 1998. *Complexity and Postmodernism: Understanding Complex Systems*. New York: Routledge.

Clayton, P., & Davies, P. 2006. *The Re-emergence of Emergence: The Emergentist Hypothesis from Science to Religion*. New York: Oxford University Pres.

Clippinger, J. H. 1999. Order from the botton up: Complex adaptive systems and their management. In J. H. Clippinger (Ed.), *The Biology of Business* (1–30). San Francisco: Jossey-Bass.

Conte, R., Edmonds, B., Moss, S. & Sawyer, K. 1998. Sociology and social theory in agent based social simulation: A symposium. *Computational and Mathematical Organization Theory*, 7: 183–205.

Contractor, N., Whitbred, R., Fonti, F., Hyatt, A., O'Keefe, B., & Jones, P. 2000. Structuration theory and self-organizing networks. Presented at Organization Science Winter Conference, Keystone, CO.

Cooper, A., Gimeno-Gascon, F. J., & Woo, C. 1994. Initial human and financial capital as predictors of new venture performance. *Journal of Business Venturing*, 9: 371–96.

Corning, P. 2002. The re-emergence of "emergence": A vernerable concept in search of a theory. *Complexity*, 7(6): 18–30.

Cowan, G., Pines, D., & Meltzer, D. (Eds.). 1994. *Complexity: Metaphors, Models, and Reality* (Vol. Proceedings, #11). New York: Addison-Wesley.

Csanyi, V., & Kampis, G. 1985. Autogenesis: Evolution of replicative systems. *Journal of Theoretical Biology*, 114: 303–21.

Csikszentmihalyi, M. 1990. *Flow: The Psychology of Optimal Experience*. New York: Harper & Row.

Csikszentmihalyi, M. 1996. *Creativity*. New York: HarperCollins.

Darley, V. 1994. Emergent phenomena and complexity. *Artificial Life*, IV: 411–6.

Davidson, R. 1982. Economic dynamics. In W. C. Schieve & P. Allen (Eds.), *Self-Organization and Dissipative Structures: Applications in Physical and Social Sciences* (339–43). Austin, TX: University of Texas Press.

Delmar, F., & Shane, S. 2003. Does business planning facilitate the development of new ventures? *Strategic Management Journal*, 24: 1165–85.

Delmar, F., & Shane, S. 2004. Legitimating first: Organizing activities and the survival of new ventures. *Journal of Business Venturing*, 19: 385–411.

Depew, D., & Weber, B. (Eds.). 1985. *Evolution at a Crossroads: The New Biology and the New Philosophy of Science*. Cambridge, MA: MIT Press.

Depew, D., & Weber, B. 1994. *Darwinism Evolving*. New York: Oxford University Press.

De Vany, A. 1996. Information, chance, and evolution: Alchian and the economics of self-organization. *Economic Inquiry*, 34: 427–42.

Dew, N., Reed, S., Sarasvathy, S., & Wiltbank, R. 2011. On the entrepreneurial genesis of new markets: Effectual transformations versus causal search and selection. *Journal of Evolutionary Economics*, 21: 231–53.

Dooley, K. 1997. A complex adaptive systems model of organization change. *Nonlinear Dynamics, Psychology, and the Life Sciences*, 1: 69–97.

Downey, A. 2009. *Think Complexity: Complexity Science and Computational Modeling*. Sebastopol, CA: O'Reilly Media.

Drazin, R., & Sandelands, L. 1992. Autogenesis: A perspective on the process of organizing. *Organization Science*, 3: 230–49.

Dyke, C. 1988. Cities as dissipative structures. In B. Weber, D. Depew, & J. Smith (Eds.), *Entropy, Information and Evolution: New Perspectives on Physical and Biological Evolution*. Cambridge, MA: MIT Press.

Ehrenfeld, J. 2007. Would industrial ecology exist without sustainability in the background? *Journal of Industrial Ecology*, 11: 73–84.

Epstein, J. M., & Axtell, R. 1996. *Growing Artificial Societies: Social Science from the Bottom up*. Cambridge, MA: MIT Press.

Ferdig, M., & Ludema, J. 2005. Transformative interactions: Qualities of conversation that heighten the vitality of self-organizing change. In R. Woodman (Ed.), *Research in Organizational Change and Development*, Vol. 15: 171–207. New York: Elsevier Press.

Fleming, L., & Sorenson, O. 2001. Technology as a complex adaptive system. *Research Policy*, 30: 1019–39.

Folke, C., Carpenter, S., Walker, B., Scheffer, M., Elmqvist, T., Gunderson, L., & Holling, C. S. 2004. Regime shifts, resilience, and biodiversity in ecosystem management. *Annual Review of Ecology, Evolution, and Systematics*, 35: 557–81.

Foster, J. 2000. Competitive selection, self-organization and Joseph A. Schumpeter. *Journal of Evolutionary Economics*, 10: 311–28.

Foster, J. 2011. Energy, aesthetics and knowledge in complex economic systems. *Journal of Economic Behavior and Organization*, 80: 88–100.

Foster, J., & Metcalfe, J. S. 2012. Economic emergence: An evolutionary economic perspective. *Journal of Economic Behavior and Organization*, 82: 420–32.

Fritz, R. 1989. *The Path of Least Resistance*. New York: Fawcett Columbine.

Ganco, M., & Agarwal, R. 2009. Performance differentials between diversifying entrants and entrepreneurial start-ups: A complexity approach. *Academy of Management Review*, 34: 228–53.

Gartner, W., Carter, N., & Reynolds, P. 2004. Business start-up activities. In W. Gartner, K. Shaver, N. Carter, & P. Reynolds (Eds.), *Handbook of Entrepreneurial Dynamics* (285–98). Thousand Oaks, CA: SAGE Publications.

Gartner, W., Shaver, K., Carter, N., & Reynolds, P. (Eds.). 2004. *Handbook of Entrepreneurial Dynamics*. Thousand Oaks, CA: SAGE Publications.

Garud, R., Jain, S., & Kumaraswamy, A. 2002. Institutional entrepreneurship in the sponsorship of comon technological standards: The case of Sun Microsystems and Java. *Academy of Management Journal*, 45(196–214).

Garud, R., & Karnøe, P. 2003. Bricolage versus breakthrough: Distributed and embedded agency in technology entrepreneurship. *Research Policy*, 32: 277–301.

Garud, R., & Nayyar, P. 1994. Transformative capacity: Continual structuring by intertemporal technology transfer. *Strategic Management Journal*, 15: 365–85.

Garud, R., & Van de Ven, A. 1992. An empirical evaluation of the internal corporate venturing process. *Strategic Management Journal*, 13: 93–109.

Gavetti, G., & Levinthal, D. 2000. Looking forward and looking backward: Cognitive and experiential search. *Administrative Science Quarterly*, 45: 113–37.

Gavetti, G., Levinthal, D., & Rivkin, J. 2005. Strategy making in novel and complex worlds: The power of analogy. *Strategic Management Journal*, 26: 691–712.

Gell-Mann, M. 1994. *The Quark and the Jaguar*. New York: W. H. Freeman.

Gemmill, G., & Smith, C. 1985. A dissipative structure model of organization transformatoin. *Human Relations*, 38(8): 751–66.

Georgescu-Roegen, N. 1971. *The Entropy Law and the Economic Process*. Cambridge, MA: Harvard University Press.

Gersick, C. 1991. Revolutionary change theories: A multilevel exploration of the punctuated equilibrium paradigm. *Academy of Management Review*, 16: 10–36.

Gibbs, J. W. 1906. *The Scientific Papers of J. Willard Gibbs*. New York: Longmans, Green.

Gilstrap, D. 2007. Dissipative structures in educational change: Prigogine and the academy. *International Journal of Leadership in Education*, 10: 49–69.

Gioia, D., Schultz, M., & Corley, K. 2000. Organizational identity, image, and adaptive instability. *Academy of Management Review*, 25: 63–81.

Gleick, J. 1987. *Chaos: Making a New Science*. New York: Penguin.

Goldstein, J. 1988. A far-from-equilibrium systems approach to resistance to change. *Organizational Dynamics*, 15(1): 5–20.

Goldstein, J. 1994. *The Unshackled Organization*. Portland, OR: Productivity Press.

Goldstein, J. 1999. Emergence as a construct: History and issues. *Emergence*, 1: 49–72.

Goldstein, J. 2000. Emergence: A concept amid a thicket of conceptual snares. *Emergence*, 2(1): 5–22.

Goldstein, J. 2011. Probing the nature of complex systems: Parameters, modeling, interventions—Part 1. *Emergence: Complexity and Organization*, 13(3): 94–121.

Goldstein, J., Hazy, J., & Lichtenstein, B. 2010. *Complexity and the Nexus of Leadership: Leveraging Nonlinear Science to Create Ecologies of Innovation*. New York: Palgrave Macmillan.

Granovetter, M. 1973. The strength of weak ties. *American Journal of Sociology*, 78: 1360–80.

Greenwood, R., & Hinings, C. R. 1996. Understanding radical organizational change: Bringing together the old and the new institutionalism. *Academy of Management Review*, 21: 1022–54.

Guastello, S. 1995. *Chaos, Catastrophe, and Human Affairs: Applications of Nonlinear Dynamics to Work, Organizations, and Social Evolution*. Mahway, NJ: Lawrence Erlbaum and Associates.

Guastello, S. 1998. Self-organization and leadership emergence. *Nonlinear Dynamics, Psychology, and Life Sciences*, 2: 301–15.

Gunderson, L., & Holling, C. S. (Eds.). 2001. *Panarchy: Understanding Transformations in Human and Natural Systems*. Washington, DC: Island Press.

Gunz, H., Lichtenstein, B., & Long, R. 2001. Self-organization in career systems: A view from complexity science. *M@n@gement*, 5(1): 63–88.

Hainsworth, F. 1986. Precision and dynamics of positioning by Canada Geese flying in formation. *Journal of Experimental Biology*, 128: 445–62.

Hazy, J., Goldstein, J., & Lichtenstein, B. (Eds.). 2007. *Complex Systems Leadership Theory: New Perspectives from Complexity Science on Social and Organizational Effectiveness*. Mansfield, MA: ISCE Publishing.

Heinzen, T. E. 1994. Situational affect: Proactive and reactive creativity. In M. Shaw & M. Runco (Eds.), *Creativity and Affect* (127–46). Westport, CT: Ablex Publishing.

Heinzen, T. E. 1999. Proactive creativity. In M. Runco & S. R. Pritzker (Eds.), *Encyclopedia of Creativity*, Vol. 1: 429–34. San Diego: Academic Press, Elsevier.

Holland, J. 1995. *Hidden Order*. Redwood City, CA: Addison-Wesley.

Holland, J. 1998. *Emergence: From Chaos to Order*. Cambridge, MA: Perseus Books.
Huber, G., & Glick, W. 1993. *Organizational Change and Redesign*. New York: Oxford University Press.
Jantsch, E. 1980. *The Self-Organizing Universe*. New York: Pergamon Press.
Johnson, N. 2009. *Simply Complexity: A Clear Guide to Complexity Theory*. Oxford, UK: Oneworld Publications.
Johnson, S. 2001. *Emergence: The Connected Lives of Ants, Brains, Cities, and Software*. New York: Scribner
Juarrero, A. 1999. *Dynamics in Action: Intentional Behavior as a Complex System*. Cambridge, MA: MIT Press.
Katz, J., & Gartner, W. 1988. Properties of emerging organizations. *Academy of Management Review*, 13: 429–41.
Kauffman, S. 1993. *The Origins of Order*. New York: Oxford University Press.
Kelly, K. 1994. *Out of Control: The Rise of Neo-Biological Civilization*. Reading, MA: Addison-Wesley.
Kimberly, J. 1971. The emergence and stabilization of stratification in simple and complex social systems. *Sociological Inquiry*, 40(Spring): 73–101.
Krugman, P. 1996. *The Self-Organizing Economy*. Cambridge, MA: Bradford Press.
Lawrence, T., Hardy, C., & Phillips, N. 2002. Institutional effects of interorganizational collaboration: The emergence of proto-institutions. *Academy of Management Journal*, 45: 281–90.
Leifer, R. 1989. Understanding organizational transformation using a dissipative structure model. *Human Relations*, 42: 899–916.
Lesourne, J. 1993. Self-organization as a process in evolution of economic systems. In R. Day & P. Chen (Eds.), *Nonlinear Dynamics and Evolutionary Economics* (150–66). New York: Oxford University Press.
Lesourne, J., & Orlean, A. (Eds.). 1998. *Advances in Self-Organization and Evolutionary Economics*. London: Economica.
Levie, J., & Lichtenstein, B. 2010. A terminal assessment of stages theory: Introducing a dynamic states approach to entrepreneurship. *Entrepreneurship Theory and Practice*, 34(2–March): 314–54.
Levinthal, D. 1991. Organizational adaptation and environmental selection—Interrelated processes of change. *Organization Science*, 2: 140–44.
Levinthal, D. 1997. Adaptation on rugged landscapes. *Management Science*, 43: 934–50.
Levinthal, D., & Myatt, J. 1994. Co-evolution of capabilities and industry: The evolution of mutual fund processing. *Strategic Management Journal*, 15(Special Issue): 45–62.
Levinthal, D., & Warglien, M. 1999. Landscape deisgn: Designing for local action in complex worlds. *Organization Science*, 10(3): 342–57.
Lewin, R. 1992. *Complexity: Life on the Edge of Chaos*. New York: MacMillan.
Lichtenstein, B. 2000a. Dynamics of rapid growth and change: A complexity theory of entrepreneurial transitions. In G. Liebcap (Ed.), *Advances in the Study of Entrepreneurship, Innovation, and Economic Growth*, Vol. 6: 161–92. Westport, CT: JAI Press.
Lichtenstein, B. 2000b. Emergence as a process of self-organizing: New assumptions and insights from the study of nonlinear dynamic systems. *Journal of Organizational Change Management*, 13: 526–44.
Lichtenstein, B. 2000c. Generative knowledge and self-organized learning: Reflecting on Don Schon's research. *Journal of Management Inquiry*, 9(9): 47–54.
Lichtenstein, B. 2000d. Self-organized transitions: A pattern amid the "chaos" of transformative change. *Academy of Management Executive*, 14(4): 128–41.
Lichtenstein, B. 2009. Moving far from far-from-equliibrium: Opportunity tension as the catalyst of emergence. *Emergence: Complexity and Organization*, 11(4): 15–25.

Lichtenstein, B. 2011a. Complexity science contributions to the field of entrepreneurship. In P. Allen, S. Maguire, & B. McKelvey (Eds.), *The SAGE Handbook of Complexity and Management* (471–93). Thousand Oaks, CA: SAGE Publications.

Lichtenstein, B. 2011b. Levels and degrees of emergence: Toward a matrix of complexity in entrepreneurship. *International Journal of Complexity in Leadership and Management*, 1(3): 252–74.

Lichtenstein, B., & Brush, C. 2001. How do "resource bundles" develop and change in new ventures? A dynamic model and longitudinal exploration. *Entrepreneurship Theory and Practice*, 25(3): 37–58.

Lichtenstein, B., Carter, N., Dooley, K., & Gartner, W. 2007. Complexity dynamics of nascent entrepreneurship. *Journal of Business Venturing*, 22: 236–61.

Lichtenstein, B., Dooley, K., & Lumpkin, T. 2006. Measuring emergence in the dynamics of new venture creation. *Journal of Business Venturing*, 21: 153–75.

Lichtenstein, B., & Jones, C. 2004. A self-organization theory of radical entrepreneurship. *Best Papers Proceedings, National Academy of Management*: OMT Division; CD format.

Lichtenstein, B., & Kurjanowicz, B. 2010. Tangibility, momentum, and the emergence of *The Republic of Tea*. *ENTER Journal*, 1: 125–48.

Lichtenstein, B., & McKelvey, B. 2011. Four types of emergence: A typology of complexity and its implications for a science of management. *International Journal of Complexity in Leadership and Management*, 1(4): 339–78.

Lichtenstein, B., & Plowman, D. A. 2009. The leadership of emergence: A complex systems leadership theory of emergence at successive organizational levels. *The Leadership Quarterly*, 20: 617–30.

Liu, J., Dietz, T., Carpenter, S., Alberti, M., Folke, C., Moran, E., Pell, A. N., Deadman, P., Kratz, T., Lubchenco, J., Ostrom, E., Ouyang, Z., Provencher, W., Redman, C., Schneider, S., & Taylor, W. 2007. Complexity of coupled human and natural systems. *Science*, 317(Sept. 14): 1513–16.

Lotka, A. 1922. Contribution to the energetics of evolution. *Proceedings of the National Academy of Sciences U S A*, 6: 147–51.

Lotka, A. 1945. The law of evolution as a maximal principle. *Human Biology*, 17: 167–94.

MacIntosh, R., & MacLean, D. 1999. Conditioned emergence: A dissipative structures approach to transformation. *Strategic Management Journal*, 20: 297–316.

Macy, M. 1991. Chains of cooperation: Threshold effects in collective action. *American Sociological Review*, 56: 730–47.

Maguire, S., & Hardy, C. 2009. Discourse and deinstitutionalization: The decline of DDT. *Academy of Management Review*, 52: 148–78.

Maguire, S., Hardy, C., & Lawrence, T. 2004. Institutional entrepreneurship in emerging fields: HIV/AIDS treatment advocacy in Canada. *Academy of Management Journal*, 47: 657–80.

Maguire, S., & McKelvey, B. 1999. Complexity and management: Moving from fad to firm foundations. *Emergence*, 1(2): 19–61.

Maguire, S., McKelvey, B., Mirabeau, L., & Oztas, N. 2006. Complexity science and organization studies. In S. Clegg, C. Hardy, W. Nord, & T. Lawrence (Eds.), *Handbook of Organization Studies* (2nd ed., 165–214). London: SAGE Publications.

March, J. 1981. Footnotes to organizational change. *Administrative Science Quarterly*, 26: 563–77.

Marinova, S., Moon, H., & Kamdar, D. 2013. Getting ahead or getting alone? The two-facet conceptualization of conscientiousness and leadership emergence. *Organization Science*, 24(4): 1257–76.

Marion, R., & Uhl-Bien, M. 2001. Leadership in complex organizations. *The Leadership Quarterly*, 12: 389–418.

Maturana, H. R., & Varela, F., J. 1980. *Autopoiesis and Cognition*. Dordrecht, Holland: D. Reidel Publishing.

McClelland, J. L., Botvinick, M., Noelle, D., Plaut, D., Rogers, T., Seidenberg, M., & Smith, L. 2010. Letting structure emerge: Connectionist and dynamical systems approaches to cognition. *Trends in Cognitive Science* 14(8): 348–56.

McKelvey, B. 1999a. Avoiding complexity catastrophe in coevolutionary pockets: Strategies for rugged landscapes. *Organization Science*, 10(3): 294–321.

McKelvey, B. 1999b. Self-organization, complexity catastrophe, and microstate models at the edge of chaos. In J. Baum & B. McKelvey (Eds.), *Variations in Organization Science* (279–310). Thousand Oaks, CA: SAGE Publications.

McKelvey, B. 2004a. MicroStrategy from MacroLeadership: Distributed intelligence via new science. In A. Lewin & H. Volberda (Eds.), *Mobilizing the Self-Renewing Organization*. New York: Palgrave Macmillan.

McKelvey, B. 2004b. Toward a 0th law of thermodynamics: Order creation complexity dynamics from physics and biology to bioeconomics. *Bioeconomics*, 6: 65–96.

McKelvey, B. 2004c. Toward a complexity science of entrepreneurship. *Journal of Business Venturing*, 19: 313–42.

McKelvey, B., Li, M., Xu, H., & Vidgen, R. 2013. Re-thinking Kauffman's NK fitness landscape: From artifact and groupthink to weak-tie effects. *Human Systems Management*, 32(1): 17–42.

Mintzberg, H., & Waters, J. 1985. Of strategies, deliberate and emergent. *Strategic Management Journal*, 6(3): 257–72.

Mitchell, M. 2009. *Complexity: A Guided Tour*. New York: Oxford University Press.

Morowitz, H. 2002. *The Emergence of Everything*. New York: Oxford University Press.

Mullins, J., & Komisar, R. 2009. *Getting to Plan B: Breaking Through to a Better Business Model*. Boston: Harvard Business Review Press.

Newey, L., & Zahra, S. 2009. The evolving firm: How dynamic and operating capabilities interact to enable entrepreneurship. *British Journal of Management*, 20(Suppl 1): S81–S100.

Nicolis, G. 1989. Physics of far-from-equilibrium systems and self-organization. In P. Davies (Ed.), *The New Physics*. New York: Cambridge University Press.

Nicolis, G., & Prigogine, I. 1989. *Exploring Complexity*. New York: W. H. Freeman.

Nonaka, I. 1988. Creating organizational order out of chaos: Self-renewal in Japanese firms. *California Management Review*, 30–Spring: 57–73.

Nowak, A., Tesser, A., Vallacher, R., & Borkowski, W. 2000. Society of self: The emergence of collective properties in self-structure. *Psychological Review*, 107: 39–61.

Obstfeld, D. 2005. Social networks, the Tertius Lungens orientation, and involvement in innovation. *Administrative Science Quarterly*, 50: 100–30.

Odum, H. 1969. The strategy of ecosystem development. *Science*, 164: 262–70.

Odum, H. 1988. Self-organization, transformity, and information. *Science*, 242: 1132–39.

Odum, H., & Odum, E. 1976. *Energy Basis for Man and Nature*. New York: McGraw Hill.

Odum, H., & Pinkerton, R. 1955. Time's speed regulator: The optimum efficiency for maximum power output in physical and biological systems. *American Scientist*, 43(2): 331–43.

Oliver, A., & Montgomery, K. 2000. Creating a hybrid organizational form from parental blueprints: The emergence and evolution of knowledge firms. *Human Relations*, 53(1): 33–56.

O'Mahony, S., & Ferraro, F. 2007. The emergence of governance in an open source community. *Academy of Management Journal*, 50: 1097–1106.

Osborn, R., & Hunt, J. 2007. Leadership and the choice of order: Complexity and hierarchical perspectives near the edge of chaos. *The Leadership Quarterly*, 18(4): 319–40.

Padgett, J., & Powell, W. 2011. *The Emergence of Organizations and Markets*. Princeton, NJ: Princeton University Press.

Pascale, R. 1999. Surfing the edge of chaos. *Sloan Management Review* (Spring): 83–94.

Pathak, S., Day, J., Nair, A., Sawaya, W., & Kristal, M. 2007. Complexity and adaptivity in supply networks: Building supply network theory using a complex adaptive systems perspective. *Decision Sciences*, 38: 547–80.

Plowman, D. A., Baker, L., Beck, T., Kulkarni, M., Solansky, S., & Travis, D. 2007a. Radical change accidentally: The emergence and amplification of small change. *Academy of Management Journal*, 50: 515–43.

Plowman, D. A., Solanksy, S., Beck, T., Baker, L., Kulkarni, M., & Travis, D. 2007b. The role of leadership in emergent, self-organization. *The Leadership Quarterly*, 18(4): 341–56.

Poirer, G., Amin, E. & Aggleton, J., 2008. Qualitatively different hippocampal subfield engagement emerges with mastery of a spatial memory task by rats. *Journal of Neuroscience*, 28(5): 1034–45.

Porter, M., & Siggelkow, N. 2008. Contextual interactions within activity systems and sustainability of competitive advantage. *Academy of Management Perspectives*, 22(2): 34–56.

Prietula, M. 2011. Thoughts on complexity and computational models. In P. Allen, S. Maguire, & B. McKelvey (Eds.), *The SAGE Handbook of Complexity and Management*: 93–110. Thousand Oaks, CA: SAGE Publications.

Prigogine, I. 1955. *Introduction to the Thermodynamics of Irreversible Processes*. New York: Wiley.

Prigogine, I., & Glansdorff, P. 1971. *Thermodynamic Theory of Structure, Stability, and Fluctuations*. New York: Wiley & Sons.

Prigogine, I., & Stengers, I. 1984. *Order out of Chaos*. New York: Bantam Books.

Purdy, J., & Gray, B. 2009. Conflicting logics, mechanisms of diffusion, and multi-level dynamics of emergence in institutional fields. *Academy of Management Journal*, 52: 355–80.

Quinn, J. B. 1989. Strategic change: Logical incrementalism. *Sloan Management Review*, Summer: 45–60.

Reid, R. 2007. *Biological Emergences: Evolution by Natural Experiment*. Cambridge, MA: Bradford Books—MIT Press.

Reuf, M., Aldrich, H., & Carter, N. 2003. The structure of founding teams: Homophily, strong ties and isolation among U.S. entrepreneurs. *American Sociological Review*, 68: 195–225.

Rivkin, J. 2000. Imitation of complex strategies. *Management Science*, 46: 824–44.

Rivkin, J., & Siggelkow, N. 2003. Balancing search and stability: Interdependencies among elements of organizational design. *Management Science*, 49: 290–311.

Rivkin, J., & Siggelkow, N. 2007. Patterned interactions in complex systems: Implications for exploration. *Management Science*, 53: 1068–85.

Romanelli, E., & Tushman, M. 1994. Organizational transformaton as punctuated equilibrium: An empirical test. *Academy of Management Journal*, 37: 1141–66.

Rosser, J. B. 1992. The dialogue between the economic and the ecologic theories of evolution. *Journal of Economic Behavior and Organization*, 17: 195–215.

Ryan, A. 2007. Emergence is coupled to scope, not level. *Complexity*, 13(2): 66–77.

Salthe, S. 1989. Self-organization of/in hierarchically structured systems. *Systems Research*, 6(3): 199–208.

Saviotti, P. P., & Mani, G. S. 1998. Technological evolution, self-organization, and knowledge. *Journal of High Technology Management Research*, 9: 255–70.

Sawyer, K. 2001. Simulating emergence and downward causation in small groups. In S. Moss & P. Davidsson (Eds.), *Multi-Agent-Based Simulation* (49–67). Berlin: Springer.

Sawyer, K. 2005. *Social Emergence: Societies as Complex Systems*. New York: Cambridge University Press.

Sawyer, K., & DeZutter, S. 2009. Distributed creativity: How collective creations emerge from collaboration. *Psychology of Aesthetics, Creativity, and the Arts*, 3(2): 81–92.

Saynisch, M. 2010. Beyond frontiers of traditional project management: An approach to evolutionary, self-organizational principles and the complexity theory—Results of the research program. *Project Management Journal*, 41(2): 21–37.

Schelling, T. 1978. *Micromotives and Macrobehavior*. New York: W. W. Norton.

Schieve, W., & Allen, P. (Eds.). 1982. *Self-Organization and Dissapative Structures: Applications in the Physical and Social Sciences*. Austin, TX: University of Texas Press.

Schneider, E., & Sagan, D. 2005. *Into the Cool: Energy Flow, Thermodynamics, and Life*. Chicago: University of Chicago Press.

Schoonhoven, C. B., & Romanelli, E. (Eds.). 2001. *The Entrepreneurship Dynamic*. Stanford, CA: Stanford Business Books.

Schrödinger, E. 1944. *What Is Life?* Cambridge, UK: Cambridge University Press.

Servat, D., Perrier, E., Treuil, J. P., & Drogoul, A. 1998. When agents emerge from agents: Introducing multi-scale viewpoints in multi-agent simulations. In J. Sichman, R. Conte, & N. Gilbert (Eds.) *Multi-Agent Systems and Agent-Based Simulation*, (183–98). Berlin: Springer-Verlag.

Siggelkow, N., & Rivkin, J. 2005. Speed and search: Designing organizations for turbulence and complexity. *Organization Science*, 16: 101–22.

Siggelkow, N., & Rivkin, J. 2006. When exploration backfires: Unintended consequences of multilevel organizational search. *Academy of Management Journal*, 49: 779–96.

Simon, H. 1955. A behavioral model of rational choice. *The Quarterly Journal of Economics*, 69(1): 99–118.

Smith, C. 1986. Transformation and regeneration in social systems: A dissipative structure perspective. *Systems Research*, 3: 203–13.

Smith, C., & Comer, D. 1994. Change in the small group: A dissipative structure perspective. *Human Relations*, 47: 553–81.

Smith, C., & Gemmill, G. 1991. Self-Organization in small groups: A study of group effectivenss within non-equilibrium conditions. *Human Relations*, 44: 697–716.

Sommer, S., Loch, C., & Dong, J. 2009. Managing complexity and unforseeable uncertainty in startup companies: An empirical study. *Organization Science*, 20: 118–13.

Sonenshein, S. 2009. Emergence of ethical issues during strategic change implementation. *Organization Science*, 20: 223–39.

Sorenson, O. 2002. Interorganizational complexity and computation. In J. Baum (Ed.), *Companion to Organizations* (664–85). Malden, MA: Blackwell Publishers.

Sorenson, O., & Audia, P. 2000. The social structure of entrepreneurial activity: Geographic concentration of footwear production in the U.S., 1940-1989. *American Journal of Sociology*, 106: 424–61.

Sorenson, O., Rivkin, J., & Fleming, L. 2006. Complexity, networks and knowledge flow. *Research Policy*, 35: 994–1017.

Stacey, R. 1995. The science of complexity: An alternative perspective for strategic choice processes. *Strategic Management Journal*, 16: 477–95.

Staudenmayer, N., Tyre, M., & Perlow, L. 2002. Time to change: Temporal shifts as enablers of organizational change. *Organization Science*, 13(5): 583–97.

Stevenson, B. W. 2012. Developing an awareness and understanding of self-organization as it relates to organizational development and leadership issues. *Emergence: Complexity & Organization*, 14(2): 69–85.

Street, C., & Gallupe, R. B. 2009. A proposal for operationalizing the pace and scope of organizational change in management studies. *Organizational Research Methods*, 12: 720–37.

Strogatz, S. 2003. *Sync: How Order Emerges from Chaos in the Universe, Nature, and Daily Life*. New York: Hyperion.

Swenson, R. 1988. *Emergence and the principle of maximum entropy production: Multi-level system theory, evolution, and nonequilibrium thermodynamics*. Paper presented at the Proceedings of the 32nd Annual Meeting of the ISGSR.

Swenson, R. 1989. Emergent attractor and the law of maximum entropy production: Foundations to a theory of general evolution. *Systems Research*, 6(3): 187–97.

Swenson, R. 1997. Thermodynamics and evolution. In G. Greenberg & M. Haraway (Eds.), *Encyclopedia of Comparative Psychology*. New York: Garland Publishers.

Tan, J. 2007. Phase transitions and emergence of entrepreneurship: The transformation of Chinese SOEs over time. *Journal of Business Venturing*, 22: 77–96.

Tapsell, P., & Woods, C. 2010. Social entrepreneurship and innovation: Self-organization in an indigenous context. *Entrepreneurship & Regional Development*, 22(6): 535–56.

Tsoukas, H., & Chia, R. 2002. On organizational becoming: Rethinking organizational change. *Organization Science*, 13: 567–83.

Uhl-Bien, M., & Marion, R. (Eds.). 2008. *Complexity Leadership. Part 1: Conceptual Foundations*. Charlotte, NC: Information Age Publishing.

Uhl-Bien, M., Marion, R., & McKelvey, B. 2007. Complexity leadership theory: Shifting leadership from the industrial age to the information era. *The Leadership Quarterly*, 18: 298–318.

Ulrich, H., & Probst, J. B. (Eds.). 1984. *Self-Organization and Management of Social Systems*. Berlin: Springer-Verlag.

Unsworth, K. 2001. Unpacking creativity. *Academy of Management Review*, 26(2): 289–97.

Van de Ven, A. 1992. Longitudinal methods for studying the process of entrepreneurship. In D. L. Sexton & J. D. Kasarda (Eds.), *The State of the Art of Entrepreneurship* (214–42). Boston: PWS-Kent Publishers

Waldrop, M. 1992. *Complexity*. New York: Touchstone/Simon & Schuster.

Wallner, T., & Menrad, M. 2012. High performance work systems as an enabling structure for self-organized learning processes. *International Journal of Advanced Corporate Learning*, 5(4): 32–37.

Weick, K., & Quinn, R. 1999. Organizational change and development. *Annual Review of Psychology*, 50: 361–86.

Weimerskirch, H., Martin, J., Clerquin, Y., Alexandre, P. & Jiraskova, S. 2001. Energy saving in flight formation. *Nature*, 413(6857): 697–8.

Whetten, D. 1989. What constitutes a theoretical contribution? *Academy of Management Review*, 14: 490–5.

Wicken, J. 1985. Thermodynamics and the conceptual structure of evolutionary theory. *Journal of Theoretical Biology*, 117: 363–83.

Wicken, J. 1986. Evolutionary self-organization and entropic dissipation in biological and socioeconomic systems. *Journal of Social and Biological Structures*, 9: 261–73.

Wicken, J. 1989. Evolution and thermodynamics: The new paradigm. *Systems Research and Behavioral Science*, 15: 365–72.

Yusuf, J.-E. 2012. A tale of two exits: Nascent entrepreneur learning activities and disengagement from start-up. *Small Business Economics*, 39(3): 783–99.

Zaror, G., & Guastello, S. 2000. Self-organization and leadership emergence: A cross-cultural replication. *Nonlinear Dynamics, Psychology, and Life Sciences*, 4: 113–20.

Zohar, A., & Borkman, T. 1997. Emergent order and self-organization: A case study of alcoholics anonymous. *Nonprofit and Voluntary Sector Quarterly*, 26: 527–52.

Zuijderhoudt, R. 1990. Chaos and the dynamics of self-organization. *Human Systems Management*, 9: 225–38.

Zurek, W. H., & Schieve, W. C. 1982. Nucleation paradigm: Survival threshold in population dynamics. In W. Schieve & P. Allen (Eds.), *Self-Organization and Dissipative Structures: Applications in the Physical and Social Sciences* (203–24). Austin, TX: University of Texas Press.

CHAPTER 2

Prototypes of Emergence

The goal of this chapter is to map out a discipline of emergence. To begin, it is necessary to present the full range of emergents that have been identified and studied by scholars across the natural, computational, and social sciences. While a complete list is infeasible, the examples here provide a comprehensive introduction to the many forms and "layers" of emergence:

- The emergence of "water" and its macroproperties out of "hydrogen + oxygen" (Corning & Kline, 1998)
- Laser light—the emergence of highly coherent light-energy waves (Haken, 1977)
- The emergence of macrostructures in far-from-equilibrium chemical systems, as studied by Prigogine and others (Prigogine, 1955; Prigogine & Stengers, 1984; Swenson, 1988; Nicolis & Prigogine, 1989)
- Symmetry-breaking processes which shift the dynamics of the macrosystem (Anderson, 1972)
- The emergence of "gliders" in the cellular automata computational system "Game of Life" (Conway, 1970)
- The emergence of ordered landscapes in NK computational modeling (Kauffman, 1993)
- In multi-agent systems, computational entities emerge which are capable of learning, decision-making, and coalition-building (Axelrod, Mitchell, Thomas, Bennett, & Bruderer, 1995; Gilbert & Conte, 1995; Axelrod, 1997; Sawyer, 2001)
- Autocatalysis—self-reinforcing catalytic networks that are central to the buildup of biological complexity (Eigen, 1971; Eigen & Schuster, 1979; Ulanowicz, 2002)
- Dynamics of slime molds—populations of multicellular organisms which, in adversity, organize into a single living column that can literally move across the forest floor, to re-generate the population in a more resource-rich place (Bonner, 1959; Nicolis & Prigogine, 1989)

- Symbiogenesis—the envelopment of separate organisms (e.g., mitochondria) into a cell, generating an emergent entity with significantly increased metabolism and capacity for adaptation (Margulis, 1967, 1981)
- Complexity that emerges within ant colonies, beehives, and termite hills, including division of labor and the construction of very large free-standing structures (Wilson & Holldobler, 1990)
- Ecological resilience—the capacity of an entire ecosystem to grow while remaining adaptive (Ulanowicz, 1980, 2002; Folke et al., 2004; Walker et al., 2006)
- Emergence of increasingly complex types of organisms in evolutionary history (Jantsch, 1980; Coren, 1998; Chaisson, 2001; Morowitz, 2002)
- Emergence of human communities and societies (Carniero, 1970, 1987)
- Traffic jams (Nagel & Paczuski, 1995; Johnson, 2001)
- Emergence of slang words, conversational routines, and other shared social practices (Lang & Lang, 1961; Giddens, 1984)
- Norms and leadership that emerge in a group or team (Guastello, 1998; Arrow & Burns, 2004)
- Entrepreneurship—the emergence of new organizations (Katz & Gartner, 1988; Gartner, 1993; Gartner, Shaver, Carter, & Reynolds, 2004; Lichtenstein, Carter, Dooley, & Gartner, 2007)
- The creation of new industries (Schumpeter, 1934; Sarasvathy & Dew, 2005; Chiles, Tuggle, McMullen, Bierman, & Greening, 2010; Dew, Reed, Sarasvathy, & Wiltbank, 2011)
- The emergence of organizational communities and aggregates (Chiles, Meyer, & Hench, 2004; Ehrenfeld, 2007; Viega & Magrini, 2009)
- The rise of social institutions and of material infrastructure in large societies (Sawyer, 2005; Padgett & Powell, 2011)

In sum, the range of emergents is remarkable—from anthills to alliances, from slime molds to societies. On first reading it may appear that there are far more differences than similarities across these types of emergence. Likewise, the very breadth of examples leads to some critical questions: Are there any core principles or qualities of emergence across this list? Can there be a definition of emergence that doesn't depend on the level of description or unit of analysis? Given my proposal for a discipline of emergence, how can these can be organized into a useful framework? Have other scholars attempted to map the contours of emergence?

George Ellis (2006) is one of a handful of scholars who have developed such a cross-disciplinary framework, in his five-level "hierarchy" of emergence. In his model, level 1 emergence includes macroproperties of gasses, liquids, and solids, as well as conductivity and heat capacity. Level 2 emergence leads to higher-level structures, as in magnetic domains, convection patterns, and cellular automata. Level 3 emergence incorporates feedback control systems that can manifest "meaningful top-down action . . . directed by implicit innate goals" (p. 100); these are, nevertheless, simple. Examples include the processes that form living cells. Level 4 emergence adds memory, thus "allowing adaptive behavior that responds to historical events" (p. 100). Here he includes animal behavior, as well as some forms of communication. Finally, with level 5 emergence comes language and "the capacity for self-conscious reflection" (p. 100). As such, this level includes the emergence of human artifacts and society.

Others have made similar attempts (Deacon, 2003, 2006). For example, Boulding (1956–see Ashmos & Huber, 1987) identified a "hierarchy of complex systems" that ranges from simple frameworks to social organizations and beyond. In the main, each of these approaches incorporates a wide swath of emergents from physics, chemistry, biology. and evolutionary theory, with a very brief nod to social emergence. At the same time, they leave out a lot of exemplars on our list of prototypes, including symbiogenesis, computational order in NK landscapes, and learning in multi-agent systems. A broader framework is needed to capture the full range of emergents for a discipline of emergence.

EIGHT PROTOTYPES OF EMERGENCE

As an alternative approach, Jeff Goldstein (2011) has suggested a framework of prototypes of emergence—essential archetypes of emergents across all levels and scope. In his view, each prototype has one or more unique drivers. Like Ellis, he identified the relational properties that aggregate in physical systems, as well as the amplification dynamics that lead to emergent structures. As another example, computational systems and collaborative emergence incorporate "rules" that guide agent interactions.

Extending this idea broadly and yet with parsimony, I propose the following eight prototypes as a starting point for a discipline of emergence. The proposal suggests that virtually all examples and types of emergence can be organized within these eight categories. My expectation is that as an emergence discipline takes shape and gains momentum, these eight prototypes may be augmented by others. Still, my hope is that with this first draft of such a framework, scholars in all disciplines can gain a foothold for exploring and clarifying the drivers of emergence and find other ways to integrate emergent phenomena.

What follows is a description of these eight prototypes and the examples of emergence that each of them incorporates. In the final section of the chapter I attempt to find some similarities across the eight categories, through an analysis of common drivers and conditions for emergence across all of the prototypes.

Prototype I—Relational Properties

When a large number of homogeneous agents—for example, atoms or molecules—are put together, the relationships between them lead to emergent properties;

examples include the thermodynamic properties of gasses, liquids, and solids. A moment of reflection will help us appreciate the type of emergence this represents. Temperature, for example, is not embodied in any one molecule but occurs as the combined effects of the entire volume of gas or liquid. Likewise, pressure is an emergent property that is only measurable as the aggregate of relationships within a container.

This prototype also includes certain mathematical relationships, such as symmetry-breaking. Symmetry-breaking refers to the recognition by Phil Anderson (1972) that quantitative increases in a substance can, if large enough, generate qualitative shifts of kind. These are qualitative breaks in the symmetry of the underlying substance, whose identification leads to new levels of analysis and a new scientific field. As one example, consider a container of atoms that can be described using quantum mechanics. As more and more atoms are introduced, at some threshold number, the law of large numbers breaks down; the system is only explainable through the laws of chemistry. Similar thresholds differentiate the fields of biology and physiology. In a somewhat similar way, power law relationships like those found by Bak and Chen (1991) may also reflect these relational properties.

To these I add an aspect of emergence that is not itself a prototype but draws from relational and cooperative effects, namely synergy.[1,2] Corning (2002) defines synergy as "the combined (cooperative) effects that are produced by two or more particles, elements, parts or organisms—effects that are not otherwise attainable" (p. 22). These effects are gained through the relationships between the elements, which is why I include them here. In addition, his synergism hypothesis (Corning 1983, 1994, 2003, 2012) shows how synergy is a driver of order throughout evolution. In the process he identifies the most common "kinds" of synergy, which I include in note 1.

Prototype II–Exo-Organization: Energy Driven into Constrained Systems

Some of the most well-known exemplars of emergence—Bérnard cells, chemical clocks, the coherence of laser light (all to be described later on)—are only achieved under very precise experimental conditions. Specifically, in each case, high amounts of energy are driven into a closed container,[3] forcing the elements (e.g., molecules) into a "far-from-equilibrium" state, which is a precursor for the emergence of order. From one perspective, it is the external and constant input of energy, combined with the constraints of the container, that lead to order creation. Here, "exo" refers to the external driver of energy, and "organization" points to the necessary constraints.

A good example of exo-organization is the formation of laser light, which can only happen in very specific conditions. A "closed" cylinder is mirrored on the inside. Outside the container is an "excitation lamp"—an external energy source that drives highly charged light into the cylinder, thus exciting the atoms. When the excited atoms return to their normal state by emitting their extra energy quanta, the mirrors reflect the light back into the atoms, inducing further cycles of emission and induction. "The repeated recycling of emitted light progressively amplifies the coherence (phase-locking) and amplitude of light... by many orders of magnitude" (Deacon 2006, p. 135).[4] The outcome is well known: Lasers are used to cut metal, weld joints, cut diamonds, carry communication signals, and act as optical scanners (Corning, 2003). But these results are wholly dependent on the externally driven force of energy and equally on the constraints of the system.

Further examples are found in the far-from-equilibrium thermodynamics of Prigogine and his colleagues (Prigogine, 1955; Nicolis & Prigogine, 1989).[5] That is, exo-organization explains the emergence of macro-level structures in the Bérnard experiment, in terms of an increasing input of heat being dissipated through a materially closed container. Other exo-organized emergent phenomena follow the same pattern. Prigogine and Stengers (1994) describe the chemical clock, and Bushev (1994, p. 63) provides a useful summary analysis. Common to all these processes is the forced input of energy flows within carefully designed constraints.

Prototype III–Computational Order: Rule-Based Interactions of Simulated Agents

Most books on emergence and nearly all the books on complexity science focus on agent-based computational order as the sin qua non of emergence. This attention on computational forms of emergence is not misplaced, for great insight about order creation has been gained by scholars associated with the Sante Fe Institute, including Kauffman (1993), Holland (1995, 1998), Gell-Mann (1994, 2002), Crutchfield (1994a, 1994b), Mitchell (2009), and many others outside the Institute, including Carley (1992, 1996, Carley & Prietula, 1994; Carley & Lee, 1998), Tesfatsion (2011), and Levinthal (1997; Levinthal & Warglien, 1999). As detailed in Chapter 3, computational science offers several methodologies for exploring emergent order "in silico," including NK landscapes, cellular automata, genetic algorithms, spin-glass models, and agent-based modeling. Importantly, the driver of pattern formation in all of these is similar; they can be captured within a specific prototype of computational order. (Jeff Goldstein was the first to make this claim; much of my description is based on his insightful analysis.)

In computational emergence, "agents" interact with neighboring agents based on a small number of rules; given the right parameters and a moderate degree of interdependence, macroscopic aggregations of agents will form as discernable patterns, groups, and simple hierarchies. Such computational order increases the agent's adaptability (Kauffman, 1993), learning capability (Holland, 1975, 1995), and performance (Carley & Prietula, 1994; Carley & Svoboda, 1996).

As the sophistication of computational simulations has grown, so too have the variegated forms and patterns of order they display (see Lichtenstein & McKelvey,

2011, for a review). As a result, these models have been usefully applied to a wide range of phenomena, including innovation (Fleming & Sorenson, 2001; Sorenson, Rivkin, & Fleming, 2006), organizational change (Levinthal, 1997; McKelvey, 1999), political alliances (Axelrod & Bennett, 1993; Axelrod et al., 1995), social segregation (Schelling, 1978), and network formation (Carley & Lee, 1998; Carley, 1999).

Like the previous prototype, computational order springs from an input of energy into a highly constrained environment; specifically, electricity fuels the computer and its software, motivating agent interactions in a specific way. But something more is involved, namely the instructions—the rules of interaction—encoded as the computational program itself. These rules provide constructive constraints for agent behavior, which, when combined with a high level of interaction, result in a unique type of emergence. Part of what distinguishes this prototype from social emergence (see discussion of prototype VI) is the origin of the rules: in computational order the rules originate outside the simulation, that is, they are programmed in by the researcher. This approach is beneficial precisely because the researcher can try out many variants of the program over many (hundreds of) runs, thus increasing validity and theoretical robustness of the model (McKelvey, 1999, 2002). The drawback, as argued earlier, is that the imposition of rules on the agents presents limitations in modeling the subtlety of social interactions.[6] In sum, since the value of computational order for understanding emergence is drawn from the particularities of programmable agents, it reflects a distinct prototype of emergence.

The next two prototypes—autocatalysis and symbiogenesis—focus on drivers of biological and evolutionary order creation. These two categories reflect distinct self-generating "engines" of organic and ecological order creation.

Prototype IV—Autocatalysis

In the broadest sense, much of emergence depends on a cycle of positive feedback within the system, which *amplifies* certain behaviors and patterns of order, transferring them from a limited regime to the system as a whole. In fact, the role of amplification in generative emergence is so important that an entire chapter is dedicated to it (see Chapter 12).

Autocatalysis, however, involves something more than amplification. In an autocatalytic system, a macromolecule produced in a chain of reactions (e.g., a polypeptide) itself becomes a *catalyst* that spurs one or more of its precursor reactions in the chain (e.g., increasing the production of its amino acid components). When this happens, the entire cycle becomes a self-amplifying system, producing far greater amounts of the products at far lower energetic costs (Weber et al., 1989; see note[7] for a fuller explanation). The result is "an autocatalytic system capable of pulling energy resources into the propagation of that polypeptide" (Weber et al., 1989, p. 386).

An intriguing metaphor for this process is given by Ulanowicz (2002), who says that an autocatalytic cycle generates a "centripetal vortex" which draws into itself the energy and resources necessary for its own growth and maintenance. He explains:

> Some form of positive feedback is responsible for most of the order we perceive in organic systems. . . . [In autocatalysis] the effect of each and every link in the feedback loop remains positive. . . . [T]he action of each and every element in the cycle quickens the activity of the next member (quicken meaning to make alive as well as to make more rapid). Any autocatalytic cycle becomes the center of a centripetal vortex, pulling as many of the needed resources as possible into its domain. . . . Autocatalytic selection pressure and the competition it engenders define a preferred direction for the system, that of ever more effective autocatalysis. (Ulanowicz, 2002, pp. 39, 42)

This last statement reveals an important corollary, namely that an autocatalytic system has a competitive advantage due to its higher efficiency. This is a core theoretical insight that bolstered research on thermodynamic extensions of neo-Darwinist evolutionary theory, which were developed by Depew and Weber (1985, 1994), Salthe (1985, 1989, 2010), Wicken (1979, 1980, 1986, 1988), and others (Coren, 1998; Morowitz, 2002). Furthermore, the engine of autocatalysis seems to operate at many levels in the biosphere (see Eigen's [1971; Eigen & Schuster, 1979] descriptions of hypercycles as one example), and is central to the other three drivers in this prototype.

Further insights into and applications of autocatalysis have been developed by John Padgett (2011) and his collaborators (Padgett & Ansell 1993; Padget, Lee & Collier, 2003; Padgett & Powell, 2011), who have developed an entire research stream applying the science of autocatalysis to the emergence of social structures and institutions. More on this approach is presented in Chapter 3.

Prototype V—Symbiogenesis

This prototype was discovered by Lynn Margulis (1971, 1981, 1992), whose careful research on the origin of eukaryotes led to her recognition of a unique mode of evolutionary emergence. Jeff Goldstein nicely summarizes symbiogenesis as

> a symbiotic *envelopment* of one microorganism by another, whereby each one retains its integrity through a radical interdependence that enhances the functioning of both. . . . Once the two systems are integrated (through absorption) the functions of both recombine, yielding an overall reduction in the number of parts within the emergent entity. (Goldstein, Hazy, & Lichtenstein, 2010, p. 87).

The "engine" of order creation here is symbiosis—the association of two or more different species that improves the functioning of both. This association can occur in several ways. The first is through "endosymbiosis," in which the two species occur within the same cell, as in the presence of mitochondria in human cells. Reid (2007, p. 98) explains the evolutionary outcome:

> In endosymbiosis there is not only an exchange of energy and molecules between the symbiotic cells, genes have been transferred, resulting in a near monopoly of protein-synthesizing information by the nucleus.

Margulis's research showed exactly how different elements of sexual reproduction were facilitated by endosymbiosis within the cell nucleus.

A second type of association occurs in "symbiocosms"—organisms that are "composed of mosaics and mixes of different symbioses that demonstrate a [very high] degree of interaction" (Reid, 2007, p. 100). One example is the cellulose-digesting microorganisms that occur in cattle and termites. Another, explained by Haines (2002—in Reid, 2007, p. 100) refers to the tsetse fly as not a single insect but "a soup of symbionts," composed of three distinct species that have a mutualistic relationship with the host.

Reid identifies a third type of association, namely the emergence of entire ecosystems through symbiogenesis. Examples include the emergence of marine phytosynthetic ecosystems such as coral reefs, the thiobios ecosystem of prokaryotes in deep-water thermal rift communities, terrestrial plant-fungus ecosystems, and nitrogen-fixing symbiosis. He summarizes his lengthy analysis:

> Symbiogenesis thus provides a way of emerging to new wholes.... The condition of new wholeness that emerges from symbiogenesis is largely due to complementarity of the biochemical, physiological, and behavioral functions of the pre-symbiotic individuals. Margulis (1981) and Douglas (1994) provide long lists of emergent metabolic properties of symbioplexes. (Reid, 2007, p. 116)

Finally, rounding out this "engine" of biological and evolutionary order creation is a quote from Margulis (1998, p. 8):

> From the long view of geological time, symbioses are like flashes of evolutionary lightening. To me symbiosis as a source of evolutionary novelty helps explain the observation of "punctuated equilibrium" of discontinuities in the fossil record.

Beyond these two prototypes of biological emergents—autocatalysis and symbiogenesis—there are other engines of self-generated order. For example, the "ascendency" of ecosystems is based on certain drivers as suggested by Ulanowicz (1980, 2002) and Odum (1969, 1988). Further, Lotka, Odum, and Swenson have made convincing arguments in favor of a law of "maximum power output" (Lotka, 1945; Odum & Pinkerton, 1955; Swenson, 1989, 1997). Together these studies may explain the source of evolutionary success for organisms and ecosystems.

Likewise, Reid (2007) includes three other categories of emergence in biological evolution, and Corning made the compelling claim that "the universe can be portrayed as a vast structure of synergies" (Corning, 2003, p. 5). Still, these two prototypes seem to be the most prevalent (accepted) and unique for the biological world, offering a good foundation for further work.

The next three prototypes focus on emergence of social structures, through collaborative emergence, generative emergence, and collective action.

Prototype VI–Collaborative Emergence: Social Structures

Perhaps the most complete analysis of social emergence in this era has been accomplished by Sawyer (2001, 2002, 2003b, 2004), whose most recent text (Sawyer, 2005) presents a detailed analysis of numerous social emergents, including integration patterns, shared social practices, social institutions, and collective behavior. By way of explaining these examples, he reviews the two prevailing sociological approaches to emergence, namely the structure paradigm and the interaction paradigm, in order to show their benefits and limitations. In doing so, he reveals several distinct levels of analysis that lie between the conventional notions of individual agency and social structure—three intermediate "levels of social reality" that explain the complexity of social emergence. Thus, his emergence paradigm presents social reality as a five-level process, shown in Box 2.1.

The intermediate three levels are related through what he calls "collaborative emergence," which refers to the dynamic interactions between individuals and social structures that constrain and are enabled by ephemeral and stable emergents. Specifically, Sawyer says (2005, pp. 210–211, his italics),

> In any social situation there is a continuing dialectic: social emergence, where individuals are co-creating and co-maintaining ephemeral and stable emergents, and downward causation from those emergents. . . . During conversation encounters, interactional frames emerge, and these are collective social facts that . . . constrain the possibilities for action. [This] frame is . . . analytically independent of those individuals, and it has causal power over them. I refer to this process (Sawyer, 2003a) as *collaborative emergence* . . . The emergence paradigm emphasizes the identification of the mechanisms of collaborative emergence that lead to ephemeral and stable emergents.

Based on this explanation, the drivers of social emergence begin to take shape. At the heart of social emergence is an ongoing stream of interactions across a large number of individuals; each interaction is enabled by the stable emergents at hand, while being simultaneously constrained by them. The result is a stream of *unintended emergent structures* that constrain behavior even as they provide meaning to human action. Although my presentation of Sawyer's work is rather simplistic, it does offer an outline of this prototype of social emergence (see Box 2.1).

> *BOX 2.1* DRIVERS OF SOCIAL EMERGENCE (FROM SAWYER, 2005)
>
> 1. **Individual:** Intention, agency, memory, personality, cognition
> 2. **Interaction level:** Discourse patterns, symbolic interaction, collaboration, negotiation
> 3. **Ephemeral emergents** (i.e., conversation theory): Topic, context, interactional frame, participation structure, relative role and status
> 4. **Stable emergents:** Group subcultures, group slang and catch phrases, conversational routines, shared social practices, collective memory
> 5. **Social structure:** Laws, regulations and institutions; material systems and infrastructure

Sawyer's drivers of social emergence can be further extended to other types of emergents. For example, consider the dynamics of traffic jams, mobs, and even fads. These emergents arise when many autonomous agents are in close proximity and are interacting at a rapid rate. The sum of all these interactions is "stochastic"—no group of agents has primacy and no individual alone can shift the stream of interactions outside of its random occurrence.

Taking a stripped-down version of Sawyer's collaborative emergence, each interaction involves a response (reaction) to the previous interaction that reflects the agent's current preference, aims or cognitive frame. Given a critical mass of agents, in some unpredictable cases these preferential actions can aggregate, perhaps becoming amplified in one direction or another. Like the symmetry-breaking of prototype I, this amplification may lead to an unpredictable emergent—a new level of analysis that is analytically distinct from the mass of agents who make it up.

This description is similar to another example of "social" emergence: the collective behavior of social insects that leads to the construction of, for example, beehives or huge termite mounds. Analysis suggests that these collective processes occur when one insect randomly drops a particle or pheromone in the same place as a previous one; this attracts the same behavior from other insects down the line, until the micro-aggregation amplifies into a physical structure. Although tiny at first, this structure orients (enables and constrains) the behavior of all agents in the colony, who use it as the foundation for an emergent tower or hive activity.

Finally, the drivers of collaborative emergence also help explain social norms and shared practices, and the rise of shared cognitive schema. As such, the same driver can be said to be at the heart of emergent institutions. Although the dynamics of collaborative emergence at the institutional level are likely to be much more complex than the creation of ant hills, institutional emergence shares the key drivers of this prototype: a large number of interactions across agents, co-created rules that guide agent behavior and some form of preferential action. At a micro level these drivers lead to the emergence of patterns between two or several people; at a macro level these drivers scale up to produce patterns of social interaction that emerge as institutional norms. Parsimony leads me to make this claim, that the dynamics underlying collaborative emergence and institutional emergence are similar enough that they can be combined within a single prototype. Institutional scholars and sociologists may disagree, sparking a conversation that can explore these similarities and differences and, more importantly, contribute to the vibrancy of an emergence discipline.

Prototype VII–Generative Emergence

The seventh prototype—generative emergence—adds a significant driver to emergence, namely intentionality. That is, generative emergence refers to the *intentional creation* of organizations, social endeavors, and other ventures. Organizations are generative social entities that emerge through the agentic actions of individuals and groups, an ongoing stream of intentional action with unpredictable results. Such organizing efforts play a fundamental role in our lives; generative emergents are ubiquitous in modern society.

It is surprising to me that organizations are not mentioned in Sawyer's typology; nor are organizations mentioned in most levels-of-analysis typologies, including those developed by systems theorists (e.g., von Bertalanffy, 1956; Ashmos & Huber, 1987; Boulding, 1988). In fact, no previous list of emergents has included organizations as a distinct category. Given how ubiquitous organizations are in society, generative emergence provides a means for understanding their creation.

Generative emergence is the result of an organizing effort directed toward certain aims. By "organizing effort" I would include any endeavor that is initiated with a specific intent, what Juarrero (1999) describes as intentional behavior. In virtually every case, an organizing effort is intended to create an emergent entity—an organization or venture—that generates value in some form for the organizer(s), for others in the community, and for the people who will become customers or clients. When the value that is created through this emergent entity generates the necessary energy and resources to sustain the entity over time, then an organization emerges. In slightly more technical terms, in generative emergence a social entity is created that generates what it needs to continuously generate itself.

There are two drivers of generative emergence that distinguish it from the other prototypes: an intent to create value and a method for doing so. The first, an intent to create value, involves a perception or belief that whatever is to be produced—whether a tangible product, an engaging activity, or a beneficial service of some kind—will be of value to others and to the organizer. This intent provides the motivation for action and the pursuit of requisite tasks for the endeavor (Juarrero, 1999); this is related to the idea of opportunity tension mentioned earlier.

To illustrate this driver of value creation, consider a small business that provides a product. In exchange for that product, customers will pay money—literally exchanging one kind of value for another. That money pays for the resources and activities that provide the value, thus resulting in a generative system. (A similar "formula" can be identified for non-profits, social innovations, and Internet-based ventures; see note[8]). The key driver here is not the money but the initial perception by the organizer(s) that the value they could generate would be found valuable by others—in cinematic terms, "If you build it they will come." Obviously, if the perception of value is not shared by others, the organization will not be sustained.

The second driver, and this is equally challenging, is enacting (developing) a method by which the value actually gets created and delivered to those who want it. In economic terms this is called the "business model," which refers to the combination of activities, resources, and skills that are needed to produce the product or service, tell others about it, and deliver the value in an exchange with the customer. In different language this refers to all of the (emergent) structures and processes that turn the intent into a reality in ways that are sustainable—at least for the organizer(s).

In a broad sense there are comparisons between these drivers and other drivers already mentioned (see Table 2.1, later in this chapter). In particular, generative emergence is infused with aspects of autocatalysis, far-from-equilibrium states, amplification, and collaborative emergence. For example, just as an autocatalytic loop emerges when the output of one reaction improves the likelihood of a previous step in the cycle, so too, generative emergence occurs when the output of an organizing effort improves the likelihood of a continuation of the previous steps in the cycle. Similar comparisons could be made with the other drivers.

The key difference, however, is the role of human intent and human agency in organizing a social entity. No such intent exists in other prototypes of emergence. For example, social emergence is "unintended" (Sawyer, 2005, p. 213), computational agents act without design or intent, and surely a tree does not grow because of an "intent" to create value for itself and its ecosystem. Nor are these actions projective; a cell doesn't perceive that by enveloping a mitochondria it will gain enormous energetic benefits. Yet in each case there are synergistic benefits whereby something valuable is produced by the emergent. Likewise in each case, there is a method for producing that value, whether through an exchange of energy resources, an aggregation that amplifies agents' individual actions, an "interaction frame" that sets the conditions for interchange between human agents, or "rules" that guide agent action and interaction.

So, in some sense the main addition in generative emergence is *agency*—a self-conscious motivation to cause order to arise. Such causal agency is anathema to virtually all formulations of self-organization; as noted in Chapter 1, an entire literature has developed that exclaims the lack of a central controller as a key insight from complexity science (Goldstein et al., 2010).[9] As mentioned earlier, one of the key moves I am making in the book is separating out the term *self-organization* from emergence, in order to capture the qualities of social order creation while giving primacy to the role of agency in the process.

By including human agency into the arena of emergence, we can finally explore one of the most prevalent and impactful forms of emergence in the world today: the creation of organizations. This is done through the use of complexity science as a tool and the other forms of emergence as a backdrop. In effect, this entire book is an effort to introduce generative emergence as a prototype with the same validity and theoretical strength as that of the other prototypes.

Prototype VIII—Collective Action: Emergence of Social Aggregates

In this first draft of the prototypes for emergence, the eighth prototype is collective action. Here, the elements of emergence are themselves semi-autonomous agents, like organizations or ventures. For example, in the SEMATECH example, a group of companies developed an emergent entity, a collaborative that was stronger than the individual firms within it. Such collectives are important and interesting, for they provide the innovations in our society, acting collectively to pursue a positive outcome.

This is a distinct prototype, because it refers to collections of organizations or social entities, which together seem to exhibit a shared intention or goal. Such aggregations can include the creation of new industries, product markets, organizational communities, and industrial ecologies (Garud, Jain, & Kumaraswamy, 2002; Garud, Kumaraswamy, & Sambamurthy, 2006; Garud, Kumaraswamy, & Karnøe, 2010; Chiles et al., 2010; Dew et al., 2011). To be clear, the breadth of interactions across organizations and institutions presents new dynamics yet to be understood.

In sociology and organization theory, researchers have been exploring such large-scale organizing efforts, in two primary ways. First, researchers of institutional entrepreneurship have explored the conditions for radical change and innovation at the institutional level (Lawrence, Hardy, & Phillips, 2002; Maguire, Hardy, & Lawrence, 2004; Maguire & Hardy, 2009; Purdy & Gray, 2009). Second, social movements theory has identified some of the dynamics that arise which lead to collective endeavors—organizing efforts that are intended to create change. These are emergent—they are emergents within a broader social ecology that continues to evolve. Exploring the dynamics of that process is the aim of collective action (Zald & Berger, 1978; Scully & Segal, 2002).

It turns out that a rigorous mapping of the five-phase process onto these macro-organizational entities reveals a strong correspondence, with some important differences that are discussed in Chapter 17. In terms of drivers, the emergence of organizational aggregates is driven first of all by the intent to create value to a much broader scope, and is augmented by some of the engines of collaborative emergence, including an ongoing stream of interactions across a large number of agents, preferential actions that aggregate into microstructures that attract and amplify further actions, and some form of "symbiosis"—mutual benefit—through association. As I suggest in Chapter 18, these thoughts provide some direction for future work.

INITIAL ANALYSIS: SIX DRIVERS OF EMERGENCE

Although the eight prototypes are distinct, there are correspondences between the drivers of emergence across all the prototypes. As a preliminary analysis, consider my descriptions of the emergence drivers within each prototype (Table 2.1), and then the sorting of these into a single set of proposed drivers and conditions (Table 2.2). In this preliminary analysis, the drivers or conditions that are most prominent across all eight prototypes are as follows:

- Interdependence of agents
- Large N of interacting agents
- Amplification
- Far-from-equilibrium state
- Rules that guide agent behavior
- Preferential action

Table 2.1 DRIVERS OF EMERGENCE ACROSS THE EIGHT PROTOTYPES

Prototype Name	Drivers Described	Initial Conditions
I: Relational properties	Large N of interacting agents	
	Relationships → Properties	
II: Exo-organization	High energy driven into system	Far-from-equilibrium state
	Closed (constrained) container	Amplification
III: Computational order	Large N of interacting agents	Ongoing stream of interactions
	A few rules guide agent behavior	Interdependence of agents
IV: Autocatalysis	A reaction chain produces its own catalyst	Far-from-equilibrium state
		Amplification
		Interdependence of agents
V: Symbiogenesis	Symbiosis through envelopment or association	
VI: Collaborative emergence	Large N of interacting agents	Ongoing stream of interactions
	Emergent rules guide agent behavior	Aggregation → amplification
		Interdependence of agents
	Preferential action	
VII: Generative emergence	Intent to create value	Far-from-equilibrium state
	Method for producing value	Collaborative emergence
		Amplification
		Interdependence of agents
VIII: Collective action	Intent to create value	Collaborative emergence
	Large N of interacting agents	Rules (local + institutional) guide agent behavior
	Ongoing stream of interactions	Preferential action
	Symbiosis through association	Interdependence of agents

Table 2.2 EMERGENCE DRIVERS AND CONDITIONS MENTIONED IN TWO OR MORE PROTOTYPES

Driver/Condition of Emergence	Mentioned in Which Prototypes
Interdependence of agents	III. Computational order
	IV. Autocatalysis
	VI. Collaborative emergence
	VII. Generative emergence
	VIII. Generative emergence—macro
Large N of interacting agents	I. Relational properties
	III. Computational order
	VI. Collaborative emergence
	VIII. Generative emergence—macro
Amplification	II. Exo-organization
	IV. Autocatalysis
	VI. Collaborative emergence
	VII. Generative emergence
Ongoing stream of interaction	III. Computational order
	VI. Collaborative emergence
	VIII. Generative emergence—macro
Far-from-equilibrium state	II. Exo-organization
	IV. Autocatalysis
	VII. Generative emergence
Rules guide agent behavior	III. Computational order
	VI. Collaborative emergence
	VIII. Generative emergence—macro

Even this cursory analysis reveals dynamics that may be helpful in gaining a deeper understanding of emergence overall, and in defining the contours for a discipline of emergence.

Toward Generative Emergence, Through Complexity Science

The rest of this book focuses on one of the eight prototypes or fields of emergence, namely generative emergence. Although much of what I will show may be valid for the other prototypes of emergence, my empirical research is based in organization science and entrepreneurship, and is thus focused on organizations and social entities as the unit of analysis. Thus, I can be confident of my findings within that arena (only), that is, within the context of generative emergence, and I am confident of applications of this work into the social sciences. At the same time, this nascent arena also holds promise for understanding the creation and re-creation of our projects, ventures, organizations, and, potentially, our collaborations, shared endeavors, alliances, cross-sector initiatives, social relations, new products, and technologies.

How can these dynamics be explored? Complexity science provides the methods for studying emergence. McKelvey (2001) was strong in his claim that complexity science is "really order-creation science." Each of the 15 sciences of complexity provide important avenues for exploring emergence. The chapter which follows provides a detailed introduction to each of the sciences—it is especially written for PhD students and scholars, with an aim to support research designs that can capture emergence and its dynamics.

NOTES

1. Peter Corning (1983, 2003, 2005) has shown how this apparently simple quality of synergy is central to the buildup of structure throughout the universe: "The universe can be portrayed as a vast structure of synergies, a many-leveled edifice in which the synergies produced at one level serve as the building blocks for the next level" (Corning, 2003, p. 5). Some examples make clear the breadth of his view: synergies are expressed in the center of gravity of an object, in the properties of "supermolecules," in the strength of metal alloys, in the success of lichen, and in the fact that the combination of two toxic molecules, chlorine and sodium, result in a molecule that is critical for life—NaCl, i.e., table salt. Overall, his categories of synergy include the following:

   Synergies of scale—large aggregates have properties that their individual parts do not (similar to prototype 1)
   Threshold effects—critical points that precipitate a change of state (see Chapter 13 in this book)
   Phase transitions—radical change of state in physical or biological systems
   Gestalt effects—the ability to form (perceive) wholes out of parts
   Functional complementarities—combined action of complementary parts, e.g., lichen symbioses; Velcro; bricks and mortar create stable dwellings
   Augmentation—e.g., catalysts encourage reactions that would otherwise be impossible
   Risk- and cost-sharing—larger groupings reduce individuals' risks and costs, in, for example, schools of fish, collective foraging, and insurance in human societies
   Combination of labor—in social insects, as well as in human organizations and society

   Although these are not drivers of emergence per se, many of them are implied in these prototypes. Equally important, they act as order-creation engines which, when combined with other drivers, lead to emergents in the biological, ecological, and social world.
2. Specifically, Corning proposes that *emergence* should *not* be used as a synonym for *synergy*. Instead, he proposes "that emergent phenomena be defined as a 'subset' of the vast (and still expanding) universe of cooperative interactions that produce synergistic effects... both in nature and in human societies" (2003, p. 16).
3. That is, materially closed, but energetically open.
4. Those familiar with this example will recognize Haken's emphasis on the phase-locking aspect, which he described as "enslavement" (Haken, 1977, 2008; Bushev, 1994).
5. In general, these reflect the "European school" of complexity science; see McKelvey (2004) and Andriani & McKelvey (2007, 2009).

6. As mentioned in Chapter 1, Sawyer notes two key limitations in computational simulations (Sawyer, 2004, pp. 165–166):

> First, the macrostructures or macroproperties do not themselves emerge from the simulation but are imposed by the designer. Yet in actual societies, macrophenomena are themselves emergent from microprocesses.... A second problem in applying these multilevel artificial societies to sociological theory is that agents do not have any perception of the emergent collective entity (Castelfranchi, 1998; Conte et al., 1998; Servat et al., 1998). In the CORMAS simulation, agents do not know that they are being taxed, nor that a quota has been imposed. In the EOS simulation of group formation ... no agent has awareness of its own group as an entity, and agents that are not in a group have no way of recognizing that the group exists or who its members are.

7. Consider the following dissipative route, described by Weber et al., 1989, Figure 1, p. 386: A proto-receptor X delivers excitation energy to an amino acid reaction, $A \sim P$, which then yields polypeptides PP. In autocatalysis, these polypeptides feed forward, i.e., they catalyze the steps that lead to their production. This illustrates an autocatalytic system, which is capable of pulling energy and resources into itself, to initiate its own continued propagation.
8. Of course, small business is the simplest case. As other examples, consider social media, where customers "pay attention" to the site, thus exchanging their time for the information or network. More complex are non-profit and governmental organizations, which offer services to people who do not pay for them. In non-profits these services are often valuable to "donors" who donate funds that maintain the organization. In governmental organizations, the value is accrued to society, which pays for it through taxes and other measures. Many other variants can be described, and shall be throughout the book.
9. Perhaps a more ingenious way to explain my addition of agency is through Alicia Juarrero's (1999) marvelously helpful reinterpretation of intentional behavior as reflecting a complex system.

REFERENCES

Anderson, P. 1972. More is different. *Science*, 177(4047): 393–96.

Andriani, P., & McKelvey, B. 2007. Beyond Gaussian averages: Redirecting organization science toward extreme events and power laws. *Journal of International Business Studies*, 38: 1212–30.

Andriani, P., & McKelvey, B. 2009. From Gaussian to Paretian thinking: Causes and implications of power laws in organizations. *Organization Science*, 20: 1053–71.

Arrow, H., & Burns, K. L. 2004. Self-organizing culture: How norms emerge in small groups. In M. Schaller & C. Crandall (Eds.), *The Psychological Foundations of Culture* (171–99). Mahwah, NJ: Lawrence Erlbaum Associates.

Ashmos, D., & Huber, G. 1987. The system paradigm in organization theory: Correcting the record and suggesting the future. *Academy of Management Review*, 12: 607–21.

Axelrod, R. 1997. *The Complexity of Cooperation: Agent-Based Models of Competition and Cooperation*. Princeton, NJ: Princeton University Press.

Axelrod, R., & Bennett, D. S. 1993. A landscape theory of aggregation. *British Journal of Political Science*, 23: 211–33.

Axelrod, R., Mitchell, W., Thomas, R., Bennett, D. S., & Bruderer, E. 1995. Coalition formation in standard-setting alliances. *Management Science*, 41: 1493–508.
Bak, P., & Chen, K. 1991. Self-organized criticality. *Scientific American*, January: 46–53.
Bonner, J. T. 1959. Differentiation in social amoebae. *Scientific American*, 201: 152–62.
Boulding, K. 1988. *The World as a Total System*. Thousand Oaks, CA: SAGE Publications.
Bushev, M. 1994. *Synergetics: Chaos, Order, Self-Organization*. Singapore: World Scientific.
Carley, K. 1992. Organizational learning and personnel turnover. *Organization Science*, 3: 20–46.
Carley, K. 1996. A comparison of artificial and human organizations. *Journal of Economic Behavior and Organization*, 31: 175–91.
Carley, K. 1999. On the evolution of social and organizational networks. In S. Andrews & D. Knoke (Eds.), *Research in the Sociology of Organizations*, Vol. 16: 3–30. Stamford, CT: JAI Press.
Carley, K., & Lee, J.-S. 1998. Dynamic organizations: Organizational adaptation in a changing environment. *Advances in Strategic Management*, 15: 269–97.
Carley, K., & Prietula, M. 1994. *Computational Organization Theory*. Hillsdale, NJ: Lawrence Erlbaum & Associates.
Carley, K., & Svoboda, D. M. 1996. Modeling organization adaptation as a simulated annealing process. *Sociological Methods and Research*, 25: 138–68.
Carniero, R. 1970. A theory of the origin of the state. *Science*, 169: 733–8.
Carniero, R. 1987. The evolution of complexity in human societies and it mathematical expression. *International Journal of Comparative Sociology*, 28: 111–28.
Castelfranchi, C. 1998. Simulating with cognitive agents: The importance of cognitive emergence. In J. Sichman, R. Conte & N. Gilbert (Eds.) *Multi-Agent Systems and Agent-Based Simulation* (26–44). Berlin: Springer-Verlag.
Chaisson, E. 2001. *Cosmic Evolution: The Rise of Complexity in Nature*. Cambridge, MA: Harvard University Press.
Chiles, T., Meyer, A., & Hench, T. 2004. Organizational emergence: The origin and transformation of Branson, Missouri's musical theaters. *Organization Science*, 15(5): 499–520.
Chiles, T., Tuggle, C. S., McMullen, J., Bierman, L., & Greening, D. 2010. Dynamic creation: Elaborating a radical Austrian approach to entrepreneurship. *Organization Studies*, 31: 7–46.
Conte, R., Edmonds, B., Moss, S. & Sawyer, K. 1998. Sociology and social theory in agent-based social simulation: A symposium. *Computational and Mathematical Organization Theory*, 7: 183–205.
Conway, J. 1970. The game of life. *Scientific American*, 223(4): 4.
Coren, R. 1998. *The Evolutionary Trajectory: The Growth of Information in the History and Future of the Earth*. Amsterdam: Gordon and Breach Publishers.
Corning, P. 1983. *The Synergism Hypothesis: A Theory of Progressive Evolution*. New York: McGraw Hill.
Corning, P. 2002. The re-emergence of "emergence": A vernerable concept in search of a theory. *Complexity*, 7(6): 18–30.
Corning, P. 2003. *Nature's Magic: Synergy in Evolution and the Fate of Humankind*: New York: Cambridge University Press.
Corning, P. 2005. *Holistic Darwinism: Synergy, Cybernetics, and the Bioeconomics of Evolution*. Chicago: Universtiy of Chicago Press.
Corning, P., & Kline, S. J. 1998. Thermodynamics, information and life revisited, part I: "To be or entropy." *Systems Research and Behavioral Science*, 15: 273–95.
Crutchfield, J. 1994a. The calculi of emergence: Computation, dynamics and induction. *Physica D: Nonlinear Phemonema*, 75(1): 11–54. Reprinted in SFI 94-03-016. Special Issue on the Proceedings of: Complex Systems—From Complex Dynamics to Artificial Reality.

Crutchfield, J. 1994b. Is anything ever new? Considering emergence. In G. Cowan, D. Pines, & D. Meltzer (Eds.), *Complexity: Metaphors, models, and Realty* (479–97). Reading, MA: Addison-Wesley.

Deacon, T. 2003. The hierarchic logic of emergence: Untangling the interdependence of evolution and self-organization. In B. Weber & D. Depew (Eds.), *Evolution and Learning: The Baldwin Effect Reconsidered* (273–308): Cambridge, MA: MIT Press.

Deacon, T. 2006. Emergence: The hold at the wheel's hub. In P. Clayton & P. Davies (Eds.), *The Re-Emergence of Emergence: The Emergentist Hypothesis from Science to Religion* (111–50). New York: Oxford University Press.

Depew, D., & Weber, B. (Eds.). 1985. *Evolution at a Crossroads: The New Biology and the New Philosophy of Science*. Cambridge, MA: MIT Press.

Depew, D., & Weber, B. 1994. *Darwinism Evolving*. New York: Oxford University Press.

Dew, N., Reed, S., Sarasvathy, S., & Wiltbank, R. 2011. On the entrepreneurial genesis of new markets: Effectual transformations versus causal search and selection. *Journal of Evolutionary Economics*, 21: 231–53.

Douglas, A. E. 1994. *Symbiotic Interactions*. Oxford, UK: Oxford University Press.

Ehrenfeld, J. 2007. Would industrial ecology exist without sustainability in the background? *Journal of Industrial Ecology*, 11: 73–84.

Eigen, M. 1971. Self-organization of matter and the evolution of biological macromolecules. *Naturwissenschaften*, 58: 465–523.

Eigen, M., & Schuster, P. 1979. *The Hypercycle: A Principle of Natural Self-Organizing; In Three Parts*. New York: Springer.

Ellis, G. 2006. On the nature of emergent reality. In P. Clayton & P. Davies (Eds.), *The Re-Emergence of Emergence: The Emergentist Hypothesis from Science to Religion* (79–110). NewYork: Oxford University Press.

Fleming, L., & Sorenson, O. 2001. Technology as a complex adaptive system. *Research Policy*, 30: 1019–39.

Folke, C., Carpenter, S., Walker, B., Scheffer, M., Elmqvist, T., Gunderson, L., & Holling, C. S. 2004. Regime shifts, resilience, and biodiversity in ecosystem management. *Annual Review of Ecology, Evolution, and Systematics*, 35: 557–81.

Gartner, W. 1993. Words lead to deeds: Towards an organizational emergence vocabulary. *Journal of Business Venturing*, 8: 231–9.

Gartner, W., Shaver, K., Carter, N., & Reynolds, P. (Eds.). 2004. *Handbook of Entrepreneurial Dynamics*. Thousand Oaks, CA: SAGE Publications.

Garud, R., Jain, S., & Kumaraswamy, A. 2002. Institutional entrepreneurship in the sponsorship of comon technological standards: The case of Sun Microsystems and Java. *Academy of Management Journal*, 45: 196–214.

Garud, R., Kumaraswamy, A., & Karnøe, P. 2010. Path dependence or path creation? *Journal of Management Studies*, 47(4): 760–74.

Garud, R., Kumaraswamy, A., & Sambamurthy, V. 2006. Emergent by design: Performance and transformation at Infosys Technologies. *Organization Science*, 17: 277–86.

Gell-Mann, M. 1994. *The Quark and the Jaguar*. New York: W.H. Freeman.

Gell-Mann, M. 2002. What is complexity? In A. Q. Curzio & M. Fortis (Eds.), *Complexity and Industrial Clusters* (13–24). Heidelberg: Physica-Verlag.

Giddens, A. 1984. *The Constitution of Society: Outline of the Theory of Structuration*. Cambridge, UK: Polity Press.

Gilbert, N., & Conte, R. (Eds.). 1995. *Artificial Societies: The Computer Simulation of Social Life*. London: Taylor & Francis.

Goldstein, J. 2011. Probing the nature of complex systems: Parameters, modeling, interventions—Part 1. *Emergence: Complexity and Organization*, 13(3): 94–121.

Goldstein, J., Hazy, J., & Lichtenstein, B. 2010. *Complexity and the Nexus of Leadership: Leveraging Nonlinear Science to Create Ecologies of Innovation* New York: Palgrave Macmillan.

Guastello, S. 1998. Self-organization and leadership emergence. *Nonlinear Dynamics, Psychology, and Life Sciences*, 2: 301–15.

Haken, H. 1977. *Synergetics*. Berlin: Springer-Verlag.

Haken, H. 2008. Self-organization. *Scholarpedia*, 3(8): 1401.

Holland, J. 1975. *Adaptation in Natural and Artificial Systems*. Ann Arbor, MI: University of Michigan Press.

Holland, J. 1995. *Hidden Order*. Redwood City, CA: Addison-Wesley.

Holland, J. 1998. *Emergence: From Chaos to Order*. Cambridge, MA: Perseus Books.

Jantsch, E. 1980. *The Self-Organizing Universe*. New York: Pergamon Press.

Johnson, S. 2001. *Emergence: The Connected Lives of Ants, Brains, Cities, and Software*. New York: Scribner.

Juarrero, A. 1999. *Dynamics in Action: Intentional Behavior as a Complex System*. Cambridge, MA: MIT Press.

Katz, J., & Gartner, W. 1988. Properties of emerging organizations. *Academy of Management Review*, 13: 429–41.

Kauffman, S. 1993. *The Origins of Order*. New York: Oxford University Press.

Lang, K., & Lang, G. E. 1961. *Collective Dynamics*. New York: Thomas Crowell Co.

Lawrence, T., Hardy, C., & Phillips, N. 2002. Institutional effects of interorganizational collaboration: The emergence of proto-institutions. *Academy of Management Journal*, 45: 281–90.

Levinthal, D. 1997. Adaptation on rugged landscapes. *Management Science*, 43: 934–50.

Levinthal, D., & Warglien, M. 1999. Landscape deisgn: Designing for local action in complex worlds. *Organization Science*, 10(3): 342–57.

Lichtenstein, B., Carter, N., Dooley, K., & Gartner, W. 2007. Complexity dynamics of nascent entrepreneurship. *Journal of Business Venturing*, 22: 236–61.

Lichtenstein, B., & McKelvey, B. 2011. Four types of emergence: A typology of complexity and its implications for a science of management. *International Journal of Complexity in Leadership and Management*, 1(4): 339–78.

Lotka, A. 1945. The law of evolution as a maximal principle. *Human Biology*, 17: 167–94.

Maguire, S., & Hardy, C. 2009. Discourse and deinstitutionalization: The decline of DDT. *Academy of Management Review*, 52: 148–78.

Maguire, S., Hardy, C., & Lawrence, T. 2004. Institutional entrepreneurship in emerging fields: HIV/AIDS treatment advocacy in Canada. *Academy of Management Journal*, 47: 657–80.

Margulis, L. 1967. On the origin of mitosing cells. *Journal of Theoretical Biology*, 14: 225–74.

Margulis, L. 1971. Symbiosis and evolution. *Scientific American*, 225(2): 49–57.

Margulis, L. 1981. *Symbiosis in Cell Evolution: Life and its Environment on the Early Earth*. New York: W. H. Freeman.

Margulis, L. 1992. Biodiversity: Molecular biological domains, symbiosis and kingdom origins. *Biosystems*, 27: 39–51.

Margulis, L. 1998. *Symbiotic Planet: A New View of Evolution*. New York: Basic Books.

McKelvey, B. 1999. Avoiding complexity catastrophe in coevolutionary pockets: Strategies for rugged landscapes. *Organization Science*, 10(3): 294–321.

McKelvey, B. 2004. Toward a complexity science of entrepreneurship. *Journal of Business Venturing*, 19: 313–42.

Mitchell, M. 2009. *Complexity: A Guided Tour*. New York: Oxford University Press.

Morowitz, H. 2002. *The Emergence of Everything*. New York: Oxford University Press.

Nagel, K. & Paczuski, M. 1995. Emergent traffic jams. *Physical Review E*, 51(4): 2909.

Nicolis, G., & Prigogine, I. 1989. *Exploring Complexity*. New York: W. H. Freeman.
Odum, H. 1969. The strategy of ecosystem development. *Science*, 164: 262–70.
Odum, H. 1988. Self-organization, transformity, and information. *Science*, 242: 1132–39.
Odum, H., & Pinkerton, R. 1955. Time's speed regulator: The optimum efficiency for maximum power output in physical and biological systems. *American Scientist*, 43(2): 331–43.
Padgett, J., & Ansell, C. 1993. Robust action and the rise of the Medici, 1400–1434. *American Journal of Sociology*, 98(6): 1259–1319.
Padgett, J., Lee, D., & Collier, N. 2003. Economic production as chemistry. *Industrial and Corporate Change*, 12(4): 843–77.
Padgett, J., & Powell, W. 2011. *The Emergence of Organizations and Markets*. Princeton, NJ: Princeton University Press.
Prigogine, I. 1955. *Introduction to the Thermodynamics of Irreversible Processes*. New York: John Wiley & Sons.
Prigogine, I., & Stengers, I. 1984. *Order out of Chaos*. New York: Bantam Books.
Purdy, J., & Gray, B. 2009. Conflicting logics, mechanisms of diffusion, and multi-level dynamics of emergence in institutional fields. *Academy of Management Journal*, 52: 355–80.
Reid, R. 2007. *Biological Emergences: Evolution by Natural Experiment*. Cambridge, MA: Bradford Books—MIT Press.
Salthe, S. 1985. *Evolving Hierarchical Systems: Their Structure and Representation*. New York: Columbia University Press.
Salthe, S. 1989. Self-organization of/in hierarchically structured systems. *Systems Research*, 6(3): 199–208.
Salthe, S. 2010. Development (and evolution) of the universe. *Foundations of Science*, 15: 357–67.
Sarasvathy, S., & Dew, N. 2005. New market creation through transformation. *Journal of Evolutionary Economics*, 15: 533–65.
Sawyer, K. 2001. Simulating emergence and downward causation in small groups. In S. Moss & P. Davidsson (Eds.), *Multi-Agent-Based Simulation* (49–67). Berlin: Springer.
Sawyer, K. 2002. Nonreductive individualsm, part 1: Supervenience and wild ddisjunction. *Philosophy of the Social Sciences*, 32: 537–59.
Sawyer, K. 2003a. *Improvised Dialogues: Emergence and Creativity in Conversation*. Westfield, CT: Greenwood Press.
Sawyer, K. 2003b. Nonreductive individualism, part 2: Social causation. *Philosophy of the Social Sciences*, 33: 203–24.
Sawyer, K. 2004. The mechanisms of emergence. *Philosophy of the Social Sciences*, 34: 260–82.
Sawyer, K. 2005. *Social Emergence: Societies as Complex Systems*. New York: Cambridge University Press.
Schelling, T. 1978. *Micromotives and Macrobehavior*. New York: W. W. Norton.
Schumpeter, J. 1934. *The Theory of Economic Development*. Boston: Harvard University Press.
Scully, M., & Segal, A. 2002. Passion with an umbrella: Grassroots activists in the workplace. In M. Lounsbury & M. Ventresca (Eds.), *Social Structure and Organizations Revisited* (19: 125–69). Oxford, UK: JAI/Elsevier Science.
Servat, D., Perrier, E., Treuil, J. P., & Drogoul, A. 1998. When agents emerge from agents: Introducing multi-scale viewpoints in multi-agent simulations. In J. Sichman, R. Conte, & N. Gilbert (Eds.), *Multi-Agent Systems and Agent-Based Simulation*, (183–98). Berlin: Springer-Verlag.
Sorenson, O., Rivkin, J., & Fleming, L. 2006. Complexity, networks and knowledge flow. *Research Policy*, 35: 994–1017.
Swenson, R. 1988. *Emergence and the principle of maximum entropy production: Multi-level system theory, evolution, and nonequilibrium thermodynamics*. Paper presented at the Proceedings of the 32nd Annual Meeting of the ISGSR.

Swenson, R. 1989. Emergent attractor and the law of maximum entropy production: Foundations to a theory of general evolution. *Systems Research*, 6(3): 187–97.
Swenson, R. 1997. Autocatakinetics, evolution, and the law of maximum entropy production: A principled foundation towards the study of human ecology. *Advances in Human Ecology*, 6: 1–47.
Tesfatsion, L. 2011. Agent-based modeling and institutional design. *Eastern Economic Journal*, 37: 13–19.
Ulanowicz, R. 1980. An hypothesis on the development of natural communities. *Journal of Theoretical Biology*, 85: 225–45.
Ulanowicz, R. 2002. Ecology, a dialog between the quick and the dead. *Emergence*, 4(1-2): 34–52.
Viega, L. B., & Magrini, A. 2009. Eco-industrial park development in Rio de Janeiro, Brazil: A tool for sustainable development. *Journal of Cleaner Production*, 145: 638–49.
von Bertalanffy, L. 1956. General system theory. *General Systems*, 1: 1–10.
Walker, B., Gunderson, L., Kinzig, A., Folke, C., Carpenter, S., & Schultz, L. 2006. A handful of hueristics and some propositions for understanding resilience in social-ecological systems. *Ecology and Society*, 11(1): 13–29.
Weber, B., Depew, B., Dyke, C., Salthe, S., Schneider, E., Ulanowicz, R., & Wicken, J. 1989. Evolution in thermodynamic perspective: An ecological approach. *Biology and Philosophy*, 4: 373–405.
Wicken, J. 1979. The generation of complexity in evolution: A thermodynamic and information-theoretical discussion. *Journal of Theoretical Biology*, 87: 9–23.
Wicken, J. 1980. A thermodynamic theory of evolution. *Journal of Theoretical Biology*, 87: 9–23.
Wicken, J. 1986. Evolutionary self-organization and entropic dissipation in biological and socioeconomic systems. *Journal of Social and Biological Structures*, 9: 261–73.
Wicken, J. 1988. Thermodynamics, evolution, and emergence: Ingredients for a new synthesis. In B. Weber, D. Depew, & J. D. Smith (Eds.), *Entropy, Information, and Evolution: New Perspectives on Physical and Biological Evolution* (139–72). Cambridge, MA: MIT Press.
Wilson, E. O., & Holldobler, B. 1990. *The Ants*. Cambridge, MA: Harvard University Press.
Zald, M. & Berger, M. 1978. Social movements in organizations: Coup d'etat, insurgency, and mass movements. *American Journal of Sociology*, 83(4): 823–61.

CHAPTER 3

Studying Emergence: 15 Fields of Complexity Science

The eight prototypes provide the structure for a discipline of emergence. Equally important to the formation of a discipline are the methods that can be used to study it. This chapter presents those methods, organized as 15 distinct fields of complexity science. Although each of these complexity sciences is unique, they all share some underlying assumptions, premises that are central to generative emergence. Thus, before presenting each of the complexity sciences, I begin by uncovering those assumptions.

The easiest way to explain these assumptions is to contrast them with the way most scientists and social scientists see the world, namely in terms of general linear reality (Abbott, 1988). In particular, traditional social analysis assumes that individual "agents" (individuals) are independent and identically distributed, that they act in a *linear* way, and that more encompassing units of analysis like organizations or institutions are merely aggregations of agents. Thus, in contrast to the assumptions of emergence, the premise of a reductionist view of the world is that all of reality can be explained by understanding its parts and their direct relationships; nothing more than that "exists" in any tangible sense.

However, just as an emergent property cannot be reduced to or solely explained by the components of the system, so too an exploration of emergence cannot be done using a reductionist paradigm. Instead, understanding emergence requires a fundamental shift in the worldview that underlies traditional scientific methodologies. This shift was the origin of the complexity sciences. In particular, this shift to a more systemic framework had begun in the natural sciences in the 1950s and was soon applied to the social sciences through the creation of general systems theory. Later these all morphed into what we now call complexity science. By reviewing the origins of that early work and how it evolved, we can gain insight into how to extend it into the study of emergence, and generative emergence in particular. This chapter begins that process.

ORIGINS OF COMPLEXITY SCIENCE

General Systems Theory: Initiating a Shift of Perspective

In the 1960s, social science applications of concepts from cybernetics (Ashby, 1956), "self-organization" (Prigogine, 1955), and ecology (Odum & Pinkerton, 1955) became integrated into general systems theory. Originators of this somewhat radical approach included Ludwig von Bertalanffy (1950, 1956), along with his colleagues Heinrich von Foerster (1960), Kenneth Boulding (1961), and Buckminister Fuller (1969).[1] These thinkers together developed a new method and approach to science which promised to identify general principles for all systems—an interdisciplinary framework for science. The comprehensive text for the new field, *General System Theory*, by von Bertalanffy (1956), became the basis of the open systems model that even today pervades modern management and underlies much of the social sciences.

The basic idea of open systems is that organizations (a) take in resources from the environment, (b) process them in a useful way, and (c) transfer the output back to the environment. In simple formulation, all natural and social systems operate according to an input → throughput → output framework.[2]

General systems theory is, in the words of von Bertalanffy (1956), "a general science of 'wholeness' based on mathematically realizable properties and propositions." The long-term goal of these theorists was a unity of the sciences, a shift from reductionism to "perspectivism," and ultimately to *organization* as a unifying principle that would guide the "physical, biological, social and moral universe." Von Bertalanffy's vision was enthusiastically embraced by his colleagues and others with great hopes—these hopes were encapsulated by von Bertalanffy in the long title of his second edition: *General System Theory—Foundations, Development, Applications: An Authoritative Introduction to One of the Most Important Theoretical and Methodological Reorientations in Contemporary Physical, Biological, Behavioral and Social Sciences.*

The most concerted effort to realize these goals was pursued by James Grier Miller (1978) in his remarkable book *Living Systems*. In this 1,000+ page text (with 3,326 footnotes!), Miller identifies 19 critical subsystems that underlie every realization of a living system at all biological levels, from cell to organ to organism to group to organization to society to global systems. In rigorous and nearly mathematical terms, he lays out sets of hypotheses that refer to the structure, process, and interactions of these subsystems, each of which could be operationalized in at least two of the seven levels of living systems. In sum, he developed 442 testable propositions that seek to explain the activity of all systems across all the sciences. Although the vast majority of these were never pursued, they reflect his vision for a truly integrated science:

> A general theory of living systems . . . implies a unity of science. It contends that the method which has advanced physical science can also advance the science of living systems. (Miller, 1978, p. 7)

Over time, this integrative vision of general systems theory was expressed in a variety of scientific modalities, some of which became unique disciplines of their own, as I show next.

Foundations of Complexity Science

The most comprehensive historical overview of complexity science is Goldstein's (1999) article on "emergence as a construct." In addition to proposing a parsimonious set of characteristics for emergence, he developed a visual "map" of the "mathematical and scientific roots of emergence" (Goldstein 1999, p. 55) which has since been updated twice (Goldstein, Hazy, & Lichtenstein, 2010, p. 7; in http://emergentfool.com/category/complex-quotes/ (see Figure 3.1). His foundations include cybernetics, game theory, autopoiesis, fractal geometry, catastrophe theory, self-organized criticality, among others.

Goldstein makes an important distinction in his analysis, namely that the early disciplines of information theory and general systems theory focused on systems that were "simple, linear and equilibrium seeking, in contrast to the complex nonlinear and nonequilibrium systems in which complexity theory is interested" (Goldstein, 1999, p. 55). This idea comes clear through disciplines that are expressly focused on complex and emergent phenomena, including nonlinear dynamical systems theory, social networks, computational theories (including cellular automata, agent-based models, and game theory), as well as synergetics, nonequilibrium thermodynamics, and biological emergence—all of which are among the 15 fields of complexity science.

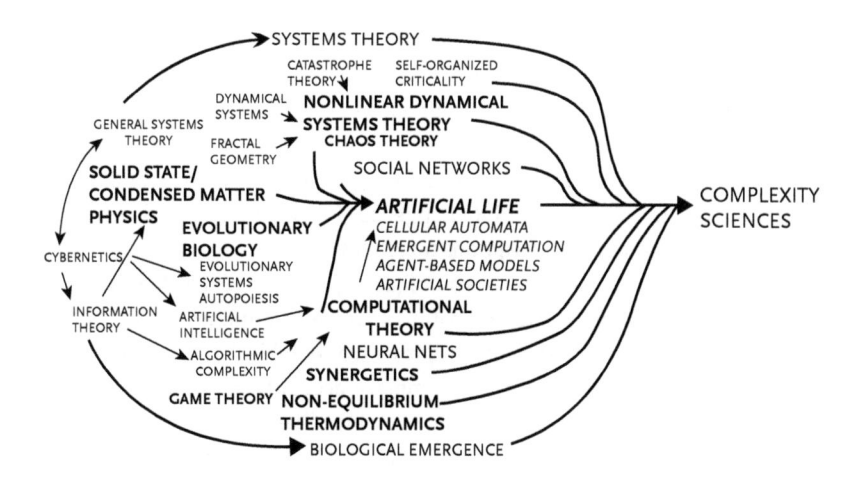

Figure 3.1: Goldstein's Origins of Complexity Science
From Goldstein, Hazy & Lichtenstein (2010), *Complexity and the Nexus of Leadership*. Also updated in http://emergentfool.com/category/complex-quotes/. Reprinted with permission from Goldstein, Hazy, and Lichtenstein (2010), *Complexity and the Nexus of Leadership*.

To take a chronological perspective, we can examine the publication dates of the main texts of complexity science—those that catalyzed a field or stream of research. These provide an inclusive list of complexity disciplines. In the decades after World War II researchers developed new nonlinear methods and models for understanding reality, the most prominent ones being

- Cybernetics (Weiner, 1948/1961)
- Non-equilibrium thermodynamics (Prigogine, 1955)
- System dynamics (Forrester, 1961; Maruyama, 1963)
- Deterministic chaos theory (Lorenz, 1963; May, 1974, 1976)
- Computational genetic algorithms (Neumann, 1966)
- Autocatalysis (Eigen, 1971a, 1971b)
- Complex adaptive systems (Holland, 1975)
- Catastrophe theory (Thom, 1975; Zeeman, 1977)
- Synergetics (Haken, 1977)
- Fractals (Mandelbrot, 1983)

With Gleick's (1987) best-selling book *Chaos: Making a New Science*, many of these approaches became known as "chaos" theories, mainly because the metaphors from deterministic chaos theory were so colorful and easy to (simplistically) apply. Some years later Lewin (1992) and Waldrop (1992) described a new synthesis of these models, based on research coming out of the Santa Fe Institute. At that point, "complexity" became known primarily as a computational science (see Axelrod & Bennett, 1993; Kauffman, 1993; Cowan, Pines, & Meltzer, 1994; Holland, 1995; Carley, 1995, Krugman, 1996; Carley 2000).

In a broad sense, what links most of this work is a worldview that understands human agents to be heterogeneous, diverse, and ever-changing. The underlying assumptions for a science of emergence focus on interdependence, agency, relationality, and entrepreneuring. Numerous authors have explored the nature of this new paradigm, including classic texts by Bateson (1980), Berman (1988), and Harre and Secord (1979), among many more (e.g., Capra, 1982; Augros & Stanciu, 1987; Rothschild, 1992; Capra, 1996; Lappe, 2011). These ideas are also expressed within the methodological descriptions that follow.

Each complexity science provides a unique approach for exploring emergence. A broad sweep across all of the originating sciences of nonlinearity yields a proposed list of 15 sciences of complexity, presented in Table 3.1. The table is based on classic and recent overviews and summary accounts of complexity science, mainly for social scientists, including the following: Gleick (1987); Lewin (1992); Waldrop (1992); Casti (1994); Cowan et al. (1994); Goerner (1994); Guastello (1995); Capra (1996); Elliott and Kiel (1996); Dooley (1997); Eve, Horsfall, and Lee (1997); Anderson, Meyer, Eisenhardt, Carley, and Pettigrew (1999); Goldstein (1999); Marion (1999); McKelvey (1999b, 1999c); Goldstein (2000); Sorenson (2002); McKelvey (2004a, 2004b), Maguire, McKelvey, Mirabeau, and

Table 3.1. FIFTEEN COMPLEXITY SCIENCES FOR UNDERSTANDING EMERGENCE

Complexity Science Discipline	Managerial Insights from Theory	Contribution to explaining Emergence	Management References
Deterministic chaos theory	Dynamic systems are highly sensitive to initial conditions (i.e., butterfly effect). Mathematical methods for measuring time series data reveal a range of order (i.e., types of attractors) in apparently random behavior. Shifts in attractors imply organizational transformation and learning.	The presence of (new) order can be discerned (measured) through rigorous mathematical techniques	Thietart & Forgues, 1995; Cheng & Van de Ven, 1996; Dooley & Van de Ven, 1999
Catastrophe theory	Emergence (transformation) can be modeled as incremental change across one parameter (variable) that creates "catastrophic" (punctuated) change across another. These nonlinear models better reflect the social world. Reanalysis of behavioral data using the higher-order polynomial models from catastrophe theory explains up to 400% more variance than the same data analyzed using linear regression models.	Higher-order polynomial regression models reveal much more behavioral order than can be found using linear methods.	Bigelow, 1982; Gresov et al., 1993; Guastello, 1995, 1998
Fractals	Natural systems exhibit self-similarity across scales, whose dimensionality can be measured using a mathematical mapping technique. Organizations exhibit self-similar behavior and/or values across levels (e.g., individual, group, company-wide).	Mathematical analysis of repeated patterns across scales reveals an underlying evolutionary process.	Zimmerman & Hurst, 1993
Positive feedback: cybernetics, increasing returns	Nonlinear systems arise in part due to positive-feedback cycles that produce rapid aggregation. When this occurs, "control" is only achieved through responsiveness and flexibility. In economic "winner-take-all" situations, small initial differences in one entity (organization) can generate a self-reinforcing cycle that produces nonproportional increases in overall returns.	Emergence often occurs through positive-feedback processes. Due to sensitivity of initial conditions, luck and location play unexpected roles in a system's emergent form.	Beer, 1981; Arthur, 1988b, 1990, 1994; Chiles & Meyer, 2001; Espinosa et al., 2004
Power laws; self-organized criticality	Many dynamic systems evolve to a state in which all changes are related through a single equation, measured as a power law. These phenomena are best explain using Pareto (rather than Gaussian) distributions, which distinguish between the 80% of instances with little influence and the 20% that capture most of the activity in the system.	Most events have virtually no impact on dynamic phenomena like earthquakes or market behavior, but those phenomena can be transformed by a tiny number of very rare events.	Stanley et al., 1996; Morel & Ramanujam, 1999; Andriani & McKelvey, 2007, 2009; Boisot & McKelvey, 2010

(continued)

Table 3.1. CONTINUED

Complexity Science Discipline	Managerial Insights from Theory	Contribution to explaining Emergence	Management References
System dynamics	Multilevel dynamic interactions across systems can be modeled as linked loops of stocks and flows. These models show how and why unexpected behavior occurs in complex systems. These models can identify "leverage" points that avoid unintended effects.	Emergent (unexpected, nonlinear) outcomes in dynamic systems can be tractable through rigorous modeling of the system's logic.	Forrester, 1961; Hall, 1976; Sterman, 2000; Rudolph & Repenning, 2002
Complex adaptive systems	Complex systems can be modeled as a set of actors or elements—"agents"—whose interactions over time can yield emergent behavior within the system as a whole. In a CAS, it is assumed that agents follow a few "simple rules" which yield collective behavior that is unpredictable even from a complete knowledge of every agent's capabilities.	Emergent outcomes can be explained (qualitatively) as the result of "self-organization" in complex adaptive systems.	Dooley, 1997; Choi et al., 2001
Cellular automata	The physical distance of simulated agents significantly affects the dynamics of system evolution. Macro-level structures are determined in part by spatial qualities of a field, including, e.g., density, proximity, and size.	This computational modeling technique shows that some emergent structural patterns are due to agent proximity.	Schelling, 1978; Lomi & Larsen, 1996; Goldenberg, Libai, & Muller, 2002
Genetic algorithms	Agents "in silico" can be programmed to share traits in such a way that aggregates of agents can form. Computationally, the traits are shared through a "genetic" process whereby specific rules (qualities) in two interacting agents are copied and shared between them.	Computational method that allows agents in silico to "share" traits and qualities, revealing complex patterns and structures over time.	Holland, 1995; Krugman, 1996; Axelrod & Cohen, 2000
NK landscapes	Levels of adaptability within a complex system are dependent on (1) the number N of nodes (agents or modules) in the system and (2) the degree of interdependence K between the agents in the system. The interaction between N and K determines the ease of adaptability: the higher the interaction, the more "rugged" the landscape, yielding more "optimal points" of adaptation but making it harder to transition from one local optimum to another.	The range (variability) of emergence and adaptation crucially depends on the degree of interdependence expressed in the system.	Levinthal, 1997; McKelvey, 1999a; Gavetti & Levinthal, 2000; Fleming & Sorenson, 2001

Topic	Description	Summary	References
Agent-based simulations; Multi-agent learning models	Multiple computational algorithms can be linked within a single model, allowing researchers to explore more complex phenomena. Simulations show that adaptation and learning evolve through moves that are conditioned by agent qualities (e.g., knowledge) and local circumstances (e.g., dynamism), which themselves change over time.	Connecting computational methods increases the rate of emergence in simulation models.	Carley, 1990; Carley & Svoboda, 1996; Epstein & Axtell, 1996; Carley, 1999b
Autogenesis; autopoiesis; autocatalysis	Self-maintaining interactions in an ecosystem. Autocatalysis explains how sets of molecules can catalyze each other, creating self-renewing resources within biosystems. Autopoietic systems maintain their identity through self-referencing of interactions within a coherent internal mental model.	Qualitative explanation for the sustainability of social and biological entities, through self-creation process.	Pantzar & Csanyi, 1991; Drazin & Sandelands, 1992; Padgett & Powell, 2011
Dissipative structures	New levels of order can spontaneously emerge in disequilibrium situations, through a self-amplifying process sparked by experiments, resulting in greater system capacity. Entities (groups, organizations) can generate new order by dissipating large amounts of energy, information, and resources.	Process theory of emergent-order creation; replicated across multiple contexts.	Smith & Gemmill, 1991; Lichtenstein, 2000b; Chiles et al., 2004; Plowman et al., 2007
Ecosystem resilience and transition	Natural ecosystems show remarkable sustainability because their "products"—the outflows from all organisms in the ecosystem—are resources necessary for maintenance and renewal. Ecological systems show the essence of complexity: high interdependence across semi-autonomous entities, and symbiotic self-organization. This resilience (Holling, 2001) can, however, make the ecosystem inflexible in periods of high environmental change, causing a "flip" to a nonadaptive state.	Research examines the conditions necessary to establish and maintain an ecosystem.	Buenstorf, 2000; Holling, 2001; Colbert, 2004; Folke et al., 2004; 2005; Liu et al., 2007; Walker et al., 2006
Ascendency in ecosystems, directionality in evolution	Applications of nonlinearity in natural systems and self-organization ideas in biology focus on systemwide generation of sustainable and growing ecosystems. Ecosystems achieve "ascendency" through a "trial-and-reinforcement" dynamic, thus increasing total flow of energy through an environment. Broadly, self-organization and other forms of non-selection-based adaptation lead to a directionality in evolution: toward greater capacity to process information.		Wicken, 1986; Dyke, 1992; Morowitz, 2002; Ulanowicz, 2002

Oztas (2006); Davis, Eisenhardt, and Bingham (2007); and Padgett and Powell (2011), among others. The entire list also reflects insights from the *Handbook for Complexity and Management* (Allen, Maguire, & McKelvey, 2011). Undoubtedly some scholars will disagree with the categorizations and brief descriptions of these fields; this list should properly be thought of as an evolving framework that provides a starting point for capitalizing on connections across complexity research, the key science in a discipline of emergence.

Each of these 15 fields of complexity explores the conditions, properties, or processes of emergence in dynamic, complex systems, and they do this in different ways. My aim in this review is to introduce each discipline briefly, with a focus on how it may contribute to a study of emergence, and to provide examples of its use by management researchers. As I will explain throughout this chapter, these are arranged in a particular order, which roughly corresponds to the amount of complexity and depth of emergence that each can explore.

15 FIELDS OF COMPLEXITY SCIENCE

Mathematical and Analytic Sciences of Complexity

Deterministic Chaos Theory

Originally developed in response to an anomaly in atmospheric science (Lorenz, 1963), this mathematical field has been used to identify stable patterns across large time-series data sets (Brown, 1995; Guastello, 1995). In particular, data that appear to be stochastic or even random may, upon analysis using tools from deterministic chaos theory, be found to be structured in complex patterns that are mathematically defined (Baker & Gollub, 1996; Sulis & Combs, 1996). However, in contrast to traditional linear frameworks, these structural patterns are not deterministic, that is, the specific location of a future data point cannot be predicted. Instead, the theory shows how to define the underlying system that generates all the data points, that is, the area within which all the data will occur. This overall area is called the "attractor" for the data. Although the trajectory that generates any specific point cannot be determined, the attractor identifies the parameters of the data, or the "farthest edges" on each dimension that data will be found.

Mathematically speaking, the nonlinearity described by deterministic chaos theory is very specific, referring to two common issues that arise in the computation of data from complex dynamic systems. The first issue involves amplification: In nonlinear systems, changes tend to be amplified (Maruyama, 1963; May, 1974; Arthur, 1988b; Brown, 1995). In deterministic systems with well-known initial conditions, these amplifications can be tracked, making the system predictable. However, nonlinearity (and lack of predictability—a foundation of general linear reality) begins to show up when these systems are measured computationally, a problem that has to do with the physical number of digits that a computer can calculate. Whatever that number, even if it can calculate up to the millionth of a unit, the very last digit of every measurement is *always* rounded up. Although this rounding may seem extremely small, in dynamic and multidimensional systems these differences are amplified and thus become larger and larger over subsequent iterations, ultimately leading to an unpredictable outcome. In these cases the deterministic model breaks down, reflecting an epistemic inability to predict the ultimate outcome of a trajectory. A common example of this problem is in predicting the weather, a very dynamic system analyzed through computations that always get rounded up; this explains why weather predictions are so often inaccurate.

Technically, this leads to the notion that complex systems have "sensitive dependence on initial conditions," because even a difference of a millionth of a part, iterated thousands of times, will amplify to generate a host of unpredictable paths. In popular writings (Gleick, 1987) this metaphor was pushed to its extreme, where the single flap of a butterfly's wings could theoretically be amplified across weather systems, leading to increased turbulence or even a storm many thousands of miles away. As a metaphor, "chaos" has been a very popular moniker for systems that do not behave in linear ways. In fact, most authors use the term *chaos* not for its mathematical meaning but to signify the presence of nonlinear and/or surprising outcomes in social systems, a habit exemplified by the metaphorical title of my first dissertation paper (Lichtenstein, 2000b).[3]

In management and the social sciences, deterministic chaos has been used to identify patterns and structures in seemingly random data; this has been well outlined by Dooley and Van de Ven (1999). Guastello (1987, 1995, 1998) has dedicated his prestigious career to presenting the value of this approach and its application in catastrophe theory (see next section), first in a compendium of his own research studies (1995), and then as founding editor of the journal *Nonlinear Dynamics, Psychology, and Life Sciences*. Others have pursued the approach to improve understanding of organizational change (Cheng & Van de Ven, 1996; Marion, 1999) and the nature of economic and other social processes (e.g., Coleman, Vallacher, Nowak, & Bui-Wrzosinska, 2007; Matilla-Garcia & Marin, 2010). More mathematical examples have been published in journals such as *Chaos; Dynamical Systems; Chaos, Solitons & Fractals*; and *International Journal of Bifurcation and Chaos in Applied Sciences and Engineering*.

In terms of emergence, deterministic chaos theory provides a mathematical approach for identifying wholesale shifts in behavior from one "attractor" to another. The paper by Cheng Van de Ven (1996) is an excellent example of this usage, and I shall describe it in more detail in Chapter 4. Marion (1999), Allen, Strathern, and Baldwin (2007), and others have adopted more general terms to extend the idea more rigorously into human systems.

Catastrophe Theory

A related set of mathematical tools has been designed to explain and track transitions between one attractor and another, especially when incremental changes across one dimension of activity result in punctuated or "catastrophic" shifts in another dimension. Thom (1975) and Zeeman (1977) developed a series of equations now known as catastrophe theory (Guastello, 1995), which describe these systemwide "catastrophic changes." The core claim of the field is that a small set of formulas can explain all types of catastrophic change. In Guastello's (1995, pp. 33–34) marvelously clear explanation:

> The central proposition of catastrophe theory is the classification theorem (Thom, 1975), which states (with qualifications) that, given a maximum of four control parameters, all discontinuous changes of events can be modeled by one of seven elementary topological forms.... The models describe change between (or among) qualitatively distinct forms of behavior, such as remaining on a job versus quitting.

Management scholars have applied the most basic of the seven models—the "fold and cusp" model—to explain organization-wide transformation (Bigelow, 1982), shifts in strategic design (Gresov, Haveman, & Oliva, 1993), and complex group level phenomena, such as leadership emergence, motivation, and personnel turnover (Guastello, 1995). As another example, Guastello (1998) used one of the four-dimensional models to describe the types of leaders that emerged in a series of four-person task groups. His "swallowtail" equation resulted in an R^2 of .9993, meaning that his nonlinear model explained more than 99% of the variance of the situation; all variables were statistically significant (at the .05 level). This degree of explanation is virtually unheard of in social science studies, many of which are happy to explain 10% or perhaps 15% of the overall outcomes. To explain nearly 100% of the factors driving a situation suggests that the underlying model is very powerful. Indeed, the experiment was expanded to incorporate cross-cultural participants, with results that replicated the earlier sample (Zaror & Guastello, 2000). Their implication is that the emergence of leadership may reflect qualities *within the internal dynamics of the system itself*, rather than being due to individual, environmental, or contextual drivers.

In terms of emergence, catastrophe theory can track significant changes in a system and is far more accurate then linear approaches for explaining oscillations and multiple modes in complex systems. Thus, if emergence occurs, catastrophe models may be used to formalize its explanation (Gresov et al., 1993; Guastello, 1998). However, like attractors in deterministic chaos theory, the presence of a catastrophe model does not reveal how new activities are generated, nor does it show the dynamics of interaction that lead to the creation of a new system.

Fractals

Just as deterministic chaos theory identifies patterns of behavior within a system, fractal mathematics allows for a careful mapping of subtle similarities across system levels, that is, similarities from one level to another (Mandelbrot, 1983). In technical terms fractals measure the "density" of a nonlinear data set, like stock market behavior or the shape of a coastline (Casti, 1994). When such measures are taken at increasing orders of magnitude, each fractal dimension is "self-similar" to the ones before and after it, meaning that the underlying patterns are the same across levels of analysis. In turn, this relationship is always governed by a power law (Cramer, 1993). This notion of "self-similarity across scales" (Bak, 1996; Krugman, 1996) has become a core tenet of complexity science.

In management, fractal analysis has helped describe and explain changes that occur with similar patterns at multiple scales, at the individual-, group-, departmental- and whole-organizational level of analysis (Zimmerman & Hurst, 1993). Recently, fractal dimensionality was used to explain subtle but important dynamics in the network TV industry (Farjoun & Levin, 2011). In associated fields, fractals have been used to determining the efficacy of a company's information technology by exploring the "continued coherence" between organizational activities and information technology (IT) capabilities across levels (Dhillon & Fabian, 2005). Moreover, economic geographers have found that self-similarity in the morphology of built-up areas in Europe is often greater across regions and nations than it is within large cities (Thomas, Frankhauser, & Badariotti, 2012).

Applications of fractals may provide intriguing insights into emergence. For example, fractal mathematics could be used to rigorously describe parallel emergences of activity patterns within a multilevel system. Admittedly, there are no interacting agents in fractal geometry, and the only thing that actually emerges from the math is the beautiful graphic images that have become iconic of chaos and complexity studies (see, e.g., Iannaccone & Khokha, 1996; Pietgen, Jurgens, & Saupe, 2004). However, the metaphor of "self-similarity" provides a framework for exploring emergent patterns at ever-deeper levels and dimensions of a complex system.

Positive Feedback Processes: Cybernetics, Increasing Returns in Economics

Many emergences are sparked by nonlinear change triggered by positive-feedback processes, whereby the inputs to a process yield outputs that themselves reinforce the inputs in a continuous cycle, earlier described in terms of autocatalysis. Unless moderated by a balancing or reducing process, this positive dynamic will lead to accelerating change, reinforcing cycles, and "snowball effects" that continually increase (May, 1976; Senge, Roberts, Ross, Smith, & Kleiner, 1994; Sterman & Wittenberg, 1999; Senge, 2006). These outcomes are the opposite of negative feedback, through which information-based systems can be maintained in a state of control. This understanding initiated the first cybernetics (Weiner, 1948/1961), which Goldstein and others include as a core antecedent to complexity science. In contrast, positive feedback leads to what Maruyama called "the second cybernetics" (Maruyama, 1963), expressing the fundamental difference between cybernetics' initial emphasis on negative feedback for control versus the amplification and sometimes uncontrollable effects of positive feedback.

Although cybernetics as such is not well integrated into management, a number of scholars continue to explore its viability, often drawing on Stafford Beer's "viable system model" as a core framework (Beer, 1981; Espinosa, Harnden, & Walker, 2004, 2008). For example, Brewis, Papamichail, and Rajaram (2011) used the "viable systems model" as a tool to explore business models, suggesting that the cybernetic model of responsiveness-as-control provides several insightful ways to intervene and improve the processes underlying the activities of the business model. In a very different way, DiRenzo and Greenhaus (2011) extended theories of voluntary turnover by suggesting that individuals consistently enact a "cybernetic" process of continuously evaluating their skills, comparing them to their ideal skill levels and job prospects, and taking action to bring their current levels up to their ideal. In both cases management becomes a process of interaction that seeks to identify and respond creatively to system changes.

Extending this basic idea of positive feedback processes into the realm of economics, Arthur was the first to show the influence of "increasing returns," in, for example, the emergence of one product over a very similar one, or the rise of one market to the exclusion of another. This endogenous process leads to reinforcing feedback dynamics that alter the system (Arthur, 1988a, 1988b, 1994). Moreover, he showed that in "winner-take-all" product situations, that is, product markets that require the choice of a single dominant design, the positive feedback process that leads to system emergence will also lead to system "lock in," making it nearly impossible to shift out of the new attractor and into another one (Arthur, 1989; Levy & Lichtenstein, 2010). An intriguing result is that the "winning" design may not be the best one, as Arthur (1994) and others have shown.

An application of increasing returns to the emergence of organizational clusters was developed by Chiles and Meyer (2001), using more data from their Branson, MO case. They suggest that although geographic attractiveness is an important consideration in the origin of a cluster, historical accident can be even more salient: "The arbitrary location decision of a pioneering firm can attract other firms that recognize the benefits of co-location. As additional firms jump on the bandwagon, momentum builds, and the location becomes locked in" (Chiles & Meyer, 2001, p. 62). These effects can be reinforced through entrepreneurs who "run in packs," pursuing cooperative strategies that "capture the benefits and minimize the costs of clustering." Their data bear out this process, showing that unplanned and unexpected events led to initial interest in the area, which was leveraged by entrepreneurs and business people who sought to capitalize on those initial "accidents" that drew tourists to the area. As will be described in detail in Chapter 4, many dozens of such positive-feedback processes were central to the emergence of the cluster.

Self-Organized Criticality, Pareto Distributions, Power Laws

Whereas fractals can measure the nonlinearity of a complex system that is in a stable form, for example, a coastline or a cauliflower, self-organized criticality developed as a means to mathematically measure the nonlinearity of a system with a constant flow of inputs and outputs. The question posed by Bak and Chen (1991; Bak, 1996) regards the variability of changes over time that maintain the system in a far-from-equilibrium state—always incorporating new inputs while remaining at a certain size. Their paradigm experiment is the now-famous "sandpile," a system composed of a stream of sand that drops onto a plate with fixed diameter. After the sand covers the plate in the form of a sandpile, the continuing input of sand leads to a series of sand avalanches in which differing amounts of sand fall off the plate and onto the floor. There is an underlying pattern to these avalanches, however. Most of the time only a few dozen grains of sand will fall off the plate, which does not affect the pile as a whole. However, occasionally a huge avalanche will occur in which thousands of grains of sand will fall away at the same time, often breaking large chasms in the sandpile.

An analysis of these sandpile drops reveals a surprising regularity: All the variance in sand drops (transformed in logarithmic form) can be fitted to a single line, where the slope explains a ratio of *size of the sand drops* compared to their *frequency*. This is a power law, and it shows that small changes—the 80% of changes that have no other impact—happen very frequently in a dynamic system, whereas the largest, 20% of changes happen only rarely.[4] Earthquakes have the same pattern: The vast majority of earthquakes are so small that we don't feel them, but a very small proportion of them are very large, causing major damage wherever they hit (Andriani & McKelvey, 2007, 2009). According to Bak and Chen (1991), the implication is that very large system changes are rare, but normal. In their terms, this state is self-organized because the system keeps adjusting "spontaneously" so as to maintain a specific angle of the pile (given system parameters, e.g., gravity, amount of sand-grain stickiness). Since this process starts as soon as the sandpile reaches a critical state, they call the phenomenon "self-organized criticality."

In terms of emergence, one can use this idea by seeing it as a way to measure the "rate" or pace of dynamics within a system. The stream of sand can represent any stream of activity or resource—inputs to a manufacturing system, for example, or personnel turnover in organizations. The model can help explain the non-uniform changes occurring over time across the system, by identifying the prevalence of seemingly insubstantial shifts punctuated by major upheavals of the entire system. One example is the study by Gunz, Lichtenstein, and Long (2002), who explored vacancy chains (chains of employee turnover) in three organizations that were all part of the timber industry in the Upper Northwest. In our application of the model, the inputs (stream of sand) were the number of vacancies at any given time across all the organizations, and the capacity (size of the plate) was the size of the organizations. As predicted by the model of self-organized criticality, our analysis found that the size and frequency of vacancy chains followed a power law. That is, most commonly, only one or two people left an organization at the same time, but occasionally there was a mass exodus, usually catalyzed by an executive who left and invited numerous people in the organization to join him or her. From a human resources (HR) perspective, the insight is that these changes are normal—they are expected within dynamic systems like organizational membership (Gunz et al., 2002), rather than caused by any missteps in HR strategy or lack of employee engagement.

It turns out that self-organized criticality is only one stream within the broader discipline of power laws, a field that has recently gained attention through a series of papers in prominent management journals (Andriani & McKelvey, 2007, 2009; Boisot & McKelvey, 2010, 2011). The basic premise in this work is that our common understanding of the world is mostly wrong, because it is based on the idea that events or activities are distributed according to a "normal" curve, the well-known Gaussian distribution basis of general linear reality. In this common paradigm, most of the events in a system fall near a "mean" or average of the distribution, with fewer and fewer occurring away from the mean. However, as demonstrated by Bak and Chen and others, natural phenomena and social dynamics may not be explainable using a Gaussian distribution. Instead, the behavior of most dynamic systems follows a power law, being captured through a Paretian distribution. As Andriani and McKelvey (2009, p. 1055) argue,

> When events are interdependent, interactive, or both, normality in distributions is not the norm. Instead, Pareto distributions dominate because positive feedback (and other) processes leading to extreme events occur more frequently than "normal" Gaussian-based statistics lead us to expect.

One of my favorite examples of this claim was accomplished by Stanley and his colleagues at Boston University (Stanley et al., 1996). They found that a single power law accounts for the relationship between growth rates and internal structuring of U.S. manufacturing companies. The finding is valid across more than seven orders of magnitude, from companies with 10 employees to those with more than two million employees. To be clear, their finding means that there is a singular pattern of structural relationships in all manufacturing firms—from the smallest businesses to the largest multinationals, a claim confirming the nonlinear nature of seemingly deterministic processes.

Others have used power laws to reanalyze important social issues that were thought to be normally distributed, including economic fluctuations (Scheinkman & Woodfordd, 1994), distribution of wealth (Pareto, 1897, in Andriani & McKelvey,

2009; Levy & Solomon, 1997), growth rate of countries' GDP (Lee, Amaral, Canning, Meyer, & Stanley, 1998), entrepreneurship and innovation (Poole, Van de Ven, Dooley, & Holmes, 2000), actor networks (Barabasi & Bonabeau, 2003), and many more—Andriani and McKelvey (2009) list 101 examples.

Perhaps an even more important result is that Pareto distributions can capture the entire spectrum of phenomena that display linear and nonlinear elements. Boisot and McKelvey (2010) showed this through an example of software firms. Many of them have linear growth, but some of them have nonlinear outcomes; the Paretian approach captures both.

The value of this connection is well seen in entrepreneurship, which includes 17,000,000 tiny mom-and-pop firms, a smaller number of medium and larger companies, and a tiny number of extraordinary corporations such as Walmart, Google, and Facebook that dominate the business landscape. A power-law analysis can examine all of these firms within one sample, a prospect that would be impossible using Gaussian distributions.

In terms of emergence, power laws reveal a system in a dynamic state and point to some qualities of its emergence. As Krugman (1996, in Andriani & McKelvey, 2010, p. 1055) says, "Power laws often appear as telltales of self-organization, emergence-in-action, and self-organizing economies." Power laws and their causal properties are embedded in emergent systems, and the tools from power-law theory provide a way to identify the regularities inherent in nonlinear phenomena.

System Dynamics

Whereas power-law mathematics reveals the flow of interactions across a dynamic system, system dynamics reveals the flows of interdependence within a system. Originally developed to uncover the roots of causality in manufacturing firms (Forrester, 1961), an early and influential application of the science was used in the *Limits to Growth Report for the Club of Rome* (Meadows, Meadows, Randers, & Behrens, 1972). Just as power-law theory shows that Gaussian distributions misspecify and thus cannot explain a great deal of complex social phenomenon, system dynamics shows how managerial perceptions of causality and change are mainly wrong. This is due to the multilayered flows of information and action in dynamic systems that human minds are unable to track on their own. In fact, managerial training, based exclusively on linear and tractable models, often results in a misspecification of causes (Sterman, 1989; 2000) and, thus, a paradox, identified by Sterman (2002, p. 501): "Thoughtful leaders increasingly recognize that we are not only failing to solve the persistent problems we face, but are in fact causing them." Sterman's insight was preceded by Forrester's, in 1959: "With a high degree of confidence we can say that the intuitive solutions to the problems of complex social systems will be wrong most of the time" (in Hall, 1976, p. 199). This finding has been well documented by numerous studies (e.g., Sterman, 1989; Repenning & Sterman, 2001; Repenning, 2002; Sterman, 2002).

Developing a system dynamics model of a specific phenomenon first requires that the analyst identify each salient stock and flow in the system, that is, the resources and information that accumulate as inputs for use in the process, and the flows of these inputs and actions from one node to the next. A key insight is the role of delays—processes and feedbacks that are sometimes postponed because of internal dynamics. These delays, even if they are short, create nonlinear effects that are usually very difficult to perceive in real time. Once the key system elements are identified, the analyst can use computational tools like STELLA and iThink to make a computational model that links all the dynamics of the system and provides a time-based simulation of how the system will evolve.

A classic application of system dynamics is Hall's (1976) study of the collapse of the *Saturday Evening Post*. By mapping the key aspects of the publishing company into a simulation model and linking the model to real data from the firm, Hall was able to explore multiple scenarios to determine what caused the dramatic fall of the nationally acclaimed magazine. He found that the normal tools for managerial control of the magazine—focusing on margins and on costs, and pursuing growth through increased trial subscriptions and decreasing advertising prices—led to an unexpected and unnoticed positive-feedback cycle: increased readership and advertising led to increased editorial pages, which led to increased costs. In an attempt to maintain margins the magazine then increased ad prices, which led to *decreased* advertising, which led to decreased editorial pages, which led to decreased subscriptions, which again led to a need to maintain margins by increasing ad prices, decreased advertising, decreased pages, decreased subscriptions, and so on. In his ingenious analysis, Hall used the system dynamics model to find a different leverage point that would have saved the company, namely to link ad prices to the number of readers, rather than to overall margins. He showed that this simple fix would have slowly but effectively increased revenues and subscriptions and balanced margins, thus creating a turnaround in the company.

More recently, system dynamics has been used to identify unexpected, nonlinear and emergent outcomes of organizational learning (Repenning & Sterman, 2001), managerial decision processes (Rudolph & Repenning, 2002), dynamic capabilities (Romme, Zollo, & Berends, 2010), and organizational evolution (Sterman & Wittenberg, 1999). Sastry (1997) applied the method to highlight an important gap in Tushman and Romanelli's (1985) theory of organizational transformation. In addition, visual system dynamics (Senge, 2006) is a powerful tool for understanding organizational learning (Kim, 1993) and increasing it in practice (Pegasus-Communications, 1999).

In the study of emergence, system dynamics makes a substantive contribution to our understanding of interdependence and feedback flows within systems, issues central to the coming-into-being of social entities. The methodology itself leads to a deep inquiry into the constituents and boundaries of a system, and it highlights the challenges of relying on our intuition to identify the multiple causalities and delayed feedback processes that are so common in human systems and which can lead to whole-system change and emergence.

Complex Adaptive Systems

Complex adaptive systems (CAS) is a general theoretical framework that broadly describes most computational models of complexity as well as a variety of rigorous applications in other management fields. The term was popularized by Holland (1995), who suggested that for complex systems, "the question of coherence under change is the central enigma," which can be explored using tools of complex adaptive systems. He continues: "This is more than terminology. It signals our intuition that general principles rule CAS behavior."

Holland identified seven key principles of CAS—four properties and three mechanisms; these are nicely illustrated in his Figure 1.16 (p. 38). His properties are (1) aggregation leading to emergent properties, (2) nonlinearity and its inherent complexity, (3) flows of resources and information, and (4) diversity which is the basis for new possibility in dynamic systems. His three mechanisms are (5) tags that identify an agent to other agents, (6) internal models or schemata through which agents perceive and act in their environment, and (7) building blocks that can be recombined in innumerable ways. Holland (1995, p. 10) defines complex adaptive systems as follows:

> [CAS are] systems composed of interacting agents described in terms of rules. These agents adapt by changing their rules as experience accumulates. In CAS, a major part of the environment of any given adaptive agent consists of other adaptive agents, so that a portion of any agent's efforts at adaptation is spent adapting to other adaptive agents.

Gell-Mann (1994, p. 18) provides a slightly different characterization of CAS: any adaptive system or set of nested adaptive systems that gathers experience and information as inputs, identifies regularities, and takes action based on an evolving schema. These actions are reflected in the schema of the agents in its environment. Another approach is taken by Anderson (1999), who argues that complex adaptive systems have four elements: agents with schemata, self-organizing networks sustained by importing energy, co-evolution, and system evolution. Even with their differences, these three approaches provide a base for careful analogies to organizational phenomena.

One active application of CAS has been in reanalyzing supply chains in terms of self-organizing "supply nets" (Choi, Dooley, & Rungtusanatham, 2001). This work focuses on the increased capacity for learning throughout a system of semi-autonomous interacting agents, instead of the traditional top-down control that has been traditionally used to manage supply chains. Others have extended this work to improving coordination and performance in supply networks (e.g., Surana, Kumara, Greaves, & Raghavan, 2005; Pathak, Day, Nair, Sawaya, & Kristal, 2007). CAS has also been used to explain organizational change (Dooley, 1997), small business management (Fuller & Moran, 2001), technology innovation (Fleming & Sorenson, 2001), and leadership (Lichtenstein et al., 2007).

In terms of emergence, CAS is a good approach for understanding computational and social emergence. CAS became enacted in a variety of computational disciplines, including cellular automata, genetic algorithms, and NK landscape models, each of which I will review next. However, the general model provides insights into the properties and mechanisms that lead to emergent patterns and levels. As such, it forms a very useful link between computational emergence and all the social fields of emergence.

Computational Models of Complexity

Over the past two decades several sophisticated computational methods have been invented which allow researchers to develop dynamic models of emergence processes and test them in highly controlled and repeatable ways. These models include cellular automata (Krugman, 1996), NK landscape models (Kauffman, 1993), genetic algorithms (Holland, 1995), and combinations of several approaches found in agent-based modeling (Carley, 1999a; Malerba, Nelson, Orsenigo, & Winter, 1999).

Cellular Automata

Cellular automata (CA) are fairly simple simulation models that explore patterns of aggregation and emergence among computational agents. The basis of the model is a linear or two-dimensional matrix, within which each agent (cell) at each time steps looks at its "nearest neighbors"—the one or two agents on either side. The agent then evaluates its neighbor agents on the basis of a single rule or "trait" or preference and then acts according to that rule—for example, move toward the agent that is "most like you." Depending on the outcome of the evaluation, each agent moves one space. Thus, at each time step all or most agents move, leading to a new and unpredictable configuration—unpredictable for the agents and unplanned from a computational point of view. From this new configuration, at the next time step all agents again pursue this evaluation, and all agents move again. The simulations continue until all agents are positioned such that no agents move.

It turns out that even very small initial differences in preferences or traits across the set of agents lead to an aggregation process that is remarkably stable over time. The classic example is Schelling's (1978) study on segregation in cities, "Micromotives and Macrobehavior." In this study, Schelling used a checkerboard model,[5] and he gave each agent a slightly different set of attributes (i.e., agents are mildly heterogeneous) and arranged them in a totally stochastic pattern across the board. He then programmed a single rule for all agents: "choose to live nearby agents who are moderately similar to you." Once the simulation started the agents aggregated toward agents who were like themselves. In a short number of steps a distinct segregation of agents emerged; these segregations remained stable for long periods of time, just as we see in real cities. The insight, however, is that neighborhood segregation may not be due to external social cues, nor to broader economic divisions, nor to any of a number of sociological principles. Instead, segregation derives from a very simple preference to be near people who are moderately like oneself (Schelling, 1978).

A similar result was obtained through a more complicated CA model, developed by Axelrod and Bennett (1993). Seeking to explain political alliances, they programmed each agent (nation) with a *propensity* to work with any other nation, based on their past experiences and current goals. Given the historically accurate assumption that political alliances generally configure nations into (only) two groups, they also programmed agents with a "frustration level" indicating their overall evaluation of being in one configuration vs. another, given their propensity to work with each of the other agents in that configuration.[6] Then at each time step, each agent was to make an internal calculation of which alliance would lead to the lowest frustration overall. Following their programming their overall aim was to choose the alliance that would maximally reduce their frustration. According to the theory, each time an agent changes alliances, the combined frustration across all agents should decrease, ultimately leading to a global minimum. The underlying model is in note [7].

A remarkable aspect of this study is their use of actual data, of political alliances from 1939. Their model allowed them to accurately predict the political alliance formation of every single nation except one during WWII. In Alexrod's words, "It is remarkable that such a simple theory and such a parsimonious operationalization of its concepts can come up with a prediction that is very close to what actually happened" (Axelrod, 1997, p. 88).

Given the strengths of cellular automata to explore issues involving close interactions, spatial structuring, and proximity between agents, the tool has been used to explore a variety of research questions at multiple levels, including strategic evolution (Lomi & Larson, 1997), the organization of supply chains (Nair, Narasimhan, & Choi, 2009), the distribution of firms (Lomi & Larsen, 1996), and the emergence of "edge cities" (Krugman, 1996).

Using a simple CA application of spatial modeling, economist Paul Krugman (1996) built on Garreau's (1992) work on the rise of edge cities in metropolitan regions through an application of the methodology used by Zipf (1949). In Krugman's edge-city simulations, agents are businesses that enjoy a certain percentage of business activity within the city's (connected) neighborhoods. He presents a spatial simulation model in which business activities, initially randomly dispersed, always evolve into a highly ordered distribution of "edge cities" around a central business district. He explained his findings through Simon's notion of near-decomposibility (Simon, 2002). Although few management researchers have taken up Krugman's model, it does exhibit hierarchical emergence: A few simple rules generate an emerging order—edge city groupings. These are ontologically distinct from their component businesses.

NK Landscape Models

By specifying two additional parameters to the cellular automata model, Kauffman (1993) developed a computational tool that shows how patterns and structures can emerge through the adaptive changes within a system or matrix of agents. In his approach, each cell in the matrix is an agent with N traits or attributes that can change over time. At every time step each agent draws from its nearby neighbors a combination of attributes that appear to be most adaptive in the local neighborhood. Across the system, agents' attributes are set to a certain level of *interdependence* (K), such that the higher the K, the more a change in one attribute will effect changes in other attributes. After a short number of iterations, an internal structure emerges in the landscape, reflecting those combinations of attributes that are most and least adaptive relative to all others. As is now well known, the degree of order in the overall landscape crucially depends on K—the degree of interdependence across the system (Kauffman, 1993). The general insight is that some measure of connectedness brings the entire system to a higher level of fitness and adaptability, but too much interconnection can lock the system into a "catastrophe" of interdependence (Sorenson, 1997; McKelvey, 1999a), stopping all adaptive change.

One exemplary use of the NK model for studying emergence is Fleming and Sorenson's (2001) study of technological invention. Treating invention as a recombination of existing components in a given field, they showed that the usefulness of an invention (measured as the six-year count of citations) "can be maximized by working with a large number of components that interact to an intermediate degree" (Fleming & Sorenson, 2001, p. 1025). These data and analysis confirm the fact that a moderate amount of interaction—measured as an "intermediate degree" of K interdependence—is the crucial determinate of innovation success. Details about this study are presented in Chapter 5.

Other management scholars have used the NK model to study a host of strategic and organization issues, including the performance contribution of cognitive vs. experiential learning (Gavetti & Levinthal, 2000; Gavetti, Levinthal, & Rivkin, 2005), the ways that organizational design and decision-making affect organizational outcomes (Rivkin & Siggelkow, 2003; Siggelkow & Rivkin, 2005), and the upper limits of strategic interconnections across firms (Levinthal, 1997; Rivkin, 2000; Sommer, Loch, & Dong, 2009). Moderate levels of interconnection can be achieved through modularization of the production process (Levinthal & Warglien, 1999; Ethiraj & Levinthal, 2004) or through adopting strategies based on the industry-wide level of firm interdependence (Baum, 1999). The NK model has been used to study a wide variety of management issues, including profits (Lenox, Rockart, & Lewin, 2006), competitive advantage (Porter & Siggelkow, 2008), and successful strategies for entrepreneurial start-ups (Ganco & Agarwal, 2009).

There is not actually very much emergence, per se, in the NK model (Lichtenstein & McKelvey, 2011). For the most part, self-organization is limited to agent connections (networks) with the nearest neighbors. In this respect, most NK models detail how patterns emerge within a specific system, rather than the creation of the system itself. This argument continues in Chapter 4.

Genetic Algorithms

An important advance in modeling emergence has occurred through the use of genetic algorithms (GA), invented by Holland (1994, 1995). In many ways these are similar to most computational models in which agents have the capacity to change their attributes over time—they can learn (Carley & Hill, 2000), innovate new products (Fleming & Sorenson, 2001), and develop new strategies (Gavetti et al., 2005). However, in cellular automata models, agents interact according to rules that are programmed into the system. Furthermore, CA models are typically limited to a relatively few rules because the landscape grows geometrically each time a rule or agent is added. In contrast, genetic algorithms allow agents to have many rules (Macy & Skvoretz, 1998), and, more importantly, they allow these complex agents to change the rule strings governing their behavior (Macy & Skvoretz, 1998). New agent formations can have varying numbers of rules from each prior agent form, thus allowing increased evolutionary fitness of complex processes such as decision-making and learning, along with recombinations of diverse skills. Over time, genetic algorithms co-evolve toward improved adaptive capability; differentiated groups emerge, and soon thereafter group norms also solidify. Holland (1998, pp. 190–191) describes how aggregates of new rules can represent "macro-laws" at a higher "level" of order—a level he calls a "constrained generating procedure," or CGP:

> Just what is a new level in a *CGP*? The answer turns on one of the basic properties of a *CGP*: the possibility of combining mechanisms to make a more complex mechanism.... [T]he resulting composite, the resulting *CGP*, can itself be characterized as a mechanism—a subassembly that can be used to form still more complex mechanisms.... We have moved up one level of description.

Genetic algorithms have been applied in a range of models. For example Paul, Butler, Pearlson, and Whinston (1996) examined the adaptation of emergent financial trading firms (groups) and found an increase in combinations of better performing agents over time.[8] Crowston's (1996) GA model showed that organizations and/or their employee agents can minimize coordination costs by organizing in particular ways.⁹ GA models can show how emergent behaviors of agents adapt and change in a co-evolving context (Holland, 1998). Further, agent moves can be viewed as leadership decisions, which enables leadership scholars to explore how agents in complex systems "adapt by changing their rules as experience accumulates" (Holland, 1995, p. 10). Likewise, "each change of strategy by a worker alters the context in which the next change will be tried and evaluated. When multiple populations of agents are adapting to each other, the result is a leadership process" (Axelrod & Cohen, 2000, p. 8). Finally, GA models can help define interaction process that hold across levels, which may allow researchers to identify similar patterns acting in macroevolution and in microevolution.

Agent-Based and Multi-Agent Learning Models

Agent-based modeling is elegantly summarized by Tesfatsion (2011, pp. 36–37):

> More precisely, each agent in an Agent-Based Model (ABM) is a software program encompassing data as well as methods that act on these data. . . . . In addition, agents can contain other agents as member data, thus permitting hierarchical constructions.
>
> The data and methods of any particular agent are encapsulated, in the sense that they can be partially or completely hidden from other agents. This encapsulation renders agents imperfectly predictable from the viewpoint of other agents in their computational world.
>
> Cognitive agents in ABMs can exhibit behavioral adaptation, goal-directed learning, social communication (talking with each other), and the endogenous formation of interaction networks. A key aspect of these cognitive agents is their autonomy relative to traditionally modeled economic agents. Cognitive ABM agents can self-activate and self-determine their actions on the basis of internal data and methods hidden from other agents. Moreover, these internal data and methods can change over time as the cognitive agents explore and interact within their world. ABM researchers . . . investigate how large-scale effects arise from the micro-level interactions of dispersed cognitive agents.

Carley and her colleagues have produced some of the more sophisticated agent-based models, by combining elements of CA, GA, and neural networks. In her CONSTRUCT (Carley, 1991) and CONSTRUCT-O (Carley & Hill, 2000) models, simulated agents have a position or role in a social network and a mental model consisting of knowledge about other agents. Agents communicate and learn from others with similar types of knowledge. CONSTRUCT-O allows for the rapid formation of subgroups and the emergence of culture, which, when it crystallizes, supervenes to alter agent co-evolution and search for improved performance. These models show the emergence of communication networks (one level) and the formation of stable hierarchical groups (two levels). They also show how higher levels of order "supervene" to influence lower-level behavior.

Quite possibly the most famous example of "bottom-up" agent-based modeling is Epstein and Axtell's growing artificial societies (Epstein & Axtell, 1996). They boil their agent behavior down to a single rule: "Look around as far as your vision permits, find the spot with the most sugar, go there and eat the sugar" (p. 6). Agents search on a CA landscape and come to hold genetic–identity–culture identification tags according to a GA. Not only does this model build social networks (one level), but also higher-level groups emerge (two levels). These groups develop cultural properties that can supervene to alter the behavior and groupings of agents (three levels).

Another sophisticated agent model is Carley's ORGAHEAD model (Carley, 1990; Carley & Lee, 1998; Carley, 1999a). This simulation consists of small groups of workers (agents) led by an executive team, which develops firm-level strategy based on environmental inputs, including decisions about design, workload, and personnel. Groups that emerge in this model have control over which agents their workers will interact with and learn from, and this higher-order control alters subsequent co-evolutionary emergence. Likewise, at a higher level, the emergent culture of the firm alters the knowledge-creation strategies of its agents. In these ways, Carley's model reflects three levels of order (or perhaps four; see Lichtenstein & McKelvey, 2011). Each of these and others provide intriguing examples of how agent moves (leadership) at one level affect the structure and context for further moves (learning and leadership) at higher levels.

Biological and Energetic Approaches in the Complexity Sciences

In contrast to the computational and mathematical approaches described thus far, the next four fields explore emergence in natural (real) dynamic systems. The specific sciences—autocatalysis, dissipative structures, resilience, and ecological ascendency—examine the creation of life and the emergence of complex order in far-from-equilibrium chemical and biological systems. When these sciences are rigorously applied to organizations and management they exhibit the features of intrinsic emergence (see Chapter 5); their tangible expression (realization) of emergence is not a model but is the actual generation of a new systemic level of order in the real world. This, along with their link to natural systems, makes these fields especially valid for understanding the emergence of social entities (Lichtenstein, 2000b; Holling, 2001; Liu et al., 2007; Padgett & Powell, 2011).

Autocatalysis, Autogenesis, and Autopoiesis

At the center of studies on the origin of life are the studies by Manfred Eigen (1971a, 1971b; Eigen & Schuster, 1979) on autocatalysis—the creation of self-producing and self-catalyzing molecular networks. This work, for which he received the Nobel Prize in chemistry, showed how sets of molecules could become "self-organized" such that the outputs of a series of reactions would include the necessary inputs and the catalysts that can amplify and sustain the reaction network over time. The overall process was hypothesized as a key to understanding how complex macromolecules like RNA, polypeptides, and enzymes could be produced even before the creation of the earliest cells (Eigen, 1992), a thesis others pursued as well (especially Morowitz, 1966, 1968, 1992; Farmer, Kauffman, & Packard, 1986).

The actual mechanism for this self-catalyzing effect, as mentioned earlier, is the cyclic nature of these interrelated reactions, whereby each molecular element or string "in the autocatalytic network is constructed out of the interactions among the other strings" (Padgett, 2011, p. 51). As to when the network will actually emerge, Padget uses Kauffman's work on random-graph theory (Kauffman, 1993, pp. 308–309) to explain that, because of the nonlinearity of the network with its connected reactions (ties) and sites of molecular production (nodes), "... sooner or later the number of ties will exceed the growing number of nodes, thereby triggering autocatalysis. . . . [T]he implication of the model is that networks of proteins alone can self-organize into and trigger life if polymer lengths can grow long enough" (Padgett, 2011, pp. 52–53).

As most social scientists will appreciate, this framing allows for a direct application to social networks, which is the theoretical aim of Padgett and Powell's (2011) work. Specifically, they define autocatalysis (on p. 8) as "a set of nodes and transformations in which all nodes are reconstructed through transformations among nodes in the set." Structurally, this definition holds for the origin of economic products, organizations, or networks (p. 8, note 23). Thus, their approach forms a powerful foundation for understanding the emergence of new organizational forms, new markets, and other network-based entities, which they and their colleagues pursue throughout their book. Their approach is highly compatible with my own, a point I shall emphasize in Chapter 18.

Two related fields that have been used in management are autogenesis and autopoiesis. Both of these theories focus on how an autonomous system produces its internal structures through a regenerative organizing process. One approach, with origins in theoretical biology, by Maturana and Valera (1980), uses the idea of "structural coupling" to explain why we experience ourselves as autonomous beings even though we are inextricably linked to an external environment. In the social sciences, a parallel approach of autogenesis (Csanyi & Kampis, 1985; Pantzar & Csanyi, 1991) focuses on identity-making processes through which an agent's core values and schemas define the rules that formulate emergent structures (Drazin & Sandelands, 1992) and social structures (Kickert, 1993). Broader implications were derived by Luhmann in his "autopoiesis of social systems" (Luhmann, 1986, 1990).

From an entrepreneurial perspective, one value of autogenesis and autopoiesis is the conceptualization of mutual causality as the "structural coupling" of resource flows and environmental potentials (Swenson, 1992a, 1997). Understanding these flows provides the capability for accessing further regimes of resources, for example, in the forms of knowledge, opportunity, or competitive advantage.

Dissipative Structures

Another key science of complexity is dissipative structures theory, based on Ilya Prigogine's Nobel Prize–winning work on how order is spontaneously created in far-from-equilibrium systems (Prigogine, 1955; Prigogine & Glansdorff, 1971; Prigogine & Stengers, 1984). According to the theory, increasing energy flows through a system (e.g., in the form of heat or energy) can cause the system to move from near-equilibrium into far-from-equilibrium dynamics. At a critical threshold, there will emerge a new "level of order"—literally, macrostructures will appear spontaneously in the system (Bénard, 1901; Prigogine, 1955; Nicolis & Prigogine, 1989). These macrostructures increase the capacity of the system to dissipate heat energy. According to one set of experiments, the emergent new level of order expands the system's processing capacity by several orders of magnitude (Swenson, 1989, 1991).

Swenson himself was an entrepreneur who created a successful business, being the first to commercially produce and sell a new kind of cereal in the 1960s: granola. Swenson's understanding of how dissipative structures link to organizational growth is comparable to many researchers' application of the dissipative structures model to entrepreneurship (Binks & Vale, 1990; Foster, 2000), innovation (Dosi & Fagiolo, 1998; Saviotti & Mani, 1998), group dynamics (Smith, 1986; Smith & Comer, 1994), and economics in general (Georgescu-Roegen, 1971; De Vany, 1996). In management, dissipative structures theory has been used to explain the emergence of order in high-growth entrepreneurial ventures (Lichtenstein, 2000a, 2000b), the emergence of a new dominant logic for strategy (Bettis & Prahalad, 1995), transformative changes in strategy (MacIntosh & MacLean, 1999; Garud & Van de Ven, 2002) and organization (Leifer, 1989; Goldstein, 1994), the emergence of industry-level collaborative ventures (Browning, Beyer, & Shetler, 1995), and the emergence of sustainable economic regions (Chiles, Meyer, & Hench, 2004).

Since dissipative structures theory is the basis for generative emergence, I will not go into further depth here. Instead, Chapter 6 reviews the empirical studies that give rise to the theory, and Chapter 7 shows how it can be rigorously applied to social systems.

Ecosystem Resilience and Transition

Long-standing studies of natural ecologies have led to a general model of resilience—systemwide dynamics that lead to the adaptive persistence of an entire ecosystem, especially in the face of "stress, strain and surprise" (Clark, Holling, & Jones, 1996, p. 1). Conceptually, the science answers the biologically critical question of how far outside its normal activity regime an ecosystem can be pushed before it loses its ability to "bounce back," ultimately leading to extinction (Holling, 1973; May 1974, 1976). Through numerous studies applying this work to coupled biological–social systems, a definition for this adaptivity was developed by Walker, Holling, Carpenter, and Kinzig (2004, p. 4): "Resilience is the capacity of a system to absorb disturbance and reorganize while undergoing change so as to still retain essentially the same function, structure, identity and feedbacks." From a complexity perspective, "resilience reflects the degree to which a complex adaptive system is capable of self-organization (versus lack of organization or organization forced by external factors)" (Folke et al., 2004, p. 559).

These studies, organized by the Resilience Alliance (www.resalliance.org; Gunderson & Holling, 2001), revealed properties that "shape the adaptive cycle" of interactive ecosystems. These include the wealth or potentiality of a system, its internal controllability, and its adaptive capacity (Holling, 2001; Folke et al., 2004). These dimensions provide a framework for the dynamics of an adaptive cycle—a generalized theory of evolution and resilience in coupled biological and social ecosystems based on temporal changes across the dimensions (Gunderson & Holling, 2001). According to investigators' research, ecosystems move through an adaptive cycle, which Holling (1973) found to be composed of four successive phases: from exploitation to conservation as resources accumulate and transform, then through shorter periods of release and reorganization—moments of ecological innovation, that lead back to the exploitation phase.

It turns out that the nonlinearities common in these coupled biological–social systems can lead to what are called thresholds—"transition points between alternate states [of a system]" (Liu et al., 2007, p. 1512). In the natural world, these shifts are often irreversible and can lead to a severe decrease in the overall capacity of the ecosystem (Anderies, Walker, & Kinzig, 2006). At the same time, collaborators have identified frameworks of governance and management that can mitigate or perhaps avoid such regime shifts (Berkes, Colding, & Folke, 2000, 2003; Folke, Hahn, Olsson, & Norberg, 2005; Olsson et al., 2006; Walker et al., 2006). Ultimately, these studies provide an innovative approach to social sustainability (Folke et al., 2010; Loorbach, 2010; Westley et al., 2011). I shall return to this research in the final chapter of the book.

Ecological Ascendency; Directionality in Evolution

The final area is perhaps more an aspiration than a formal field, being a connection of insights that extend the fields of autocatalysis, dissipative structures, and ecological resilience. The core claim is that there is an inherent directionality of order creation in natural systems. Specifically, autocatalytic networks, dissipative structures, and ecological systems tend to *maximize* their capacity for processing energy flows, thereby fueling growth (Lotka, 1922, 1945; Odum & Pinkerton, 1955; Odum, 1969; Ulanowicz, 1980, 1987, 2002).

Lotka, for example, proposed a "law of maximum energy" for biological organisms (Lotka 1922, p. 147), which asserts that selective advantages "must go to those organisms whose energy-capturing devices are most efficient" (see Schneider & Sagan, 2005, p. 147). Pursuing that thinking, Odum and Pinkerton (1955, pp. 331, 332) developed a proposition: "natural systems tend to operate at that efficiency which produces a maximum power output . . . the greatest useful energy per unit time." Ulanowicz coupled this concept with Eigen's (1971) work on autocatalysis, to argue that autocatalytic networks are "growth enhancing" (Ulanowicz, 2002)—in formal terms, "an increase in the output of any element in an [energy] cycle when traced around the loop will engender a further increase in the starting flow" (Ulanowicz, 1983, p. 220).

Although these claims do not appear momentous in and of themselves, they lead to a rather surprising conclusion: When autocatalytic loops draw on the same pool of resources, they will be inherently competitive. Further, the one with greater efficiency will grow to its maximum output. Ulanowicz (1980, 1987) refers to this as "ascendency" and draws on Odum (1969) to claim that "in the absence of major perturbations, ecosystems have a propensity to increase in ascendency. Increasing ascendency [refers to] the tendency for [autocatalytic systems] to reinforce each other to the exclusion of nonparticipating members" (Ulanowicz, 2002, p. 47).

A cadre of scholars have pursued this idea, developing a "thermodynamic" approach to evolution that significantly extends the traditional neo-Darwinian model (Wicken, 1979, 1980, 1981; Depew & Weber, 1985; Wicken, 1985; Salthe, 1989; Weber, Depew, & Smith, 1990; Salthe, 1993; Depew & Weber, 1994). These studies were formally integrated in a collaboration among Weber, Depew, Dyke, Salthe, Schneider, Ulanowicz, and Wicken (1989), who presented an ecological, relational model of evolution in which "the self-organizing principles that lead to life's emergence . . . [are] entirely consistent with the broad Darwinian schema" (p. 377). In propositions P10—P15 (p. 380), they argue that "ecosystems favor species that increase the total energy flow through the ecosystem, [thus realizing] a maximization of energy flow into organizational propagation and a minimum of metabolic costs. [The result is] a continual hyperbolic increase in complicatedness [in evolution]."

This claim to a *natural* increase in complicatedness—what Swenson called "an inexorable increase" (Swenson, 1989, 1992b, 1997)—leads to a proposition that there is a directionality in evolution. Evolutionary adaptation follows increases in the capacity to process information or "complexity." Several very worthy endeavors to describe this new view include *The Evolutionary Trajectory* (Coren, 1998), *Cosmic Evolution* (Chaisson, 2001), and *The Emergence of Everything* (Morowitz, 2002). Chaisson (2001, p. 52) summarizes these efforts in his recognition that dissipative structures can build on themselves in "successive" cycles of reordering. Since each cycle yields the dissipation of more energy, further cycles generate greater complexity:

> Since each successive reordering causes more complexity than the preceding one, such systems become even more susceptible to fluctuations.... The resulting phenomenon—termed "order through fluctuations"—is a distinctly evolutionary one.[10]

Operationally, Chaisson extends the Shannon-Weaver formulation of biological ecosystems to calculate the "free energy rate density" of an ecosystem (2001, p. 138); his measure is "ergs per second per gram." With some moderate assumptions about the gram-density of structures like plants, animals, brains, and society, he shows an unmistakable logarithmic (hockey stick) amplification of "complexity," that is, increases in the free energy rate density, which progresses from the origin of the universe to the complex societies of today.

What this nonlinear increase in complexity and energy flux means is hard to say. Still, the ideas may be usefully combined with any other of the 15 sciences of complexity.

Applying the Sciences to Organization

In summary, these 15 fields present perhaps the most inclusive categorization of complexity sciences. Some will suggest that other fields should be added to the list. For example, Austrian economics is closely related to complexity science (see, for example, Chiles, Tuggle, McMullen, Bierman, & Greening, 2010), and the non-predictive processes underlying effectuation are quite consonant with these ideas as well (see the work of Dew, Reed, Sarasvathy, & Wiltbank, 2011). On the other hand, others would claim that the list is too broad, including fields like deterministic chaos theory and fractals that only measure emergence without producing it (see Lichtenstein and McKelvey, 2011). More important than these distinctions, however, is the conversations they initiate that help clarify and formalize a discipline of emergence.

Each of these 15 fields provide a perspective for understanding the emergence of order in physical, chemical, computational, biological, and ecological systems. Nearly all of them have been applied in organization science (Anderson et al., 1999; Maguire et al., 2006), entrepreneurship (Lichtenstein, 2011), and leadership (Lichtenstein, 2007). At the same time, the value of each applications differs, depending on the degree to which the science is well suited to the problem being explored, and on the rigor of the analogy from the science to social phenomena. The next chapter provides a framework for evaluating those analyses, with the goal of improving complexity science applications to organizations.

NOTES

1. Buckminister Fuller's classic *Operating Manual for Spaceship Earth* (1996) provided a compelling social narrative around the limits of our open system. This vision has evolved into the sustainability movement.
2. In particular, the two major texts that helped originate the academic field of management, Thompson's (1967) *Organizations in Action* and Katz and Kahn's (1978) *The Social Psychology of Organization*, were themselves based on the principles of open system theory. Their proposal, that open systems theory should underlie a field of management, was driven in part by their "radical" claim—now taken for granted—that system-level effects should be accounted for in understanding organizations, as much or more so than individual-level properties. Further, Katz and Kahn's description of the self-renewing quality of open systems is extremely consonant with generative emergence. Today the open systems framework underlies a vast segment of literature in organization science (see Scott, 1981, for the classic introduction). Curiously, the value of this nascent field was not heralded. In a 1972 special issue of *The Academy of Management Journal* on general system theory in organizations (see Von Bertalanffy, 1972) several of the papers focused on the limitations of the effort and on ways that general systems theory duplicated existing theory (e.g., Duncan, 1972; Kast & Rosenzweig, 1972; Thayer, 1972). Still, the stage had been set for an approach that would capture the dynamics and qualitative shifts within open systems.
3. Here are some further examples: Prigogine & Stengers, 1984; Zunderhoudt, 1990; Lewin, 1992; Begun, 1994; Dubinskas, 1994; Levy, 1994; Thietart & Forgues, 1995; Eoyang, 1997; Holland 1998; Lindberg et al., 1998; Pascale, 1999.
4. Mathematically, a power law is the rank/frequency expression, $F \sim N^{-\beta}$, where F is frequency, N is rank (the variable), and β, the exponent, is constant. A power law is simply a set of Pareto-distributed data points plotted on log X- and Y-axes.
5. This CA model is now available as a free download from Northwestern University: http://ccl.northwestern.edu/netlogo/
6. The program itself is more interesting in that it accounts for the distances between countries, such that frustration is a calculation that includes the propensity (desire, or lack thereof) to work with a country, as well as the distance between the two countries. Thus, a country could have high frustration by being in an alliance (configuration) with a certain other country, but that frustration would be mitigated if the countries are far away from each other. Moreover, the program accounts for the size of each country, weighting the larger countries to indicate their broader political power.
7. [From Axelrod and Bennett, 1993]. The symmetry of propensities guarantees that if one nation reduces its frustration by switching sides then the energy for the whole system will be reduced. Here is the proof. Without loss of generality, let $X = A'$ versus B where $A' = A \cup \{k\}$, and let $Y = A$ versus B' where $B' = B \cup \{k\}$. To shorten the notation let $K = \{k\}$ and $r_{ij} = s_i s_j p_{ij}$. $E(X) = \Sigma_{A'} \Sigma_B r_{ij} + \Sigma_B \Sigma_{A'} r_{ij}$ since $d_{ij}(X) = 0$ for $i \in A'$, $j \in A'$ or $i \in B, j \in B$; and $d_{ij}(X) = 1$ for $i \in A, j \in B'$ or $i \in B, j \in A'$. Likewise $E(Y) = \Sigma_A \Sigma_{B'} r_{ij} + \Sigma_{B'} \Sigma_A r_{ij}$. So $E(X) - E(Y) = \Sigma_{A'} \Sigma_B r_{ij} - \Sigma_A \Sigma_{B'} r_{ij} + \Sigma_B \Sigma_{A'} r_{ij} - \Sigma_{B'} \Sigma_A r_{ij} = \Sigma_K \Sigma_B r_{ij} - \Sigma_A \Sigma_K r_{ij} + \Sigma_B \Sigma_K r_{ij} - \Sigma_K \Sigma_A r_{ij}$ since $\Sigma_{A'} \Sigma_B r_{ij} = \Sigma_A \Sigma_B r_{ij} + \Sigma_K \Sigma_B r_{ij}$. But $\Sigma_K \Sigma_B r_{ij} = \Sigma_B \Sigma_K r_{ij}$ and $\Sigma_A \Sigma_K r_{ij} = \Sigma_K \Sigma_A r_{ij}$ since $p_{ij} = p_{ji}$. So $E(X) - E(Y) = \left(\Sigma_K \Sigma_B r_{ij} - \Sigma_K \Sigma_{A'} r_{ij}\right) = 2\left(s_k \Sigma_B s_j p_{kj} - s_k \Sigma_A s_j p_{kj}\right) = 2s_k \left(F_k(X) - F_k(Y)\right)$, since $d_{kj}(X) = 0$ for $j \in A$, $d_{kj}(X) = 1$ for $j \in B$, $d_{kj}(Y) = 0$, for $j \in B$ and $d_{kj}(Y) = 1$ for $j \in A$. But $s_k > 0$. So for adjacent configurations, X and Y, differing only by nation k, if $F_k(X) - F_k(Y) > 0$ then $E(X) - E(Y) > 0$.

8. Details of the simulation are instructive. Their trading firms operate in a financial market; each may have from one to nine constituent agents, and each agent has a different rule set for buying and selling financial instruments or doing nothing. Firms may activate or deactivate their agents, or form combinations of seemingly better-performing agents from prior periods. In an efficient market performance climate with a 50% probability of success, their model firms beat the market 60% of the time.
9. Specifically, Crowston (1996) simulates organizations of agents within in subgroups, acting in a market with task interdependency. Bottom-level agents have to perform their tasks in a specific length of time. Agents who coordinate may expedite their tasks, but the cost of coordination means a lessening of their time allotment according to the following rule: if an agent were to "talk" to all the other agents all the time there would be no time left to accomplish any tasks. Results show that organizations and/or their employee agents do in fact minimize coordination costs through organizing in particular ways.
10. Note that Chaisson uses the term developed by Prigogine and his collaborators, "order through fluctuations" (see Prigogine & Stengers, 1984, Chapter 6, pp. 177–209).

REFERENCES

Abbott, A. 1988. Transcending general linear reality. *Sociological Theory*, 6(2): 169–86.

Abbott, A. 1992. From causes to events: Notes on narrative positivism. *Sociological Methods and Research*, 20: 428–55.

Allen, P., Maguire, S., & McKelvey, B. (Eds.). 2011. *The SAGE Handbook of Complexity and Management*. Thousand Oaks, CA: SAGE Publications.

Allen, P., Strathern, M., & Baldwin, J. 2007. Complexity and the limits to learning. *Journal of Evolutionary Economics*, 17(4): 401–31.

Anderies, J., Walker, B., & Kinzig, A. 2006. Fifteen weddings and a funeral: Case studies and resilience-based management. *Ecology and Society*, 11(1): 21–32.

Anderson, P. 1999. Complexity theory and organization science. *Organization Science*, 10: 216–32.

Anderson, P., Meyer, A., Eisenhardt, K., Carley, K., & Pettigrew, A. 1999. Introduction to the special issue: Application of complexity theory to organization science. *Organization Science*, 10(3): 233–36.

Andriani, P., & McKelvey, B. 2007. Beyond Gaussian averages: Redirecting organization science toward extreme events and power laws. *Journal of International Business Studies*, 38: 1212–30.

Andriani, P., & McKelvey, B. 2009. From Gaussian to Paretian thinking: Causes and implications of power laws in organizations. *Organization Science*, 20: 1053–71.

Anonymous. 1996. Consumers turning over "new leaf" with emergence of premium tea. *Business Wire*: InfoTrack article #A17986914.

Arthur, B. 1988a. Competing technologies: An overiew. In G. Dosi, C. Freeman, R. Nelson, G. Silverberg, & L. Soete (Eds.), *Technical Change and Economic Theory*. London: Pinter Press.

Arthur, B. 1988b. Self-reinforcing mechanisms in economics. In P. Anderson, K. Arrow, & D. Pines (Eds.), *The Economy as an Evolving Complex System*. Reading, MA: Addison-Wesleuy.

Arthur, B. 1989. Competing technologies, increasing returns, and lock-in by historcial events. *Economic Journal*, 99: 116–31.

Arthur, B. 1990. Positive feedbacks in the economy. *Scientific American*, February: 92–99.

Arthur, B. 1994. *Increasing Returns and Path Dependence in the Economy*. Ann Arbor, MI: University of Michigan Press.

Ashby, R. 1956. *An Introduction to Cybernetics*. New York: John-Wiley & Sons.
Augros, R., & Stanciu, G. 1987. *The New Biology: Discovering the Wisdom of Nature*. Boston: Shambhala Press.
Axelrod, R. 1997. *The Complexity of Cooperation: Agent-Based Models of Competition and Cooperation*. Princeton, NJ: Princeton University Press.
Axelrod, R., & Bennett, D. S. 1993. A landscape theory of aggregation. *British Journal of Political Science*, 23: 211–33.
Axelrod, R., & Cohen, M. 2000. *Harnessing Complexity*. New York: Free Press.
Bak, P. 1996. *How Nature Works: The Science of Self-Organized Criticality*. New York: Springer-Verlag.
Bak, P., & Chen, K. 1991. Self-organized criticality. *Scientific American*, January: 46–53.
Baker, G., & Gollub, J. 1996. *Chaotic Dynamics, An Introduction* (2nd ed.). Cambridge, UK: Cambridge University Press.
Barabasi, A.-L., & Bonabeau, E. 2003. Scale-free networks. *Scientific American*, 288(May): 60–69.
Bateson, G. 1980. *Mind and Nature—A Necessary Unity*. New York: Bantam Books.
Baum, J. 1999. Whole-part coevolutionary competition in organizations. In J. Baum & B. McKelvey (Eds.), *Variations in Organization Science* (113–36). Thousand Oaks, CA: Sage Publications.
Beer, S. 1981. *The Brain of the Firm: A Development in Management Cybernetics*. Chinchester, UK: John Wiley & Sons.
Begun, J. 1994. Chaos and complexity: Frontiers of organization science. *Journal of Management Inquiry*, 3: 329–35.
Bénard, H. 1901. Les tourbillons cellulaires dans une nappe liquide transportant de la chaleur par convection en régime permanent. *Annales de Chimie et de Physique*, 23: 62–114.
Berkes, F., Colding, J., & Folke, C. 2000. Rediscovery of traditional ecological knowledge as adaptive management. *Ecological Applications*, 10: 1251–62.
Berkes, F., Colding, J., & Folke, C. (Eds.). 2003. *Navigating Social-Ecological Systems: Building Resilience for Complexity and Change*. Cambridge, UK: Cambridge University Press.
Berman, M. 1988. *The Reenchantment of the World*. New York: Bantam Books.
Bertalanffy, V. 1950. The theory of open systems in physics and biology. *Science*, 111(January 13): 23–28.
Bettis, R., & Prahalad, C. K. 1995. The dominant logic: Retrospective and extention. *Strategic Management Journal*, 16: 5–14.
Bigelow, J. 1982. A catastrophe model of organizational change. *Behavioral Science*, 27: 26–42.
Binks, M., & Vale, P. 1990. *Entrepreneurship and Economic Change*. London: McGraw-Hill.
Boisot, M., & McKelvey, B. 2010. Integrating modernist and postmodernist perspectives on organizations: A complexity science bridge. *Academy of Management Review*, 35: 415–34.
Boisot, M., & McKelvey, B. 2011. Connectivity, extremes and adaptation: A power-law perspective on organizational effectiveness. *Journal of Management Inquiry*, 20(2): 119–33.
Boulding, K. E. 1961. *The Image*. Ann Arbor, MI: Ann Arbor Paperbooks.
Brewis, S. J., Papamichail, K. N., & Rajaram, V. 2011. Decision-making practices in commercial enterprises: A cybernetic intervention into a business model. *Journal of Organizational Transformation and Social Change*, 8(1): 35–49.
Brown, C. 1995. *Chaos and Catastrophe Theories*. Newbury Park, CA: SAGE Publications.
Browning, L., Beyer, J., & Shetler, J. 1995. Building cooperation in a competitive industry: Sematech and the semiconductor industry. *Academy of Management Journal*, 38: 113–51.
Buenstorf, G. 2000. Self-organization and sustainability: Energetics of evolution and implications for ecological economics. *Ecological Economics*, 33: 119–34.
Capra, F. 1982. *The Turning Point*. New York: Bantam Books.

Capra, F. 1996. *The Web of Life*. New York: Anchor Books.
Carley, K. 1990. Group stability: A socio-cognitive approach. In B. M. E. Lawler, C. Ridgeway, & H. Walker (Ed.), *Advances in Group Processes*, Vol. 7: 1–44. Stamford, CT: JAI Press.
Carley, K. 1991. A theory of group stability. *American Journal of Sociology*, 56(3): 331–54.
Carley, K. 1995. Computational and mathematical organization theory: Perspective and directions. *Computational and Mathematical Organization Theory*, 1: 39–56.
Carley, K. 1999a. Learning within and among organizations. *Advances in Strategic Management*, 16: 33–53.
Carley, K. 1999b. On the evolution of social and organizational networks. In S. Andrews & D. Knoke (Eds.), *Research in the Sociology of Organizations* (Vol. 16: 3–30). Stamford, CT: JAI Press.
Carley, K. 2000. *Intra-organizational computation and complexity*. Working paper, Carnegie Mellon University.
Carley, K., & Hill, V. 2000. Structural change and learning within organizations. In A. Lomi (Ed.), *Dynamics of Organizational Societies; Models, Theories, and Methods*. Cambridge, MA: MIT Press.
Carley, K., & Lee, J.-S. 1998. Dynamic organizations: Organizational adaptation in a changing environment. *Advances in Strategic Management*, 15: 269–97.
Carley, K., & Svoboda, D. M. 1996. Modeling organization adaptation as a simulated annealing process. *Sociological Methods and Research*, 25: 138–68.
Casti, J. 1994. *Complexification*. New York: Harper Perennial.
Chaisson, E. 2001. *Cosmic Evolution: The Rise of Complexity in Nature*. Cambridge, MA: Harvard University Press.
Cheng, Y., & Van de Ven, A. 1996. The innovation journey: Order out of chaos? *Organization Science*, 6: 593–614.
Chiles, T., & Meyer, A. 2001. Managing the emergence of clusters: An increasing returns approach to strategic change. *Emergence*, 3(3): 58–89.
Chiles, T., Meyer, A., & Hench, T. 2004. Organizational emergence: The origin and transformation of Branson, Missouri's musical theaters. *Organization Science*, 15(5): 499–520.
Chiles, T., Tuggle, C. S., McMullen, J., Bierman, L., & Greening, D. 2010. Dynamic creation: Elaborating a radical Austrian approach to entrepreneurship. *Organization Studies*, 31: 7–46.
Choi, T., Dooley, K., & Rungtusanatham, M. 2001. Supply networks and complex adaptive systems: Control vs. emergence. *Journal of Operations Management*, 19: 351–66.
Clark, W., Holling, C. S., & Jones, D. D. 1996. Towards a structural view of resilience: 31. International Institute of Applied Systems Analysis.
Colbert, B. 2004. The complex resource-based view: Implications for theory and practice in strategic human resource management. *Academy of Management Review*, 29: 341–58.
Coleman, P., Vallacher, R., Nowak, A., & Bui-Wrzosinska, L. 2007. Intractable conflict as an attractor: A dynamical systems approach to conflict escalation and intractability. *American Behavioral Scientist*, 50(11): 1454–75.
Coren, R. 1998. *The Evolutionary Trajectory: The Growth of Information in the History and Future of the Earth*. Amsterdam: Gordon and Breach Publishers.
Cowan, G., Pines, D., & Meltzer, D. (Eds.). 1994. *Complexity: Metaphors, Models, and Reality*. Vol. Proceedings, #11. New York: Addison-Wesley.
Cramer, F. 1993. *Chaos and Order: The Complex Structure of Living Things* (D. L. Loewus, Trans.). New York: VCH.
Crowston, K. 1996. An approach to evolving novel organizational forms. *Computational and Mathematical Organization Theory*, 2: 29–47.

Csanyi, V., & Kampis, G. 1985. Autogenesis: Evolution of replicative systems. *Journal of Theoretical Biology*, 114: 303–21.

Davis, J., Eisenhardt, K., & Bingham, C. 2007. Developing theory through simulation methods. *Academy of Management Review*, 32: 480–99.

Depew, D., & Weber, B. (Eds.). 1985. *Evolution at a Crossroads: The New Biology and the New Philosophy of Science*. Cambridge, MA: MIT Press.

Depew, D., & Weber, B. 1994. *Darwinism Evolving*. New York: Oxford University Press.

De Vany, A. 1996. Information, chance, and evolution: Alchian and the economics of self-organization. *Economic Inquiry*, 34: 427–42.

Dew, Reed, Sarasvathy & Wiltbank, 2011. On the entrepreneurial genesis of new markets: Effectual transformations versus causal search and selection. *Journal of Evolutionary Economics*, 21: 231–53.

Dhillon, G., & Fabian, F. 2005. A fractal perspective on competencies necessary for managing information systems. *International Journal of Technology Management*, 31(1/2): 129–39.

DiRenzo, M., & Greenhaus, J. 2011. Job search and voluntary turnover in a boundaryless world: A control theroy perspective. *Academy of Management Review*, 36(3): 567–89.

Dooley, K. 1997. A complex adaptive systems model of organization change. *Nonlinear Dynamics, Psychology, and the Life Sciences*, 1: 69–97.

Dooley, K., & Van de Ven, A. 1999. Explaining complex organizational dynamics. *Organization Science*, 10(3): 358–72.

Dosi, G., & Fagiolo, G. 1998. Exploring the unknown. On entrepreneurship, coordination and innovation-driven growth. In J. Lesourne & A. Orlean (Eds.), *Advances in Self-Organization and Evolutionary Economics* (308–52). London: Economica.

Drazin, R., & Sandelands, L. 1992. Autogenesis: A perspective on the process of organizing. *Organization Science*, 3: 230–49.

Dubinskas, F. 1994. On the edge of chaos: A metaphor for transformative change. *Journal of Management Inquiry*, 3: 355–66.

Duncan, D. M. 1972. James G. Miller's living systems theory: Issues for management thought and practice. *Academy of Management Journal*, 15(4): 513–23.

Dyke, C. 1992. From entropy to economy: A thorny path. *Advances in Human Ecology*, 1: 149–76.

Eigen, M. 1971a. Molecular self-organization and the early stages of evolution. *Quarterly Reviews of Biophysics*, 4: 149–212.

Eigen, M. 1971b. Self-organization of matter and the evolution of biological macromolecules. *Naturwissenschaften*, 58: 465–523.

Eigen, M. 1992. *Steps Toward Life: A Perspective on Evolution* Oxford, UK: Oxford University Press.

Eigen, M., & Schuster, P. 1979. *The Hypercycle: A Principle of Natural Self-Organizing; In Three Parts*. New York: Springer.

Elliott, E., & Kiel, D. (Eds.). 1996. *Chaos Theory in the Social Sciences: Foundations and Applications*. Ann Arbor, MI: University of Michigan Press.

Eoyang, G. 1997. *Coping with Chaos*. Cheyanne, WY: Laguno Corporation.

Epstein, J. M., & Axtell, R. 1996. *Growing Artificial Societies: Social Science from the Bottom up*. Cambridge, MA: MIT Press.

Espinosa, A., Harnden, R., & Walker, J. 2004. Cybernetics and participation: From theory to practice. *Systemic Practice and Action Research*, 17(6): 573–89.

Espinosa, A., Harnden, R., & Walker, J. 2008. A complexity approach to sustainability: Stafford Beer revisited. *Eurpoean Journal of Operational Research*, 187: 636–51.

Ethiraj, S. K., & Levinthal, D. 2004. Modularity and innovation in complex systems. *Management Science*, 50: 159–73.

Eve, R., Horsfall, S., & Lee, M. 1997. *Chaos, Complexity, and Sociology*. Thousand Oaks, CA: SAGE Publications.

Farjoun, M., & Levin, M. 2011. A fractal approach to industry dynamism. *Organization Studies*, 32(6): 825–51.

Farmer, J. D., Kauffman, S., & Packard, N. 1986. Autocatalytic replication of polymers. *Physica D*, 22: 5–67.

Fleming, L., & Sorenson, O. 2001. Technology as a complex adaptive system. *Research Policy*, 30: 1019–1039.

Folke, C., Carpenter, S., Walker, B., Scheffer, M., Chapin, T., & Rockstrom, J. 2010. Resilience thinking: Integrating resilience, adaptability and transformability. *Ecology and Society*, 15(4): 20–8.

Folke, C., Carpenter, S., Walker, B., Scheffer, M., Elmqvist, T., Gunderson, L., & Holling, C. S. 2004. Regime shifts, resilience, and biodiversity in ecosystem management. *Annual Review of Ecology, Evolution, and Systematics*, 35: 557–81.

Folke, C., Hahn, T., Olsson, P., & Norberg, J. 2005. Adaptive governance of social-ecological systems. *Annual Review of Environmental Resources*, 30: 441–73.

Forrester, J. 1961. *Industrial Dynamics*. Cambridge, MA: MIT Press.

Foster, J. 2000. Competitive selection, self-organization and Joseph A. Schumpeter. *Journal of Evolutionary Economics*, 10: 311–28.

Fuller, R. B. 1969. *Operating Manual for Spaceship Earth*. New York: Simon and Schuster.

Fuller, T., & Moran, P. 2001. Small enterprises as complex adaptive systems: A methdological question? *Entrepreneurship and Regional Development*, 13: 47–63.

Ganco, M., & Agarwal, R. 2009. Performance differentials between diversifying entrants and entrepreneurial start-ups: A complexity approach. *Academy of Management Review*, 34: 228–53.

Garreau, J. 1992. *Edge City*. New York: Anchor Books.

Garud, R., & Van de Ven, A. 2002. Strategic organizational change processes. In H. Pettigrew, H. Thomas, & R. Whittington (Eds.), *Handbook of Strategy and Management* (206–31). London: SAGE Publications.

Gavetti, G., & Levinthal, D. 2000. Looking forward and looking backward: Cognitive and experiential search. *Administrative Science Quarterly*, 45: 113–37.

Gavetti, G., Levinthal, D., & Rivkin, J. 2005. Strategy making in novel and complex worlds: The power of analogy. *Strategic Management Journal*, 26: 691–712.

Georgescu-Roegen, N. 1971. *The Entropy Law and the Economic Process*. Cambridge, MA: Harvard University Press.

Gleick, J. 1987. *Chaos: Making a New Science*. New York: Penguin.

Goerner, S. 1994. *Chaos and the Evolving Ecological Universe*. Langhorn, PA: Gordon & Breach.

Goldenberg, J., Libai, B., & Muller, E. 2002. Riding the sadddle: How cross-market communications can create a major slump in sales. *Journal of Marketing*, 66: 1–66.

Goldstein, J. 1994. *The Unshackled Organization*. Portland, OR: Productivity Press.

Goldstein, J. 1999. Emergence as a construct: History and Issues. *Emergence*, 1(1): 49–72.

Goldstein, J. 2000. Emergence: A concept amid a thicket of conceptual snares. *Emergence*, 2(1): 5–22.

Goldstein, J., Hazy, J., & Lichtenstein, B. 2010. *Complexity and the Nexus of Leadership: Leveraging Nonlinear Science to Create Ecologies of Innovation*. New York: Palgrave Macmillan.

Gresov, C., Haveman, H., & Oliva, T. 1993. Organizational design, inertia and the dynamics of competetive response. *Organization Science*, 4: 181–208.

Guastello, S. 1987. A butterfuly catastrophe model of motivation in organizations. *Journal of Applied Psychology*, 72: 165–82.

Guastello, S. 1995. *Chaos, Catastrophe, and Human Affairs: Applications of Nonlinear Dynamics to Work, Organizations, and Social Evolution*. Mahway, NJ: Lawrence Erlbaum & Associates.

Guastello, S. 1998. Self-organization and leadership emergence. *Nonlinear Dynamics, Psychology, and Life Sciences*, 2: 301–15.

Gunderson, L., & Holling, C. S. (Eds.). 2001. *Panarchy: Understanding Transformations in Human and Natural Systems*. Washington, DC: Island Press.

Gunz, H., Lichtenstein, B., & Long, R. 2002. Self-organization in career systems: A view from complexity science. *M@n@gement*, 5(1): 63–88.

Haken, H. 1977. *Synergetics*. Berlin: Springer-Verlag.

Hall, R. 1976. A system pathology of an organization: The rise and fall of the old *Saturday Evening Post*. *Administrative Science Quarterly*, 21: 185–211.

Harre, R., & Secord, P. F. 1979. *The Explanation of Social Behaviour*. Totowa, NJ: Littlefield, Adams & Company.

Holland, J. 1975. *Adaptation in Natural and Artificial Systems*. Ann Arbor, MI: University of Michigan Press.

Holland, J. 1994. Echoing emergence: Objectives, rough definitions, and speculations of ECHO-class models. In G. Cowen, D. Pines, & D. Meltzer (Eds.), *Complexity: Metaphors, Models, and Reality*: 309–43. Sante Fe, NM: Sante Fe Institute.

Holland, J. 1995. *Hidden Order*. Redwood City, CA: Addison-Wesley.

Holland, J. 1998. *Emergence: From Chaos to Order*. Cambridge, MA: Perseus Books.

Holling, C. S. 1973. Resilience and stability of ecological systems. *Annual Review of Ecology and Systematics*, 4: 1–23.

Holling, C. S. 2001. Understanding the complexity of economic, ecological, and social systems. *Ecosystems*, 4: 390–405.

Iannaccone, P. M., & Khokha, M. 1996. *Fractal Geometry in Biological Systems*. Boca Raton, FL: CRC Press.

Kast, F., & Rosenzweig, J. 1972. General systems theory: Applications for organization and management. *Academy of Management Journal*: 15(4): 447–65.

Kauffman, S. 1993. *The Origins of Order*. New York: Oxford University Press.

Kickert, W. 1993. Autopoiesis and the science of (public) administration: Essence, sense and nonsense. *Organization Studies*, 14: 261–78.

Kim, D. 1993. The link between individual and organizational learning. *Slaon Management Review*, Fall: 37–50.

Krugman, P. 1996. *The Self-Organizing Economy*. Cambridge, MA: Bradford Press.

Lappe, FM. 2011. *EcoMind: Changing the Way We Think, To Create the World We Want*. New York: Nation Books.

Lee, Y., Amaral, L. A. N., Canning, D., Meyer, M., & Stanley, E. 1998. Universal features in the growth dynamics of complex organizations. *Physical Review (Amerian Physical Society)—Letters*, 81(15): 3275–82.

Leifer, R. 1989. Understanding organizational transformation using a dissipative structure model. *Human Relations*, 42: 899–916.

Lenox, M., Rockart, S., & Lewin, A. 2006. Interdependency, competition and the distribution of firm and industry profits. *Management Science*, 52: 757–72.

Levinthal, D. 1997. Adaptation on rugged landscapes. *Management Science*, 43: 934–50.

Levinthal, D., & Warglien, M. 1999. Landscape deisgn: Designing for local action in complex worlds. *Organization Science*, 10(3): 342–57.

Levy, D. 1994. Chaos theory and strategy. *Strategic Management Journal*, 15: 167–78.

Levy, D., & Lichtenstein, B. 2010. Non-linear meltdowns and the potential for emergence: Complex systems theory and social-environmental sustainability. In

A. Hoffman & M. T. Dacin (Eds.), *Oxford Handbook on Business and the Environment* (591–610). New York: Oxford University Press.

Levy, M., & Solomon, S. 1997. New evidence for the power-law distribution of wealth. *Physica A: Statistical Mechanics and its Applications*, 242(1): 90–4.

Lewin, R. 1992. *Complexity: Life on the Edge of Chaos*. New York: MacMillan.

Lichtenstein, B. 2000a. Emergence as a process of self-organizing: New assumptions and insights from the study of nonlinear dynamic systems. *Journal of Organizational Change Management*, 13: 526–44.

Lichtenstein, B. 2000b. Self-organized transitions: A pattern amid the "chaos" of transformative change. *Academy of Management Executive*, 14(4): 128–41.

Lichtenstein, B. 2007. A matrix of complexity for leadership. In J. Hazy, J. Goldstein, & B. Lichtenstein (Eds.), *Complex Systems Leadership Theory* (285–304). Boston: ISCE Press.

Lichtenstein, B. 2011. Complexity science contributions to the field of entrepreneurship. In P. Allen, S. Maguire, & B. McKelvey (Eds.), *The SAGE Handbook of Complexity and Management* (471–93). Thousand Oaks, CA: SAGE Publications.

Lichtenstein, B., & McKelvey, B. 2011. Four types of emergence: A typology of complexity and its implications for a science of management. *International Journal of Complexity in Leadership and Management*, 1(4): 339–78.

Lichtenstein, B., Uhl-Bien, M., Marion, R., Seers, A., Orton, D., & Schreiber, C. 2007. Complexity leadership theory: Explaining the interactive process of leading in complex adaptive systems. *Emergence: Complexity and Organization*, 8(4): 2–12.

Lindberg, C., Herzog, A., Merry, M., & Goldstein, J. 1998. Life at the edge of chaos. *Physician Executive*, 24(1): 6–21.

Liu, J., Dietz, T., Carpenter, S., Alberti, M., Folke, C., Moran, E., Pell, A. N., Deadman, P., Kratz, T., Lubchenco, J., Ostrom, E., Ouyang, Z., Provencher, W., Redman, C., Schneider, S., & Taylor, W. 2007. Complexity of coupled human and natural systems. *Science*, 317(Sept. 14): 1513–16.

Lomi, A., & Larsen, E. 1996. Interacting locally and evolving globally: A computational approach to the dynamics of organizational populations. *Academy of Management Journal*, 39(5): 1287–321.

Lomi, A., & Larson, E. 1997. A computational approach to the evolution of competitive strategy. *Journal of Mathematical Sociology*, 22: 151–76.

Loorbach, D. 2010. Transition management for sustainable development: A prescriptive, complexity-based governance framework. *Governancee*, 23: 161–83.

Lorenz, E. 1963. Deterministic nonperiodic flow. *Journal of the Atmospheric Sciences*, 20: 130–41.

Lotka, A. 1922. Contribution to the energetics of evolution. *Proceedings of the National Academy of Sciences USA*, 6: 147–51.

Lotka, A. 1945. The law of evolution as a maximal principle. *Human Biology*, 17: 167–94.

Luhmann, N. 1986. The autopoiesis of social systems. In F. Geyer & J. van der Zouwen (Eds.), *Sociocybernetic Paradoxes: Observation, Control and Evolution of Self-Steering Systems* (172–92). Thousand Oaks, CA: SAGE Publications.

Luhmann, N. 1990. *Essays on Self-Reference*. New York: Columbia University Press.

MacIntosh, R., & MacLean, D. 1999. Conditioned emergence: A dissipative structures approach to transformation. *Strategic Management Journal*, 20: 297–316.

Macy, M., & Skvoretz, J. 1998. The evolution of trust and cooperration between strangers: A computational model. *American Sociological Review*, 63: 683–60.

Maguire, S., McKelvey, B., Mirabeau, L., & Oztas, N. 2006. Complexity science and organization studies. In S. Clegg, C. Hardy, W. Nord, & T. Lawrence (Eds.), *Handbook of Organization Studies* (2nd ed., 165–214). London: SAGE Publications.

Malerba, F., Nelson, R., Orsenigo, L., & Winter, S. 1999. "History-friendly" models of industry evolution: The computer industry. *Industrial and Corporate Change*, 8: 3–40.
Mandelbrot, B. 1983. *The Fractal Geometry of Nature*. New York: Freeman Press.
Marion, R. 1999. *The Edge of Organization*. Thousand Oaks, CA: SAGE Publications.
Maruyama, M. 1963. The second cybernetics. *American Scientist*, 51: 164–79.
Matilla-Garcia, M., & Marin, M. R. 2010. A new test for chaos and determinsm based on symbolic dynamicsk. *Journal of Economic Behavior and Organization*, 76(3): 600–14.
Maturana, H. R., & Varela, F., J. 1980. *Autopoiesis and Cognition*. Dordrecht, Holland: D. Reidel Publishing.
May, R. 1974. Biological populations with nonoverlapping generations: Stable points, stable cycles, and chaos. *Science*, 186: 645–47.
May, R. 1976. Simple mathematical models with very complicated dynamics. *Nature*, 26: 455–67.
McKelvey, B. 1999a. Avoiding complexity catastrophe in coevolutionary pockets: Strategies for rugged landscapes. *Organization Science*, 10(3): 294–321.
McKelvey, B. 1999b. Complexity theory in organization science: Seizing the promise or becoming a fad? *Emergence*, 1(1): 5–32.
McKelvey, B. 1999c. Toward a Campbellian realist organization science. In J. Baum & B. McKelvey (Eds.), *Variations in Organization Science* (383–412). Thousand Oaks, CA: SAGE Publications.
McKelvey, B. 2004a. Toward a 0th law of thermodynamics: Order creation complexity dynamics from physics and biology to bioeconomics. *Bioeconomics*, 6: 65–96.
McKelvey, B. 2004b. Toward a complexity science of entrepreneurship. *Journal of Business Venturing*, 19: 313–42.
Meadows, D., Meadows, D., Randers, J., & Behrens, W. 1972. *The Limits to Growth: A Report to the Club of Rome*. New York: Universe Press.
Miller, J. G. 1978. *Living Systems*. New York: McGraw-Hill.
Morel, B., & Ramanujam, R. 1999. Through the looking glass of complexity: The dynamics of organizations as adaptive and evolving systems. *Organization Science*, 10(3): 278–93.
Morowitz, H. 1966. Physical background of cycles in biological systems. *Journal of Theoretical Biology*, 13: 60–62.
Morowitz, H. 1968. *Energy Flow in Biology: Biological Organization as a Problem in Thermal Physics*. New York: Academic Press.
Morowitz, H. 1992. *Beginnings of Cellular Life: Metabolism Recapitulates Biogenesis*. New Haven, CT: Yale University Press.
Morowitz, H. 2002. *The Emergence of Everything*. New York: Oxford University Press.
Nair, A., Narasimhan, R., & Choi, T. 2009. Supply networks as a complex adaptive system: Toward simulation-based theory building on evolutionary decision making. *Decision Sciences*, 40(4): 783–815.
Neumann, J. V. 1966. *Theory of Self-Reproducing Automata*. Champaign, IL: University of Illinois Press.
Nicolis, G., & Prigogine, I. 1989. *Exploring Complexity*. New York: W. H. Freeman.
Odum, H. 1969. The strategy of ecosystem development. *Science*, 164: 262–70.
Odum, H., & Pinkerton, R. 1955. Time's speed regulator: The optimum efficiency for maximum power output in physical and biological systems. *American Scientist*, 43(2): 331–43.
Olsson, P., Gunderson, L., Carpenter, S., Ryan, P., Lebel, L., Folke, C., & Holling, C. S. 2006. Shooting the rapids: Navigating transitions to adaptive governance of social-ecological systems. *Ecology and Society*, 11(1): Article 18.
Padgett, J. 2011. Autocatalysis in chemistry and the origin of life. In J. Padgett & W. Powell, *The Emergence of Organizations and Markets* (33–70). Princeton, NJ: Princeton University Press.

Padgett, J., & Powell, W. 2011. *The Emergence of Organizations and Markets*. Princeton, NJ: Princeton University Press.

Pantzar, M., & Csanyi, V. 1991. The replicative model of the evolution of the business organization. *Journal of Social and Biological Structures*, 14: 149–63.

Pareto, V. 1897. *Cours d'Economie Politique*. Paris: Rouge and Cie.

Pascale, R. 1999. Surfing the edge of chaos. *Sloan Management Review*, Spring: 83–94.

Pathak, S., Day, J., Nair, A., Sawaya, W., & Kristal, M. 2007. Complexity and adaptivity in supply networks: Building supply network theory using a complex adaptive systems perspective. *Decision Sciences*, 38: 547–80.

Paul, D. L., Butler, J. C., Pearlson, K. E., & Whinston, A. B. 1996. Computationally modeling organizational learning and adaptability as resource allocation. *Computational and Mathematical Organization Theory*, 2: 301–24.

Pegasus-Communications. 1999. *Organizational Learning at Work*. Waltham, MA: Pegasus Communications.

Pietgen, H. O., Jurgens, H., & Saupe, D. 2004. *Chaos and Fractals: New Frontiers of Science* (2nd ed.). New York: Springer-Verlag.

Plowman, D. A., Baker, L., Beck, T., Kulkarni, M., Solansky, S., & Travis, D. 2007. Radical change accidentally: The emergence and amplification of small change. *Academy of Management Journal*, 50: 515–43.

Poole, M. S., Van de Ven, A., Dooley, K., & Holmes, M. 2000. *Organizational Change and Innovation Processes: Theory and Methods for Research*. New York: Oxford University Press.

Porter, M., & Siggelkow, N. 2008. Contextual interactions within activity systems and sustainability of competitive advantage. *Academy of Management Perspectives*, 22(2): 34–56.

Prigogine, I. 1955. *Introduction to the Thermodynamics of Irreversible Processes*. New York: John Wiley & Sons.

Prigogine, I., & Glansdorff, P. 1971. *Thermodynamic Theory of Structure, Stability, and Fluctuations*. New York: John Wiley & Sons.

Prigogine, I., & Stengers, I. 1984. *Order out of Chaos*. New York: Bantam Books.

Repenning, N. 2002. A simulation-based approach to understanding the dynamics of innovation implementation. *Organization Science*, 13(2): 109–27.

Repenning, N., & Sterman, J. 2001. Nobody ever gets credit for fixing problems that never happened: Creating and sustaining process improvement. *California Management Review*, 43(4): 64–88.

Rivkin, J. 2000. Imitation of complex strategies. *Management Science*, 46: 824–44.

Rivkin, J., & Siggelkow, N. 2003. Balancing search and stability: Interdependencies among elements of organizational design. *Management Science*, 49: 290–311.

Romme, G., Zollo, M., & Berends, P. 2010. Dynamic capabilities, deliberate learning and environmental dynamism: A simulation model. *Industrial and Corporate Change*, 19(4): 1271–99.

Rothschild, M. 1992. *Bionomics: Economy as Ecosystem*. New York: Holt & Company.

Rudolph, J., & Repenning, N. 2002. Disaster dynamics: Understanding the role of quantity in organizational collapse. *Administrative Science Quarterly*, 47: 1–30.

Salthe, S. 1989. Self-organization of/in hierarchically structured systems. *Systems Research*, 6(3): 199–208.

Salthe, S. 1993. *Development and Evolution: Complexity and Change in Biology*. Cambridge, MA: Bradford—MIT Press.

Sastry, A. 1997. Problems and paradoxes in a model of punctuated organizational change. *Administrative Science Quarterly*, 42(2): 237–75.

Saviotti, P. P., & Mani, G. S. 1998. Technological evolution, self-organization, and knowledge. *Journal of High Technology Management Research*, 9: 255–70.

Scheinkman, J., & Woodfordd, J. 1994. Self-organized criticality and economic fluctuations. *American Economic Review*, 84: 417–21.
Schelling, T. 1978. *Micromotives and Macrobehavior*. New York: W. W. Norton.
Schneider, E., & Sagan, D. 2005. *Into the Cool: Energy Flow, Thermodynamics, and Life*: Chicago: University of Chicago Press.
Scott, R. 1981. *Organizations: Rational, Natural, and Open Systems*. Saddlebrook, NJ: Prentice-Hall.
Senge, P. M. 2006. *The Fifth Discipline* (revised ed.). New York: Doubleday.
Senge, P. M., Roberts, C., Ross, R., Smith, B., & Kleiner, A. 1994. *The Fifth Discipline Fieldbook*. New York: Currency/Doubleday.
Siggelkow, N., & Rivkin, J. 2005. Speed and search: Designing organizations for turbulence and complexity. *Organization Science*, 16: 101–22.
Simon, H. 2002. Near decomposability and the speed of evolution. *Industrial and Corporate Change*, 11: 587–99.
Smith, C. 1986. Transformation and regeneration in social systems: A dissipative structure perspective. *Systems Research*, 3: 203–13.
Smith, C., & Comer, D. 1994. Change in the small group: A dissipative structure perspective. *Human Relations*, 47: 553–81.
Smith, C., & Gemmill, G. 1991. Self-organization in small groups: A study of group effectiveness within non-equilibrium conditions. *Human Relations*, 44: 697–716.
Sommer, S., Loch, C., & Dong, J. 2009. Managing complexity and unforseeable uncertainty in startup companies: An empirical study. *Organization Science*, 20: 118–13.
Sorenson, O. 1997. *The complexity catastrophe: Interdependence and adaptability in organizational evolution*. Ph.D. dissertation, Stanford University, Palo Alto, CA.
Sorenson, O. 2002. Interorganizational complexity and computation. In J. Baum (Ed.), *Companion to Organizations* (664–85). Malden, MA: Blackwell Publishers.
Stanley, M., Amaral, L., Buldyrev, S., Havlin, S., Leschhorn, H., Maass, P., Salinger, M., & Stanley, E. 1996. Scaling behavior in the growth of companies. *Nature*, 379: 804–806.
Sterman, J. 1989. Misperceptions of feedback in dynamic decision making. *Organizational Behavior and Human Decision Processes*, 43(3): 301–44.
Sterman, J. 2000. *Business Dynamics*. Chicago: Irwin-McGraw-Hill.
Sterman, J. 2002. All models are wrong: Reflections on becoming a systems scientist. *System Dynamics Review*, 18(4): 501–32.
Sterman, J., & Wittenberg, J. 1999. Path dependence, competition, and succession in the dynamics of scientific revolutions. *Organization Science*, 10: 322–41.
Sulis, W., & Combs, A. (Eds.). 1996. *Nonlinear Dynamics in Human Behavior*. Singapore: World Scientific Press.
Surana, A., Kumara, S., Greaves, M., & Raghavan, U. N. 2005. Supply-chain networks: A complex adaptive systems perspective. *International Journal of Production Research*, 43(20): 4235–265.
Swenson, R. 1989. Emergent attractor and the law of maximum entropy production: Foundations to a theory of general evolution. *Systems Research*, 6(3): 187–97.
Swenson, R. 1991. End-directed physics and evolutionary ordering. In F. Geyr (Ed.), *Cybernetics of Complex Systems*. Salinas, CA: Intersystems Press.
Swenson, R. 1992a. Autocatakinetics, yes—Autopoiesis, no: Steps toward a unified theory of evolutionary ordering. *International Journal of General Systems*, 21: 207–28.
Swenson, R. 1992b. Order, evolution, and natural law: Fundamental relations in complex system theory. In C. Negoita (Ed.), *Cybernetics and Applied Systems* (125–47). New York: Marcel Dekker.

Swenson, R. 1997. Autocatakinetics, evolution, and the law of maximum entropy production: A principled foundation towards the study of human ecology. *Advances in Human Ecology*, 6: 1–47.

Tesfatsion, L. 2011. Agent-based modeling and institutional design. *Eastern Economic Journal*, 37: 13–19.

Thayer, F. 1972. General system(s) theory: The promise that could not be kept. *Academy of Management Journal*, 15(4): 481–93.

Thietart, R., & Forgues, B. 1995. Chaos theory and organization. *Organizational Science*, 6: 19–31.

Thom, R. 1975. *Structural Stability and Morphogenesis*. Reading, MA: Addison-Wesley.

Thomas, I., Frankhauser, P., & Badariotti, D. 2012. Comparing the fractality of European urban neighborhoods: Do national contexts matter? *Journal of Geographic Systems*, 14(2): 189–208.

Thompson, J. 1967. *Organizations in Action*. New York: McGraw Hill.

Tushman, M., & Romanelli, E. 1985. Organizational evolution: A metamorphosis model of convergence and reorientation. *Research in Organizational Behavior*, 7: 171–222.

Ulanowicz, R. 1980. An hypothesis on the development of natural communities. *Journal of Theoretical Biology*, 85: 225–45.

Ulanowicz, R. 1983. Identifying the structure of cycling in ecosystems. *Mathematical Biosciences*, 65: 219–37.

Ulanowicz, R. 1987. Growth and development: Variational principles reconsidered. *European Journal of Operational Research*, 30: 173–78.

Ulanowicz, R. 2002. Ecology, a dialog between the quick and the dead. *Emergence*, 4(1-2): 34–52.

von Bertalanffy, L. 1956. General system theory. *General Systems*, 1: 1–10.

von Bertalanffy, L. 1972. The history and status of general systems theory. *Academy of Management Journal*, 15(4): 407–26.

von Foerster, H. 1960. On self-organizing systems and their environments. In M. Yovitz, & S. Cameron (Eds.), *Self-Organizing Systems*. New York: Pergamon Press.

Waldrop, M. 1992. *Complexity*. New York: Touchstone/Simon & Schuster.

Walker, B., Gunderson, L., Kinzig, A., Folke, C., Carpenter, S., & Schultz, L. 2006. A handful of hueristics and some propositions for understanding resilience in social-ecological systems. *Ecology and Society*, 11(1): 13–29.

Walker, B., Holling, C. S., Carpenter, S., & Kinzig, A. 2004. Resilience, adaptability and transformability in social-ecological systems. *Ecology and Society*, 9(2): 5.

Weber, B., Depew, B., Dyke, C., Salthe, S., Schneider, E., Ulanowicz, R., & Wicken, J. 1989. Evolution in thermodynamic perspective: An ecological approach. *Biology and Philosophy*, 4: 373–405.

Weber, B. H., Depew, D. J., & Smith, J. D. (Eds.). 1990. *Entropy, Information, and Evolution*. Cambridge, MA: MIT Press.

Weiner, N. 1948/1961. *Cybernetics*. Cambridge, MA: MIT Press.

Westley, F., Olsson, P., Folke, C., Homer-Dixon, T., Vredenburg, H., Loorbach, D., Thompson, J., Nilsson, M., Lambin, E., Sendzimir, J., Banerjee, B., Galaz, V., & van der Leeuw, S. 2011. Tipping toward sustainability: Emerging pathways of transformation. *Ambio*, 40: 762–80.

Wicken, J. 1979. The generation of complexity in evolution: A thermodynamic and information-theoretical discussion. *Journal of Theoretical Biology*, 77(3): 349–65.

Wicken, J. 1980. A thermodynamic theory of evolution. *Journal of Theoretical Biology*, 87: 9–23.

Wicken, J. 1981. Evolutionary self-organization and the entropy principle: Teology and mechanism. *Nature and System*, 3: 129–41.

Wicken, J. 1985. Thermodynamics and the conceptual structure of evolutionary theory. *Journal of Theoretical Biology*, 117: 363–83.

Wicken, J. 1986. Evolutionary self-organization and entropic dissipation in biological and socioeconomic systems. *Journal of Social and Biological Structures*, 9: 261–73.

Zaror, G., & Guastello, S. 2000. Self-organization and leadership emergence: A cross-cultural replication. *Nonlinear Dynamics, Psychology, and Life Sciences*, 4: 113–20.

Zeeman, E. 1977. *Catastrophe Theory: Selected Papers*. Reading, MA: Addison-Wesley.

Zimmerman, B., & Hurst, D. 1993. Breaking the boundaries: The fractal organization. *Journal of Management Inquiry*, 2: 334–54.

Zipf, G. K. 1949. *Human Behavior and the Principle of Least Effort*. New York: Hafner.

Zuijderhoudt, R. 1990. Chaos and the dynamics of self-organization. *Human Systems Management*, 9: 225–38.

CHAPTER 4
Defining Emergence and Generative Emergence

The previous chapter presented a set of methods that can facilitate the study of emergence for a given unit of analysis. Like the eight prototypes described in Chapter 2, these complexity sciences provide a structure for gaining insight into the phenomenon of emergence, a means for exploring what emergence is and how it occurs. In this sense we are following the advice of Kuhn (1970), who noted that all new scientific paradigms (or disciplines) have at their root (1) a *framework* and (2) a *methodology* that provides a unique view into the world, both of which facilitate new questions and open new arenas of understanding. By linking the methods of complexity science to the eight prototypes of emergence, we make a good deal of progress toward developing a discipline of emergence.

A third critical component of any new scientific discipline (Kuhn, 1970) is a core *definition* for the phenomenon being studied. Thus, the present chapter takes up the challenge of defining emergence. The approach I will take in this chapter is to review the most comprehensive meanings of emergence, drawing on long-standing efforts to define emergence in evolutionary studies and philosophy, with support from more recent explorations in sociology, biology, and complexity science. This analysis reveals five specific qualities that are common across these disciplines and are at the heart of most recent definitions of emergence.

Bear in mind that my primary academic contribution is to social scientists.[1] Thus, the definition I am proposing has a focus on human phenomena of emergence, through a review of the history and key philosophical questions that emergence scholars have been exploring for well over 100 years.[2] To be fair, the summary that follows cannot hope to capture all the subtlety and critical detail of these literatures; however, I hope to have identified the main themes and insights.

My analysis is based on a number of key papers and books, whose authors include Sawyer (2005), Corning (2002), Juarraro (1999), Goldstein (2000, 2001, 2003), Depew and Weber (1994), Bar-Yam (2004), Ryan (2007), Bechtel and Richardson

(1992), Blitz (1992), Kim (1992), Newman (1996), Kim (1999), De Wolf and Holvoet (2005), and others listed in the next sections. All errors in interpretation are my own responsibility. As a discipline of emergence becomes stronger, my hope is that others can expand on this definition, to incorporate weak emergence and subtle emergence dynamics such as symmetry-breaking (Anderson, 1972) and computational emergence.

EVOLUTIONARY STUDIES—THE "EMERGENTISTS"

Most informed historical sketches of emergence credit George H. Lewes (1875) as the originator of the term. His distinction between "resultants" and "emergents" was aimed at understanding how qualitative shifts in evolution, especially the creation of "mind" and consciousness, could possibly emerge in light of Darwin's (then recently developed) incrementalist theory of evolution. Lewes outlines the basic claim, that emergence—the arising of qualitatively distinct forms in biological evolution—is not the same as what he calls "resultants." By my reading, resultants are outcomes due to *aggregation*, that is, incremental additions or subtractions of forces (what he calls "a sum or a difference"), rather than a reorganization of the forces themselves:

> Every resultant is either a sum or a difference of the cooperant forces.... Further, every resultant is clearly traceable in its components, because these are homogeneous and commensurable.... It is otherwise with emergents.... The emergent is unlike its components in so far as these are incommensurable, and it cannot be reduced to their sum or their difference. (Lewes, 1875, p. 413, in Corning, 2002)

Here Lewes offers a pair of definitional qualities: Emergents are "incommensurable"—they "cannot be reduced" to a sum or difference. By incommensurable he means that emergent properties do not correspond to their components, nor can they be explained by the components alone. Instead, emergent properties reflect *a new dimension* in the system, a dimension or continuum that is not describable in the terms used to describe the components themselves.

A good example of incommensurability is the emergent property of "wetness" in water. Wetness is not commensurate with the molecules of hydrogen and oxygen, because wetness is not defined in quantum mechanics, the discipline that studies atomic properties. Even studying the interactions of hydrogen and oxygen through chemistry will not reveal wetness per se (although a good organic chemist can discern absorption from the structure of the molecules), just as a mere aggregation of these two gasses doesn't necessarily create water. What makes water wet is, in part, the presence of an external system or organism that can experience water as wet. Rather than a property that can be explained solely through an understanding of the atoms themselves, wetness requires an interaction between water and another system or ecology.³ Thus wetness is an emergent, not a simple resultant.

Over time, Lewes' approach was distilled to what is now a defining feature of emergence, namely qualitative novelty. His distinction also became the touchpoint for a long and continuing argument within evolutionary theory about "higher levels" of biologically complexity. Specifically, do "higher levels" actually exist? This question led to a deeper theoretical question as to whether the qualitative novelty so often displayed in evolution can in principle be generated out of incremental change, as claimed by Darwin's theory, or whether it reflects an underlying "teleological" direction in evolution. This argument is still active in evolutionary theory (see, e.g., Simpson 1944; Laporte 1982; Gandhi, 1983; Laszlo, 1987; Hoffman, 1989; Mayr, 1991; Swenson, 1992; Salthe, 1993; Goerner 1994; Dennett, 1995; Swenson, 1997; Coren, 1998; Chaisson, 2001; Morowitz 2002). Moreover, as mentioned in Chapter 3, scholars of ecological ascendency make as their central claim the directionality of evolution (Coren, 1998; Chaisson, 2001).

For early writers in this genre, qualitative novelty was explained as being caused by some kind of *additional* force in evolution, Bergson's (1911) *elan vital* being the best known example. These forces had no material basis but somehow "caused" the emergence of life. However, such dualistic and nonmaterial approaches became "increasingly difficult for serious scientists to maintain . . . as science became more firmly detached from metaphysics" (Sawyer, 2005, p. 29). In its place, a rising group of scholars pursued an "evolutionary emergentist" approach which aimed to validate emergence as a real (ontological) causal force that originates in material reality, even if it cannot be explained by being reduced to its component parts. Emergentists thus found ways to present emergence in nonmetaphysical terms while also claiming that the mechanisms of emergence were not reducible to the system's components.

Perhaps the leading emergentist of his day was Conrad Lloyd Morgan (1923, 1926, 1933), who saw evolution in terms of the creation of qualitative novelty. His central claim was that incremental changes can generate qualitative shifts in evolution that are not reducible to the system's elements. Morgan then strengthened his claim by introducing what he called "return action." Later, Sperry and others (Sperry, 1969, 1986, 1991; el-Hani & Pereira, 2000) called this quality "downward causation," whereby higher-order processes literally "act on" lower-level ones. A hallmark for emergentists was the idea that higher-level emergents *causally influence* their lower level constituents, such that "lower level processes proceed 'differently'—in a sense not further analyzed—under the influence of the higher level emergents" (Blitz, 1992, p. 102).⁴ According to this view, two key elements of emergence are qualitative novelty and downward causation.

Another viewpoint on emergence had been taken up by philosophers of science, starting with Broad (1929), who was committed to an understanding of emergence that would be "contrasted with mechanistic theories which are too neat, and with vitalistic theories which are too mysterious" (Newman, 1996, p. 246). In Broad's view emergence exists when the rules that underlie emergent properties cannot be traced analytically back to their components. Specifically, Broad defined emergence in terms of a whole composed of constituents A, B, and C in a relation R to each other, in which "the characteristic properties of the whole R(A,B,C) cannot, even in theory, be deduced from the most complete knowledge of the properties of A, B, and C in isolation" (Broad, 1929, p. 61, in Newman, 1996, p. 245). In this way, Broad introduced another key definitional quality emergence, non-deducibility.

In summary, the evolutionary emergentists identified three core, definitional qualities of emergence. First, emergence leads to qualitative novelty. Second, higher-order emergent properties affect their lower-level components through downward causation. Third, the properties of emergent systems are not deducible from the properties that make up those systems. These three qualities are also central to the definitions of emergence from philosophy.

EMERGENCE IN PHILOSOPHY

Whereas the evolutionary emergentists are concerned about the origins of novelty in biological evolution, the central questions about emergence for philosophers (including the philosophy of science) focus on how we can understand *causality* at the deepest level, and where the locus of causality is. In a philosophical sense, the world is knowable because we can isolate specific causes and their results, and we understand these causes in terms of mechanisms that operate at the physical base of reality—through atoms, molecules, and organisms. This reductionist argument is the bedrock of general linear reality (Abbott, 1988) and is embedded in most of the natural sciences and many of the social sciences as well (see Sawyer, 2005, for examples). However, when the tangible basis of a cause cannot be located, as is the case with emergent qualities, the common response is not to deny the reductionist frame but instead to argue that we simply don't have the tools to see or understand the mechanisms—they are present, but hidden. Philosophically, then, a claim for emergent system properties is, according to reductionists, merely a mistake based on a lack of knowledge (Corning, 2012, p. 299). Wimsatt (1997, p. S372) presents this argument:

> A traditional philosophical reductionist might suppose that emergence will be a thing of the past—reductionistic explanations for phenomena [will] demonstrate that they are not emergent. As science progresses, emergence claims will be seen as nothing more than temporary confessions of ignorance (e.g., Nagel, 1961).

The importance of such reductionist claims cannot be overstated. If all reality can be explained *solely* with recourse to the material aspects of a system, then anything that appears emergent *is not really so*. Such an outcome would denigrate emergence to being an epiphenomenon only, a symptomatic or "secondary phenomenon" (Webster's Dictionary) that can be explained with recourse to the micro-level dynamics alone. In this view, emergence is not real except in our perceptions and beliefs, and ultimately its material basis will be found (Corning, 2002; Sawyer, 2004; Clayton & Davies, 2006). In fact, a so-called emergent property could be validated (called real) only if it was tangible—material, concrete, and with ontological existence. For those of us who study emergence, this is a relatively high bar to reach.

Fortunately, this problem has been addressed by philosophers and others, who have successfully argued for an ontological basis of emergence. Their arguments shed light on how a formal definition of emergence might be constructed.

Weak Emergence

There are two ways to deal with the claims of reductionism while retaining the existence of emergence. The first is to argue for a slightly diminished form of emergence, called "weak" emergence. According to this view, new properties do emerge in a system, and these properties are not contained within any of the systems parts. However, these properties do not lead to the existence of an entirely independent entity. Instead, the source of emergence is in the interaction or organization of the system's parts, thus allowing for emergence to be traced to its material base. By making this modified claim to reductionism, an emergence philosopher can argue for the existence (reality) of an emergent property, while grounding it solely in material sources. As Wimsatt (1994, p. S373) posits, "An emergent property is—roughly—a system property which is dependent upon the mode of organization of the systems parts, without being embedded within any of the parts per se." Similar definitions are provided by Bedau (1997) and Chalmers (2006). Bar-Yam (2004, p. 16) presents a very intuitive and helpful description of weak emergence:

> Consider a brick wall that is impervious to penetration: the wall would not be impervious if it was missing any one of its many parts [i.e., bricks]. The property of being impervious is an emergent property that can be readily understood from the wall's structure but does not reside in any one of its parts, a property known as weak emergence.

Other examples of weak emergence include the classic discovery by Huygens (according to Wimsatt, 1994, p. S374), that

> pendulum clocks hung together on a beam became synchronized and kept better time than either did alone.... This system is a 'virtual metronome' regulating each clock but not located in any of them.... There is nothing antireductionist here.

He also mentions McClintock's (1971) discovery of "menstrual synchrony" that emerges among women who are closely connected, as, for example, women living in the same dormitory (McClintock, 1971, 1984; Whitten & McClintock, 1999). Again, so long as the emergent property can be "found" in the interactions within the system, the causal process is neither mysterious nor outside the traditional scientific mode of explanation. At the same time, it is not predictable simply from a knowledge of the components, just as one might not predict that a pile of bricks will be a wall.

Strong Emergence

On the other hand, many emergence scientists argue for a stronger view of emergence—for the *ontological* basis of emergence. They argue that the emergent system is a real "entity" unto itself, with its own causal forces that are distinct from the causal properties of its components. From a philosophical perspective, *strong emergence* is defined as an emergent property that (a) cannot be reduced to the system's parts nor to their interactions and (b) has "downward" causal properties that affect the parts themselves.

Bar-Yam (2004) gives an example that is helpful for distinguishing strong emergence. He describes an experimental situation in which money is being allocated to several individuals; each person is allowed a range of allocation, but the total amount to all players is constrained by a maximum. The result is a set of emergent allocations that is "caused" by the global constraint yet cannot be derived from it. As Bar-Yam (2004, p. 16) states,

> The global constraint (e.g., total amount of money) impacts the behavior of all subsystems [individuals] of the system, because allocating a value to any one individual subsystem impacts the possible allocations to the other subsystems. Interestingly, this constraint cannot be seen from the allocations given to any individual or subgroup over time.

By "cannot be seen" Bar-Yam highlights how the global emergent property—the actual set of allocation amounts—is not "located" in the parts of the system, nor in their interactions. It can only be "found" with recourse to the whole system, which includes the global constraint. This claim ingeniously invalidates a reductionist argument against emergence and thus exemplifies strong emergence.

Moreover, Bar-Yam shows how the global constraint has a direct causal influence on the behavior of the parts (2004, p. 16): "These strongly emergent properties imply a global-to-local causality that is conceptually disturbing (but allowed!) in the context of conventional science."[5] Bar-Yam's mathematical proof (in his 2004 paper and in Bar-Yam, 1997) shows that although uncomfortable, strong emergence is perfectly acceptable within the tenets of modern science and philosophy and provides an important complement to the weaker form.[6]

A different but equally compelling way to identify strong emergence is to ask whether the scientific language (discipline) that is needed to describe the emergent property can also describe the system's parts. For example, the language of "permeability" can be applied to a single brick as well as to the whole wall; on the other hand the dynamics of consciousness are not likely to be fully be understood solely through an understanding of neurobiology.

If a single discipline suffices to explain both levels, then the quality is weakly emergent. If, in contrast, a separate discipline is needed for a full explanation of the emergent phenomenon, then strong emergence is present. Using a previous example, understanding the emergent "wetness" of water requires more than one discipline—at a minimum, quantum mechanics, chemistry, and physiology. Strong emergence leads to properties and entities that are not describable at the same level or discipline as the parts. As Bechtel and Richardson argue (Bechtel & Richardson, 1992, p. 263): "Very often there will not only be different vocabularies for discussing the parts and the wholes, but also different disciplines that investigate them and different research tools employed in performing these investigations."

A comprehensive example of this idea was provided by Corning (2002) in his analysis of water as an exemplar of strong emergence. Essentially, he describes how the many emergent properties of water can only be understood with recourse to disciplines and macro-level principles that go beyond the quantum mechanical explanations of its molecular components (Corning, 2002, p. 24):

> But the properties of water also entail numerous macro-level physical principles . . . [including its] compressibility, surface tension, cohesion, adhesion, and capillarity. . . . [In a broader sense,] principles relating to density and specific gravity must be invoked to account for, say, the buoyancy of a rowboat. Hydraulics are needed to understand how water reacts to a force exerted on it . . . whereas hydrodynamics is required to explain the behavior of water flowing through a pipe or in a river bed.

Here Corning shows that the properties of "truly emergent phenomena" represent strong emergence precisely because they incorporate or "co-create" additional (higher-level) dimensions that cannot be reduced to the components on their own.

An even stronger definition was offered by Ryan (2007), based on Checkland's (1981) description of emergent properties: "Indeed, more than the fact that they [emergent properties] 'do not exist' at the lower level, emergent properties are *meaningless* in the language appropriate to the lower level." Here the ontological existence of emergence—that it's realness is proven by the need to use more than one discipline (level) to explain it—can be linked to the non-deducibility of emergence—being unpredictable even with a complete knowledge of its components. For the emergent properties represent new dimensions in the system, dimensions that the components themselves don't express. Thus, at the core of strong emergence is the quality of non-deducibility, as well as ontological existence.

In sum, what philosophers add to the definition of emergence is a claim to its existence as a "strong" or real quality. Although this claim is harder to uphold in human and social contexts, a number of researchers have brought this idea into the social sciences, especially sociology that has since its inception struggled to identify the connection between individual action and social institutions. I now turn to that dialogue.

EMERGENCE OF SOCIAL ENTITIES

"Realness" is a central issue in sociological analyses of emergence, which revolve around whether the social world is merely the aggregate sum of individual behaviors or whether there are social laws and social entities which are non-reducible to the individuals who are affected by their emergence. Here I present two exemplary approaches for understanding the core features of emergent social patterns. The first is Sawyer's (2005) summary of emergence in sociology and psychology (his Chapters 3, 4, and 5), based on his numerous studies of emergence in groups, in creativity, and in social systems (Sawyer, 2001, 2002, 2003, 2004).

Sawyer's argument in favor of strong emergence is based on the philosophical claim of multiple realizability, that is, that emergent phenomena in the biological and social world can be realized by a host of different individual components. For example, the mental state of "pain" might be realized by a wide range of neurobiological states, such that any instance of pain cannot be reduced to a specific set of neurons.[7] As such, pain is an emergent property that is caused by the neurological system but is irreducible to its neural base. Another example, more sociological in nature, is the case of "being a church" (Sawyer, 2005, p. 68). A church is made up of a collection of individually held beliefs and intentions, the sum total of which "are (in some sense) constitutive of the social property 'being a church.' Yet the [emergent] property of 'being a church' can be realized by a wide range of individual beliefs and dispositions. The same is true of properties such as 'being a family' and 'being a collective movement.'"

In other words, "being a church" exemplifies strong emergence, for every individual church community has an existence that goes beyond the aggregate of individuals who are its members. Moreover, as this example illustrates, there are literally thousands of different combinations of people who could bring into existence, *realize* or *instantiate*, a church. Sawyer argues that there is an important disjunction between "being a church" and the specific combination of individuals who make it up. He then adopts a technical term, *wild disjunction,* to describe this lack of conjoining of macroproperties to their microstates. Sawyer summarizes his argument as follows:[8]

> A social property may be said to be emergent when it is multiply realized in wildly disjunctive complex systems of individuals. Such emergent social properties participate irreducibly in causal relations.... In the terms used by philosophers of science, this is an argument for *strong emergence* (e.g., Bedau, 2002; Pihlström, 2002). Many philosophers

instead choose to argue for various versions of weak emergentism that do not allow for downward causal powers. But these philosophers have not addressed the nonreductive argument for higher-level property realism outlined here. (Sawyer 2005, pp. 71, 72; his italics and citations)

These arguments lead to a version of sociological emergence based in "nonreductive individualism," which incorporates downward causation. Both of these qualities are central to the definition of emergence being presented here.

One additional framework for understanding strong emergence comes from economics, in the work of Harper and Endres (2012). Through their careful analysis of emergent macroeconomic systems, they have identified an "anatomy of emergence" that consists of seven elements (p. 354). Note how most of these are embedded in our assumptions of emergence and in the qualities described thus far:

> E1—*Material realization:* emergent patterns are realized in physical structures and processes;
>
> E2—*Coherence:* the pattern is not a mere aggregate but a systemic whole ("a network") whose components are connected and interact;
>
> E3—*Non-distributivity of systemic properties:* the entire pattern possesses at least one systemic (i.e., global) property that none of its components has;
>
> E4—*Structure-dependence of systemic properties:* systemic properties of the pattern depend on the composition of the system (the set of its elements) and its connective structure (the organization of its elements).

They continue:

> These core features are common to all forms of emergence in economics.... [E]conomic patterns exhibiting extra-strength versions of emergence that are particularly relevant to evolutionary economics must possess one or more of the following additional features:
>
> E5—*Genuine novelty:* the pattern is a genuinely novel structure that is qualitatively different from the patterns from which it emerges;
>
> E6—*Unpredictability in principle:* the first-time appearance of a new type of economic pattern cannot be predicted (i.e., logically deduced) through a rational procedure;
>
> E7—*Irreducibility:* the systemic properties of the pattern do not follow from the properties of the system components in isolation or in simpler systems.

The main differences between these seven elements and the five-part definition that I give next is their focus on macroeconomic systems, instead of my focus on generative emergence. The latter, being intentionally created, requires two aspects that go beyond the definitions given up until now.

FURTHER QUALITIES OF STRONG EMERGENCE

Following the arguments above, strong emergence includes the creation of a system with higher-order properties that are (a) qualitatively novel, (b) not reducible to the system's components or their interactions, and (c) display downward causality, that is, these emergent properties affect the system's components. Two additional elements are crucial to a comprehensive definition of emergence for social scientists: the constructional nature of emergence, and increased capacity.

Self-Transcending Construction

Emergence, according to Goldstein, is better understood as a self-transcending construction (Goldstein, 2001, 2002, 2003, 2007). By "self-transcending" Goldstein (2007) refers to the well-known principle that "emergent order *arises out of* yet *transcends* lower level and antecedent conditions" (p. 73). This claim is based on the theory of nested systems, which shows how emergence "transcends but includes" its components (see von Bertalanffy, 1968; Koestler, 1979; Ashmos & Huber, 1987; Wilber, 1995). As such, an emergent entity incorporates existing system components into itself[9] and yet transcends them by introducing something radically new. This quality of transcendence is what defines radical novelty for Goldstein (2007, p. 73):

> *Self-transcending constructions* (STCs) place attention on how pre-existing order is transformed into emergent order. . . . [A]lthough emergent phenomena may be radically novel with respect to what they are generated out of, they are not magical appearances out of the blue but rather build on lower level components. Hence, self-transcendence includes the two fundamental requirements for emergence: building blocks, and a simultaneous transcendence of the same building blocks.

This process is expressed in the "constructional" nature of emergence (Goldstein, 2001, p. 156):

> [C]onstructional activity is self-transcending in its ability to *generate* radical novelty. New levels arise not as higher classes of lower level regularities but as new creative integrations . . . that recombine, alter relations between wholes and parts . . . intensify under some kind of containment . . . and include some element of negation operations that open a space for radical novelty.

Goldstein's mathematical logic and new notation for self-transcending constructions is well worth exploring in depth.[10] Importantly, it is very close to the definition of emergence presented by Corning (2002), who argues that in emergence, "constituent parts with different properties are modified, reshaped, or transformed by their participation in the whole" (p. 24). Both scholars thus recognize that emergence is multiply transformative: The emergent level alters the components, just as the components (re)shape the emergent. At the same time, the whole is modified and reorganized through the constructional process. All of this can be embedded in the idea that an emergent system *includes, transcends,* and *transforms* its components.[11]

As important as these three ideas are to understanding emergence, parsimony would favor attempting to incorporate them into aspects into the already presented categories: Can they be subsumed within the qualities of qualitative novelty, nonreducibility, or downward causation?

Indeed, upon reflection, the first two of these additional qualities, "includes" and "transcends," are already reflected in (a) *qualitative novelty* and (b) *nonreducibility*, because both of those qualities rely on the idea that the emergent system is unique; it can not be deduced from its components. Both qualities reveal how an emergent transcends its components even as it includes them by being supervenient on those components.

The third new quality, "transforms," could be incorporated into the meaning of downward causation, if that category was expanded to incorporate the multiple directionality of influence. In other words, causation in emergent systems is downward, as well as upward (transforms) and lateral. As a means of incorporating this expanded frame, the third quality (c) is best described as *mutual causality*.

However, there is still something fundamentally new in Goldstein's analysis that requires its own core quality. This idea is embodied in Goldstein's term "structioning." Structioning is an unusual mixture of construction (a noun) and structuring (a verb), which exactly reflects his recognition that emergence is both a compositional outcome and a dynamic process. In this view, emergence is a constructive and co-creative process in which the drive to create is interdependent with the building blocks that are available and at hand; it is in their *interaction* that these components can be transformed into something more than they have been.

This interdependence of agency and resources is increasingly discussed in studies of emergence within the organization sciences. For example, entrepreneurship and management scholars have studied this interdependence in terms of effectuation (Sarasvathy, 2001), bricolage (Garud & Karnøe, 2003; Baker & Nelson, 2005), and co-creative methods of organizing (Gartner et al., 1992; Gartner, 1993; Weick, Sutcliffe, & Obsfeld, 2005). In an entrepreneurial sense the resources and skills of the founders drive the potentiality of the venture, just as the responses from customers and other stakeholders define the potentiality of the venture, evoking new resources and skills. This recursive process reveals the constructed-but-spontaneous nature of emergence, it being a combination of planned moves and unstructured usage and "creation" of available resources.

Furthermore, and this is perhaps more important, the idea of structionings refers to *constraints* on the process—that is, it recognizes that that co-creative agency can only generate emergence in the presence of constraints, within a container that directs, informs, organizes, and structures that agency. A good deal more will be said about constraints in Chapter 17, where I will claim that the entire theory, the entire process model of emergence, depends on there being constraints within which the system can emerge. Suffice it to say there is good reason to add a new category to the more traditional definitions of emergence, a category that places attention on the co-creative, mutual interactive ecologies within which all emergence occurs. Although its meaning is not yet complete, this meaning-in-process is central to a fourth quality for defining strong emergence, namely (d) *structionings*.

Increased Capacity

Finally, the agentic quality of structionings leads to a fifth quality of emergence, *increased capacity*. Increased capacity refers to the functional benefits of emergence, or the ways in which emergence leverages components in new ways, adding capacity to a system's functioning. This fifth quality of strong emergence is perhaps its most influential one, for within it we see the ever-expanding effects of our social creations.

Corning helps frame the quality of increased capacity by presenting it within a much broader approach, called the synergism hypothesis (Corning, 1983, 2002, 2003, 2005, 2012). His studies show that all of the types of synergy—and all examples of emergence—provide highly positive outcomes for the entities involved. One of the many examples he cites is the collective behavior of Emperor penguins to huddle together in the bitter cold of the Antarctic winter, a phenomenon that was captured in the movie *March of the Penguins* (Jacquet, 2005). One study (Le Maho, 1977) showed that "these animals were thereby able to reduce their individual energy expenditures by up to 50%" (Corning 2002, p. 23), allowing them to stay alive and propagate amidst average temperatures of −70°F. Such positive effects have significant evolutionary advantage, as he describes (Corning 2002, p. 27):

> The synergism hypothesis [is] an economic (or better said, bioeconomic) theory of complexity; it is the functional "payoffs" produced by synergistic phenomena that have been responsible for the "progressive" complexification of living systems (and human societies as well).

Another example he cites is the eukaryotic cell, an evolutionary "triumph" of symbiogenesis which allows these simple organisms to grow several thousand times the size of their prokaryotic precursors, in part because the now-incorporated mitochondria and chloroplasts allow the cell to produce 1,500% to 2,000% more energy than a typical bacteria can. "In short, emergence often 'pays' in evolutionary terms" (Corning 2002, p. 27).

In Corning's view, emergence is a subset of synergetic effects; specifically, "all emergent phenomena produce synergistic effects, but many synergies do not entail emergence." Specifically, as we have seen, emergence leads to qualitative novelty, a quality that goes beyond synergy by adding the sense of systemwide capacity. Goldstein (2001, p. 145) provides another good explanation, in reference to the design outcomes from a creativity exercise he does with his students:

> These novel outcomes are emergent in the sense that the students did not predict them from just looking at the parts. It is as if all the possibilities of parts don't even come into existence until they are combined with other parts in varied relations. In this way the whole brings out more in the parts than the parts alone. This is another way to understand the often-heard remark that emergent wholes are greater than the sum of their parts: They're greater since they help to bring out potencies of the parts that were not manifest before.

From an empirical perspective, the quality of increased capacity was the core insight that Prigogine brought to thermodynamics, and the one that helped him achieve the Nobel Prize. He showed how and why some systems, when pushed up to and beyond their critical threshold of capacity, will generate new order—what he called "self-organize"—so as to increase the overall capacity of the system. As I shall show in Chapter 6, experiments on these emergent structures reveal that order creation can generate "orders of magnitude more capacity within the system" (Swenson 1988, 1989, 1991, 1992). Thus, increased capacity is central to complexity understandings of emergence and finds a central place in my list of qualities of emergence.

In sum, strong emergence refers to the arising of higher-order system properties that (a) are *qualitatively novel*—the properties transcend (but include) the system components; (b) are *not reducible* to the system's components, nor to interactions across the components, and (c) effect *mutual causality*—emergent properties have upward, downward, and lateral influence on all system components, as the components do on the whole. These (d) *structionings* reflect an ongoing interdependency of agency and constraint, and they lead to (e) *increased capacity* within the emergent system.

Many other aspects of emergence have been highlighted by scholars, some of whom have presented lists of what should be included in a definition of emergence; see note[12] for examples by Sawyer (2005), Goldstein (2000), and DeWolf and Holvoet (2005). A close look at all of these will show that each element is contained within the five main qualities I have identified so far. On the basis of this analysis, I have developed a formal definition of strong emergence, to which I shall add some important elements.

DEFININING STRONG EMERGENCE

In strong emergence the outcomes would include these five qualities:

(a) **Qualitative novelty**—includes but transcends components
(b) **Nonreducible** to the components nor to their interactions alone

(c) **Mutual causality**—downward, upward, and lateral (agent-to-agent) causation
(d) **Structionings**—co-creative coordinations of the process within its ecosystem
(e) **Confers additional capacity**—to the components and within the system

When all five qualities are present in an emergent, the outcome is defined as *strong emergence.*

My sense is that these five qualities represent only part of the story. That is, my definition only refers to the *outcomes* of emergence. It does not yet refer to the *process* by which emergence arises.

Emergence as Process and Outcomes

The distinction between the process and outcomes of emergence has been made only recently, mainly in studies of the creation of social emergents with temporal dynamics that have been analyzed in detail. A few recent definitions of emergence make this distinction between its process and its outcomes. For example, Mihata (1977) distinguishes between the process of "arising" that leads to emergence, and its outcomes: "The concept of emergence is most often used today to refer to the process by which patterns or global-level structures arise from interactive local-level processes" (Mihata, 1997, p. 31).

This distinction is also central to Goldstein's (1999, p. 49) definition of emergence, which appeared in the inaugural issue of the journal *Emergence*: "Emergence, as in the title of this new journal, refers to the *arising* of novel and coherent *structures, patterns, and properties* in complex systems." Here, as in Mihata's work, "arising" refers to the dynamics of order creation, which Goldstein distinguishes from its possible outcomes. This distinction between process and outcome is mentioned by other complexity scholars, including Crutchfield (1994), Holland (1998), and McKelvey (2004).

These scholars do not clearly separate weak from strong emergence; in the definition I have proposed, any given outcome would be assessed as strong emergence if it displays all five qualities. By "strong" I am implying that the emergent is semi-autonomous within its social ecology; it is a recognized agent within its society and social network. A good example occurs in organizational emergence—the organizing by a nascent entrepreneur that leads to new company. As has been shown by Gartner and his colleagues (Gartner, Bird, & Starr, 1992; Gartner, 1993; Gartner, 2010), there is a moment when the entrepreneurial process turns from being a series of organizing behaviors—activities that all nascent entrepreneurs do in creating a start-up (Carter, Gartner, & Reynolds, 1996; Lichtenstein, Carter, Dooley, & Gartner, 2007)—to being an organization, a formal entity that "acts" and is perceived as a true social fact (Delmar & Shane, 2003, 2004). Like all examples of strong emergence, the "facticity" of the emergent is precisely its strength and leads to its ability to wield agency.

In sum, the five qualities refer to strong emergence as an outcome, and they represent the outcomes aspect of emergence. Before delving into the process aspect, which is the focus of most of the rest of this book, I will present a few important notes about outcomes that are important to my argument as a whole.

A Continuum of Outcomes

Is there only one "type" of outcome? Or, more to the point, are all outcomes of emergence the same? Based on the definitions above, most scholars have suggested that there are multiple possible outcomes of emergence. Mihata, for example, refers to two types. First he mentions emergent *patterns*—new order created within a specific level of analysis; for example, the patterns of agent order in a computer simulation. Second, he refers to *global-level structures*—the emergence of whole systems; for example, the emergence of a new organization. Mihata thus distinguishes emergence *within* a system from emergence *of* a system. That dual notion is also reflected in Goldstein's (1999, p. 49) definition, in which *coherent structures* refers to systemwide entities (e.g., organizations), whereas *patterns and properties* refers to new order that emerges within a system.

These examples and others suggest that emergent outcomes may be arrayed on a continuum, from simple patterns at one end, to complex whole-system entities on the other. This idea is parallel to the "hierarchies of emergence" approach taken by Ellis (2006) and described in Chapter 2. In Goldstein's case this continuum runs from properties, to patterns, to coherent structures, the latter having the most systemwide effects. Likewise, Bedau (2002) describes three types: *nominal emergence*, *weak emergence*, and *strong emergence*, each one conferring greater complexity and reflecting more of the five qualities mentioned earlier.[13] A similar continuum is given by Bar-Yam (2004), who identifies four steps in a continuum: type 0 emergence, type 1 weak emergence, type 2 strong emergence, and type 3 strong emergence.[14]

In my study of generative emergence, I have also found it helpful to distinguish a continuum of outcomes. Bill McKelvey has offered significant value to me and others in this regard (see McKelvey & Lichtenstein, 2007; Lichtenstein & McKelvey, 2011; McKelvey, Lichtenstein, & Andriani, 2012). As a result, and drawing on all of these scholars, I define outcomes in terms of four degrees of emergence (Lichtenstein & Kurjanowicz, 2010; Lichtenstein, 2011):

(0) Zero-degree no emergence—reflecting the lack of new order creation
(1) First-degree order emergence
(2) Second-degree systemic emergence
(3) Third-degree radical emergence

These outcomes are described in depth in Chapter 9 but are mentioned briefly here.

The most common outcome of emergent process is *no outcome*. In fact, it is rare that an organizing effort or the prospect of emergence actually leads to a new regime of order. Entrepreneurs experience this when they dissolve an organizing venture that is just not working out. We are all familiar with goals that are unfulfilled or initiatives that don't succeed.

First-degree order emergence refers to the creation of patterns within systems, exemplified in most agent-based modeling studies and in small-scale emergences within social organizations. A new order emerges, but it is within a broader and continuous social ecology, a pattern within the system.

Second-degree systemic emergence is rare; it refers to the case of an emergent system that doesn't display downward causation. An example might be a new product line within a retail environment; it is a "new entry" (Lumpkin & Dess, 1996), but it doesn't alter the systems and components within which it emerged.

Third-degree radical emergence is strong emergence; it is the core topic of this book and the intended outcome of generative emergence. In radical emergence, the emergent "takes on a life of its own," by becoming a semi-autonomous member of the surrounding social ecology. This perception of existence goes beyond the entrepreneurial individuals who make it up.

In sum, I propose a definition for emergence as a process, likely to be unique for each prototype, that leads to an outcome—either dissolution or order creation. The outcome would be assessed as strong emergence if it exemplifies radical emergence and the five qualities of qualitative novelty, nonreducibility, mutual causality, structioning, and increased capacity. By making this definition general, each of the eight prototypes or "fields" of emergence will, over time, specify the processes and outcomes that are unique to their context.

Coda: A Discipline of Emergence

This definition is meant to complement the two other aspects for an emergence discipline—the eight prototypes, and the 15 fields of complexity science. Together these three frameworks provide a general definition of the phenomenon, a set of complementary methods to study it, and a way to understand its drivers. This can be the initial basis for a new discipline.

In a discipline of emergence, each field (prototype) would explore its phenomenon by developing studies that help specify the drivers, processes, and outcomes of relevance. Over time, scholarship within each of these fields could be synthesized and integrated across fields, thus generating insights into the overall phenomenon of emergence—how it arises and what its effects are across all fields.

My primary contribution to this endeavor, beyond providing a proposed structure for the discipline itself, is an in-depth introduction to one of its fields, namely generative emergence. My interest is spurred by the fact that this is the only type of emergence that is driven by intentionality and agency (Juarrero, 1999; also Lichtenstein, 2009). This framework provides for an entrepreneurial analysis of emergence, how new ventures and organizations are organized by intentional agents called entrepreneurs, in the service of a specific goal or aim.

At the core of this framework is a five-phase process model of generative emergence. These five phases form the middle chapters of the book, Chapters 10 through 14. To gain perspective on those phases and the case study analysis that helped reveal them, I now turn to a summary of management literature on emergence (Chapter 5), a description of the underlying science of generative emergence, dissipative structures theory (Chapter 6), and a rigorous mapping of dissipative structures onto organizing structures (Chapters 7 and 8). Chapter 9 finishes setting the stage, by presenting the four categories of outcomes that can be seen in generative emergence.

NOTES

1. My aim is to support the exploration of emergent phenomena in psychology, sociology, anthropology, organization science and management, policy studies, entrepreneurship, social innovation, communications, cultural studies, economics, education, history, human geography, international relations, linguistics, political science, social work, and more.
2. As mentioned later in this chapter, the earliest citation I have found is Lewes' 1875 text; other early work includes Morgan (1923), Popper (1926), Fisher (1930), and Mead (1938). The issues have been deepened by scholars such as Klee (1984), Sperry (1986), Kim (1992), Blitz (1992), and Schröder (1998). For an excellent compilation of recent thinking in physics, biology, cognition, and religion see Clayton and Davies (2006).
3. In a philosophical sense, wetness can only be perceived through the sense of touch, which is described through the disciplines of physiology and neuropsychology.
4. In philosophy the term for this is "supervenience" which reflects a more technical understanding of "acting upon." *Supervenience* is a complicated term with a complex history. According to Sawyer's (2005) account, there is a strict difference between supervenience and downward causation. The former refers to a mapping of emergent properties onto the tangible parts of the system that create them. Downward causation is a stronger term that implies a motive force, by which the emergent properties of a system tangibly affects the system's parts. Sawyer's analysis is extremely helpful, and I strongly recommend his chapter-long description of these philosophical issues. In my treatment I shall avoid confusion by simply using downward causation.
5. By admitting "disturbing but allowed," Bar-Yam recognizes the discomfort that unseen causal influences pose for traditional science. A very similar sentiment is given by Bedau (1997, p. 377) in his arguments against strong emergence:

> Although strong emergence is logically possible, it is uncomfortably like magic. How does an irreducible but supervenient downward causal power arise, since by definition it cannot be due to the aggregation of the micro-level potentialities. Such causal powers would be quite unlike anything within our scientific ken. This not only indicates how they will discomfort reasonable forms of materialism. Their mysteriousness will only heighten the traditional worry that emergence entails illegitimately getting something from nothing.

6. A surprising example of this idea is Bar-Yam's description of a lock and a key (2004, p. 18):

> The properties of a key in opening a door are not contained in a description of the parts of the key. Instead they are contained in the relationship between the components of the key and the components of the lock. This relationship is not present in the description of the parts of the key by themselves. We can note that when viewing a system that includes both the key and lock, their relationship is that of a constraint that is not contained in the description of the parts themselves but rather in the description of the relationships between them.

7. The argument is far more specific. Sawyer (2005, p. 67) draws from Fodor's (1974) "influential argument against reductionist physicalism," by explaining the technical meaning of multiple realizability, "the observation that although each mental state must be supervenient on some physical state, each token instance of that mental state might be implemented, grounded, or realized by a different physical state." Supervenience, in turn, is defined as "a relation between two levels of analysis [such that] if a collection of lower-level components with a given set of relations causes higher-level property E to emerge at time t, then on every other occasion when that same collection of components in that same set of relations occurs, E will again emerge." With this idea in place, Sawyer concludes his proof: "each token instance of 'pain' might be realized by a different supervenience base," that is, by a different set of neurons and their relations. If so, "reduction would be difficult if the neurobiological equivalent of a psychological term was a ... combination of many neurobiological concepts and terms." Thus, since the psychological term *pain* can refer to a combination of different neurobiological states, the higher-level emergent could never be convincingly reduced to its neurobiological base. According to Sawyer (2005, p. 67), "Fodor termed such a realization 'wildly disjunctive.'" See note 8 as well.
8. Sawyer continues:

> In fact, most social properties of interest to sociologists seem to have wildly disjunctive individual-level descriptions, just as most of the properties of interest to other sciences have wildly disjunctive lower-level realizations, including biology, psychology, and geology; see Fodor (1997). [In sum, emergentism claims that] only in cases where the relation between higher- and lower-level properties is wildly disjunctive beyond some threshold of complexity will the higher-level property not be lawfully reducible (see Sawyer, 2004; 2005, p. 67)

Sawyer thus provides a defendable definition of the nonreducibility of emergence. Moreover, he uses the same foundation of wild disjunction to argue that irreducible emergence can logically entail downward causation, that a social property S could "lawfully be identified as the cause of social property S* and the individual property I* ... due to wild disjunction." He acknowledges that some theorists have argued against the "lawful causality of emergent properties," or downward causation. However, he carefully shows how their claims can be countered due to wild disjunction.

9. Perhaps this could be expanded: The emergent system "takes on" all of the components within its immediate ecology; "takes responsibility for" and ultimately is the "caretaker" of the underlying stream of resources and opportunity.
10. See especially Goldstein's (2000) paper. The following papers provide a well-rounded summary of STCs: Goldstein (2001, 2002, 2007). More recent work, which I will review later, focuses on the containers and constraints that are essential to emergent order (Goldstein, 2003, 2011).

11. Goldstein has gone farther than any other emergence researcher to explore the complexity of "system levels" by showing how emergence "entangles" levels rather than distinguishes them. "In emergence, upper levels influence lower levels and lower levels influence upper levels, and there's lateral interaction, and so on" (Goldstein, 2001, p. 153). The result is a truly unique view of emergence. Again, I quote:

> The intriguing thing here is that the very arising of the new emergent level is characterized by just this transgression of the level distinction itself. [The construction] of a new emergent level [comes with] the radically novel property that they transgress their very assignment to this new distinct level. . . . That is, once the higher level is reached, the lower level has been subsumed into it so that the lower level components are now parts of this higher level coherence. [There is thus a] paradox that the new [and so-called distinct] emergent level is characterized by the transgression of level distinctions!

12. For example, Sawyer (2005, p. 95) identified four qualities that are inherent in emergence—non-aggregativity (itself composed of four elements), near-decomposability, non-localization, and complex interactions. More broadly, Goldstein (2000) identified eight "broad issues" that must be "encountered" when explaining emergence—these are causality; spontaneity; predictability; ontology; prevalence; levels; coherence; and outcomes. Perhaps the most comprehensive list was offered by DeWolf and Holvoet (2005), in a special issue, *Engineering Self-Organized Systems*. Based on "an extensive literature study" they identified the most "important characteristics" of emergence and self-organization (the latter denoted with *). In the eight that follow, note the similarity with what we have already seen:

- Micro-macro effect, i.e., global emergent properties
- Radical novelty
- Increase in order*
- Autonomy*
- Coherence
- Interacting parts
- Dynamical, i.e., evolving over time
- Adaptability or robustness with regard to changes

13. Specifically (Bedau, 2002), *nominal emergence* refers to a system-level property that arises merely as an aggregation of its components. A simple example is a circle, which is indeed a macro-level property that does not inhere in any of its points; however, it is nothing more than the combination of the points themselves—it is a "resultant" in Lewes' terms. The second type is *weak emergence*, which refers to "aggregate global behaviors" that can be derived from micro-level processes but which involve interactions so complicated that "the global behavior has no simple explanation" (Bedau, 2002, p. 12). Third, *strong emergence* adds the additional qualities of "irreducible causal powers," especially downward causation; these "give emergent properties the dramatic form of ontological novelty that many people associate with the most puzzling kinds of emergent phenomena" (Bedau, 2002, p. 10).

14. Bar-Yam's (2004) *type 0 emergence* is fully coincident with Bedau's nominal emergence; it refers to whole-system properties derived solely from its components. *Type 1 weak emergence* refers to collective system behaviors such as pressure, temperature, phase transition properties, patterns of traffic jams, and other "structural, dynamic or

response properties of systems" (p. 19)—these exactly correspond to the first categories given by Deacon (2006) and Ellis (2006). Here the difficulty of explaining the system behavior is due to the resolution of the system; only by reducing the scope and scale can the dynamics be explained—a point well presented by Ryan (2007). *Type 2 strong emergence* refers to the strong emergence we encountered earlier, where the properties of the system may determine the properties of a part, but only when those constraints are defined for the entire collective rather than for each part separately. Last, *type 3 strong emergence* refers to properties that are emergent only in the relationship between two or more components such that emergence can only be understood as a fully systemic issue. His example is of a lock and a key—mentioned in note 6—where the emergent property of "key fitting into lock" is only realized when both components are in direct relationship.

REFERENCES

Abbott, A. 1988. Transcending general linear reality. *Sociological Theory*, 6(2): 169–86.
Anderson, P. 1972. More is different. *Science*, 177(4047): 393–6.
Ashmos, D., & Huber, G. 1987. The system paradign in organization theory: Correcting the record and suggesting the future. *Academy of Management Review*, 12: 607–21.
Baker, T., & Nelson, R. 2005. Creating something from nothing: Resource construction through entrepreneurial bricolage. *Administrative Science Quarterly*, 50: 239–366.
Bar-Yam, Y. 1997. *Dynamics of Complex Systems*. Reading, MA: Addison-Wesley—Advanced Book Program.
Bar-Yam, Y. 2004. A mathematical theory of strong emergence using mutliscale variety. *Complexity*, 9(6): 15–24.
Bechtel, W., & Richardson, R. 1992. Emergent phenomena and complex systems. In A. Beckermann, H. Flohr, & J. Kim (Eds.), *Emergence or Reduction? Essays on the Prospects of Nonreductive Physicalism* (257–88). Berlin: Walter de Gruyter.
Bedau, M. 1997. Weak emergence. *Philosophical Perspectives*, 11(Mind, Causation, and World): 375–99.
Bedau, M. 2002. Downward causation and the autonomy of weak emergence. *Principia*, 6(1): 5–50.
Bergson, H. 1911. *Creative Evolution (originally L'evolution Creatrice, 1907)*. New York: Henry Holt.
Blitz, D. 1992. *Emergent Evolution: Qualitative Novelty and the Levels of Reality*. Boston: Kluwer Academic.
Broad, C. D. 1929. *Mind and Its Place in Nature*. New York: Harcourt, Brace.
Carter, N., Gartner, B., & Reynolds, P. 1996. Exploring start-up event sequences. *Journal of Business Venturing*, 11: 151–66.
Chaisson, E. 2001. *Cosmic Evolution: The Rise of Complexity in Nature*. Cambridge, MA: Harvard University Press.
Chalmers, D. 2006. Strong and weak emergence. In P. Clayton, & P. Davies (Eds.), *The Re-Emergence of Emergence: The Emergentist Hypothesis from Science to Religion* (244–56). New York: Oxford University Press.
Checkland, P. 1981. *Systems Thinking, Systems Practice*. Chinchester, UK: John Wiley & Sons.
Clayton, P., & Davies, P. 2006. *The Re-Emergence of Emergence: The Emergentist Hypothesis from Science to Religion*. New York: Oxford University Pres.
Coren, R. 1998. *The Evolutionary Trajectory: The Growth of Information in the History and Future of the Earth*. Amsterdam: Gordon and Breach Publishers.

Corning, P. 1983. *The Synergism Hypothesis: A Theory of Progressive Evolution.* New York: McGraw Hill.
Corning, P. 2002. The re-emergence of "emergence": A vernerable concept in search of a theory. *Complexity*, 7(6): 18–30.
Corning, P. 2003. *Nature's Magic: Synergy in Evolution and the Fate of Humankind*: New York: Cambridge University Press.
Corning, P. 2005. *Holistic Darwinism: Synergy, Cybernetics, and the Bioeconomics of Evolution.* Chicago: Universtiy of Chicago Press.
Corning, P. 2012. The re-emergence of emergence, and the causal role of synergy in emergent evolution. *Synthese*, 185(2): 295–317.
Crutchfield, J. 1994. The calculi of emergence: Computation, dynamics and induction. *Physica D: Nonlinear Phemonema*, 75(1): 11–54. Reprinted in SFI 94-03-016. Special Issue on the Proceedings of: Complex Systems—From Complex Dynamics to Artificial Reality
Deacon, T. 2006. Emergence: The hold at the wheel's hub. In P. Clayton & P. Davies (Eds.), *The Re-Emergence of Emergence: The Emergentist Hypothesis from Science to Religion* (111–50). New York: Oxford University Press.
Delmar, F., & Shane, S. 2003. Does business planning facilitate the development of new ventures? *Strategic Management Journal*, 24: 1165–85.
Delmar, F., & Shane, S. 2004. Legitimating first: Organizing activities and the survival of new ventures. *Journal of Business Venturing*, 19: 385–411.
Dennett, D. 1995. *Darwin's Dangerous Idea: Evolution and the Meanings of Life.* New York: Touchstone.
Depew, D., & Weber, B. 1994. *Darwinism Evolving.* New York: Oxford University Press.
De Wolf, T., & Holvoet, T. 2005. Emergence versus self-organization: Different concepts but promising when combined. *Lecture Notes in Computer Science*, 2464(Special issue on Engineering Self-Organizing Systems): 77–91.
el-Hani, C., & Pereira, A. 2000. Higher level descriptions: Why should we preserve them? In P. Andersen, C. Emmeche, N. Finnemann, & P. V. Christiansen (Eds.), *Downward Causation: Minds, Bodies and Matter* (118–42). Aarhus, Denmark: Aarhus University Press.
Ellis, G. 2006. On the nature of emergent reality. In P. Clayton & P. Davies (Eds.), *The Re-Emergence of Emergence: The Emergentist Hypothesis from Science to Religion* (79–110). New York: Oxford University Press.
Fisher, R.A. 1930. *The Genetical Theory of Natural Selection.* Oxford, UK: Clarendon Press.
Fodor, J. 1997. Special sciences: Still autonomous after all these years. *Philosophical Perspectives*, 11: 149–63.
Gandhi, K. (Ed.). 1983. *The Evolution of Consciousness.* New York: Paragon House.
Gartner, W. 1993. Words lead to deeds: Towards an organizational emergence vocabulary. *Journal of Business Venturing*, 8: 231–39.
Gartner, W. (Ed.). 2010. *ENTER—Entrepreneurial Narrative Theory Ethnomethodology and Reflexivity.* Clemson University: Spiro Institute for Entrepreneurial Leadership.
Gartner, W., Bird, B., & Starr, J. 1992. Acting as if: Differentiating entrepreneurial from organizational behavior. *Entrepreneurship Theory and Practice*, 16(3): 13–30.
Garud, R., & Karnøe, P. 2003. Bricolage versus breakthrough: Distributed and embedded agency in technology entrepreneurship. *Research Policy*, 32: 277–301.
Goerner, S. 1994. *Chaos and the Evolving Ecological Universe.* Langhorn, PA: Gordon & Breach.
Goldstein, J. 1999. Emergence as a construct: History and issues. *Emergence*, 1(1): 49–72.
Goldstein, J. 2000. Emergence: A concept amid a thicket of conceptual snares. *Emergence*, 2(1): 5–22.

Goldstein, J. 2001. Emergence, radical novelty, and the philosophy of mathematics. In W. Sulis & I. Trofimova (Eds.), *Nonlinear Dynamics in the Life and Social Sciences* (133–52), NATO Science Series, Vol. 320. Amsterdam: IOS Press.

Goldstein, J. 2002. The singular nature of emergent levels: Suggestions for a theory of emergence. *Nonlinear Dynamics, Psychology and Life Sciences*, 6: 293–309.

Goldstein, J. 2003. The construction of emergent order, or, how to resist the temptation of hylozosim. *Nonlinear Dynamics, Psychology, and Life Sciences*, 7(4): 295–314.

Goldstein, J. 2007. A new model for emergence and its leadership implications. In J. Hazy, J. Goldstein, & B. Lichtenstein (Eds.), *Complex Systems Leadership Theory* (61–92_. Mansfield, MA: ISCE Publishing.

Goldstein, J. 2011. Probing the nature of complex systems: Parameters, modeling, interventions—Part 1. *Emergence: Complexity and Organization*, 13(3): 94–121.

Harper, D., & Endres, A. 2012. The anatomy of emergence, with a focus on capital formation. *Journal of Economic Behavior and Organization*, 82: 352–67.

Hoffman, A. 1989. *Arguments on Evolution—A Paleontologist's Perspective*. New York: Oxford University Press.

Holland, J. 1998. *Emergence: From Chaos to Order*. Cambridge, MA: Perseus Books.

Jacquet, L. 2005. *March of the Penguins*. Warner Brothers.

Juarrero, A. 1999. *Dynamics in Action: Intentional Behavior as a Complex System*. Cambridge, MA: MIT Press.

Kim, J. 1992. "Downward causation" in emergentism and nonreductive physicalism. In A. Beckermann, H. Flohr, & J. Kim (Eds.), *Emergence or Reduction? Essays on the Prospects of Nonreductive Physicalism* (119–38). Berlin: Walter de Gruyter.

Kim, J. 1999. Making sense of emergence. *Philosophical Studies*, 95: 3–36.

Klee, R. 1984. Micro-determinism and concepts of emergence. *Philosophy of Science*, 51: 44–63.

Koestler, A. 1979. *Janis—A Summing Up*. New York: Random House.

Kuhn, T. S. 1970. *The Structure of Scientific Revolutions*. Chicago: University of Chicago Press.

Laporte, L. (Ed.). 1982. *The Fossil Record and Evolution*. San Francisco: W. H. Freeman.

Laszlo, E. 1987. *Evolution—The Grand Synthesis*. Boston, MA: Shambhalla.

Le Maho, Y. 1977. The emperor penguin: A strategy to live and breed in the cold. *American Scientist*, 65: 680–93.

Lewes, G. H. 1875. *Problems of Life and Mind, Volume 2*. London: Kegan Paul, Trench & Turbner.

Lichtenstein, B. 2009. Moving far from far-from-equliibrium: Opportunity tension as the catalyst of emergence. *Emergence: Complexity and Organization*, 11(4): 15–25.

Lichtenstein, B. 2011. Levels and degrees of emergence: Toward a matrix of complexity in entrepreneurship. *International Journal of Complexity in Leadership and Management*, 1(3): 252–74.

Lichtenstein, B., Carter, N., Dooley, K., & Gartner, W. 2007. Complexity dynamics of nascent entrepreneurship. *Journal of Business Venturing*, 22: 236–61.

Lichtenstein, B., & Kurjanowicz, B. 2010. Tangibility, momentum, and the emergence of The Republic of Tea. *ENTER Journal*, 1: 125–48.

Lichtenstein, B., & McKelvey, B. 2011. Four types of emergence: A typology of complexity and its implications for a science of management. *International Journal of Complexity in Leadership and Management*, 1(4): 339–78.

Lumpkin, G. T., & Dess, G. 1996. Clarifying the entrepreneurial orientation construct and linking it to performance. *Academy of Management Review*, 21: 135–72.

Mayr, E. 1991. *One Long Argument: Charles Darwin and the Genesis of Modern Evolutionary Thought*. Cambridge, MA: Harvard University Press.

McClintock, M. 1971. Menstrual synchrony and suppression. *Nature*, 229(January 22): 244–45.

McClintock, M. 1984. Estrous synchrony: Modulation of ovarian cycle length by female pheromones. *Physiology & Behavior*, 32(5): 701–705.
McKelvey, B. 2004. Toward a 0th law of thermodynamics: Order creation complexity dynamics from physics and biology to bioeconomics. *Bioeconomics*, 6: 65–96.
McKelvey, B., & Lichtenstein, B. 2007. Leadership in the four stages of emergence. In J. Hazy, J. Goldstein, & B. Lichtenstein (Eds.), *Complex Systems Leadership Theory*: 93–108. Boston: ISCE Publishing.
McKelvey, B., Lichtenstein, B., & Andriani, P. 2012. When organizations and ecosystems interact: Toward a law of requisite fractality in firms. *International Journal of Complexity in Leadership and Management*, 2(1/2): 104–36.
Mead, H. 1938. *The Philosophy of the Act*. Chicago: University of Chicago Press.
Mihata, K. 1997. The persistence of emergence. In R. Eve, S. Horsfall, & M. Lee (Eds.), *Chaos, Complexity, and Sociology: Myths, Models and Theories* (30–38). Thousand Oaks, CA: SAGE Publications.
Morgan, C. L. 1923. *Emergent Evolution*. London: Williams & Norgate.
Morgan, C. L. 1926. *Life, Mind and Spirit*. London: Williams & Norgate.
Morgan, C. L. 1933. *The Emergence of Novelty*. New York: Henry Holt & Co.
Nagel, E. 1961. *The Structure of Science*. New York: Harcourt Brace and World.
Newman, D. 1996. Emergence and strange attractors. *Philosophy of Science*, 63: 245–61.
Pihlström, S. 2002. The re-emergence of the emergence debate. *Principia*, 6: 133–81.
Popper, S. 1926. Emergence. *Journal of Philosophy*, 23: 241–5.
Ryan, A. 2007. Emergence is coupled to scope, not level. *Complexity*, 13(2): 66–77.
Salthe, S. 1993. *Development and Evolution: Complexity and Change in Biology*. Cambridge, MA: Bradford—MIT Press.
Sarasvathy, S. 2001. Causation and effectuation: Toward a theoretical shift from economic inevitability to entrepreneurial contingency. *Academy of Management Review*, 26: 243–63.
Sawyer, K. 2001. Simulating emergence and downward causation in small groups. In S. Moss & P. Davidsson (Eds.), *Multi-Agent-Based Simulation* (49–67). Berlin: Springer.
Sawyer, K. 2002. Nonreductive individualsm, part 1: Supervenience and wild disjunction. *Philosophy of the Social Sciences*, 32: 537–59.
Sawyer, K. 2003. Nonreductive individualism, part 2: Social causation. *Philosophy of the Social Sciences*, 33: 203–24.
Sawyer, K. 2004. The mechanisms of emergence. Philosophy of the Social Sciences(34).
Sawyer, K. 2005. *Social Emergence: Societies as Complex Systems*. New York: Cambridge University Press.
Schröder, J. 1998. Emergence: Non-deducibility or downwards causation? *Philosophical Quarterly*, 48(193): 433–52.
Simpson, G. G. 1944. *Tempo and Mode in Evolution*. New York: Columbia University Press.
Sperry, R. 1969. A modified concetp of consciousness. *Psychological Review*, 76: 532–36.
Sperry, R. 1986. Discussion: Macro- versus micro-determinism. *Philosophy of Science*, 53: 265–70.
Sperry, R. 1991. In defense of mentalism and emergent interaction. *Journal of Mind and Behavior*, 122: 221–46.
Swenson, R. 1992. Order, evolution, and natural law: Fundamental relations in complex system theory. In C. Negoita (Ed.), *Cybernetics and Applied Systems* (125–47). New York: Marcel Dekker.
Swenson, R. 1997. Autocatakinetics, evolution, and the law of maximum entropy production: A principled foundation towards the study of human ecology. *Advances in Human Ecology*, 6: 1–47.
von Bertalanffy, L. 1968. *General Systems Theory*. New York: Braziller Books.

Weick, K., Sutcliffe, K., & Obstfeld, D. 2005. Organizing and the process of sensemaking. *Organization Science*, 16: 409–21.

Whitten, W., & McClintock, M. 1999. Pheromones and regulation of ovulation. *Nature*, 401(6750): 232–33.

Wilber, K. 1995. *Sex, Ecology, Spirituality*. Boston: Shambhalla Publications.

Wimsatt, W. 1994. The ontology of complex systems: Levels of organization, perspectives, and causal thickets. *Canadian Journal of Philosophy*, 24(Supplement1): 207–74.

Wimsatt, W. 1997. Aggregativity: Reductive hueristics for finding emergence. *Philosophy of Science*, 64(Suppl): S372–84.

CHAPTER 5

Types of Emergence Studies in Management

Over the past two decades, scholars of organization science have been drawing on complexity science to explore and explain emergence in organizational change, entrepreneurship, strategy, and organizational behavior. Given the range and fuzziness of definitions given for emergence up until now, and the numerous approaches that complexity science offers for exploring emergence, it makes sense that the scope of these applications to management is quite broad. In order to provide some coherence to these complexity science writings, some researchers have organized the field and its applications into two or a few "types of complexity," so as to more carefully delineate the contributions and applications of their work. A types-of-complexity framework also allows one to compare the qualities of one type to another, and to see how different perspectives and approaches to complexity can be divergent but complementary.

The most well-recognized framework for types-of-complexity was articulated by McKelvey (2004), who distinguished the "European school" from the "American school" of complexity. The former type originates in the work of Prigogine, Haken, and others, who explored how new order is generated in systems that are pushed into "far-from-equilibrium" conditions—exo-organizing in my prototype framework. This contrasts with the American school, led by researchers at the Santa Fe Institute, which has explored how order is generated across agents in computational models. In his analysis McKelvey says, "both European and American perspectives are important.... Neither seems both necessary and sufficient by itself, especially in social settings. [They] are *coproducers*" (McKelvey 2004, p. 321).

A more detailed "map" of the field was provided by Maguire, McKelvey, Mirabeau, and Oztas (2006), in their review of complexity science for the *SAGE Handbook of Organization Studies* (Clegg, Hardy, Nord, & Lawrence, 2006). Their key distinction was between "objectivist" work that includes models and rigorous analogies for understanding complex systems, and "interpretivist" work that informs narrative studies of complex systems. This distinction leads to five types of complexity applications: (1) models—computational but also qualitative, (2) metaphors, and (3) meaning, which are supported by (4) introductions that offer general overviews of complexity in management, and (5) reflections that review and consider the import of complexity studies. This analysis is useful for integrating postmodern and modernist applications of the complexity sciences; see also Boisot and McKelvey (2010).

An alternative approach is to organize complexity science applications in terms of their capability for understanding emergence. This would require a framework that examines what each complexity science can actually do analytically; in other words, given a particular methodology, what type of emergence can be discerned by any given field or author. One such framework was initially suggested by McKelvey (in Lichtenstein & McKelvey, 2011). It distinguishes two dimensions of explanation that complexity thinking can provide,[1] leading to a 2 × 2 design with four types of emergent outcomes. Our explanation reveals the normative edge to this typology:

> The first two types of emergence comprise simple upward causality and homogeneous agents. The second two types comprise coevolving heterogeneous agents with increasing degrees of causal complexity. Each type of emergence is progressively more intricate and multifaceted than its predecessor. More importantly, each successive type defines emergence in a more stringent way, such that what is considered "emergence" of the first type would not be defined so in types two through four, and so on. In the same way, the four types range along a continuum of analytic intricacy and arduousness, such that each successive type presents more challenges to researchers and modelers. . . . Our implicit argument is that the higher the degree (type) of emergence, the more complete will be its explanation of the underlying dynamics of self-organization leading to emergent structuring. (Lichtenstein & McKelvey, 2011, pp. 344, 349)

In that paper, our focus was primarily on computational emergence. In contrast, my aim in this chapter is to widen the arc of analysis so as to include all the disciplines of complexity science, to examine how well each of them has been used to explore and explain emergence. My approach here is based on a framework developed by one of the originators of the Santa Fe Institute, James Crutchfield (1994a, 1994b). Crutchfield distinguished three types of complexity science: discovery, modeling, and intrinsic complexity. In addition to those three, management researchers have used *metaphors* from one (or more) of the complexity sciences to help elucidate some of the nonmechanistic, nonlinear dynamics of a particular organizational phenomenon. This leads to four types of emergence studies: type I complexity *metaphors* for emergence, type II *discovering* emergence, type III *modeling* emergence, and type IV generating *intrinsic* emergence. What follows is a brief explanation and exemplars for each type.

FOUR TYPES OF EMERGENCE APPLICATIONS IN MANAGEMENT

Type I—Complexity Metaphors for Emergence

Rather than being based on a particular complexity science or a method per se, complexity metaphors for emergence aim for a shift in perspective, a change in our cognitive maps, to produce a more dynamic understanding of complex systems in general. Like Gartner's (1993) "vocabulary" for emergence, a shift in perspective can be expressed through qualities of dynamic systems that can be applied (metaphorically) to organizations. Familiar phrases that show up in type I metaphors include self-organization, far-from-equilibrium, nonlinear dynamics, sensitive dependence on initial conditions, and edge of chaos. Although each of these terms has specific scientific meaning within one or more complexity sciences, outside of that scientific context these terms are metaphors because they are not operationalized, nor are they linked to the mechanisms or underlying drivers that give them rigorous scientific meaning.

In formal terms, type 1 complexity metaphors are *not* metaphors within their theoretical domain. For example, the unpredictable and cascading effects of "nonlinear dynamics" are well understood through the complexity sciences of system dynamics (e.g., Hall, 1976) and through certain aspects of deterministic chaos theory (Bygrave, 1989b); both fields give operationalized definitions that are confirmed through repeatable experiments. Likewise, the mathematical meaning of "sensitive dependence on initial conditions" is well defined by deterministic chaos theory (Lorenz, 1963; May, 1976; Wolf, Swift, Swinney, & Vastano, 1985). However—and this is the important point—once these constructs are taken out of their broader theory, used in isolation from their nomological net and separated from their scientific and methodological grounding, they become metaphors, not constructs. Metaphors can be very useful (Tsoukas, 1991) for helping us picture the world in a more holistic, dynamic, and unpredictable way. Yet, even the most artful use of metaphors should not be confused as a direct application of a complexity science per se (Maguire & McKelvey, 1999).

One of the most successful uses of complexity metaphors is in one of the earliest top-tier journal articles to use "complexity theory," Brown and Eisenhardt's (1997) study on "continuous change." Using an in-depth qualitative approach, the researchers explored organizing and innovation processes in six project-based organizations—this was part of a broader analysis reported in their book, drawn from Brown's dissertation (Brown & Eisenhardt, 1998). By dividing their sample into three successful vs. three unsuccessful product portfolios, a cross-case analysis allowed them to identify key differences between the successful and unsuccessful cases. These differences were highlighted through a series of metaphors that draw from but are not direct analogies to specific complexity sciences.

For example, one of the overall patterns they found in successful projects was "semistructures"—a "balance" between strict mechanistic structures and loose organic structure. Successful projects had clear responsibilities, a characteristic of formal bureaucracy; at the same time these characteristics allowed developers to "improvise," a characteristic of organic structures. This combination of mechanistic and organic is unusual, as is the capability of finding the balance between them. According to Brown and Eisenhardt (1997, p. 15),

> True improvisation relies on . . . (1) performers instinctively communicating in real time with one another, yet (2) doing so within a structure of a few, very specific rules. Managers of successful portfolios relied on structures that were neither too extensive nor chaotic.

Describing these as semistructures that "lie between the extremes of very rigid and highly chaotic organization" (1997, p. 28), they summarize:

> Perhaps closest to our research is work on complexity theory (Gell-Mann, 1994; Kauffman, 1993). Like organizations, complex systems have large numbers of independent yet interacting actors. Rather than ever reaching a stable equilibrium, the most adaptive of these complex systems . . . keeps changing continuously by remaining at the poetically termed "edge of chaos" that exists between order and disorder. By staying in this intermediate zone, these systems . . . exhibit the most prolific, complex, and continuous change (Waldrop, 1992; Kelly, 1994; Kauffman, 1995).
>
> Continuously changing organizations are likely to be complex adaptive systems with semistructures that poise the organization on the edge of order and chaos. (Brown & Eisenhardt, 1997, pp. 31, 32)

Their analysis is useful for highlighting the nonmechanistic and nonlinear qualities of successful organizing. The concepts are metaphors because the study itself is not grounded in one of the complexity sciences per se, that is, the theory and methods are not derived from NK landscapes nor from self-organized criticality, nor do they use genetic algorithms. Further, the "edge of chaos" concept is itself a metaphor drawn from certain computational modeling experiments by Langton (1986, 1990) that were mentioned by Kauffman in his book (see Maguire et al., 2006 for a strong critique of this term). In formal terms, there is no one-to-one correspondence between these concepts' origins in computational complexity science and their application in management theory. At the same time, the metaphors provide a valuable access point to understanding the dynamics of a nontraditional mode of organizing, an access point so effective as to help catapult complexity science into the field well before the 1999 special issue of *Organization Science*. Thus, although metaphors are not science per se, they provide an intuitive grasp of complex system dynamics.

Another good example of the application of complexity metaphors is a little-known but intriguing paper by Biggiero (2001), on "self-organizing processes in building entrepreneurial networks." His analysis of emergent networks within emerging industrial districts is based on his many-decades of study of the

"Biomedical Valley" district in the province of Modena in Italy. After introducing the broad set of networks and social systems there, and reviewing several papers in which the area is described as a "self-organizing network," Biggiero says (2001, pp. 213–214),

> The self-organizing nature of Industrial Districts gives them the property of complex adapting systems, which implies at least three main characteristics:
> 1. Being cases of order from noise or, in Kauffman's (1993) terms, creating order at the *edge of chaos*
> 2. Showing positive and negative externalities, *positive-feedback mechanisms*, and the consequent lock-in phenomena (Arthur, 1988a, 1994; Biggiero, 2002)
> 3. Manifesting high *sensitivity to initial conditions*, and thus having a highly unpredictable behavior because of the presence of many bifurcations and *strange attractors* in their dynamics (Waldrop, 1992; Casti, 1994)

Biggiero's metaphorical use of these terms is very helpful as a description. At the same time, these should be considered as metaphors, because of the way each term is only loosely related to the mathematics of the field it draws from. His reference to the "edge-of-chaos" is Langton's work (Langton, 1986, 1990) on cellular automata models of emergence. *Positive-feedback mechanisms* are a reference to Arthur's work in economics; they refer to ideas initially presented by Maruyama (1963). *Sensitivity to initial conditions* and *strange attractors* are concepts from deterministic chaos theory. Within their own disciplines each of these concepts is well explained. However, each discipline does so in a very different way, using specific methods and mathematics. Moreover, drawing together three different fields is risky, although it does lead to striking metaphors, which is precisely what this and other authors intend and achieve.

Many other examples could be given; my chapter in the *SAGE Handbook for Complexity Studies* is a good place for further examples (Lichtenstein, 2011a). However, a final one is useful to show why using metaphors alone may limit the degree of insight that can be gained. In this example the goal is laudable: a call for complexity science to create a new paradigm for strategic entrepreneurship (Schindehutte & Morris, 2009). Throughout the paper the authors mention terms as loose metaphors from a host of complexity disciplines, borrowing concepts from complex adaptive systems, dissipative structures, cybernetics, deterministic chaos, morphogenetic fields (Sheldrake, 1981, 1988), self-organized criticality, fractals, and self-organization. Although they provide an inspiring vision for strategic entrepreneurship, the metaphoric use of these sciences makes it difficult to operationalize them into specific concepts. Thus, the illustrations are vivid, but the applications for new work are somewhat limited. In sum, metaphors are useful to a point, as an informal way of presenting emergent properties.

Type II—Discovering and Describing Complexity

Crutchfield's (1994a) "discovering complexity" refers to a post-hoc analysis that measures or defines something that has emerged in a complex system, whether an emergent pattern or an emergent level of order. Importantly, the discovery of emergence in type II is, as Crutchfield says, is in the eye of an observer: "Surely, the system state doesn't know its behavior is unpredictable" (Crutchfield, 1994a, p. 517). That is, the discovery of emergence involves a post-hoc analysis of time series data (e.g., system behaviors), using mathematical and conceptual tools that allow scholars to verify the existence of emergence in dynamic systems. In addition to *discovering* emergence, this type includes *describing* emergence, which refers to cohesive qualitative frameworks for describing order creation in complex systems. Such descriptions, although less rigorous than the mathematical tools for discovering complexity, provide a systemic model that coherently explains how emergence can be studied or identified in entrepreneurial settings.

An exemplar of type II is Cheng and Van de Ven's (1996) discovery of emergence in two high-tech innovation ventures. The analysis draws from a longitudinal study of internal corporate venturing at 3M, a research project led by Andy Van de Ven and his group of doctoral students, now esteemed scholars in the field (Van de Ven, Angel, & Poole, 1989; Van de Ven & Poole, 1990; Garud & Van de Ven, 1992; Van de Ven, Pooley, Garud, & Venkataramen, 1999). In previous analyses, the research group had shown that early innovation dynamics in these ventures were random, unpredictable, and "faulty" (Van de Ven & Pooley, 1992; Garud & Van de Ven, 1992). However, Ven de Ven thought there might be more to the story, and this instinct was borne out in the book-length compilation of the entire research project (Van de Ven et al., 1999).

A most intriguing part of these secondary analyses was his use of deterministic chaos theory, the mathematics of which could explore for the presence of a "chaotic attractor" in the data. (These data can be submitted to such an analysis because they include 96 and 152 months of event-coded data, which is enough to run the statistical analyses that show chaotic patterns in the time series [Guastello, 1995; Dooley & Van de Ven, 1999]). Pursuing that hypothesis, Cheng and Van de Ven (1996) used the three statistical tests that can reveal the presence of a "chaotic attractor." The first test, a Lyapunov exponent, explores whether two data points that are contiguous at the start of the series will diverge exponentially; this tests whether the data are sensitive to initial conditions and therefore chaotic. The second test, the correlation dimension, explores whether the data are random or if they display a "strange attractor," i.e. whether the location of each data point is unpredictable but all the data exist within a well-defined set of parameters. The third test, a BDS statistic, determines if the data set is nonlinear, by testing whether or not the data points are independent and identically distributed (IID), a premise underlying linear statistical analyses.

Their findings contrasted with earlier analyses of the same data, by showing that the earlier innovation phases were not random but were chaotic, that is, they were nonlinear and nonpredictable but occurred within a specific region of action. This led to a re-evaluation of the process, to an expectation that actions and outcomes were chaotic at the beginning of the process and periodic at the end. Specifically, Cheng and Van de Ven concluded (1996, p. 609):

> From these results we tentatively conclude that the actions taken and outcomes experienced... began in chaos and ended in order, while exogenous context events occurred randomly throughout time.

By discovering chaos, they showed that what appears to be random may, under closer scrutiny, show an underlying order that transcends the apparent unpredictability of the process, a point very well explored by Dooley and Van de Ven (1999). In addition, their study confirmed the presence of a punctuated shift in the dynamics of both ventures, linking chaos theory with Prigogine's dissipative structures theory: "Transitions between chaotic and periodic patterns of learning... can be explained by the fact that our dynamic system is a dissipative structure" (Cheng & Van de Ven, 1996, p. 609).

The discovery of a strange attractor and its shift to a new strange attractor does not, in and of itself, reveal emergence. At the same time, this approach goes well beyond a metaphor, for in this case it applies chaos mathematics to organizational data in a way that preserves every element of deterministic chaos theory. To my mind, their study is an exemplar use of complexity science and provides wonderful insight into some of the outcomes of emergence.

Another instance of discovering complexity in entrepreneurship is the early work of Bill Bygrave, a theoretical physicist who became a successful entrepreneur and venture capitalist, later applying his knowledge as an entrepreneurship professor and scholar (Bygrave, 1989a, 1989b, 1993, 1997; Bygrave & Hofer, 1991). An early paper (Bygrave, 1989b) is one of the first applications of chaos and complexity theory to management. Bygrave starts by advocating the use of catastrophe theory to model the start-up process as a "disjointed, discontinuous, unique event" (Bygrave 1989b, p. 9). He then explores how deterministic chaos theory could generate new insights into entrepreneurial phenomena such as flows of venture capital and the emergence of high-growth companies. In particular, he shows how such flows can become increasingly variable, with sharp peaks and valleys that get closer and closer together. Like Cheng and Van de Ven (but seven years earlier), Bygrave argues that these apparently random occurrences reflect an underlying order that may exist over time. Although he is skeptical about more direct applications, his outlook is prescient: "[C]atastrophe and chaos provide us with useful metaphors for the entrepreneurship process [that can] help us form and sharpen our philosophy and methodology" (Bygrave 1989b, p. 28).

A final example of describing complexity is a research study of emergence dynamics in a start-up venture, which began from a serendipitous conversation in which the entrepreneur said that, as of that week, she was starting to organize "HealthInfo"—an online health-based information service (Lichtenstein, Dooley, & Lumpkin, 2006). The data consist of our interviews with the entrepreneur every other week for two years, along with her financial information (costs, projections), marketing plans, and other related materials. Our analysis identified three modes of organizing: business vision, strategic organizing, and tactical organizing. *Business vision* was tracked biweekly, and its dynamics were analyzed using "centering resonance analysis," a semantic language software that identifies the most salient issues in a qualitative data set. *Strategic organizing* was analyzed through an event time series analysis of "organizing moves" in the data, where different "epochs" could be discovered through a quality control analysis. *Tactical organizing* was identified through a visual analysis of start-up behaviors, where a shift would show up as a punctuated change in the data chart.

Our post-hoc analysis found that all three modes of organizing did undergo a punctuated shift within a six-week span of time; each coded time series shows a statistically significant change in that period. We identified the combination of these as an "emergence event" in this venture—a distinct and punctuated shift across all three modes of organizing that led to a new and more inclusive opportunity for the business.

Here again, tools from complexity science provide a means for discovering when emergence happens and describing what actually unfolds. These tools for discovering emergence are important precursors to modeling emergence or identifying its drivers.

Type III—Complexity Models of Emergence

Type III refers to computational or formal modeling of emergence. In the main, these are agent-based programs designed to explore emergence "in silico," that is, through a computer simulation. Virtually all modeling emergence studies are achieved through one of the computational approaches summarized in Chapter 3. Computational models and simulations allow researchers to explore how specific rules and ongoing interactions between agents, operationalized as algorithms in a computer program, can lead to unexpected emergence over time. Further, computational modeling provides an unprecedented experimental environment in which a continuous range of values in key variables can be tested for their influence, without interference from spurious or external effects (Davis, Eisenhardt, & Bingham, 2007). As such, complexity modeling presents a powerful context for understanding and developing theories of emergence in organizations (McKelvey, 1997, 1999b, 2002), as the following examples show.

An exemplar of complexity modeling is Fleming and Sorenson's (2001) study of technology innovation. They begin with a well-accepted theory of innovation as a recombination of existing and new technologies, such that invention is a process of "recombinant search for better combinations and configurations of constituent technologies (Fleming & Sorenson, 2001, p. 1020). To explore this idea, they used a computational model of recombinant search processes, the NK landscape model. Note that this application is particularly strong because the theoretical content and research question are directly linked to the method's underlying theory. Theirs is one of the few NK landscape studies based on research questions that are linked to the underlying biological theory that gave rise to the method itself (Wright, 1932; Kauffman, 1993).

Following Kauffman's method, Fleming and Sorenson modeled the "fitness" or effectiveness of an innovation as an interaction between the number of components N in the innovation and their degree of interdependence, K. The resulting model translates the structure of the components into a topography, a visual and mathematical "landscape" in which the configuration of components corresponds to a specific location on the landscape, and its fitness is translated as the "height" of the topography at that point. Kauffman showed that the topography mainly depends on K, where low interdependence (low K) yields a single optimal fitness configuration, while the higher the K, the more "rugged" the landscape and the more varied the fitness of any given configuration. Overall, an intermediate level of K yields the highest overall fitness across the landscape.

In the Fleming and Sorenson model, innovation is measured in terms of patents, where N refers to the number of components being combined into a potential innovation (measured through the number of subclasses listed); K refers to their interdependence (measured as the "ease of combining a particular technology"); and *fitness* refers to the number of citations the patent receives in following years. Each of these variables was counted across 17,264 patents granted during May–June, 1990; subclass data were derived through 70,000 subclasses identified in patents from 1790 to 1989, and citations were counted across six years. Note that these operationalizations are extremely close to the original theoretical design of the method.

Their results confirm the hypothesis that beyond a minimal level, higher K leads to reduced fitness regardless of the number of components. Overall, they found that the usefulness (fitness) of an invention "can be maximized by working with a large number of components that interact to an intermediate degree" (Fleming & Sorenson, 2001, p. 1030). In addition, whereas increasing the number of components leads to increased citation counts (at a decreasing rate), it is also true that an increase in components decreases the certainty of outcomes, given a high K (p. 1032).

Their analysis provides practical and strategic insight for inventors. Fleming and Sorenson recognized that the "haphazard" nature of sexual recombination in nature is fundamentally different from the intelligence of human inventors who can decompose the search space to identify the key forces that shape it and thus "become increasingly 'foresighted' and able to predict the outcomes of previously untried combinations. . . . Thus, the effective difficulty of using interdependent technologies declines with time and experience" (Fleming & Sorenson, 2001, p. 1035). All of this adds to the theory underlying NK landscapes, and highlights important distinctions and insights for technology innovation.

A second example of complexity modeling is Ganco and Agarwal's (2009) study of new entry, in which the potential for successful entry into existing or new markets by entrepreneurial start-ups is contrasted with entry by existing companies that diversify into new areas. Empirical research into the performance differential between these two types of firms has generated contradictory results. Some show that start-ups' flexibility leads to higher innovation; others show that the much higher resource base of existing companies leads to a performance advantage. The authors suggest that a rigorous modeling approach that allows for modifications of certain parameters without changing the entire situation may provide a more subtle understanding of the factors that lead to performance.

Ganco and Agarwal used Kauffman's NKC model, an extension of his other work. Specifically, they distinguished start-ups from existing firms by using the concept of internal (intrafirm) "coupling" to represent K, arguing that start-ups have a lower level of internal coupling than diversifying entrants (Ganco and Agarwal, 2009, p. 236). Further, they incorporated industry turbulence by arguing that C refers to interfirm coupling; high levels of C correspond to an industry with high interdependence and turbulence. Finally, following the accepted tenet that the level of K is far more impactful than N, they operationalized N in terms of a firm's size of decision space, which is kept constant across the types of firms and across time.

Their findings show that in highly turbulent conditions, new entry by an existing firm will be more successful than new entry by a start-up company; however start-ups will generally perform better when turbulence is lower and when the capability for industry learning is greater. The authors state, "The likelihood that entrepreneurial start-ups will outperform diversifying entrants (among late entrants) increases with the strength of the learning mechanisms the entrants can employ... [such that] with sufficiently strong learning, late entrepreneurial start-ups are likely to become the best-performing cohort" (Ganco and Agarwal, 2009, p. 244). Based on additional findings, several other propositions are forwarded as well.

A different form of complexity modeling includes studies that develop formal hypotheses based on complexity theory and test them using a particular analytic model on a relatively large data set. One example is our (Lichtenstein, Carter, Dooley, & Gartner, 2007) study of nascent entrepreneurship, the activities of individuals who were in the process of starting a new business. The study drew on complexity science to explore the temporal dynamics of entrepreneurial organizing, dynamics that are not well characterized using traditional linear models from strategy and economics.

In particular, we identified three temporal parameters relevant to entrepreneurs and discussed by complexity researchers—rate, concentration, and timing of organizing. By linking those parameters to predictions about the successful emergence of nascent ventures, we developed a formal model with three hypotheses based on entrepreneurship and complexity science. A brief summary will help demonstrate how such a formal model works.

First, we predicted that the higher the rate of organizing, the more likely a new venture will emerge (McKelvey, 2004). This relationship had already been shown for nascent entrepreneurs by Carter, Gartner, and Reynolds (1996), who found that successful emergence was directly related to a higher number of organizing activities completed. Second, the lower the concentration of activities—the more spread out over time—the more likely a new venture will emerge. This claim is based on NK landscape models that show how too high interdependence between agents can lead to a "complexity catastrophe" that freezes up the entire system (Kauffman, 1993; Sorenson, 1997; McKelvey, 1999a). We argue that because organizing activities are interdependent as well, spreading out organizing activities—a lower concentration—should lead to higher success. Third, given a low threshold of concentration, the later the timing of activities, the more likely a new venture will emerge. From a complexity science perspective, later timing allows for the creation of a "scaffold of emergence in the system (Holland, 1995), providing a catalyst for further activities to be enacted" (Lichtenstein et al., 2007, p. 244). This also draws on the accumulating effects of positive feedback processes in complex systems (Maruyama, 1963; Arthur, 1988b, 1990) and momentum in organizational change (Jansen, 2004; Lichtenstein & Kurjanowicz, 2010).

We tested this model on the Panel Study of Entrepreneurial Dynamics, which tracked 1,000 nascent ventures over four years, drawn from a random sample of Americans. In order to focus on emergence, Kevin Dooley developed a type of reverse logistic regression model that, instead of identifying firms that drop out of the pool at each stage, identified those ventures which emerged. Our statistical analysis confirmed the three hypotheses and uncovered a general pattern of temporal dynamics for new venture creation: "Our findings demonstrate that the ventures which emerged, compared with those that did not, pursued organizing activities at a faster rate, with lower concentration, and with timing that was later in the process" (Lichtenstein et al., 2007, pp. 253–254).

In sum, computational modeling or formal models can be a valuable way to understand emergence. Models provide replicable frameworks that can push theory and improve practice, given their limitations.

Type IV—Generative Complexity

In type IV generative complexity, the agents in the system are themselves able to capitalize on the order that emerges within it, thus leading to additional functionality to the system (Crutchfield, 1994b, p. 518). Beyond a description of emergent order (type II) and computational models of emergent structure (type III), generative complexity occurs when a system agent "has the requisite information processing capability with which to take advantage of the emergent patterns" (Crutchfield,

1994b, p. 518). Crutchfield labels this "intrinsic emergence," since the effects of order creation are discernable to agents within the system, rather than due to post-hoc analyses by external observers (Crutchfield, 1994a, p. 4):

> In the emergence of coordinated behavior, though, there is a closure in which the patterns that emerge are important *within* the system.... Since there is no external referent for novelty or pattern, we can refer to this process as "intrinsic" emergence.

Thus, the crucial element and importance of type IV generative complexity is that the newly created order generates additional and unforeseen capabilities and capacities within the system. "What is distinctive about intrinsic emergence is that the patterns formed confer additional functionality which supports global information processing" (Crutchfield, 1994b, p. 518). Thus, when generative complexity occurs, the system gains the capacity to create and capitalize on new opportunities, generate new resources, increase efficiency, and expand its overall potential to generate value. Like "generative leadership" (Goldstein, Hazy, & Lichtenstein, 2010), which increases the capacity of all individuals in an organization, this ultimate type of emergence generates numerous benefits to the agents and the system as a whole.

This increased capacity is not available to computational agents in simulation models, except perhaps for agent-learning models (e.g., Carley 1998; Carley & Hill, 2001), although Sawyer (2005) strongly disagrees with even this possibility (see pp. 157–169). Likewise, these generative qualities exist at a completely different level than the data used for discovering emergence, or in metaphors for emergence that simply describe new capacities rather than generate them. Instead, this last type of complexity study tends to provide the highest leverage for explanation and, more importantly, for action (Lichtenstein & Kurjanowicz, 2010; Lichtenstein, 2011b). Not surprisingly, it focuses only on emergence in and of biological and social entities—humans, groups, organizations, communities, and ecosystems. Thus, qualitative and narrative research on real social systems is the only arena in which generative emergence can be accomplished.

One of the best studies of this type is the dissertation research of Todd Chiles (Chiles, Meyer, & Hench, 2004), who pursued a 100-year study of emergence in Branson MO, now one of the most visited tourist areas in the United States. Using dissipative structures theory as a framework, their analysis explored the dynamics underlying the "punctuated emergences" that transformed the region from a small town to a thriving organizational collective. In the context of generative emergence, they do an excellent job of showing how emergences in the region generated more capacity for growth, leading to further emergences over time. In particular, they identify a series of positive feedback processes through which emergent structures generated increased capacity in the area, which itself led to more emergence. As one example, improvements in regional infrastructure—new and expanded highways, two new dams that created accessible lakes, and improvements to sewage, water, and electricity service—led to increased accessibility and activities for tourists and retirees. The more tourists in the area, the more businesses were started, primarily theaters and other music venues; these in turn brought more tourists. Likewise, with more tourists came more performers; their success led others to do the same, ultimately leading to the arrival of the Presleys, Roy Clark, and Andy Williams.

An even more direct expression of increased capacity within Branson, MO is seen in the role of retirees, who streamed into the area throughout the 1940s, 1950s, and 1960s. It turns out that their retirement portfolios were almost uniformly deposited in one of the few local banks in town; this money then became available to potential theater owners as capital with which to start their businesses. Here again, the more activities and the better the infrastructure, the more retirees and the more capital, leading to yet further cycles of business development and economic growth.

A further demonstration of increased capacity there came in the form of national media attention, through a popular movie and TV show episodes set in Branson. Later, the rise in theater foundings led to a *60 Minutes* episode on the area. Chiles et al. (2004, p. 509; words in quotes are from the regional marketing council) report:

> A *60 Minutes* segment that aired in 1991 and 1992 was "a real catalyst" for a "major explosion" that brought more tourists, theaters, and businesses, and even bigger stars, according to informants, and it took Branson to "a whole different level."

The depth of their analysis is impressive, incorporating interviews from 38 informants, 1,200 pages of coded textual data from a wide of sources, and enough quantitative data to run 12 different Poisson regression models across 40 years of time series data. The findings reflect organizing and emergence at multiple levels, including individual entrepreneurs, key families, organizations and businesses, community-wide associations, and regional and national effects. Through this detail they were able to show how emergence was generative at each level, leading to greater capacity in future eras.

Since his dissertation, Chiles has led a series of scholars in examining generative complexity and emergence of markets through a "radical subjectivist" model of dynamic creation. After extending Lachman's radical subjectivist approach to the current economic climate (Chiles, Bluedorn, & Gupta, 2007), they identified three processes that generate order-creating market dynamics: empathy, modularizing, and "self-organization" (Chiles, Tuggle, McMullen, Bierman, & Greening, 2010). The latter study argues that entrepreneurs' future expectations lead to market *divergence*—an economic process that is stronger than the *convergence* toward imitation. Divergence serves to increase heterogeneity, which pushes the market farther from equilibrium, which sparks further divergence, in a self-amplifying loop. At a critical point the market as a whole will "self-organize," creating new regimes of order through "punctuated dis-equilibrium."

According to this theory, the fluctuations that drive divergence and novelty are *endogenous to the firm*—they come from the entrepreneur's imagination and foresight into how to provide "creative value" for potential customers. When competing entrepreneurs in this far-from-equilibrium market continuously produce divergence in relation to each other, endogenous entrainment helps catalyze the self-organization of economic order (Chiles et al., 2010, p. 28). This emergence of coherent market order also increases the capacity of the ecosystem, by engendering new alliances, identifying new opportunities, and opening unexpected resources and prospective new business models—the benefits of which are shared. In these ways Chiles and his colleagues used type IV generative emergence, showing how agent organizing leads to new capabilities and energies in the system.

Summary

Virtually all complexity research papers in management can be categorized as one of the four types: complexity metaphors, discovering complexity, modeling complexity, and generative complexity. In effect, these four types provide a framework for assessing the kinds of questions and answers that are being developed in any given research project.

For Crutchfield (1994b), this assessment was implicitly normative, with later types providing a more effective or useful analysis then earlier ones. In a study by Lichtenstein and McKelvey (2011), we affirmed such a hierarchy of value, making an argument that the later types can be more integrative and inclusive, and that they present findings which are more easily applied by social scientists. However, the normative argument can be deflected in two ways. First, some of the most impactful complexity research has been metaphorical rather than intrinsic—consider Brown and Eisenhardt's (1997) research, which has been very influential in the field of management.[2] More importantly, a key principle of effective research design is to focus first on the research question and then choose the method that best explores and answers the question at hand (Edmondson & McManus, 2007). In our case, the first choice is the emergence prototype to be explored, and the particular phenomenon of interest there. Next is the choice of the type of complexity one is after—metaphor, discovery, modeling, or intrinsic emergence. These two choices would then direct a scholar to choose the complexity science that is ideally suited to explore the question at hand. In all likelihood the value of the study would be based on these choices and on the quality of the project, rather than on which type of complexity explanation is pursued.

Moving Forward: The Dynamics of Dissipative Structures

Up to now I have introduced emergence, defined it, and categorized the range of emergent phenomena into eight prototypes, with the aim of providing a foundation for a discipline of emergence. In addition, I have introduced the entire range of complexity sciences and reviewed how researchers have used complexity science for understanding emergence.

With this as a foundation, I now move toward an explanation of generative emergence, based on the insights from dissipative structures theory. Specifically, the next four chapters introduce the science of dissipative structures (Chapter 6), develop a rigorous analogy of the science to organizations (Chapter 7), reveal and resolve the key differences between order creation in thermodynamics and emergence in social systems (Chapter 8), and outline the four main outcomes of emergence in the social world (Chapter 9). This orientation sets the stage for my main goal in the book, which is to describe the process by which social entities come into being—the five phase process model of generative emergence.

NOTES

1. One dimension is agent heterogeneity, which refers to the degree of differentiation across agents in a complex system. This dimension ranges from (a) homogeneous—agents in the system are mainly similar, to (b) heterogeneous—agents have clear distinctions across one or more characteristics. The second dimension is causal intricacy, which refers to the influences that agents have on higher- and lower-level groupings of agents. In a basic form, this ranges from (a) simple, linear, equilibrium, and deducible causality, to (b) multilayered, nonlinear, supervenient and nondeducible causality (Lichtenstein & McKelvey, 2011, p. 344).
2. As of February 2014 the paper has been cited 3,051 times in Google Scholar.

REFERENCES

Arthur, B. 1988a. Competing technologies: An overiew. In G. Dosi, C. Freeman, R. Nelson, G. Silverberg, & L. Soete (Eds.), *Technical Change and Economic Theory* (590–607). London: Pinter Press.

Arthur, B. 1988b. Self-reinforcing mechanisms in economics. In P. Anderson, K. Arrow, & D. Pines (Eds.), *The Economy as an Evolving Complex System* (9–31). Reading, MA: Addison-Wesleuy.

Arthur, B. 1990. Positive feedbacks in the economy. *Scientific American*, February: 92–99.

Arthur, B. 1994. *Increasing Returns and Path Dependence in the Economy*. Ann Arbor, MI: University of Michigan Press.

Bigelow, J. 1982. A catastrophe model of organizational change. *Behavioral Science*, 27: 26–42.

Biggiero, L. 2001. Self-organizing processes in building entrepreneurial networks: A theoretical and empirical investigation. *Human Systems Management*, 20: 209–22.

Biggiero, L. 2002. The location of multinationals in industrial districts: Knowledge transfer in biomedical. *Journal of Technology Transfer*, 27(1): 111–22.

Brown, S., & Eisenhardt, K. 1997. The art of continuous change: Linking complexity theory and time-based evolution in relentlessly shifting organizations. *Administrative Science Quarterly*, 42: 1–34.

Brown, S., & Eisenhardt, K. 1998. *Competing on the Edge*. Boston: Harvard Business School Press.

Bygrave, W. 1989a. The entrepreneurship paradigm (I): A philosophical look at its research methodologies. *Entrepreneurship Theory and Practice*, 14(1): 7–26.

Bygrave, W. 1989b. The entrepreneurship paradigm (II): Chaos and catastrophes among quantum jumps. *Entrepreneurship Theory and Practice*, 14(2): 7–30.

Bygrave, W. 1993. Theory building in the entrepreneurship paradigm. *Journal of Business Venturing*, 8: 255–80.

Bygrave, W. 1997. The entrepreneurial process. In W. D. Bygrave (Ed.), *The Portable MBA in Entrepreneurship* (2nd ed., 1–26). New York: John Wiley & Sons.

Bygrave, W., & Hofer, C. 1991. Theorizing about entrepreneurship. *Entrepreneurship Theory and Practice*, 16(2): 13–23.

Carley, K. 1998. Organizational adaptation. *Annuls of Operations Research*, 75: 25–47.

Carley, K., & Hill, V. 2001. Structural change and learning within organizations. In A. Lomi & E. Larson (Eds.), *Dynamics of Organizations: Computational Modeling and Organizational Theories* (63–92). Cambridge, MA: MIT Press/AAAI Press.

Carter, N., Gartner, B., & Reynolds, P. 1996. Exploring start-up event sequences. *Journal of Business Venturing*, 11: 151–66.

Casti, J. 1994. *Complexification*. New York: HarperPerennial.

Cheng, Y., & Van de Ven, A. 1996. The innovation journey: Order out of chaos? *Organization Science*, 6: 593–614.

Chiles, T., Bluedorn, A., & Gupta, V. 2007. Beyond creative destruction and entrepreneurial discovery: A radical Austrian approach to entrepreneurship. *Organization Studies*, 28: 267–493.

Chiles, T., Meyer, A., & Hench, T. 2004. Organizational emergence: The origin and transformation of Branson, Missouri's musical theaters. *Organization Science*, 15(5): 499–520.

Chiles, T., Tuggle, C. S., McMullen, J., Bierman, L., & Greening, D. 2010. Dynamic creation: Elaborating a radical Austrian approach to entrepreneurship. *Organization Studies*, 31: 7–46.

Clegg, S., Hardy, C., Nord, W., & Lawrence, T. (Eds.). 2006. *Handbook of Organization Studies*. London, UK: SAGE Publications.

Crutchfield, J. 1994a. The calculi of emergence: Computation, dynamics and induction. *Physica D* (SFI 94-03-016. Special issue on the Proceedings of: Complex Systems—From Complex Dynamics to Artificial Reality).

Crutchfield, J. 1994b. Is anything ever new? Considering emergence. In G. Cowan, D. Pines, & D. Meltzer (Eds.), *Complexity: Metaphors, Models, and Realty*. Reading, MA: Addison-Wesley.

Davis, J., Eisenhardt, K., & Bingham, C. 2007. Developing theory through simulation methods. *Academy of Management Review*, 32: 480–99.

Dooley, K., & Van de Ven, A. 1999. Explaining complex organizational dynamics. *Organization Science*, 10(3): 358–72.

Edmondson, A., & McManus, S. 2007. Methodological fit in management field research. *Academy of Management Review*, 32: 1155–79.

Fleming, L., & Sorenson, O. 2001. Technology as a complex adaptive system. *Research Policy*, 30: 1019–1039.

Ganco, M., & Agarwal, R. 2009. Performance differentials between diversifying entrants and entrepreneurial start-ups: A complexity approach. *Academy of Management Review*, 34: 228–53.

Garud, R., & Van de Ven, A. 1992. An empirical evaluation of the internal corporate venturing process. *Strategic Management Journal*, 13: 93–109.

Gell-Mann, M. 1994. *The Quark and the Jaguar*. New York: W. H. Freeman.

Goldstein, J., Hazy, J., & Lichtenstein, B. 2010. *Complexity and the Nexus of Leadership: Leveraging Nonlinear Science to Create Ecologies of Innovation* New York: Palgrave Macmillan.

Guastello, S. 1995. *Chaos, Catastrophe, and Human Affairs: Applications of Nonlinear Dynamics to Work, Organizations, and Social Evolution.* Mahway, NJ: Lawrence Erlbaum and Associates.

Hall, R. 1976. A system pathology of an organization: The rise and fall of the old *Saturday Evening Post. Administrative Science Quarterly*, 21: 185–211.

Holland, J. 1995. *Hidden Order.* Redwood City, CA: Addison-Wesley.

Jansen, K. 2004. From persistence to pursuit: A longitudinal examination of momentum during the early stages of strategic change. *Organization Science*, 15: 276–95.

Kauffman, S. 1993. *The Origins of Order.* New York: Oxford University Press.

Kelly, K. 1994. *Out of Control: The Rise of Neo-biological Civilization.* Reading, MA: Addison-Wesley.

Langton, C. 1986. Studying artificial life with cellular automata. *Physica D: Nonlinear Phenomena*, 22(1): 120–49.

Langton, C. 1990. Computation to the edge of chaos: Phase transitions and emergent computation. *Physica D: Nonlinear Phenomena*, 42(1): 12–37.

Lichtenstein, B. 1998. *Self-Organized Change in Entrepreneurial Ventures: A Dynamic, Non-linear Model.* Doctoral dissertation, Boston College/UMI.

Lichtenstein, B. 2011a. Complexity science contributions to the field of entrepreneurship. In P. Allen, S. Maguire, & B. McKelvey (Eds.), *The SAGE Handbook of Complexity and Management* (471–93). Thousand Oaks, CA: SAGE.

Lichtenstein, B. 2011b. Levels and degrees of emergence: Toward a matrix of complexity in entrepreneurship. *International Journal of Complexity in Leadership and Management*, 1(3): 252–74.

Lichtenstein, B., Carter, N., Dooley, K., & Gartner, W. 2007. Complexity dynamics of nascent entrepreneurship. *Journal of Business Venturing*, 22: 236–61.

Lichtenstein, B., Dooley, K., & Lumpkin, T. 2006. Measuring emergence in the dynamics of new venture creation. *Journal of Business Venturing*, 21: 153–75.

Lichtenstein, B., & Kurjanowicz, B. 2010. Tangibility, momentum, and the emergence of The Republic of Tea. *ENTER Journal*, 1: 125–48.

Lichtenstein, B., & McKelvey, B. 2011. Four types of emergence: A typology of complexity and its implications for a science of management. *International Journal of Complexity in Leadership and Management*, 1(4): 339–78.

Lorenz, E. 1963. Deterministic nonperiodic flow. *Journal of the Atmospheric Sciences*, 20: 130–41.

Maguire, S., & McKelvey, B. 1999. Complexity and management: Moving from fad to firm foundations. *Emergence*, 1(2): 19–61.

Maguire, S., McKelvey, B., Mirabeau, L., & Oztas, N. 2006. Complexity science and organization studies. In S. Clegg, C. Hardy, W. Nord, & T. Lawrence (Eds.), *Handbook of Organization Studies* (2nd ed., 165–214). London: SAGE Publications.

Maruyama, M. 1963. The second cybernetics. *American Scientist*, 51: 164–79.

May, R. 1976. Simple mathematical models with very complicated dynamics. *Nature*, 26: 455–67.

McKelvey, B. 1997. Quasi-natural organization science. *Organization Science*, 8: 351–80.

McKelvey, B. 1999a. Avoiding complexity catastrophe in coevolutionary pockets: Strategies for rugged landscapes. *Organization Science*, 10(3): 294–321.

McKelvey, B. 1999b. Toward a Campbellian Realist Organization Science. In J. Baum & B. McKelvey (Eds.), *Variations in Organization Science* (383–412). Thousand Oaks, CA: SAGE Publications.

McKelvey, B. 2002. Model-centered organization science epistemology. In J. Baum (Ed.), *Companion to Organizations* (752–80). Thousand Oaks, CA: SAGE Publications.

McKelvey, B. 2004. Toward a complexity science of entrepreneurship. *Journal of Business Venturing*, 19: 313–42.

Sawyer, K. 2005. *Social Emergence: Societies as Complex Systems*. New York: Cambridge University Press.

Schindehutte, M., & Morris, M. 2009. Advancing strategic entrepreneurship research: The role of complexity science in shifting the paradigm. *Entrepreneurship Theory and Practice*, 33(1): 241–76.

Sheldrake, R. 1981. *A New Science of Life*. Los Angeles: J.P. Tarcher.

Sheldrake, R. 1988. *The Presence of the Past*. New York: Time Books.

Sorenson, O. 1997. *The complexity catastrophe: Interdependence and adaptability in organizational evolution*. Ph.D. dissertation, Stanford University, Palo Alto, CA.

Thom, R. 1975. *Structural Stability and Morphogenesis*. Reading, MA: Addison-Wesley.

Tsoukas, H. 1991. The missing link: A transformational view of metaphors in organizational science. *Academy of Management Review*, 16(3): 566–85.

Van de Ven, A., Angel, H., & Poole, M. S. 1989. *Research on the Management of Innovation*. New York: Ballanger Books.

Van de Ven, A., & Poole, M. S. 1990. Methods for studying innovation development in the Minnesota Innovation Research Program. *Organization Science*, 1: 313–35.

Van de Ven, A., & Pooley, D. 1992. Learning while innovating. *Organization Science*, 3: 91–116.

Van de Ven, A., Pooley, D., Garud, R., & Venkataramen, S. 1999. *The Innovation Journey*. New York: Oxford University Press.

Waldrop, M. 1992. *Complexity*. New York: Touchstone/Simon & Schuster.

Wolf, A., Swift, J. B., Swinney, H. L., & Vastano, J. A. 1985. Determining Lyapunov exponents from a time series. *Physica*, 16D: 285–317.

Wright, S. 1932. The roles of mutations, inbreeding, crossbreedding and selection in evolution. Paper presented at the 11th International Conference of Genetics.

CHAPTER 6

Dissipative Structures—Theory and Experiments

Of the 15 sciences of complexity, dissipative structures theory is the one that comes closest to explaining the order-creation dynamics of generative emergence. Dozens of studies make an analogy between the emergence of dissipative structures in thermodynamics and the emergence of structures in organizations. The goal of this chapter is to explain how such an analogy actually works. Unfortunately, this not as easy as it may sound. Some scholars have complained that dissipative structures are so different from social entities that the analogy simply cannot, and should not, be made. Their argument is that the dynamics driving molecules in a closed container are not at all similar to the dynamics facing heterogeneous, intelligent, proactive agents like entrepreneurs and executives. In short, how can we make a viable comparison between a molecule in a chemical experiment and a human social agent?

It turns out that the only way to proceed toward a convincing analogy is through a very careful isomorphic mapping between dissipative structures and organizational emergence. In order to accomplish this, we need a detailed understanding of the thermodynamic science underlying dissipative structures theory (Chapter 6). This in-depth scientific explanation can then be carefully applied to social systems, through a rigorous homology between exo-organizing in thermodynamics and generative emergence in the social world (Chapter 7). Finally, our careful analysis of the differences between these two frameworks forms the basis for the five-phase model, which is introduced in Chapter 7 and developed further in Chapters 10–14.

A "PARADIGM SHIFT" IN THERMODYNAMICS

Prigogine's career-long effort to expand the boundaries of thermodynamics through the study of dissipative structures can be best appreciated through an introduction to the core premises of the field, the first and second laws of thermodynamics. The first law of thermodynamics is an extension of the conservation of energy law. Simply put, in an isolated system such as our universe, the total energy of the system—from input, work, and output—is always constant. The sum of all energy is fixed; energy itself can be neither created nor destroyed, even though it can change into different forms (Chaisson, 2001; see also Swenson, 1989 and McKelvey, 2004).

This latter point was pursued by Carnot (1824; see Swenson, 1998), even before the formulation of the second law. In seeking to understand what happens when energy does change form, Carnot saw that the fall of water that turns a mill wheel is similar to the "fall or flow of heat from higher to lower temperatures," which is what motivates a steam engine.[1] Thus, although potential energy is destroyed in each case—measured as an increase in "entropy"—a corresponding "motive force" is created that generates change. Carnot's insight was that the irreversible destruction of "motive force" in the world—the entropy that's produced when energy flows from higher to lower potentials—is indeed the force that causes all change. Further, his experiments showed the process to be *inexorable:* not only does entropy always increase, it always increases to a maximum. This idea was formalized by Clausius in 1865: "Die Entropie der Welt strebt einem Maximum zu"—entropy always strives to a maximum (Prigogine & Stengers, 1984, p. 119; Swenson 1998, p. 211).[2]

Closer explorations of these ideas revealed a powerful pattern, that systems with more internal order can dissipate entropy far more effectively than disordered ones. Thus, as Swenson claims, "the world is in the order-production business because ordered flow produces entropy faster than disordered flow" (Swenson, 1998, p. 215). This idea has become central to dissipative structures theory. Moreover, as mentioned in Chapter 3, these interpretations lead to a view of evolution as an inexorable process of ecological ascendency.

New paradigms, like far-from-equilibrium thermodynamics, are accepted because of the solutions they provide; as well, they reveal new questions which further push the boundaries of the discipline (Kuhn, 1970). In thermodynamics, these key questions led to the advances developed by Prigogine and others. The first is based on the Clausius' early definition of entropy, and the other is based on the empirical gap between entropy in natural systems and order in biological systems.

Clausius said that entropy naturally strives "to a maximum." One step beyond this assertion is an intriguing prospect: Can the *production* of entropy be maximized as well? What if one intentionally pushes the amount of entropy production to a maximum in a closed system—what would happen? This question was explored at the turn of the century (Bénard, 1901) through a new experimental setup that allows the system to move farther- and farther- away from equilibrium. This was also the core of Prigogine's study of far-from-equilibrium thermodynamics, which has deepened our understanding of the order-creation dynamics of emergence.[3]

Another question revealed by the second law of thermodynamics soon because a conundrum for biological science: If energy always dissipates, how is it that highly ordered biological entities can continue to exist? Although this seemed to be a philosophical question, it was powerfully framed as problem for thermodynamics by Erwin Schrödinger (1944) in his wonderful masterpiece, *What is Life?* Although somewhat afield of our main journey, his explanation about the buildup of order in a constantly dissipating universe is worth visiting, for it reveals the essential value of a far-from-equilibrium approach. In the quote that follows, "negative entropy" refers to an ordered substance, or one that accrues from the buildup of energy rather than its dissipation as directed by the second law.

> It is by avoiding the rapid decay into the inert state of "equilibrium" that an organism appears so enigmatic . . . How does the living organism avoid decay? . . . It can only keep aloof [from] maximum entropy, which is death . . . by continually drawing from its environment negative entropy. . . . What an organism feeds upon is negative entropy . . . attracting, as it were, a stream of negative entropy upon itself, to compensate [for] the entropy increase it produces by living. . . . Thus the device by which an organism maintains itself stationary at a fairly high level of orderliness (= fairly low level of entropy) really consists in continually sucking orderliness from its environment. (Schrödinger, 1944, pp. 70, 71, 73)

Up to that time and for another decade beyond, neither physics, chemistry, nor thermodynamics had a means of exploring what it could mean to "continually suck orderliness from the environment." However, Prigogine and his colleagues helped figure it out, enacting their understanding in two experiments—the Bérnard cell experiment, and the Belousov-Zhabotinsky reaction. Since these are the two experiments underlying dissipative structures theory, I will go into each of them at some length.

EXPERIMENT 1: THE BÉRNARD EXPERIMENT

The basic experiment showing far-from-equilibrium thermodynamic effects, published by French scientist H. Bérnard (1901), has since been replicated by numerous researchers. The experiment starts with a cylindrical container that is filled with viscous (thick) fluid. The bottom of the container is a metallic plate that is a heat source. The top of the container is a corresponding heat sink; it draws heat energy away from the fluid and back out to the surrounding environment.[4] This experiment has since become the model for a natural open system—it includes an input of energy in the form of heat, a throughput of energy from the bottom to the top of the cylinder, and an output of the energy through the heat sink at the top of the apparatus.

Here is how the process is described by Nicolis and Prigogine (1989): Initially, before the heat is turned on, the system settles into equilibrium such that the fluid is homogenous throughout the container; following the second law of thermodynamics, the fluid will remain at equilibrium unless perturbed. One can test the apparatus by initiating a small perturbation, for example, by touching the top plate of the container with one finger (p. 10). At that place the fluid in the container will increase in temperature by a few degrees, by an amount that is proportional to the difference between the fluid at room temperature and the heat from the finger—usually a difference of about 28° Fahrenheit.[5] Then, as predicted by the second law, the system will immediately seek equilibrium by dissipating that spot of heat energy throughout the container, until the fluid is again homogenous. A close examination will show that the heat is dissipated through *conduction currents*—flows of molecular interactions that disperse the temperature differences through propagating interactions across the system. Until the fluid is fully homogenous the experimental system is in a "near-equilibrium" state; once the perturbation is lifted, that state always resolves to a full equilibrium state, as predicted by statistical mechanics.

The question, and the impetus for the experiment, is what happens when a perturbation is *not* lifted, but continues and even increases, such that the system cannot resolve back to equilibrium. To explore that case, the experiment begins by turning on the source plate, which produces a small amount of heat energy that is infused into the fluid. As before, the system responds by generating conduction currents—local interactions (molecule-to-molecule) that dissipate the heat through vibrational exchanges that extend throughout the container.

In addition, as soon as the source begins to radiate heat, the "sink" is activated, drawing out heat from the fluid at the very top of the container. Thus, the same amount of heat energy that is inputted from the bottom of the container is removed from the top of the container by the sink. Experimentally, this makes the fluid at the top of the cylinder cooler than the fluid at the base. As such, the dissipation of heat is directed from the bottom to the top of the cylinder: energy is dissipated most quickly by rising through the container and out the sink. In metaphorical terms, the conduction currents "carry" heat energy through the fluid and out the top at a rate that is exactly proportional to the rate of heat input from the source.

What happens when the energy from the source continues to increase? It turns out that the heat can be turned up to a rather large degree, with normal convection currents being able to dissipate that heat throughout the container. However, at a certain level of energy input, convection currents on their own are not sufficient for dissipating all of the excess energy through the system. That is when the predictability of the second law begins to break down.

At this point the chemical system will spontaneously produce *fluctuations*. In physical terms these fluctuations involve large groups of molecules that aggregate together. This aggregation can incorporate (encapsulate) a greater amount of heat than the individual molecules can on their own. The fluctuation then transports the heat energy up through the container and releases it to the sink. From the perspective of statistical mechanics and near-equilibrium thermodynamics, such fluctuations are completely unexpected; there is no theory in the previous paradigm that would explain why and how such an event would occur.

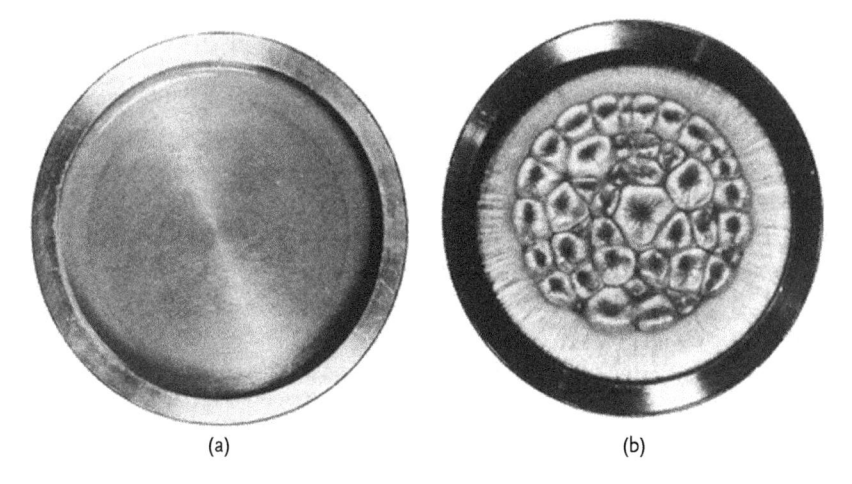

Figure 6.1:
Homogeneity of dissipative structures system → critical threshold → macro order out of micro components.
From Swenson (1989); also in Swenson (2010). Reprinted with permission from Rod Swenson, 'Selection Is Entailed by Self-Organization and Natural Selection Is a Special Case', *Biological Theory*, 5:2 (Spring, 2010), pp. 167–181. © 2010 by Konrad Lorenz Institute for Evolution and Cognition Research.

As the applied heat continues to increase, the rate of these fluctuations also increases, until the system reaches a critical threshold, when another unprecedented event occurs. At a specific upper limit X_{crit}, one of these fluctuations produces enough upward force to initiate an unbroken current of heat energy from the bottom of the container to the top and then back down again. These macroscopic cycles are huge—the molecules are traveling a distance equivalent (at our scale) to the circumference of the earth. These emergent macroscopic structures are much more efficient at producing entropy than the same molecules were on their own, as the continuous rotational motion significantly increases the dissipation of heat in the system.

These macroscopic rotational structures are visible to the naked eye; images are presented in Figure 6.1. Just beyond the threshold X_{crit}, one sees the spontaneous emergence of first one, then two, then three and more of these macroscopic "structures" which order the fluid. As more of them fill the container, they maximize their volume through closest packing by forming hexagons, that is, each one becomes shaped into a hexagonal current that fits perfectly to its neighbors. These hexagonal structures will remain intact for as long as the heat energy continues to pour into the container.

Several important processes are present in this order-creation phenomenon, each of which become vitally important for understanding the emergence of macroscopic structures in the experiment. First, the emergence process is initiated when the system moves away from equilibrium and into a far-from-equilibrium state. Second, this state leads to fluctuations and an amplification process within the entire system. Third, the emergent order—each rotating hexagonal structure—is only a reaggregation of elements (molecules) that are already in the system. Fourth, the emergent structures are stable, remaining organized for as long as the energy continues to flow through the system. Finally, emergence results in two important outcomes. First, what emerges is a new "level" of order in the system, for it now contains the fluid and the structures within it. Second, emergent order increases the *capacity* of the system to do "work"—to dissipate energy—a point that will become very relevant in the application of the theory to social systems. Each of these processes and outcomes are described next.

Far-From-Equilibrium Dynamics

An essential aspect of pushing systems into a far-from-equilibrium state is that virtually all physical and chemical systems have to be *pushed* into that state: the common experimental starting point for these dynamics is equilibrium. In fact, the vast majority of physics, chemistry and mechanics is based on the Newtonian (idealized) world of equilibrium and homogeneity, in which any differences across the system are quickly dissipated, returning the system to its equilibrium state. In equilibrium, the laws of physics are linear and "reversible," allowing for mathematical tractability and predictable results. In thermodynamics, equilibrium refers to a state in which there are no net fluxes across the system—neither energy nor matter are exchanged between the system and its environment (Nicolis & Prigogine, 1989, p. 55). This is the essence of the second law of thermodynamics, that natural systems will always return to a stable state of equilibrium. In both cases equilibrium is the "norm"—the basis of physical science and the state toward which all systems proceed. Note how this assumption also underlies general linear reality (Abbott, 1988).

Moving away from equilibrium thus requires some constant force applied to the system. In technical terms this force is called a "constraint" (Nicolis & Prigogine, p. 56; see also Chapter 17 in this book), for such a force constrains the system's degrees of freedom, in this case pushing it toward a nonlinear state. In the Bérnard experiment the force being added is heat energy; in the BZ reaction, described next, the influx is the continuous pumping of chemicals into the experimental container, as well as the mechanical energy that stirs all the components to ensure their interaction.

Once outside the region of equilibrium these fluxes can increase. Initially, a small input of energy into the system will push it into a "near-equilibrium" state; as described earlier, the system will then seek resolution back to equilibrium. Likewise, in normal, near-equilibrium conditions, any fluctuations are dampened by the equilibrium-seeking behavior of the system, as dictated by the second law of thermodynamics.

However, a flux of energy or material inputs may be pushed through the system at a rate that goes beyond this normal range, that is, beyond the functional capacity of the system to remain at or near equilibrium. As the amount of energy input goes beyond a critical threshold, the system will move into a new state, a state that remains far-from-equilibrium. As noted by Prigogine and Stengers (1984, p. 140), "when the thermodynamic forces acting on a system become such that the linear region is exceeded,…the stability of the stationary state … can no longer be taken for granted." This far-from-equilibrium state generates surprising dynamics.

Amplification of Fluctuations

A driver of these dynamics, and the second aspect of this exo-emergence process, revolves around fluctuations in the system, which begin when the system moves toward a far-from-equilibrium state. Note that in the near-equilibrium condition any natural fluctuations in the system will be dampened, as the system "strives" for equilibrium. However, as the system moves into a far-from-equilibrium state, natural fluctuations may become amplified. "In such a state, certain fluctuations, instead of regressing, may be amplified and invade the entire system, compelling it to evolve toward a new regime that may be qualitatively quite different from the stationary states" (Prigogine & Stengers, 1984, pp. 140–141). Dissipative structures theory thus explains when and why linear systems can become nonlinear ones, and at what point negative feedback can shift to positive feedback and amplification.

A more mathematical explanation of the onset of nonlinearity is presented by Nicolis and Prigogine (1989, p. 59). They describe the striking difference between linear and nonlinear laws using the idea of superposition, for example, of waves in a system. When a system is acting linearly, two waves will superimpose *additively* on one other, often muting the outcome. But beyond a specific threshold this pattern shifts: "In a nonlinear system, adding a small cause to one that is already present can induce dramatic effects that have no common measure with the amplitude of the cause" (Nicolis & Prigogine, 1989, p. 59). In other words, a nonlinear system often expresses "nonproportionality," where the strength of a perturbation—a "cause"—is not proportional to its effect.

Another description focuses on condensation to explain how a system shifts from a linear state to a nonlinear one. Nicolis and Prigogine (1989) begin with the fact that in a gas, condensation droplets often form and evaporate over and over. But there is also a well known critical state—a critical droplet size where the liquid state becomes stable. If the size of a droplet exceeds this "nucleation threshold," the gas almost instantaneously transforms into a liquid. This shift to nonlinearity comes with a rapid amplification of a microscopic fluctuation occurring at the "right moment," resulting in favoring one reaction path over a number of equally possible paths. Thus, although the particular outcomes cannot be predicted, reaching a critical threshold always leads to amplification processes that rapidly alter the internal order.

Nucleation Mechanism

An intriguing aspect of nonlinearity is reflected in what Prigogine calls a "nucleation mechanism" (Prigogine & Stengers, 1984; Nicolis & Prigogine, 1989). This idea responds to the question, How can a single fluctuation turn into an entire macroscopic structure? Likewise, how does one of the fluctuations become amplified into an emergent order (hexagon), which then diffuses across the entire space?

Prigogine and Stengers (1984) provide a "slow-motion" example of this initiation process, involving the emergence of very large pillars in termite nests. At a microscopic level, purely stochastic forces can result in one area point in the nest gaining a very slight increase in its concentration of deposits, tiny bits of earth. Because of the pheromones released, this area will attract more termites, who will dump their earth in that spot, thus creating a positive feedback cycle that amplifies the inputs. Quickly this spot becomes the foundation for a new macrostructure.

In their terms, this exemplifies a "nucleation mechanism"—a process whereby a tiny differentiation becomes the "nucleus" of an amplifying process. Here, the slight emphasis of one element over another becomes a seed that "nucleates" the order-creation process, initiating a cascade of emergence in the system. According to the theory, this initial difference leads to the emergence of a dissipative structure that slowly overtakes and transforms the entire system. Prigogine and Stengers (1984, p. 187) note:

> When a new structure results from a finite perturbation, the fluctuation that leads from one regime to the other cannot possibly overrun the initial state in a single move. It must first establish itself in a limited region and then invade the whole space: There is a nucleation mechanism.... [If] the structural fluctuation successfully imposes itself... the whole system will adopt a new mode of functioning: Its activity will be governed by a new 'syntax.'

In Swenson's experiments (see Figure 6.2), two structures initially arise. Swenson explains, these "Bérnard cells ... arise from two separate origin events." As his photo shows, the entire fluid is "on the verge" of emergence; these two structures then influence their closest neighbors, leading to the ordering of the entire system.

Emergence as Recombination

Although it may appear obvious, it is useful to reflect on the fact that the emergent order makes no material change in the system—no new molecules are imported into the Bérnard experiment. A similar but more subtle point refers to the heat energy within the system. Here, too, a close examination shows that only the flow of energy through the system is heightened; in the experiment, the source and the sink are increased at the same rate. In other words, the amount of heat remains

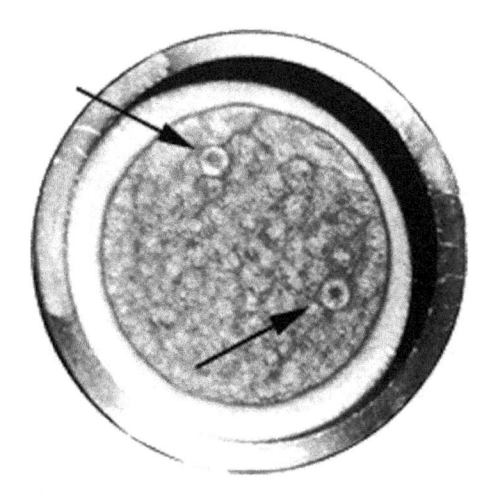

Figure 6.2: Origins of Order in Dissipative Structures System
"The figure shows a time slice in the Bérnard cell experiment right after the minimum threshold of X is crossed and the production of macroscopic order ... has begun. Here ... two individual autocatakinetics [arrows] or self-organizing systems (Bérnard cells) emerge. Here it is important to note that these arise from two separate origin events ... Macro is preferentially and opportunistically selected ... because, relative to the ... micro mode, it greatly increases the dissipative rate" (Swenson, 2010, p. 178). Figure from Swenson (1989); also in Swenson (2010). Reprinted with permission from Rod Swenson, 'Selection Is Entailed by Self-Organization and Natural Selection Is a Special Case', *Biological Theory*, 5:2 (Spring, 2010), pp. 167–181. © 2010 by Konrad Lorenz Institute for Evolution and Cognition Research.

proportional throughout the process. Mathematically what increases is the *energy flux*, the rate of energy flow through the system.

In an intriguing sense, it is this flux itself that is organizing the molecules in the system, or to put it another way, the dynamics of the system are the "causal agent" of the outcome of emergence. In the theory of emergence, existing elements in the system are reorganized and reaggregated through the high energy flux. Recombination puts the emphasis of emergence on existing elements and explores how they are reorganized, such that the new order is "nothing but" what's in the system, even as the emergence brings with it properties and outcomes that go beyond the components themselves.

Stability of the Newly Emerged State

Once they emerge, these hexagonal structures will remain stable, in what Nicolis and Prigogine called a state of "stationary disequilibrium." This term highlights the inherent dynamic tension in the system, which I call a dynamic state (Levie & Lichtenstein, 2010). On the one hand, the dissipative structure emerges and remains in place because of the rapid and amplified inputs through the system, which push it into a disequilibrium state. On the other hand, this disequilibrium doesn't change; it somehow remains stationary, even amidst ongoing perturbations within the system.

An exemplar of "stationary disequilibrium" is the vortex that forms when water is let out of a bath tub. To explain, consider the vortex as a dissipative structure: Its emergence begins when the stopper is lifted from the tub, thereby inducing the water to rapidly run down the drain. The entire volume of water in the bathtub exerts pressure on the small drain, pushing the system into a far-from-equilibrium state. According to the second law of thermodynamics, the molecules of water will attempt to dissipate through the drain as quickly as possible. Given the right conditions, a "fluctuation" will occur in this system, leading to the emergence of a macroscopic structure: A vortex materializes in the water—a "tornado" that aims right down to the drain. As explained by dissipative structures theory, the vortex will form as soon as the system reaches a critical point, at which point the system "somehow" figures out that the rate and volume of dissipation can increase through the creation of a vortex.

In terms of stability, think about perturbing the structure by sticking a finger into the vortex. The macrostructure is remarkably hard to dislodge—the little water-tornado continuously reforms itself after being poked, always seeking to "circumvent" the constraining influence of the finger. The continuous presence of the vortex, up until the entire tub is drained, reflects the stability of dissipative structures in the disequilibrium conditions.

The vortex suggests something more: What is creating the "form" of the vortex, the shape of the tornado, and likewise the boundaries of the hexagonal structures in the Bérnard experiment? In each case these are "nothing but" the molecules that comprise them—the vortex is nothing but the water draining through it, and the hexagonal structures are nothing but the molecules rotating through the container. And yet, when the structures are perturbed, they re-form almost immediately. What is it that re-forms the structure or form? The molecules that were there moments ago are either far down the drain or far removed from the initial point of impact. Clearly, the emergent order is something more than the molecules that comprise it. But what?

The only way to answer this question is to take into account the entire system, including the ongoing flow of energy through the system, the containers surrounding the order, and the laws of dissipation that operate in far-from-equilibrium conditions. Like all definitions of emergence, these systemwide influences are "causes" of order creation, and these systemic qualities help define the nature and properties of the order that comes into being. Importantly, the order emerges and remains stable *only through the constant and rapid flow of energy through the system.*

Outcomes: Emergence is a New "Level" of Order

In terms of general systems theory, a new level of order has emerged in the container. Up until now, the internal system—the fluid—could be described in terms of chemistry, that is, the fluid is composed of molecules that are stochastically moving as a fluid. Once the shift happens, however, the fluid can only be described in terms of two distinct levels, the second one being an ordered structure that is composed of hundreds of millions of molecules all acting in a coherent manner. Following the precedence from general systems theory, these new structures are a distinct unit of analysis, a "higher" level of order.

One way to define this higher level is that it "transcends but includes" its lower level components. "Includes" here means that the higher level is "nothing but" the molecules, whereas "transcends" means that the higher level has properties and qualities that go beyond the properties of the molecules. By "going beyond," I mean at least three things—(1) a shift in dissipation process, (2) a dramatic increase in capacity, and (3) an ordered stability. The first of these I will explain here, the other two in subsequent sections.

In thermodynamic terms, the hexagonal structures have transformed the dissipation process from conduction into convection—a difference in *kind* that deserves a bit of explanation. Recall from chemistry that at a molecular level, an increase in energy (e.g., through heat) is expressed as an increase in the vibration of a given molecule. This vibrational energy can be dissipated in two main ways. In conduction, the additional energy is dissipated through *vibrational* contact with adjacent molecules; as the higher energy molecule interacts with another of lower energy, it literally "gives up" some of that vibration, thus spreading it out across the field. As an example think of the molecules of iron that make up the outside of a woodstove. When the wood in the stove is lit and the stove gets hot, the heat is transferred from the wood to the iron frame. As each molecule vibrates, those vibrations get transferred to adjacent molecules in the iron, slowly heating up the entire stove. This conduction energy dissipates the energy by spreading it out across the entire frame. Although effective, the process is somewhat slow.

A second kind of dissipation process is convection, whereby energy is dissipated through "mass transfer" that is effected across the entire system. In our wood stove example, the air surrounding the wood stove gets hot. Because heat rises, these hotter molecules of air push upward, toward the ceiling of the room. As more hot air rises, cooler air in the room takes its place; this air then gets hotter and rises as well. Soon a flow of hot air is rotating through the entire room, instigated by the heat from the stove. Thus, in convection, the heat is being transferred "en mass," through the massive number of air molecules that dissipate the heat throughout the room. This is in contrast to conduction, in which the energy is dissipated molecule by molecule, through vibrational contact. For this reason, convection currents are far more efficient at transferring heat than are conduction currents.[6]

Here we have a difference in kind: Conduction currents operate at the level of individual molecules, whereas convection operates across an entire system of molecules, through the room, or through the container in the Bérnard experiment. In this way, the shift in dissipation represents a new level of order—the emergence of a new unit of analysis.

Outcomes: Increased Coherence and Capacity

A remarkable aspect of these convection currents is that they are composed of hundreds of billions of molecules that somehow "coordinate" their activity. Swenson (1989, 1991) helps reveal the enormity of this event. He shows that initially the molecules are interacting in distances on the order of 10^{-8} cm—about four millionths of an inch—and in time scales of 10^{-15} seconds—about a trillionth of a second. After the transition, however, these interactions can be measured on the order of centimeters and minutes. To get a human feel for the tremendous difference this represents, he compares an individual molecule to an individual person and translates the degree of difference in human terms:

> Relative to a component of human size and lifespan . . . this variability [is] equivalent to changes [that are] orders of magnitude greater than the circumference of the earth, and over time scales greater than the full 4 billion year history of bioevolution. (Swenson 1989, p. 217)

To translate: In normal circumstances we generally pursue actions that last a matter of seconds and occasionally minutes. Likewise, our immediate interface with the world occurs within arm's length, over a few meters. In comparison, the emergent structures here exist in time scales of hundreds of millions of years and interact in distances of more than 25,000 miles.

But equally remarkable is that these emergent structures are *coherent* throughout this expanded time and space. That means, in comparison, that our singular actions would be synchronously coordinated across hundreds of millions of people across the entire planet, and that coherence would last far beyond the evolutionary history of *Homo sapiens*. These are the measured findings from this experiment, which has been repeated numerous times with the same results.

Another remarkable outcome from these macroscopic structures is the increase in capacity that they provide to the system. Swenson shows that the emergent convection structures are able to dissipate *orders of magnitude* more heat through the system than the linear "conduction currents." Swenson (1991, see Figure 6.3), for example, shows the discontinuous increase in energy flux that corresponds to the "transformation from disorder to order." According to his rigorous measurements of these increases in "field potential" the capacity of the system to dissipate energy "increase[s] by orders of magnitude."[7] This increase in capacity confirms the original notion that all systems strive for maximum entropy production. The insight from dissipative structures theory is that the most effective way to maximize entropy production is to create structural order. This claims is foundational to the complexity field of ecological ascendency (in Chapter 3).

Another good example of this process is demonstrated by the Belousov-Zhabotinsky (B-Z) reaction, the second paradigm experiment of emergence in far-from-equilibrium conditions.

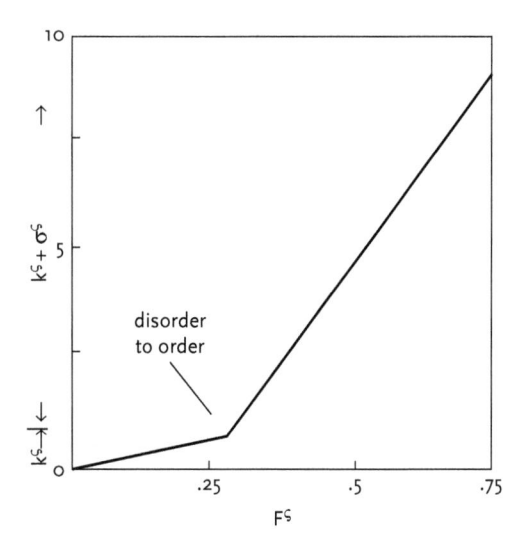

Figure 6.3: Increased Capacity through Emergence
Here, outcomes of emergence are measured here as increased entropy production. The figure shows the dramatic discontinuous increase in entropy production (in this case corresponding to the increase in heat transferred from source to sink) that occurs during the transition from disordered (micro) to ordered (macro) mode.

Photos and text from Swenson (2010, p. 178). Reprinted with permission from Rod Swenson, 'Selection Is Entailed by Self-Organization and Natural Selection Is a Special Case', *Biological Theory*, 5:2 (Spring, 2010), pp. 167–181. © 2010 by Konrad Lorenz Institute for Evolution and Cognition Research.

EXPERIMENT 2: THE B-Z REACTION—A CHEMICAL CLOCK

Whereas the first experiment of dissipative structures involves the ordering of molecules in space, the second experiment, known as the Belousov-Zhabotinsky (B-Z) reaction, examines how order can spontaneously emerge over time. Although the experimental situation produces far-from-equilibrium behavior in a different way, the mechanisms and processes of order creation are rather similar.

The setup begins by putting four distinct chemical compounds—call them A, B, X, and Y—into a container and stirring them together. According to traditional chemistry, given the right compounds, the chemicals will react together, producing a product that is some combination of the compounds, while at the same time moving the entire system toward equilibrium.

In order to explore the potential nonlinear behavior of these reactions, two additions are made to this customary setup. First, the container is turned into an open system: The compounds A, B, X, and Y are continuously pumped into the container, and the equivalent amount of excess mixture is drained out of the container in order to keep the total volume of liquid constant. In addition, an automatic stirring device insures that the compounds in the solution fully interact with each other. Although the openness of the system doesn't cause nonlinear reactions in and of itself, the continuous flow of highly interacting elements pushes the system into a far-from-equilibrium state, which is a necessary condition of order creation, as it was in the Bérnard experiment.

The second key to this experiment is that two of the compounds are catalysts, that is, their presence in the solution "encourages" (amplifies) the other two chemicals to interact. In fact, these compounds exemplify a special type of catalysis, one in which the presence of the product is required for its own synthesis. This is autocatalysis, which was described in Chapter 5. Specifically, in order to produce the molecule X through a chemical reaction, the solution already has to have the product X. Prigogine gives as an example the reaction scheme: $A + 2X \rightarrow 3X$; in the presence of molecule X, the molecule A is converted into another X. Thus, X is needed to produce more X.

What Prigogine found is that an autocatalytic reaction will shift the system from a linear to a nonlinear regime: "One important feature of systems involving such 'reaction loops' is that the kinetic equations describing the changes occurring in them are *nonlinear* differential equations" (Prigogine & Stengers, 1984, p. 134). The combination of far-from-equilibrium conditions and autocatalytic loops turns the system into an order-creating regime, by shifting it out of its initial stationary state. Prigogine emphasized that the only way that a chemical reaction can be shifted out of a stationary state is through this unique combination. Likewise, Prigogine found that the only way to disrupt the stationary state of a thermodynamic system is through the presence of "catalytic loops," where the product of a chemical reaction is involved in its own synthesis (Prigogine & Stengers, 1984, p. 145). Autocatalysis (Eigen, 1971; Eigen & Schuster, 1979) is thus a core driver of exo-organizing.

Emergence of Order—Systemwide Oscillations

What occurs in this far-from-equilibrium regime? Prigogine and his collaborators found that beyond a certain "critical threshold"—a certain ratio of one of the autocatalytic molecules compared to the others—the entire system will "abruptly" change from one state to another, producing an oscillation that takes over the entire solution. They report (1984, p. 147):

> Instead of remaining stationary, the concentrations of X and Y begin to oscillate with a well-defined periodicity. . . . We therefore have a periodic chemical process—a chemical clock.

In one particular version of the experiment, called the Brusselator, the actual color of the solution in the container changes from being all yellow to being colorless to being all yellow and back again, in a regular periodicity. (Nicolis and Prigogine [1989] provide the chemical constituents and their initial concentrations for the Brusselator on pp. 19 and 23; see more helpful descriptions and schematics at Scholarpedia.org/Belousov-Zhabotinsky reaction. Current research is being pursued by the Fraden Group at Brandeis, among other places [http://fraden.brandeis.edu/research/bz.html]. For further videos, search YouTube for Belousov-Zhabotinsky.)

Another version of the BZ reaction, described as "surface catalysis," retains the same setup of chemicals but leaves out the continuous stirring. The result is a visual expression of these internal processes—regular patterns still emerge, but they propagate in space and time in the form of wave fronts. In their words (Nicolis & Prigogine, 1989, p. 22),

> In each case the wave fronts propagate over macroscopic distances of space, without distortion and at a prescribed speed; they both represent and transmit the "message" released by the chemistry at the center from which the whole pattern emanates.... As in the Bérnard problem, we can associate the formation of wave fronts with space symmetry breaking.

These spiral wave fronts have become well-known images showing "order out of chaos" (see Figure 6.4). Prigogine and Stengers used them to illustrate the cover of their book of that name. Several videos on YouTube illustrate the spiral effect as well.[8]

As in the Bérnard cell, this new regime is in a state of "stationary disequilibrium"—the oscillations will continue as long as the inputs remain the same. Even if this state is disturbed, for example, by briefly increasing the concentration of one of the reagents, or raising the temperature of the container for a few moments, the system will return to the same pattern of oscillations. In formal terms, "after ... applying a slight concentration or temperature pulse in the BZ reagent...[it] will resume an oscillatory mode of exactly the same amplitude and period as before. This is the property of asymptotic stability" (Nicolis & Prigogine, 1989, p. 20).

PARALLELS BETWEEN THE TWO EXPERIMENTS

In many ways the two experiments are similar. Summarizing these parallels will lead to a set of processes and outcomes, and experimental conditions, that lead to the emergence of order in dissipative structures. In Chapter 7 these will become the basis for a direct analogy between emergence of a dissipative structure and emergence of social entities.

Processes and Outcomes

- **Once initiated, the system is pushed into a far-from-equilibrium state.** As energy is inputted into the system, the system transitions from equilibrium to a far-from-equilibrium state, a state that is maintained as long as the energy is imported into the system.

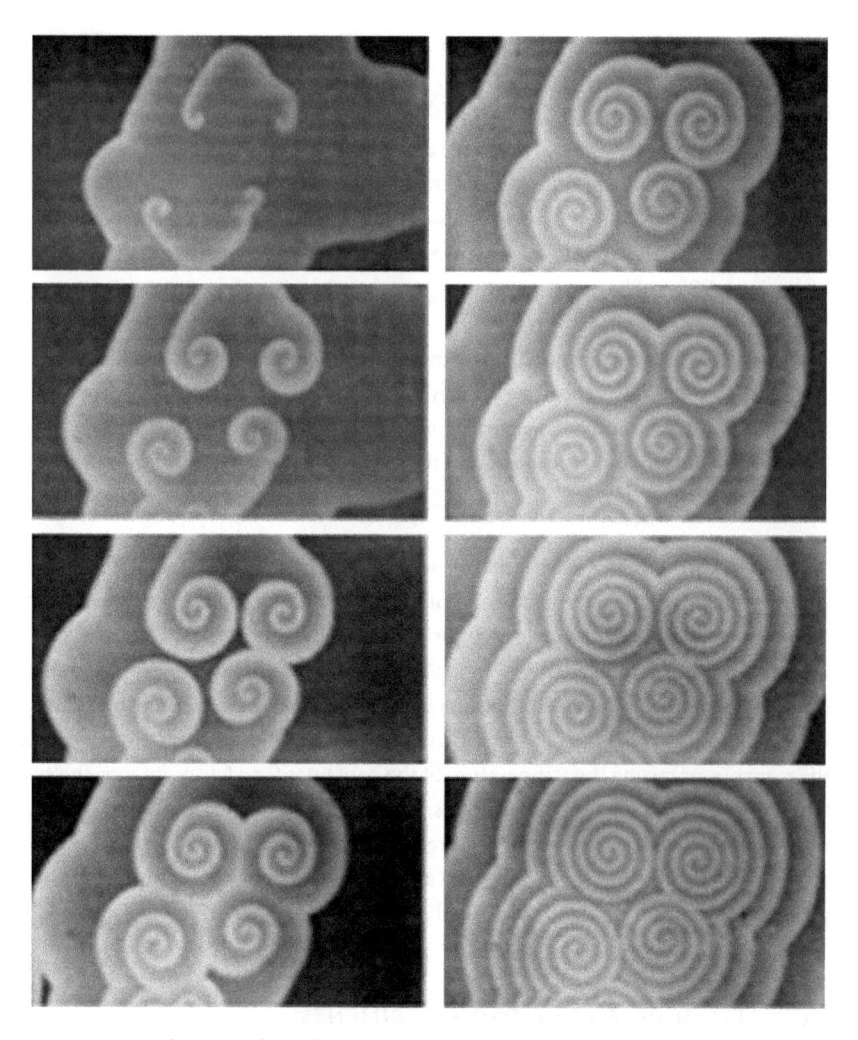

Figure 6.4: Development of Spiral Waves in the BZ Reaction.
These occur after hydrodynamic breaking of a concentric wave (Zhabotinsky & Zaikin, 1971).
From: http://www.scholarpedia.org/article/Belousov-Zhabotinsky_reaction Reprinted with permission from the Zhabotinsky family.

- **Fluctuations near a threshold.** In the Bérnard experiment, as the inputs move the system farther away from equilibrium to a critical threshold, natural "fluctuations" will emerge in the fluid. Something similar but less dramatic occurs in the B-Z reaction, just before the onset of periodic oscillation (see Nicolis & Prigogine, 1989; p. 19). These fluctuations are the seed of new order.
- **At the threshold, nonlinearity and amplifications.** Both systems have a well-defined threshold point. Before reaching that threshold the system's elements interact in a linear way. In contrast, as the system is pushed to its

threshold, it begins to act in nonlinear ways, often accelerating fluctuations and other processes in the system. In addition, the onset of order is not instantaneous throughout the system. Instead, it starts in one specific area, then diffuses outward to surrounding areas of the container.

- **Emergent order is a recombination of existing elements.** The new order is a recombination of elements already in the system. That is, a dissipative structure reorganizes itself without recourse to external ingredients. In addition, emergence is unexpected and unpredictable even with a complete knowledge of the components, and it occurs relatively rapidly once the threshold is passed.
- **Emergent order remains stable.** In both experiments the newly emergent order remains stable for as long as the input levels remain the same. Experimentally, when the input is reduced, the system will leave its far-from-equilibrium state. The emergent order will then dissipate and the entire system will become homogeneous as it was at the outset of the experiment.
- **Outcomes: Emergent order increases systemic capacity.** In the Bérnard experiment, the emergent order dramatically increases the capacity of the system to dissipate heat. In the B-Z reaction, the new order produces the maximal amount of catalysis across the compounds. Visually (to an observer) the chemical system shifts from monotonic to oscillating colors, or from homogeneous to visibly spiraled.
- **Outcomes: Emergent order "transcends but includes" the components.** These emergences generate a new level or layer of order in the system, with its own properties, patterns, and integrity that cannot be reduced to its components. In this way the emergent order "transcends but includes" its components—the hexagonal structures generate outcomes that are well beyond what can be produced by the molecules alone, yet these structures are made up solely by those molecules. Likewise, the chemical clock's colors or shapes are expressed at a "higher" level than the molecules—the colors can only be "seen" by humans outside the system, yet the entire system is "nothing but" the compounds.

Experimental Conditions

- **Strong container.** Dissipative structures emerge within well-defined containers. Both experiments are designed around containers—cylinders with specific boundaries on all sides, and with carefully arranged points of interaction where the system is open to the environment. The characteristics of the container constrain and support the emergence of order. For example, in the Bérnard experiment the heat energy is channeled by the sides of the cylinder; the number and size of the hexagonal structures depend on the size of the cylinder. Thus, having a strong container is a requisite condition of these experiments.

- **Agents are homogeneous.** The components of the systems are homogeneous molecules; agents are totally undifferentiated.
- **Agent behavior is linear and deterministic.** The component agents are subject to the laws of statistical mechanics and traditional thermodynamics, namely each agent's local actions are linear and predictable. Likewise, the entire system is deterministic, that is, the components follow specific laws that always determine their behavior.
- **Initiated by an "external" agent.** Both experiments start when energy or resources are imported (pushed) into the system, either in the form of heat or through the input of chemical compounds into the solution. Importantly, someone outside the system has to literally turn the experiment "on." Without this external agent there is no order creation.
- **Inputs are exogenous to the system.** The energy or resources that are imported into the system during the experiment are drawn from the "environment," from a seemingly unlimited stock of energy and resources that exists "outside" the formal experiment. Like the existence of a container in these experiments, this condition is assumed. .
- **Outputs are discarded into the environment.** Like the inputs, the energy and resources that flow out of the sink become exogenous to the system; they provide no additional "value" in the experiment. Specifically, the heat energy in the Bérnard experiment is exported out of the system and is unused after that. The excess chemicals in the B-Z reaction are also transferred out of the system.

Each of these elements must be accounted for if we are to make true analogy between dissipative structures in natural systems and emergent order in human systems. Can such an analogy be developed? Answering that question is the goal of the next chapter.

NOTES

1. Carnot's derivation of the second law was based on his exploration of efficiency in steam engines, which he found was improved when energy was transferred in the form of heat and pressure rather than through the more common mode of mechanical motion. This "Carnot engine" was engineered by Watt into the modern steam engine, which literally "powered" the Industrial Revolution, along with a number of other important innovations.
2. Swenson has extended this idea through the law of maximum entropy production, which claims that the any natural system will "select the path or assembly of paths, out of otherwise available paths, that minimize the potential or maximize the entropy *at the fastest rate,* given the constraints" (my italics). It turns out that order flow is far more efficient at dissipating energy than disordered flow. In my terms, emergents have much greater capacity to dissipate energy. Thus, the world (evolution) will select for greater order (or capacity for order creation).
3. Nicolis and Prigogine (1989, p. 16) use the term "stationary nonequilibrium state" to reflect the unusual properties of the nonequilibrium system, namely that the concentrations of

chemical elements are constant but are not at equilibrium, a situation that is anathema in classical chemistry.
4. According to Nicolis and Prigogine (1989), an important constraint of the experiment is the relative largeness of the parallel plates compared to the width of the entire cylinder. Specifically, they describe the fluid in a container "between two horizontal parallel plates whose dimensions are much larger than the width of the layer" (p. 9). Essentially, the container has to be "stout," or have a relatively large diameter compared to its height. Swenson's photographs of the Bérnard experiment also suggest the same ratio. More on that distinction in reference to "containers and constraints" is provided in Chapter 17.
5. Assuming a body temperature of 98°F and room temperature of 70°F.
6. It turns out that this is especially true for a viscous fluid, which allows for further heat conduction through gravitational drag properties from the viscosity of the fluid.
7. Swenson continues: Order occurs spontaneously and inexorably as soon as the field force F is at the minimum level that will support it. Swenson's claim is that order will emerge "as soon as" the minimum threshold is reached. See Swenson (1989, 1991, 1997).
8. A good example is: http://www.youtube.com/watch?v=IBa4kgXI4Cg&feature=channel. Others can be found by searching "Belousov Zhabotinsky," including http://www.youtube.com/watch?v=bH6bRt4XJcw&feature=related

REFERENCES

Abbott, A. 1988. Transcending general linear reality. *Sociological Theory* 6(2): 169–86.
Bénard, H. 1901. Les tourbillons cellulaires dans une nappe liquide transportant de la chaleur par convection en régime permanent. *Annales de Chimie et de Physique*, 23: 62–114.
Carnot, S. 1824. Reflections on the motive power of fire, and on machines fitted to develop that power. *The Second Law of Thermodynamics Benchmark Papers on Energy*, 5.
Chaisson, E. 2001. *Cosmic Evolution: The Rise of Complexity in Nature*. Cambridge, MA: Harvard University Press.
Eigen, M. 1971. Self-organization of matter and the evolution of biological macromolecules. *Naturwissenschaften*, 58: 465–523.
Eigen, M., & Schuster, P. 1979. *The Hypercycle: A Principle of Natural Self-Organizing; In Three Parts*. New York: Springer.
Kuhn, T. S. 1970. *The Structure of Scientific Revolutions*. Chicago: University of Chicago Press.
Levie, J., & Lichtenstein, B. 2010. A terminal assessment of stages theory: Introducing a dynamic states approach to entrepreneurship. *Entrepreneurship Theory and Practice*, 34(2–March): 314–54.
McKelvey, B. 2004. Toward a 0th law of thermodynamics: Order creation complexity dynamics from physics and biology to bioeconomics. *Bioeconomics*, 6: 65–96.
Nicolis, G., & Prigogine, I. 1989. *Exploring Complexity*. New York: W. H. Freeman.
Prigogine, I., & Stengers, I. 1984. *Order out of Chaos*. New York: Bantam Books.
Schrödinger, E. 1944. *What is Life?* New York: Cambridge University Press.
Swenson, R. 1989. Emergent attractor and the law of maximum entropy production: Foundations to a theory of general evolution. *Systems Research*, 6(3): 187–97.
Swenson, R. 1991. End-directed physics and evolutionary ordering. In F. Geyr (Ed.), *Cybernetics of Complex Systems* (41–60). Salinas, CA: Intersystems Press.
Swenson, R. 1997. Autocatakinetics, evolution, and the law of maximum entropy production: A principled foundation towards the study of human ecology. *Advances in Human Ecology*, 6: 1–47.

Swenson, R. 1998. Thermodynamics, evolution, and behavior. In G. Greenberg & M. Haraway (Eds.), *Encyclopedia of Comparative Psychology* (207–18). New York: Garland Publishers.

Swenson, R. 2010. Selection is entailed by self-organization, and natural selection is a special case. *Biological Theory*, 5(2): 167–81.

Zhabotinsky, A. M., & Zaikin, A. 1971. Spatial effects in a self-oscillating chemical system, In E. E. Sel'kov (Ed.) *Oscillatory Processes in Biological and Chemical Systems II.* Moscow: Science Publishers.

CHAPTER 7

Applying Dissipative Structures to Organizations

Having explicated the molecular dynamics in far-from-equilibrium thermodynamic systems—the Bérnard experiment and the B-Z reaction—we are challenged to find how these dynamics are analogous to emergence in human and social systems. Pursuing such an analogy requires vigilance about the constraints necessary to preserve the essential science while applying it to human ecologies. As will become clear in what follows, I am an optimist around these questions, but only because I take very seriously the charge of rigor—the need for very high integrity in making a strict analogy.[1]

There are actually two very different approaches for applying dissipative structures theory to order-creation processes in biological and social contexts. The first approach claims that the same mathematics of negative entropy in chemical systems can be used by extension to explain the buildup of order in organisms, ecosystems, evolution, and in economies. This approach has been pursued by a host of researchers over the past 30 years, and in the next section I will briefly review that effort.

A second approach is to make a "transformative metaphor" (Tsoukas, 1991) between these two contexts—an analogical mapping of core processes and relationships from the source to the target, in our case from a dissipative structure to its parallel in human systems. This second approach will form the main body of this chapter.

EXTENDING THERMODYNAMICS INTO ECOLOGY AND ECONOMY

Well before Prigogine explored the dynamics of dissipative structures, scholars were proposing ways to use the second law of thermodynamics as the basis for explaining the buildup of order in all biological, social, and evolutionary contexts. Specifically, researchers looked for a connection between energy dissipation and the presence of order by extending statistical mechanics from thermodynamics to biological and ecological systems. These extensions took several forms.

"Negentropy" in Biology and Economics

Gibbs (1906) and Lotka (1922, 1945) led this effort. Later, the link to biological organization was pursued by Schrödinger (1944); his work is helpfully summarized by Corning and Kline (1998b), among others. Schrödinger's idea led to a wide range of extensions into the emergence and development of "negentropy" in biological systems. Given the highly technical nature of this work, I have placed the summary of these extensions in the Appendix to this chapter.

Others drew the entropy concept further, to help explain the disequilibrium processes of economics. Important early approaches were developed by Georgescu-Roegen (1971) and Boulding (1978, 1980, 1981), as well as Odum and Odum (1976). More recently, Dyke (1992) has presented a careful argument in favor of integrating the entropy concept into a broader definition of economics, which

> sets the boundaries [of economics] in such a way that our continuity with natural processes, and our utter dependence on them, is emphasized. . . . Economies become aspects of ecosystems, reminding us of our inescapable place within the biota of the earth. (pp. 149–150)

In a separate essay entitled "Cities as Dissipative Structures," Dyke explores "the material conditions for the emergence of an economy as a dissipative structure" (Dyke, 1988, p. 364). Similar conclusions are made by J. Barkley Rosser, in his essay entitled "The Dialogue Between the Economic and the Ecologic Theories of Evolution" (Rosser, 1992, p. 195). There is merit in each of these attempts to extend thermodynamics to biological and social systems.

Problems with These Extensions

At the same time, there are many risks and problems with this entire approach. Dyke (1992) recognizes these challenges in the very title of his essay, "From Entropy to Economy: A Thorny Path." His concluding paragraph summarizes some of the key issues: "The most important entropy considerations for systems like economic systems is the entropy stored in structure and, quite frankly, nobody knows how to measure that entropy" (p. 174). Without adequate measures, how can a mathematical pursuit be effective? Perhaps more problematic are the conceptual challenges in applying the original measures of entropy in closed physical systems to much broader applications such as organisms and economies. These applications have led, in the words of Corning and Kline (1998a, p. 274), to

> many loose and inaccurate renderings of the Second Law...[causing a] confusion that has ... infected the disciplines of information theory, economics and biology, where terms like "entropy, "negentropy" and even the concept of "information" are used in a bewildering variety of ways.

For these reasons and others, I have decided to follow a different overall approach, which remains true to the core science of dissipative structures theory and applies these processes as an analogue to organizational emergence. At the core of this approach is a general principle that all systems that do work can be described as sets of resources (material and energetic) which are organized to accomplish that task. Such systems are sustained through a continuous loop of inputs, transformations, and output as described by general systems theory. Specifically, resources are input into the system, transformed to accomplish their work, then turned into outputs; these outputs then catalyze further inputs (Adams, 1988; Boulding, 1988; Kaufmann, 1991). Here the focus is on the transformation and exchange of "energy" through systems, rather than on the nonlinear statistical analysis of entropy production within them. As such, this approach allows for rigorous metaphors that don't get constrained by computational complexity and varying interpretations of entropy. Although this necessarily limits a mathematical analysis of order creation in social system, it exchanges that type of rigor for a clear correspondence to organizations and other social entities.

DISSIPATIVE STRUCTURES AS A MODEL FOR EMERGENCE

The model of dissipative structures and concepts from far-from-equilibrium system change have long been used as analogies for how order is created within social and economic entities. Some examples include work by Schieve and Allen (1982); Ulrich and Probst (1984); Artigiani (1987); Adams (1988); Dyke (1988); Goldstein (1988); Leifer (1989); Zuijderhoudt (1990); Smith and Gemmill (1991); Barton (1994); Goldstein (1994); Smith and Comer (1994); De Vany (1996); Zohar and Borkman (1997); Saviotti and Mani (1998); Weisbuch, Kirman, and Herreiner (1998); MacIntosh and MacLean (1999); Foster (2000); Biggiero (2001); Fuller and Moran (2001); and Gilstrap (2007). My own work has also emphasized this approach (Lichtenstein, 1995, 2000a, 2000b, 2000c, 2002; Lichtenstein & Jones, 2004; Lichtenstein, 2009; Lichtenstein & Plowman, 2009). Most of this work takes for granted that one can make a rigorous analogy between order creation in dissipative structures and in organizations. My aim here is to critically examine this assumption so as to clarify the ways in which it holds, and how any differences should be resolved.

The Making of a Rigorous Analogy

In order to analyze the validity of a proposed analogy between dissipative structures theory and its social parallel, I will use Tsoukas' (1991) method for making a "transformational metaphor." This approach works by making four successively in-depth links between a source (dissipative structures) and a target (organizations); these are at the levels of insight, analogy, isomorphism, and identity. The level of *insight* comes from a metaphor that proposes a useful link between two phenomena. In this case, the insight is that dissipative structures may be a useful metaphor for understanding organizational order creation. Next, the level of *analogy* is a conceptual model which claims that the emergence of an organization, and by extension any social entity, is analogous to the emergence of order in a dissipative structure, for example, to the materialization of hexagonal structures in a Bérnard experiment. At the third level of *isomorphism*, the analogy is shown to be valid through an isomorphic mapping, or by showing how the processes and conditions of emergence in dissipative structures can be systemically mapped onto the processes and conditions of emergence in social entities. Finally, the deepest connection is at the level of *identity*, which claims that a single generalized theory explains the "cause" of emergence in both contexts. In the summary by Garud and Kotha (1994, p. 675), this last level "provides a theoretical rationale for how the source and target are identical." To date, such a rigorous analysis of dissipative structures has not appeared in the literature.

Tsoukas explains that the third level of analogical mapping is perhaps the most critical: "the metaphor breaks down, usually when it is not possible to create an isomorphic mapping between the two ... models" (Tsoukas 1991, p. 576). In point of fact, most previous researchers have adopted the first two levels but have not been rigorous about this third level; perhaps this is why the social sciences have so many definitions and usages of emergence and self-organization. In contrast, the previous chapter has provided the tools for making a rigorous isomorphic mapping, by summarizing the distinct processes and outcomes and the experimental conditions for the emergence of order in dissipative structures. In order to make the mapping as clear as possible, I will start by making the analogy to the processes and outcomes of emergence. In a second analysis I will examine the degree to which the experimental conditions for dissipative structures are isomorphic to the conditions that lead to emergence of a social entity. In Chapter 8 I will focus on the *differences* between dissipative structures and social systems. Figure 7.1 summarizes all these layers of a transformative metaphor, including the isomorphic mapping of the phases of the process in dissipative structures emergence and how they would relate to phases of emergence in social entities. Details about those phases are presented next.

Metaphor:
    Emergence of hexagonal structures   *is like*   Emergence of "social structures"
    in Bérnard experiment   e.g., organizations

Conceptual Model:
    Emergence process of a   *is analogous to*   Emergence process of a
    dissipative structure   new social entity

Isomorphic Mapping:

System is pushed toward a far-from-equilibrium state	System is pushed toward a far-from-equilibrium state
Fluctuations appear near a threshold	Experiments appear near a threshold
At the threshold, nonlinearity	At the threshold, nonlinearity
Emergence is a recombination of existing elements	Emergence is a recombination of existing elements
Stability of the newly emerged state	Stability of the newly emerged state
Outcomes: Emergence of a new level of order that increases systemic capacity	Outcomes: Emergence of a new level of order that increases systemic capacity

Theoretical Identity:
    both processes express   **Generative Emergence**

Figure 7.1: Transformative Metaphor of Emergence Processes

Mapping the Process of Emergence from Dissipative Structures to Social Entities

1. A System Is Pushed Toward a Far-From-Equilibrium State

The Bérnard experiment and the B-Z reaction begin in an equilibrium state, with no exogenous inputs and no internal order. This state changes as soon as energy in the form of heat or chemical compounds is inputted into the system. As described earlier, initially the physical system moves into a near-equilibrium state as it seeks to dissipate these additional resources. However, as more and more energy enters the system, the system moves farther and farther away from equilibrium, toward a state of high dynamism and turbulence—what Prigogine called "far-from-equilibrium."

In an analogy to social entities, the process of generative emergence begins with an input of energy or resources into the system. In entrepreneurial terms, this refers to "organizing" (Gartner & Brush, 2007)—developing a vision and starting to pursue it by bringing new resources into the system (Gartner, 1993). These inputs push the system away from its normal ("equilibrium") state and into a state of higher dynamism, activity, and intensity, into a "far-from-equilibrium state" (Leifer,

1989; MacIntosh & MacLean, 1999; Chiles, Meyer, & Hench, 2004; Lichtenstein, 2009).[2] This state is highly dynamic and turbulent; it is laden with new expectations for higher productivity, greater creativity, and much more energy. In McKelvey's terms (McKelvey, 2004), the farther away from normal that the entrepreneur seeks to push the venture, the farter from equilibrium it operates, leading to high levels of fervency, uncertainty, and extremely long work days. The move into a far-from-equilibrium state sets the stage for emergence.

2. Near a Threshold, Fluctuations

In the Bérnard experiment, as heat energy is pushed into the system from the source, conduction currents allow the flow of heat to dissipate effectively through the fluid and out the source. However, as explained in the previous chapter, at some point those linear flows are unable to keep up with the amount of heat being input into the system; this is the threshold of far-from-equilibrium dynamics. Just beyond this threshold the system begins to produce "fluctuations"—rapid aggregations of molecules that transport a higher amount of heat through the system. Each fluctuation can be seen as an *experiment*—an attempt by the system to "keep up with" the increasing demands of heat dissipation.

In social entities, the farther away from "normal" the system is pushed, the less likely that existing routines and tried-and-true practices will be able to keep up with the rising intensity and expectations. As the system moves into a far-from-equilibrium state, individuals face increasing challenges, issues that cannot be solved using "standard operating procedures." They invariably try new things—experiments—that are aimed at solving the problems at hand. These innovations are attempts to deal with the growing intensity, by increasing productivity, enhancing creativity, or in some way extending the limits of what can be done in the organization. Although the outcome of each experiment is not assured, each one represents a test to see if a new "mode of organizing" can satisfy the aspiration and increased flow of energy through the system.

3. At the Threshold, Nonlinearity

As the energy inputs continue to rise, and the normal conduction currents are less and less able to dissipate the requisite level of heat, the whole system moves toward a threshold—a critical point of imminent change. Up to this point, the system operates in a linear mode; negative feedback loops serve to dampen any fluctuations that arise, in order to maintain stability as close to equilibrium as possible. According to Prigogine's explanation, this critical threshold defines the point where the system can no longer follow the laws of near-equilibrium thermodynamics, precisely because the amount of heat to be dissipated goes beyond the capacity of the system to do so. Thus, when this threshold is approached, the system shifts into a nonlinear mode, where positive feedback loops amplify rather than dampen fluctuations. These amplifications lead to the emergence of order.

All dynamic social entities have nonlinear qualities—positive feedback loops interact with negative feedback loops to generate a dynamic balance of activity. However, as described earlier, when the system moves toward a far-from-equilibrium state this "balance" is disrupted; the resulting experiments seek to maintain some kind of order amidst what feels like an increasing state of "chaos." The closer the system is to this critical threshold of intensity, the more it reveals nonlinearity, whereby ideas and actions that were previously "dampened" or disregarded now become amplified and reinforced. New positive feedback loops appear that catalyze specific resources and magnify certain causes in nonproportional ways. In this nonlinear mode there is less and less control but more and more innovation, opportunity, and room for creation.

4. Emergence Involves a Recombination of Existing Elements

The emergence of order in a dissipative structure occurs through a reorganization of elements that already exist in the system; the emergent hexagonal structures are formed only by the molecules that exist in the container. Thus, in the Bérnard experiment, no additional material resources are necessary for emergence; emergence is based on a recombination of current components. In the B-Z reaction, this correspondence is somewhat more complicated, since the far-from-equilibrium state is achieved by increasing the concentration of one of four chemical compounds in the system. Further, the flow of chemicals through the container produces a series of linear and catalytic reactions that yield a set of products that remain in the system. Even so, the order that emerges is due to an increase of interactions already within the container, rather than to a totally new substance brought in from the environment.

In social entities, emergence is also based on a recombination of existing components. Similar to the B-Z reaction, recombination may also mean the incorporation of resources that have been accessed or produced by the system during the organizing process. In this way, emergence involves a reorganizing of existing components, taking into account that some of those elements—new resources, skills, and partners, for example—may have been generated or brought into the system along the way, as a means of expanding the potentiality of the enterprise. In formal terms to be explained later in the chapter, the resources accessed are part of the *social ecology* out of which the entire endeavor is formed. Thus, when needed resources are accessed and integrated into the system, they become part of the entity, incorporated as existing components. Even though some examples of emergence involve elements that may be drawn into the system as last-minute experiments, the order-creation process will only work if these "new" elements are assimilated in a way that preserves the integrity of all system elements.[3] Much more will be said about this later on.

5. Stability of the Newly Emerged State

As explained in the previous chapter, the order that emerges in dissipative structures remains stable as long as the system stays in a far-from-equilibrium state. This has been shown empirically (Prigogine & Glansdorff, 1971; Prigogine & Stengers, 1984; Swenson, 1988; Swenson, 1992, 1997) and theoretically (Nicolis & Prigogine, 1989). Further, like the state of the system at equilibrium, any external perturbation is resisted; even if disturbed, the system will quickly return to its ordered state.

Emergent social entities are also stable, to the degree that they remain in a far-from-equilibrium state. However, remaining in this state is not so easy, for it requires the same amount and quality of resources (customers, supplies, relationships) to be continuously available and that their flow through the system remain uninterrupted. As any entrepreneur or event organizer will tell you, this assumption is never assured; maintaining the stability of an emergent entity is always a hard-won effort.

Even so, the impetus of emergent entities is to remain organized, a fact that has been well shown in a variety of contexts (Staw, 1981; DeTienne, Shepherd, & deCastro, 2008; Walsh & Bartunek, 2011). Whereas stability in physical systems is generated through the "laws" of order creation, stability in social entities is derived through further experimentation and learning of ways to improve the reliability and efficiency of the system.

Outcomes: Emergence of a New Level of Order that Increases Systemic Capacity

Two outcomes are endemic to dissipative structures, so much so that they generally are not even mentioned in scientific analyses, nor in most applications. The first is definitional, namely that emergence leads to a new level of order; it creates a new tangible layer of systemic activity that is distinct from its components. An example from biology makes this point strongly. A cell is solely a combination of molecules, but that combination yields properties and characteristics that operate at a completely different level than the molecules, generating new functions that are self-sustaining and can be aggregated into even larger units of functionality. Likewise in a dissipative structure, the emergent order introduces a new unit of analysis into the system; each hexagonal structure is an "entity" with properties and functionality that cannot be understood from the level of the molecules that make them up.

Second, an important measure of this new functionality is that it generates greater capacity for the system to do its work. Since the "work" in the Bérnard experiment is to dissipate the excess energy pouring into the system, the emergence of a dissipative structure—the creation of the hexagonal structures in the fluid—leads to much higher capacity of the system to dissipate heat. As mentioned in Chapter 6, Swenson (1988, 1989, 1991) measured this increase and found that the capacity of the system to dissipate energy was improved "by orders of magnitude."

The emergence of social entities yields exactly similar outcomes. The first, that emergence leads to a new layer of analysis, has been clearly presented by Ashmos and Huber (1987), who have shown how groups are a new level of order composed of individuals; organizations are a new level of order composed of groups; and partnerships, alliances, and industrial ecosystems are even broader units of analysis composed of organizations. Similarly, in the entrepreneurship literature, organizational emergence is defined by the perception that a new organization has come into being which is more than simply an entrepreneur doing work. The organization is seen—it is a tangible "member" of society that acts in valid and trusted ways (Gartner, 1985; Gartner, Bird, & Starr, 1992; Gartner, 1993; Sarasvathy & Dew, 2005; Sarasson, Dean, & Hilliard, 2006; Gartner & Brush, 2007; Santos & Eisenhardt, 2009).

The second outcome revolves around the purpose of organizing, which is to accomplish things that individuals working alone cannot accomplish. From the perspective of emergence, this refers to the fact that the new venture has far greater capacity to create value (through products and services) than the individuals did before it emerged (Robb, 1990; Lichtenstein, 2000c; Nicholls-Nixon, 2005; Lichtenstein, Dooley, & Lumpkin, 2006; Lichtenstein & Kurjanowicz, 2010). In fact, this new capacity is at the core of all organizing efforts.

Summary: Five Phases of Emergence

There are five key processes that lead to emergence, and two outcomes of the process. As just described, these processes and outcomes in physical systems are analogous to the processes and outcomes in social systems. To summarize, the process of dissipative structures emergence begins when energy is pushed into the system, moving it toward a far-from-equilibrium state. As it reaches a threshold of change, fluctuations occur—experiments that aim to keep the system intact by increasing its ability to dissipate the extra energy. If these processes continue, the system will reach a threshold, beyond which one or more of the fluctuations can be amplified, becoming the seed around which a new order can emerge. This emergent order is a recombination of existing elements that confers two key outcomes: a new level of order, and a greater capacity to dissipate heat. This newly emerged state will remain stable for as long as the higher rate of energy is inputted into the system.

From the viewpoint of entrepreneurship this process has strong parallels to the start-up of a new venture. The emergence of an entrepreneurial venture starts with an aspiration—a vision for a new company, the perception of a viable business opportunity, and an internal motivation to create an enterprise. This vision and motivation lead to organizing: the entrepreneur takes action toward the idea, pushing the social ecology out of its "norm" and into a disequilibrium state. As things start to get intense, she and her associates start coming up with experiments— ideas and possibilities to help catalyze the process. If this organizing continues, the entire endeavor will reach a critical threshold; given a host of good fortune and hard work, at some hard-to-define point the venture may emerge. At this point, its components become organized (recombined) into a broader whole as the vision comes into focus and reality. Products and services become produced, customers buy them and ask for more. The business begins to take on a life of its own, becoming a distinct entity in the business ecosystem. The entrepreneur quickly solidifies the enterprise through some basic systems and procedures, perhaps by hiring the first employee, setting up a bank account, and so on. The company has started up and now is primed for development and growth.

THE FIVE PHASES IN ENTREPRENEURIAL TERMS

After working with this basic model for more than 20 years, I have found that these five phases and the outcomes they confer can be generalized in ways that expand their application and utility. Thus, what follows is a presentation of the five phases,[4] using terminology that will be more familiar to those studying organizations. Given that these phases form the foundation for everything that follows, I will describe them in some detail, drawing on the work of many colleagues in the field. First I present a summary, which is then extended in Chapters 10–14.

Phase 1: Disequilibrium Organizing

Creating and maintaining a disequilibrium state of organizing has long been recognized as a driver of emergence (Schieve & Allen, 1982; Prigogine & Stengers, 1984). Empirical studies have described emergence in disequilibrium markets (Tan, 2007), in industries and institutions facing disequilibrium circumstances (Baker & Nelson, 2005; Purdy & Gray, 2009), and in organizations experiencing far-from-equilibrium states (Plowman et al., 2007). A useful way to think about disequilibrium is to consider how far outside the norm an organization is operating (McKelvey, 2004)—how unique and unprecedented the events and activities are that agents are experiencing (Andriani & McKelvey, 2009). For example, empirical studies of emergence show how the system gets pushed beyond its reference state, outside of its common range of behavior and experience, and into a new, highly dynamic state (Anderson, 1999). Sustaining this disequilibrium organizing state for some period of time seems to be a requisite of emergent order creation (Meyer, Gaba, & Colwell, 2005).

What causes disequilibrium? A key concept of generative emergence is that new order creation begins with an *aspiration* (Simon, 1955)—the vision of an entrepreneur or entrepreneurial team to dramatically extend or radically enhance the organization. This aspiration is not the result of a crisis but arises out of the creativity, passion, and engagement of the entrepreneur. This internal drive is an "opportunity tension;" it is what happens when an entrepreneur aspires to push the organization to a new level of capacity. *Opportunity* refers to economic potentials that can be realized through entrepreneurial action (McMullan, Plummer & Acs, 2007); *tension* reflects the personal passion and creative tension (Fritz, 1989) that makes the opportunity real (Adler & Obstfeld, 2006; Baron, 2008; Cardon, Wincent, Singh, & Drnovsek, 2009). Opportunity tension is the proactive drive that starts new entrepreneurial firms, that leads companies to grow to the next level, and that pursues the creation of a new institution. This drive of opportunity tension is critical for emergence; it will be explained much more fully in Chapter 10.

For a working entrepreneur or any successful business person, the voiced expression of an aspiration is quickly followed by specific actions that would accomplish the new aspiration and goals. As will be described in Chapter 10, these "organization-building" activities often increase dramatically, thus pushing the organization into a non-normal state of "disequilibrium organizing."

Phase 2: Stress and Experiments

Pushing the venture into disequilibrium organizing leads to several challenges, including a rapid rise in work intensity as well as a frustration with the currently existing routines, systems, and relationships, which are unable to manage the increased levels of activity in the system. Formally, these existing structures and relationships evolved to facilitate and support a "normal" rate of organizational action. Thus, as the organizing effort first attempts to shift away from its reference state, the inertia of existing routines is still present while new routines or processes have not yet emerged to take their place (Goldstein, 1988). As the system moves farther into a non-normal state with intensity and short-term goals shifting into high gear, current routines and relationships may come up short and begin to fail. This increase of pressure in the organization leads to higher degrees of stress, intensity, and interpersonal conflict. More about these qualities will be described in Chapter 11.

With this increase in stress comes an increase in experiments, that is, new ideas and initiatives that arise across the organization, each of which aims to solve one or more of the problems and stressors that agents are facing in their disequilibrium organizing. Experiments are expected from every angle of the organization, not just the founder. Experiments are happening all the time in organizations, although in normal conditions these suggestions and ideas generate relatively little change (Leifer, 1989; Dooley, 1997). In contrast, when the venture is pushed into disequilibrium, there's a likelihood that the rate of new experiments will increase, as will their ingenuity, as agents are themselves pushed to find solutions for problems they've never experienced before.

Phase 3: Amplifications to a Critical Threshold or Event

As the system moves farther away from its reference state into disequilibrium, there is an increase in positive reinforcement cycles within the organization (Anderson, 1999), also termed "deviation amplification" (Maruyama, 1963). With this increase in positive feedback the occurrence of one action or event increases the likelihood that other similar events will emerge in the system (Arthur, 1988, 1990; Krugman, 1996), thus pushing the system toward further change. Amplification is thus a natural result of the nonlinear dynamics of disequilibrium.

In many cases, at the peak of these interdependent processes of disequilibrium, experiments, and amplification, the system reaches a threshold, a critical tipping point toward emergence. Virtually every discipline of complexity science recognizes the importance of critical thresholds or "bifurcation points." A good theoretical explanation is given by Kevin Dooley (1997, p. 87), who draws on thermodynamics to show how experiments and amplifications are precursors to a threshold of emergence. "Below a certain threshold level, change is unlikely and perturbations [i.e., experiments] are dampened. Above the threshold value, change is imminent and perturbations are magnified" (Dooley, 1997, p. 87). Similar descriptions are given in works by Bigelow (1982), Bygrave (1989), Anderson (1999), and Rudolph and Repenning (2002). Chapter 12 explains these dynamics.

In generative emergence this bifurcation point occurs at the apex of (1) disequilibrium organizing, (2) stress and experiments, and (3) amplification to a critical threshold or event. On the other side of this threshold, the organization will either dissolve and collapse, or, if the conditions are right, the system will generate (4) new order through a recombination of its elements, leading to a distinct entity with greater capacity, which then (5) is stabilized as an ongoing dynamic state (see Chapter 8).

Phase 4: New Order Through Recombinations

Threshold events mark the coming-into-being of new order in the system—a recombination (Chiles et al., 2004), reorganization (Leifer, 1989), or redesign (MacIntosh & MacLean, 1999) of the internal structures and properties of the organization that generates a new system state (Morel & Ramanujam, 1999). At this point the pieces are brought together, the system is tried for the first time, roles are shifted to deal with the new offering, and existing resources are releveraged or reused to fit new needs. Researchers have identified numerous ways that recombination can occur, including bricolage (Levi-Strauss, 1967), resequencing

(Fleming & Sorenson, 2001), and symbiogenesis of organisms (Margulis, 1971). These and other aspects of new order creation are described in Chapter 13.

Phase 5: Stabilizing Feedback

New emergent order, if it creates value, will stabilize itself in short order by finding parameters that best increase its overall sustainability in the ecology. Stabilizing feedback anchors the change by slowing down the nonlinear processes that led to the amplification of emergence in the first place (Sastry, 1997). These actions help institutionalize the change throughout the system (Chiles et al., 2004), by slowly increasing the legitimacy of the new entity or structure. From an entrepreneurial perspective, if the emergence of a new dynamic state leads to positive outcomes, the founder and employees will find ways to sustain it by developing new processes, routines, and relationships that support the new system to continuously achieve its goals. Through these feedbacks the dynamic state is stabilized and can sustain itself. Chapter 14 summarizes these dynamics.

Outcomes: Autonomous Entity with Greater Capacity

The emergent dynamic state will exhibit a greater capacity than the system had before. Here there is a strong mapping between these outcomes in a dissipative structure and in a social entity; only the measures need adapting to the context. Note that the emergent dissipative structures increase the heat flux through the system, far beyond its initial capacities. Similarly, the emergent order in a social entity increases the capacity of its members to produce, market, and sell products and services, thus increasing the flow of revenues and costs through the business entity. For example, emergent partnerships might generate unexpected sources of revenues, new collaborations might expand capabilities, and/or a new product line might also reveal a social innovation that solves a problem or closes a gap in the broader community.

Further, what also emerges is an external perception that the new entity "exists"—that the new venture or enterprise has an independent integrity that goes beyond the actions of its founder and that others can engage and trade with as a full partner. This new level of analysis in the system is more than a pattern or a combination; it represents the creation of a new set of properties that can act on the external environment.

Of course, emergence is not assured; an equally likely outcome is the lack of creation, the collapse of the effort. That is, proceeding through a cycle of emergence does not ensure a positive outcome. There are two theoretical reasons for the potential of collapse after self-organization. The first, mentioned earlier, focuses on the challenges of (re)creating an entire system all at once, which involves an unprecedented amount of internal processing that can (and often does) overwhelm the system as a whole. The second reason refers back to the theoretical claim cited earlier, that new order will stabilize itself *if it is creating value*. That is, when emergence leads to new value creation for the firm, it is likely to be sustained. However, the creation process can just as likely lead to lower resource capacity and a lack of connection to existing resources, leading to the organization's demise. Overall the effectiveness of emergence can rarely be predicted, although there may be certain managerial moves that can increase the likelihood of positive emergence (Uhl-Bien, Marion, & McKelvey, 2007).

Validity of the Analogy

A final aspect of Tsoukas' method is one that is particularly intriguing in our case, namely, testing the validity of the isomorphic mapping. He argues that only through empirical research can we determine if the two phenomena are homomorphic, that is, whether the mapping preserves the essential relationships among the elements of the analogy and thus renders a valid and useful transformation of one to the other:

> There can be no a priori guarantees that a transformation has indeed been homomorphic or not. This can be ascertained only through a comparison of the homomorphic model with real situations. Such a comparison may refute the proclaimed homomorphism and, thus, render the model useless. . . . Simply stated, any object can be mapped onto anything else under some transformation, but whether it is a useful mapping or not will have to be settled empirically. (Tsoukas, 1991, p. 577)

It turns out that a fairly large number of management scholars have applied the dissipative structures theory to organizational emergence, transformation, and change. The most central studies are summarized in Table 7.1, which compares nine of these commonly cited studies across the five phases just presented. In almost every case the studies use parallel wording to describe each of the phases; in fact, these phases are often used as section headings in these papers. As the table shows, these studies, pursued separately and with only minimal reference to each other, all share the same understanding about how dissipative structures can be applied in organizations.

The most convincing part of this examination shown in Table 7.1 is the fact that all of the empirical examples (except Lichtenstein et al., 2007) are *inductive* theory-development studies—research studies that seek to create new theory based on rich longitudinal data. Although these scholars were familiar with Prigogine's work, each group entered the field with no formally defined constructs. They collected large amounts of qualitative and quantitative data. These data were organized temporally, and their analysis produced a description and theoretical modeling of transformational and emergent change. By design, inductive theoretical

Table 7.1 PRESENCE OF THE FIVE PHASES (CONDITIONS) AND THEIR OUTCOMES IN COMPLEXITY STUDIES OF EMERGENCE

Research Study; Unit of Analysis	Phase 1: Disequilibrium Organizing	Phase 2: Stress/ Experiments	Phase 3: Amplification, Threshold	Phase 4: New Order: Recombination	Phase 5: Stabilizing Feedback	Outcomes: New Level; Higher Capacity
Nonaka, 1988* *Organizational knowledge creation*	CREATION OF CHAOS	AMPLIFICATION OF FLUCTUATION		THE NEW ORDER RESTRUCTURING KNOWLEDGE	COOPERATIVE PHENOMENON FOR RESOLVING DISCREPANCIES	More knowledge, more dissemination
Leifer, 1989 *Organizational transformation*	FAR-FROM-EQUILIBRIUM CONDITIONS	EXPERIMENTATION	Bifurcation point or trigger event	TRANSFORMATION RESYNTHESIS	STABILITY	More adaptive, flexible
Smith & Gemmill, 1991 *Team evolution*	NON-EQUILIBRIUM STATE	EXPERIMENTATION PROCESS	SYMMETRY BREAKING	SELF-REFERENCING	RESONANCE, REPARATION	More adaptability
Browning, Beyer, & Shetler, 1995* *Industry alliance*	IRREVERSIBLE DISEQUILIBRIUM	SELF-ORGANIZING PROCESSES		A NEW ORDER	Unintended consequences†	Saved the U.S. industry; major growth
MacIntosh & MacLean, 1999* *Strategic renewal*	CREATING FAR-FROM-EQUILIBRIUM CONDITIONS	CONDITIONING	Positive feedback; Decision point	The organization...formulate[s] a new deep structure	MANAGING THE FEEDBACK PROCESS	Positive outcomes when process followed
Lichtenstein, 2000a* *New venture growth*	INCREASED ORGANIZING	TENSION (EXPERIMENTS)	THRESHOLD	NEWLY EMERGING CONFIGURATION	—	Outcomes from the transitions
Chiles, Meyer, & Hench, 2004* *Regional aggregation*	FLUCTUATION DYNAMICS	ORDER THROUGH FLUCTUATION	POSITIVE FEEDBACK	RESOURCE RECOMBINATIONS	STABILIZATION DYNAMICS	More tourists, more shows, higher reputation of area
Lichtenstein et al., 2007* *New venture creation*	ADAPTIVE TENSION	INTERDEPENDENCE		Scaffolding of emergence	—	System takes on a "life of its own"
Plowman et al., 2007* *Organizational renewal*	FAR-FROM-EQUILIBRIUM STATE	ACTIONS AMPLIFY SMALL CHANGES		ACQUIRING NEW AND REARRANGING EXISTING RESOURCES	NEGATIVE FEEDBACK	Rapid, new growth of the congregation

Notes: Constructs in SMALL CAPS refer to actual section headings in the papers. Most other entries are quotes taken from their text. * = empirical study. † = in this one case, only a limited connection between the construct in that paper and the listed sequence.

models are necessarily unique, since they are individually generated through the particular data analysis. Thus it is quite surprising that all of these research teams came up with essentially the *same five processes* to describe their cases. Furthermore, in many instances they arranged these in the same sequence. The fact that these different authors, looking at emergence across very different contexts, found the same processes through their exploratory analysis provides a high degree of empirical validation and face validity for the model. This claim is presented in Table 7.1.

Next Steps

With this analysis, we are half-way to making the full analogy between dissipative structures and social entities. While the analysis in this chapter found strong correlation between the processes and outcomes of emergence in dissipative structures and organizations, the analysis in the next chapter will identify many important differences between the conditions of order creation in dissipative structures, and the conditions that lead to emergence in social systems. It turns out that these differences provide important insights into generative emergence.

APPENDIX—DISSIPATIVE STRUCTURES IN EVOLUTION

Schrödinger's idea led to a wide range of extensions into the emergence and development of "negentropy" in biological systems. Perhaps the best known of these was achieved by Howard Odum, who sought to explain this buildup of energy and order by finding a way to literally compute the flows and transformations of energy within ecological systems (Odum & Pinkerton, 1955; Odum, 1971; Odum & Odum, 1976; Odum, 1988). One of his key insights was to define the "hierarchy" of energy transformations, which is composed of "large flows of low-quality energy being converged and transformed into smaller and smaller volumes of higher and higher quality types of energy" (Odum, 1988, p. 1135). Next, to make possible a direct calculation of these energy transformations from one form to another, he coined the term *EMERGY*, defined as the total energy—in "solar emjouls per joule"—needed to produce any specific entity in an ecosystem.[5] When this "transformity process" is calculated across all ecosystems—from simple organisms to complex humans to the growth of information and knowledge—he can show that the greatest amount of EMERGY is produced through the higher levels of education and more effective uses of knowledge in society.[6]

To other researchers, the "negentropy" caused by the dissipation of energy flows became a foothold for extending thermodynamics into evolution itself. Jeffrey Wicken (1979, 1985, 1986, 1988) was one of a large group of researchers (including Wiley & Brooks, 1983, Depew & Weber, 1985; Brooks & Wiley, 1986; Weber et al., 1989; Weber, Depew, & Smith, 1990; Depew & Weber, 1994) who pursued this idea in a mathematical way. Wicken proposed that thermodynamics could be extended into biological and social ecosystems (see Wicken, 1988, pp. 156–160), by substituting the "thermodynamic information content" $I_M = -k \ln P_i$ into Gibbs' equation for calculating the free energy gradients in any canonical ensemble of macrostates, $P_i = W_i e^{(a-ei)/kT}$.[7] He then showed that each of these macrostates $W_i e$ "... are factorable into configurational [structural, i.e., order-producing] and thermal components." By arguing that positive entropy production is equivalent to the dissipation of thermodynamic information content,[8] this leads to a general proposition: "The flow of thermodynamic information from its energetic and configurational modes to its thermal mode constitutes the tie between the evolutionary and thermodynamic arrows." This tie is described more generally in his 1981 paper (Wicken, 1981, pp. 135–136):

> [A] thermodynamics of evolution comes [out of] a growing body of work over the past two decades[9] [which] has shown evolutionary self-organization to be a necessary consequence of energy flow and entropy production. . . . Because the particular forces of nature through which dissipation occurs are for the most part associative ones, irreversible processes tend to increase the overall structuring of the Universe toward increasing levels of complexity. . . . Dissipation is the driving force of the building-up or anamorphic tendency in the Universe. . . . Structuring through dissipation is therefore an evolutionary first principle.

This strong claim was part of a chorus of researchers who were all explaining how the new science of far-from-equilibrium thermodynamics could become the core to a theory of evolution that supplants "The Poverty of Neo-Darwinism" (Wicken, 1989, p. 369) with a new "paradigm" for a thermodynamics of evolution. As mentioned earlier, this overall framework was first enunciated by Jantsch (1980) and Laszlo (1987), and summarized in a series of edited and co-authored volumes, especially those by Depew and Weber (1985), Weber et al. (1990), and Depew and Weber (1994), as well as in a general statement by the leaders of this small but tenacious intellectual "movement" (Weber et al., 1989).

Not everyone agrees with this approach. Corning and Kline (1998b) summarize the opposing view. In particular they reveal inconsistencies—and strongly critique—the use of entropy and its application in biology and evolution by Wicken, Brooks and Wiley, Schrodinger, and others. In a similar way, Kenneth Bailey (1987) critiqued Odum's use of order and entropy, claiming that they lead to untenable anomalies in direct contradiction to empirical reality.

In fact, Corning and Kline (1998a, p. 274) assert: "All the equations of physics taken together cannot describe, much less explain, living systems." This is followed by several strong reasons for why the physics of dissipative structures cannot and should not be applied to biological or human systems (see note[10]). Even Adams (1988), whose book is subtitled "Social Evolution as the Self-Organization of Energy," critiques the mathematical approach: "Various scientists have objected because the ability to measure the creation of entropy has meaning in a closed system but becomes questionable in an open system. Indeed, the whole notion of entropy is of doubtful utility in the present analysis" (Adams, 1988, p. 33). A final summary by Corning and Kline (1998a, p. 476) makes the point clear:

> We believe the entire strategy associated with various attempts to reduce biological evolution and the dynamics of living systems to the principles of either classical, or irreversible thermodynamics...that is to say, to manifestations of simple, one-level physical systems—is a theoretical cul de sac.

NOTES

1. As will become clear, the term *analogy* here draws on Tsoukas' definition of "homology" i.e., a process that is exactly parallel in two (or more) contexts. In addition, the term will be drawn out (below) to incorporate the meaning ascribed by Garud and Kotha (1994, pp. 674–675), in which a one-to-one mapping is accomplished through (1) metaphor, (2) analogy, and (3) identity.
2. Although social systems are never at "equilibrium" as defined by thermodynamics, they can operate in a state of dynamic stability—what I'll later define as a dynamic state—in which inputs and outputs remain relatively consistent over time.
3. Here we come perilously close to the issues of self-reference, that the new system must have high self-reference to the original form. This point was made strongly made by Smith (1986) with his advisor (Gemmill & Smith 1985; Smith & Gemmill 1991). It follows earlier work on autopoiesis which emphasizes the retention of identity in system change (Varela, 1979; Pantzar & Csanyi, 1991; Drazin & Sandelands, 1992). I emphasized this idea as an outcome variable in my main dissertation paper (Lichtenstein, 2000).
4. Technically, each phase represents a "sequence of change" in Abbott's (1988) frame, for each phase incorporates a series of process, qualities and characteristics. However, to capture the dynamics of the process in clear terms, I have decided to use the term *phase*.
5. The EPA has a short course on EMERGY—see http://www.epa.gov/aed/html/collaboration/emergycourse/presentations/index.html. This provides an accessible entry into the following conversation on the link between EMERGY and economics.
6. Much more can be said about this calculation, which is based on an annual EMERGY share per individual per year of 38,000,000,000 J/person/year—see his Figure 9 (Odum 1988, p. 1138). Further details are in his Figure 1, "Energetics of Energy Transformation Hierarchy" (Odum 1988, p. 1135), and his Table 1, "Typical Solar Transformaties" (p. 1136).
7. Obviously I'm glossing over his explanations and the embedded jargon of thermodynamics. This summary is drawn from his 1988 chapter. His more substantive introductions to this idea are well explained in Wicken (1979, 1981, 1985, 1986, 1988).
8. Specifically, he argues that "the positive entropy production ($dS_1 > 0$) is equivalent to the dissipation of thermodynamic information ($dI_M < 0$)." He continues:

    > If we are dealing with dissipation of energy from a closed system . . . then $\Delta S_e = Q/T = \Delta E/T = \Delta I_e$. Then replacing ΔS by $-\Delta i_{th}$—Δi_c allows one to write the second law in thermodynamic terms as: $dI_c + dI_{th} + dI_e < 0$ (equation 10)

Evidently, increases in one of these parameters must be tied to decreases in another. *The flow of thermodynamic information from its energetic and configurational modes to its thermal mode constitutes the tie between the evolutionary and thermodynamic arrows* (Wicken 1988, p. 159, italics in original).

9. Here, in his footnote 16, he cites the following: Morowitz (1968), Prigogine, Nicolis, and Babloyantz (1972), Black (1978), and Wicken (1980).
10. Continuing their quote, Corning and Kline (1988b, p. 287) explain:

> It is comparable to characterizing jet engines—which are painstakingly designed and manufactured with extremely precise dimensional properties and tolerances—as dissipative structures. They are neither self-designed nor are their dissipative properties among their most salient features.... This is also an example of the fallacy of using one-level analytical systems to explain multi-level processes. Finally, and most serious, the domain of irreversible thermodynamics is restricted to states where the ordinary temperature and pressure can still be defined locally, but many biological processes do not satisfy this criterion. An illustration is the process that initiates the capture of available energy and the miracle of photosynthesis in living systems—namely, the activation of high energy states within atoms via irradiation by sunlight. This fundamental life-creating process cannot even be described by irreversible thermodynamics (on this point, see also Morowitz, 1968).

REFERENCES

Abbott, A. 1988. Transcending general linear reality. *Sociological Theory*, 6(2): 169–86.
Adams, R. N. 1988. *The Eighth Day: Social Evolution as the Self-Organization of Energy*. Austin, TX: University of Texas.
Adler, P., & Obstfeld, D. 2006. The role of affect in creative projects and exploratory search. *Industrial and Corporate Change*, 16: 19–50.
Anderson, P. 1999. Complexity theory and organization science. *Organization Science*, 10: 216–32.
Andriani, P., & McKelvey, B. 2009. From Gaussian to Paretian thinking: Causes and implications of power laws in organizations. *Organization Science*, 20: 1053–71.
Arthur, B. 1988. Self-reinforcing mechanisms in economics. In P. Anderson, K. Arrow, & D. Pines (Eds.), *The Economy as an Evolving Complex System* (9–31). Reading, MA: Addison-Wesley.
Arthur, B. 1990. Positive feedbacks in the economy. *Scientific American*, February: 92–99.
Artigiani, R. 1987. Revolution and evolution: Applying Prigogine's dissipative structures model. *Journal of Social and Psychological Structures*, 10: 249–64.
Ashmos, D., & Huber, G. 1987. The system paradigm in organization theory: Correcting the record and suggesting the future. *Academy of Management Review*, 12: 607–21.
Bailey, K. 1987. Restoring order: Relating entropy to energy and information. *Systems Research*, 4(2): 83–92.
Baker, T., & Nelson, R. 2005. Creating something from nothing: Resource construction through entrepreneurial bricolage. *Administrative Science Quarterly*, 50: 239–366.
Baron, R. 2008. The role of affect in the entrepreneurial process. *Academy of Management Review*, 33: 328–40.
Barton, S. 1994. Chaos, self-organization, and psychology. *American Psychologist*, 49: 5–14.

Bigelow, J. 1982. A catastrophe model of organizational change. *Behavioral Science*, 27: 26–42.
Biggiero, L. 2001. Self-organizing processes in building entrepreneurial networks: A theoretical and empirical investigation. *Human Systems Management*, 20: 209–22.
Black, S. 1978. On the thermodynamics of evolution. *Perspectives in Biology and Medicine*, 21: 348–56.
Boulding, K. 1978. *Ecodynamics: A New Theory of Societal Evolution*. Newbury Park, CA: SAGE Publications.
Boulding, K. 1980. Equilibrium, entropy, development, and autopoiesis: Towards a disequilibrium economics. *Eastern Economic Journal*, 6(3-4): 179–88.
Boulding, K. 1981. *Evolutionary Economics*. Thousand Oaks, CA: SAGE Publications.
Boulding, K. 1988. *The World as a Total System*. Thousand Oaks, CA: SAGE Publications.
Brooks, D., & Wiley, E. O. 1986. *Evolution as Entropy: Toward a Unified Theory of Biology*. Chicago: University of Chicago Press.
Browning, L., Beyer, J., & Shetler, J. 1995. Building cooperation in a competitive industry: SEMATECH and the semiconductor industry. *Academy of Management Journal*, 38: 113–51.
Bygrave, W. 1989. Theory building in the entrepreneurship paradigm. *Journal of Business Venturing*, 8: 255–80.
Cardon, M., Wincent, J., Singh, J., & Drnovsek, M. 2009. The nature and experience of entrepreneurial passion. *Academy of Management Review*, 34(3): 511–32.
Chiles, T., Meyer, A., & Hench, T. 2004. Organizational emergence: The origin and transformation of Branson, Missouri's musical theaters. *Organization Science*, 15(5): 499–520.
Corning, P., & Kline, S. J. 1998a. Thermodyamics, information and life revisited, part 2: "Thermoeconomics" and "control information." *Systems Research and Behavioral Science*, 15: 453–82.
Corning, P., & Kline, S. J. 1998b. Thermodynamics, information and life revisited, part I: "To be or entropy." *Systems Research and Behavioral Science*, 15: 273–95.
Depew, D., & Weber, B. (Eds.). 1985. *Evolution at a Crossroads: The New Biology and the New Philosophy of Science*. Cambridge, MA: MIT Press.
Depew, D., & Weber, B. 1994. *Darwinism Evolving*. New York: Oxford University Press.
DeTienne, D., Shepherd, D., & deCastro, J. O. 2008. The fallacy of "only the strong survive": The effects of extrinsic motivatin on the persistence decisions for underperforming firms. *Journal of Business Venturing*, 23(5): 528–46.
De Vany, A. 1996. Information, chance, and evolution: Alchian and the economics of self-organization. *Economic Inquiry*, 34: 427–42.
Dooley, K. 1997. A complex adaptive systems model of organization change. *Nonlinear Dynamics, Psychology, and the Life Sciences*, 1: 69–97.
Drazin, R., & Sandelands, L. 1992. Autogenesis: A perspective on the process of organizing. *Organization Science*, 3: 230–49.
Dyke, C. 1988. Cities as dissipative structures. In B. Weber, D. Depew, & J. Smith (Eds.), *Entropy, Information and Evolution: New Perspectives on Physical and Biological Evolution* (355–68). Cambridge, MA: MIT Press.
Dyke, C. 1992. From entropy to economy: A thorny path. *Advances in Human Ecology*, 1: 149–76.
Fleming, L., & Sorenson, O. 2001. Technology as a complex adaptive system. *Research Policy*, 30: 1019–39.
Foster, J. 2000. Competitive selection, self-organization and Joseph A. Schumpeter. *Journal of Evolutionary Economics*, 10: 311–28.
Fritz, R. 1989. *The Path of Least Resistance*. New York: Fawcett Columbine.
Fuller, T., & Moran, P. 2001. Small enterprises as complex adaptive systems: A methdological question? *Entrepreneurship and Regional Development*, 13: 47–63.

Gartner, W. 1985. A conceptual framework for describing the phenomonon of new venture creation. *Academy of Management Review*, 10: 696–706.

Gartner, W. 1993. Words lead to deeds: Towards an organizational emergence vocabulary. *Journal of Business Venturing*, 8: 231–39.

Gartner, W., Bird, B., & Starr, J. 1992. Acting as if: Differentiating entrepreneurial from organizational behavior. *Entrepreneurship Theory and Practice*, 16(3): 13–30.

Gartner, W., & Brush, C. 2007. Entrepreneurship as organizing: Emergence, newness and transformation. In T. H. M. Rice (Ed.), *Praeger Perspectives on Entrepreneurship*, Vol. 3: 1–20. Westport, CT: Prager Publishers.

Garud, R., & Kotha, S. 1994. Using the brain as a metaphor to model flexible production systems. *Academy of Management Review*, 19(4): 671–98.

Gemmill, G., & Smith, C. 1985. A dissipative structure model of organization transformatoin. *Human Relations*, 38(8): 751–66.

Georgescu-Roegen, N. 1971. *The Entropy Law and the Economic Process*. Cambridge, MA: Harvard University Press.

Gibbs, J. W. 1906. *The Scientific Papers of J. Willard Gibbs*. New York: Longmans, Green.

Gilstrap, D. 2007. Dissipative structures in educational change: Prigogine and the academy. *International Journal of Leadership in Education*, 10: 49–69.

Goldstein, J. 1988. A far-from-equilibrium systems approach to resistance to change. *Organizational Dynamics*, 15(1): 5–20.

Goldstein, J. 1994. *The Unshackled Organization*. Portland, OR: Productivity Press.

Jantsch, E. 1980. *The Self-Organizing Universe*. New York: Pergamon Press.

Kaufmann, H. 1991. *Time, Chance and Organizations*. Chatham, NJ: Chatham House.

Krugman, P. 1996. *The Self-Organizing Economy*. Cambridge, MA: Bradford Press.

Laszlo, E. 1987. *Evolution—The Grand Synthesis*. Boston: Shambhalla.

Leifer, R. 1989. Understanding organizational transformation using a dissipative structure model. *Human Relations*, 42: 899–916.

Levi-Strauss, C. 1967. *The Savage Mind*. Chicago: University of Chicago Press.

Lichtenstein, B. 1995. Evolution or transformation: A critique and alternative to punctuated equilibrium. *Best Papers Proceedings, National Academy to Management*: 291–295.

Lichtenstein, B. 2000a. Emergence as a process of self-organizing: New assumptions and insights from the study of nonlinear dynamic systems. *Journal of Organizational Change Management*, 13: 526–44.

Lichtenstein, B. 2000b. Generative knowledge and self-organized learning: Reflecting on Don Schon's research. *Journal of Management Inquiry*, 9(9): 47–54.

Lichtenstein, B. 2000c. Self-organized transitions: A pattern amid the "chaos" of transformative change. *Academy of Management Executive*, 14(4): 128–41.

Lichtenstein, B. 2002. *Entrepreneurship as emergence: Insights and methods from philosophy and complexity science*. Paper presented at the Lally-Darden Entrepreneurship Theory Retreat, Arlie, VA.

Lichtenstein, B. 2009. Moving far from far-from-equliibrium: Opportunity tension as the catalyst of emergence. *Emergence: Complexity and Organization*, 11(4): 15–25.

Lichtenstein, B., Carter, N., Dooley, K., & Gartner, W. 2007. Complexity dynamics of nascent entrepreneurship. *Journal of Business Venturing*, 22: 236–61.

Lichtenstein, B., Dooley, K., & Lumpkin, T. 2006. Measuring emergence in the dynamics of new venture creation. *Journal of Business Venturing*, 21: 153–75.

Lichtenstein, B., & Jones, C. 2004. A self-organization theory of radical entrepreneurship. *Best Papers Proceedings, National Academy of Management*: OMT Division; CD format.

Lichtenstein, B., & Kurjanowicz, B. 2010. Tangibility, momentum, and the emergence of The Republic of Tea. *ENTER Journal*, 1: 125–48.

Lichtenstein, B., & Plowman, D. A. 2009. The leadership of emergence: A complex systems leadership theory of emergence at successive organizational levels. *The Leadership Quarterly*, 20: 617–30.

Lotka, A. 1922. Contribution to the energetics of evolution. *Proceedings of the National Academy of Sciences U S A*, 6: 147–51.

Lotka, A. 1945. The law of evolution as a maximal principle. *Human Biology*, 17: 167–94.

MacIntosh, R., & MacLean, D. 1999. Conditioned emergence: A dissipative structures approach to transformation. *Strategic Management Journal*, 20: 297–316.

Margulis, L. 1971. Symbiosis and evolution. *Scientific American*, 225(2): 49–57.

Maruyama, M. 1963. The second cybernetics. *American Scientist*, 51: 164–79.

McKelvey, B. 2004. Toward a complexity science of entrepreneurship. *Journal of Business Venturing*, 19: 313–42.

McMullan, J., Plummer, L., & Acs, Z. 2007. What is an entrepreneurial opportunity? *Small Business Economics*, 28: 273–83.

Meyer, A., Gaba, V., & Colwell, K. 2005. Organizing far from equilibrium: Nonlinear change in organizational fields. *Organization Science*, 16: 456–73.

Morel, B., & Ramanujam, R. 1999. Through the looking glass of complexity: The dynamics of organizations as adaptive and evolving systems. *Organization Science*, 10(3): 278–93.

Morowitz, H. 1968. *Energy Flow in Biology: Biological Organization as a Problem in Thermal Physics*. New York: Academic Press.

Nicholls-Nixon, C. 2005. Rapid growth and high performance: The entrepreneur's "impossible dream?" *Academy of Management Executive*, 19(1): 77–89.

Nonaka, I. 1988. Creating organizational order out of chaos: Self-renewal in Japanese firms. *California Management Review*, 30(Spring): 57–73.

Nicolis, G., & Prigogine, I. 1989. *Exploring Complexity*. New York: W. H. Freeman.

Odum, H. 1971. *Environment, Power & Society*. New York: Wiley Interscience.

Odum, H. 1988. Self-organization, transformity, and information. *Science*, 242: 1132–39.

Odum, H., & Odum, E. 1976. *Energy Basis for Man and Nture*. New York: McGraw Hill.

Odum, H., & Pinkerton, R. 1955. Time's speed regulator: The optimum efficiency for maximum power output in physical and biological systems. *American Scientist*, 43(2): 331–43.

Pantzar, M., & Csanyi, V. 1991. The replicative model of the evolution of the business organization. *Journal of Social and Biological Structures*, 14: 149–63.

Plowman, D. A., Baker, L., Beck, T., Kulkarni, M., Solansky, S., & Travis, D. 2007. Radical change accidentally: The emergence and amplification of small change. *Academy of Management Journal*, 50: 515–43.

Prigogine, I., & Glansdorff, P. 1971. *Thermodynamic Theory of Structure, Stability, and Fluctuations*. New York: John Wiley & Sons.

Prigogine, I., Nicolis, G., & Babloyantz, A. 1972. A thermodynamics of evolution. *Physics Today*, 23: 23–8

Prigogine, I., & Stengers, I. 1984. *Order out of Chaos*. New York: Bantam Books.

Purdy, J., & Gray, B. 2009. Conflicting logics, mechanisms of diffusion, and multi-level dynamics of emergence in institutional fields. *Academy of Management Journal*, 52: 355–80.

Robb, F. 1990. On the application of the theory of emergence and of the law of maximum entropy production to social processes. *Systems Practice*, 3: 389–99.

Rosser, J. B. 1992. The dialogue between the economic and the ecologic theories of evolution. *Journal of Economic Behavior and Organization*, 17: 195–215.

Rudolph, J., & Repenning, N. 2002. Disaster dynamics: Understanding the role of quantity in organizational collapse. *Administrative Science Quarterly*, 47: 1–30.

Santos, F., & Eisenhardt, K. 2009. Constructing markets and shaping boundaries: Entrepreneurial power in nascent fields. *Academy of Management Journal*, 52: 643–71.

Sarasson, Y., Dean, T., & Hilliard, B. 2006. Entrepreneurship as the nexus of individual and opportunity: A structuration view. *Journal of Business Venturing*, 21: 286–305.
Sarasvathy, S. 2001. Causation and effectuation: Toward a theoretical shift from economic inevitability to entrepreneurial contingency. *Academy of Management Review*, 26: 243–63.
Sarasvathy, S., & Dew, N. 2005. New market creation through transformation. *Journal of Evolutionary Economics*, 15: 533–65.
Sastry, A. 1997. Problems and paradoxes in a model of punctuated organizational change. *Administrative Science Quarterly*, 42(2): 237–75.
Saviotti, P. P., & Mani, G. S. 1998. Technological evolution, self-organization, and knowledge. *Journal of High Technology Management Research*, 9: 255–70.
Schieve, W., & Allen, P. (Eds.). 1982. *Self-Organization and Dissapative Structures: Applications in the Physical and Social Sciences*. Austin, TX: University of Texas Press.
Schrödinger, E. 1944. *What is Life?* New York: Cambridge University Press.
Simon, H. 1955. A behavioral model of rational choice. *The Quarterly Journal of Economics*, 69(1): 99–118.
Smith, C. 1986. Transformation and regeneration in social systems: A dissipative structure perspective. *Systems Research*, 3: 203–13.
Smith, C., & Comer, D. 1994. Change in the small group: A dissipative structure perspective. *Human Relations*, 47: 553–81.
Smith, C., & Gemmill, G. 1991. Self-Organization in small groups: A study of group effectivenss within non-equilibrium conditions. *Human Relations*, 44: 697–716.
Staw, B. 1981. The escalation of commitment to a course of action. *Academy of Management Review*, 6: 577–87.
Swenson, R. 1988. *Emergence and the principle of maximum entropy production: Multi-level system theory, evolution, and nonequilibrium thermodynamics*. Paper presented at the Proceedings of the 32nd Annual Meeting of the ISGSR.
Swenson, R. 1989. Emergent attractor and the law of maximum entropy production: Foundations to a theory of general evolution. *Systems Research*, 6(3): 187–97.
Swenson, R. 1991. End-directed physics and evolutionary ordering. In F. Geyr (Ed.), *Cybernetics of Complex Systems*. Salinas, CA: Intersystems Press.
Swenson, R. 1992. Order, evolution, and natural law: Fundamental relations in complex system theory. In C. Negoita (Ed.), *Cybernetics and Applied Systems* (125–47). New York: Marcel Dekker.
Swenson, R. 1997. Autocatakinetics, evolution, and the law of maximum entropy production: A principled foundation towards the study of human ecology. *Advances in Human Ecology*, 6: 1–47.
Tan, J. 2007. Phase transitions and emergence of entrepreneurship: The transformation of Chinese SOEs over time. *Journal of Business Venturing*, 22: 77–96.
Tsoukas, H. 1991. The missing link: A transformational view of metaphors in organizational science. *Academy of Management Review*, 16(3): 566–85.
Uhl-Bien, M., Marion, R., & McKelvey, B. 2007. Complexity leadership theory: Shifting leadership from the Industrial Age to the Information Era. *The Leadership Quarterly*, 18: 298–318.
Ulrich, H., & Probst, J. B. (Eds.). 1984. *Self-Organization and Management of Social Systems*. Berlin: Springer-Verlag.
Varela, F. 1979. *Principles of Biological Autonomy*. New York: North Holland.
Walsh, I., & Bartunek, J. 2011. Cheating the fates: Organizational founding in the wake of demise. *Academy of Management Journal*, 54(5): 1017–44.
Weber, B., Depew, B., Dyke, C., Salthe, S., Schneider, E., Ulanowicz, R., & Wicken, J. 1989. Evolution in thermodynamic perspective: An ecological approach. *Biology and Philosophy*, 4: 373–405.

Weber, B. H., Depew, D. J., & Smith, J. D. (Eds.). 1990. *Entropy, Information, and Evolution.* Cambridge, MA: MIT Press.

Weisbuch, G., Kirman, A., & Herreiner, D. 1998. Market organization. In J. Lesourne & A. Orlean (Eds.), *Advances in Self-Organization and Evolutionary Economics* (160–82). London: Economica Ltd.

Wicken, J. 1979. The generation of complexity in evolution: A thermodynamic and information-theoretical discussion. *Journal of Theoretical Biology,* 77(3): 349–65.

Wicken, J. 1980. A thermodynamic theory of evolution. *Journal of Theoretical Biology,* 87(1): 9–23.

Wicken, J. 1981. Evolutionary self-organization and the entropy principle: Teology and mechanism. *Nature and System,* 3: 129–41.

Wicken, J. 1985. Thermodynamics and the conceptual structure of evolutionary theory. *Journal of Theoretical Biology,* 117: 363–83.

Wicken, J. 1986. Evolutionary self-organization and entropic dissipation in biological and socioeconomic systems. *Journal of Social and Biological Structures,* 9: 261–73.

Wicken, J. 1988. Thermodynamics, evolution, and emergence: Ingredients for a new synthesis. In B. Weber, D. Depew, & J. D. Smith (Eds.), *Entropy, Information, and Evolution: New Perspectives on Physical and Biological Evolution* (139–72). Cambridge, MA: MIT Press.

Wicken, J. 1989. Evolution and thermodynamics: The new paradigm. *Systems Research and Behavioral Science,* 15: 365–72.

Wiley, E. O., & Brooks, D. 1983. Victims of history—A nonequilibrium approach to evolution. *Systemic Zoology,* 31: 1–24.

Zohar, A., & Borkman, T. 1997. Emergent order and self-organization: A case study of Alcoholics Anonymous. *Nonprofit and Voluntary Sector Quarterly,* 26: 527–52.

Zuijderhoudt, R. 1990. Chaos and the dynamics of self-organization. *Human Systems Management,* 9: 225–38.

CHAPTER 8

From Dissipative Structures to Dynamic States

In the last chapter I showed how the process by which dissipative structures emerge is isomorphic to the process by which a social entity emerges, and I used generative emergence as the linking theory, the general model that explains both sides of the analogy. At the same time, I have expressed some caution about this analogy, specifically because the theoretical link refers only to process and outcomes, but not to the conditions of emergence. In order to develop a valid and reliable metaphor, these differences have to be examined and resolved.

The present chapter takes up that issue, examining the dissimilarities between the experimental conditions that lead to the emergence of dissipative structure and the ecosystem conditions that lead to the emergence of a social entity. This analysis leads to important distinctions between generative emergence and exo-organizing, distinctions that are resolved through the dynamic state model of organizing in social systems (Levie & Lichtenstein, 2010).

EXAMINING THE METAPHOR FROM DISSIPATIVE STRUCTURES

A specific set of experimental conditions are required for producing a dissipative structure. As presented in Chapter 6, these conditions were found for the Bérnard experiment and for the BZ reaction. To review, the conditions for exo-organizing are as follows:

- **Strong container.** Dissipative structures emerge within well-defined, nonporous containers, whose characteristics constrain and support the emergence of order. Having a strong container is a requisite condition of these experiments.
- **Agents are homogeneous.** The components of the system are homogeneous molecules. In the Bérnard experiment every element is indistinguishable;

likewise, in the BZ reaction the molecules of each chemical are totally the same. Thus agents (molecules) are undifferentiated; neither diversity nor heterogeneity is present.
- **Agent behavior is linear and deterministic.** Agents are subject to the physically determined laws of thermodynamics, that is, they behave in ways that are linear and predictable. Further, agents in dissipative structures display neither learning nor cognition of any kind. Instead, the entire system is deterministic; components follow specific laws that determine their behavior.
- **Process is started by an "external" agent.** From the perspective of molecular agents in the system, the process starts "out of nowhere," when energy in the form of heat or chemicals starts pouring into the system. Of course, both experiments are actually started by a researcher outside the container system, who has to literally turn the experiment on. A full accounting of this initiating agency would have to include the intention and goals of the researcher, the effort in setting up the lab and apparatus, and other factors.
- **Inputs are exogenous to the system.** The energy and resources imported into the system during the experiment are drawn from the "environment," that is, from a seemingly unlimited stock of energy and resources that exist "outside" the formal experiment. Like the existence of a container in these experiments, this condition is assumed but never mentioned.
- **Outputs are discarded into the environment.** Like the inputs, the energy and resources that flow out of the sink become exogenous to the system; they provide no additional "value" in the experiment. Specifically, the heat energy in the Bérnard experiment is exported out of the system and is unused after that; the excess chemicals in the B-Z reaction are also transferred out of the system.

As in the previous chapter, each of these elements will be drawn out. In preparation, Figure 8.1 outlines the prospect of an ideographic analogy between the experimental conditions that give rise to dissipative structures, and the sociopersonal conditions that give rise to social entities. In contrast to the processes and outcomes, comparing the conditions reveals important differences between the two contexts.

COMPARING THE CONDITIONS FOR DISSIPATIVE STRUCTURES VS. SOCIAL ENTITIES
Container and Boundaries

As was clear from my description of the Bérnard experiment and the B-Z reaction, one of the requirements for the emergence of a dissipative structure is a strong container, which in chemistry means a nonporous vessel within which the components of the system are held and maintained. Researchers have shown that the container itself plays an important role in the formation of the hexagonal structures in the

Metaphor:		
Emergence of order in Bérnard experiment	*is like*	Emergence of "social entities," e.g., organizations
Conceptual Model:		
Experimental conditions for emergence of dissipative structure	*is analogous to*	Sociopersonal conditions for emergence of a social entity
Isomorphic Mapping...?		
Strong container		Container is shared vision + focused action
		Boundaries co-evolve with emergent entity
Agents are homogeneous		Agents are diverse
Agents are linear and deterministic		Agents are self-directed
Process is started by an external agent		Process is started from within
Inputs are exogenous to the system		Inputs are endogenous, through social ecology
Outputs are discarded into the environment		Outputs become inputs: key is sustainability
Theoretical Identity:		
Exo-Organization Emergence	← / ? / →	Generative Emergence

Figure 8.1: Transformative Metaphor of Conditions For Emergence.

Bérnard experiment. In reviewing these studies, Goldstein (2011) presented a series of reasons for why the size and shape of the vessel provide constraints necessary to the emergence of dissipative structures. Using the term "self-organization" as a general frame for dissipative structures, Goldstein (2011, pp. 107–108) explains that

> processes of self-organization require and reveal a host of constraints, innate and emergent.... And it is the constraints brought about by the containment in self-organizing systems which channel the "ordered flow" of energy.

His analysis of previous research provides compelling explanations for why a strong container is necessary for dissipative structures emergence.

Whereas dissipative structures are contained by a defined physical vessel, social entities emerge out of personal interactions across a social ecology[1] and within social networks whose boundaries are inherently undefined. From an entrepreneurial perspective, one can say that the dynamics that give rise to social entities are "contained" within a social ecology, through those individuals that engage with the entrepreneur's vision. The contours of that engagement provide a focus that helps direct entrepreneurial action toward more a defined market and more specific outcomes. In this way, the emerging focus provides boundaries that reduce the scope of possible choices, allowing entrepreneurs to channel their efforts in a more effective way. Likewise, these boundaries decrease the uncertainty of the organizing effort and increase the likelihood of success. This process leads to the well-known finding that the clearer the focus around specific customers and markets, the more likely a business will start up and succeed (Bhide, 2000; Morris, Schindette, & Allen, 2005; Shane, 2005; Mullins, 2006).

At the same time, since opportunities emerge and change over time, a founder's focus needs to be flexible, incorporating feedback from individuals and events (Gartner, Bird, & Starr, 1992; Sarasvathy, 2001). Furthermore, researchers have shown that entrepreneurial firms are more successful when they allow for rapid redefinitions of the proposed boundaries and scope of the company, based on evolving perceptions of need and opportunity and on the reframing of what resources are easily accessible and at hand (Dew, Read, Sarasvathy, & Wiltbank, 2008, 2009).

Thus, although constraints are necessary in dissipative structures and in social entities, the nature of these constraints is quite different. In the exo-organization of dissipative structures, the container is a nonpermeable constraint built into the apparatus in preparation for the experiment. In social entities, by contrast, the container is a conceptual boundary initially expressed by the founders as the focus and scope of the organizing effort, which becomes more focused as they engage with their social ecology. The boundaries start as an initial sketch that gets explored and tested over time, becoming more solidified and defined through the feedback with customers and stakeholders, leading to greater momentum and legitimacy for the endeavor. In this sense, the entity's boundary co-evolves with its emergence.[2]

Agents: Homogeneous and Deterministic vs. Diverse and Self-Directed

In dissipative structures the physical components of the system—its "agents"—are molecules, each of which follows the deterministic laws of chemistry and statistical mechanics. Using the Bérnard experiment as the paradigm case, all of the molecules start out being strictly homogeneous with no discernable differences in chemical constitution or valence. Although this homogeneity is not a theoretical requirement for dissipative structures,[3] it is a reflection of the simplicity of the experimental system which limits alternative processes and explanations. Homogeneity is also evident in many instances of computational emergence and interactional emergence, where the emphasis is on the "simple rules" and iterative interactions that lead to emergent order.

Of course, agents in a social system are not at all homogeneous; in fact, diversity is key to the enactment of variations and innovations (see Page, 2007, for the most comprehensive review of these literatures). Diversity has long been linked to higher performance in teams and organizations, especially when moderating factors are accounted for (e.g., Boone & Hendricks, 2009; Kearney, Gebert, & Voelpel, 2009; Mitchell, Parker, & Giles, 2012). Likewise, research on innovation teams suggests that homogeneity yields a premium through more diverse sets of expertise and experience, access to broader social networks, and the ability to access alternative resources (e.g., (Knott, 2003; Xu, 2011). Furthermore, some entrepreneurship researchers have long argued that heterogeneity across individuals explains why some people identify and pursue business opportunities whereas others do not (Hayek, 1945, 1967), and how differences in business experience lead to differences in how opportunities are interpreted and acted upon (Shane, 2000). In these ways, and in contrast with dissipative structures experiments, diversity is central to the emergence of social entities.

Similarly, there is an important distinction between the behavior of agents in dissipative structures and that in social structures. In the former, molecular constituents of dissipative structures display deterministic behavior—their actions can be fully explained by the conditions and lawful interactions they undergo.[4] In the latter, human agents are hardly deterministic: indeed, it is our creative and "nonlinear" thinking and action that often lead to innovation (Finke & Bettle, 1996; Sulis & Combs, 1996; Groves, Vance, & Choi, 2011; Gemmill, Boland, & Kolb, 2012). Moreover, founders of new organizations are highly self-directed, and their behavior is not determined by the perceptions of others (Baron, 1998, 2004; Baron & Markman, 2003).

This is perhaps the biggest difference between exo-organizing and generative emergence, namely that individuals are goal-seeking, internally and externally motivated agents who are sometimes unpredictable in their decisions and actions. Rather than having a set of conditions that always lead to a predictable outcome, as is the case in dissipative structures, the emergence of social entities has a much wider range of drivers and obstacles and thus is not predictable.

Initiated by Agent(s) Outside vs. Inside the System

In the experiments of dissipative structures theory, there must be a researcher who sets up the apparatus, then turns on the electricity to start the flow of energy through the container. Except for the heat or chemical energy that drives the system into a far-from-equilibrium state, the "agency" that initiates emergence is outside the system itself. Exactly the same situation occurs in computational emergence: the agents are activated only because the software program is programmed by the researcher and then started by a human agent outside the system.[5]

In contrast, the emergence of a social entity is initiated by agency *within* the system, specifically by one or more human agents within their social ecology; the founder and team start a process of organizing. In entrepreneurial terms, the founders identify or create a viable opportunity, then marshal and access resources to enact it (Gartner, 1993; Gartner & Brush, 2007). In dynamic systems language, the founders identify an untapped cache of resources—an unmet need, unsolved problem, or an innovation that can create a new source of value—and they begin to push energy and resources toward that goal through their organizing efforts (Slevin & Covin, 1997; McKelvey, 2004; Lichtenstein, 2009).

Thus, the agency that drives generative emergence is always endogenous to the system. In this sense there is no "outside" of an entrepreneurial organizing process. Instead, a key element of being a successful entrepreneur is the ability to distinguish the organizing endeavor from its social context by *creating the boundaries* of a new organization (Aldrich, 1979; Katz & Gartner, 1988). Contrast this with other prototypes of emergence, especially computational emergence and exo-organizational emergence, in which the agency of order creation is always outside the system. This difference has a considerable influence on the dynamics of emergence.

Inputs: Exogenous vs. Endogenous Sources of Energy

In dissipative structures experiments, the energy and resources that are imported into the system are exogenous to the container, being drawn from the environment into the focal system. Commonly, we say that energy is imported into the system from the environment, a frame developed through the "open systems" model (von Bertalanffy, 1956; Miller, 1978) that remains central to organization science (Thompson, 1967; Scott, 1981; Ashmos & Huber, 1987).[6]

Where do these energy inputs come from, that is, what does "from the environment" mean in the context of dissipative structures? At a simple level, the energy used to run the experiment is accessed though the electrical outlet on the wall of the laboratory; more specifically, the energy is "from" the electrical wires and the energy grid in that region. In a real sense this energy source is external to the experiment; it is also external to the lab, to the building, to the encompassing institution (university, research center), and to the research context itself.[7]

In contrast, consider the energy and resources that go into the creation of a new social entity. Minimally these include time, money, and expertise (existing knowledge, new learning); relationships and alliances (social networks); supplies for manufacturing or inventory; and personal effort, among other things. These and other types of resources are directly from the founders or are accessed through the founders' social ecology. Examples include financing—most new ventures are started with money from the founder or their friends and family; the same is true of the time, effort, and much of the expertise that goes into creating a new company. Similarly, the social networks that give rise to possible partners, including suppliers and distributors, collaborators, advisory board members, and key hires, are by and large directly linked to someone on the core organizing team. Overall, the resources needed to start a venture are accessed through founders' social ecology, through sources that are not easily distinguished from the emerging entity itself.[8]

As such, the vast majority of energy inputs to an emerging social entity are internal to the organizing effort and thus endogenous to the system.[9] For similar reasons, agents of generative emergence can be described as being "self-determined," for they exhibit strong internalized agency that draws toward itself the opportunities, resources, and support for creating new social entities (Katz & Gartner, 1988; Bird, 1992; Busenitz & Barney, 1997; Baron & Markman, 2003; Baron, 2008; Brush, Manolova, & Edelman, 2008; Dew et al., 2008; Casrud & Brannback, 2011). The very directionality of this flow—from the inside out rather than the outside in—clearly distinguishes generative emergence from exo-organization, and from computational emergence as well.

Outputs: Discarded to the Environment vs. Used to Sustain the System

In the same way that the inputs to a dissipative structure are exogenous to the system, so too the outputs of energy and resources become exogenous. Specifically, the heat energy in the Bérnard experiment is exported out of the system through the sink and is unused after that. Likewise, the excess chemicals in the B-Z reaction are transferred out of the system. Once exported out of the container these sources of energy are not used again in the experiment. In real terms, the outputs are discarded, providing no value to the system.

By contrast, the outputs to a social system are never discarded; instead, they are actively exchanged by proximate agents. That is, the core effort in a social entity is to transform energy and resources into valuable outputs. These outputs are designed to bring value to the social system, through specific products and services that certain customers will find valuable. In economic terms, the value provided by the venture—the system's output—is exchanged for an equivalent source of value, namely money. This exchange of value for value is at the core of all economic and social entities.[10]

Thus, in generative emergence the outputs of the system are a critical source of inputs for the venture, because the money that is exchanged goes to fund the operations of the organization. In this sense, a successful venture is an "energy conversion system" (Slevin & Covin, 1997, p. 55), converting resources and effort into a valued product or service, which, through an exchange, is converted into further resources that fuel the organization. The entire process is generative, with entrepreneurial action generating opportunities, resources, and organizing that generates new value. The value that is produced generates resources (money), which is channeled back into the venture as a source of energy that sustains and grows the entity. Hence the term generative emergence.

Implications and Summary

In sum, the differences between generative emergence and exo-organization are significant. All the sociopersonal conditions of generative emergence are endogenous, self-directed, and co-creative. The container is a fluid boundary rather than a predesigned vessel. Agents are diverse and self-directed, far different from the homogeneous deterministic molecules of dissipative structures. The process is initiated by an agent who expects to be central to the venture; likewise, the inputs of energy and resources he or she accesses are endogenous to the social ecology from which the venture emerges. Finally, in contrast to dissipative structures that discard outputs into the environment, generative emergence produces outputs that are wanted by its customers, who exchange them for money that becomes a key input to the venture, allowing it to be sustained and grow.

In these ways, the conditions that lead to dissipative structures are substantively different from the conditions that lead to generative emergence. These differences allow for a clear distinction of generative emergence as a separate prototype from exo-organizing.

It turns out that this proposition can be formalized, through a framework that explains the internal dynamics of all emergent social entities—from entrepreneurial ventures and new organizations, to programs, projects, initiatives, enterprises, collaborations, new departments, and work units. This model is called a dynamic state; the outcome of a five-phase process of generative emergence is the creation of a dynamic state. In formal terms, every social entity that arises from generative emergence can be described in terms of a dynamic state (Levie & Lichtenstein, 2010).

GENERATIVE EMERGENCE OF A DYNAMIC STATE

Organizing as Value Creation

A meaningful explanation of the dynamic state model starts at the end: the reason that any social entity arises is to provide value of some kind. Value means something of worth for a specific group of people—customers, clients, companies, a neighborhood or social group, and for the organizers. In entrepreneurial terms, value is generated through products, services, experiences, or interactions that satisfy a need, solve a problem, make something easier or less expensive, improve a situation, or in some way provide satisfaction. Although we each experience value in different ways, we all turn to organizations, events, and communities to provide us with the things that we value and the products that we want.

How is value "created?" My claim is that value is always created through a dynamic state, whether an organization or venture, a project or program, an event or interaction, a community or social network—really, any social entity. As a construct, a dynamic state models (represents) an engine of value creation. A dynamic state takes in resources and energy (inputs), "transforms" them and adds value, and then offers the value to clients and customers in the form of products, services, activities, and events. For example, a grocery store takes in (purchases inputs of) bulk supplies of food; they add value through their ability to source and offer a wide selection of items that are kept fresh, organized, and easy to find. Each shopper chooses which items will bring them value; in economic terms the price of each item represents the value the individual receives as a result of the transaction.[11]

In this case the money received by the grocery store is used to maintain its value-creation processes—to fund the cost of the food; to pay employees who distribute, stock, and sell the merchandise; to pay the costs of the building and necessary technology and advertising. All of these processes are necessary to provide the valued service, and the revenues received are used to maintain all of the processes. The unit of analysis is not the product or service but the entire organization, the entire dynamic state.

In a tangible sense the organization as a whole generates value to the customer, who exchanges it for value in the form of money, which is used to maintain the activities that generate more value. This systemic process is represented by a dynamic state—it is the outcome of generative emergence, which refers to the creation of a dynamic state.

Before describing the various elements of a dynamic state, a few tangible examples will help express the generality of the model. Consider a concert you have recently attended. The organizers of the event believed that enough people would value the music and decide to attend, and thus they booked the band and the venue, made arrangements with a ticket agency and a marketing group, and hired staff to manage the event. The value of the concert was reflected in the value (price) of the tickets. The revenues received were allocated to pay for all the activities that generated the value itself, including the organizers. Note, too, that the concert has other outcomes as well, mainly the positive feelings that participants experienced, experiences that help build the reputation of the band, which raises its value in the future.

As a slightly more interesting example of the value creation in a dynamic state, consider this book you're reading now, whether in print or e-book format. You purchased the book on the basis of the value you believed you would gain by reading it; in exchange, you paid money. The money is being used by the publisher to generate this book and others like it. In this example, the book project is a dynamic state, which is fueled by my motivation to generate value through these ideas, in concert with Oxford University Press's commitment to bring unique and valuable books to the marketplace of ideas. If all goes well, the total costs of producing this book are recovered through purchases of the book. At the same time, the publishing house operates within a broader level dynamic state; the value they create is in the aggregation of all their titles, and the value exchanged goes toward sustaining the production of individual texts as well as in providing more capacity to contract and produce additional texts. In both of these examples, dynamic states provide a generalized model of value creation.

Value creation is also at the heart of social innovations, whether produced by non-profits, non-governmental organizations (NGOs), or for-profit companies. For example, organizations like CARE or Lifestraw generate life-saving value for people and societies; many of us value their tangible good work by donating to organizations like these. Here, the tangible value being received by one group is funded by another group, the donors, who gain a type of moral or emotional value from their donations. Increasingly, exemplars of social innovation elide the old distinction between for-profit and non-profit organizations (see, for example, Boyd, Henning, Reyna, Wang, & Welch, 2009; Dacin, Dacin, & Matear, 2010; Ellis, 2010).

Although these examples are somewhat simplistic, they make a key point: The generative emergence of any dynamic state is initiated by a perception that value can be created, it is organized around the production of that value, and it is sustained by the exchanges made on behalf of the created value. However, value creation is only the end of the process; understanding the other elements of a dynamic state can reveal further insights about generative emergence.

ELEMENTS OF A DYNAMIC STATE

A dynamic state involves three main elements: opportunity tension, an organizing model, and value creation; these are held within a broader context which I refer to as a social ecology. Before introducing those elements of a dynamic state, a brief description of the term itself is required.

On the surface, the term *dynamic state* is an internal contradiction: *state* refers to a stable mode of activity—literally "the particular condition that something is in at a specific time" (Oxford Dictionary), the outcome of a series of events. We think of a state as a static quality that remains relatively permanent over time. In contrast, *dynamic* is characterized by "constant change, activity or progress" (Oxford Dictionary), usually through temporal processes and interactions. Dynamic, as it is used here, means constantly "becoming," as Tsoukas and Chia (2002) suggest. Being the opposite of equilibrium, *dynamic* seems to contradict its adjacent term, *state*. Together they express an inherent tension between stability and change, formation and existence, which is at the heart of this complexity-inspired approach.

Social Ecology as the Substrate for Emergence

Dynamic states do not emerge out of nothing; like every prototype of emergence, order arises out of a substrate: the material, energetic, and informational ecosystem that contains the components and resources that get organized into an emergent entity. In the Bérnard experiment, for example, the substrate is the viscous fluid through which heat energy flows from a source to a sink. In organizations the substrate is a "thick" social network of colleagues, friends, and acquaintances; the substrate includes social capital (relationships), human capital (skills, experience), knowledge and technology, societal infrastructure, and business connections to commercial and social entities within and across a given industry.

"Energy" flows through this social ecology in the form of new ideas, innovations in business models, changes in the business and social landscape, longer-term demographic and social trends, capital resources, and social support—all the elements that go into the creation of any social entity. For entrepreneurs, their social ecology is the fabric of their professional life, the source of resources and potential that have helped them organize all previous endeavors up to the present and that continuously present new opportunities to consider. Figure 8.2 suggests several categories of these resources, including people, culture, technology, local and regional economy, markets or industries and sectors, and all the relationships within and between those categories. Further categories could be added as well.

These resources provide the sources of new ideas and organizing efforts in two ways. Most broadly, any individual who organizes something—any entrepreneur—is deeply influenced by the social and cultural environment of their childhood and early adulthood, a point that is well acknowledged in the literature (Carland, Hoy, & Carland, 1988; Shaver & Scott, 1991; Aldrich & Martinez, 2001; Baron & Markman, 2003). This long-term influence conjoins with proximal issues in the development of a *core logic* for the organizing effort—a set of shared beliefs and values that guide decisions about the new venture, similar to a dominant logic (Prahalad & Bettis, 1986; Bettis & Prahalad, 1995; Obloj, Obloj, & Pratt, 2010). In most cases this core logic remains rather stable in the long term (Drazin & Sandelands, 1992), and it forms a blueprint for the firm (Baron, Burton, & Hannan, 1996). Thus, the core logic for the organizing effort is derived from the experience and social ecology of the entrepreneur or organizer.

The social ecology is the raw source of ideas and opportunities that lead to new organizations and organizing efforts. In an entrepreneurial sense, virtually all opportunities arise out of changes in the social milieu, including shifts in regulations, innovations to technologies, demographic and social trends, and changes in norms and expectations that guide social activity as well as our individual goals

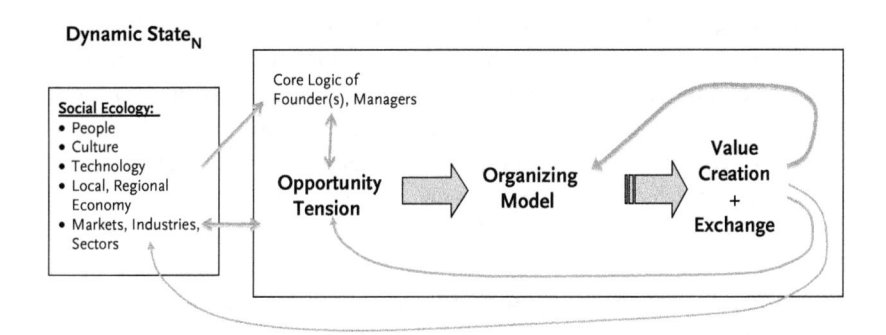

Figure 8.2: Elements of a Dynamic State

(Timmons, 1999; Morris et al., 2005). Thus, one's social ecology is always the source for potential business ideas and the resources to pull it off.[12]

Opportunity Tension as the Driver of Generative Emergence

In the Bérnard experiment, the five-phase emergence process begins when the researcher "turns up the heat" in the container, pushing it toward a far-from-equilibrium state. Likewise, generative emergence is initiated when a leader, organizer, or founder begins to push the system out of its norm, beyond its reference state and toward disequilibrium organizing. What does it mean for someone to "turn up the heat" in their social ecology?

As mentioned earlier, an entrepreneurial agent is an enterprising individual who has the passion to pursue a new business idea *and* comes up with a way to generate new value in their ecology. This idea, this interest, this potential for enacting an opportunity is exactly analogous to the heat that begins to flow through the container. However, in contrast to emergence of dissipative structures, the *agency* that initiates the process is within the system—humans have agency in ways that molecules do not.[13] Thus, generative emergence is always driven by agency, in the form of a vision for how to improve the social ecology by creating new value, and an aspiration—a motivation and intention—to pursue that vision. In more formal terms this combined driver of vision and motivation is called opportunity tension, and it is central to the emergence of all dynamic states (Lichtenstein, 2009; Levie & Lichtenstein, 2010).

Opportunity tension integrates an individual's perception for how to capitalize on an opportunity to create value, with the motivation and passion to do so. This motivation to act is expressed as "creative tension" (Fritz, 1989), a state of dynamic energy often found in artists and performers. Creative tension occurs when the artist gains a vision or an inspiration for a new work, a creative insight that seeks expression. Immediately the artist will feel a gap between his or her vision and the current state of things; this gap is literally a tension between the potentiality of a finished creative work and the actuality of the creative work that does not yet exist.

According to Fritz's lifetime career of performance and research, creative tension is "an internal creative energy that seeks resolution." Artists "resolve" their creative tension through making or performing their art. In this way, the term *tension* also refers to the term *intention*, which is defined as "resolve ... [or] determination to act in a certain way" (Webster's, 1996). Intention describes a motive force for action—a purpose or aim to bring something about.

Just as artists express their creative tension through their artwork, entrepreneurs express their creative tension through their organizing, in the creation of a new company. For all creative social beings, opportunity tension is the passion and motivation to do whatever it takes to enact an idea into a viable enterprise (Lichtenstein, 2009). It starts with an aspiration for a dynamic state, tethered to the current situation, and amplified by the potential customers who may gain value through the endeavor. The impetus to create leads to entrepreneurial action—the initiation of new ventures, projects, social innovations, events, and conferences.

The term *opportunity* indicates the potential value and revenue that may be gained by providing a new product or service. In a business sense opportunity reflects the likelihood that people will exchange value (in the form of money) for the value that is being proposed by the entrepreneur and his or her organization. Going back to the language of thermodynamics, opportunity refers to the prospect of accessing unused "energy potentials" by transforming inputs into valued outputs, a process McKelvey (2004) described as "adaptive tension." This meaning emphasizes the potentiality that entrepreneurs see in a business opportunity, based on their judgment that a potential group of customers—a target market—would find value in a product or service that the entrepreneur could create (Mullins, 2006). In a sense, the art of entrepreneurship is to identify that potential within the social ecology and enact it through the passion of the entrepreneur—this is reflected in the term *opportunity tension*.

Opportunity tension thus links a potential business opportunity with the drive to make it happen. Whereas entrepreneurial scholars are hotly debating the origin of opportunities (Shane & Venkataraman, 2000; Sarasson, Dean, & Hilliard, 2006; Alvarez & Barney, 2007, 2013; McMullan, Plummer, & Acs, 2007; Garud & Giuliani, 2013), my sense is that these arguments can be resolved in action: The success of any organizing endeavor is based on the effort that is put into it and the value that can be generated by it (Gartner, 1988, 1993; Gartner et al., 1992), amidst a host of mediating factors. At the same time, the motivation to act is often based on the perceived scope of the opportunity—the greater the market potential, the greater the motivation to act. That is, an entrepreneur's aspiration reflects an educated guess about the ultimate size of the market, or the perceived pool of potential resources, *and* their ability to create an organization to capitalize on this anticipated energy potential in a sustainable way.[14] Likewise, the degree of opportunity tension is based on a recursive testing of an emerging business concept: The more confirmation of the opportunity, the more amplified the entrepreneur's belief that it can and must be exploited.

Opportunity without tension is merely a good idea; tension without opportunity is not likely to generate a sustainable dynamic state. Together, opportunity tension drives virtually all organizing efforts that lead to generative emergence. This is why opportunity tension is one of the central components of dynamic states. Formally, when there is opportunity *and* (in)tension, the organizing process begins (Lichtenstein et al., 2007).

An Organizing Model Is the Method for Creating Value

How does an organization transform an opportunity tension into a reliable system for creating value? The answer is to use an organizing model, the core activities and processes that convert resource and energy inputs into valued products and services, and make these available to customers. Scholars seeking to understand this process have used the term *business model*, which describes "the set of activities which a firm performs, how it performs them, and when it performs them so as to offer its customers benefits they want" (Afuah, 2004, p. 2). Although many definitions of a business model have been proposed (Morris et al., 2005; Zott & Amit, 2007; George & Bock, 2011; Lindgren, 2012), the approach that is most connected to the dynamic states framework is the model by Osterwalder and Pigneur (2010, p. 15):

> A business model describes . . . how an organization creates, delivers and captures value . . . The business model is like a blueprint for a strategy to be implemented through organizational structures, processes, and systems.

Osterwalder and Pigneur present a business model as a combination of nine "building blocks"—core elements that describe how an organization creates value and how customers receive that value. These building blocks form a parsimonious explanation for the process, whether in for-profit companies or in non-profit social innovations, whether in corporate settings or in hybrid entrepreneurial situations (Osterwalder, 2010; Osterwalder & Pigneur, 2010; see http://www.slideshare.net/Alex.Osterwalder/presentations). Since not all of these are businesses per se, I have adopted the more generalized term *organizing model*, which can be applied to any version of a dynamic state.

A powerful application of the Osterwalder approach is the Lean Business Canvas, popularized by Steven Blank (2012). These versions all focus on the same thing: what is the minimum basis for creating value. As shown in Figure 8.3, the first five building blocks of the Osterwalder model are customer focused, reflecting

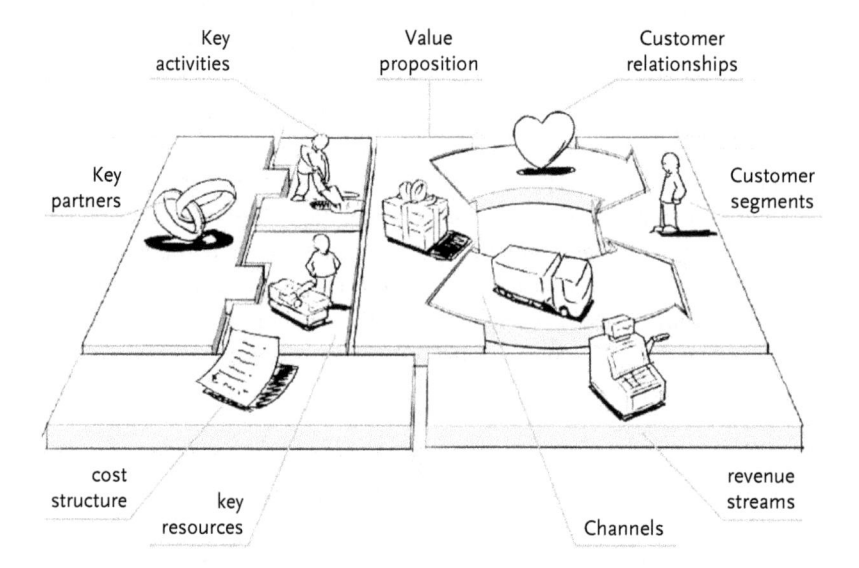

Figure 8.3 Osterwalder's Images for a Business Model
From Osterwalder (2010). Reprinted with permission from Osterwalder, A., & Pigneur, Y. 2010. *Business Model Generation: A Handbook for Visionaries, Game Changers, and Challengers*. Hoboken, NJ: John Wiley & Sons.

how customer needs can be fulfilled by delivering a unique value proposition to a specific target market. The next four building blocks are organization focused, describing what has to be done to provide that value. Osterwalder' business model, which includes the entire set, is shown in Figure 8.4, and it is discussed in detail in Osterwalder (2010) and Osterwalder and Pigneur (2010). The basic logic of the organizing model is as follows:

How an organization generates value:

(1) An organization, endeavor, or initiative serves one or more **customer segments,** through a
(2) **Value proposition** that seeks to solve a problem and satisfy the needs of the client or customer.
(3) Value propositions are delivered through **channels** that communicate (market), distribute, and sell the product or service.
(4) **Customer relationships** have to be built and maintained for each customer segment.
(5) **Revenue streams** are gained when a value proposition is successfully offered and received.

How the organization produces that value:

(6) **Key activities** are the tasks and systems needed to produce value. These require
(7) **Key resources**—assets and inputs required to offer and deliver the value to customers, and
(8) **Key partnerships**—suppliers and alliances that provide unique resources, avenues for outsourcing noncritical tasks, and that help the organization gain legitimacy and support.
(9) Each of these three processes has costs. The **cost structure** describes the fixed and variable costs, as well as economies of scope or scale, that yield value-driven vs. cost-driven business models.

It is important to recognize that any dynamic state must incorporate all of these building blocks in order to create and provide value in a sustainable way. To return to the Oxford University Press example, their *value proposition* involves publishing books that provide insight and innovative knowledge to intelligent readers. Like most large book publishers, they deliver their books through broad *distribution channels*—catalogues, book stores, and online. Customers and libraries exchange money for the value they receive, thus generating *revenue streams* for the company. These revenues go to offsetting the company's *costs*, mainly for the *activities* that go into printing the books and managing projects, and for key *resources* which include printing presses and materials and also the knowledge and relationships that generate valuable offerings. Some of these relationships are developed through

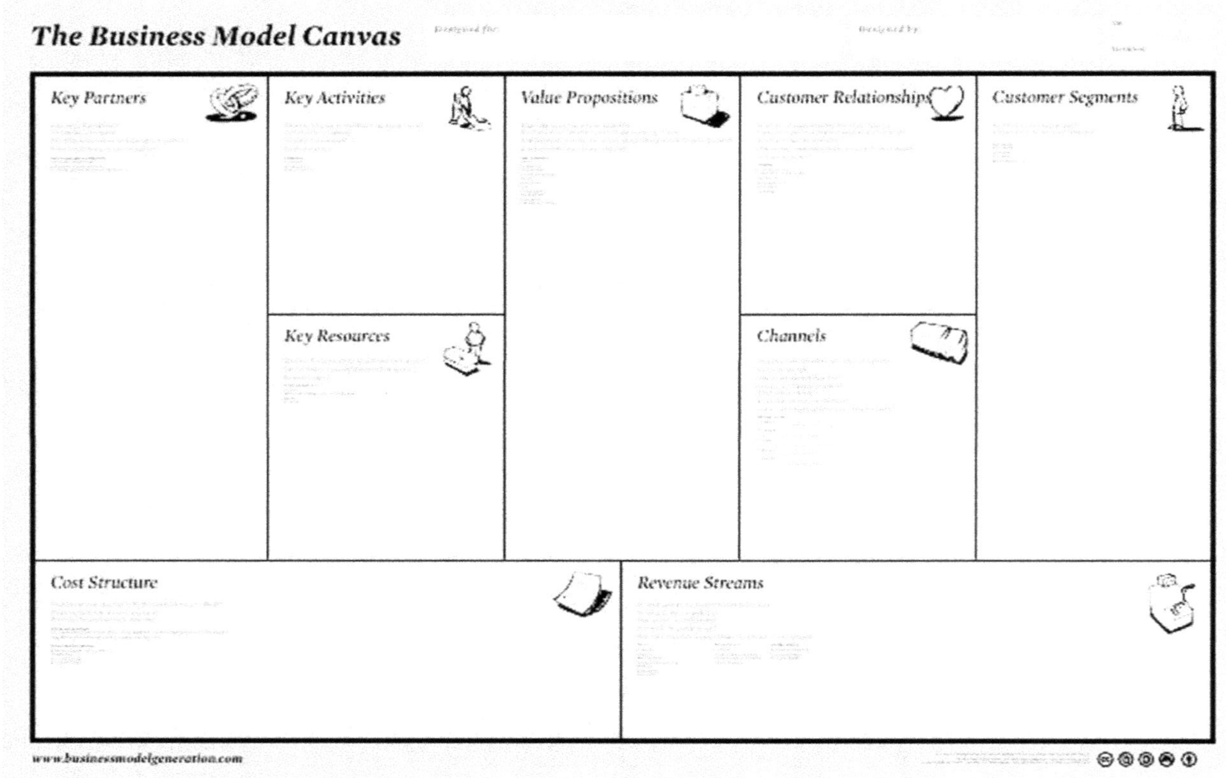

Figure 8.4: Osterwalder's Business Model Canvas
From www.businessmodelgeneration.com. Reprinted with permission from Osterwalder, A., & Pigneur, Y. 2010. *Business Model Generation: A Handbook for Visionaries, Game Changers, and Challengers.* Hoboken, NJ: John Wiley & Sons.

partnerships that support key aspects of the endeavor. As a whole, the organizing model describes how the dynamic state generates value, and how that value regenerates the dynamic state.

Osterwalder (2009) has shown how the same building blocks explain non-profit enterprises, such as the Grameen Bank or the Kiva Foundation. In these cases there are two value propositions—one for the beneficiaries of the service, and the other for the funders; each of these customer segments receives a different type of value. In the case of Grameen Bank, revenues are gained through very small profit margins on the loans to householders. In the Kiva Foundation, revenues are gained through donations. In both cases, the revenues go to the activities that generate value for clients, the resources needed to accomplish those activities, and the international partnerships that support the process. Similar examples could be developed for any kind of social innovation. For a fuller explanation, see Osterwalder (2009).

In short, an organizing model provides a parsimonious explanation for how value is created and distributed in a sustainable way.

Value Creation and Its Influence to the Dynamic State

From an open systems perspective, inputs to the system are encoded in its opportunity tension; transformation of those inputs happens through the organizing model, and outputs are based on the value creation. As Figure 8.2 shows, value creation influences the dynamic state in three specific ways, designated by the feedback loops in the figure.

First, as mentioned earlier, the value created is exchanged for value transacted, that is, the product or service is exchanged for money.[15] The money collected from the revenue streams is primarily allocated to offset the costs of producing value; some is used for further research or development and expansion of the organizing effort, or it is retained as profit. This link between value creation and revenues is a positive feedback loop that allows the organization to sustainably fulfill its value propositions and pursue new ones.

A second feedback loop involves the information and meaning that the entrepreneur gleans from the rate and pace of sales of their offering. That is, the size of the revenue stream is one reflection of the size of the opportunity itself, and the rate of increase (or decrease) of that stream provides more information on the ultimate size and scope of the opportunity. In this case, the feedback loop connects the revenue stream with the opportunity tension, informing the entrepreneur(s) about the validity and long-term viability of the opportunity itself.

Adroit organizers use this information to continuously improve the value proposition, adding features, benefits, and extensions to the product or service, the relationships they generate with clients, and the marketing and distribution channels they've chosen. Likewise, this information feeds back to the activities side, providing clues for decreasing costs or increasing activities, shifting the use of partners, and altering resource bases. Ideally, in this way the value feeds back to the opportunity tension, which leads to constant improvements to the business concept and its expression through the organizing model (Miles, Miles, & Snow, 2006; Bucherer, Eisert, & Gassmann, 2012).

Last, value creation feeds back to the social ecology through the interactions customers have with their own social networks around the benefits (or drawbacks) of the product or service they've recently purchased. These conversations lead to dissemination of the offering, which in some cases alters some structures or institutions in the broader social ecology, especially when new products have a role in creating an industry, as described by Rindova and Fombrun (2001); Garud, Jain, and Kumaraswamy (2002); Chiles, Tuggle, McMullen, Bierman, and Greening (2010); Garud, Kumaraswamy, and Karnøe (2010); and Dew, Reed, Sarasvathy, and Wiltbank (2011).

In sum, all organizing efforts that succeed can be described in terms of a dynamic state. The origins and resources of new endeavors start in the social ecology of the system or organizer. This social ecology contributes to an opportunity tension—the creative aspiration of an entrepreneur or organizer who identifies an opportunity or need that can be capitalized on or solved by enacting a specific organizing model. The goal of this process is value creation; the value that's exchanged is used to regenerate the dynamic state. As such, a dynamic state provides a useful representation of the outcomes of generative emergence.

To be fair, not all organizing efforts lead to a dynamic state. Most endeavors are less successful than their founders would want. As I will detail in the next chapter, a good portion of entrepreneurial endeavors "fail"—the organizer does not create the value he or she had hoped, and in most cases the initiative stops. Thus, by no means does my description of a dynamic state suggest that this is the most common outcome of organizing. At the same time, all organizing efforts are driven by opportunity tension and have as their goal the creation of a sustainable entity—a dynamic state. This idea will be expanded through examples in most of the chapters that follow.

CONNECTING DYNAMIC STATES TO THE CONDITIONS FOR GENERATIVE EMERGENCE

In summary, Table 8.1 (from Figure 8.1) reviews the differences between the experimental conditions that lead to dissipative structures and the conditions that lead to the generative emergence of a dynamic state.

These conditions for generative emergence are well connected to the elements of a dynamic state. Making this connection helps summarize the essence of the dynamic states model. These connections between generative emergence and a dynamic state are summarized in Table 8.2.

Table 8.1. DIFFERENCES BETWEEN DISSIPATIVE STRUCTURES AND GENERATIVE EMERGENCE

Conditions for Dissipative Structures	Conditions for Generative Emergence
Strong container	Container is shared vision + focused action
	Boundaries co-evolve with emergent entity
Agents are homogeneous	Agents are heterogeneous and diverse
Agents are linear and deterministic	Agents are self-directed
Process is started by an external agent	Process is started from within
Inputs are exogenous to the system	Inputs are endogenous, through social ecology
Outputs are discarded into the environment	Outputs become inputs: key is sustainability

Note that these conditions for generative emergence are operative at the start of any organizing effort. In effect, these conditions describe the qualities that are necessary but not sufficient for accomplishing generative emergence. In a similar way, several elements of a dynamic state are present from the start of an organizing endeavor, providing the motivation, agency, and resource base from which generative emergence can proceed. As a set, these conditions and elements are essential for the emergence of any sustained social entity.

As mentioned before, the outcomes of the process are emergent when the value that is created is sufficient to sustain the dynamic state over time. However, such positive outcomes are not at all assured; the effort may not be able to create value, and thus will not yield a self-generating system. This negative case is perhaps much more common then the positive one. Thus, I shall describe it at the start of the next chapter, on outcomes of generative emergence.

Table 8.2. CONNECTIONS BETWEEN GENERATIVE EMERGENCE AND DYNAMIC STATES

Conditions for Generative Emergence	Elements of a Dynamic State
Container is shared vision + focused action	Opportunity tension provides focus for vision and action
Boundaries co-evolve with emergent entity	Boundaries and concept evolve through interactions
Agents are diverse	Agents in the social ecology are diverse
Agents are self-directed	Founder and members of the organizing team are self-directed
Process is started from within	Opportunity tension is generated by founder/organizer within the social ecology
Inputs are endogenous, through social ecology	Resources, information, and energy for venture are accessed through social networks and social ecology of the organizer
Outputs become inputs; sustainability is essential	Value creation outputs become the inputs for costs, resources, and sustainability of the venture

NOTES

1. Social ecologies refer to the structure of our social environment and the substrate within which we conduct our daily lives. Social ecologies can be described according to seven main features, which were summarized in Goldstein, Hazy, and Lichtenstein (2010, pp. 27–36):

    1. Ecologies are systems of difference.
    2. Diversity is the source of adaptability.
    3. An ecology is a *nexus* of interacting ecosystems, in which interdependence permeates.
    4. Ecosystems require interaction resonance.
    5. Ecosystems co-evolve through cooperative strategies.
    6. Ecosystems thrive in a *dis*equilibrium world.
    7. Ecosystems exist at multiple levels.

2. For a good example, see Lichtenstein, Dooley, and Lumpkin (2006). Philosophically, this connection between the nature (identity) of the entity and the definition of its boundary is at the core of the autopoiesis theory, as initially presented by Varela (1979) and later adapted to organizations by Csanyi and Kampis (1985), Drazin and Sandelands (1992) and Pantzar and Csanyi (1991).
3. Specifically, in Nicholis and Prigogine (1989) there is virtually no mention of homogeneity of molecules in the experimental fluid, except in regard to temperature.
4. Deterministic here does not mean predictable, rather it means fully determined by the internal and external situation. The question of predictability becomes complicated as soon as the system moves into a far-from-equilibrium state, where linear causal relations break down. At that point, agent behavior can be best explained in terms of an attractor in deterministic chaos theory, that is, there are clear parameters—tangible boundaries—within which all agents will be found. However, the actual position of any given molecule at any given moment is virtually (or completely) impossible to predict, because of the high degree of complexity of the entire system.
5. Much more can and should be said about this difference. As an extension of the same point, "self-organization" in simulation models is only possible because programmers—human agents outside the system—generate the contextual rules, agent characteristics, and interaction processes that lead to aggregation and emergence, a point carefully made by Sawyer and reviewed in Chapter 2. Thus, although the order that emerges is spontaneous, it is hardly free, for it relies on hours and hours of programming effort to arrange, and on the electricity and the entire experimental setup to produce.
6. Note that the apparatus in the Bérnard experiment forms a *materially closed system* but an *energetically open system*. That is, the agents in the fluid are located inside the container and they remain there throughout the process. In contrast, energy in the form of heat is inputted into and through the system and then is "pulled" out through the sink. Thus the system is open to energy flow, but it is closed to material flow. In the B-Z reaction this equation is somewhat different. There the molecular compounds remain closed within the container, whereas the inputted energy—the addition of additional fluid into the system—is offset by a concomitant output of fluid so as to keep the system from overflowing.
7. As mentioned earlier, the same can be said for the energy that animates computational emergence.

8. As a detail, the similarity between the terms *source* and *resource* is intriguing. Etymologically, they derive from the same root: the Latin *surgere*—to "lead up from below," from something that has "surged up" (Ayto, 1991).
9. Some "exceptions" to this rule include changes to regulations or large-scale institutional shifts that may set the stage for a business opportunity, as well as trends or events at a national or regional level. One might also include unelicited support from organizations or individuals who hear about the venture from "outside sources," although here again the distinction between "inside" and "outside" may be purely perceptual. Finally, I would hasten to include the role of social infrastructure—electricity, roads, the rule of law, the Internet—which is certainly external to the firm, but which I would not include in terms of agency per se.
10. A similar logic can be applied to non-profit organizations, and all endeavors that don't "sell" their outputs to customers. This will be discussed in the next section.
11. More formally, the value created is *exchanged* through a transaction between the seller and the buyer. In this language the price someone pays for an item should be *equivalent to the value they receive* as a result of the transaction. Of course, price is not the only determinant of value. Some activities, like playing in a park with the kids, are valuable in part because they are free; some activities provide so much value that, as one credit card commercial says, they are "priceless."
12. This link is iterative (represented by the double-sided arrow in Figure 8.2), because as entrepreneurs assess the validity of the idea by testing it in the market—in their social ecology—their conversations evoke alterations and additions that are tested again and again. A good concept is thus co-created in the process of organizing.
13. This apparently simple act is actually not so simple, for it appears to be occurring outside the container. And in all classic experimental situations, the turning on of the experiment is an externality, not counted within the activity of the container. But how can this be so? Without a motivation to explore these order-creation processes we would not know that they exist in this way. Thus, the experiment begins with *agency*—an agent turns up the heat to the container. To carry the analogy to its conclusion we would ask *why* the agent is pursuing this experiment. The answer is that some *value* is being generated through it; the experiment and its finding generate value in terms of knowledge to the researchers and to the academic and social community who reads their work. This perceived value is an internal driver of agency, it's the motivation for the P.I. to pursue the experiment and write up the results. In some real and profound way this agency cannot be separated from the increase in heat energy through the container.
14. Suffice it to say that the bottom line of generative emergence must be sustainability, that is, the ongoing sustenance of the dynamic state through the value that's received for the value that's produced. Likewise, the notion of ecological sustainability is necessarily embedded in the dynamic states model, in ways that are familiar to those who attend to more systemic models of economics (Odum & Odum, 1976; Boulding, 1978; Rothschild, 1992; Clippinger, 1999; Esty & Winston, 2006; Espinosa, Harnden, & Walker, 2008; Senge, Smith, Krushwitz, Laur, & Schley, 2008). I will say much more about this in Chapter 18.
15. Although most economic exchanges use money, many do not. Consider the growing phenomenon of formal online bartering—community-based initiatives through which individuals can gain services or products and exchange them for time or services that they or others offer within a kind of virtual "bank." Examples include International Monetary Systems—https://www.imsbarter.com/, Tradebank—http://tradebank.com/, and TimeBanks—http//www.timebanks.org, the latter being described as a way to use "time as currency [to] promote equality and build caring community economies through inclusive exchange of time and talent."

REFERENCES

Afuah, A. 2004. *Business Models: A Strategic Management Approach*. Boston: McGraw Hill Irwin.

Aldrich, H. 1979. *Organizations and Environments*. Englewood Cliffs, NJ: Prentice-Hall.

Aldrich, H., & Martinez, M. A. 2001. Many are called, but few are chosen: An evolutionary perspective for the study of entrepreneurship. *Entrepreneurship Theory and Practice*, 25(4-Summer): 41–56.

Alvarez, S., & Barney, J. 2007. Discovery and creation: Alternative theories of entrepreneurial action. *Strategic Entrepreneurship Journal*, 1: 11–27.

Alvarez, S., & Barney, J. 2013. Epistemology, opportunities, and entrepreneurship: Comments on Venkataraman et al. (2012) and Shane (2012). *Academy of Management Journal*, 38(1): 154–56.

Ashmos, D., & Huber, G. 1987. The system paradign in organization theory: Correcting the record and suggesting the future. *Academy of Management Review*, 12: 607–21.

Ayto, J. 1991. *Dictionary of Word Origins: Histories of More than 8,000 English-Language Words*. New York: Arcade/Skyhorse Publishing.

Baron, J., Burton, D., & Hannan, M. 1996. The road taken: The origins and evolution of employment systems in emerging high-technology companies. *Industrial and Corporate Change*, 5: 239–76.

Baron, R. 1998. Cognitive mechanisms in entrepreneurship: Why and when entrepreneurs think differently than other people. *Journal of Business Venturing*, 13: 275–24.

Baron, R. 2004. The cognitive perspective: A valuable tool for answering entrepreneurship's basic "why?" questions. *Journal of Business Venturing*, 19: 221–40.

Baron, R. 2008. The role of affect in the entrepreneurial process. *Academy of Management Review*, 33: 328–40.

Baron, R., & Markman, G. 2003. Beyond social capital: The role of entrepreneurs' social competence in their financial success. *Journal of Business Venturing*, 18: 41–60.

Bettis, R., & Prahalad, C. K. 1995. The dominant logic: Retrospective and extention. *Strategic Management Journal*, 16: 5–14.

Bhide, A. 2000. *The Origin and Evolution of New Businesses*. New York: Oxford University Press.

Bird, B. 1992. The operations of intentions in time: The emergence of new ventures. *Entrepreneurship Theory and Practice*, Fall: 11–20.

Blank, S. 2012. Why the lean start-up changes everything. *Harvard Business Review*, 91(5): 63–72.

Boone, C., & Hendricks, W. 2009. Top management team diversity and firm performance: Moderators of functional-background and locus of control diversity. *Management Science*, 55(2): 165–80.

Boulding, K. 1978. *Ecodynamics: A New Theory of Societal Evolution*. Newbury Park, CA: SAGE Publications.

Boyd, B., Henning, N., Reyna, E., Wang, D., & Welch, M. 2009. *Hybrid Organizations: New Business Models for Environmental Leadership*. Sheffield, UK: Greenleaf Publishing.

Brush, C., Manolova, T., & Edelman, L. 2008. Properties of emerging organizations: An empirical test. *Journal of Business Venturing*, 23: 547–66.

Bucherer, E., Eisert, U., & Gassmann, O. 2012. Towards systematic business model innovation: Lessons from product innovation management. *Creativity and Innovation Management*, 21(2): 183–98.

Busenitz, L., & Barney, J. 1997. Differences between entrepreneurs and managers in large organizations: Biases and hueristics in strategic decision-making. *Journal of Business Venturing*, 12(1): 9–30.

Carland, J., Hoy, F., & Carland, J. A. 1988. "Who is an entrepreneur" is a question worth asking. *Amercian Journal of Small Business*, 12(4): 33–39.

Casrud, A., & Brannback, M. 2011. Entrepreneurial motivations: What do we still need to know? *Journal of Small Business Management*, 49(1): 9–26.

Chiles, T., Tuggle, C. S., McMullen, J., Bierman, L., & Greening, D. 2010. Dynamic creation: Elaborating a radical Austrian approach to entrepreneurship. *Organization Studies*, 31: 7–46.

Clippinger, J. H. (Ed.). 1999. *The Biology of Business: Decoding the Natural Laws of Enterprise*. San Francisco: Jossey-Bass.

Csanyi, V., & Kampis, G. 1985. Autogenesis: Evolution of replicative systems. *Journal of Theoretical Biology*, 114: 303–21.

Dacin, P., Dacin, M. T., & Matear, M. 2010. Social entrepreneurship: Why we don't need a new theory and how we move forward from here. *Academy of Management Perspectives*, 24(3): 37–57.

Dew, N., Read, S., Sarasvathy, S., & Wiltbank, R. 2008. Outlines of a behavioral theory of the entrepreneurial firm. *Journal of Economic Behavior and Organization*, 66(1): 37–59.

Dew, N., Read, S., Sarasvathy, S., & Wiltbank, R. 2009. Effectual versus predictive logics in entrepreneurial decision-making: Differences between experts and novices. *Journal of Business Venturing*, 24: 287–309.

Dew, N., Reed, S., Sarasvathy, S., & Wiltbank, R. 2011. On the entrepreneurial genesis of new markets: Effectual transformations versus causal search and selection. *Journal of Evolutionary Economics*, 21: 231–53.

Drazin, R., & Sandelands, L. 1992. Autogenesis: A perspective on the process of organizing. *Organization Science*, 3: 230–49.

Ellis, T. 2010. *The New Pioneers: Sustainable Business Success through Social Innovation and Social Entrepreneurship*. West Sussex, UK: John Wiley & Sons.

Espinosa, A., Harnden, R., & Walker, J. 2008. A complexity approach to sustainability: Stafford Beer revisited. *Eurpoean Journal of Operational Research*, 187: 636–51.

Esty, D., & Winston, A. 2006. *Green to Gold*. New Haven, CT: Yale University Press.

Finke, R., & Bettle, J. 1996. *Chaotic Cognition: Principles and Applications*. Mahwah, NJ: Lawrence Erlbaum and Associates.

Fritz, R. 1989. *The Path of Least Resistance*. New York: Fawcett Columbine.

Gartner, W. 1988. "Who is an entrepreneur" is the wrong question." *American Journal of Small Business*, 12(4): 11–32.

Gartner, W. 1993. Words lead to deeds: Towards an organizational emergence vocabulary. *Journal of Business Venturing*, 8: 231–39.

Gartner, W., Bird, B., & Starr, J. 1992. Acting as if: Differentiating entrepreneurial from organizational behavior. *Entrepreneurship Theory and Practice*, 16(3): 13–30.

Gartner, W., & Brush, C. 2007. Entrepreneurship as organizing: Emergence, newness and transformation. In T. H. M. Rice (Ed.), *Praeger Perspectives on Entrepreneurship*, Vol. 3: 1–20. Westport, CT: Prager Publishers.

Garud, R., & Guiliani, A. P. 2013. A narrative perspective on entrepreneurial opportunities. *Academy of Management Review*, 38(1): 157–60.

Garud, R., Jain, S., & Kumaraswamy, A. 2002. Institutional entrepreneurship in the sponsorship of comon technological standards: The case of Sun Microsystems and Java. *Academy of Management Journal*, 45: 196–214.

Garud, R., Kumaraswamy, A., & Karnøe, P. 2010. Path dependence or path creation? *Journal of Management Studies*, 47(4): 760–74.

Gemmill, G., Boland, R., & Kolb, D. 2012. The socio-cognitive dynamics of entrepreneurial ideation. *Entrepreneurship Theory and Practice*, 36(5): 1053–73.

George, G., & Bock, A. 2011. The business model in practice and its implications for entrepreneurship research. *Entrepreneurship Theory and Practice*, 35(1): 83–111.

Goldstein, J. 2011. Probing the nature of complex systems: Parameters, modeling, interventions—Part 1. *Emergence: Complexity and Organization*, 13(3): 94–121.

Goldstein, J., Hazy, J., & Lichtenstein, B. 2010. *Complexity and the Nexus of Leadership: Leveraging Nonlinear Science to Create Ecologies of Innovation.* New York: Palgrave Macmillan.

Groves, K., Vance, C., & Choi, T. 2011. Examining entrepreneurial cognition: An occupational analysis of balanced linear and nonlinear thinking and entrepreneurship success. *Journal of Small Business Management*, 49(3): 438–66.

Hayek, F. 1945. The use of knowledge in society. *American Economic Review*, 35: 519–30.

Hayek, F. 1967. *Studies in Philosophy, Politics and Economics.* Chicago: University of Chicago Press.

Katz, J., & Gartner, W. 1988. Properties of emerging organizations. *Academy of Management Review*, 13: 429–41.

Kearney, E., Gebert, D., & Voelpel, S. 2009. When and how diversity benefits teams: The importance of team members' need for cognition *Academy of Management Journal*, 52(3): 581–98.

Knott, A. M. 2003. Persistent heterogeneity and sustainable innovation. *Strategic Management Journal*, 24(8): 687–705.

Levie, J., & Lichtenstein, B. 2010. A terminal assessment of stages theory: Introducing a dynamic states approach to entrepreneurship. *Entrepreneurship Theory and Practice*, 34(2–March): 314–54.

Lichtenstein, B. 2009. Moving far from far-from-equliibrium: Opportunity tension as the catalyst of emergence. *Emergence: Complexity and Organization*, 11(4): 15–25.

Lichtenstein, B., Dooley, K., & Lumpkin, T. 2006. Measuring emergence in the dynamics of new venture creation. *Journal of Business Venturing*, 21: 153–75.

Lindgren, P. 2012. Business model innovation leadership: How do SMEs strategically lead business model innovation? *Journal of Business and Management*, 7(14): 53–66.

McKelvey, B. 2004. Toward a complexity science of entrepreneurship. *Journal of Business Venturing*, 19: 313–42.

McMullan, J., Plummer, L., & Acs, Z. 2007. What is an entrepreneurial opportunity. *Small Business Economics*, 28: 273–83.

Miles, R., Miles, G., & Snow, C. 2006. Collaborative entrepreneurship: A business model for continuous innovation. *Organizational Dynamics*, 35(1): 1–11.

Miller, J. G. 1978. *Living Systems.* New York: McGraw-Hill.

Mitchell, R., Parker, V., & Giles, M. 2012. Open-mindedness in diverse team performance: Investigating a three-way interaction. *International Journal of Human Resource Management*, 23(17): 3652–72.

Morris, M., Schindette, M., & Allen, J. 2005. The entrepreneur's business model: Towards a unified perspective. *Journal of Business Research*, 58(6): 726–35,

Mullins, J. 2006. *The New Business Road Test.* New York: Financial Times Press.

Nicolis, G., & Prigogine, I. 1989. *Exploring Complexity.* New York: W. H. Freeman.

Obloj, T., Obloj, K., & Pratt, M. 2010. Dominant logic and the entrepreneurial firms' performance in a transition economy. *Entrepreneurship Theory and Practice*, 34(1): 151–71.

Odum, H., & Odum, E. 1976. *Energy Basis for Man and Nture.* New York: McGraw Hill.

Osterwalder, A. 2009. How to systematically build business models beyond profit. SlideShare.com. http://www.slideshare.net/Alex.Osterwalder/business-models-beyond-profit-social-entrepreneurship-lecture-wise-etienne-eichenberger-iqbal-quadir-grameen-bank-grameen-phone

Osterwalder, A. 2010. What is a business model. SlideShare.com. http://www.slideshare.net/Alex.Osterwalder/what-is-a-business-model

Osterwalder, A., & Pigneur, Y. 2010. *Business Model Generation: A Handbook for Visionaries, Game Changers, and Challengers.* Hoboken, NJ: John Wiley & Sons.

Page, S. 2007. *The Difference: How the Power of Diversity Creates Bettter Groups, Firms, Schools, and Societies*. Princeton, NJ: Princeton University Press.

Pantzar, M., & Csanyi, V. 1991. The replicative model of the evolution of the business organization. *Journal of Social and Biological Structures*, 14: 149–63.

Prahalad, C. K., & Bettis, R. 1986. The dominant logic: A new lingage between diversity and performance. *Strategic Management Journal*, 7: 485–501.

Rindova, V., & Fombrun, C. 2001. Entrepreneurial action in the creation of the specialty coffee niche. In C. B. Schoonhoven & E. Romanelli (Eds.), *The Entrepreneurship Dynamic* (236–61). Palo Alto, CA: Stanford University Press.

Rothschild, M. 1992. *Bionomics: Economy as Ecosystem*. New York: Holt & Company.

Sarasson, Y., Dean, T., & Hilliard, B. 2006. Entrepreneurship as the nexus of individual and opportunity: A structuration view. *Journal of Business Venturing*, 21: 286–305.

Sarasvathy, S. 2001. Causation and effectuation: Toward a theoretical shift from economic inevitability to entrepreneurial contingency. *Academy of Management Review*, 26: 243–63.

Scott, R. 1981. *Organizations: Rational, Natural, and Open Systems*. Upper Saddle River, NJ: Prentice-Hall.

Senge, P., Smith, B., Krushwitz, N., Laur, J., & Schley, S. 2008. *The Necessary Revolution*. New York: Doubleday.

Shane, S. 2000. Prior knowledge and the discovery of entrepreneurial opportunities. *Organization Science*, 11: 448–69.

Shane, S. 2005. *Finding Fertile Ground: Identifying Extraordinary Opportunities for New Ventures*. Upper Saddle River, NJ: Wharton School/Pearson Education.

Shane, S., & Venkataraman, S. 2000. The promise of entrepreneurship as a field of research. *Academy of Management Review*, 25: 217–26.

Shaver, K., & Scott, L. 1991. Person, process, choice: The psychology new venture creation. *Entrepreneurship Theory and Practice*, 16(2): 23–46.

Slevin, D., & Covin, J. 1997. Time, growth, complexity, and transitions: Entrepreneurial challenges for the future. *Entrepreneurship Theory and Practice*, 22(2 Winter): 53–68.

Sulis, W., & Combs, A. (Eds.). 1996. *Nonlinear Dynamics in Human Behavior*. Singapore: World Scientific Press.

Thompson, J. 1967. *Organizations in Action*. New York: McGraw Hill.

Timmons, J. 1999. *New Venture Creation* (5th ed.). Homewood, IL: Richard D. Irwin.

Tsoukas, H., & Chia, R. 2002. On organizational becoming: Rethinking organizational change. *Organization Science*, 13: 567–83.

Varela, F. 1979. *Principles of Biological Autonomy*. New York: North Holland.

von Bertalanffy, L. 1956. General system theory. *General Systems*, 1: 1–10.

Webster's. 1996. *Merriam-Webster's Collegiate Dictionary* (10th ed.). Springfield, MA: Merriam-Webster, Inc.

Xu, Y. 2011. Entrepreneurial social capital and cognitive model of innovation. *Management Research Review*, 34(8): 910–26.

Zott, C., & Amit, R. 2007. Business model design and the performance of entrepreneurial firms. *Organization Science*, 18(2): 181–99.

CHAPTER 9

Outcomes of Generative Emergence

The process that leads to generative emergence will result in one of several outcomes. Emergence scholars have for many years identified a continuum of emergence outcomes (e.g., Crutchfield, 1994; Bedau, 1997; Holland, 1998; Goldstein, 2000, 2002; McKelvey, 2001, 2004; Bar-Yam, 2004; Andriani & McKelvey, 2009). Drawing on this work, I have identified four "points" on a continuum of emergence outcomes. The first point is dissolution, a lack of emergence. This outcome (or lack of an outcome) is rarely described in the literature, but it is perhaps the most likely to occur. So as the first possible outcome, an organizing effort may end in dissolution. This, and the other three outcomes, are described in the present chapter.

NOT EMERGENCE—DISSOLUTION

Perhaps the most likely outcome of an emergence process is *no* emergence, due to a dissolution of the system or a cessation the effort to create a new dynamic state. Given how often this occurs, it seems surprising that management research has rarely explored the dynamics of failure or the dissolution of emerging systems. Virtually every description of emergence or self-organization focuses on the positive outcomes of the process—this is true for my own work as well.[1] The implication from this complexity literature is that only positive outcomes will accrue from emergence; however, the opposite is also likely. As one of my dissertation advisers adjured about any owner or executive, "You can self-organize your company right off a cliff!"

Of course, this lack of attention to failure is part of the pervasive bias for success that is endemic to management in general, and entrepreneurship in particular. A success bias leads to limitations in decision-making ability and cognitive acuity (Kahneman, Slovic, & Tversky, 1982) and in a lack of learning or action (Levinthal & March, 1993; Denrell, 2003). In entrepreneurship this problem is ubiquitous because of the problem of "sampling on the dependent variable," whereby researchers choose existing—successful—companies as the basis of their samples, thus disregarding the failures and all that failure can teach.

In the same way that many innovations and organizations fail, so too emergence as a whole is not the panacea that many complexity science authors would have us believe. Instead, a more robust theory of emergence would acknowledge that the (re)creation of the system involves so many uncertainties and challenges that positive outcomes, or results that are adaptive for the organization, are hardly guaranteed. Thus, dissolution is an equally likely outcome of the emergence process. For these reasons and more, I include failure as the "0th degree" of emergence.

Lichtenstein (2000) provides a good example of how "self-organization" can lead to a catastrophic outcome, in my description of ApplySci, a venture-capitalized high-potential start-up. There, the peak of tension was well expressed by one senior project manager: "I think we're standing at the edge of a precipice, and the earth is crumbling beneath us" (Lichtenstein, 2000, p. 135). In this case, the reorganization was unsuccessful: The newly appointed CEO pursued a blue-sky strategy that was not well connected to the venture's strengths, she made a series of cost-cutting moves that severely limited the firm's capacity to respond to potential new orders, and her strong decision-making style disenfranchised the remaining employees. "The result was a feeling of discouragement, frustration and chaos" (Lichtenstein, 2000, p. 136), which led to an abrupt acquisition of the venture and subsequent loss of nearly $8,000,000 in investments. Thus, there was no "re-emergence" at ApplySci; instead it experienced a dramatic loss of value-creation activities and the dissolution of the organization.

If a new dynamic state does arise, there are several different types of possible outcomes of emergence. Following Goldstein's (1999) definition, I argue that there is a continuum of emergence outcomes that reflects three degrees of emergence. These are first-degree order emergence, second-degree systemic emergence, and third-degree radical emergence.

FIRST–DEGREE ORDER EMERGENCE: AGENT INTERACTIONS THAT LEAD TO INTERNAL ORDER

The first-degree of emergence—the initial level of complexity that can arise from an emergence process—is the creation of a persistent pattern or structure within a dynamic system. In first-degree emergence the system remains constant; no new system emerges. Instead, what emerges is an internal pattern or structure, which remains relatively stable over time. An emergent structure does not create a new *level* of order; it simply adds to the richness of the system under observation. As Crutchfield (1994) noted, a first-degree emergent pattern is usually measured and modeled post hoc—after its creation and from outside the system. Further, the system and its participants (agents) may be unaware that something has actually emerged (Crutchfield, 1994).

Almost all NK studies exemplify first-degree emergence. For example, Dan Levinthal and his collaborators have shown how adaptation and innovation are affected by certain patterns of interdependence, whether within firms (Levinthal, 1997; Levinthal & Warglien, 1999) or across them (Levinthal & Myatt, 1994; Baum, 1999). Nicolaj Siggelkow and his colleagues have shown how patterns of innovation success and competitive advantage can rely on the right balance of exploration and exploitation (Siggelkow & Rivkin, 2005, 2006; Porter & Siggelkow, 2008). Ganco and Agarwal (2009) show how entrepreneurial firms generate internal structures on the basis of their strategic choices—what emerges are structural components in existing ventures. Fleming and Sorenson (2001) identified the internal pattern of innovation that distinguishes which patent-based inventions were likely to be successful. As with the other examples, the pattern represents an internal and post-hoc order that is not, in and of itself, a unique "level" of organizing. McKelvey and I summarized this research (Lichtenstein & McKelvey, 2011, p. 355):

> There is not actually very much emergence, per se, in the *NK* model. For the most part, self-organization is limited to agent connections (networks) with nearest neighbors. For example, when Kauffman studies the effects of species of varying size, S, he does so by changing S as a control parameter, not by allowing the size of S (groups) to emerge from agent interactions. In this respect most *NK* models represent a sophisticated example of Type 1 emergence.

Sawyer (2005) is far more critical of computational studies, focusing on their inability to model mutual causality, let alone an emergence of macro-level properties:

> In those simulations in which macroproperties influence individual action, those macroproperties do not themselves emerge from the simulations but are specified in advance by the designers.... A second problem ... is that agents do not have any perception of the emergent collective entity.... No agent has awareness of its own group as an entity, and agents that are not in a group have no way of recognizing that the group exists or who its members are.[2] (pp. 162–163, 165–166)

Qualitative researchers have identified first-degree emergence. The most prominent example is the formation of "semistructures" that were found in the most successful new product development teams (Brown & Eisenhardt, 1997, 1998). These were described as patterns of organizing, configurations of activity and communication that emerged (or didn't) in response to the dynamic environment for innovation in the firm. A similar referent is the "self-organization" of structures in high-growth entrepreneurial companies (Nicholls-Nixon, 2005), which appear to improve performance without generating a distinct level or unit of organizing in the firm.

In all of these examples, the outcomes of emergence are an internal order or pattern that improves the functioning of the system but without adding a new level of order.[3]

Power Laws as First-Degree Emergence

A stronger version of first-degree emergence occurs when a single process, rule, or algorithm generates a "macro-pattern" of order across many scales (Casti, 1994), leading to a "power law." A power law is a mathematical description of dynamics that are invariant across many orders of magnitude (Andriani & McKelvey, 2007, 2009). In technical terms, when the log-log distribution of two system dimensions is a straight line—as Zipf (1949) found for the rank vs. size of all U.S. cities—the emergent outcomes represent a "power law" which reflects some process that is invariant across scales. As Andriani and McKelvey (2007) describe,

> If plotted on double-log paper, Pareto distributions show the distinctive *"power law"* signature—a negatively sloping straight line. Power laws seem ubiquitous.... They apply to earthquakes, web hits, phone calls, wealth . . . cities, and firms. Power law phenomena call for *"scale-free theories"* because the same cause and explanation apply to each of the different levels. They exhibit the *power law signature* because they shrink by a fixed ratio.

Their 2007 paper identifies more than 80 power law phenomena, many of which are social processes. Two further examples confirm the point. As mentioned in Chapter 3, Stanley et al. (1996), found that a single scaling law was able to fully explain the relationship between size and structure across *seven orders of magnitude*. In biology, West, Brown, and Enquist (1997) demonstrated a power law relationship between the mass and metabolism of virtually any organism and its components, across 27 orders of magnitude (of mass).

These power laws are more pervasive than first-degree emergence; however, they still occur *within* one level of analysis, rather than across more than one level. That is, the emergent phenomena that Stanley et al. found pertain to structuring within manufacturing firms; in other words, the firm is the unit of analysis. Thus, even though the same pattern was found across seven orders of magnitude, the power law relationship is found *within* the firm, not between structures within work teams, or structures of manufacturing alliances, or patterns of relationships across industries.

Overall, power laws represents a strong type of first-degree emergence, a type that is critical for understanding dynamic systems. In particular, Brock (2000, p. 30) suggested that power laws are *the* key contribution of complexity science, observing that the study of complexity "tries to understand the forces that underlie the patterns or scaling laws that develop as newly ordered systems emerge."

SECOND-DEGREE SYSTEMIC EMERGENCE: CREATION OF A NEW LEVEL OF ORDER

The second degree of emergence refers to the creation of a new level of order or unit of analysis. It relies on qualitative novelty—the creation of a coherent system that is qualitatively different from the components that make it up—but without an expectation that the emergent entity will display downward causation that can affects its components. Similarly, second-degree emergence refers to the creation of a macro-level of order, but with less emphasis on nonreducibility. As such, second-degree emergence has parallels to weak emergence (Salthe, 1985; Bedau, 1997, 2002; Wimsatt, 1997; Schröder, 1998; Chalmers, 2006).

Examples of second-degree emergence include some organizational innovations, some projects and initiatives, some product launches, and some internal ventures. Studies of second-degree emergence highlight the creation of new systems without determining if and how those systems lead to changes in the components themselves. A good example is the way that Shane (2000) and others showed how distinct business opportunities are developed and enacted over time. For these researchers, business opportunities are relatively objective entities whose emergence presents distinct possibilities for entrepreneurs (Lumpkin & Lichtenstein, 2005; Alvarez & Barney, 2007), allowing them to capitalize on their skills, social networks, and resource bases without making substantive changes. Such entities reflect second-degree emergence.

Second-degree emergence can also occur during the new-venture organizing process, in which the entrepreneur conceptualizes a new business context or idea or product. For example, Lichtenstein, Dooley, and Lumpkin (2006) showed how one entrepreneur completely redefined her product, market, and organizing context in the midst of her start-up, creating a new "level" of organizing for the venture. Specifically, the original venture, HealthInfo, became subsumed within a newly emergent corporate structure, HealthUSA (Lichtenstein et al., 2006, p. 161):

> [T]he entrepreneur has reinterpreted her organizing efforts by creating a corporate entity HealthUSA, with HealthInfo being one of the component businesses. HealthUSA is a broader, more encompassing business concept than HealthInfo; it re-contextualizes the business opportunity.... The birth of HealthUSA involves the creation of a qualitatively new level of order within her organizing, for a corporation with several member companies is a more encompassing business concept than just one of those companies alone.

Intriguingly, this "emergence event" did not lead to any conscious shifts in her activities nor in her long-term values, although our analysis revealed subtle but significant changes in her organizing efforts. In this way, the new level was created but did not generate discernable downward causal effects.

A similar example was uncovered by Cheng and Van de Ven (1996) in their reanalysis of organizing shifts in an innovation project. They used post-hoc methods for measuring emergence, applying deterministic chaos theory to test for the emergence of a new "strange attractor" in the data. They found such a wholesale shift reflecting the emergence of a new "epoch" in the organizing process—a new system of behavior and outcome arose in the project. Here again, although a new system emerged, it did not seem to alter the longer-term results of the project, nor did it seem to have causal influence on the members of the venture. Thus, I suggest that this shift may be an example of second-degree emergence.

In corporate settings, studies have explained how "new entry" can be enacted (Burgelman, 1983; Lumpkin & Dess, 1996) by mid-level managers. Yet, these two studies do not present evidence that the emergence of the new entity leads to substantive changes in its champions or in the components of the product or its design. Other examples include the emergence and re-emergence of formal organizing systems (Garud, Kumaraswamy, & Sambamurthy, 2006) which also represent new systemwide changes but which don't fundamentally alter the behavior of the employees within them.

THIRD-DEGREE RADICAL EMERGENCE: A NEW LEVEL WITH MUTUAL CAUSALITY

The third and strongest form of emergence adds the property of mutual causality, through downward causation, whereby the newly emergent entity exerts a discernable influence on its components, but also through upward causation, whereby the components of the system—the individuals and certain resources—play a role in determining what the emerging system will become. Third-degree generative emergence emphasizes all five qualities that define emergence, including higher degrees of qualitative novelty, less reducibility, higher mutual causality, more agency and structurations, and greater amounts of increased capacity (see Chapter 4).

A prime example of third-degree radical emergence is the successful start-up of a new entrepreneurial venture. As scholars have shown, the organizing period of new venture creation is composed of a stream of start-up behaviors intended to make the organization "known" to its environment (Gartner, 1993; Gartner & Starr, 1993; Gartner & Carter, 2003). At a critical point of momentum and positive feedback (Lichtenstein & Kurjanowicz, 2010), the entrepreneur denotes that the nascent company has "started" (Bygrave & Hofer, 1991; Gartner, Carter, & Reynolds, 2004; Gartner, Shaver, Carter, & Reynolds, 2004). At that point the business firm emerges as a semi-autonomous agent within a particular industry (Brush, Manolova, & Edelman, 2008), reflecting third-degree emergence.

The creation of the firm represents true qualitative novelty, as described by Gartner, Bird, and Starr (1992, pp. 15, 17):

> The differences between emerging and existing organizations are not "differences in degree" across certain dimensions, but quantum differences between the two types.... The process of change from the emerging organization to the existing organization is not the "growth" of certain variables, but an entirely new reconstitution, a "gestalt."

Moreover, in radical emergence the new entity gains an *identity* that cannot be reduced to the founder, the employees, or the value they create. Instead, the venture now enacts wholly new behaviors, including, for example, being legally recognized, becoming a competitor within the industry, and having a credit rating. Likewise, third-degree emergence causes, and is caused by, changes in the perceptions and behaviors of its employees, customers, suppliers, and other stakeholders. The organization from that point on encompasses a kind of agency—it "behaves" in tangible ways, and as predicted in the idea of structionings, it is very hard to identify where the components are and where the organization is as a whole. Finally, the viability of the venture is due to the increased capacity that is achieved—something more is added because of its emergence.

A different example of third-degree emergence and mutual causation at its heart is the study by Donde Plowman and her students (Plowman et al., 2007), of radical emergence at "Mission Church." According to their data the emergent was sparked by an informal idea from a member's friend, to produce a one-time initiative for feeding local homeless people. However, this action became the catalyst for dramatic changes that emerged within the initiative and throughout the church itself. In particular, the success of the first Sunday breakfast sparked an unexpected enthusiasm among its organizers, leading to a year-long series of self-organized and self-funded events. As the visibility of the initiative grew, its leaders altered their tactics and modes of organizing, focusing first on resource acquisition (e.g., creating new space, gaining volunteers with specific expertise) and later on broader efforts to institutionalize the effort. Moreover, the attitude of the church leaders also transformed as the initially innocuous project soon became the focal point for a dramatic shift in the mission of the entire organization.

Over time, the behaviors and decisions of the community and its pastors were strongly influenced by the growing legitimacy and publicity of the initiative, leading to even more radical moves by the leaders, significant shifts in church membership, and changes in the way the community related to the church as a whole. The emergent outcomes (e.g., the growth of the initiative; the reformulation of the church's mission around the initiative) and their impact on agent behaviors (e.g., the internal development of the organizing committee; dramatic public actions by the pastors) were interdependent and co-evolving, creating a accelerating feedback loop that strengthened both the system and its components, exemplifying radical emergence.

Another example of third-degree emergence can be shown in some studies of industry creation, in which a new population comes into being as a distinct unit of order, *and* that new order generates sociological and institutional properties that constrain and govern the behavior of its component firms. For example, Aldrich (1999) and Aldrich and Reuf (2006, Chapter 9) have suggested how the strategies facilitating industry emergence can impact organizational-level processes of learning and legitimacy. Likewise, Low and Abrahamson (1997) showed how an emerging firm's organizing tactics and internal structure may be determined by the rate at which a new industry is forming. Note that these mutually causal effects occur as the industry is emerging (co-evolving), long before the effects of institutional norms (DiMaggio & Powell, 1983), industry archetypes (Greenwood & Hinings, 1993), and the dynamics of density dependence (Carroll, 1985, 1988) become salient. In these ways the co-evolutionary creation of a new industry illustrates the third degree of emergence.

SUMMARY AND NEXT STEPS

In sum, the process of generative emergence leads to a range of outcomes—in many cases failure, and if success, then either first-degree order emergence, second-degree systems emergence, or third-degree radical emergence. These outcomes thus complete the introduction to generative emergence. What remains is a full presentation of the *process* of generative emergence—the five phases that lead to third-degree radical emergence. In the following five chapters, each of the phases will be explored in depth, starting with disequilibrium organizing.

NOTES

1. As a few examples, consider Allen (1982); Smith and Gemmill (1991); Goldstein (1994); Smith and Comer (1994); Carley (1990, 1999); Zohar and Borkman (1997); Choi, Dooley, and Rungtusanatham (2001); Fuller and Moran (2001); Chiles, Meyer, and Hench (2004); Garud, Kumaraswamy, and Sambamurthy (2006); Plowman et al. (2007); and Fuller, Warren, and Argyle (2008). In contrast, note the more balanced views of Brian Arthur (1989, 1990), for example, who takes a more agnostic view of the outcomes of a self-reinforcing process.
2. The same result can be seen through the lens of qualitative novelty. As I described earlier, a key element of qualitative novelty is that describing the emergent requires the use of a different language or discipline than that used to describe the agents. However, this is not the case for computational emergence. For example, in order to describe coherent structures in cellular automata, such as "gliders" in the Game of Life, one needs to compare them to the noncoherent patterns in the simulation. Thus the *same language* is necessary to identify the emergent properties as is used to describe the nonemergent ones. As another example, note how Holland (1998, p. 191) defines the "new levels" that emerge from a constrained generating procedure: "[T]he resulting composite . . . can itself be

characterized as a mechanism—a subassembly that can be used to form still more complex mechanisms." Here he characterizes the mechanism using a singular language that defines the set of states, inputs, and transition functions used to generate the more complex level. As such, all three "levels" require the same scientific language; thus they represent somewhat less novel forms of emergence, i.e., first-degree emergence.
3. That is, an emergent pattern in a computational system may add functional capability in terms of information processing, but it does not lead to a new "level" in the system, nor to the transformation of the system components themselves. Computational modeling of emergence is highly successful and has given social scientists useful insights, but it studies only the first degree of possible outcomes of emergence. We (McKelvey & Lichtenstein, 2007; Lichtenstein & McKelvey, 2011) have identified some instances of higher-order organizing that computational emergence does achieve. Likewise, Sawyer (2005, Chapter 8) provides a variety of computational templates that may yet evolve to reveal emergence. Still, the challenges explain why I am introducing generative emergence, which captures far more dimensions of creation than computational models have been able to accomplish. Whether computational modeling will ever accomplish further degrees of specification remains to be seen. Many scholars believe that agent-based models have the potential to offer very sophisticated results (Sawyer, 2005). In particular, several key studies have shown how computational results have parallel findings in the real world (see Axelrod, Mitchell, Thomas, Bennett, & Bruder, 1995; Carley, 1996; Carley & Svoboda, 1996).

REFERENCES

Aldrich, H. 1999. *Organizations Evolving*. Newbury Park, CA: SAGE Publications.
Aldrich, H., & Reuf, M. 2006. *Organizations Evolving* (2nd ed.). Thousand Oaks, CA: SAGE Publications.
Alvarez, S., & Barney, J. 2007. Discovery and creation: Alternative theories of entrepreneurial action. *Strategic Entrepreneurship Journal*, 1: 11–27.
Andriani, P., & McKelvey, B. 2007. Beyond Gaussian averages: Redirecting organization science toward extreme events and power laws. *Journal of International Business Studies*, 38: 1212–30.
Andriani, P., & McKelvey, B. 2009. From Gaussian to Paretian thinking: Causes and implications of power laws in organizations. *Organization Science*, 20: 1053–71.
Axelrod, R., Mitchell, W., Thomas, R., Bennett, D. S., & Bruderer, E. 1995. Coalition formation in standard-setting alliances. *Management Science*, 41: 1493–508.
Bar-Yam, Y. 2004. A mathematical theory of strong emergence using mutliscale variety. *Complexity*, 9(6): 15–24.
Baum, J. 1999. Whole-part coevolutionary competition in organizations. In J. Baum & B. McKelvey (Eds.), *Variations in Organization Science* (113–36). Thousand Oaks, CA: SAGE Publications.
Bedau, M. 1997. Weak emergence. *Philosophical Perspectives*, 11 (Mind, Causation, and World): 375–99.
Bedau, M. 2002. Downward causation and the autonomy of weak emergence. *Principia*, 6(1): 5–50.
Brock, W. A. 2000. Some Santa Fe scenery. In D. Colander (Ed.), *The Complexity Vision and the Teaching of Economics* (29–49). Chelternham, UK: Edward Elgar.
Brown, S., & Eisenhardt, K. 1997. The art of continuous change: Linking complexity theory and time-based evolution in relentlessly shifting organizations. *Administrative Science Quarterly*, 42: 1–34.

Brown, S., & Eisenhardt, K. 1998. *Competing on the Edge.* Boston: Harvard Business School Press.
Brush, C., Manolova, T., & Edelman, L. 2008. Properties of emerging organizations: An empirical test. *Journal of Business Venturing,* 23: 547–66.
Burgelman, R. 1983. A process model of internal corporate venturing in the diversified major firm. *Administrative Science Quarterly,* 28: 223–44.
Bygrave, W., & Hofer, C. 1991. Theorizing about entrepreneurship. *Entrepreneurship Theory and Practice,* 16(2): 13–23.
Carley, K. 1996. A comparison of artificial and human organizations. *Journal of Economic Behavior and Organization,* 31: 175–91.
Carley, K., & Svoboda, D. M. 1996. Modeling organization adaptation as a simulated annealing process. *Sociological Methods and Research,* 25: 138–68.
Carroll, G. 1985. Concentration and specialization: The dynamics of niche width in organizational populations. *American Journal of Sociology,* 90: 1262–83.
Carroll, G. (Ed.). 1988. *Ecological Models of Organization.* Cambridge, MA: Ballinger.
Casti, J. 1994. *Complexification.* New York: Harper Perennial.
Chalmers, D. 2006. Strong and weak emergence. In P. Clayton & P. Davies (Eds.), *The Re-Emergence of Emergence: The Emergentist Hypothesis from Science to Religion* (244–56). New York: Oxford University Press.
Cheng, Y., & Van de Ven, A. 1996. The innovation journey: Order out of chaos? *Organization Science,* 6: 593–614.
Crutchfield, J. 1994. Is anything ever new? Considering emergence. In G. Cowan, D. Pines, & D. Meltzer (Eds.), *Complexity: Metaphors, Models, and Realty* (479–97). Reading, MA: Addison-Wesley.
Denrell, J. 2003. Vicarious learning, understmpling of failure, and the myths of management. *Organization Science,* 14(3): 227–43.
DiMaggio, P., & Powell, W. 1983. The iron cage revisited: Institutional isomorphism and collective rationality in organizational fields. *American Sociological Review,* 48: 147–60.
Fleming, L., & Sorenson, O. 2001. Technology as a complex adaptive system. *Research Policy,* 30: 1019–39.
Ganco, M., & Agarwal, R. 2009. Performance differentials between diversifying entrants and entrepreneurial start-ups: A complexity approach. *Academy of Management Review,* 34: 228–53.
Gartner, B., & Starr, J. 1993. The nature of entrepreneruial work. In S. Birley, & I. MacMillan (Eds.), *Entrepreneurship Research: Global Perspectives.* Amsterdam: North-Holland.
Gartner, W. 1993. Words lead to deeds: Towards an organizational emergence vocabulary. *Journal of Business Venturing,* 8: 231–39.
Gartner, W., Bird, B., & Starr, J. 1992. Acting as if: Differentiating entrepreneurial from organizational behavior. *Entrepreneurship Theory and Practice,* 16(3): 13–30.
Gartner, W., & Carter, N. 2003. Entrepreneurial behavior and firm organizing processes. In Z. J. Acs & D. B. Audretsch (Eds.), *Handbook of Entrepreneurship Research* (195–221). Boston: Kluwer.
Gartner, W., Carter, N., & Reynolds, P. 2004. Business start-up activities. In W. Gartner, K. Shaver, N. Carter, & P. Reynolds (Eds.), *Handbook of Entrepreneurial Dynamics* (285–98). Thousand Oaks, CA: SAGE Publications.
Gartner, W., Shaver, K., Carter, N., & Reynolds, P. (Eds.). 2004. *Handbook of Entrepreneurial Dynamics.* Thousand Oaks, CA: SAGE Publications.
Garud, R., Kumaraswamy, A., & Sambamurthy, V. 2006. Emergent by design: Performance and transformation at Infosys Technologies. *Organization Science,* 17: 277–86.

Goldstein, J. 2000. Emergence: A concept amid a thicket of conceptual snares. *Emergence*, 2(1): 5–22.
Goldstein, J. 2002. The singular nature of emergent levels: Suggestions for a theory of emergence. *Nonlinear Dynamics, Psychology and Life Sciences*, 6: 293–309.
Greenwood, R., & Hinings, C. R. 1993. Understanding strategic change: The contribution of archetypes. *Academy of Management Journal*, 36: 1052–81.
Holland, J. 1998. *Emergence: From Chaos to Order*. Cambridge, MA: Perseus Books.
Kahneman, D., Slovic, P., & Tversky, A. (Eds.). 1982. *Judgment under Uncertainty: Hueristics and Biases*. New York: Cambridge University Press.
Levinthal, D. 1997. Adaptation on rugged landscapes. *Management Science*, 43: 934–50.
Levinthal, D., & March, J. 1993. The myopia of learning. *Strategic Management Journal*, 14(Special Winter Issue): 95–112.
Levinthal, D., & Myatt, J. 1994. Co-evolution of capabilities and industry: The evolution of mutual fund processing. *Strategic Management Journal*, 15(Special Issue): 45–62.
Levinthal, D., & Warglien, M. 1999. Landscape deisgn: Designing for local action in complex worlds. *Organization Science*, 10(3): 342–57.
Lichtenstein, B., Carter, N., Dooley, K., & Gartner, W. 2007. Complexity dynamics of nascent entrepreneurship. *Journal of Business Venturing*, 22: 236–61.
Lichtenstein, B., Dooley, K., & Lumpkin, T. 2006. Measuring emergence in the dynamics of new venture creation. *Journal of Business Venturing*, 21: 153–75.
Lichtenstein, B., & Kurjanowicz, B. 2010. Tangibility, momentum, and the emergence of The Republic of Tea. *ENTER Journal*, 1: 125–48.
Lichtenstein, B., & McKelvey, B. 2011. Four types of emergence: A typology of complexity and its implications for a science of management. *International Journal of Complexity in Leadership and Management*, 1(4): 339–78.
Low, M., & Abrahamson, E. 1997. Movements, bandwagons, and clones: Industry evolution and the entrepreneurial process. *Journal of Business Venturing*, 12: 435–58.
Lumpkin, G. T., & Dess, G. 1996. Clarifying the entrepreneurial orientation construct and linking it to performance. *Academy of Management Review*, 21: 135–72.
Lumpkin, T., & Lichtenstein, B. 2005. The role of organizational learning in the opportunity recognition process. *Entrepreneurship Theory and Practice*, 29(4): 451–72.
McKelvey, B. 2001. What is complexity science? It is really order creation science. *Emergence*, 3(1): 137–57.
McKelvey, B. 2004. Toward a 0th law of thermodynamics: Order creation complexity dynamics from physics and biology to bioeconomics. *Bioeconomics*, 6: 65–96.
McKelvey, B., & Lichtenstein, B. 2007. Leadership in the four stages of emergence. In J. Hazy, J. Goldstein, & B. Lichtenstein (Eds.), *Complex Systems Leadership Theory* (93–108). Boston: ISCE Publishing.
Nicholls-Nixon, C. 2005. Rapid growth and high performance: The entrepreneur's "impossible dream?" *Academy of Management Executive*, 19(1): 77–89.
Plowman, D. A., Baker, L., Beck, T., Kulkarni, M., Solansky, S., & Travis, D. 2007. Radical change accidentally: The emergence and amplification of small change. *Academy of Management Journal*, 50: 515–43.
Porter, M., & Siggelkow, N. 2008. Contextual interactions within activity systems and sustainability of competitive advantage. *Academy of Management Perspectives*, 22(2): 34–56.
Salthe, S. 1985. *Evolving Hierarchical Systems: Their Structure and Representation*. New York: Columbia University Press.
Schröder, J. 1998. Emergence: Non-deducibility or downwards causation? *Philosophical Quarterly*, 48(193): 433–52.

Shane, S. 2000. Prior knowledge and the discovery of entrepreneurial opportunities. *Organization Science*, 11: 448–69.
Siggelkow, N., & Rivkin, J. 2005. Speed and search: Designing organizations for turbulence and complexity. *Organization Science*, 16: 101–22.
Siggelkow, N., & Rivkin, J. 2006. When exploration backfires: Unintended consequences of multilevel organizational search. *Academy of Management Journal*, 49: 779–96.
Stanley, M., Amaral, L., Buldyrev, S., Havlin, S., Leschhorn, H., Maass, P., Salinger, M., & Stanley, E. 1996. Scaling behavior in the growth of companies. *Nature*, 379: 804–806.
West, B., Brown, J. H., & Enquist, B. J. 1997. A general model for the origin of allometric scaling laws in biology. *Science*, 274(4, #5309): 122–26.
Wimsatt, W. 1997. Aggregativity: Reductive hueristics for finding emergence. *Philosophy of Science*, 64(Supplement): S372-S384.
Zipf, G. K. 1949. *Human Behavior and the Principle of Least Effort*. New York: Hafner.

CHAPTER 10

Phase 1: Disequilibrium Organizing

In the previous several chapters I have pursued a rigorous mapping of emerging dissipative structures onto emerging social structures, with two key results. On the one hand, my analysis found a strong dissimilarity in the *conditions* that give rise to each type of emergence. Specifically, the emergence of dissipative structures in thermodynamic systems are an example of exo-organizing, whereas the emergence of social entities is based in the prototype of generative emergence. That difference clarifies the distinct drivers of exo-organizing versus generative emergence.

My analysis also showed strong similarities in the *process* by which emergence occurs in both contexts. That process includes five phases of generative emergence; these are as follows:

Phase 1: disequilibrium organizing
Phase 2: stress and experiments
Phase 3: amplification to a critical threshold or event
Phase 4: new order through recombination
Phase 5: stabilizing feedback

The next five chapters will explore each of these phases more fully. Each will present a description of the phase, and connect it to research literature in entrepreneurship, strategy, sociology, complexity science, organization theory, and management in general. Then, examples of each phase of change will be presented, mainly from unpublished data in my dissertation,[1] as well as other published studies.

The first phase, disequilibrium organizing, has several key elements that need to be explained. The first is the driver of disequilibrium, namely opportunity tension. A second element of disequilibrium organizing is operational, namely, the metrics that would allow for a convincing presentation of the process. Third is the container itself—the boundary, the system within which disequilibrium organizing takes place.

OPPORTUNITY TENSION: THE ORIGIN OF EMERGENCE

What is it that motivates someone to start an organizing process? In more precise terms, what *drives* the origin of generative emergence? What motivates a person's actions to create an organization, or any social initiative, any value-creating endeavor? A useful way to explore these questions is through the literature of entrepreneurship, which was the first social science to explore emergence (Schumpeter, 1934). Entrepreneurship is also a useful entry point because it has had the longest history of using complexity science to explain social organizing (Bygrave, 1989; Stevenson & Harmeling, 1990; see Lichtenstein, 2011).

Entrepreneurship researchers have focused on two drivers of emergence. The first is the organizing behaviors themselves—the actions entrepreneurs take to create new organizations. Many studies have explored this behavioral framework; some key examples include Katz and Gartner (1988); Gartner, Bird, and Starr (1992); Gartner (1993); Delmar and Shane (2003, 2004); Gartner and Brush (2007); Lichtenstein, Carter, Dooley, and Gartner (2007); and Brush, Manolova, and Edelman (2008) (also see Davidsson, 2006). A second driver for emergence that has been well explored is the role of *opportunity* in entrepreneurship (Long & McMullan, 1984; Kirzner, 1997; Shane, 2000; Shane & Venkataraman, 2000; Ardichvili, Cardozo, & Ray, 2003; Chiasson & Saunders, 2005; McMullan, Plummer, & Acs, 2007) and, in concert to this, the role of passion and emotion in pursuing organizing (Baron, 2008; Cardon, Wincent, Singh, & Drnovsek, 2009). These drivers are all integrated into opportunity tension.

Is Entrepreneurial Opportunity Recognized or Created?

A good deal of progress has been made in understanding the nature of entrepreneurial opportunity (McMullen et al., 2007); however, a central dichotomy remains in the literature: Are opportunities *recognized*, or are they *created*? (Alvarez & Barney, 2013; Eckhardt & Shane, 2013; Garud & Gaiuliani, 2013). In more formal terms, is economic opportunity an "objective" phenomenon that can be recognizable by anyone with the right information (Kirzner, 1997; Shane, 2000)? Or is opportunity fundamentally a creative phenomenon that gets enacted by an entrepreneur through her or his interactions in a specific context (Sarasvathy, 2001a; Chiasson and Saunders, 2005; Chiles et al., 2010)? On the surface, of course, it is both (see Alvarez & Barney, 2007; also Garud & Gaiuliani, 2013; and Eckhardt & Shane, 2013). However, this solution leaves out a very important issue.

The problem with focusing on opportunities as the driver of new venture creation is the implication that the main impetus for creating new value is the entrepreneur's goal to satisfy the needs of a particular market or external constituency. Indeed, this is precisely the advice given in every entrepreneurship textbook, to use information from the market to guide the development of a new product or service (Timmons,

1999; Shane, 2005; Mullins, 2006). Likewise, theories arguing that opportunities are co-created by entrepreneurs and their environments are also based on the importance of focusing on external needs that can be filled through one's own skills and resources (Sarasvathy, 2001b; Sarasvathy & Dew, 2005; Sarasson, Dean, & Hilliard, 2006).

However, other researchers have shown that the perception of a business opportunity is not enough to spark persistent effort toward its fulfillment (McMullan et al., 2007; Dimov, 2011). Instead, the entrepreneur has to experience a motivation to pursue it (Eckhardt & Shane, 2006; Lichtenstein et al., 2007). Likewise, research has shown that only individuals with requisite knowledge and motivation can recognize and subsequently exploit those opportunities (Grégoire, Barr, & Shepherd, 2010; Mitchell & Shepherd, 2010). The problem is, these notions of motivation have not been integrated into the idea of opportunity.

A more expansive explanation would lie in a construct that integrates opportunity perception with the internal drives of the entrepreneur—the personal motivation to create something new (Cardon et al., 2009; Prottas, 2011; Hechavarria, Renko, & Matthews, 2012). Internal motivation has been shown to be critical to creativity (Heinzen, 1994, 1999; Amabile, Conti, Coon, Lazenby, & Herron, 1996; Unsworth, 2001), and motivation is central to understanding organizational behavior in general. Up to now, the role of endogenous drive has not been explored in much of the recent theorizing on entrepreneurial opportunity, even though studies have shown how internal motivation and personal drives predict entrepreneurial activity (Collins, Hanges, & Locke, 2004).

Internal Motivation, or "External" Opportunity

As a thought experiment, consider taking a random sample of American adults, to find those who are actively attempting to start a new business, and ask them what the major driver is of their activities. Entrepreneurship scholars will recognize this allusion to the Panel Study of Entrepreneurial Dynamics—the PSED (Gartner, Shaver, Carter, & Reynolds, 2004), which has been increasingly applied to understand the dynamics of entrepreneurial activity.[2] One question in that survey asked individuals to identify the driver of their business activity, whether it was the business idea—an opportunity—or their decision to start any business—their internal goals. The question reads: "Which came first for you, the business idea or your decision to start some kind of business?"

The answers to this question were unexpected: Nearly two-thirds of all respondents said that rather than opportunity per se, it was their "decision to start" a business that was the primary driver, or was simultaneous to their identification of a specific business opportunity. Only 36.9% replied that the opportunity alone came first (Hills & Singh, 2004, p. 266). This result argues against the notion that opportunity alone is the main driver for entrepreneurial activity. These findings and others suggest that the driver of entrepreneurial action is a combination of opportunity perception and internal motivation. These two facets can be integrated through the construct of opportunity tension. This idea was introduced briefly in Chapter 8, and will be discussed in more detail here.

Integrating Opportunity + Intention

Opportunity tension represents an internal drive—the entrepreneur's intention—that arises in conjunction with his or her perception of a business opportunity, a market need that can be filled through entrepreneurial action (Lichtenstein, 2009). Opportunity tension starts when an entrepreneur perceives or enacts a pool of potential resources, creating an opportunity and simultaneously constructing a way to capitalize on that economic potential, through a unique and sustainable organizing model. The combination of perception and enactment is highly intentional, for these are closely connected in real time, a truism expressed in the entrepreneurial quip, "Ready, Fire, Aim." Being entrepreneurial is the capability to draw forth a cache of potentiality by identifying and enacting a felt need in a market, and the resource cache that comes with it (McKelvey, 2004; Chiles, Tuggle, McMullen, Bierman, & Greening, 2010).

When any creative individual gets inspired to create, their aspiration or vision generates a creative tension (Fritz, 1989, 1991) within them, the felt desire to pursue the project. The farther away the vision is from the current reality, the higher the creative tension of the artist or creator. In this sense, the *rate* of opportunity tension is equivalent to the size of the gap between the entrepreneur's aspiration and their current situation (Senge, 2006).

At the same time, this combination of intention, aspiration, and commitment to pursue a venture is based on a clear perception of a market potential. As before, the clearer and more feasible the opportunity appears, the higher the motivation to pursue it (Baron & Markman, 2003; Baron, 2008). If it feels viable and possible for the entrepreneur, the opportunity initiates a creative tension within the individual that spurs him or her into action (Gartner, 1993). Thus, when there is opportunity and creative tension, the organizing process begins.[3] Although opportunity tension doesn't capture every possible driver of entrepreneurship, it does reflect a consensus around agency. Further, it links to an intriguing literature exploring entrepreneurship as a co-creative process (Sarasvathy, 2001b; Chiasson & Saunders, 2005; Chiles, Bluedorn, & Gupta, 2007; Chiles et al., 2010; Sarasvathy & Venkataramen, 2011; Garud & Guiliani, 2013).

DISEQUILIBRIUM ORGANIZING: ACTIONS FOR CREATING ORGANIZATIONS

What does opportunity tension generate? The answer is *organizing*: taking entrepreneurial action toward, in favor of, the prospect of creating a new dynamic state. Organizing as a construct originated in the work of Karl Weick and his colleagues (Weick, 1977, 1995; Weick & Roberts, 1993; Weick, Sutcliffe, & Obstfeld, 2005) and was adapted to entrepreneurial action by Bill Garter (1985, 1988, 2001). Building on their work, I start by describing the *organizing* element of disequilibrium organizing.

Organizing in Entrepreneurship

According to entrepreneurial scholars, the process of emergence is driven by the "enactment" of entrepreneurial behaviors, a concept that links to scholarship on "self-organizing" (Weick, 1977), "acting as if" (Gartner et al., 1992), "effectuation" (Sarasvathy, 2001a, 2001b; Sarasvathy & Venkataramen, 2011), and "entrepreneuring" (Steyaert, 2007; Rindova, Barry, & Ketchen, 2009). All of these refer to an agentic-sensemaking-learning process of entrepreneurial behavior. In research terms, these intentional actions (Juarrero, 1999) have been operationalized into a set of "organizing activities" pursued by entrepreneurs (Gartner, Carter, & Reynolds, 2004; Gartner & Brush, 2007). Specifically, scholars have identified 27 major tasks that cover the range of activity enacted by "nascent entrepreneurs," those individuals who are in the process of starting a business (Reynolds & Miller, 1992; Reynolds, 2000; Gartner, Shaver, Carter, & Reynolds, 2004). These include, for example:

- Developing a prototype
- Doing marketing activities
- Drawing up financials
- Taking a business course
- Getting a telephone number
- Finding and negotiating with suppliers
- Becoming a legal entity

Taken one by one, these organizing activities would not lead to disequilibrium, but together, with each building on the other in a dynamic pattern, they can predict which nascent start-ups will be successful (Lichtenstein et al., 2007).

From Organizing to Disequilibrium

How can one track or measure how much organizing it takes to push the system into disequilibrium? One solution is given by McKelvey (2004), namely to examine how far outside the "norm" (for that system) the organizing process leads. Another framework is to examine how unique and unprecedented the events and activities are that are being enacted (see, e.g., Andriani & McKelvey, 2007).

Empirical studies of emergence have shown how, when an entrepreneur or entrepreneurial team starts gaining momentum, their organizing pushes the existing system away from its common (normal) state and into a state of higher dynamism, activity, and intensity, that is, into a "far-from-equilibrium state" (Leifer, 1989; MacIntosh & MacLean, 1999; Chiles, Meyer, & Hench, 2004; Lichtenstein, 2009). This state is highly dynamic and turbulent; it is laden with new expectations for higher productivity, greater creativity, and much more energy. The move into a far-from-equilibrium state sets the stage for emergence.

A good example of this disequilibrium organizing effect was presented by Chiles and his colleagues, in their description of how entrepreneurial aspirations by individuals in and around Branson, MO, ultimately led to the emergence of the region as a national center for musical theater (Chiles & Meyer, 2001; Chiles et al., 2004). Their study shows how momentum and disequilibrium grew over time—through increased tourism, a steady growth of theaters, the publication of a best-selling book, two *60-Minutes* episodes about Branson's theatrical explosion, and later from the introduction of big-name stars like Andy Williams. Aspirations like these propelled the region farther and farther away from its original roots, into disequilibrium, thus creating the conditions for emergence (Chiles et al., 2004, p. 509):

> The opening of Andy Williams's theater in 1992 marked a "distinct break" [that] "went against the norm," said his manager. . . . It changed the "frame of reference," broke the "mindset" of Branson as a country music venue, and ushered in a new regime of order.

In these ways the emerging agglomeration of entertainment venues expanded, incorporating new theaters, restaurants, shops, fun activities for children and families, and so on. The entire region thus moved into a state of *continuous* disequilibrium organizing, setting the stage for further emergence over time.

McKelvey (2001) offers a complementary view of disequilibrium organizing, through the example of Jack Welch as chief executive officer (CEO) of General Electric. According to McKelvey, Welch catalyzed far-from-equilibrium dynamics—what he calls adaptive tension—in every business there, by giving them only *one* success metric: "Be #1 or #2 in your industry, or be reorganized, split up, or sold." This charge is not an average, normal event; it is extreme, perhaps one of the most extreme challenges ever given to a group of companies. And the result, conditioned by Welch's leadership, was also extreme, as GE became one of the most financially successful corporations in the past 100 years.

Here the link between opportunity tension and disequilibrium organizing is clear: Welch as entrepreneurial leader created an *internal* tension in each of his divisional executives by using an *external* "bar" that sparked a new kind of thinking—an entrepreneurial, opportunity-driven mindset (Lumpkin & Lichtenstein, 2005). Welch was essentially charging them with breaking out of their own internal mindsets, going against the norm, beyond expectations, by creating and acting on new business opportunities. This translated to an increased drive by the division heads, who pushed this to their direct reports and onto the entire organization. If this drive can be effectively channeled into pursuing new actions that yield unique, creative, and successful new products and business concepts, the disequilibrium organizing will have ultimately led to generative re-emergence.

In order to understand how this drive is channeled into disequilibrium organizing, I will expand on one of the core qualities of generative emergence, namely structioning.

CREATING THE CONTAINER FOR ACTION

Dissipative structures theory describes how an increasing flow of energy through a container pushes the system into a far-from-equilibrium state, ultimately leading to the emergence of new order within the container. In the Bérnard experiment and the in B-Z reaction, the increased energy that sparks order creation must be *driven into and through the system*—thus, there must be a container that defines and bounds the system as a whole. As mentioned earlier, advanced studies show that the characteristics of the container play an unmistakable role in the quality of order creation within it (Finke, Ward, & Smith, 1995; Goldstein, 2003, 2011). For this reason and others, one of the five qualities I include in generative emergence is "structioning," the co-creative energizing of agency and a parallel formation of constraints that can contain and direct that energy. In other words, for generative emergence to happen, a container must be (co)created that can channel the opportunity tension and entrepreneurial action of disequilibrium organizing. How does such a container arise, and from what is it formed?

Consider an individual entrepreneur with an opportunity tension for creating a small company with a mission for environmental sustainability. In this simplified example, our entrepreneur is compelled by an internal motivation to create a company that will play a positive role in the environment. In this case she is driven by a vision for how her expertise can solve a problem that certain companies are facing in their operations. How does she create a "container" within which her organizing efforts can be channeled and contained, thereby to accelerate and grow?

Note that already at this early stage, our entrepreneur has identified several tangible characteristics about her nascent company; these are "constraints" that focus and direct her organizing efforts. For example, she has identified a potential industry, potential skills and resources she can access, and a potential problem she can solve. She has probably spoken with a number of people in the industry—colleagues, clients or suppliers, advisers, and peers. These people help her discern the boundaries and scope of her potential company. In fact, each interaction she has helps to clarify and further contain her organizing activity.

Thus, the container for her business is derived from her social ecology; it comes into being through her ongoing interactions with every agent she meets—potential customers, suppliers and collaborators, bankers and legal council, possible partners and competitors, governmental agencies, and so on. In this way, the emergence of a container is an iterative co-creative process that parallels the emergence of the business concept and organizing model, as well as the acquisition of resources that can make the venture work. In some ways this reflects the well-known correspondence between boundary creation and new venture creation, the legitimation of a new venture by key stakeholders who then acknowledge the company as "existing" in a social sense (Zimmerman & Zeitz, 2002; Delmar & Shane, 2004; Aldrich & Reuf, 2006).

As another metaphor, consider an interaction between the entrepreneur and a potential supplier. As the supplier gets a clearer feel for the entrepreneur's idea and needs, the business she is attempting to start becomes more tangible in a cognitive sense; through ongoing interactions this supplier starts to "see" a "real" company. The more real and tangible this perception, the more the container has emerged in that space. The more that a "real" company is perceived, by more and more stakeholders and others, the more the empty container becomes "filled in," such that the image of a sole individual becomes replaced by a "going concern"—a company that can reliably produce value and fulfill its commitments. Using this metaphor, the more the container is filled in, the "stronger" the container for organizing, and the more energy the entrepreneur can channel through the container to produce more viability, growth, and sustainability. In this dynamic systems perspective, the formation of the container generates a nonlinear affect, which the entrepreneur often feels as momentum and acceleration. More of this process will be teased out through the examples presented next.

EXAMPLES OF DISEQUILIBRIUM ORGANIZING FROM FOUR COMPANIES

The main focus of these five chapters is a presentation of data on each of the five phases, drawn from my dissertation research. In contrast to most case-study data in which the company's story is described all the way through, these data are presented by each of the five phases. Thus, in this chapter I give examples of disequilibrium organizing within each venture; in the next chapter I present each venture's stress and experiments, and so on. These will all be brought together in Chapters 15 and 16, which review the entire scope of the generative emergences in these four firms.

Before presenting my data, a brief review of my research methods is in order; scholars may be interested in the detailed account in the Appendix to this chapter. My year-long study pursued a "quasi-experimental interrupted time series design" (Cook & Campbell, 1979, pp. 209–214), by tracking four small ventures that were "on the verge" of a transition to a new stage. My methods are based on Van de Ven and colleagues' Minnesota Innovation Research Program (MIRP) study (Van de Ven, 1992; Van de Ven, Pooley, Garud, & Venkataramen, 1999), as well as work by Yin (1989), Barley (1990), and others. The data comprise weekly interviews of at least 50% of all employees (averaging up to 32 interviews per week across all four ventures) for 52 consecutive weeks—amounting to 750 interviews and 1,000 hours of on-site observation. Important methodological aspects are presented in the Appendix. Following is a short summary for each venture.

At **DevelopNet,** the high aspiration of the entrepreneur led to his vision of building one of the most sophisticated technologies available (nearly new-to-the-world) for improving simulation capabilities and dynamic access to real-time company data. Having supported himself through Department of Defense-based Small Business Innovation Research Grants (SBIRs), the founder—we'll call him Mark—identified a new opportunity that he felt he could capitalize on in a big way, leading to a remarkable re-emergence that ultimately tripled their revenues.

ApplySci was founded by an MIT scientist who had developed a new-to-the-world technology with applications in advanced materials and in pharmaceutics and drugs that would allow for self-regulation of their absorption in the body. After several years of lab-based development, the scientist's group pursued a major push to scale up and sell the technology in a series of rapidly growing markets. Unfortunately they didn't realize that, when scaled up, the technology failed in critical ways, making it unattractive for consumers and physicians. After a board shake-up, 60% of the employees were fired, including the CEO and his chief technology officer. Ultimately the venture collapsed leaving the board with a loss of $6,000,000 of their investment.

ServiceCo originated as an application of the call to "privatize government," through a contract to print and distribute an often-used government form in exchange for permission to sponsor advertisers on the brochure. This approach allowed micro-local advertising in specific zip code districts (by choosing franchises as partners), years before the Internet became a viable alternative. Although I heard about them only just before their relaunch, I did collect follow-up data and retrospective accounts of the re-emergence they experienced.

AgencyInc was a small local insurance company, a six-person, tech-enabled family-run business with aspirations to grow significantly through acquisition. During the eight months I was there, the key aspiration opportunity unfolded, only to collapse at the final meeting. No recognizable patterns of change are visible in any of the time series for AgencyInc. Note that only a few years later, a much more substantive acquisition was developed. The founder is now one of the senior vice-presidents of one of the most esteemed financial institutions in the United States.

A summary of the characteristics of these ventures is presented in Table 10.1. Table 10.2 presents examples of disequilibrium organizing in the four ventures.

Disequilibrium Organizing at DevelopNet

From my very first interview with the CEO, it was clear that he was passionate about his business and very focused on achieving its main goal: to receive venture capital

Table 10.1. CHARACTERSITICS OF THE FOUR VENTURES IN THE STUDY

	DevelopNet	ApplySci.	AgencyInc.	ServiceCo.
Opportunity/value proposition	Apply proprietary computer application as a tool for allowing real-time access to relational data sets, via Internet/Intranet[†]	Formulate patented technology for specific applications in industrial, commercial, and biomedical markets	Use leading-edge technology to gain an advantage through enhanced customer service	Pursue a public–private partnership through product(s) that help individual citizens while saving money for the U.S. Government
Industry/product-market	Internet/Web development; applied to large financial institutions	Chemical science start-up with venture capital, applications in "unlimited" areas	Insurance agency, serving mainly commercial clients	For-profit public service company, pursuing consumer services markets
Size (employees)	8 (downsized to 4)	24 (failed—shut down)	9 (stayed same size)	25 (grew to 45)
Size (annual gross revenue)	$500,000	$435,000 ($4,000,000 annual costs)	$1,000,000	$1,000,000
Venture age	6 years	3 years	5 years	4 years
Initial dominant logic	Trying to become a "100,000,000 company" through VC-backed expansion into local sales offices that would offer mainly turnkey technology	Research and development venture aiming to commercialize unique products through contracts with large consumer-focused companies	Continue to leverage technology to expand reputation around customer service. Aiming for large-scale growth through acquisitions of other agencies	Use current product as a "cash cow" that would fund the development of a second, unique product that would serve a very different market
Entrepreneur's Experience	Started several companies	Started multiple companies	First start-up	First company for all four partners

Age of entrepreneur/ Employees	Entrepreneur = 55 Employees = ~ 30	Entrepreneur = 45 Employees = ~ 35	Entrepreneur = 36 Employees ≈ 45	Entrepreneurs = 30 Employees = ~ 36
Core group of weekly interview participants	CEO, CFO, operations manager, lead programmer, other programmer (70% of total) Interviewed 100% of all employees at least once	CEO, CTO, VP Technology;[a] 3 marketing managers, 3 lab scientists, office manager, receptionist (65% of total) Interviewed 95% of all employees at least once	CEO, co-owner, executive manager, service team leader, system administrator, accounting manager (60% of total) Interviewed 100% of all employees at least once	CEO, president, COO, 2 product development managers, 4 area managers, 2 sales managers; 4 project associates, 2 administrators (48% of total) Interviewed 90% of all employees at least once
Weeks	47 DCPs	43 DCPs; biweekly interviews continued to week 55	32 DCPs (no evidence of any change)	40 DCPs, but all follow-up started *after* the major shift

[a]Note that in 1996 this was a relatively unique and leading-edge capability.

CEO, chief executive officer; CFO, chief financial officer; CTO, chief technology officer; DCP, data collection period; VP, vice-president.

Table 10.2. DISEQUILIBRIUM ORGANIZING IN THE FOUR VENTURES

Venture	Qualitative Evidence	Quantitative Measure	Time-Series Dynamics
DevelopNet	"Our goal is to become a $100,000,000 company in six years." (CEO) "Pressure to have a great web site, since that's our business.... [We're] always at the edge of capacity." (Product manager)	Hours worked, coded from weekly billing-time cards: Organization-building activities = [Marketing + Administration hours]	Organization-building activities increase to a peak of 571% over a 30-week period, with only one additional staff person hired. Then within 3 weeks that category of work decreases by 87%, where it remains for the rest of the case.
ApplySci	"ApplySci has made major strides. In 1996 it plans to bring its commercialization efforts to fruition." (Business plan) "We've just got so much going on. We don't have time to be careful." (Lab scientist)	Lab work, coded as all formulations and experiments logged in all lab books, every week	Lab work more than doubles (up by 133%) over a 35-week period; in the final 3 months the lab work increases by 466%. Then within just 4 weeks the lab activity decreases by 67%, where it remains for the rest of the case.
AgencyInc	"If I'm not growing through new accounts I have to grow somewhere else. That...is acquisitions." (Founder) "Some days are crazy and busy. Other days are routine." (Service team member)	All account activity by each employee, reported weekly	No evidence of increase or decrease over time. High variance on a month-to-month basis can be accounted for by seasonal deadlines and random (stochastic) factors.
ServiceCo	"Take [the company] to the next level... from about $7.5 million in sales to...$300 million over the next five years. (Founder)	No real-time measure identified	Project employee salaries increase by 200% over a 24-week period and another 560% over the next 12 weeks.

that would fund the creation of regional sales offices across the United States, all of which would sell his technology to the largest and fastest-growing financial services companies in their area. In the words of the CEO: "Our goal is to become a $100,000,000 company in six years." The business plan showed that this was possible, given the rapidly growing market. In 1996, financial services companies were just starting an era of major growth. With the capabilities of its technology, and only a small amount of application programming, this was an exciting opportunity that would fulfill the life-time ambitions of its founder/CEO.

A very fortunate source of data in this firm was the weekly, hand-filled time cards that were transcribed and used for monthly billing of clients. In addition to client hours, the time cards included client support, new product development, marketing, administrative, and other information. These were easy to transfer from the weekly billing time-cards, providing seven distinct categories of work activity for each employee for every week in the study.

Those time cards showed that client billing rapidly dropped to zero once the organizing effort was initiated. In exchange, each employee significantly increased their hours on marketing activities, which included introductory small-group workshops, sales meetings, and website development time. The other useful category was "Admin," which referred to non-sales time spent on the prospective venture. These two were combined into an index of "Organization-Building" activities, which captured the hours spent on organizing the venture's emergence to a new level.

The data are presented in the charts in Figures 10.1–10.3. As shown in Figure 10.1, organization building activities increased to a peak—an increase of 571% over a 30-week period. Note in Figure 10.2 the corresponding decrease in client billing. With only four staff available to pursue this work, that reflects a nearly full-time effort by the entire staff, with further additions by the CFO and CEO. However, Figure 10.3 shows that within a short four-week period starting at data collection period (DCP) 13 and extending to DCP 17, organization building decreased dramatically (by 87%); it remained at nearly zero for the rest of the case. Clearly something significant happened at DCP 13 in this case. More of this case is told in the following chapters.

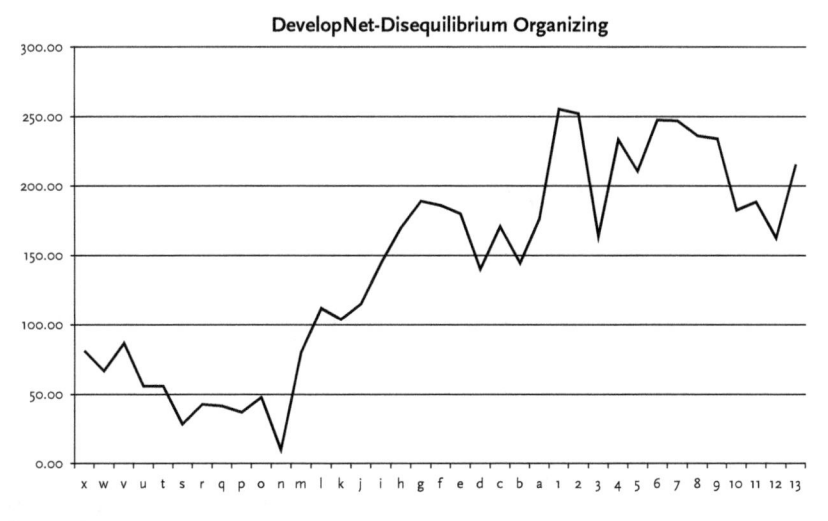

Figure 10.1:
DevelopNet Disequilibrium Organizing, from 24 Weeks before DCP 1 through DCP 13

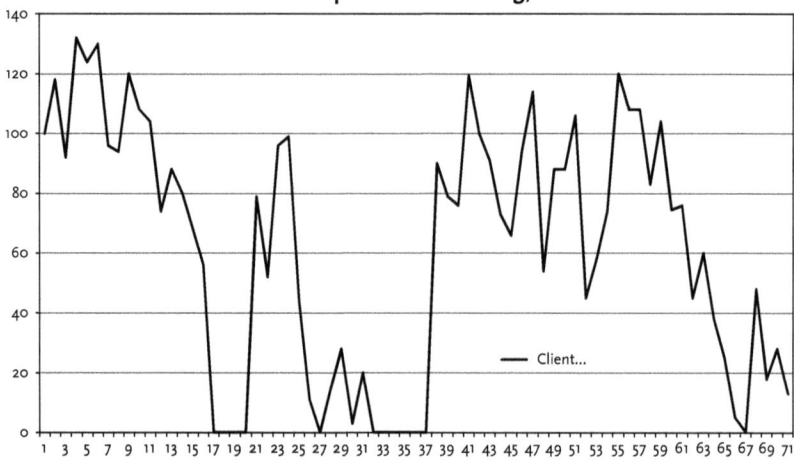

Figure 10.2:
DevelopNet Consulting Time, from DCP 1 through DCP 71
Note decrease in client billing corresponds to increase in organization building activities.

Disequilibrium Organizing at ApplySci

The opportunity tension at ApplySci had for many years been expressed in two parallel sides of the venture: an applied material side and a biomedical side. The biomedical business had become a spin-off venture for a time, but "rejoined" the firm two years before I started collecting data there. Their next step was announced in the business plan they had developed just a few months before I arrived: "ApplySci

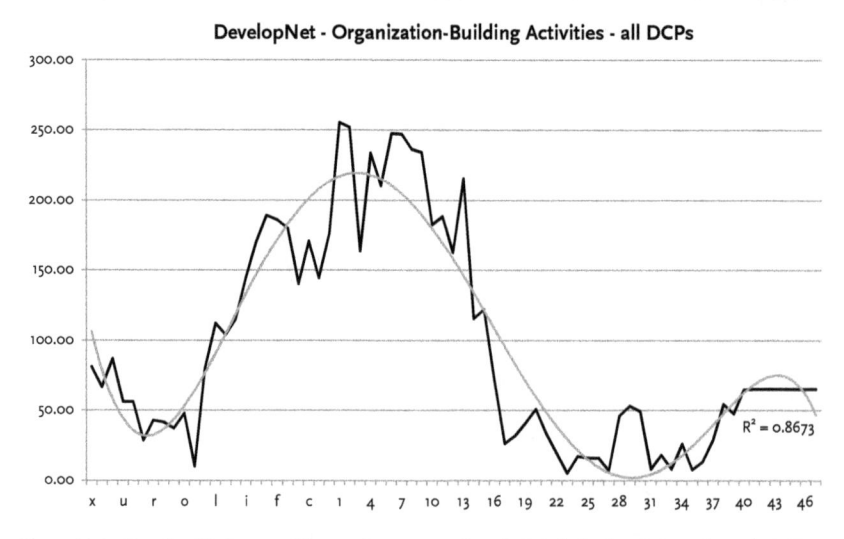

Figure 10.3: DevelopNet Disequilibrium Organizing, from 24 Weeks before DCP 1 through DCP 47
Included is a second-order polynomial (curved) trend-line, which reflects the main rise in organization building, followed by a second rise later on in the case. Note that the trend-line captures (explains) 86% of the variance of the time-series data.

Generative Emergence

has made major strides. In 1996 it plans to bring its commercialization efforts to fruition." In a quote that was prescient about the problems it would later have to face, one lab scientist reported to me, "We've just got so much going on. We don't have time to be careful."

A good view of the rapid increase in organizing activities can be gained by examining all progress on the technology itself: the development, analysis, and formulations of the core technology that was done in labs. This laboratory-based effort was fully recorded in the lab notebooks of the employees; all scientific employees kept these notebooks as standard practice. As previously arranged, I had access to these data, which were kept by nearly half of all employees in the company, including the CEO, chief financial officer (CFO), chief technical officer (CTO), and senior managers. Thus, lab work provided an inside view into the key organizing activities at the center of the organization.

An analysis of the lab work activities shows that for 35 weeks from when their goal was announced—to commercialize the technology—the total amount of lab work increased by 133% (more than doubling). Moreover, in the final 12 weeks that figure rose by 466%. Then, after a major shift, lab activity dropped by 67% and ultimately down to zero, where it remained. These dynamics are shown in Figures 10.4 and 10.5.

A simple interpretation, which will be expanded as we move through the phases of this company's attempts at generative emergence, is that disequilibrium organizing rises to a peak in DCP 29, then drops precipitously. This suggests that DCP 29 is the point at which we will find a critical event of some kind leading to the emergence—or non-emergence—of a new dynamic state.

Work Activity at ApplySci - All Lab Work

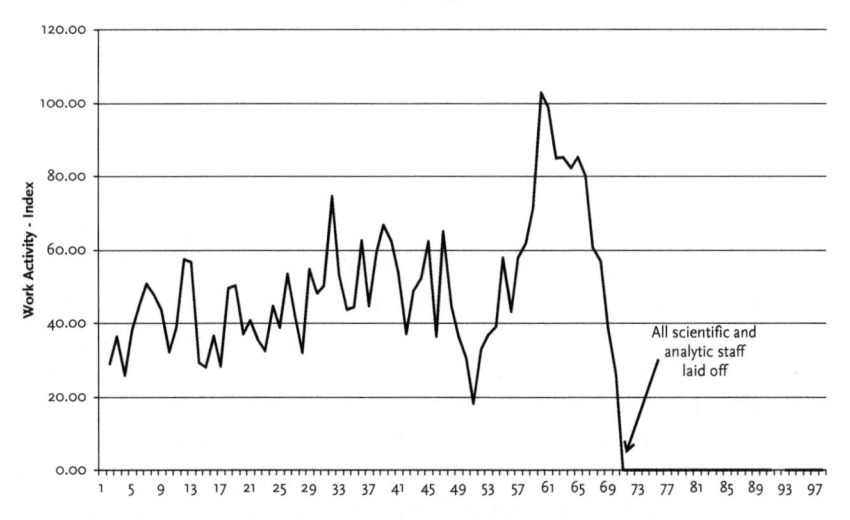

Figure 10.4: ApplySci Organization Building Activities, from 32 Weeks before DCP 1 to DCP 65
Here the daily count is "lab work" + "experiments" (e.g., for stability) + "formulations" for testing by commercial businesses, + analytic information. In sum, work activity captures any test of the technology's development and consistency. Informal trend-lines are added to show the major effort that started in data collection period (DCP) 18 and continued through DCP 29, when all scientific and analytic staff were laid off.

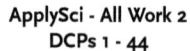

Figure 10.5: ApplySci Organization Building Activities, from DCP 1 to DCP 42
Note that these are archival data, which I was able to collect from 32 weeks before my first data collection period (DCP). Added to the 44 DCPs analyzed in this graph, the time series is 76 weeks long, nearly 18 months of daily entries across four lab technicians. The data are derived in the same way as in Figure 10.4, that is, "lab work" + "experiments" + commercial "formulations" + analytic information.

Disequilibrium Organizing at ServiceCo

As mentioned earlier, the data for this company are mainly retrospective. They had carefully kept me from entering the process during the critical moments of change; only after their major shift did they invite me to pursue interviews with the cofounders, executive team, and employees. Still, these qualitative data and some archival information provide a sense of the dramatic increase in efforts that preceded the emergence of a new dynamic state.

Their aspiration to become a nationally recognized company was originated in the initial collaboration between the two founders, one of whom wanted to grow the MarketServe product, while the other agreed that his goal to start PeopleServe would wait until they gained some venture capital (these product names are pseudonyms). Once the MarketServe product had been started, this secondary goal was clearly expressed by the founder, who declared his intent to "take ServiceCo to the next level—from about $7.5 million to $300 million in sales over the next five years." That commitment led to a significant push in hiring and organizing; within nine months the company had more than doubled its workforce; the number of project-based employees increased by 300%. In the words of one of the cofounders:

> We had made a ... decision ... to pursue PeopleServe in a big way. We had money behind it, we had people working on it, we had contracts and verbal commitments with outside partners. (ServiceCo cofounder; DCP 1)

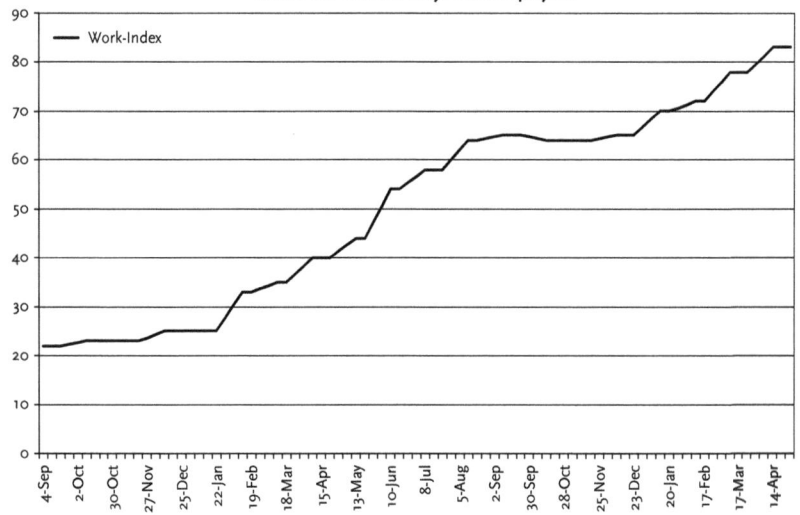

Figure 10.6: ServiceCo Total Employees

The plan was strong, the potential market was huge, and the effort started with great enthusiasm. The increase in project personnel is represented in Figure 10.6 for ServiceCo.

AgencyInc—A Lack of Disequilibrium Organizing

A contrasting example is AgencyInc, whose founder introduced his company as a fast-growth, leading-edge broker of residential and commercial insurance, poised to move into a new era. His enthusiasm mitigated my own wariness of including the venture into my sample, for two reasons. First, it is a technology-enhanced venture rather than a technology-focused venture like the others. Second, it had been virtually the same size for its entire seven years. However, the CEO's passion and vision were captivating, especially for an insurance company, and his perceived opportunity tension convinced me that I should track their progress to a high-growth venture through acquisitions.

Among the benefits of tracking this firm was a remarkable metric for work activity, a count of *all account activity by all employees, calculated daily*. This metric was possible because their company-wide computer program kept track of every activity that was done by each employee. By multiplying these activities by a calculation of the minutes spent on each one, I was able to develop a variable that identified the amount of work each employee performed every day, including the founders (CEO and CFO). As Figure 10.7 for AgencyInc shows, these data appear to be nearly random, with a good deal of variation around a stable mean. Trend lines were unable to demonstrate any discernable increase or decrease across the months of data collection. This suggests that there was virtually no disequilibrium organizing in this firm.

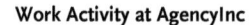

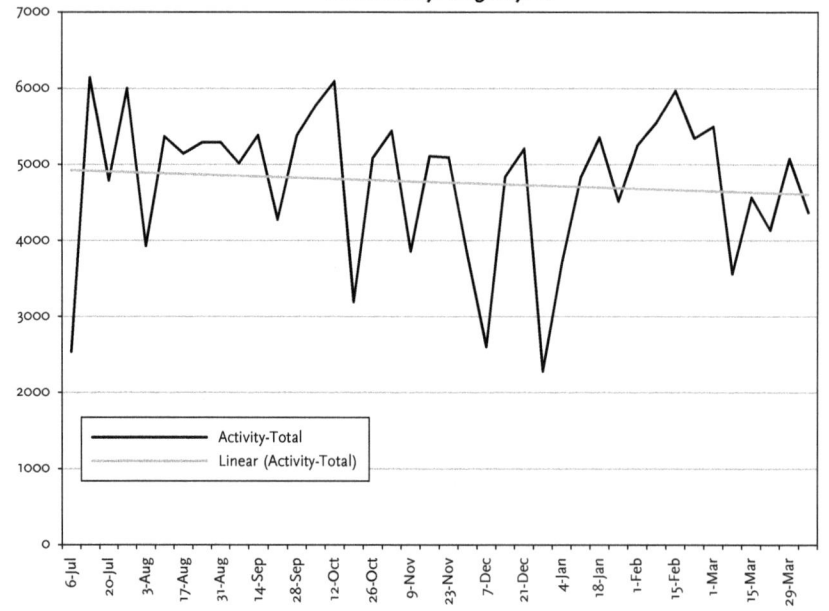

Figure 10.7: AgencyInc Work Activity
Included is a linear trend-line, showing no distinct trend or statistically significant pattern.

Do these instances of disequilibrium organizing lead to parallel increases in stress and experiments? That is the question for the next chapter.

APPENDIX

METHODS FOR CAPTURING DATA FOR EMERGENCE

Data Collection and Sampling

In order to capture the dynamic process of generative emergence in entrepreneurial firms, I followed the recommendations of scholars in management (Eisenhardt, 1989; Van de Ven, Angel, & Poole, 1989) and entrepreneurship (Stevenson & Harmeling, 1990; McKelvey, 2004), who recommend a longitudinal, comparative case study design.[a] Identifying the ordering of sequences of re-emergence and capturing the subtle dynamics within those sequences required *real-time* tracking of small ventures while they were undergoing a major transformation. In formal terms, I pursued a "quasi-experimental interrupted time series design" (Cook & Campbell, 1979, pp. 209–214), which translates to a real-time "experiment" involving an ongoing collection of data; the "interruption" is the hypothesized re-emergence of a venture's dynamic state. This "change point" (Poole, Van de Ven, Dooley, & Holmes, 2000) would provide a foundation for comparing the sequences and their dynamics across cases. The quasi-experimental approach was risky in that it was impossible to know ahead of time whether any of the organizations I was tracking would make a shift or what its outcome would be. However, if they did, I would gain access to data of a type rarely collected in the field.[b]

These aims led to four criteria for choosing my cases (i.e., the sample frame). First, scholars suggest that rapid nonlinear shifts associated with opportunity creation and reformation are more likely in high-potential ventures (Bhide, 2000) such as high-tech entrepreneurial start-ups; this became my first selection criterion. Second, to maximize the potential of tracking an actual transformative shift I looked for entrepreneurial ventures that were, in the words of their founders, "on the verge of a transition" from one growth stage to the next (Eggers, Leahy, & Churchill, 1994). Third, complexity researchers have recognized the distributed and multilevel nature of complex adaptive systems such as entrepreneurial firms (Salthe, 1989; McKelvey, 2004) while at the same time recognizing that each element of the system plays a unique and crucial role in the whole system's evolution (Holland, 1995). Therefore, the firms to be chosen for the study would have to be large enough to have developed some clear distinctions in roles and managerial responsibilities, yet small enough so that I could interview at least 50% of all organizational members on each visit; that meant that firms needed to be 10 to 25 employees in size. Finally, in order to capture the subtle interactions in complex systems, I required full access to the organization, its financials, and its participants on a weekly basis.

This criterion-based sampling procedure was carried out through judgment sampling (Emery & Cooper, 1991). Thirty-five organizations were contacted, four of which met all these criteria and agreed to participate in the intensive research effort.[c] My research sites are identified by the pseudonyms DevelopNet, ApplySci, ServiceCo, and AgencyInc; characteristics are provided in Table 10.1.

I wanted to maximize my on-site presence in these firms in order to support validity and reliability in the theory-building process, and to capture the richness of internal sensemaking that is at the heart of emergent change (Stevenson & Harmeling, 1990; Maguire & Hardy, 2009). Thus, I spent one day a week in each of these ventures for 9 to 12 months of data collection. In addition to my weekly interviews with a core group of managers, line personnel, administrative staff, and the CEO, I interviewed 95% of all members of all organizations at least once during the study. Other primary data collected included all financial information, business plans, organizational charts, company memos, board of directors' minutes, marketing materials, e-mails, and technology analyses. In total, I spent over 1,000 hours of on-site observation and collected over 750 interviews throughout the full study (across all four organizations).

I developed a "brief-question" approach for this research—a single question that could be answered by each participant in as little as 2 to 5 minutes. The goal of the brief-question format was to focus attention on current and upcoming activities rather than on retrospective events, and to make it easy for the members of these busy entrepreneurial firms to participate week after week in the research study. The basic question was: "What is happening this week? From your perspective, what are the key issues the company is facing right now?" In order to reduce repeated response bias I sometimes included a follow-up question, for example, about resources, changes, and other salient issues. Employees were assured of strict confidentiality of all responses, and all organizations have remained completely anonymous. To facilitate a rapid development of trust I did not tape-record interviews. For the first several weeks I used a small notepad to record answers (Barley, 1990). After the fifth week the interviews were typed directly into a laptop computer.[d] Each interview was carefully reviewed, correcting spelling and grammar and adding words or phrases that had been missed in the initial transcriptions. My typing abilities (which approached 110 wpm with mistakes), in conjunction with reviewing and correcting each interview immediately or in some cases within 24 hours, resulted in virtually verbatim transcripts.

I transcribed my quantitative data into an Excel spreadsheet,[e] which allowed me to run charts that displayed the week-to-week dynamics of any operationalized variable. All the data for the study were organized by week within each organization. Each week is a data collection period (DCP); a valid DCP includes real-time interview data that can be coded into all requisite variables (see next section). Table 10.2 includes the number of DCPs in each case, which range from 8 months of weekly data at AgencyInc to 11 months at DevelopNet with two years of follow-up.

Operationalizing and Measuring—Every Variable, Every Week in Every Organization

During the real-time collection of interviews I sought to operationalize (measure) each of the five sequences into one or more variables that could be mapped as a time series (Monge, 1990; Van de Ven et al., 1989; Van de Ven & Poole, 1990; Van de Ven, 1992). An operationalization was acceptable if (a) the variable could be identified in every organization and (b) the variable could be distinguished qualitatively or tracked or coded into a quantitative variable that showed variance from week to week in all firms.

My primary goal was to develop operationalizations that would be relatively generalizable in other cases and in other industries (Eisenhardt, 1989). Another goal was to allow for a falsification of the analysis. In an analytic check I tested each variable for construct validity (Miles & Huberman, 1994), internal validity (Cook and Campbell, 1979), and reliability and trustworthiness (Denzin, 1989; Erlandson, Harris, Skipper, & Allen, 1993). Initially I identified 21 variables that were measurable in all four companies. In my secondary analysis, I reduced these to a parsimonious set of one or two variables per sequence; these are the variables used in my dissertation.

Next, I developed *time series* for each of the quantitative variables. Specifically, I used a validated technique of operational coding (Van de Ven et al., 1989; Stake, 1994; Poole et al., 2000) in which transcripts are manually searched for mentions of specific constructs in the theory. Then, on a week-by-week basis, all mentions of a given variable were identified for each organization by two separate coders (the author and a graduate researcher), including all instances of stress/experiments, critical events, emergents, and stabilizing feedback. Initially, our interrater reliability ranged between 60% and 70%; every code was discussed by both individuals until 100% agreement was reached. Each phrase and its coding became a row in a master Excel spreadsheet; the full database includes nearly 2,000 codes.

Visual Time-Series Analysis of the Data

Following the coding model developed by Van de Ven and his colleagues, these weekly codes were entered in a separate workbook for each organization, in which each variable is a row and each week is a column. *Every completed row is thus considered a time series* whose length is the total number of weeks that data were collected and coded. Once the basic time series were entered, I expanded the data by incorporating ratios of variables, cumulative counts, and other combinations. Initially I used a total of 86 unique time series for my analysis; about 30 of these became most relevant, most of which are presented in Chapters 10–14.

Each of these time series was turned into a chart (in Microsoft Excel), and a visual trend analysis was done according to the dimensions suggested by Monge (1990), including rates of change, magnitude, duration, and lag effects to other variables. My primary focus on rates of change draws from methodological and philosophical developments in complexity theory (e.g., Dooley & Van de Ven, 1999); time series were used to develop and confirm the overall model. Later these time-series charts were simplified into temporal graphs that emphasize the start-week and end-week for each phase in the cycle, and a complete graph for every organization that reveals the combined (scaled) time-series dynamic for all five phases on one sheet. This helped determine key timing differences, which were then plotted.

After my initial analysis I wrote case studies for each organization (carefully edited to hide all employee identities), which were sent to each of the founder/CEOs for clarification and critical feedback (Denzin, 1989). Their feedback was integrated into the analyses.

Like other longitudinal studies of change, my understanding evolved through multiple iterations of data collection, theory development, and preliminary interpretations of the qualitative and quantitative data (Barley, 1986; Gersick, 1988; Van de Ven et al., 1989). More importantly, the overall model has matured in the years since the data were originally collected (Brown & Eisenhardt, 1997).

In historical terms, these events occurred in 1996–1997, well before the dot-com bubble. Contextually the venture capital market for these firms was somewhat similar to the current situation faced by clean-tech organizations in the United States, in that it focused much more on later-stage ventures, an issue that was important in two of the three cases I examined. Given the very in-depth nature of the interview data, my assumption is that the interactive dynamics of entrepreneurs and employees in these firms represent general patterns of behavior which should remain valid over time.

NOTES

1. The case studies from my dissertation have been a catalyst for many publications, including Lichtenstein (2000) and Lichtenstein and Brush (2001). However, no publication has included the time series charts and associated in-depth data. As such, I am exceedingly grateful to Oxford University Press to give me the book-length space to present them.
2. Carter, Reynolds, and Gartner (1996) were involved in the early exploration of this challenge: how to create a truly randomized sample of nascent entrepreneurs, before they have actually "started" the business. Carter, Gartner, and Reynolds found that to identify 1,000 such individuals, making phone calls to a representative random sample of 64,000 Americans was required. The Panel Study of Entrepreneurial Dynamics (PSED) and PSED 2 are maintained by the University of Michigan; go to: http://www.psed.isr.umich.edu/psed/home. By 2012, there had been more than 100 papers published that analyze PSED data.
3. This idea is drawn in part from McKelvey's (2004) "adaptive tension," which for him describes externally induced "energy differentials" in the system (i.e., opportunities). Opportunity tension is meant to be more entrepreneurially focused by capturing the combination of external and internal drivers for action (Chiles et al., 2010). Opportunity tension expresses the internal drive to capitalize on a potential energy differential across a system, and it expresses the expectation that new resources can be captured as a means of bringing the opportunity to fruition.

APPENDIX NOTES

a   At the time, before I understood that I had examined instances of re-emergence, my literature base was organizational change and transformation (Bartunek, 1984; Tushman & Romanelli, 1985; Leifer, 1989; Stevenson & Harmeling, 1990).
b   I also credit my dissertation committee for their willingness to support me in this unconventional research design.
c   The fourth organization, known as "ServiceCo," initially appeared to satisfy the criteria; however, after some months I realized that they had already undergone their major transition in the weeks before I arrived. For this paper I include relevant data from ServiceCo, some of which is retrospective.
d   Most participants were unwilling to have me tape-record their thoughts, however, none were uncomfortable with me typing as they spoke. Perhaps they perceived that tape-recording was more risky than typing, or perhaps the placement of my laptop, which

was outside of their direct visual field (on my lap, generally on the other side of their desk), made them feel more at ease.

e Following common guidelines, each organization had its own workbook. Data were organized in columns, with each following week being the next column to the right. Variables or processes were listed as rows. In two cases, the number of quantitative categories that were already being collected by the organization numbered 30 to 40 rows (e.g., detailed weekly time-card data). Data were added from week 1 (DCP 1 = data collection period 1) through to the end of data collection in the case, either 9 or 12 months, depending on the venture. Charts were then developed, through ChartWizard using cleaned data across the spreadsheet; i.e., one main worksheet with all data, then individual worksheets for time series charts on the variables.

REFERENCES

Aldrich, H., & Reuf, M. 2006. *Organizations Evolving* (2nd ed.). Thousand Oaks, CA: SAGE Publications.

Alvarez, S., & Barney, J. 2013. Epistemology, opportunities, and entrepreneurship: Comments on Venkataraman et al. (2012) and Shane (2012). *Academy of Management Review*, 38(1): 154–56.

Amabile, T., Conti, R., Coon, H., Lazenby, J., & Herron, M. 1996. Assessing the work environment for creativity. *Academy of Management Journal*, 39: 1154–84.

Andriani, P., & McKelvey, B. 2007. Beyond Gaussian averages: Redirecting organization science toward extreme events and power laws. *Journal of International Business Studies*, 38: 1212–30.

Ardichvili, A., Cardozo, R., & Ray, S. 2003. A theory of entrepreneurial opportunity identification and development. *Journal of Business Venturing*, 18: 105–24.

Barley, S. 1986. Technology as an occasion for structuring. *Administrative Science Quarterly*, 31: 220–47.

Barley, S. 1990. Images of imaging: Notes on doing longitudinal field work. *Organization Science*, 1: 220–47.

Baron, R. 2008. The role of affect in the entrepreneurial process. *Academy of Management Review*, 33: 328–40.

Baron, R., & Markman, G. 2003. Beyond social capital: The role of entrepreneurs' social competence in their financial success. *Journal of Business Venturing*, 18: 41–60.

Bartunek, J. 1984. Changing interpretive schemes and organizationl restructuring: The example of a religious order. *Administrative Science Quarterly*: 224–41.

Bhide, A. 2000. *The Origin and Evolution of New Businesses*. New York: Oxford University Press.

Brown, S., & Eisenhardt, K. 1997. The art of continuous change: Linking complexity theory and time-based evolution in relentlessly shifting organizations. *Administrative Science Quarterly*, 42: 1–34.

Brush, C., Manolova, T., & Edelman, L. 2008. Properties of emerging organizations: An empirical test. *Journal of Business Venturing*, 23: 547–66.

Bygrave, W. 1989. The entrepreneurship paradigm (II): Chaos and catastrophes among quantum jumps. *Entrepreneurship Theory and Practice*, 14(2): 7–30.

Cardon, M., Wincent, J., Singh, J., & Drnovsek, M. 2009. The nature and experience of entrepreneurial passion. *Academy of Management Review*, 34(3): 511–32.

Carter, N., Gartner, B., & Reynolds, P. 1996. Exploring start-up event sequences. *Journal of Business Venturing*, 11: 151–66.

Chiasson, M., & Saunders, C. 2005. Reconciling diverse approaches to opportunity research using the structuration theory. *Journal of Business Venturing*, 20: 747–68.

Chiles, T., Bluedorn, A., & Gupta, V. 2007. Beyond creative destruction and entrepreneurial discovery: A radical Austrian approach to entrepreneurship. *Organization Studies*, 28: 267–493.

Chiles, T., Meyer, A., & Hench, T. 2004. Organizational emergence: The origin and transformation of Branson, Missouri's musical theaters. *Organization Science*, 15(5): 499–520.

Chiles, T., Tuggle, C. S., McMullen, J., Bierman, L., & Greening, D. 2010. Dynamic creation: Elaborating a radical Austrian approach to entrepreneurship. *Organization Studies*, 31: 7–46.

Collins, C., Hanges, P., & Locke, E. 2004. The relationship of achievement motivation to entrepreneurial behavior: A meta-analysis. *Human Performance*, 17(1): 95–117.

Cook, T., & Campbell, D. 1979. *Quasi-Experimentation*. Boston: Houghton Mifflin.

Davidsson, P. 2006. Nascent entrepreneurship: Empirical studies and developments. *Foundations and Trends in Entreprenuership*, 2(1): 1–76.

Delmar, F., & Shane, S. 2003. *Does the order of organizing activiites matter for new venture performance?* Paper presented at the Frontiers of Entrepreneurship, Babson College.

Delmar, F., & Shane, S. 2004. Legitimating first: Organizing activities and the survival of new ventures. *Journal of Business Venturing*, 19: 385–411.

Denzin, N. 1989. *The Research Act* (3rd ed.). Englewood Cliffs, NJ: Prentice Hall.

Dimov, D. 2011. Grappling with the unbearable elusiveness of entrepreneurial opportunities. *Entrepreneurship Theory and Practice*, 35(1): 57–81.

Dooley, K., & Van de Ven, A. 1999. Explaining complex organizational dynamics. *Organization Science*, 10(3): 358–72.

Eckhardt, J. T., & Shane, S. 2006. Opportunities and entrepreneurship. *Journal of Management*, 29(3): 333–49.

Eckhardt, J. T., & Shane, S. 2013. Response to the commentaries: The individual-opportunity (IO) nexus integrates objective and subjective aspects of entrepreneurship. *Academy of Management Review*, 2013(1): 160–62.

Eggers, J., Leahy, K., & Churchill, N. 1994. Stages of small business growth revisited. *Frontiers of Entreprenuerial Research*, 14: 131–44.

Eisenhardt, K. 1989. Building theories from case study research. *Academy of Management Review*, 14: 532–50.

Emery, C. W., & Cooper, D. R. 1991. *Business Research Methods* (4th ed.). Homewood, IL: Irwin.

Erlandson, D., Harris, E., Skipper, B., & Allen, S. 1993. *Doing Naturalistic Inquiry*. Newbury Park, CA: SAGE Publications.

Finke, R., Ward, T., & Smith, S. (Eds.). 1995. *The Creative Cognition Approach*. Cambridge, MA: MIT Press.

Fritz, R. 1989. *The Path of Least Resistance*. New York: Fawcett Columbine.

Fritz, R. 1991. *Creating*. New York: Fawcett Columbine.

Gartner, B. 2001. Is there an elephant in entrepreneurship research? Blind assumptions in theory development. *Entrepreneurship Theory and Practice*, 25(4): 27–40.

Gartner, W. 1985. A conceptual framework for describing the phenomonon of new venture creation. *Academy of Management Review*, 10: 696–706.

Gartner, W. 1988. "Who is an entrepreneur" is the wrong question." *American Journal of Small Business*, 12(4): 11–32.

Gartner, W. 1993. Words lead to deeds: Towards an organizational emergence vocabulary. *Journal of Business Venturing*, 8: 231–39.

Gartner, W., Bird, B., & Starr, J. 1992. Acting as if: Differentiating entrepreneurial from organizational behavior. *Entrepreneurship Theory and Practice*, 16(3): 13–30.

Gartner, W., & Brush, C. 2007. Entrepreneurship as organizing: Emergence, newness and transformation. In T. H. M. Rice (Ed.), *Praeger Perspectives on Entrepreneurship*, Vol. 3: 1–20. Westport, CT: Prager Publishers.

Gartner, W., Carter, N., & Reynolds, P. 2004. Business start-up activities. In W. Gartner, K. Shaver, N. Carter, & P. Reynolds (Eds.), *Handbook of Entrepreneurial Dynamics* (285–98). Thousand Oaks, CA: SAGE Publications.

Gartner, W., Shaver, K., Carter, N., & Reynolds, P. (Eds.). 2004. *Handbook of Entrepreneurial Dynamics*. Thousand Oaks, CA: SAGE Publications.

Garud, R., & Guiliani, A. P. 2013. A narrative perspective on entrepreneurial opportunities. *Academy of Management Review*, 38(1): 157–60.

Gersick, C. 1988. Time and transition in work teams. *Academy of Management Journal*, 29: 9–41.

Goldstein, J. 2003. The construction of emergent order, or, how to resist the temptation of Hylozosim. *Nonlinear Dynamics, Psychology, and Life Sciences*, 7(4): 295–314.

Goldstein, J. 2011. Probing the nature of complex systems: Parameters, modeling, interventions—Part 1. *Emergence: Complexity and Organization*, 13(3): 94–121.

Grégoire, D., Barr, P., & Shepherd, D. 2010. Cognitive processes of opportunity recognition: The role of structural alignment. *Organization Science*, 21(2): 413.

Hechavarria, D., Renko, M., & Matthews, C. 2012. The nascent entrepreneurship hub: Goals, entrepreneurial self-efficacy and start-up outcomes. *Small Business Economics*, 39(3): 685–701.

Heinzen, T. E. 1994. Situational affect: Proactive and reactive creativity. In M. Shaw & M. Runco (Eds.), *Creativity and Affect* (127–46). Westport, CT: Ablex Publishing.

Heinzen, T. E. 1999. Proactive creativity. In M. Runco & S. R. Pritzker (Eds.), *Encyclopedia of Creativity*, Vol. 1: 429–34.

Hills, G., & Singh, R. 2004. Opportunity recognition. In W. Gartner, K. Shaver, N. Carter, & P. Reynolds (Eds.), *Handbook of Entrepreneurial Dynamics* (259–72). Thousand Oaks, CA: SAGE Publications.

Holland, J. 1995. *Hidden Order*. Redwood City, CA: Addison-Wesley.

Juarrero, A. 1999. *Dynamics in Action: Intentional Behavior as a Complex System*. Cambridge, MA: MIT Press.

Katz, J., & Gartner, W. 1988. Properties of emerging organizations. *Academy of Management Review*, 13: 429–41.

Kirzner, I., M. 1997. Entrepreneurial discovery and the competitive market process: An Austrian approach. *Journal of Economic Literature*, 35: 60–85.

Leifer, R. 1989. Understanding organizational transformation using a dissipative structure model. *Human Relations*, 42: 899–916.

Lichtenstein, B. 2000. Self-organized transitions: A pattern amid the "chaos" of transformative change. *Academy of Management Executive*, 14(4): 128–41.

Lichtenstein, B. 2009. Moving far from far-from-equliibrium: Opportunity tension as the catalyst of emergence. *Emergence: Complexity and Organization*, 11(4): 15–25.

Lichtenstein, B. 2011. Complexity science contributions to the field of entrepreneurship. In P. Allen, S. Maguire, & B. McKelvey (Eds.), *The SAGE Handbook of Complexity and Management* (471–93). Thousand Oaks, CA: SAGE Publications.

Lichtenstein, B., & Brush, C. 2001. How do 'resource bundles' develop and change in new ventures? A dynamic model and longitudinal exploration. *Entrepreneurship Theory and Practice*, 25(3): 37–58.

Lichtenstein, B., Carter, N., Dooley, K., & Gartner, W. 2007. Complexity dynamics of nascent entrepreneurship. *Journal of Business Venturing*, 22: 236–61.

Long, W., & McMullan, W. E. 1984. *Mapping the new venture opportunity identification process*. Paper presented at the Frontiers of Entrepreneurship Research, Wellesley, MA.

Lumpkin, T., & Lichtenstein, B. 2005. The role of organizational learning in the opportunity recognition process. *Entrepreneurship Theory and Practice*, 29(4): 451–72.

MacIntosh, R., & MacLean, D. 1999. Conditioned emergence: A dissipative structures approach to transformation. *Strategic Management Journal*, 20: 297–316.

Maguire, S., & Hardy, C. 2009. Discourse and deinstitutionalization: The decline of DDT. *Academy of Management Review*, 52: 148–78.

McKelvey, B. 2001. What is complexity science? It is really order creation science. *Emergence*, 3(1): 137–57.

McKelvey, B. 2004. Toward a complexity science of entrepreneurship. *Journal of Business Venturing*, 19: 313–42.

McMullan, J., Plummer, L., & Acs, Z. 2007. What is an entrepreneurial opportunity. *Small Business Economics*, 28: 273–83.

Miles, M. B., & Huberman, A. M. 1994. *Qualitative Data Analysis*. Thousand Oaks, CA: SAGE Publications.

Mitchell, J., & Shepherd, D. 2010. To thine own self be true: Images of self, images of opportunity, and entrepreneurial action. *Journal of Business Venturing*, 25(1): 138.

Monge, P. 1990. Theoretical and analytical issues in studying organizational processes. *Organization Science*, 1: 406–30.

Mullins, J. 2006. *The New Business Road Test*. New York: Financial Times Press.

Poole, M. S., Van de Ven, A., Dooley, K., & Holmes, M. 2000. *Organizational Change and Innovation Processes: Theory and Methods for Research*. New York: Oxford University Press.

Prottas, D. 2011. Person–environment fit and self-employment: Opportunities and needs for achievement, affiliation, autonomy and dominance. *North American Journal of Psychology*, 13(3): 403–26.

Reynolds, P. 2000. National panal study of U.S. business start-ups: Background and methodology. In J. K. R. Brockhaus (Ed.), *Advances in Entrepreneurship, Firm Emergence, and Growth*, Vol. 4: 153–227. Stamford, CT: JAI Press.

Reynolds, P., & Miller, B. 1992. New firm gestation: Conception, birth, and implications for research. *Journal of Business Venturing*, 7: 405–71.

Rindova, V., Barry, D., & Ketchen, D. 2009. Entrepreneuring as emancipation. *Academy of Management Review*, 34(3): 477–91.

Salthe, S. 1989. Self-organization of/in hierarchically structured systems. *Systems Research*, 6(3): 199–208.

Sarasson, Y., Dean, T., & Hilliard, B. 2006. Entrepreneurship as the nexus of individual and opportunity: A structuration view. *Journal of Business Venturing*, 21: 286–305.

Sarasvathy, S. 2001a. Causation and effectuation: Toward a theoretical shift from economic inevitability to entrepreneurial contingency. *Academy of Management Review*, 26: 243–63.

Sarasvathy, S. 2001b. Effectual rationality in entrepreneurial strategies: Existence and bounds. *Academy of Management Best Papers Proceedings*, Vol. 61: ENT, D1–D7.

Sarasvathy, S., & Dew, N. 2005. New market creation through transformation. *Journal of Evolutionary Economics*, 15: 533–65.

Sarasvathy, S., & Venkataramen, S. 2011. Entrepreneurship as method: Open questions for an entrepreneurial future. *Entrepreneurship Theory and Practice*, 35(1): 113–35.

Schumpeter, J. 1934. *The Theory of Economic Development*. Boston: Harvard University Press.

Shane, S. 2000. Prior knowledge and the discovery of entrepreneurial opportunities. *Organization Science*, 11: 448–69.

Shane, S. 2005. *Finding Fertile Ground: Identifying Extraordinary Opportunities for New Ventures*. Upper Saddle River, NJ: Wharton School/Pearson Education.

Shane, S., & Venkataraman, S. 2000. The promise of entrepreneurship as a field of research. *Academy of Management Review*, 25: 217–26.

Smith, C. 1986. Transformation and regeneration in social systems: A dissipative structure perspective. *Systems Research*, 3: 203–13.

Stake, R. 1994. Case studies. In N. Denzin & Y. Lincoln (Eds.), *Handbook of Qualitative Studies*. Newbury Park, CA: SAGE Publications.

Stevenson, H., & Harmeling, S. 1990. Entrepreneurial management's need for a more "chaotic" theory. *Journal of Business Venturing*, 5: 1–14.

Steyaert, C. 2007. Entrepreneuring as a conceptual attractor? A review of process theories in 20 years of entrepreneurship studies. *Entrepreneurship and Regional Development*, 19(6): 453–77.

Timmons, J. 1999. *New Venture Creation* (5th ed.). Homewood, IL: Richard D. Irwin.

Tushman, M., & Romanelli, E. 1985. Organizational evolution: A metamorphosis model of convergence and reorientation. *Research in Organizational Behavior*, 7: 171–22.

Unsworth, K. 2001. Unpacking creativity. *Academy of Management Review*, 26(2): 289–97.

Van de Ven, A. 1992. Longitudinal methods for studying the process of entrepreneurship. In D. L. Sexton & J. D. Kasarda (Eds.), *The State of the Art of Entrepreneurship* (214–42). Boston: PWS-Kent Publishers.

Van de Ven, A., Angel, H., & Poole, M. S. 1989. *Research on the Management of Innovation*. New York: Ballanger Books.

Van de Ven, A., & Poole, M. S. 1990. Methods for studying innovation development in the Minnesota Innovation Research Program. *Organization Science*, 1: 313–35.

Weick, K. 1977. Organization design: Organizations as self-designing systems. *Organizational Dynamics*, 6(2): 30–46.

Weick, K. 1995. *Sensemaking in Organizations*. Newbury Park, CA: SAGE Publications.

Weick, K., & Roberts, K. 1993. Collective mind in organizations: Heedful interrelating on flight decks. *Administrative Science Quarterly*, 38: 357–81.

Weick, K., Sutcliffe, K., & Obstfeld, D. 2005. Organizing and the process of sensemaking. *Organization Science*, 16: 409–21.

Zimmerman, M., & Zeitz, G. 2002. Beyond survival: Achieving new venture growth by building legitimacy. *Academy of Management Review*, 27(3): 414–31.

CHAPTER 11

Phase 2: Stress and Experiments

With the enthusiasm and passion of opportunity tension, the entrepreneur moves into intense activity that pushes the system into a disequilibrium state. At the same time, the increased intensity of disequilibrium organizing produces increased stress in the system, which then sparks a series of experiments that seek to reduce that stress. These two dynamics, stress and experiments, are intertwined in phase 2 of the generative emergence process.

INCREASED STRESS IN THE SYSTEM

Definitionally, *stress* is the result of applying pressure or constraints to a system. For example, in physics the application of a force or torque to an object yields a stress, measured in pounds per square inch. Psychologically, stress is a tension, a felt strain due to factors that can "alter an existing equilibrium" (Webster's Dictionary), usually due to "adverse or demanding circumstances" (Oxford Dictionary).

In this case the force being applied is in the intensity of activity, the disequilibrium organizing, of entrepreneurs and leaders as they take direct action in their pursuit of an opportunity tension. As this pursuit "heats up," gaining strength and momentum, the pressure and constraint on the system increases as well. Thus, the higher the disequilibrium, the more likely stress will be present (expressed) in the system.

Consider again the analogy from dissipative structures theory. Phase 1 disequilibrium organizing refers to "turning up the heat" in the Bernard cell experiment. Up to a point this increase is paralleled by an increase in convection currents, that is, the heat energy is able to flow unimpeded from the source to the sink. Within this normal range conduction currents are sufficient for continuously dissipating the energy through the system and out to the environment. However, as the heat increases, the system begins to reach its upper range of capacity, beyond which the container will exhibit turbulence. Essentially, turbulence is an expression of stress;

it reflects the combination of thermodynamic constraint as the conduction currents in the fluid reach the upper range of their capacity, and the growing pressure being pushed into the system through the continuous increase in energy. These increases in pressure and constraint will lead to an internal stress or tension, the core of phase 2.

In human systems, stress and tension represent the system's "autopoietic" nature, namely that all social systems, and all biological systems, have an inherent drive to remain alive, to continue sustaining themselves. When the system moves beyond the "norm," beyond the commonly known limits of activity, the system itself will strive to keep its organizing process intact—this is a key finding from autopoiesis and autocatalysis (Pantzar & Csanyi, 1991; Padgett, 2011). As the system moves farther away from its normal adaptive state, it begins to express stress.

Types of Stress in Generative Emergence

Stress and tension can be well illustrated by a simple example. Consider again our entrepreneur with an opportunity tension to create a small business. Her aim is to solve a particular sustainability issue that some companies she knows are facing. Her idea and its prospects are motivating; she feels energized by the potential, puts some ideas on paper, and starts to share her vision with others. After some initial positive feedback, she's ready to take entrepreneurial action to realize her aspiration.

In this example, the entrepreneur's actions take place within her social ecology, and within her current dynamic state, which can be envisioned as the existing structures of work, family, friends, profession, community, and personal activities that make up her busy life. As she moves into action, into disequilibrium organizing, she is literally pushing more energy through her existing system, her existing dynamic state. The more energy she generates and the more activities she successfully enacts, the more her current situation shifts into a disequilibrium state, out of its "normal" or current situation and into a period of high intensity and rapid change. From even this simple description, it is possible to spot several types of personal stress that are likely to be expressed in periods of high disequilibrium organizing.

The first is due to *increased workload*: Beyond her current commitments she is adding more and more hours of additional effort, entrepreneurial organizing activities for understanding her market, accessing new resources, expanding her network, developing a product or service, getting support and help from business professionals and advisors, pursuing marketing, and drawing up some initial financials. Workload increase is one of the most common types of organizational stress, although studies show that some people deal with it better than others (Hunter & Thatcher, 2007; Gilboa, Shirom, Fried, & Cooper, 2008). In fact, recent research shows that entrepreneurs and elite athletes in high-performance situations tend to respond to stress in mainly positive ways (Schindehutte, Morris, & Allen, 2006; Savage & Torgler, 2012).

Increased workload may lead to a personal challenge of spending less time and attention on maintaining oneself and one's personal relationships given the time required to pursue the project at hand. Not only can this result in negative reactions by those who are most affected, but it can also mean that the entrepreneur receives less emotional support during a period when she or he needs it most. In a similar way, the "extra" time spent in disequilibrium organizing is sometimes drawn from activities that are personally nurturing, for example, spending less time doing workouts, limiting special events because of a lack of time, reducing commitments to groups and communities. The overall effect is increased tension and stress in all these arenas.

A second type of stress is *cognitive and emotional stress*, often caused by ambiguity and uncertainty. Will the project work? How best to accomplish the goal? How do I convert the initial vision into a working prototype? Who are my ideal collaborators, and is there anyone I should avoid? Where can find answers to my key questions? The ambiguity of these questions generates innumerable possible paths and directions; sorting through the options can lead to even more questions. Of course, most of these questions don't have clear answers, since the very nature of entrepreneurial action is to act without knowing what the result will be (Gartner, Bird, & Starr, 1992; Gartner, 2001).

Uncertainty is increasingly understood to be at the core of entrepreneurship (McMullan & Shepherd, 2006; Sommer, Loch, & Dong, 2009), based in part on the Nobel prize–winning efforts of Khanaman and Tverski (1979; Kahneman, Slovic, & Tversky, 1982; Tversky & Kahneman, 1992), among others. Uncertainty is a key form of cognitive stress, and like the other forms of cognitive stress, it can be felt also in an emotional way.

Pursuing new projects also means rapid learning and action without having everything sorted out. Entrepreneurial circles, as mentioned earlier, express this as "Ready, Fire, Aim" (Masterson, 2008)—act first, see if the action works, and adjust as you go along. This idea has been formalized in the theory of effectuation (Sarasvathy, 2001a, 2001b; Sarasvathy & Venkataramen, 2011), which explains how and why entrepreneurs can effect innovation by working with what's at hand, responding endogenously to create the venture based on the results of these experiments.

Although most seasoned entrepreneurs operate in this bottom-up way, every entrepreneur starts with an aspiration, an intention, and direction they're aiming for. However, the innovation or technology may not work as originally designed. The ambiguity and uncertainty over technological innovations can lead to a third type of stress: *innovation challenges*, significant tangible obstacles for developing the technology, applying it in the way it was envisioned, and constructing an effective organizing model. What if the basic idea doesn't go as planned? What if the invention works at the prototype stage but when scaled up the technology behaves differently—in other words, if it doesn't work in practice? This type of stress is inherent in any pursuit of novelty and represents the gap between hopes for the innovation and its true viability in the applied context.

Another common type of innovation challenge shows up as low sales, often with results that are far below expectations. In many cases this is due to a limitation in the innovation; either it does not work as well as expected, or it is encapsulated in a business model that customers aren't willing to switch to or don't understand. Of course, sometimes innovation challenges are simply due to a poor market analysis—the projected customers really didn't have that need, or they don't need it enough to justify the price and switching costs. But whatever the case, the uncertainty about the innovation and/or its lack of acceptance are a type of stress that has immediate bottom-line implications.

Stress is also sometimes a *systemic resistance*; this fourth kind of stress arises from the changes occurring in structures and from alterations of current patterns of relationship. These are first of all the internal systems and processes that sustain the current dynamic state, routines and practices that have evolved to be as efficient as possible (Gersick & Hackman, 1990; Cohen & Bacdayan, 1994; Pentland & Rueter, 1994). As such, they are the fabric of the system, allowing the dynamic state maintain itself ongoingly (Csanyi & Kampis, 1985; Drazin & Sandelands, 1992).

However, in the pursuit of a new initiative—the drive to create a new dynamic state—at least some these existing structures may be impediments or obstacles to the effort, mainly because they were not designed according to the needs of the emerging venture but to maintain the current dynamic state in the most efficient way possible.[1] With the influx of energy from disequilibrium organizing, the system begins to reach its upper range of capacity, beyond which the "old" structures and routines just don't work any more. As disequilibrium organizing intensifies, the entire system generates stress, as the needs of the not-yet-emerged dynamic state bump up against the constraints of the currently existing system. In management terms this is felt as a resistance to change; in institutional theory it is diagnosed as the challenge of creating change in existing schema and practices. In Lewin's classic model of organizational development, this stress is reflected in the forces of resistance to an organizational change. It tends to be highly frustrating and difficult to deal with (Goldstein, 1988).

Related to systemic resistance is a fifth type of stress, *financial stress*, and more generally the challenge of pursuing a project with extremely limited resources. A lack of cash is a common entrepreneurial complaint, even though most new businesses are started with small amounts of money (Bhide, 1992), most of which comes from equity investments by the founding team, as well as credit cards, bank debt, and loans (Stauder & Kirchhoff, 2004). Still, "Cash is King"—gaining the capital to develop the technology and organize the business without running out of money for ongoing expenses is known to be one of the biggest challenges that entrepreneurs face.

Financial stress is especially high when an entrepreneur is striving to create a new dynamic state while maintaining their current business, or when re-creating their business—moving to plan B (Mullins & Komisar, 2009) or striving to "get to the next level" in the company's climb (Lichtenstein, 2000a, 2000b). In this situation, revenues from ongoing sales are now channeled toward the new business offering, thus directing money away from activities that sustain the existing business. In some cases this is exacerbated by a *reduction* in revenues, as the entrepreneur focuses away from current customers and toward this new opportunity. In addition, technology companies striving to emerge (or re-emerge) often experience "fiscal tension"— the performance gap between business plan forecasts and actual income (March, 1994; Romanelli & Tushman, 1994). In other cases the financial stress occurs as the investment capital is reduced toward zero. This is well known in high-tech firms as the challenge of "jumping the chasm" from initial prototype to a validated version that venture capitalists can then justify investing in (Moore, 2002).

In any of these five ways—increased workload, cognitive stress, innovation challenges, systemic resistance, or financial stress—organizational stress is felt keenly by the entrepreneur and her core team, and often by all the individuals involved in the project. This can lead to a sixth type of stress, which is often the type that is the most salient, namely *interpersonal conflict*. Conflict may arise in response to any of the other forms of stress, but it adds a layer of emotional anxiety as well, due to harmful effects it can have in personal relationships at work. In some cases this conflict can be productive, as when the problems lead to integrative solutions, or when complex issues initially reveal difficult emotions but these are worked through in ways that generate positive learning (Kegan & Lahey, 2001; Smith, 2011). However, the unproductive form of interpersonal conflict can reduce the quality of relationships, decrease learning and interaction, and limit progress in a shared venture. These will not serve the long-term goals of emergence. Nonetheless, unproductive conflict is very often felt in growing ventures, especially when they are facing financial stress and technological challenges.

Contrasts with the Literatures on Organizational Stress

This list of six types of stress is by no means meant to be exhaustive, nor is there an implicit order to the list. Equally, I am not proposing any underlying theory or basis for identifying these types of stress. Instead, they are empirically founded from my research. Intriguingly, academic management scholars view "organizational stress" in a very specific way that contrasts with my categorizations. In particular, the central reviews and meta-analyses of the literature focus on how work stress affects job performance and satisfaction, key issues for human resources and organizational behavior (Sullivan & Bhagat, 1992; Hunter & Thatcher, 2007; Gilboa et al., 2008). And as one might expect, there is a sizable literature on interpersonal conflict, which is often held as a result of stress. The other five forms of stress are studied in a much more limited way.

For example, a smaller set of research has explored how stress is impacted by organizational change (Vakola & Nikolaou, 2005; Dahl, 2011). These studies explore how change efforts can spark stress, and how employee attitudes toward change can either support or diminish change efforts. One in-depth study (Robinson & Griffiths, 2005) explored the ways that transformational change caused stress for employees. The authors found five "sources of change stress," including increased workload, uncertainty/ambiguity and interpersonal conflict, as well as perceived unfairness and loss. Although these components are a useful complement to the six categories described earlier, the generative emergence model proposes stress and experiments as *agents* of change, key drivers of the emergence process, rather than the traditional view of stress as a *result* of change.

Separately, my categories of stress are comparable to, but distinct from, the literature on "problems" that entrepreneurs face, especially those that have been identified in technology ventures (Kazanjian, 1988; Terpstra & Olson, 1993). For example, Terpstra and Olsen interviewed seven CEOs to learn about their key problems. The top five categories in their list are (a) internal financial management; (b) sales/marketing; (c) general management and human resources; (d) production/operations; and (e) organization design.

My data include these types: I have data on financial stress, sales/marketing challenges, technology/production, and some general management issues. However, my study also showed many more personal examples of stress, which include emotional tension, conflict, and felt limitations in resources. In some measure, these differences reflect different methodological choices; while others' studies are based on responses from CEOs only, my data are drawn from all organizational members. Also, whereas previous research used surveys to capture broad issues across a wide sample, my method focuses on personal perceptions in the moment. Another reason for these differences is that my findings spring from a very different view of stress, as a cause and positive indicator that real change is happening, that the disequilibrium organizing is moving the system out of its norm in an effective way.

EMPIRICAL EXAMPLES OF STRESS IN NEW VENTURES

My data reveal these six categories of stress in ventures I studied—these are presented in Table 11.1, which includes a few examples of each category from the four firms.

Tangible measures of stress were gleaned through financial data, especially through performance challenges as a metric for fiscal stress. These data were often available for up to a year before I began collecting data (in projections of business plans and archived income statements). They provide a measure with significant face validity to the founders and implications for all members of the firm. Examples

Table 11.1. SRESS IN THE FOUR VENTURES (REPRESENTATIVE EXAMPLES)

Increased Workload

Pace is frantic. The pulse is nearly dead! *(Marketing Manager, DevelopNet)*

I feel nervous. There's a lot of stuff in the air; concentrating at once. *(CEO, ApplySci)*

Stress levels [are high]. Putting out fires constantly. *(Project Employee, ServiceCo)*

Cognitive Stress

Tough beginning of the week; lots of grumblings, raised waves. Bit of a tough week—a lot of tension. *(Administrator, ApplySci)*

Our analytic tools: We really are not learning—no noticeable level. Why is one batch different from another? *(Analytic Scientist, ApplySci)*

I feel in limbo right now. Until we have a firm answer where the project's going, I feel on shaky ground. *(Lab Technician, ApplySci)*

Innovation Challenges

It pissed me off. . . . I built in as many preventions as I could think of—it didn't help. *(Programmer, DevelopNet)*

These are hard questions. No one has asked them in just this way, in this combination. We're facing tremendous pressure. Can these problems be solved—absolutely. Can they be solved in time? That's a tougher question. *(CTO, ApplySci)*

It did it again: Fatal Error. . . . That means no database backups for all of last week. I'm kind of in a panic about this. *(Office Manager, AgencyInc)*

It wasn't a lay-up; there were still things we needed to figure out. It was kind of like we were a big jet airplane going up the runway but we still had mechanics fixing one of the engines. *(Cofounder, ServiceCo)*

We were falling down on the job, we had defects, every time you turned around there was [another problem]. *(Cofounder, ServiceCo)*

Marketing/Sales Challenges

Marketing is the key now. Tough problem. *(CEO, DevelopNet)*

Not sure who to call—my lists get longer, they don't seem to get shorter. *(CEO, ApplySci)*

At this stage the balls are in the air, things are still looking good, but nothing has dropped yet. It's frustrating. *(Senior Manager, AgencyInc)*

Financial Stress (Organizational Resource Limitations)

At the nub, there's a limited number of really skilled people, who are being cut up too many ways. We've got to close contracts. *(CTO, ApplySci)*

The resource thing is a battle. . . . Right now is a critical time. . . . I don't know how the shift is going to work. 70%/30% kills me. *(Senior Manager, ApplySci)*

We don't have enough people to do it—29 people, most of them doing repetitive [lab work] that doesn't work anyhow. *(Senior Manager, ApplySci)*

So there were probably too few resources, and too little time . . . to really get a lot of things done. *(Controller, ServiceCo)*

(continued)

Table 11.1. CONTINUED

Fiscal Stress

Key issue is: generate sales. That's our problem. We don't have enough success, and we're burning cash. *(CFO, DevelopNet)*

Cash is becoming more critical . . . that's beginning to weigh more heavily. *(Marketing Manager, DevelopNet)*

Can we stay alive? Not the way we're structured financially. The hourglass is running out. I don't know what [the founder] has up his sleeve. *(Senior Scientist, ApplySci)*

Now just keeping the cash flow moving. That's always a challenge. We get into scary situations, but something always pulls us out. *(Office Manager, AgencyInc.)*

Interpersonal Conflict

It's been a bit of a frustrating week. [The manager] and I think it should be going one way. [The founder] wants it to go another. *(Programmer, DevelopNet)*

Part of an ongoing frustration. That same level of intensity over the weekend with the new [web]site. *(Programmer, DevelopNet)*

The bosses contradict each other. . . . The outcomes of meetings, interpretations are very different by [founder] and [executive manager medical]. If we are going to continue engineering in medical stuff, we have a tremendous problem. It is a problem basically of management. *(Senior Scientist, ApplySci)*

---

of these are presented in the figures for DevelopNet and ApplySci, presented later in the chapter.

Cognitive and emotive descriptions of stress occurred throughout the cases, and as one would expect, these are heightened in the most intense moments of organizing. This became evident in my analysis of the stress metrics for each company, through the words that were being said by individual employees. At ApplySci, for example, employees often expressed anxiety about the venture. One senior scientist related: "Can we stay alive? . . . The hourglass is running out. I don't know what [the founder] has up his sleeve." Another staff member commented, "The mood here is tense. . . . People are running all over the place, trying to catch up." The chief technology officer was blunt about the challenges they were facing with the technology itself:

> These are hard questions. . . . We're facing tremendous pressure. Can they be solved—absolutely. Can they be solved in time? That's a tougher question.

Equally intriguing were the changes in stress over time. In order to capture these dynamics, I developed an "index" of stress, which was a count of all specific expressions of stress across all the interviews in a venture for a given week, divided by the total number of employees interviewed that week. The index thus balances out the degree of stress, "averaging" it across the organizations members. The stress index for each venture is presented in Figures 11.1, 11.2, and 11.3.

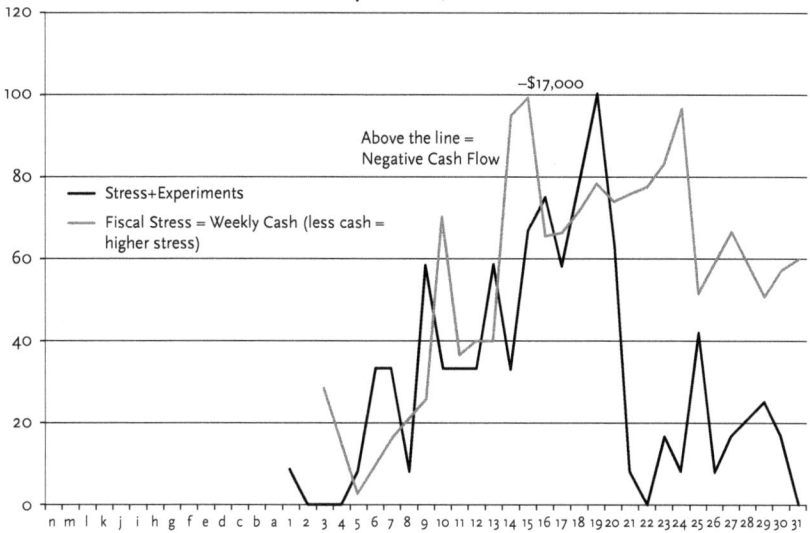

Figure 11.1: Stress Metrics for DevelopNet

This metric allows a visualization of the dynamics of stress over time in each company. As an example, note the rise and fall of stress at ApplySci—the three main peaks of stress there (see Figure 11.2). Initially, the stress index rises for three months in a row, to a peak at data collection period (DCP) 13. Then, after returning to a moderate level, the stress index rises again to a peak at DCP 24. After this

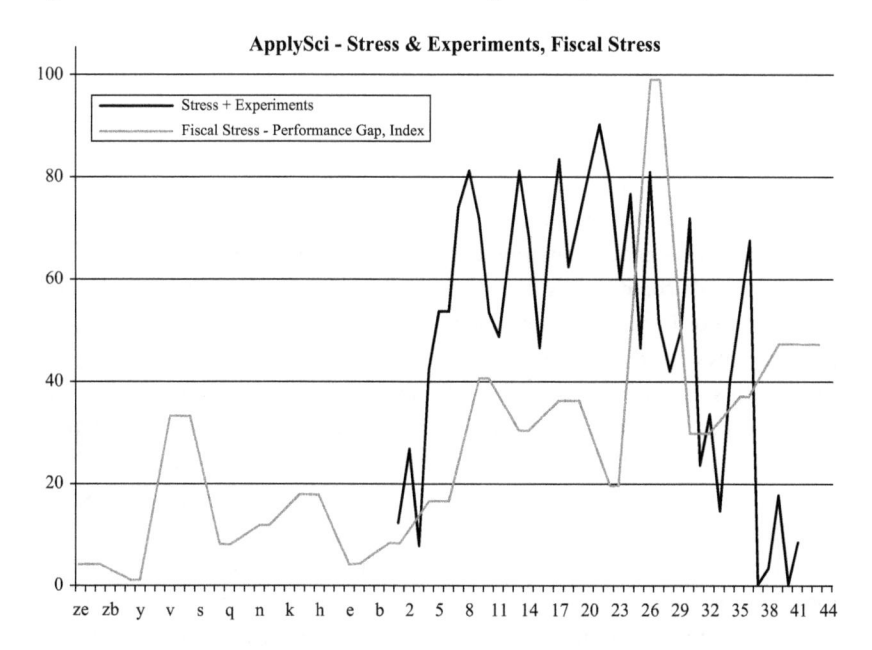

Figure 11.2: Stress Metrics for ApplySci

PHASE 2: STRESS AND EXPERIMENTS

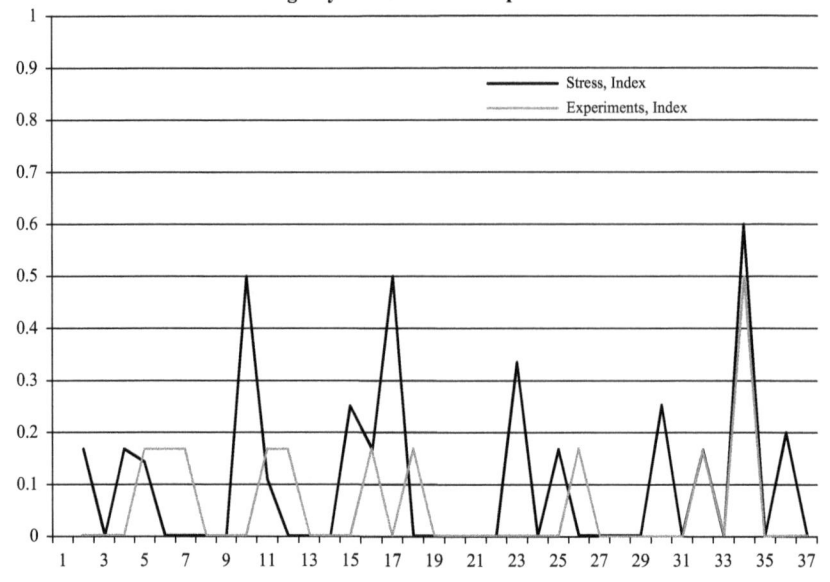

Figure 11.3: Stress Metrics for AgencyInc

second peak, stress appears to decrease over the next eight weeks or so, but then the data show a third sharp rise in stress from DCP 30 through DCP 36. After a brief reprieve this continues right through to the end of the case.

These dynamics are often parallel to the dynamics of experiments, described next.

EXPERIMENTS—SEEDS OF EMERGENCE

In generative emergence, stress is rarely a deterrent; instead, it acts as a motivator whereby the challenges brought on by disequilibrium organizing are met by a stream of creative solutions, ways to resolve the stress. These ideas and innovations are experiments—enacted attempts to resolve the stressful situation(s) being faced.

Experiments come in all shapes and sizes: from a new file system on the computer, to importing current contacts into a professional CRM system, to coming up with a new marketing strategy, to a reformulation of the product platform. Experiments also include pursuing a collaboration that significantly increases value or reduces costs, marketing a validated idea toward a new target or in a new industry, accessing a new distribution system, rethinking the financing for the venture, or drawing up a patent application. The key criterion is that an experiment should somehow increase the capability of the part of the system it impacts.

This criterion is clear from the Bérnard experiment, where the experiments are the perturbations that arise in the system. In thermodynamic terms, perturbations are massive agglomerations of molecules that hold themselves together and rise as a group from the bottom to the top of the container. What's remarkable about these perturbations is that they can "carry" and thus dissipate significantly more heat, up through the container from source to sink, compared to what can be dissipated through conduction currents alone. Thus, each perturbation is a kind of experiment, an attempt by the system to solve the impending problem of continuously increasing heat energy. According to the science, these experiments continue until the system reaches a threshold, at which point one of the perturbations becomes the seed for the emergence of new order.

Management scholars have described experiments in a variety of ways. In strategic terms they occur as cognitive and experiential search mechanisms (Gavetti & Levinthal, 2000; Siggelkow & Rivkin, 2006) that are pursued by agents aiming to solve specific (local) problems. From an evolutionary perspective (Aldrich & Reuf, 2006), experiments are variations that provide novelty and change to social systems and that can lead to organizational founding (Aldrich & Kenworthy, 1999). Experiments play a role in individual and organizational learning as well (Herriott, Levinthal, & March, 1985; Lichtenstein, Lumpkin, & Schrader, 2003; Corbett, 2005; Li & Tesfatsion, 2012). These latter cases reflect a kind of "trial and reinforcement" model that is common in nonlinear ecological systems (Ulanowicz, 1987, 2002).

Management researchers have also documented the importance of experiments in organizational emergence, an approach founded by Smith and his colleagues (Smith, 1986; Smith & Gemmill, 1991; Smith & Comer, 1994) that is based on data from groups and teams in emergence situations. As well, Goldstein's early work (Goldstein, 1988) emphasized the role of experiments in the emergence process, and Goldstein (1994) innovated the idea that experiments could be a tool to support organizational development interventions—an idea that has been expanded by others (Eoyang, 1997; Olson & Eoyang, 2001). Experiments play a key role in a wide range of empirical articles on organizational emergence, including classic works by Chiles, Meyer, and Hench (2004) and Plowman et al. (2007), and innovative studies by Boyatzis and Kolb (2000), Biggiero (2001), Boyatzis (2006, 2008), and Fuller, Warren, and Argyle (2008).

Origins of Experiments

Experiments come from a host of sources, as suggested by the robust literatures on idea generation (De Bono, 2009), product innovation (Henderson & Clark, 1990; Leonard & Sensiper, 1998; Knott, 2003; Link & Siegel, 2007), and organizational creativity (Nystrom, 1979; Brown & Duguid, 1991; Amabile, Conti, Coon, Lazenby, & Herron, 1996; Dosi & Fagiolo, 1998; Lounsbury & Crumley, 2007). A complement to these individual-level examples are organization-wide experiments presented by entrepreneurship scholars who have studied organizational emergence (Bygrave & Hofer, 1991; Gartner, 1993; Bhave, 1994; Aldrich & Kenworthy,

1999; Bhide, 2000) and the creation of new markets (Schumpeter, 1934; Chiles, Bluedorn, & Gupta, 2007; Chiles, Tuggle, McMullen, Bierman, & Greening, 2010; Dew, Reed, Sarasvathy, & Wiltbank, 2011).

In terms of process, some complexity theorists argue that experiments are happening all the time in organizations; in normal conditions these suggestions and ideas generate relatively little change (Leifer, 1989; Dooley, 1997). Since solutions will rise in parallel to a rise in stress, the farther the system moves from equilibrium to disequilibrium organizing, the more likely it is that experiments will be enacted in the system. This idea was first posited by Prigogine and Stengers (1984) and expanded by Nonaka (1988, p. 62):

> The enterprise as an open system carries on a self-renewal character [which is] continuously ... creating fluctuations. [These] rapid ... changes ... can raise the rate at which innovations occur.

The role of stress to catalyze experiments is shown in my data. A good example occurred during a period of high intensity at DevelopNet. As the following interchange between the CFO and the founder suggests, the fiscal foundations of the company were rapidly crumbling, and they needed to quickly figure out the right market and positioning for their technology.

CFO: How was the sales call?
CEO: It was a waste of time! It looks like that contract management idea isn't going to fly.... What if we strip the [simulation] portion of the software, and sell that in an exclusive [licensing] contract? The money is in [those] contracts, [and] it's an exclusive marketplace..... And we retain the commercial [software] piece.
CFO: It's a good idea. The pricing needs to be carefully done. But it gives us the money we need to get things done.

The conversation begins with an acknowledgment that the current business model wasn't working, instead, "the contract management idea" was leading to a lot of fiscal stress that the CFO and CEO talked about frequently. In this case, however, the CEO enacted a kind of modular thinking (de Bono, 2009): By "striping" the core technology (around simulation) off of the current system, they could sell it directly to customers through a licensing revenue model. His experiment was based on his sense that the revenues were in the licensing, not in the application they had designed for it—in his words, the "money is in those contracts." This experiment did end up as the seed for a new order there, albeit after further iterations.

Another origin of experiments is from the diversity of the social ecology: ideas, collaborations, and options that come from the less-connected, "weak tie" elements of social networks that are so important to innovation (Granovetter, 1973; Reuf, 2002). In this case, heterogeneity and diversity are key drivers of experiments, leading to entrepreneurial innovation and emergence (Page, 2007; Kearney,

Gebert, & Voelpel, 2009). Their importance is demonstrated by the fact that heterogeneous agents are an essential ingredients to all models of computational emergence and "self-organization" (see, e.g., Holland, 1995, 1998; McKelvey, 1999, 2002; Gavetti & Levinthal, 2000; Sorenson, 2002; Gavetti, Levinthal, & Rivkin, 2005; Maguire, McKelvey, Mirabeau, & Oztas, 2006; McKelvey, Li, Xu, & Vidgen, 2010).

Another source of experiments is the application of "lateral" and "analogical thinking"—taking a process from one context and trying it out in another (Gassmann & Zeschky, 2008; Mullins & Komisar, 2009). A simple example occurred at ApplySci, in the midst of their dawning realization that the technology had a fundamental flaw, a true innovation challenge that was becoming more and more evident over time. In response, a junior lab technician suggested that the lab scientists meet together once a week without the common flank of managers and the CTO. This experiment was quickly adopted, and it did increase the capacity of the group to keep track of the hypothesis-testing processes for the technology. Of course, this was one of many such experiments and exemplifies the fact that most experiments do not substantively alter the dynamic state. Still, as a whole, they play a role significant in generative emergence.

EXPERIMENTS IN THE NEW VENTURES

My close-up investigation of these four firms revealed a range of experiments, including shifts in the technology/business model, new processes or approaches in marketing and product development, and small changes in internal routines or equipment. A representative list is in Table 11.2.

An intriguing quality to note in Table 11.2 is the range of employees who describe experiments. Most of the experiments in the data are described by junior or mid-level employees; far fewer are from the CEO and executive team. In sum, employees other than the founder are responsible for 86.8% of all experiments across the data set. This confirms the notion that experiments are a systemwide phenomenon, not due solely to top-down leadership moves by the CEO (Goldstein, Hazy, & Lichtenstein, 2010). At the same time in these founder-led companies, the CEO and the board were often the ones whose experiments had the most power and efficacy to break through the current dynamic state and initiate a new one, suggesting a power-law dynamic.

As closely as I examined these companies, it was still very hard to identify one particular experiment that was the seed or source of new order. In some ways, the experiments helped create the conditions for emergence, adding to the disequilibrium and the stress—fluctuations—that were already growing in these systems. In reference to my claim that experiments are a seed of generative emergence into a proposition, a good deal of further analysis and study will be needed before this proposition can be properly confirmed.

Table 11.2. EXPERIMENTS IN THE FOUR VENTURES (REPRESENTATIVE EXAMPLES)

Experiments: Process

Happy about sales rep. Takes us into a whole new area.... Out of DOD, into manufacturing, financial, banks—industry. Going where the money is. *(Senior Programmer, DevelopNet)*

The goal of the seminar has changed focus/content slightly. We're using it as purely supporting, not primary lead-generation. We get that from direct contact sales, with Ralph especially. *(Market Manager, DevelopNet)*

Experiments: Business Strategy

We've refined our materials. We're aiming for a solution sell. Not software but solutions to customer problems.... Whether or not that will translate into sales remains to be seen. *(CFO, DevelopNet)*

Trying to team up with the "big boys"—[DOD companies with] multi-billion dollar contracts. *(Marketing Manager, DevelopNet)*

Andrew is off in Boston to check on a totally different world [i.e., new business model idea]: The multi-media world *(CFO, DevelopNet)*

We had a meeting yesterday where we laid out ... a plan where the business is going to go.... There's going to be some movement of resources—taking away from research and development. It will still continue, just on a reduced scale. *(Senior Scientist, DevelopNet)*

Experiments: Technology/Product

I've been trying to ... add to our page for simulations/gaming.... The technology is pretty new. It's safe to experiment on a game[ing] page. *(Lead Programmer, DevelopNet)*

We're trying a bunch of different things [in the synthesis]. [For example] we're pulling from the Y-reaction.... We're now experimenting with 'X'-levels directly after exothermic. *(Lab Technician, ApplySci)*

My goal is to get a kilogram out this week.... In the process, I'm changing some variables, to outline a process that we're going to follow. *(Lab Technician, ApplySci)*

[Thinking about a new] ... card to go into Product A or Product B; a shopping list of 40 different things—[you can] check off things like: government forms, catalogues for this and that; that we then fulfill.... We don't know [details yet]; its a concept *(Senior Manager, ServiceCo; week 10)*

Experiments: Learning, New Routines, New Equipment

I've been having trouble getting stuff done ... So, I'm learning how to do them [the formulations] myself. *(Marketing Manager, AppySci; previously all formulations were done by scientific/lab staff)*

We're thinking about renting a dryer [i.e., instituting a new method for handling the technology]. You can do 50 lbs./day with it *(Formulations Scientist, ApplySci)*

I'm the fist person to respond to an internal opening. If I got this job I'd basically be the first person to totally change their job description in the company *(Marketing Associate, ServiceCo; week 5)*

Combining Stress and Experiments: Amplification

Stress and experiments are not separate processes but interact reciprocally, each providing momentum for the other. In the next chapter I link these interdependencies with the parallel driver of disequilibrium organizing. Together, all of these increases lead to amplification, a leading edge of generative emergence. In the next chapter I will make this connection more clear.

NOTE

1. According to Odum (Odum & Pinkerton, 1955, Odum, 1969) the defining characteristic of ecosystem health is "flux" that is, the total amount of energy that can flow through the system. In contrast, organizational routines are selected for efficiency, the fewest total resources expended.

REFERENCES

Aldrich, H., & Kenworthy, A. 1999. The accidental entrepreneur: Campbellian antinomies and organizational foundings. In J. Baum & B. McKelvey (Eds.), *Variations in Organization Science* (19–24). Thousand Oaks, CA: SAGE Publications.

Aldrich, H., & Reuf, M. 2006. *Organizations Evolving* (2nd ed.). Thousand Oaks, CA: SAGE Publications.

Amabile, T., Conti, R., Coon, H., Lazenby, J., & Herron, M. 1996. Assessing the work environment for creativity. *Academy of Management Journal*, 39: 1154–84.

Bhave, M. P. 1994. A process model of entrepreneurial venture creation. *Journal of Business Venturing*, 9: 223–42.

Bhide, A. 1992. Bootstrap finance: The art of start-ups. *Harvard Business Review*, 70(6): 109–17.

Bhide, A. 2000. *The Origin and Evolution of New Businesses*. New York: Oxford University Press.

Biggiero, L. 2001. Self-organizing processes in building entrepreneurial networks: A theoretical and empirical investigation. *Human Systems Management*, 20: 209–22.

Boyatzis, R. 2006. An overview of intentional change from a complexity perspective. *Journal of Management Development*, 25: 607–23.

Boyatzis, R. 2008. Leadership development from a complexity perspective. *Consulting Psychology Journal: Practice and Research*, 60: 298–313.

Boyatzis, R., & Kolb, D. 2000. Performance, learning and development as modes of growth and adaptation throughout our lives and careers. In M. Peiperl, M. Arthur, R. Goffee, & T. Morris (Eds.), *Career Frontiers* (76–98). New York: Oxford University Press.

Brown, J. S., & Duguid, P. 1991. Organizational learning and communities-of-practice: Toward a unified view of working, learning, and innovation. *Organization Science*, 2: 40–57.

Bygrave, W., & Hofer, C. 1991. Theorizing about entrepreneurship. *Entrepreneurship Theory and Practice*, 16(2): 13–23.

Chiles, T., Bluedorn, A., & Gupta, V. 2007. Beyond creative destruction and entrepreneurial discovery: A radical Austrian approach to entrepreneurship. *Organization Studies*, 28: 267–493.

Chiles, T., Meyer, A., & Hench, T. 2004. Organizational emergence: The origin and transformation of Branson, Missouri's musical theaters. *Organization Science*, 15(5): 499–520.

Chiles, T., Tuggle, C. S., McMullen, J., Bierman, L., & Greening, D. 2010. Dynamic creation: Elaborating a radical Austrian approach to entrepreneurship. *Organization Studies*, 31: 7–46.

Cohen, M., & Bacdayan, P. 1994. Organizational routines are stored as procedural memory: Evidence from a laboratory study. *Organization Science*, 5(4): 554–68.

Corbett, A. 2005. Experiential learning within the process of opportunity identification and exploitation. *Entrepreneurship Theory and Practice*, 29(4): 473–92.

Csanyi, V., & Kampis, G. 1985. Autogenesis: Evolution of replicative systems. *Journal of Theoretical Biology*, 114: 303–21.

Dahl, M. 2011. Organizational change and employee stress. *Management Science*, 57(2): 240–56.

De Bono, E. 2009. *Lateral Thinking: A Textbook of Creativity*. New York: Penguin.

Dew, N., Reed, S., Sarasvathy, S., & Wiltbank, R. 2011. On the entrepreneurial genesis of new markets: Effectual transformations versus causal search and selection. *Journal of Evolutionary Economics*, 21: 231–53.

Dooley, K. 1997. A complex adaptive systems model of organization change. *Nonlinear Dynamics, Psychology, and the Life Sciences*, 1: 69–97.

Dosi, G., & Fagiolo, G. 1998. Exploring the unknown. On entrepreneurship, coordination and innovation-driven growth. In J. Lesourne & A. Orlean (Eds.), *Advances in Self-Organization and Evolutionary Economics* (308–52). London: Economica.

Drazin, R., & Sandelands, L. 1992. Autogenesis: A perspective on the process of organizing. *Organization Science*, 3: 230–49.

Eoyang, G. 1997. *Coping with Chaos*. Cheyenne, WY: Laguno Corporation.

Fuller, T., Warren, L., & Argyle, P. 2008. Sustaining entrepreneurial business: A complexity perspective on processes that produce emergent practice. *International Entrepreneurship Management Journal*, 4: 1–17.

Gartner, B. 2001. Is there an elephant in entrepreneurship research? Blind assumptions in theory development. *Entrepreneurship Theory and Practice*, 25(4): 27–40.

Gartner, W. 1993. Words lead to deeds: Towards an organizational emergence vocabulary. *Journal of Business Venturing*, 8: 231–39.

Gartner, W., Bird, B., & Starr, J. 1992. Acting as if: Differentiating entrepreneurial from organizational behavior. *Entrepreneurship Theory and Practice*, 16(3): 13–30.

Gassmann, O., & Zeschky, M. 2008. Opening up the solution space: The role of analogical thinking for breakthrough product innovation. *Creativity and Innovation Management*, 17(2): 97–106.

Gavetti, G., & Levinthal, D. 2000. Looking forward and looking backward: Cognitive and experiential search. *Administrative Science Quarterly*, 45: 113–37.

Gavetti, G., Levinthal, D., & Rivkin, J. 2005. Strategy making in novel and complex worlds: The power of analogy. *Strategic Management Journal*, 26: 691–712.

Gersick, C., & Hackman, R. 1990. Habitual routines in task-performing groups. *Organizational Behavior and Human Decision Processes*, 47: 65–97.

Gilboa, S., Shirom, A., Fried, Y., & Cooper, C. 2008. A meta-analysis of work demand stressors and job performance: Examining main and moderating effects. *Personnel Psychology*, 61(2): 227–71.

Goldstein, J. 1988. A far-from-equilibrium systems approach to resistance to change. *Organizational Dynamics*, 15(1): 5–20.

Goldstein, J. 1994. *The Unshackled Organization*. Portland, OR: Productivity Press.

Goldstein, J., Hazy, J., & Lichtenstein, B. 2010. *Complexity and the Nexus of Leadership: Leveraging Nonlinear Science to Create Ecologies of Innovation* New York: Palgrave Macmillan.

Granovetter, M. 1973. The strength of weak ties. *American Journal of Sociology*, 78: 1360–80.

Henderson, R., & Clark, K. 1990. Architectural innovation: The reconfiguration of existing product technologies and the failure of established firms. *Administrative Science Quarterly*, 35: 9–30.

Herriott, S., Levinthal, D., & March, J. 1985. Learning from experience in organizations. *American Economic Review*, 75: 298–302.

Holland, J. 1995. *Hidden Order*. Redwood City, CA: Addison-Wesley.

Holland, J. 1998. *Emergence: From Chaos to Order*. Cambridge, MA: Perseus Books.

Hunter, L., & Thatcher, S. 2007. Feeling the heat: Effects of stress, commitment, and job experience on job performance. *Academy of Management Journal*, 50(4): 953–68.

Kahneman, D., Slovic, P., & Tversky, A. (Eds.). 1982. *Judgment under Uncertainty: Hueristics and Biases*. New York: Cambridge University Press.

Kahneman, D., & Tversky, A. 1979. Prospect theory: An analysis of decision under risk. *Econometrica*, 47(2): 263–92.

Kazanjian, R. 1988. Relation of dominant problems to stages of growth in technology-based new ventures. *Academy of Management Journal*, 31: 257–79.

Kearney, E., Gebert, D., & Voelpel, S. 2009. When and how diversity benefits teams: The importance of team members' need for cognition *Academy of Management Journal*, 52(3): 581–98.

Kegan, R., & Lahey, L. 2001. *How the Way We Talk Can Change the Way We Work: Seven Languages for Transformation*. San Francisco: Jossey-Bass.

Knott, A. M. 2003. Persistent heterogeneity and sustainable innovation. *Strategic Management Journal*, 24(8): 687–705.

Leifer, R. 1989. Understanding organizational transformation using a dissipative structure model. *Human Relations*, 42: 899–916.

Leonard, D., & Sensiper, S. 1998. The role of tacit knowledge in group innovation. *California Management Review*, 40(3): 112–32.

Li, H., & Tesfatsion, L. 2012. Co-learning patterns as emegent market phenomena: An electricity market illustration. *Journal of Economic Behavior and Organization* 82(2): 395–419.

Lichtenstein, B. 2000a. Dynamics of rapid growth and change: A complexity theory of entrepreneurial transitions. In G. Liebcap (Ed.), *Advances in the Study of Entrepreneurship, Innovation, and Economic Growth*, Vol. 6: 161–92. Westport, CT: JAI Press.

Lichtenstein, B. 2000b. Self-organized transitions: A pattern amid the "chaos" of transformative change. *Academy of Management Executive*, 14(4): 128–41.

Lichtenstein, B., Lumpkin, T., & Schrader, R. 2003. Organizational learning by new ventures: Concepts, applications and opportunities. In J. Katz & D. Shepherd (Eds.), *Advances in Entrepreneurship, Firm Emergnece and Growth*, Vol. 6: 11–36. Westport, CT: JAI Press.

Link, A., & Siegel, D. 2007. *Innovation, Entrepreneurship and Technological Change*. New York: Oxford University Press.

Lounsbury, M., & Crumley, E. 2007. New practice creation: An institutional perspective on innovation. *Organization Studies*, 28: 993–1012.

Maguire, S., McKelvey, B., Mirabeau, L., & Oztas, N. 2006. Complexity science and organization studies. In S. Clegg, C. Hardy, W. Nord, & T. Lawrence (Eds.), *Handbook of Organization Studies* (2nd ed., 165–214. London: SAGE Publications.

March, J. 1994. The evolution of evolution. In J. Baum & J. Singh (Eds.), *Evolutionary Dynamics of Organizations* (39–52). New York: Oxford University Press.

Masterson, M. 2008. *Ready, Fire, Aim: Zero to $100 Million in No Time Flat*. New York: John Wiley & Sons.

McKelvey, B. 1999. Toward a Campbellian realist organization science. In J. Baum & B. McKelvey (Eds.), *Variations in Organization Science* (383–412). Thousand Oaks, CA: SAGE Publications.

McKelvey, B. 2002. Model-centered organization science epistemology. In J. Baum (Ed.), *Companion to Organizations* (752–80). Thousand Oaks, CA: SAGE Publications.

McKelvey, B., Li, M., Xu, H., & Vidgen, R. 2013. Re-thinking Kauffman's NK fitness landscape: From artifact and groupthink to weak-tie effects. *Human Systems Management*, 32(1): 17–42.

McMullan, J., & Shepherd, D. 2006. Entrepreneurial action and the role of uncertainty in the theory of the entrepreneur. *Academy of Managment Review*, 31: 132–52.

Moore, G. 2002. *Crossing the Chasm: Marketing and Selling Disruptive Products to Mainstream Customers*. New York: HarperBusiness.

Mullins, J., & Komisar, R. 2009. *Getting to Plan B: Breaking Through to a Better Business Model*. Boston: Harvard Business Review Press.

Nonaka, I. 1988. Creating organizational order out of chaos: Self-renewal in Japanese firms. *California Management Review*, 30(Spring): 57-73.
Nystrom, H. 1979. *Creativity and Innovation*. New York: John Wiley & Sons.
Odum, H. 1969. The strategy of ecosystem development. *Science*, 164: 262-70.
Odum, H., & Pinkerton, R. 1955. Time's speed regulator: The optimum efficiency for maximum power output in physical and biological systems. *American Scientist*, 43(2): 331-43.
Olson, E., & Eoyang, G. 2001. *Facilitating Organization Change*. San Francisco: Jossey-Bass.
Padgett, J. 2011. Autocatalysis in chemistry and the origin of life. In *The Emergence of Organizations and Markets* (33-70). Princeton, NJ: Princeton University Press.
Page, S. 2007. *The Difference: How the Power of Diversity Creates Bettter Groups, Firms, Schools, and Societies*. Princeton, NJ: Princeton University Press.
Pantzar, M., & Csanyi, V. 1991. The replicative model of the evolution of the business organization. *Journal of Social and Biological Structures*, 14: 149-63.
Pentland, B., & Rueter, H. 1994. Organizational routines as grammars of action. *Administrative Science Quarterly*, 39: 484–510.
Plowman, D. A., Baker, L., Beck, T., Kulkarni, M., Solansky, S., & Travis, D. 2007. Radical change accidentally: The emergence and amplification of small change. *Academy of Management Journal*, 50: 515–43.
Prigogine, I., & Stengers, I. 1984. *Order out of Chaos*. New York: Bantam Books.
Reuf, M. 2002. Strong ties, weak ties and islands: Structural and cultural predictors of organizational innovation. *Industrial and Corporate Change*, 11(3): 427–49.
Robinson, O., & Griffiths, A. 2005. Coping with the stress of transformational change in a government department. *Journal of Applied Behavioral Science*, 41(2): 204–21.
Romanelli, E., & Tushman, M. 1994. Organizational transformaton as punctuated equilibrium: An empirical test. *Academy of Management Journal*, 37: 1141–66.
Sarasvathy, S. 2001a. Causation and effectuation: Toward a theoretical shift from economic inevitability to entrepreneurial contingency. *Academy of Management Review*, 26: 243–63.
Sarasvathy, S. 2001b. Effectual rationality in entrepreneurial strategies: Existence and bounds. *Academy of Management Best Papers Proceedings*, Vol. 61: ENT, D1–D7.
Sarasvathy, S., & Venkataramen, S. 2011. Entrepreneurship as method: Open questions for an entrepreneurial future. *Entrepreneurship Theory and Practice*, 35(1): 113–35.
Savage, D., & Torgler, B. 2012. Nerves of steel? Stress, work performance and elite athletes. *Applied Economics*, 44(19): 2423–35.
Schindehutte, M., Morris, M., & Allen, J. 2006. Beyond achievement: Entrepreneurship as extreme experience. *Small Business Economics*, 27(4/5): 349–68.
Schumpeter, J. 1934. *The Theory of Economic Development*. Cambridge, MA: Harvard University Press.
Siggelkow, N., & Rivkin, J. 2006. When exploration backfires: Unintended consequences of multilevel organizational search. *Academy of Management Journal*, 49: 779–96.
Smith, C. 1986. Transformation and regeneration in social systems: A dissipative structure perspective. *Systems Research*, 3: 203–13.
Smith, C., & Comer, D. 1994. Change in the small group: A dissipative structure perspective. *Human Relations*, 47: 553–81.
Smith, C., & Gemmill, G. 1991. Self-organization in small groups: A study of group effectivenss within non-equilibrium conditions. *Human Relations*, 44: 697–716.
Smith, D. M. 2011. *The Elephant in the Room: How Relationships Make or Break the Success of Leaders and Organizations*. San Francisco: Jossey-Bass.
Sommer, S., Loch, C., & Dong, J. 2009. Managing complexity and unforseeable uncertainty in startup companies: An empirical study. *Organization Science*, 20: 118–13.

Sorenson, O. 2002. Interorganizational complexity and computation. In J. Baum (Ed.), *Companion to Organizations* (664–85). Malden, MA: Blackwell Publishers.

Stauder, M., & Kirchhoff, B. 2004. Funding the first year of business. In W. Gartner, K. Shaver, N. Carter, & P. Reynolds (Eds.), *Handbook of Entrepreneurial Dynamics* (352–71). Thousand Oaks, CA: SAGE Publications.

Sullivan, S., & Bhagat, R. 1992. Organizational stress, job satisfaction and job performance: Where do we go from here. *Journal of Management*, 18(2): 353–75.

Terpstra, D., & Olson, P. 1993. Entrepreneurial start-up and growth: A classification of problems. *Entrepreneurship Theory and Practice*, 17(3): 5–20.

Tversky, A., & Kahneman, D. 1992. Advances in prospect theory: Cumulative representation of uncertainty. *Journal of Risk and Uncertainty*, 5(4): 297–323.

Ulanowicz, R. 1987. Growth and development: Variational principles reconsidered. *European Journal of Operational Research*, 30: 173–78.

Ulanowicz, R. 2002. Ecology, a dialog between the quick and the dead. *Emergence*, 4(1–2): 34–52.

Vakola, M., & Nikolaou, L. 2005. Attitudes towards organizational change: What is the role of employees' stress and commitment. *Employee Relations*, 27(2): 160–74.

CHAPTER 12
Phase 3: Amplification and a Critical Event

Our entrepreneur is making a passionate effort toward capitalizing the opportunity, putting hours upon hours of time and effort into making this idea happen. Her influx of energy "turns up the heat" in her social ecology, pushing the system into disequilibrium, out of the norm, aiming toward the envisioned state. In the process, she's facing some stress. Not just the tiredness from working 60 to 70 hours a week, but also from the uncertainty, the challenges in developing a prototype and an organizing model that work, the push-back from those who don't get the idea or think its worthy. At the same time, her optimism and fortitude allow her to meet these challenges with experiments—new ideas and internally generated attempts to reduce the stress in the system.

And so we arrive at phase 3—amplification and a critical threshold. These two qualities are sequential and build on each other. Each is described separately, then with examples I will show how they are linked.

AMPLIFICATION OF THE SYSTEM

According to studies in a several complexity science fields, as a system moves farther away from its reference state into disequilibrium, there is an increase in positive reinforcement cycles within it (Anderson, 1999). This has been termed "deviation amplification" by Maruyama (1963), and the dynamic has been noted by a host of scholars (Eigen, 1971; May, 1974, 1976; Haken, 1977; Eigen & Schuster, 1979; Prigogine & Stengers, 1984; Arthur, 1990). With this increase in positive feedback, the occurrence of one action or event increases the likelihood that other similar events will occur in the system (Arthur, 1988, 1994; Krugman, 1996; Sterman, 1989), thus pushing the system toward further change. Amplification is thus a natural result of the nonlinear dynamics of disequilibrium, a point (Dooley, 1997, p. 87) expresses clearly:

> Below a certain threshold level, change is unlikely and fluctuations are dampened. Above the threshold value, change is imminent and fluctuations are magnified.

For social entities, a powerful shift occurs during the increase in disequilibrium organizing and stress, amidst a rise in experiments and other fluctuations in the system. Up to a specific threshold a dynamic state will naturally dampen fluctuations so as to remain in its current structure. However, at a threshold point the system moves into a regime of amplification, where experiments can become magnified and extended throughout the system. In system dynamics language, the system shifts from a dampening mode into a reinforcing mode. Usually this starts in specific pockets and then extends throughout the venture.

Amplification is closely correlated to stress, as nicely explained by Rudolph and Repenning (2002), in their analysis of disaster dynamics. They start by showing how increasing information requires a higher capability for processing it; this can be heightened by stress, leading to higher performance. However, if the stress rises too high,[1] a secondary process unfolds whereby performance is reduced, thus increasing stress, which further reduces performance, in an amplifying positive feedback loop that ultimately leads to a system crash (Rudolph & Repenning, 2002, p. 12–14):

> If the stress level rises enough . . . the system's response changes considerably. Added stress causes a decline in the net resolution rate [the rate at which people can resolve interruptions to the system]. . . . Rather than offsetting the change in the number of unresolved interruptions . . . the system amplifies it . . . in a reinforcing feedback process.

Their system dynamics model can predict the actual timing of this amplification process: "Once the net resolution rate falls below the steady-state arrival rate . . . the stock of interruptions pending shoots up, raising stress and causing the system to collapse."

Many empirical studies of emergence likewise connect experiments and amplifications, showing how these two phases are interdependent and interconnected. For example, at Mission Church (Plowman et al., 2007), "the tension the organization was experiencing . . . made it all the more likely that a small change could emerge and be amplified into something much larger" (Plowman et al., 2007, p. 537). At Mission Church, that small change was a seemingly simple idea by a few young adult members and their friends to provide free meals for neighborhood homeless people during one Sunday morning service. Given the "silk and stockings" heritage of the membership, such an idea would normally by quickly quashed. But in the context of emerging disequilibrium conditions in the church, their experiment became amplified in unpredictable ways, ultimately becoming the seed for the re-emergence of the institution.

In that case, the pace of amplification was remarkable: the upstart group's original goal, one breakfast for 75 marginalized customers, was quickly followed by breakfasts served every week, for up to 200 customers. At one of the weekly breakfasts a doctor arrived with a small table for informal check-ups, initiating what became a large-scale free medical clinic at the church. Over time, the breakfasts were further amplified into a full-day program for marginalized individuals in the community; additional services, some funded through public grants, were added as well. Each of these "experiments" supports a positive feedback process through which the momentum of the entire endeavor increases, faster and stronger.

In these ways the system moves farther into disequilibrium, with stress and experiments being amplified. As many an entrepreneur can attest, the venture is pushed to the brink of its capacity, the entrepreneur is doing all she can, stretching beyond her (imagined) capability, while working out the details and facing critical pressures in many directions. Will the venture take off? Will the opportunity get capitalized on? Those questions are "decided" at the critical event.

CRITICAL EVENTS

Empirical studies strongly suggest that at the peak of these dynamics there is a critical event, a kind of systemwide moment of decision. This may happen at a meeting with the strongest prospect, with the aim of closing the first major deal. It may be, like at DevelopNet, the final meeting with the final possible venture capital firm, the result of which would determine if there was any outside funding to be had for their projected growth plan. In other cases the critical event becomes the straw that breaks the camel's back—a piece of information or a result or a relationship that finally turns the venture in one direction or the other. In all cases these reflect the culmination of the process that leads to a final decision, a clear commitment to go one way or the other.

Many disciplines of complexity science recognize the importance of critical thresholds and phase transitions. For example, Kauffman (2000, pp. 56–57) builds on random graph theory to describe the increase of links within a network as an incremental process, until the ratio of links to nodes passes a specific point, when

> a giant cluster suddenly forms. . . . [A]ll of a sudden most of the [small] clusters have become cross-connected into one giant structure. The rapid increase is the signature of something like a phase transition.

Likewise, critical thresholds, and the transitions they generate to new organizing regimes, are central to the theory of self-organized criticality (Bak & Chen, 1991; Morel & Ramanujam, 1999), as well as to the processes that lead to power law dynamics (Stanley et al., 1996; Andriani & McKelvey, 2007). Similar language is used to describe the bifurcation point in nonlinear dynamical systems (May,

1976) and the *control parameter*, which "measures the moment when the system diverges into two or more directions" (Guastello, 1995, p. 24). Guastello continues: "All bifurcations share a common trademark, which is the existence of a critical point, or *bifurcation point*" (italics in original). Meyer and his colleagues (Meyer, Gaba, & Colwell, 2005, p. 470) extend this idea in the context of nonlinear change:

> In our own studies of organizational fields, we described non-linear changes as jolts, step functions, oscillations, and emergence. Others have used the terms turning points (Abbott, 2001), thresholds or tipping points (Granovetter, 1978), phase transitions (Prigogine & Stengers, 1984), increasing returns (Arthur, 1989) and network externalities (Katz & Shapiro, 1985).

Similar descriptions of critical thresholds are given by management scholars exploring organizational transformation (Golembiewski, Billingsley, & Yeager, 1975; Bigelow, 1982; Leifer, 1989), momentum in change and emergence (Jansen, 2004; Lichtenstein & Kurjanowicz, 2010), and ways in which complexity science can advance our understanding of entrepreneurship and innovation (Bygrave, 1989; Cheng & Van de Ven, 1996; Anderson, 1999). Organization scientists have explored the role and importance of thresholds in collective behavior (Granovetter, 1978; Granovetter & Soong, 1986; Macy, 1991). In the context of generative emergence, amplification dynamics lead to critical thresholds, with a result that may or may not reflect the original goals for the venture.

In the thermodynamic analogy and in system dynamics, the timing of this critical event is relatively precise; researchers can specify that point at which the system will shift into the new regime of order. McKelvey (2004, pp. 319–320) refers to these threshold points in his distinction between the two main school's of complexity science, the American school and the European school:

> [According to the European school,] a phase transition occurs because an imposing energy differential, what I term adaptive tension (McKelvey, 2004), exceeds what is called the first critical value, R_{c1}, which defines the lower bound of the region of emergent complexity.... Phase transitions are often required to overcome the threshold-gate effects characteristic of most human agents. This, in turn, requires the adaptive tension driver to rise above R_{c1}. Once these stronger than normal instigation effects overcome the threshold gates, then, assuming the other requirements are present (heterogeneous, adaptive learning agents, and so forth), coevolution starts. Neither seems both necessary and sufficient by itself, especially in social settings.
>
> American complexity scientists tend to focus on R_{c2}—the "edge of chaos" (Kauffman, 1993; 2000; Lewin, 1999), which defines the upper bound of the region of emergent complexity. What happens at R_{c1} is better understood; what happens at R_{c2} is more obscure.

In sum, critical thresholds play a major role in all dynamic systems, and complexity science studies show that these thresholds are catalyzed by positive feedback and amplification dynamics. Translating those findings into the present model, amplification and a critical threshold event will occur (only) when there has been a continued increase in disequilibrium organizing *and* a concomitant increase in stress and experiments.

Two data sets help make clear the dynamics of amplification and of critical thresholds. One is a case study based on an in-depth analysis of Republic of Tea, a start-up company in the high-end retail tea market. The second draws on my data from the four ventures.

AMPLIFICATION IN THE REPUBLIC OF TEA

The Republic of Tea was founded in 1992 as a national distributor of premier teas and tea-making items, advocating an American "Tea Mind" by encouraging consumers to slow down and take life "sip by sip, rather than gulp by gulp" (Mitchell, 1992). The venture started in conversation between strangers in an airplane. Over the following 18 months their cross-country organizing process was enacted through hundreds of fax transmissions back and forth, detailing the conception and realization of the business concept. These faxes were reproduced into a best-selling business book, titled *The Republic of Tea* (Ziegler, Ziegler, & Rosenzweig, 1994). Since these fax transmissions were their nearly exclusive mode of communicating, they reveal the internal dynamics of the organization's emergence. As part of a larger project designed by Bill Gartner in which these data were analyzed in a variety of perspectives by entrepreneurship scholars (Gartner, 2010), a colleague and I (Lichtenstein & Kurjanowicz, 2010) pursued a time-series analysis of organizing behaviors that led to the emergence of the new firm. The full methodology is in note[2]; it corresponds to the approach used for my dissertation and other work.

The transmissions include letters, notes, idea descriptions, and visible progress, along with sketches and other elements. In our analysis and coding of the transcripts, we looked for specific actions that either of the entrepreneurs took, what we called entrepreneurial "moves" made by the founders (Lichtenstein, Dooley, & Lumpkin, 2006). Our analysis revealed three categories of moves: idea generation, planning, and tangible moves. Our qualitative time-series analysis showed that the more *tangible* the actions, the more likely the venture was to gain momentum (Lichtenstein & Kurjanowicz, 2010).

Here, my aim is to highlight the momentum process itself, to illustrate amplification. To do so, I simply aggregated all three types of entrepreneurial moves into a total count of moves each week. These are graphed in Figures 12.1 and 12.2.

A close look at the time axis on both figures will suggest that the organizing process was not continuous; instead, we found three distinct epochs or periods of organizing. The first period, shown in Figure 12.1, extends from the first week after their inspiring airplane conversation about their new business idea, through a flurry of activity for a few months, then to week 12 when all organizing activity stops. Nearly two-thirds of

Republic of Tea - Phase 1
Ideation, Planning & Tangible Moves

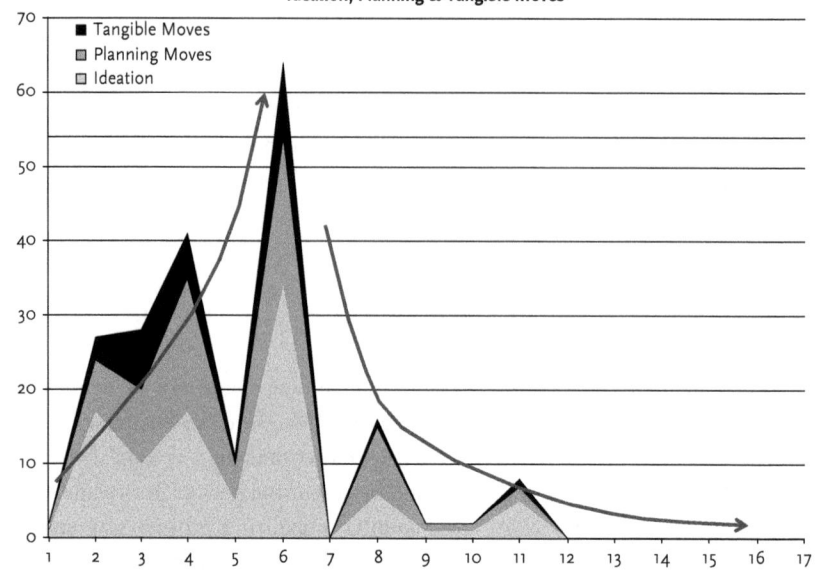

Figure 12.1: Republic of Tea—Period 1, Total Entrepreneurial Moves

all transmissions occur in these first three months. At the same time, the pattern of organizing is unmistakable: a huge immediate increase, followed by a just-as-rapid drop, leading to a flat line when no further organizing moves are made at all.

A look at the three *types* of moves shows why this may be the case. Figure 12.1 shows that the primary moves in phase 1 are idea generation—coming up with ideas, sharing visions, and describing the possibilities for the business. In contrast, planning and tangible moves take a back seat, each averaging about a quarter of the total ideas in period 1. For this reason and others, the organizing effort gains short-term momentum but quickly dissipates to nothing. Note that this pattern of rapid early momentum has been shown to be rather common in nascent firms; our study on the complexity dynamics of nascent entrepreneurs (Lichtenstein et al., 2007) found that this pattern predicts failed emergence across a large sample of nascent firms.

What follows is nearly a year of no organizing activity at all; there are no recorded transmissions between the founders from week 12 through week 64. In all respects it appears that the venture is "dead," although the book suggests that some intriguing behind-the-scenes activity was still going on (Ziegler et al., 1994). Then the effort starts up again; however, the resulting pattern is nearly opposite from its first iteration. Specifically, in this phase the majority of moves are in planning, with some key peaks in tangibility that seem to pave the way for bursts of activity in week 70, weeks 75–77, weeks 81–84, and finally in weeks 89–90 (see Figure 12.2). At the same time, idea generation becomes less and less important, reflecting only 26% of the total period 3 process.

[284] *Generative Emergence*

Republic of Tea - Phase 3
Ideation, Planning, and Tangible Moves

■ Tangibility
■ Planning Moves
■ Ideation

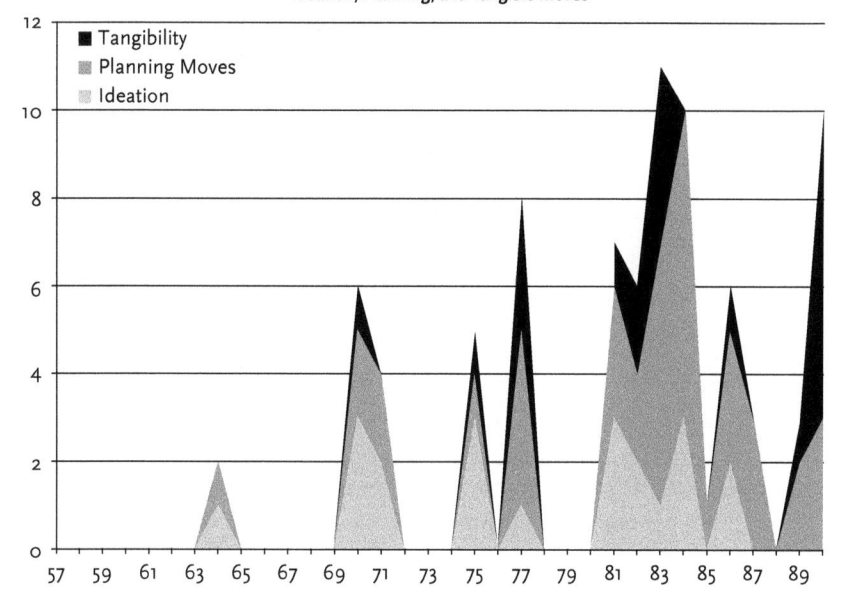

Figure 12.2: Republic of Tea—Period 3, Ideation, Planning, and Tangible Moves

For these and other reasons (see Lichtenstein & Kurjanowicz 2010), we suggest that tangibility does catalyze momentum: The more tangible the entrepreneurial moves, the more likely the venture will gain acceleration and the more likely it will emerge, as does Republic of Tea. In fact, the start-up organization surpassed its revenue projections by 200% for each of the first three years, leading to remarkable 30% annual growth rate. Thus, momentum in this case not only led to emergence, but to initial financial success as well.

EXAMPLES OF AMPLIFICATION IN THE FOUR VENTURES

DevelopNet's Amplification

DevelopNet's main effort extended for six and a half months, from the announcement of its new vision in a March 1996 business plan to the founder's decision to quit the project. This progress is clear in the chart in Figure 12.3, which shows disequilibrium organizing growing dramatically from data collection period (DCP) "n" (corresponding to mid-March 1996), through DCP 13, just before the founder's final decision. Likewise, stress and experiments, now a combined variable to emphasize momentum-building, grow dramatically from DCP 1 through DCP 16 and beyond, continuing upward to a peak at DCP 19. Added to this is a measure of fiscal stress, an index of weekly cash flow position. This is taken from the week-by-week accounting report which calculates all revenues minus all expenses for that

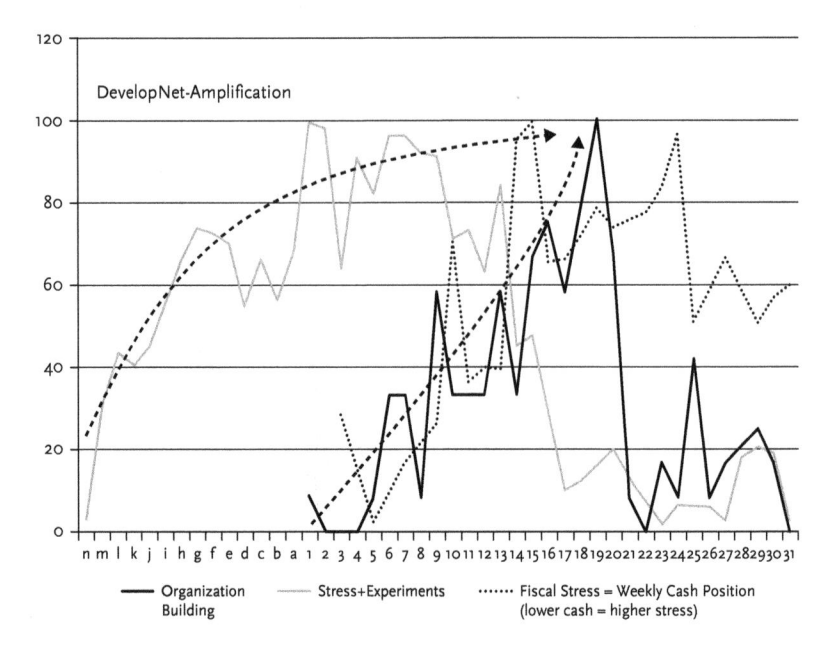

Figure 12.3: Amplification at DevelopNet

week. Importantly, at the peaks, DCP 14–16 and DCP 24, net cash is negative. When cash is negative, a small business will disband very soon thereafter.

From the chart in Figure 12.3, the amplification of stress is unmistakable: The rise in fiscal stress is parallel to the rise in stress and experiments, even though the two measures are functionally distinct. Disequilibrium organizing rises during this time as well; an informal trend-line analysis suggests that organization building activities grew consistently and in parallel to stress and experiments, both rising toward a culmination at DCP 16, which was the week of the critical event, as I will describe later.

To the question of why disequilibrium organizing does not continue through DCP 16, a closer look at the data reveals a significant decision by the CEO that was not apparent by observation. According to the time-card data, the week after a "final" peak of organization-building activity at DCP 14, the founder completed the deal for a short-term consulting contract, the first one he had entertained since March 1996. Because of his projected negative cash flow he decided to take on the work, having his programmers pursue client work instead of organization-building activities. Thus, for the next three weeks and beyond, from DCP 14 to DCP 19, two programmers were pulled off the project; together they put in 73+ hours per week on the contract, and a third programmer pitched in as well. By this analysis the founder knew the inevitable would happen and thus brought in the contract to stem the negative cash flow even before pulling the plug on the entire project.

In sum, the dual increases in disequilibrium organizing and stress and experiments generated an amplification of the system, to a peak at DCP 16, the critical

[286]   *Generative Emergence*

event in the system. As I will present in Chapter 13, this critical event sparks the emergence a new dynamic state; new order emerges in DCP 15–DCP 20.

Amplification at ApplySci

Initially at ApplySci, their slow steady increase in work activity stayed within the "norm" for the new venture; there is no evidence of ongoing fiscal stress until about DCP 8. However, my coding of stress and experiments shows a jump at DCP 5 through DCP 8, with continued high peaks through DCP 27 (see Figure 12.4). Similarly, fiscal stress makes a huge jump after DCP 23, peaking at DCP 26.

At the same time, note the significant jump in work activity from DCP 18 through DCP 27. Even disregarding the dip during the holidays (DCP 17 through DCP 19 is the end of December), once January arrived work activity soared to a peak at DCP 27, exactly meeting the peaks of fiscal stress and stress and experiments. Together these three metrics show a major amplification of disequilibrium organizing *and* stress and experiments, portending a major shift to come.

Amplification at ServiceCo

Even in retrospective interviews, a sense of amplification was quite clear at ServiceCo. The rise in project employees, a 300% increase over nine months, is evidence of disequilibrium organizing. Everyone was deeply engaged in pursuing the

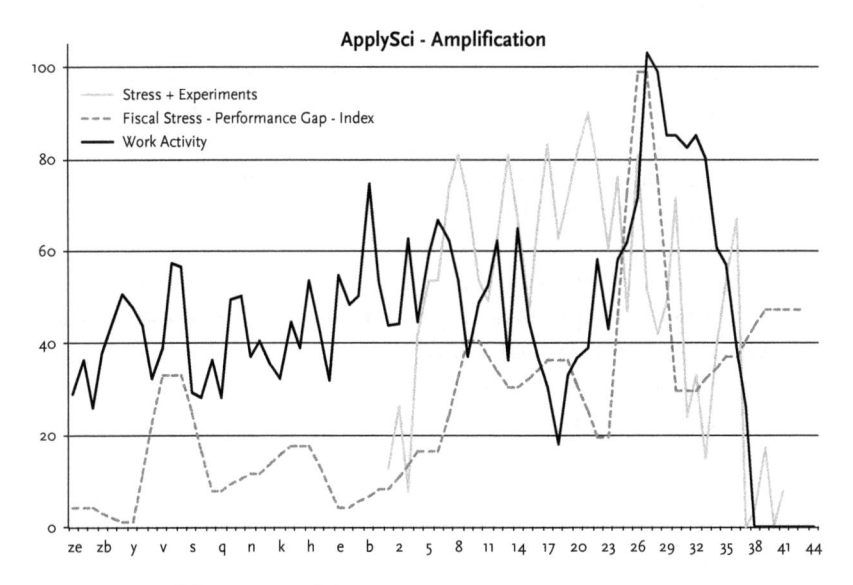

Figure 12.4: Amplification at ApplySci

new PeopleServe project; the small company was pushing forward at top speed. Unfortunately, the roll-out of the new product was not nearly as successful as they had hoped. Not only were fewer people signing up, but additional problems with the organizing model presented the founders and executive team with some worrying questions. A good view of these accelerating problems is given by the acting CFO of the company:

> In the first year we expected to get 30,000 members, and we probably got 13,000. And although we were able to sell [local] advertising, the problem is we weren't focusing on national.... [W]e had said we wanted to get ten advertisers, and we had two. So then that became a problem.... Then, doing the resource directories [we found an] issue: if someone buys one, they don't need one the next year. So I'm not sure if PeopleServe is a good idea... a lot of pieces needed to be figured out. (Acting CFO, ServiceCo)

According to the director of the project, these challenges seemed to accumulate, becoming worse and worse over time, until they called the entire organizing model into question:

> [The problems became clear] pretty quickly, as we went from [a roll-out of] 100 cities, to 50 cities, to 25 cities, to 10 cities. And as the time frame in which this was to be accomplished went from 9 months, to 12 months, to 18 months, to some day. The formula around which PeopleServe was originally designed, and the way they were staffing it [didn't work]; it was inadequately staffed to accomplish those goals, both in number and in quality.... And then it became pretty clear, finally, to more and more people, that the formula around PeopleServe ... was not going to work. (Director, PeopleServe)

A marvelous illustration of the amplifying problems at ServiceCo was given by the senior marketing manager, who was heavily involved in the PeopleServe project while maintaining his marketing leadership for MarketServe. In his quote he starts by identifying a central cultural value of PeopleServe—that everyone should work as hard (or harder!) than possible to achieve it:

> So there was this mentality which was, you know, we always strive to achieve 150%.... We go after that idea and we make it happen and we do it 150%. And what ended up happening was, we were continually going up the mountain, but as we were going up the mountain some of the rocks underneath us were falling.... We could have still gotten to the top ... but the question was, did we want the mountain to keep disintegrating as we got to the top? (Senior Marketing Manager, PeopleServe)

Finally, the amplification to a critical event was well expressed by the cofounder of ServiceCo, the one who came up with the PeopleServe idea. Here he uses an airplane metaphor to describe the peak of amplification in disequilibrium organizing and stress and experiments, which led to a shared decision to cut the project:

> [My cofounder] was very closely involved in [the decision]. Because we still had some unanswered questions around the product. It wasn't a lay-up; there were still things we needed to figure out. It was kind of like we were a big jet airplane going up the runway but we still had mechanics fixing one of the engines. . . . It was not a good way of doing things. But we have eternal optimism that we can figure things out; and sometimes we have too much optimism and we don't have enough counterbalancing forces.

As I will detail in the next chapter, this decision led to a nearly complete reordering of the company, establishing a new dynamic state that has been essentially retained to the present.

AgencyInc.

The amplification chart (Figure 12.5) for AgencyInc suggests a lack of amplification, even a lack of correlation between work activities and stress. Statistically, this disconnection is proven: the Pearson correlation coefficient comparing the two is close to zero, $a = 0.018$. Thus far in the case we find no momentum for emergence; that will be confirmed for the final two phases as well.

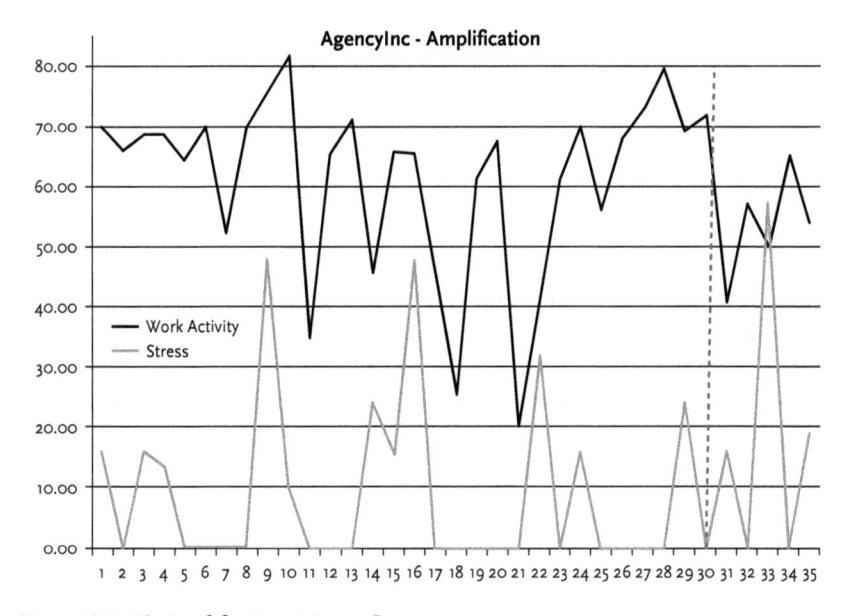

Figure 12.5: No Amplification at AgencyInc.

EXAMPLES OF CRITICAL EVENTS IN THE FOUR VENTURES

Examples of amplification are relatively easy to track with my dissertation data. What was more challenging was to identify the critical events in these ventures. In each case there was a specific incident that directly preceded a major shift; this critical event was later described as a catalyst for change. Critical events most often were long-anticipated meetings between the entrepreneur(s) and a key stakeholder—a major client, a board member, an adviser (see Table 12.1). This critical meeting led to a decision, made either by the founder or by the stakeholder on behalf of (or against) the entrepreneur, a decision that had a significant effect on the identity and direction of the venture. The meeting thus functions as a symbolic change point that distinguishes what the company is *before* the meeting from what the company is *after* the meeting.

Another feature of these meetings is that although they were planned, their outcome was unpredictable, and in most of the cases the decision was a surprise. This quality of "planned but unpredictable" reflects an intriguing middle ground between teleological change and the uncertainly inherent to complex adaptive systems change. Finally, these meetings were indeed threshold moments; as the case study results show, each was highly correlated to significant changes in the other variables.

In some cases the entrepreneur(s) and senior managers were well aware of the criticality of the situation. In fact, it appears that they used the critical event as a leverage point for shifting their overall direction. That is, although the timing and specification of the critical event may be unpredictable, it seems to occur as a kind of culmination of effort, occurring at the climax of organizing activities and stress. In this way the entrepreneur latches on to the critical event as tangible evidence of a shift, a shift he or she had been considering for some time.

A good example of this occurred at DevelopNet, where the stress index—total mentions of stress each week divided by the number of employees I interviewed—increased by 523% over a 15-week period, to a peak in DCP 19. Near the apex of this rise, in the midst of a period of severe negative cash flow, the founder reported the end of the effort.

> We've hit the trip wire. . . . Retrenching. We're going off the financial markets. (CEO, DevelopNet; DCP 16).

The "trip wire" was a key meeting with the only venture capital firm still exploring the prospect of early-stage financing. "When HT ventures said they weren't going to fund this. That was the critical event."

He elaborated soon thereafter (DCP 20),

> I decided we're going to put the whole thing on hold. . . . We've abandoned the charge-up-the-hill-to-the-$100-million-dollar-company. . . . Rather than charge up the hill, is to license the technology, and keep them busy with consulting.

Table 12.1 CRITICAL EVENTS IN THE FOUR VENTURES—REPRESENTATIVE EXAMPLES

DevelopNet

We're up against it; quickly running out of cash. We can't meet payroll next week unless we can maximize our line of credit. And Peter doesn't want to do that now. That's a critical thing now. *(CFO, DevelopNet; DCP 15)*

We have a follow-up meeting [this week] with the VCs at HT-Ventures.... They want a real review of the technology.... The key person we have to face is just coming into the conversation, and the main high jump has not been completed. *(CFO, DevelopNet; DCP 15)*

Really worried about cash. Focus on passing this hurdle with the VC.... *(CEO, DevelopNet; DCP 15)*

We hit the trip wire. Today is the day. We're going off the financial markets.... HT-Ventures [said they] will not move forward until they've seen several successes. *(CEO, DevelopNet; DCP 16)*

ApplySci

We are in a crucial point in terms of business deal making *(Senior Manager, ApplySci; DCP 21)*

I just got off the phone with [contact] at BigCo.... The IPO is killing them. They don't have time to do anything but that.... We can't expect anything in short term. What is short term? The next three weeks. He said, "I don't want to be blowing you off, we're still very interested." *(Market Manager, ApplySci; DCP 22)*

I have this impending sense of doom. We don't have BigCo, and IND-Inc is still being a huge multi-billion dollar corporation (i.e., very slow in their decision-making process) *(Senior Scientist, ApplySci; DCP 23)*

[The CEO] is right now having some difficult discussions with the board. He was essentially told if there is not a $1m deal on the table by the 14th of March, starting on 15th they'll begin a shutdown of the company. That's the context in which we're working. *(Senior Manager, ApplySci; DCP 27)*

ServiceCo

(Board member sets up a meeting with a key industry star). To put [him] in perspective, I'm a basketball fan. If I could have lunch with Michael Jordan, it would be like that. It was big—Big Time. *(Cofounder, ServiceCo)*

I think the lunch acted as a huge catalyst. We had these nagging suspicions. Can we really pull it off?... And then he basically said to us, "You're not going to be able to pull this all off." *(Cofounder, ServiceCo)*

So we didn't come back [from the meeting] and say, "O.K. let's pick one and go." ... And I think it was the night before the advisory board meeting, [the co-founder] and I went out for beers, in my mind I had picked that we needed to do this (i.e., choose one of the two major projects.). *(Cofounder, ServiceCo)*

And so, essentially the decision was made to abandon [the second project].... Once that was made then there were a series of core decisions ... that then shaped everything else. *(Controller, ServiceCo)*

AgencyInc

I was away, he [CEO of potential acquisition] has been away. So we met today. Lunch was around the appraisal, maybe with another company.... He decided I was not the guy capable of succeeding him. *(Senior Manager, AgencyInc)*

We got the word yesterday that InsureX is a dead issue. I'd say the mood after that was pretty disappointing.... I see it as a major setback. When you lose an opportunity to grow like that; I'm just disappointed. *(Office Manager, AgencyInc)*

The founder and his CFO had been anticipating this event for many weeks; in fact, it was the culmination of the overall (new) strategy for the firm, the entire basis of which required a large capital investment that would fund regional sales offices for their technology all over the United States. After weeks and months of unsuccessful follow-ups with dozens of other venture capital firms, the CEO knew that the outcome of this meeting would determine the viability of the entire vision. Without outside cash there was no way he could keep the company running in this way. The decision by the venture capital firm to not fund the project thus catalyzed his decision to "abandon" the large-scale endeavor and shift to a much more patient approach that was based on a totally different business model. This shift was based on one of the experiments proposed by him and the CFO, which ended up as the seed for a generative emergence. The idea was pursued with great success for nearly a year, at which point a new application for the technology was found that led to a higher revenue stream. In this way the critical event was the cap to one era, and the origin of the next.

Another clear exemplar of a critical event occurred at ServiceCo; the event was described by the two founders and a senior manager within weeks of its occurrence. The event was a meeting that the ServiceCo board had set up between the two enthusiastic but inexperienced entrepreneurs and one of the most senior people in the entire field, a highly visible entrepreneur in the industry. The importance of the meeting was partly due to the remarkable opportunity, which makes sense in light of one founder's description (back in 1996):

> To put [him] in perspective, I'm a basketball fan. If I could have lunch with Michael Jordan, it would be like that. It was big—Big Time.

At that meeting the industry star sized up the two business models that ServiceCo had initiated—MarketServe and PeopleServe—and he discerned that the very large market potential of each made it virtually impossible to launch both projects at the same time. Already the development and roll-out of PeopleServe were not going as planned. The other founder explained the situation and the outcome:

> I think the lunch acted as a huge catalyst. We had these nagging suspicions. Can we really pull it off? ... And then he basically said to us, "You're not going to be able to pull this all off."

As a catalyst, the lunch became a line in the sand for the two founders. The "nagging suspicions" were mainly voiced by this founder, in contrast to his co-founder who had originated the PeopleServe idea and was the lead in the project—he left the meeting talking about his enthusiasm for the project over the past year.[3] Still, the conversation went deep, especially over beers that night together and in executive-wide decision-making meetings over the next several weeks:

> And I think it was the night before the advisory board meeting, [the cofounder] and I went out for beers, in my mind I had picked that we needed to do this (i.e., choose one of the two major projects).

Their strategic analysis revealed that PeopleServe was not ready for prime-time; the proposed partnerships at the core of the organizing model were far harder to engender than anyone had expected. Thus, as the controller told me:

> And so, essentially the decision was made to abandon [the second project].... Once that was made then there were a series of core decisions . . . that then shaped everything else.

Thus, one significant meeting became a critical event that caused the dramatic upheaval in the organization. No employee was fired, a decision that significantly slowed down investment in further growth opportunities. The company expanded its highly successful MarketServe product and found other, smaller applications for new services. In the end, the company was purchased in a highly favorable deal and is now owned by a national office systems company.

Table 12.1 presents further data on critical events. On reflection, each of these was known to represent a significant break-point in the company's history, although given the uncertainty of emergence none of the entrepreneurs could have predicted how the outcome would affect the venture. Still, as the theory suggests, when a concomitant rise in disequilibrium organizing and stress and experiments leads to amplification dynamics in the venture, the occurrence of a critical event is only a matter of time.

NOTES

1. Specifically, into the "downward sloping" portion of the Yerkes-Dodson curve. Yerkes-Dodson law posits an inverted U-shaped relationship between stress and performance on moderate to difficult tasks (see, e.g., Miller, 1978; Mandler, 1984; Fisher, 1986; all in Rudolph & Repenning, 2002).
2. These data represented decisions and actions—tangible "moves" (Pentland, 1992) the entrepreneur made as she organized her business. Each *organizing move* is a tangible, "mentionable event" (Pentland, 1992, p. 259) that was coded from the interview transcripts. Like the organizing moves analyzed by Lichtenstein, Dooley, and Lumpkin (2006), each move represents a moment of organizing, through which the entrepreneur seeks to make the concept more real, more tangible, more viable, and/or more clear.

    To identify these data, the second author read through the entire book, then outlined each fax individually to insure that all possible moves would be included. Next, she examined every transcript (fax transmission) phrase by phrase and paragraph by paragraph, looking for all the distinguishable *ideas, plans,* or *actions* that were enacted by the two founders. Each of these were defined as organizing moves, and were summarized and listed in a table. The first author re-examined large sections of the data and the coding, making his own additions and alterations, each of which were agreed upon by both authors.

    At that point, the two authors worked together to code this set of *organizing moves* into three categories: ideation, planning, and tangibility. Ideation incorporates all the values, visions, and conceptual ideas that were expressed by one or both founders, for example, core values for the business, initial ideas for products, and the qualities they want to represent in the market. Planning incorporates more tangible tasks of industry research, market definition, and specific decisions regarding products, marketing or strategic entry that have implications for further organizing. Tangibility refers to actions that reach beyond the two entrepreneurs: meetings with potential suppliers and distributors; conversations with potential mentors and competitors; purchases of sample products or industry research reports; meetings with lawyers, and so on. The total data set encompasses more than 375 unique moves across 138 faxes during the 89-week start-up process.

After doing a final round of validity checks, we aggregated each category by weeks, to generate a week-by-week account of the organizing process of Republic of Tea. This method is based on Van de Ven and Poole's (1990) coding framework to analyze start-up ventures, and draws from the approach of Lichtenstein et al. (2006). In addition to charting the raw count of organizing moves, we analyzed the momentum of each category of organizing by calculating the week-to-week percentage of increase for each of the three types. Then, to make the shifts in momentum even more visually evident, we graphed the cumulative percentage of change, week to week, within the two key phases of organizing. These data transforms give us a better view into the temporal dynamics of the organizing processes (Dooley & Van de Ven, 1999).

3. Recall that these are *retrospective interviews,* the only such retrospective data in the study.

REFERENCES

Abbott, A. 2001. *Time Matters*. Chicago: University of Chicago.
Anderson, P. 1999. Complexity theory and organization science. *Organization Science*, 10: 216–32.
Andriani, P., & McKelvey, B. 2007. Beyond Gaussian averages: Redirecting organization science toward extreme events and power laws. *Journal of International Business Studies*, 38: 1212–30.
Arthur, B. 1988. Self-reinforcing mechanisms in economics. In P. Anderson, K. Arrow, & D. Pines (Eds.), *The Economy as an Evolving Complex System* (9–31). Reading, MA: Addison-Wesleuy.
Arthur, B. 1989. Competing technologies, increasing returns, and lock-in by historcial events. *Economic Journal*, 99: 116–31.
Arthur, B. 1990. Positive feedbacks in the economy. *Scientific American*, February: 92–99.
Arthur, B. 1994. *Increasing Returns and Path Dependence in the Economy*. Ann Arbor, MI: University of Michigan Press.
Bak, P., & Chen, K. 1991. Self-organized criticality. *Scientific American*, January: 46–53.
Bigelow, J. 1982. A catastrophe model of organizational change. *Behavioral Science*, 27: 26–42.
Bygrave, W. 1989. The entrepreneurship paradigm (II): Chaos and catastrophes among quantum jumps. *Entrepreneurship Theory and Practice*, 14(2): 7–30.
Cheng, Y., & Van de Ven, A. 1996. The innovation journey: Order out of chaos? *Organization Science*, 6: 593–614.
Dooley, K. 1997. A complex adaptive systems model of organization change. *Nonlinear Dynamics, Psychology, and the Life Sciences*, 1: 69–97.
Eigen, M. 1971. Self-organization of matter and the evolution of biological macromolecules. *Naturwissenschaften*, 58: 465–523.
Eigen, M., & Schuster, P. 1979. *The Hypercycle: A Principle of Natural Self-Organizing; in Three Parts*. New York: Springer.
Gartner, W. (Ed.). 2010. *ENTER—Entrepreneurial Narrative Theory Ethnomethodology and Reflexivity*. Clemson University: Spiro Institute for Entrepreneurial Leadership.

Golembiewski, R., Billingsley, K., & Yeager, S. 1975. Measuring change and persistance in human affairs. *Journal of Applied Behavioral Science*, 12: 133–57.

Granovetter, M. 1978. Threshold models of collective behavior. *American Journal of Sociology*, 83: 1420–43.

Granovetter, M., & Soong, R. 1986. Threshold models of interpersonal effects in consumer demand. *Journal of Economic Behavior and Organization*, 7: 83–100.

Guastello, S. 1995. *Chaos, Catastrophe, and Human Affairs: Applications of Nonlinear Dynamics to Work, Organizations, and Social Evolution*. Mahway, NJ: Lawrence Erlbaum and Associates.

Haken, H. 1977. *Synergetics*. Berlin: Springer-Verlag.

Jansen, K. 2004. From persistence to pursuit: A longitudinal examination of momentum during the early stages of strategic change. *Organization Science*, 15: 276–95.

Katz, M. L., & Shapiro, C. 1985. Network externalities, competition and compatibility. *American Economic Review*, 75: 424–40.

Kauffman, S. 1993. *The Origins of Order*. New York: Oxford University Press.

Kauffman, S. 2000. *Investigations*. New York: Oxford University Press.

Krugman, P. 1996. *The Self-Organizing Economy*. Cambridge, MA: Bradford Press.

Leifer, R. 1989. Understanding organizational transformation using a dissipative structure model. *Human Relations*, 42: 899–916.

Lewin, A. 1999. Application of complexity theory to organization science. *Organization Science*, 10(3): 215.

Lichtenstein, B., Carter, N., Dooley, K., & Gartner, W. 2007. Complexity dynamics of nascent entrepreneurship. *Journal of Business Venturing*, 22: 236–61.

Lichtenstein, B., Dooley, K., & Lumpkin, T. 2006. Measuring emergence in the dynamics of new venture creation. *Journal of Business Venturing*, 21: 153–75.

Lichtenstein, B., & Kurjanowicz, B. 2010. Tangibility, momentum, and the emergence of The Republic of Tea. *ENTER Journal*, 1: 125–48.

Macy, M. 1991. Chains of cooperation: Threshold effects in collective action. *American Sociological Review*, 56: 730–47.

Maruyama, M. 1963. The second cybernetics. *American Scientist*, 51: 164–79.

May, R. 1974. Biological populations with nonoverlapping generations: Stable points, stable cycles, and chaos. *Science*, 186: 645–47.

May, R. 1976. Simple mathematical models with very complicated dynamics. *Nature*, 26: 455–67.

McKelvey, B. 2004. Toward a 0th law of thermodynamics: Order creation complexity dynamics from physics and biology to bioeconomics. *Bioeconomics*, 6: 65–96.

Meyer, A., Gaba, V., & Colwell, K. 2005. Organizing far from equilibrium: Nonlinear change in organizational fields. *Organization Science*, 16: 456–73.

Mitchell, R. 1992. You are relaxed. You are content. You are approaching "tea mind," *Business Week*: 44–45.

Morel, B., & Ramanujam, R. 1999. Through the looking glass of complexity: The dynamics of organizations as adaptive and evolving systems. *Organization Science*, 10(3): 278–93.

Plowman, D. A., Baker, L., Beck, T., Kulkarni, M., Solansky, S., & Travis, D. 2007. Radical change accidentally: The emergence and amplification of small change. *Academy of Management Journal*, 50: 515–43.

Prigogine, I., & Stengers, I. 1984. *Order out of Chaos*. New York: Bantam Books.

Rudolph, J., & Repenning, N. 2002. Disaster dynamics: Understanding the role of quantity in organizational collapse. *Administrative Science Quarterly*, 47: 1–30.

Stanley, M., Amaral, L., Buldyrev, S., Havlin, S., Leschhorn, H., Maass, P., Salinger, M., & Stanley, E. 1996. Scaling behavior in the growth of companies. *Nature*, 379: 804–806.

Sterman, J. 1989. Misperceptions of feedback in dynamic decision making. *Organizational Behavior and Human Decision Processes*, 43(3): 301–44.

Ziegler, M., Ziegler, P., & Rosenzweig, B. 1994. *The Republic of Tea: The Story of the Creation of a Business, as Told Through the Personal Letters of Its Founders*. New York Currency-Doubleday.

CHAPTER 13

Phase 4: New Order through Recombinations

After the critical threshold, catalyzed by the critical event, the entire system will shift out of the previous dynamic state and into a new one, resulting either in first-degree, second-degree, or third-degree emergence, or in dissolution whereby the organizing effort (the system) begins to unravel, lose momentum, and ultimately disband. In the brightest outcomes—a third-degree generative emergence—what arises is an all-encompassing dynamic state, incorporating a new opportunity tension and core logic for venture. As mentioned earlier, generating this new value creation means creating (or re-creating) the entire organizing model for producing that value. When that is accomplished the entrepreneur usually expresses a sense that the venture is "up and running" (Gartner & Carter, 2003). However, getting to that emergence is challenging, for this new order is far more effective while utilizing nearly all the same components as the old one. Thus, gaining this new capacity means that the system has to be organized or reorganized, (re)combined into—as—the newly emergent system.

In the following sections I will define and present examples of new order and recombinations, and then show how these were enacted in the four new ventures.

NEW ORDER CREATION

Although threshold events can be quite subtle, they mark the creation of new order through a recombination (Chiles, Meyer, & Hench, 2004) or reorganization (Leifer, 1989) of the internal structures and properties of the organization (Morel & Ramanujam, 1999). For example, MacIntosh and MacLean (1999) suggest that "*a new order* based on the new deep structure will seek to impose itself." Browning et al. (1995 p. 142) use "A New Order" as their section heading: "Complexity theory suggests that, following a bifurcation point, an old system may disintegrate amid disorder to attain a more complex and appropriate alignment—a new order."

As I described in Chapter 9, the outcomes of emergence can arise along a continuum, "degrees of emergence." In a formal sense, the higher the degree of emergence, the more capacity may be generated by the emergence (Swenson, 1989; Lichtenstein, 2009; Lichtenstein & Kurjanowicz, 2010; Lichtenstein & McKelvey, 2011). After a brief review of the three degrees of emergence, this chapter provides tangible examples of those outcomes in reference to their initial dynamic state.

Three Degrees of Emergence in Dynamic States

Several complexity scientists define emergence outcomes as a continuum of types, including Bedau (1997), Goldstein (1999), and Bar-Yam (2004); my three-degree approach is built from their insights. As described in Chapter 9, in first-degree order emergence, novel properties and simple structures arise *within* the focal system. Second-degree systemic emergence refers to the arising of a new and distinct "level of analysis" that expands the definition of the system in some way. The most comprehensive outcome is third-degree radical emergence. Here an entirely new system comes into being with properties that have causal influence on the components of the system. Radical emergence thus features downward causation: The emergent system has causal power that "governs" the behavior, activity, or dynamic relationships of the system's elements.

How do these three degrees of emergence get expressed new order creation of a new dynamic state? Recall that a dynamic state incorporates three main categories: (1) an opportunity tension that envisions a core logic for the endeavor; (2) an organizing model that tangibly explains how value is to be created, that is, the activities, resources, and collaborations required to generate sustainable revenue streams; and (3) the value creation itself: the product, service, or offering that provides value to customers. In a general sense, the higher the degree of change, the more of these elements are affected.

First-degree order emergence occurs when one aspect or system within the organizing model is created (or substantively transformed), signifying the emergence of a new structure or process *within* the current dynamic state. Examples could include an emerging relationship between a new partner and a key supplier, an emergent routine (process, system) for managing activities, a new strategy for marketing or distribution, or the presentation of an alternative way to position the offering. In all these cases what emerges is a structure or pattern that informs the existing system and hopefully improves the efficacy of the current dynamic state, but does not lead to the coming-into-being of an entirely new level in system.

In some cases this (re)design leads to a product upgrade, such that the outcome of value creation is improved or extended in some way. Such product improvements are useful and often represent the culmination of much research and development.

However, these do not lead to a new system per se, only to a change in the current system, first-degree order emergence.

Examples of first-degree order emergence can be found in Sonenshein's (2009) study of ethical issue emergence in the change process at "Retail Inc." The nationwide store embarked on a strategic shift that included redesign and remodeling, new uniforms, and additional "upgrades" to certain mall stores. The emergence was successful at recreating the store's presentation and gaining more alignment in structure and routines across the stores. These represent emergences in the company's activities and resources, and in distribution channels (marketing the change) (Osterwalder & Pigneur, 2010). These emergents did not, however, effect a shift in the core logic of the firm, nor in the value creation, nor in the opportunity tension itself.

Second-degree system emergence occurs when an entire category of the dynamic state is (re)made, but still without recreating the entire system. For example, an organizer may realize that the existing product or service can be of value to a completely different market, thus initiating a "new entry" of the offering without changing the basic operations of the organization as a whole. Here the value creation is aimed at an entirely new market or industry, while much of the organizing model may be left intact. This sometimes occurs in periods of intensity, when the company is struggling to find an organizing model that works without starting from scratch.

Alternatively, a founder may decide that the organizing model could be dramatically improved, by restructuring and reconfiguring its processes. This sometimes occurs in organizational transformation, when there are shifts in the design, structure, and internal activities of a company but not in the core logic or opportunity tension, and not in the underlying value creation that the organization has been focused on. Such internal transformations may solve ongoing issues and may pave the way for broader emergence, but they do not reflect a wholesale creation or re-creation of the organization.

A useful example of second-degree system emergence comes from the wonderful paper on bricolage by Ted Baker and Reed Nelson (2005). Of the many cases they provide, one (pp. 339–340) reveals how a recombination of resources may lead to a new (emergent) product without altering the nature of the dynamic state.

> After the market for his electronics repair service went soft, Jim Roscoe (#10) found himself with a miscellany of testing equipment, power transformers, and various [electronic] components.... Aware [of the challenges of maintaining]... high-voltage underground power lines... in coal mines... he [and a friend] combined several electronic components from Roscoe's collection to create a simple and rugged tool that permitted technicians to test the underground cables, with the great advantage of not having to move or disconnect them. Roscoe sold a few of these devices to local firms and then moved on to unrelated projects. This instance of bricolage provided a temporary source of income but did not alter his overall business activities in any substantial way.

In this example Roscoe's new idea was an expansion of his current opportunity tension, applying it to a new potential market. Although new resources and activities were invented, the basic tasks were similar enough to his existing dynamic state that nothing fundamentally new appeared to emerge. Instead, the system generated a temporary revenue stream while allowing him to maintain his larger operation intact. Thus, it exemplifies second-degree system emergence.

Third-degree radical emergence is more than the others, for it is based on the creation of a new core logic for generating a sustainable dynamic state. This core logic pervades the entire firm: Radical emergence initiates a new opportunity tension that gets expressed in a new (or redesigned) organizing model for the venture, that produces a new, valuable product or service for a specific market. In the combination of these fundamental aspects of a dynamic state, there arises one or more systemwide, macro-level properties—tangible qualities that influence all the components in some way. More informally, in radical emergence the system "takes on a life of its own." Likewise, the new dynamic state becomes *seen* by others—it literally emerges as a new, independent entity in its social ecology even as it influences that social ecology.

One vibrant example of this process, and one which incorporates the "recombination" of resources, is also from Baker and Nelson's (2005) article (pp. 341–342). They describe how a farmer created an entirely new business—a dynamic state that was totally independent of his current operation—through the exploration of an opportunity tension, leading to a series of experiments that were combined into an organizing model that generated multiple revenue streams:

> Tim Grayson was a farmer whose land was crisscrossed by abandoned coal mines. He knew that the tunnels—a nuisance to farmers because of their tendency to collapse, causing mammoth sinkholes in fields—also contained large quantities of methane. Methane is another nuisance, a toxic greenhouse gas that poisons miners and persists in abandoned mines for generations. Grayson and a partner drilled a hole from Grayson's property to an abandoned mine shaft, then acquired a used diesel generator from a local factory and crudely retrofitted it to burn methane…[and thus] produce electricity, most of which he sold to the local utility, using scavenged switchgear. Because Grayson's generator also produced considerable waste heat, he built a greenhouse for hydroponic tomatoes, which he heated with water from the generator's cooling system. . . . [Expanding on his resources again], the availability of a greenhouse [with] trenches of nutrient-rich water heated "for free" [led] Grayson to realize [that] he might be able to raise tilapia, a tropical delicacy increasingly popular in the U.S. He introduced the fish to the waters that bathed the tomato roots and used the fish waste as fertilizer. Finally, with abundant methane still at hand, Tim began selling excess methane to a natural gas company.

This wonderful example offers many insights. First, each round of organizing—each cycle of emergence—generated a new offering and revenue stream, thus creating its own dynamic state. These were new products and services that had become visible (Gartner, Bird, & Starr, 1992; Gartner, 1993) to the public, tangible outcomes from the organization (not the entrepreneur per se). In marketing terms, the product becomes associated with a company that has a specific image and growing and changing reputation. The company is more than the entrepreneurial farmer; the company makes transactions, pays taxes, is covered by insurance, and so on.

In addition, these outcomes have a causal effect on the components of the system, that is, each new offering and revenue stream influences the system in unexpected ways. For example, the outputs of the initial initiative—electricity, heat, and water—were new resources that could be recombined with other existing skills and activities, thus leading to the greenhouse for tomatoes. Here again the greenhouse structures the resources within it, presenting constraints—high water volume and need for fertilizer—that influence the resources available. This influence generates a further recombinations, in which the water and fertilizer become organized into their own habitat for raising tilapia.

As is common in emergence, none of these outcomes were visible in Grayson's initial moves to capture the methane from beneath his own farm. Yet, the more emergence in the system, the more these outcomes became possible and prescient.

This summary of degrees of order creation offers a foundation for the examples of new order creation and recombination that follow. Before turning to those, I present examples of dissolution in the following short case on Iridium.

The Other Possibility: Dissolution

As mentioned earlier, proceeding through a cycle of emergence does not at all ensure a positive outcome. There are two theoretical reasons for the potential of collapse in emergence. One involves the challenges of (re)creating an entire system all at once, which involves an unprecedented amount of internal processing that can (and often does) overwhelm the system as a whole. A second reason refers back to the theoretical claim cited earlier, that new order will stabilize *as long as it is creating value*. That is, when emergence leads to new value creation for the firm, value that generates income, it is likely to be sustained. However, the creation process can just as likely lead to lower resource capacity and a lack of connection with market demand. That is, since the experiments by the system are unpredictable, and because the outcomes of order emergence are determined by a host of internal and ecological forces, some outcomes will not yield the expected value. This would cause the organization's demise.

The Collapse at Iridium

A good example involves Iridium (Dooley, Daneke, & Pathak, 2005), a high-profile spin-out venture from Motorola that in 1989 promised the very first and only worldwide, satellite-enabled telecommunications system. The system was to be sold to corporations and individuals (Finkelstein & Sanford, 2001). Originated from Motorola's early research efforts into cellular telephony, Iridium promised "the freedom to communicate—anytime, anywhere," through a unique technology that "would be orders of magnitude more effective than the emerging technology of cellular with its patchy network" (MacCormack & Herman, 2001, pp. 1, 4).

From its inception in 1989, the huge perceived global market potential of the project sparked massive amounts of disequilibrium organizing, first as an internal corporate venture, and then as an independent venture heavily supported by Motorola's chairman, Bob Galvin. Within six years, Iridium, Inc. had secured $1.9 billion in outside equity financing (Inkpen, 2001) and key contracts with strategic partners willing to develop new-to-the-world systems and processes for the venture (MacCormack & Herman, 2001).

Iridium had also accomplished a feat of international organizing: In order to gain the regulatory approval needed to operate in 170 countries, it garnered support from dozens of countries representing "most of the world's population" (Inkwell, 2001, p. 6). By mid-1998 Iridium's stock price had soared to $72/share, the entire constellation of 66 satellites had been launched, and the first Iridium call had been placed, from Vice President Al Gore to Alexander Graham Bell's great-grandson.

Iridium's initial success was paralleled with increased stress and numerous experiments designed to mitigate growing problems. Their $140 million global marketing campaign in 1998 "failed to distinguish Iridium from other wireless companies" (Inkpen, 2001), and most of the 1,000,000 sales contacts it generated were not followed up on because of logistical and tactical errors (Cauley, 1999). Iridium's potential market continued to erode in the face of unexpected increases in cellular capabilities, while early users reported blocked access, rampant interference, and dropped calls (MacCormack & Herman, 2001). By the end of 1998, Iridium had only 3,000 subscribers—just 5% of their projections—and analysts predicted 1999 losses would total more than $1.68 billion.

The initial negative response triggered a constellation of experiments in marketing and strategy. The product was repositioned to combine global cellular service with its worldwide satellite capability. This resulted in a new design for the telephone that expanded its range and its ability to connect with virtually any cellular network in the world. At the same time, Iridium revamped its marketing strategy to focus on corporate/industrial users in specific industry niches such as oil exploration, construction, and shipping (Daneke & Dooley, 2007).

Amidst continued increases in organizing and continued increases in stress and experiments, a trigger event occurred in March of 1999, when Iridium failed to meet a set of covenants promised to the banks that held the company's $800 million in debt. This failure triggered a rapid restructuring of the company: the CEO quit and was replaced; the company named a new CFO and a new V.P. of marketing/sales, while also cutting 15% of its staff. The new market strategy led to a huge cut in prices and a dramatic overhaul of their global advertising campaign.

Unfortunately, the results of this emergent structuring were highly disappointing. In August 1999 Iridium filed for Chapter 11 bankruptcy; less than a year later commercial service ended and the entire system was turned off forever, the satellites to be slowly destroyed by dropping them one by one into the oceans around the globe.

Here we see the same phases of emergence: opportunity tension leading to extremely high levels of disequilibrium organizing, and a concomitant increase in stress and experiments. These accelerate to a critical event, a reorganization that itself doesn't stem the losses. The ultimate outcome is dissolution—the destruction of the system and the loss of nearly $2 billion.

ORDER CREATION AS (RE)COMBINATIONS OF SYSTEM COMPONENTS

Order creation occurs through recombination. As important as the outcomes of emergence are, so too is the process of order creation—the *way* that the system is composed through a combining and/or recombining of resources. Thus, this section provides an overview and some examples of how, in third-degree radical emergence, the system components (resources) and their patterns of relationship have to be acquired, organized, purposed, and assimilated into a new dynamic state.

Some of the best descriptions of how resources can be recombined in generative emergence appeared in Chiles et al.'s (2004) study of the creation of a regional aggregation of organizations in Branson, MO, all focused around family-oriented musical entertainment. For example, they showed how theater facilities were constantly changing hands; these empty theaters provided easy upgrades for growing theater companies, and decreased risk for unsuccessful acts. "Theaters never stand empty for long in Branson.... If an act folds in mid-season... there will be another to take up the lease in a week or two" (Chiles et al., 2004, p. 513). The recombination of easy-to-access resources is part of what accelerates the cycles of emergence there.

Chiles and his colleagues confirmed how failures became unique opportunities for recombination. For example, one founder claimed, "We built the theater so that if it didn't work, we could put in boat storage for the lakes. That's why we built it with no slope, with a flat floor" (Chiles et. al. 2004, p. 514). In this sense the recombinatory nature of emergence had become embedded into the mental models of Branson entrepreneurs, who incorporated possible reconfigurations into their initial designs.

Donde Plowman and her colleagues (2007) also showed how new combinations of resources played a significant role in the re-emergence of a new dynamic state at "Mission Church." One of the key drivers of this re-creation was the spontaneous emergence of a free medical clinic during the daily breakfasts for the homeless. Plowman et al. use the term "amplification" to describe the positive feedback effect of new resources and how existing resources were commandeered so as to enable the overall emergence (Plowman et al., 2007, pp. 530–531):

> The first amplification occurred when the physician unexpectedly began seeing people with medical problems at the breakfasts. This new set of resources—the physician's expertise and the medicine he brought—pushed the Sunday morning event in a new and unplanned direction. About a year after the breakfasts started, the originators of the idea took it to the official church council for placement in the church's budget....
>
> Seeking a way to help pay for the renovations needed to expand the medical clinic and the Sunday breakfasts, the church applied for and received some grants from the city. The church's budget and the city's grant money represented new resources that made it possible to not only continue, but also grow the Sunday morning program in ways unanticipated before the money was received. For example, a vesting room was turned into an eye clinic, and another dressing room became showers. An organist's room became a doctor's office, and part of a classroom became a clothes closet.

Here the recombinations are unmistakable: One new resource—the physician's willingness to donate his time—led to the initial emergence of a medical clinic in the church. Services were expanded through an acquisition and reorganization of resources, including the repurposing of existing rooms and the transfer of money from previously budgeted activities to these new ones. By combining underutilized resources in a new way, new sources of value were created that served clients and the church community.

Further examples can be drawn from Baker and Nelson's (2005) mini-cases mentioned earlier. In the first example, existing electronic components were reconfigured and repurposed to solve a new problem. In the second example, a single new component, a used diesel generator, became the core for a series of new applications, recombinations, and reframing of wastes into resources that generated multiple streams of value creation in an emergent dynamic state.

ORDER CREATION AND DISSOLUTION IN THE FOUR NEW VENTURES

The four ventures show numerous examples of emergents, examples of first-degree, second-degree, and third-degree order (see Table 13.1). More importantly, they show specific emergences of new dynamic states that occur at the peak of amplification and a critical event.

Table 13.1. EMERGENTS IN THE FOUR VENTURES (REPRESENTATIVE EXAMPLES)

Core Logic; Identity—Third-Degree Emergence

I decided we're going to put the whole thing on hold.... Restructuring, downsizing, retrenchment. We've abandoned the charge-up-the-hill-to-the-$100-million-dollar-company.... Rather than charge up the hill is to license the technology, and keep them busy with consulting. *(CEO, DevelopNet)*

There's an abrupt change in thinking that's happening now.... We're switching our orientation. It has happened in the last month. It's based upon knowing we have a stable product, that appears to have tremendous capability. *(Senior Manager, ApplySci)*

We are a medical company trying to stay industrial, and fighting it very hard. *(Senior Manager, ApplySci)*

I think it's even more than the beginning of a new stage. I think it's a redefinition of the ServiceCo world as we know it. *(Project Manager, ServiceCo)*

Opportunity Tension; Value Creation—Second- /Third-Degree Emergence

[We're going to] build up our local regional webserver activity, bundling webservers for medium-sized organizations. *(CEO, DevelopNet)*

We've been coming out.... So we are a leader in nasal delivery of these. [New VP development] says what's the market for those—that's about $20b. Why are we the leader? Because we have high-tech [application]. *(CEO, ApplySci)*

We're a very focused drug delivery company. Try to get in a shape very fast. That's where we are. *(Senior Manager, ApplySci)*

The InfoServe product (which had just been launched) is by far where the money and the people and our prominence in the world are going to come from.... We're going to ride the InfoServe wave to either be a medium-sized company or a large company over the next five years. *(Project Employee, ServiceCo)*

Organizing Model—First Degree Emergence

DevelopNet put on a seminar yesterday—our first public event around the Internet. Invited 60 people; 9 showed up! 15% is amazing. Pretty successful. They'll do one/month.... This signifies an important dimension, and a direction they'll continue. *(Marketing Manager, DevelopNet)*

Happy about the sales rep (who had just been hired). We've never had a full-time permanent salesman. *(CFO, DevelopNet)*

Website—it's ready to go! Up and stable. It's a nice feeling of satisfaction. It's installed. *(Lead Programmer, DevelopNet)*

[We] brought in (hired) different people from different experience and different industries [to create the analytic department]. *(Senior Analytic Scientist, ApplySci)*

Given the whole reorganization I think it's coming out pretty interesting.... You saw the meeting of the non-managers. We're cohering. Last week, we kind of all gelled: if we're going to do this, let's do this together. We all stepped out of individual roles. *(Lab Technician, ApplySci)*

I think some of the activities, predicated on closing some deals, like WJ, and the need to get in place manufacturing operations are consistent with regulatory nature of product. To that extent, analytical, QA, document control, looking at mfg. sites ... are all part of the infrastructure required for being a player in this type of a business. So that's where some of focus is in terms of hiring and organizing. *(Senior Scientist, ApplySci)*

DevelopNet

Following the "trip wire" at data collection period (DCP) 16, a series of emergents were revealed over a four-week period, ultimately describing a complete re-creation of the core logic of the venture and its opportunity tension. Within just a few weeks several key elements of the organizing model were reformed and recombined, yielding a new strategy, product line, market, and radically changed design (structure). In one fell swoop a new dynamic state was created.

Tables 13.2 and 13.3 present these data in the form of comments by the CEO, CFO, lead programmer, and marketing manager about the shift. Note that I have tentatively assigned each comment a "degree" of emergence: first-degree improvements in products (E-1), second-degree shifts in opportunity tension and wholesale re-creations of the organizing model (E-2), and comprehensive shifts due to new core logics, third-degree emergents (E-3). My claim is that re-emergence is driven by the dramatic shift in "who we are" and what the company is about, reflected in the comments labeled E-3. In these comments we see a total reconceptualization of the company, moving away from the dream of becoming a nationwide product-sales company leveraging technology to large financial companies toward being a small, "specialist consulting organization" that gives away software as a way to encourage sales and pursues consulting—"solving problems"—for a different set of organizations.

Second-degree emergents are significant as well. Their downsizing was dramatic given their size, resulting in the shutting down of three "departments": outside sales, new project development, and the CFO role. The founder also cut the programmer group in half. However, as is usual with second-degree emergence, cutting the team in half did not decimate its knowledge base. As the lead programmer said, "We only lost about a quarter of our knowledge." Finally, first-degree emergence is reflected in the proposal to pursue computer gaming, to apply the technology in a new way without altering the system as a whole.

A close look again at the amplification chart for DevelopNet (Figure 12.3 in Chapter 12) reveals a secondary pattern of change, a slight but unmistakable increase in stress and experiments starting at DCP 23 with a peak at DCP 25, paralleled by a peak in new organization building activities at DCP 28–30. Here there is a second "round" of emergence, more like clarity on the emerging dynamic state and some moves that emphasize aspects which seem to be working. It turned out that the "ABC Leasing" proposal did take them into a new area, which later became central to their long-term business model. Over time, they built on these changes, adapting to feedback and leveraging their resources as best they could. Within about 18 months they had quadrupled their revenues and captured a growing market with their customization of an existing product.

Table 13.2. EMERGENTS LEADING TO A NEW DYNAMIC STATE AT DEVELOPNET

New Logic/ Identity/Opportunity Tension

E-3	We've run out of cash. So we're curtailing operations. The new focus is on increasing billings.... We have a good piece of technology, but we're having difficulty finding an economic advantage for it.... We have to regroup and recover.	DCP 16—CFO
E-3	So we've abandoned the attempt to do a nationwide sales thing, because we don't have the deep pockets.... So we're shifting back to being a specialist consulting organization.	DCP 19—CEO
E-3	I decided we're going to put the whole thing on hold.... Restructuring, downsizing, retrenchment. We've abandoned the charge-up-the-hill-to-the-$100-million-dollar-company.... Rather than charge up the hill, is to license the technology, and keep them busy with consulting. Hopefully the interesting stuff has ended for now. Probably ... we'll settle into a rut as a regional consulting company, that is also making money out of its licensing. I'm relieved, not having to climb up that hill with no end.	DCP 20—CEO
E-3	I feel better about what we're doing, as far as essentially focusing finally on just consulting. Not trying to sell a product, because it never seemed to work. Licensing seems like a better deal. I think our strength is using it as a simulation and modeling tool. Whereas in the visual marketplace, it's not as easy a sell. We're not that. What we do is solve problems. We don't, by selling you a product.	DCP 20—Lead Programmer

New Organizing Model

E-2	Roger will look for a new job (end of CFO). Ralph as well (end of Sales). Andrew let go. (End of Product Category). Terry new job—reduce programmers by 1/2. [In sum, 60% of employees left or were let go.]	DCP 16—CEO
E-2	We're also thinking of changing our marketing strategy. If the company is going to use our services, we'll give them the software. The new track is, you buy our labor. That cuts down on some of the profit, but it makes the sale enormously easier. On a longer-term basis, it gives us credibility. We have formalized a decision to hand out software for free to our consulting clients, as a way to generate consulting business.... formalized the strategy	DCP 16—CEO (Later formalized)
E-2	Out of financial markets	DCP 16—CEO
E-2	A couple of "game" things we're putting funding proposals in for. One is doing ... a string of video games. The other is ... an Internet game.	DCP 20—CEO

Table 13.3. EMERGENTS LEADING TO CLARIFICATION OF THE NEW DYNAMIC STATE AT DEVELOPNET

New Logic/ Identity / Opportunity Tension

E-3	One is to build up our local regional webserver activity, bundling webservers for medium-sized organizations.... We'll be building that business starting Jan 2. It's a shift we've been aiming for for a while. It's time to complete that shift.	DCP 27—CEO

New Organizing Model — DCP 34—CEO

E-2	I'd like to have 50% of my business to be in commercial.... Because I want to get away from DOD.	
E-1	We've just submitted a proposal to ABC Leasing. It's small—a $290k job. Commercial marketplace, having to upgrade our presentation. I got a favorable reaction.... We've taken a stab at this market. We're getting serious about this market. We are starting to position ourselves.	DCP 36—CEO
E-1	This is really our first commercial proposal. [ABC Leasing]	DCP 36—Lead Programmer
E-1	As part of our financial model—to achieve 90% billing ratios for people.... What we're doing is a billings bonus policy. For everybody, if they exceed 90% billable hours in a month, they get 20% of the billings. This is driving compensation off our financial model.	DCP 29—CEO

ApplySci

The re-emergence at ApplySci is highly complex, for reasons that will be revealed here and in Chapter 14. To get a sense of the process, look at the amplification chart for ApplySci (Figure 13.1). Work activity shows a gradual (and "chaotic") increase from the start of the data (32 weeks before my DCP 1) all the way through DCP 15, and then at a much faster rate through a major peak at DCP 27. Likewise, note the fast and then equally "chaotic" increase in stress and experiments, with a series of rising peaks on DCP 8, 13, 17, and 21, then again at DCP 26. As well, its clear that "financial stress" is rising—by DCP 26 it reaches a "peak," then keeps rising (worsening) until DCP 29. These increases suggest momentum toward a critical event of some kind.

My data show evidence of a series of major emergents arising in DCP 22 and 23; these were formalizations of a set of emergents that arose at DCP 12. Together these shifts were aimed at refocusing the company, bearing down on a smaller number of commercial markets, and restructuring the organization to support that aim. Table 13.4 presents much of these data; I've combined the two rounds of emergence into a single one, because my on-site observations led me to see the earlier emergents as being formalized in the latter. In sum, an "attempted" re-emergence occurred at DCP 22–23, as the company was nearing a peak of disequilibrium organizing, stress, and experiments. What actually "emerged" at this point?

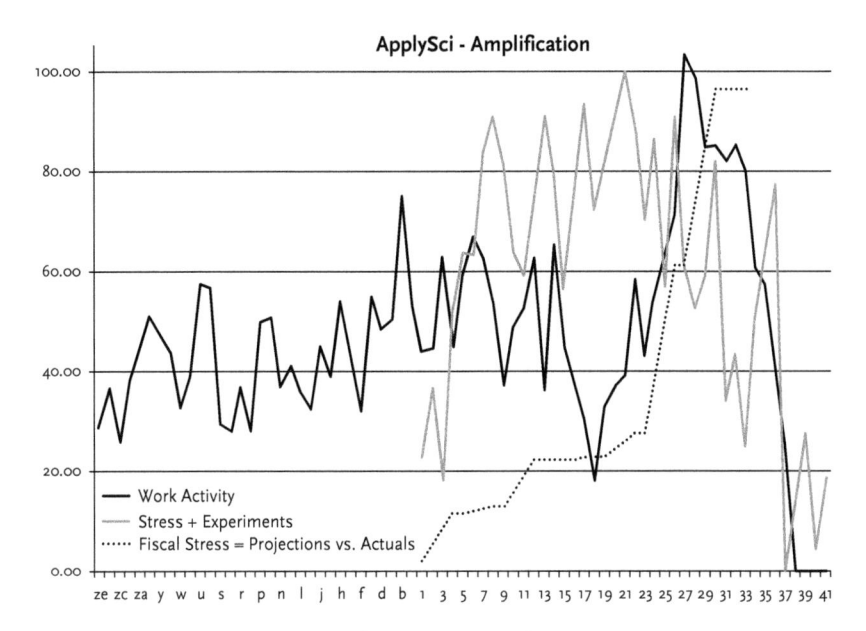

Figure 13.1: Amplification to New Order Creation at ApplySci

Pushed by the board, the CEO made a strong decision to organize the entire company around a medical/personal care products focus, rather than materials science. One of the drivers of this shift was a contract with one of the nation's largest personal care companies (BigCo), which would come to fruition by DCP 23. The dynamic state would be realized through a major redesign, whereby a project manger would manage most of the scientific and commercialization staff, according to the guidelines set out in the BigCo contract. A new lab was installed and offices were remodeled to accommodate a major shift in location for many of the personnel. Two of the new hires were long-awaited senior scientists who quickly took up their responsibilities within the emerging structure and strategy. If everything worked, the company could make the jump to high profits.

Unfortunately, things didn't work as well as everyone had hoped. Much of the problem was due to long-standing issues with the technology that had not been solved, even as the CEO had turned the corner from research to commercialization. Worse, a single inquiry from a materials company impelled the V.P. of industrial applications to "borrow" a host of lab technicians to try to get out one more formulation for that potential client. This destabilizing feedback had ramifications throughout the firm. Finally, the BigCo contract did *not* come through, leaving the organization with much more heat than light—no significant revenues and a higher "burn rate" than could reasonably be covered by the board.

Thus, a second shift happened, at DCP 38 and 39. The board, being disappointed with the outcomes up to then, fired the CEO. They had already placed a high-level V.P. of development in the company; she became the CEO, and attempted a major

Table 13.4. EMERGENTS LEADING TO A NEW DYNAMIC STATE AT APPLYSCI

New Logic/ Identity / New Opportunity Tension

E-3	... we're becoming more and more a medical company. That's been a gradual progression. At some point, he (George) made a bigger leap than I would have thought possible. // Making more of a medical strategy has been helpful.	DCP 12—Senior Marketing Manager
E-3	If there's an abrupt change in thinking that's happening now, it will be in place then (by Jan. 1). Now, where the ferment is happening—we're switching our orientation. It has happened in the last month. It's based upon knowing we have a stable product, that appears to have tremendous capability.	DCP 12—Senior Operations Manager
E-3	There is a real market. The big companies are involved. Sometimes you think it's just niche players. We met with people who were from a division of UpJohn, and ElyLilly is working on osteoporosis. I just though it was just little players. But no, it's bigger than that. So, we think there's something.	DCP 15—Senior Technical Specialist

Organizing Model

E-2	Trying to hit customers hard, to get applications through. It's a shift of focus throughout.... Get samples to people, get them interested; may lead to develop a business deal—whether a merger, partnership, whatever. We're really seeking that move.	DCP 12—Senior Technical Specialist
E-2	We were focusing on R&D; there was lab-scale development. Now backing out of that and how to move toward large-scale manufacturing. This is just a push now to commercialization.	DCP 13—Senior Technical Specialist
E-2	We're in the process of hiring four new people. One is Tiffany's replacement.... One is a stability person. We need an analytic group—that's where we're the weakest.	DCP 13—Lead Lab Scientist
E-2	We're doing a shift dividing into industrial and medical sides; people will be moved one way or the other.	DCP 13—Senior Lab Scientist
E-2	It's changing the whole structure.... We're entering the next stage, hopefully. Keep your fingers crossed!	DCP 14—Marketing Manager
E-2	Barry is maintaining the whole function of core technology and moving forward [with it], and Stan will be managing the ... product development for [BigCo].	DCP 21—Senior Lab Scientist
E-2	[B: Does this represent a major change?] Yeah, oh yeah. The whole company, except five people, are working together for one goal. Never happened here. This is two-thirds of the company.... That's a major shift in the corporation, to concentrate on one thing.	DCP 22—V.P. Medical

re-emergence of the company. Half the personnel were let go that week; all others were pushed to complete whatever sales they could. She gave it her best shot, but found no ways to solve the problems that had existed for many months already. After a few near-misses, the board decided to sell the company; the technology rights were purchased by a mid-sized personal care company, although none of the remaining employees were retained. The sale, for stock, led to the projected loss of $8,000,000 in board investments, representing half of the money they had put into ApplySci. In the end, ApplySci re-emerged into dissolution.

ServiceCo

The re-emergence at ServiceCo was remarkable, for within just six weeks the entire company of 65 people had gotten behind the decision to abandon their highly promising PeopleServe product and pursue a new core logic focused around MarketServe and related opportunities.

The exit from PeopleServe was especially challenging, because that project held a tremendous emotional appeal for all the ServiceCo members. It was a visionary way to help people's lives, improve society, and make a profit at the same time. For most of the employees who were young and optimistic, this project offered the unique prospect of work that really mattered in the world. Thus its demise signaled more than a strategic change, it reflected a new direction, a new era in the company:

> I think it's even more than the beginning of a new stage. I think it's a redefinition of the ServiceCo world as we know it. (Project Manager, ServiceCo)

In this new ServiceCo, MarketServe was no longer a "cash cow" that could fund the "real" growing edge of the company. Instead, MarketServe became the model of their success, the template for further attempts at innovation and new product development. Thus the end of PeopleServe was not simply a "chopping off" of the smaller of the two company branches, it was a reformulation of what the company was, of what it could be. While this limited overall possibilities for the firm, it also provided a new avenue for innovation, designed around the basic organizing model that had made MarketServe so successful.

This new core logic led to numerous shifts in the company, not the least of which was a reframing of opportunity tension to a more focused set of markets, all of which relied on collaborations with a major U.S. government agency. Likewise, the value creation was redefined—constrained—to product and resource offers rather than the "information-aggregation" goal that was central to PeopleServe. This constraint took advantage of core competencies that were already well developed. These two major shifts were embodied in a new shared function of the top executive team, who started weekly innovation meetings to explore new projects that were similar to MarketServe. These were closed meetings—the only "secret" gatherings in the company's short history—and were supported by one or two project assistants who pursued research ideas and followed up on product ideas. In effect, this team became the new engine of innovation for the company.

As one would expect, the new core logic led to dramatic reformulations in the organizing model. Most important was the decision to not lay anyone off;

instead, all of the PeopleServe employees were redistributed to new roles on the MarketServe business. Some of the roles were parallel and some were employee-requested shifts that took advantage of latent expertise and interests. The two founders created an "office of the CEO," who worked with the HR director to develop goal and growth plans for every employee, thus providing formal accountability and control for the first time. Although most of the activities stayed the same, the newly assigned employees enacted a flourish of improvements and extensions in systems, target markets, collaborations, and content for the MarketServe product.

In sum, the whole company was re-created: A new dynamic state emerged and then remained relatively stable for the following year and longer. Table 13.5 presents specific details regarding this process.

AgencyInc: Emergents but No New Order

At AgencyInc there were three emergents that arose during my eight months of data collection. Each one was the outcome of an acquisition, two small ones that were successfully done, and one large one which wasn't. One of these involved the solo insurance broker next door, the other was the father of one of the senior agents. Both individuals were near retirement and appreciated the offer to fold their "book of business" into the larger firm. AgencyInc took over their routine customer service and billing and gave the agents a full workspace in the company, which allowed them to keep up with their major accounts and pursue new business as they chose. Financially these were low-risk deals; each acquisition expanded AgencyInc's business by only about 10%. Likewise, given the high-tech capabilities of the employees at AgencyInc, adding these new books of business required no changes to existing systems or routines, nor was a new employee needed.

The third emergent was the loss of their major deal, the end of negotiations with a larger "competitor" who was seeking to be purchased. The importance of the loss was emphasized by the office manager, who said it was

> ... pretty disappointing.... I see it as a major setback. When you lose an opportunity to grow like that; I'm just disappointed. (Office Manager, AgencyInc)

A similar feeling of defeat was expressed by the CEO:

> It would have worked.... It would have been a good deal for us. But it didn't work out.... I'm disappointed, John [senior partner] is disappointed. The whole staff is disappointed. (CEO, AgencyInc)

This was the extent of formal change in the company during the time I collected data. Two years later they engineered a large acquisition; soon afterward they were

Table 13.5. EMERGENTS IN A NEW DYNAMIC ORDER AT SERVICECO

New Logic/ Identity / New Opportunity Tension

E-3	I think it's even more than the beginning of a new stage. I think it's a redefinition of the ServiceCo world as we know it. *(Project Manager, ServiceCo)*	From retrospective interview
E-3	New core logic—MarketServe as foundation for all new initiatives	From retrospective interview
E-3	New opportunity tension—applying MarketServe to parallel markets. Extensions to be made by Innovation Team, with weekly closed meetings	Observation, interviews

New Organizing Model

E-2	PeopleServe product abandoned	From retrospective interview
E-2	All PeopleServe employees—50% of total company—receive new roles and new reporting relationships	Observation, interviews
E-2	Employee accountability system introduced through goal and growth plans	Observation
E-2	Office of the CEO, shared leadership	Observation, interviews

acquired by a nationally known insurance firm, a move that achieved the goals they had initiated long before.

In the three ventures that experienced emergence and transformation, these changes were followed by stabilizing feedback or destabilizing feedback, processes described in the next chapter.

REFERENCES

Baker, T., & Nelson, R. 2005. Creating something from nothing: Resource construction through entrepreneurial bricolage. *Administrative Science Quarterly*, 50: 239–366.

Bar-Yam, Y. 2004. A mathematical theory of strong emergence using mutliscale variety. *Complexity*, 9(6): 15–24.

Bedau, M. 1997. Weak emergence. *Philosophical Perspectives*, 11(Mind, Causation, and World): 375–99.

Cauley, L. 1999. Losses in space—Iridium's downfall, *Wall Street Journal*. August 18, p. A1.

Chiles, T., Meyer, A., & Hench, T. 2004. Organizational emergence: The origin and transformation of Branson, Missouri's musical theaters. *Organization Science*, 15(5): 499–520.

Daneke, G., & Dooley, K. 2007. *The life-cycle revisited: Stage transitions and the failure of the Iridium project*. Paper presented at the IEEE Portland International Center for Management of Engineering and Technology.

Dooley, K., Daneke, G., & Pathak, S. 2005. *Iridium's house of cards: The nature of entrepreneurial stages and stage transition*. Arizona State University.

Finkelstein, S., & Sanford, S. 2001. Learning from corporate mistakes: The rise and fall of Iridium. *Organizational Dynamics*, 29(2): 138–48.

Gartner, W. 1993. Words lead to deeds: Towards an organizational emergence vocabulary. *Journal of Business Venturing*, 8: 231–39.

Gartner, W., Bird, B., & Starr, J. 1992. Acting as if: Differentiating entrepreneurial from organizational behavior. *Entrepreneurship Theory and Practice*, 16(3): 13–30.

Gartner, W., & Carter, N. 2003. Entrepreneurial behavior and firm organizing processes. In Z. J. Acs & D. B. Audretsch (Eds.), *Handbook of Entrepreneurship Research* (195–221). Boston: Kluwer.

Goldstein, J. 1999. Emergence as a construct: History and issues. *Emergence*, 1(1): 49–72.

Inkpen, A. 2001. *The Rise and Fall of Iridium*. Glendale, AZ: Thunderbird, Garvin School of International Management.

Leifer, R. 1989. Understanding organizational transformation using a dissipative structure model. *Human Relations*, 42: 899–916.

Lichtenstein, B. 2009. Moving far from far-from-equliibrium: Opportunity tension as the catalyst of emergence. *Emergence: Complexity and Organization*, 11(4): 15–25.

Lichtenstein, B., & Kurjanowicz, B. 2010. Tangibility, momentum, and the emergence of The Republic of Tea. *ENTER Journal*, 1: 125–48.

Lichtenstein, B., & McKelvey, B. 2011. Four types of emergence: A typology of complexity and its implications for a science of management. *International Journal of Complexity in Leadership and Management*, 1(4): 339–78.

MacCormack, A., & Herman, K. 2001. *The Rise and Fall of Iridium*. Boston: Harvard Business School Press.

Morel, B., & Ramanujam, R. 1999. Through the looking glass of complexity: The dynamics of organizations as adaptive and evolving systems. *Organization Science*, 10(3): 278–93.

Osterwalder, A., & Pigneur, Y. 2010. *Business Model Generation: A Handbook for Visionaries, Game Changers, and Challengers*. Hoboken, NJ: John Wiley & Sons.

Plowman, D. A., Baker, L., Beck, T., Kulkarni, M., Solansky, S., & Travis, D. 2007. Radical change accidentally: The emergence and amplification of small change. *Academy of Management Journal*, 50: 515–43.

Sonenshein, S. 2009. Emergence of ethical issues during strategic change implementation. *Organization Science*, 20: 223–39.

Swenson, R. 1989. Emergent attractor and the law of maximum entropy production: Foundations to a theory of general evolution. *Systems Research*, 6(3): 187–97.

CHAPTER 14

Phase 5: Stabilizing Feedback and Sustaining the System

STABILIZING FEEDBACK IN EMERGENCE

New emergent order, if it creates value, will stabilize itself by finding parameters that best increase its overall sustainability in the ecology. In social systems, as soon as emergents arise they "test" and adapt their efficacy and legitimacy, so as to become embedded into the core logic and organizing model of the dynamic state. Each of these tests is an instance of stabilizing feedback; each test seeks to anchor the emergent by slowing down the nonlinear processes that amplified emergence in the first place (Sastry, 1997). These actions help "institutionalize" the change in the system (Chiles, Meyer, & Hench, 2004), such that the emergents as a whole, and the emergence of the dynamic state, are seen as "real" and legitimate. As stabilizing feedback takes hold, what was the *new* dynamic state slowly becomes *the* dynamic state, and the cycle of emergence is completed. There is also the prospect of *destabilizing* feedback with negative effects, as occurred at ApplySci (discussed later in the chapter).

In a systems dynamics sense, stabilizing feedback produces balancing loops in a system; these are crucial to the sustained success of groups, organizations (Hall, 1976; Sterman, 1989, 2000; Repenning & Sterman, 2001), and whole ecologies (Ulanowicz, 1980; Buenstorf, 2000). Likewise, research shows how the sustainability of living and social systems is based on an integration of negative and positive feedback processes (Drazin & Sandelands, 1992); this insight is also well developed in the work of Rosen (1971, 1973). Most computational models of complexity incorporate stabilization feedback processes within their design.

A couple of basic examples will help clarify the nature of stabilizing feedback. Chiles and his colleagues (2004) described how the emergence of the Branson Mall was usefully kept in check by a strong set of common cultural values, long-standing pro-business policies, and a coordination of marketing efforts, through the actions of collective organizations in the area. Each of these stabilizing feedbacks "channeled individual action into the well-worn grooves of Branson's value system, helping stabilize each new order" (Chiles et al., 2004, p. 513). They called this institutionalizing behavior "Bransonizing," and described it clearly (2004, p. 512):

> [L]ocals counseled newcomers on the importance of fully reflecting local cultural values in their performances and maintaining the cultural consistency that had become central to Branson's national image.

A similar process was identified by Anand, Gardner, and Morris (2007), who showed how the emergence of a new practice area requires an "embedding step" in which the new design becomes "completely enmeshed into the structure of a firm" (Anand et al., 2007, p. 417), through administrative legitimacy, resource commitments, and organizational support.

In practice, individuals (employees, founders) are testing for legitimacy and viability all the time, thus it is somewhat difficult in a fast-moving social system to tease out the stabilizing feedbacks vs. expressions of stress, or experiments, or amplification. However, the processes of embedding a routine or institutionalizing a new system is somewhat unique in that it mainly occurs (is enacted and discussed) *after* the emergence of the new routine or system. Thus, timing has an important influence in capturing these subtle feedbacks. Most examples of feedback that I coded in my data occurred in response to a specific emergent, being members' perceptions on the value and viability of the shift or emergence in light of their understanding of what is *really* going on.

Examples of Stabilizing Feedback

Good examples of this post-emergence stabilizing feedback can be gleaned from the case of DevelopNet. The first example is an immediate shift from negative cash positions in DCP 14–15 to positive cash flow in DCP 16+, immediately after the retrenchment and shift to a new dynamic state. This is easy to see in the amplification for DevelopNet, shown in Figure 14.1. Leading up to the shift, the company experienced a major decrease in cash flow (shown as a *leap* in the red line to its peak at DCP 15). In real terms this amounted to a decrease in cash position from $23,241 to negative $14,195 in a single week, and to negative $17,106 in the week before the shift. However, the very week of the shift, cash flow came back to the black: $5,727 at DCP 16 and 17. Even though their cash flow didn't become consistently positive until a major contract hit at DCP 25, the shift in attention and focus did come with an immediate stabilizing feedback.

The CEO reflected on this stabilization in subsequent weeks, starting with what appears to be a rationale that helped *him* accept the current reality, then

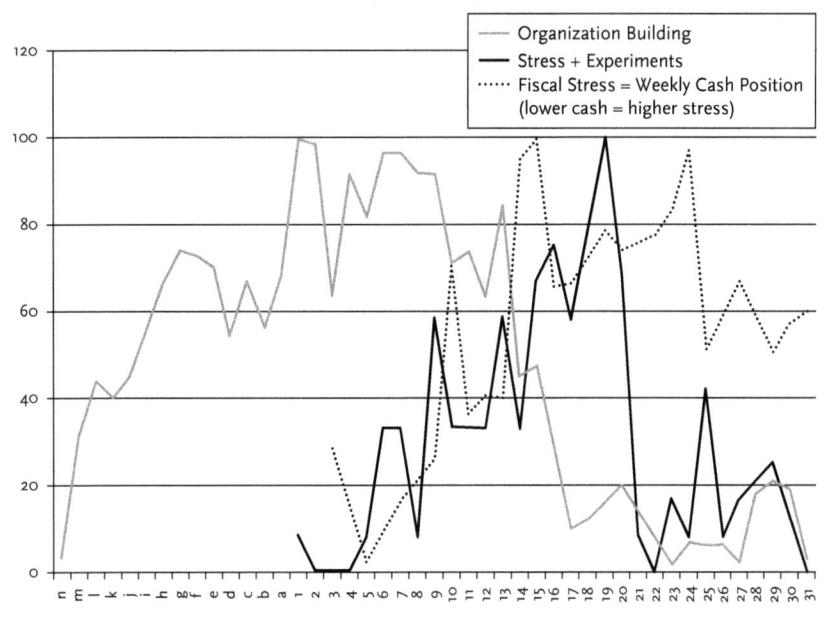

Figure 14.1: Stabilization of Cash Flows at DevelopNet

turning into perceptions of how the shift was being embedded into the routines of the company:

> So, we're retrenching—to do consulting. Billing on someone else's nickel is easier; so we'll get back into a sustaining mode. . . . On a longer-term basis, it gives us credibility. If they don't have to buy the software, there's basically no difficult decision to make. It's a no-brainer. They need to buy our labor anyway. This gives us labor billings. . . . Selling bodies is always an easy sell. If you have skilled people, you can always find a place to fill them. [DevelopNet CEO; DCP 16]
>
> So now I'm focused much more into turning this [business] into a cash cow . . . particularly through these licensing deals. Rather than charge up the hill, is to license the technology, and keep them busy with consulting. [DevelopNet CEO; DCP 20]
>
> So, basically we have stemmed the tide and hopefully the tide is going the other way. [DevelopNet CEO; DCP 22]

Although these are somewhat "weak" examples of stabilizing feedback, what they exemplify is the ongoing enactment of a new core logic for the firm that the CEO is describing to himself and ultimately to his employees and customers. Whereas the actual coded example of stabilizing feedback is the shift to positive cash flow, these comments show how the CEO is putting energy into a sustainable mode of operations, that is, stabilizing the emergence. In this sense, stabilizing feedback acts as a "brake" on the amplification process, as a means to reduce the

Table 14.1. STABLIZING FEEDBACKS AT DEVELOPNET AND APPLYSCI (REPRESENTATIVE EXAMPLES)

DevelopNet

Shift from negative cash flow (2+ weeks) to positive cash flow (2+ weeks). *(DevelopNet, Cash Flow Time Series; DCP 16)*

Also, there's this licensing deal with DOD providers. That's starting to go well.... The interest level seems high. *(DevelopNet CEO; DCP 16)*

We have more appointments [i.e. interest in the new idea]. *(Lead Programmer, DevelopNet; DCP 19)*

Also, we're closing up the hanging government contract ... In closing it out we're closing out a whole line of business ... Saying, O.K., we really are out of the DOD business.... It's time to complete that shift. *(DevelopNet CEO; DCP 27)*

ABC-Leasing called yesterday.... We got it! (i.e., they accepted DevelopNet's proposal—the first one for a new product in a new market). *(Lead Programmer, DevelopNet; DCP 43)*

We got a verbal [from ABC-Leasing]; I'll get a contract next week. *(DevelopNet CEO; DCP 43)*

ApplySci

Today we completed an [intellectual property transfer] agreement with MedicalCareInc.... He said, "We want exclusivity in the area of [x]." *(ApplySci CEO; DCP 15)*. (Note: this is a major advance for the Medical Area, which had been hoping for such a contract for some time.)

We're going into full-scale production [for SportCo] starting next week.... That's really a first for the company. *(Senior Operations Manager, ApplySci; DCP 16)* (Note: In other words, this commercialization represents the first real sale for the company, confirming their efforts on the materials side.)

[CEO] adjusted the budget to accommodate either structure. And [market manager's] job will be to prevent it from creeping back. *(Senior Manager, ApplySci; DCP 22)*

---

increasing spiral of positive feedback, by enacting balancing loops that stabilize and "linearize" the system (see, e.g., Senge, 2006). Further examples are in Table 14.1.

A more formal type of stabilizing feedback includes the responses by other companies to the emerging dynamic state, that is, contracts, conversations, and agreements with partners, customers, and other organizations that confirm the new direction. This kind of stabilizing feedback reflects the need to be sustainable within the social ecology—in a business sense, to produce value that is needed and considered viable.

One example of this kind of positive response occurred in the first round of emergence at DevelopNet, when their main goal was to find short-term clients to tide them over for a couple of months while they developed a new opportunity tension. Some weeks before, sensing the lack of progress in the financial markets, the CEO had proposed a first version of his new plan to license or give away software in exchange for an exclusive customization contract. Initially, he sent this idea out to his U.S. Department of Defense (DOD) clients, and they reacted positively:

> Also, there's this licensing deal with DOD providers. That's starting to go well. At this point we have seven companies that have expressed interest. [Describes an extension

to this concept, which I coded as an experiment.] ... The interest level seems high. (DevelopNet CEO; DCP 16)

A more promising example of stabilizing feedback was hard-won at DevelopNet, but ultimately paved the way for their long-term viability. After the second round of emergence they got busy pursuing their new strategy of giving away their core software system to new commercial customers, who would then retain the firm as a consulting company to customize the program for their needs. It turns out that the shift from DOD providers to commercial companies was harder than they had hoped, but they sent out their first proposal on DCP 36 to "ABC-Leasing," who verbally approved it a couple of months later, on DCP 43. Both the CEO and the lead programmer were enthused about that feedback, which confirmed that their direction had merit; it helped motivate their continued focus in that direction:

> ABC-Leasing called yesterday.... We got it! (Lead Programmer, DevelopNet; DCP 43)
> We got a verbal [from ABC-Leasing]; I'll get a contract next week. (DevelopNet CEO; DCP 43]

Another example of stabilizing feedback occurred at about the same time, as a result of their emergent strategy to give away software for free—a core element of the organizing model that would drive the new value creation. After a good bit of work on their website to incorporate the new strategy, the CEO wrote up a press release. Then, according to the lead programmer:

> I posted [the PR message] to a bunch of news groups ... and things have been busier. Yesterday we had one of our busiest days we've had.... But now we said "Free Software" and we have 10 users today.... It's getting some exposure, so that's kind of cool. (Lead Programmer, DevelopNet; DCP 45)

Bear in mind that in 1997, having 10 people register to work with a new website was a solid accomplishment for a small company like DevelopNet. More than anything it represents clear positive response to the idea.

DESTABILIZING FEEDBACK

Alternatively, a system may respond to an emergent by expressing destabilizing feedback—comments and actions that call into question the new emergent and/or negate the process of concretizing a new dynamic state. This finding, which goes beyond the analogies to dissipative structures, was salient at ApplySci, due in part to its decentralized culture that gave all employees license to react openly about the situation they faced. One clear example of destabilizing feedback at ApplySci occurred, as I mentioned in the Chapter 13, when the V.P. of Industrial Applications made a unilateral decision to temporarily "borrow" most of the lab technicians in order to resolve an urgent client request. In this case, the young V.P. felt a professional loyalty to work out this issue; he also may have been reacting to the fact that the new reorganization had excluded industrial applications, which was his side of the firm. In any event, the unintended consequence was to dislodge the new design by taking everyone off their newly assigned jobs and placing them temporarily on this "urgent" problem. The backlash was made worse because he made this move on the very first week that the new design was to take hold. Thus, his move was very confusing and disrupting, especially for the mid-level scientists and line-level technicians. One technician told me:

> We jumped, shifted gears, everything was thrown at that problem. . . . In a matter of a day everyone was working on the project, which detracts from [commercialization] which is probably our main focus. The structure's not sound enough yet; it disrupts what organization we're trying to form. (Senior Technical Manager; DCP 26)

A line-level lab technician shared her view in even stronger terms:

> What do you want to focus me on?? I refocused my efforts, but got nothing done before we switched! . . . Don't tell me, "This is your primary job function," then switch before it started. . . . At some point you have to get something out, or there won't be a company! (Lab Technician; DCP 24)

Unfortunately, the lab technician was more right than she would have preferred. The disruption reduced the initial solidity of the new structure, putting a brake on the entire emergence attempt. The result was no product for either customer, and a huge amount of frustration that was experienced by nearly everyone on the team, including the senior lab scientist, the senior operations manager (who was "livid" about the distraction), another lab technician, the Industrial Applications V.P., and the analytic manager.

Of course, one disruption does not eradicate an entire emergence process; however, it does exemplify destabilizing feedback, by making the emergence harder to realize and hold onto. Further, this "jumping around" was the more endemic habit in the organization, as the lab technician said: "At some point the company always jumps around; that's what gets thrown back at you." The habitual nature of these last-minute changes was reiterated by the senior operations manager:

> We do this over and over and over again. . . . This is the umpteenth time this has happened. . . . I don't understand why we keep on doing this time and time again. [Senior Operations Manager; DCP 24].

Further examples of destabilizing feedback are presented in Table 14.2.

Table 14.2. DESTABLIZING FEEDBACKS AT DEVELOPNET AND APPLYSCI (REPRESENTATIVE EXAMPLES)

DevelopNet

No luck at all [with the consortium]. No one seems to want to bite on that. So we're abandoning that.... When they were told how much the consortium would cost in the long term they lost interest, even though there was a lot of interest initially. It was a price point issue. *(DevelopNet CEO; DCP 30)*

We didn't get as much response to our mailing as I would have wanted. [He expected 1% return on 1,000 postcards]. One person called in (0.1% response rate), and I have a message that maybe a second person was interested. *(DevelopNet CEO; DCP 43)*

ApplySci

I just got off the phone with [key contact] at BigCo..... The IPO is killing them. They don't have time to do anything but that.... We can't expect anything in short term, [in]the next three weeks. He said, "I don't want to be blowing you off, we're still very interested." *(Senior Marketing Manager, ApplySci; DCP 22).* (Note: ApplySci had understood that their deal was to be *part* of the IPO; ultimately, this news was the start of the end of the entire deal with BigCo).

We've been a bit frustrated in the company itself. We've seen this division [in structure, between Marketing and Development] but didn't realize how much of a line has been drawn.... We talked as if we're willing to help each other out. But actually we don't want to mix the two sides. Which is extremely frustrating for all of us working on either side. *(Senior Scientist, ApplySci; DCP 26)*

We seem to be more chaotic and more divided than we ever had been. Having the business thing up front, it's horrible. It creates a clique. Us versus them. No communication—there's some but it's just not good. I have the same conversation five different times, in all these little circles. So I think that's one of the worst things we've done. *(Lab Scientist, ApplySci; DCP 28)*

Why do we have the big organization we have now? Why have we increased cash burn by 50%?? The reason was, that in order to meet the September checkpoint of the deal we were proposing with HealthCo we had to have commercialization compete.... We didn't have deal with HealthCo, so we said we will fund ourselves. So we are racing to meet the checkpoint on a timeline we have established, that they've never agreed to, and now it looks like they aren't going to give us the money even if we do pass the checkpoint! *(ApplySci CTO; DCP 31)*

First you pick a drug, then they couldn't decide on a drug. It basically fell apart from there. *(Senior Scientist, ApplySci; DCP 47)*

The Role of Stabilizing Feedback in Dissipative Structures Theory

Those familiar with the Bérnard experiment may be curious about how stabilizing feedbacks operate in far-from-equilibrium dissipative structures. Looking closely at the analogy, the stability of a Bérnard experiment is maintained as long as the heat continues to pour into the container. However, this is not the same as suggesting that emergent structures generate stabilizing feedback that keeps them in their ordered state. How are the two related?

This question references my long-standing attempts to explain the analogy between dissipative structures and entrepreneurial ventures, in my dissertation and the papers that immediately followed (Lichtenstein, 1998; Lichtenstein, 2000a, 2000b, 2000c). In all of those papers I presented four "stages" of emergence; these are the first four phases, without the fifth phase of stabilizing feedbacks.

It was only in my later effort to integrate the work of other qualitative researchers pursuing this approach (especially Chiles et al., 2004; and Plowman et al., 2007; along with a re-examination of Leifer, 1989; Smith & Gemmill, 1991; and MacIntosh & MacLean, 1999), that I came to see that a full description of generative emergence would have to include a fifth phase. My first incorporation of this phase was in my paper with Donde Plowman, on the leadership of emergence (Lichtenstein & Plowman, 2009), which was the basis for Figure 7.1 in Chapter 7. Thus, the idea of stabilizing feedbacks is based on management applications of complexity, not on thermodynamic science per se.

In fact, this addition was motivated by a single sentence in one of the few studies, by Garud and Kotha (1994), to use Tsoukas' (1991) approach for using "transformative metaphors" to gain insight into management phenomena. In summarizing Tsoukas' (2001) approach, Garud and Kotha extend the value of analogies by explaining how insights from the target phenomenon—in my case, insights about the emergence of a dynamic state—may be *reapplied* to the source phenomenon—in this case, applied back to dissipative structures theory to gain insight there. In their words (1994, p. 675):

> This "transformational" process also is based on the possibility that what constitutes a source and a target can [be reversed] over time (Arbib, 1989; Gentner, 1989). An object, such as the brain, can inform our understanding of another object, such as the computer, at one point in time. [However,] as our understanding of the computer increases over time, it can reciprocally influence our understanding of the brain.

In other words, is it possible that the presence of stabilizing feedbacks in social systems may reveal isomorphic structures in dissipative structures? Consider that in generative emergence the main source of stabilizing feedback is the agents in the system, who are motivated by a perception about the contribution that the emergent product will make to customers and the community. My sense is that the source of stabilization in dissipative structures is the external agent who is running the experiment. That is, the researcher is the one who maintains the influx of heat energy; the continuous flux is what leads to the ongoing structuring.

Thus, stabilizing feedbacks are caused by the researcher's interest in maintaining the emergent order, to generate knowledge and value from his or her work. The only difference is that the researcher's goal is not "in" the Bérnard cell experiment, but in the broader social (scientific) ecology within which the experiment is run. This broader social ecology, the context for the experiment, includes the research stream that the researcher is engaged with and the findings that she or he believes will generate value and knowledge for the field.

Thus, in both contexts, stabilizing feedbacks are produced by an agent—the only difference is how far "in" the system the agent resides. Such questions are intriguing, especially for those studying the philosophy of science.[1] For now, suffice it to suggest that just as complexity science has informed management, so too may organizational science's applications of complexity science provide important insights into emergence of all kinds.

NOTE

1. This research stream is itself a dynamic state, for the scientist is, like an entrepreneur, gathering resources and pursuing activities to create value, while covering the costs of the(se) endeavor(s) through grants, contracts, or a salary—each of these being stabilizing feedback that assures the researcher that he or she *is* creating value. Thus, inadvertently, we have come to a situation where the successful outcome of a Bérnard cell experiment is an emergent within the broader dynamic state of the scientist's research.

REFERENCES

Anand, N., Gardner, H., & Morris, T. 2007. Knowledge-based innovation: Emergence and embedding of new practice areas in management consulting firms. *Academy of Management Journal*, 50: 406–28.

Arbib, M.A. 1989. A view of brain theory. In E.F. Yates (Ed.) *Self-Organizing Systems: The Emergence of Order* (279–311). New York: Plenum Press

Buenstorf, G. 2000. Self-organization and sustainability: Energetics of evolution and implications for ecological economics. *Ecological Economics*, 33: 119–34.

Chiles, T., Meyer, A., & Hench, T. 2004. Organizational emergence: The origin and transformation of Branson, Missouri's musical theaters. *Organization Science*, 15(5): 499–520.

Drazin, R., & Sandelands, L. 1992. Autogenesis: A perspective on the process of organizing. *Organization Science*, 3: 230–49.

Garud, R., & Kotha, S. 1994. Using the brain as a metaphor to model flexible production systems. *Academy of Management Review*, 19(4): 671–98.

Gentner, D. 1989. The mechanisms of analogical learning. In S. Vosnidou & A. Ortony (Eds.), *Similarity and Analogical Reasoning* (199–241). New York: Cambridge University Press.

Hall, R. 1976. A system pathology of an organization: The rise and fall of the old *Saturday Evening Post*. *Administrative Science Quarterly*, 21: 185–211.

Leifer, R. 1989. Understanding organizational transformation using a dissipative structure model. *Human Relations*, 42: 899–916.

Lichtenstein, B. 1998. *Self-Organized Change in Entrepreneurial Ventures: A Dynamic, Non-linear Model*. Doctoral dissertation, Boston College/UMI.

Lichtenstein, B. 2000a. Dynamics of rapid growth and change: A complexity theory of entrepreneurial transitions. In G. Liebcap (Ed.), *Advances in the Study of Entrepreneurship, Innovation, and Economic Growth*, Vol. 6: 161–92. Westport, CT: JAI Press.

Lichtenstein, B. 2000b. Emergence as a process of self-organizing: New assumptions and insights from the study of nonlinear dynamic systems. *Journal of Organizational Change Management*, 13: 526–44.

Lichtenstein, B. 2000c. Self-organized transitions: A pattern amid the "chaos" of transformative change. *Academy of Management Executive*, 14(4): 128–41.

Lichtenstein, B., & Plowman, D. A. 2009. The leadership of emergence: A complex systems leadership theory of emergence at successive organizational levels. *The Leadership Quarterly*, 20: 617–30.

MacIntosh, R., & MacLean, D. 1999. Conditioned emergence: A dissipative structures approach to transformation. *Strategic Management Journal*, 20: 297–316.

Repenning, N., & Sterman, J. 2001. Nobody ever gets credit for fixing problems that never happened: Creating and sustaining process improvement. *California Management Review*, 43(4): 64–88.

Rosen, R. 1971. Some realizations of (M,R)-systems and their interpretation. *Bulletin of Mathematical Biophysics*, 33: 309–19.

Rosen, R. 1973. On the dynamical realization of (M,R)-systems. *Bulletin of Mathematical Biology*, 35: 1–9.

Sastry, A. 1997. Problems and paradoxes in a model of punctuated organizational change. *Administrative Science Quarterly*, 42(2): 237–75.

Senge, P. M. 2006. *The Fifth Discipline* (revised ed.). New York: Doubleday.

Smith, C., & Gemmill, G. 1991. Self-Organization in small groups: A study of group effectivenss within non-equilibrium conditions. *Human Relations*, 44: 697–716.

Sterman, J. 1989. Misperceptions of feedback in dynamic decision making. *Organizational Behavior and Human Decision Processes*, 43(3): 301–44.

Sterman, J. 2000. *Business Dynamics*. Chicago: Irwin-McGraw-Hill.

Tsoukas, H. 1991. The missing link: A transformational view of metaphors in organizational science. *Academy of Management Review*, 16(3): 566–85.

Ulanowicz, R. 1980. An hypothesis on the development of natural communities. *Journal of Theoretical Biology*, 85: 225–45.

CHAPTER 15
A Cycle of Emergence

DOES EMERGENCE HAPPEN IN CYCLES?

The past five chapters have detailed the process that leads to generative emergence—five phases of change that are a direct analogy to the microprocesses of order creation in dissipative structures. As my examples have shown, these phases have long been identified by management scholars studying organizational emergence and transformation; four- or five-phase models are found in Smith (1986); Smith and Gemmill (1991); Browning, Beyer, and Shetler (1995); Chiles, Meyer, and Hench (2004); and Plowman et al. (2007). But none of these studies has proposed a progression of phases; none have focused on the logic of action that links the phases one to the next.

In contrast, my claim is that these five phases operate sequentially, as a cycle of emergence. This logic has been expressed multiple times throughout the book: A cycle of generative emergence is initiated by an opportunity tension that generates disequilibrium organizing, which gives rise to stress and experiments. If these qualities continue to increase, the system will reinforce and amplify experiments and other energy, toward a critical event—the system reaches a tipping point. On the other side of this threshold, new order will emerge, through a recombination of components. In virtually every successful case, this emergent order results in a *more adaptive system.* If the emergence is successful, the system will produce stabilizing feedbacks that institutionalize the changes into a sustainable dynamic state. This entire process, one cycle of generative emergence, is represented in Figure 15.1.

To say that these phases operate strictly sequentially is somewhat of a misnomer, a point carefully expressed in Figure 15.1. Theoretically, the key insight is that these phases are *interdependent* and mutually causal: The more correlation there is between the dynamics of each grouping, the higher the likelihood that the sequence will progress. Figure 15.1 emphasizes the interdependence of process through the two-way interactions between phases 1 and 2, phases 4 and 5, and in

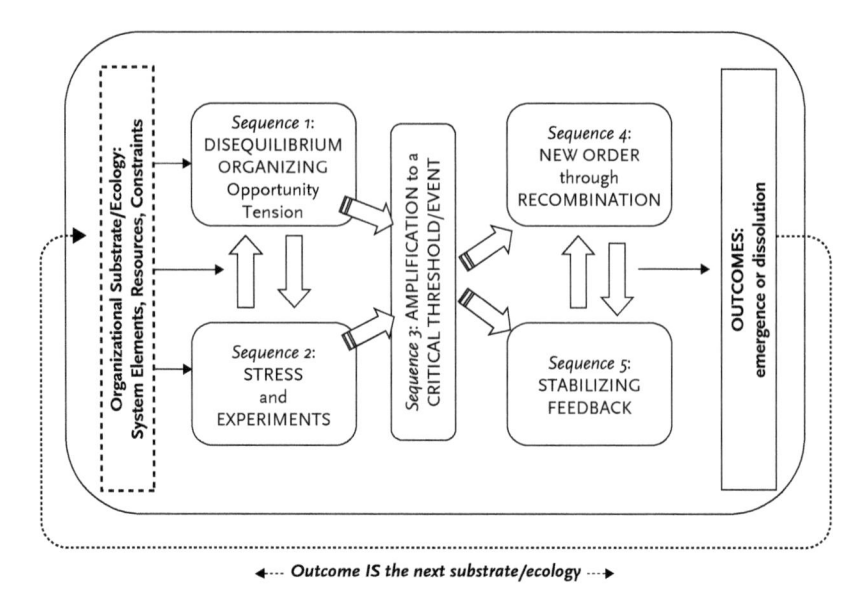

Figure 15.1: One Cycle of Emergence—Idealized Diagram of Five-Phase Emergence Sequence

the feedback between the outcomes and the substrate of emergence. As is true in complexity science more generally, these recursive interactions reflect the interdependence of agents/processes in complex systems, interdependence that leads to emergence (Holland, 1995, 1998; Cilliers, 1998; Anderson, 1999; Johnson, 2001; Maguire, McKelvey, Mirabeau, & Oztas, 2006; Rivkin & Siggelkow, 2007; Goldstein, Hazy, & Lichtenstein, 2010).

My research suggests that this interdependence across phases is particularly strong for the phases before the threshold and after the threshold. For example, disequilibrium organizing leads to increased stress in the system, generating experiments that may push the system further toward disequilibrium organizing. Similarly, this co-creative increase is a driver for amplification: The more the momentum (amplification), the more likely that further experiments will be enacted. Likewise, for new order to be sustainable it must create adaptive value; increasing value creation may lead to additional recombinations of resources and order. Moreover, the value created may spark further aspiration—opportunity tension—which can drive another round of disequilibrium organizing.

Most of my colleagues who have explored emergence empirically using a dissipative structures approach describe these phases as *conditions* (Chiles et al., 2004; Plowman et al., 2007), *elements* (Smith, 1986), and *processes* (Nonaka, 1988; Browning et al., 1995), rather than phases per se (but see MacIntosh & MacLean, 1999). In this way they explicitly recognize the intricate interactions between each aspect of the process and avoid the pitfalls of assuming a strictly progressive sequence. Like them I am balancing my claim of "sequential" by recognizing the interactive and iterative nature of the process. However, I do see generative emergence as a progression of energy and intensity in and through a system, which results in a shift of state and outcomes from that shift. This is necessarily a progressive story—the progressive sequence of phases brings with it a developmental progression of the social ecology within which it starts.

In addition, there are clear benefits from framing the progressive process of generative emergence as a cycle. In particular, it provides an answer to the problem of origins: From *what* does a dynamic state emerge? What is the substrate or ecology out of which generative emergence begins? The answer is that the outcome of a cycle of emergence *is* the substrate from which a new dynamic state can emerge.

A Cycle of Emergence

Several empirical studies have emphasized this cyclic nature of emergence. For example, Chiles et al. (2004, p. 505) theorize the evolution of Branson, Missouri as cycles of "punctuated emergences," through which four distinct historical eras are "initiated and periodically reinitiated by fluctuations . . . each of which qualitatively transformed the system, ushering in one new regime of order after another." The outcome of each cycle provides the context from which the next discontinuity arises, triggering the next cycle of emergence.

Leifer (1989) presaged this understanding in his dissipative structures analysis of organizational transformation. His model of dissipative structures (Figure 2, p. 907) is drawn as a circle, with trigger events leading to a cycle that includes reframing and visioning, experimentation, transformation, resynthesis, and then— sometime later[1]—a move from stability to the disequilibrium conditions that precede another trigger event. He explains that organizations with more "openness to the environment" can allow for "a greater openness to the next cycle of transformation" (Leifer 1989, p. 911). This leads to his claim that a dissipative organization is "constantly renewing itself, albeit inefficiently, [toward a] more effective way of operating," such that "the normal evolution of organizations proceeds from transformation to transformation," in an ongoing cycle of emergence.

In a similar way, Katz (1993, Figure 1, p. 99) models organizational emergence as a cyclic process, whereby

> Individuals, partners, teams and/or firms engage in → A combinatorial revolution to create a proto-organization . . . → Which works until it reaches a trigger . . . creating a revolution → Leading to a possibly new combination of properties . . . for a relatively stable period. → And so on, the process goes.

The cycle of emergence here is embedded in the concluding phrase: "and so on the process goes"—from one "combinatorial revolution" to the next, in an unceasing drive to optimize the capabilities of the venture to the needs and desires of its customers. According to Browning, Beyer, and Shetler (1995, p. 139), this concept is central to "complexity theory" as a whole—the study of

> emergent orders as self-organizing systems in which innovative cultural patterns and increasingly complex structures repeatedly emerge. These structures may stabilize, continue to evolve, self-destruct, or do all three—in cycles.

Understanding these cycles and their dynamics is a core goal of our work. Before exemplifying these dynamics, it is important to appreciate how each cycle is related to the next.

Emergence Outcomes Are the Substrate for a New Cycle

In Figure 15.1, a dotted line expresses the crucial link between one cycle and the next; the line represents a temporal feedback loop between the outcomes of emergence (at time N) and the social substrate/ecology (at time $N + 1$). A somewhat better visualization is Figure 15.2, which aims to show that the emerged dynamic state *is* (becomes) an integrated social ecology of its own. This may, over time, become the substrate out of which yet another process of generative emergence may be initiated.

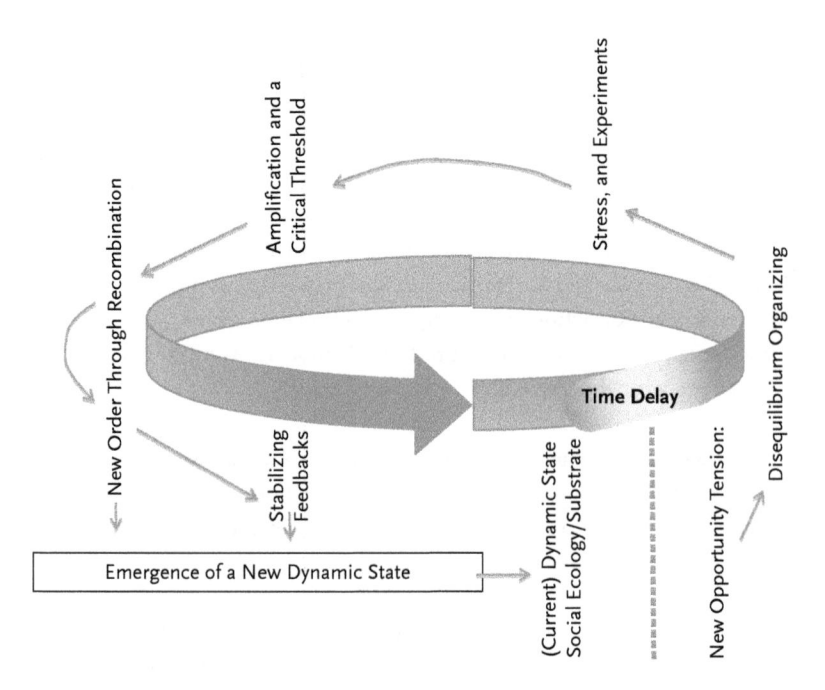

Figure 15.2: One Cycle of Emergence—Temporal Image

Generative Emergence

The ecology of a system is forever altered by the emergence process, because that process, whether it leads to success or dissolution, creates a new set of conditions out of which the system (e.g., organization) operates. It is the *interdependence* in emergence, and in its interactive process, which alters the components of the systems ecology, regardless of the degree of emergence outcome. Like the notion of *path creation* (Garud & Karnoe, 2001; Garud, Kumaraswamy, & Karnøe, 2010), emergence is a truly creative process that does more than affect the existing ecology: Emergence (re)makes the substrate within which it occurs, generating a new ecology out of which a new developmental level may arise (see also Salthe, 2010). This is true for a single cycle of emergence, and as I describe in Chapter 16, for a cycle of re-emergence.

EXAMPLES OF A CYCLE OF EMERGENCE

A number of studies have collected and analyzed data that reveal an entire cycle of emergence, showing the sequential progression of all five phases. Two cases in particular exemplify how a cycle of emergence operates: the early rise of Starbucks (Lichtenstein & Jones, 2004), and the creation of the SEMATECH alliance (Browning et al., 1995). These examples highlight an interdependence across phases and reveal a coherent flow of change across the entire process. After presenting these, I will summarize other studies that reveal cycles of emergence—at HealthInfo (Lichtenstein, Dooley & Lumpkin 2006) and at the Republic of Tea (Lichtenstein & Kurjanowicz, 2010). A similar progression occurs in re-emergence, as examples from my dissertation companies in the next chapter will show.

A Cycle of Emergence at Starbucks

A Substrate for Generative Emergence

The context for the emergence of Starbucks was the coffee industry in the 1970s, a product market that was dominated by a few major brands of medium-quality ground coffee. These mass-marketed products were purchased in grocery stores and drunk at home. In the early 1980s these large companies started to lose market share as consumers started seeking higher-quality morning beverages (Rindova & Fombrun, 2001). This shift started with few small specialty coffee shops offering fresh roasted beans and high-quality coffee to limited regional markets, by maintaining a kind of "avant-garde" model of takeout coffee for a select population (Koehn, 2001). Over a 10-year period, from 1979 to 1989, this shift in consumer preference took hold, evidenced by the dramatic increase in microroasters of premium coffee, which jumped from 40 to 385, equivalent to a 1,000% increase during this time (Andrews, 1992, in Rindova & Fombrun, 2001, p. 245). By 1996 there were nearly

7,000 specialty coffee shops in the United States (Rindova & Fombrom, 2001, p. 267), a growth that drove, and was driven by, the rapid expansion of Starbucks. Clearly, there was opportunity; the question was whether it could be captured. This is where the vision and emergence of Starbucks begins.

Phase 1: Disequilibrium Organizing at Starbucks

Howard Schultz, the founder of Starbucks, started to feel opportunity tension soon after he was hired as the director of marketing and operations for the original Starbucks stores in Seattle—there were less than six at the time. In a now oft-told story, through his 1983 buying trip to Milan Italy, he "saw an enormous opportunity for Starbucks [by] recreating the Italian coffee bar culture in the U.S." (Koehn, 2001, p. 8). Finding that his bosses were not interested in his vision, he left there to found *Il Giornale*, a gourmet coffee bar in downtown Seattle. Within a year the growing venture had three stores and $1.5 million in annual revenue.

Schultz's infusion of organizing energy continued in 1988 with the purchase of the original Starbucks stores for $3.8 million; within three years the entrepreneur and his partner had grown Starbucks to 75 retail stores. The initial emergence of Starbucks was thus clearly marked by the drive and intensity of opportunity tension:

> Schultz and his team thought that they *had* to move quickly. They believed that the potential market for specialty coffee was enormous.... To exploit this appeal, he and his colleagues would have to make the Starbucks experience available to millions of consumers [and] speed was essential. (Koehn, 2001, p. 11)

Phase 2: Stress and Experiments at Starbucks

As Starbucks grew from 1987 through 1991, it faced an increasing mismatch between its high aspirations to become *the* leading high-quality coffee bar in the United States, and the real limitations of its resources and operations. Perhaps the best example of this stressful mismatch is Schultz's early expansion into Chicago, 2,000 miles away from their roasting plant; the expansion had commenced *before* the company had an infrastructure capable of supporting that expansion. Because of this, "many of the problems that Schultz and his advisers had foreseen did, in fact, materialize" (Koehn, 2001, p. 13), leading to increased stress throughout the company. Fiscal stress also increased during this period: "[D]espite growing sales, losses also mounted.... Starbucks lost money in fiscal 1987, 1988, and 1989—more than $1.1 million in 1989 alone" (Koehn, 2001, p. 13).

This growing stress in the face of continued expansion at Starbucks generated a stream of organizational experiments. At a corporate level the organization experimented with a unique word-of-mouth marketing strategy: Instead of advertising their new locations they relied on superior service to catalyze customer recognition and sales growth. Also, in 1988 Starbucks issued its first mail-order catalogue, an experiment in building an alternative distribution channel that would help identify the needs and locations of its core customers. In addition, every new store was seen as an experiment of sorts, particularly due to Starbucks' strategy of "store clustering," which "increased consumer awareness of the brand, but often at the cost of cannibalizing existing business" (Koehn, 2001, p. 19).

In sum, the opportunity tension felt by Howard Schultz led to a dramatic rise in disequilibrium organizing, starting in 1983 and continuing through the 1980s. As their goals for growth outstripped their capacity, stress grew throughout the company. In response, a series of experiments were made—ingenious attempts to deal with the "chaos" and make the leap to a viable company. This became realized at the peak of these increases, in 1991.

Phase 3: Amplification and a Critical Event

A specific trigger point seemed to happen at Starbucks in 1991, during its high-paced expansion into yet another new market, Southern California. Like its entry into other markets the company relied on consumers' endorsements rather than advertising to initiate growth. However, this time things were different (Koehn, 2001, pp. 13–14):

> Word-of-mouth spread quickly, and lines formed outside stores ... Hollywood notables, such as director David Lynch ... frequented company outlets. [According to Schultz,] "almost overnight, Starbucks became chic."

This "overnight" transition to critical mass is captured by Starbucks' CFO Orin Smith:

> One day it seemed [that] a critical mass of customers discovered Starbucks and stayed with the company. "We had been working for a long time," he continued. . . . "But we did not know exactly when it would bear fruit. Then virtually overnight, it just popped."

Phase 4: New Order Through Recombination

What "popped" was the emergence of Starbucks as a national brand—the "lift-off" of a high-potential company into a period of sustained growth and expansion (Bhide, 1992). In our terms, a dynamic state emerged—the opportunity tension had become enacted through an effective organizing model that creates value, enough by customers to continuously sustain the operation.

This emergence was supported by the creation and recombination of structures and systems to expand the long-term capacity of the company. At the corporate level, for example, Schultz and his executive team "worked to develop a range of systems—financial, accounting, legal, planning, and logistics—that the company would require . . . to become a national business" (Koehn, 2001, p. 13). An IT network was installed, which finally linked all stores to a central database with shared computer systems. A new roasting plant was built, and corporate offices were expanded. During this same period Starbucks experienced other emergent outcomes, including becoming a distributor for major corporate accounts, including Horizon Air, Nordstrom's, and later Barnes and Noble.

These structural changes were linked to an acceleration of brand recognition that furthered the momentum of growth. As Koehn describes (2001, p. 14), "The markets that the company had been trying to build by opening stores and educating consumers in [Los Angeles, San Francisco, Chicago and other cities] took off, attaining new, sustained momentum."

Phase 5: Stabilizing Feedbacks

In a broader sense, the *meaning* of Starbucks expanded to a new level as well, as the chain developed a "near-cult status" (Koehn, 2001, p. 14). This expansion reflected a cultural legitimacy earned by Starbucks, which was seen as the originator of this new kind of retail establishment (Koehn, 2001, p. 20).

> By the early 1990s Starbucks had become a recognized "third place"—a location apart from home or work where people congregated for social interaction, refreshment, or a few moments of communal solitude.

This belief became a key source of stabilizing feedback, as Starbucks became seen as an "institution" more than simply a business. In addition, the value creation at Starbucks was stabilized by the demographics of its clientele, 85% of whom were repeat customers, many of whom came in several times a week. Their ongoing purchases went hand-in-hand with the long-term relationships they were able to build with the barristers due to another type of stabilizing feedback, namely Starbucks has the lowest employee turnover of any similar retail store, in part because they offer salaries up to three times higher than the average for the food service industry, with a benefits package that outstrips all competitors. Their focus on *retaining* employees leads to a high-quality customer experience that grows through repeat visits—the essence of a stabilizing feedback loop. Note the additional stabilization: with this degree of repeat visits advertising was unnecessary, thus the company gladly traded higher labor costs for a marketing budget that is close to zero.

Outcomes of Emergence

In terms of outcomes, the emergences at Starbucks demonstrate a remarkable expansion of capacity. From 1990 to 1992, from the mid-point of their process to their generative emergence, Starbucks nearly doubled in size, to 154 stores and 2,000 employees. In the same period sales increased by almost 300% to $103 million, with net income growing 70%–100% annually. This dramatic expansion continued for several years; by 1995 more than 3,000,000 people per week visited Starbucks, and the average customer frequented a company store 18 times per month (Koehn, 2001, p. 2).

These outcomes are all part of a cycle of emergence at Starbucks, which culminated in its ultimate emergence into a public company. Although my thoughts here are inconclusive (without having studied the original data), the rapidly rising success and reputation of the company led to a growing interest by others to invest in the new phenomenon. Ultimately, this resulted in the generative emergence of Starbucks as a public corporation. The Starbucks IPO in July of 1992 yielded $29 million in investments (Koehn, 2001, p. 20). With this capital, Starbucks began a very different era of organizing, reaching out to international markets.[2]

A Cycle of Emergence at SEMATECH

Another case that reveals a cycle of emergence is drawn from Browning, Beyer, and Shetland's (1995) analysis of the founding of SEMATECH, a 25-year old consortium of U.S. companies in the semiconductor industry that cooperate by pooling knowledge and resources in order to continuously extend the technological frontier for the industry and its member companies. Its origin, according to the detailed analysis by Browning et al. (1995), reflects a cycle of emergence.

Context for the Emergence of SEMATECH

Prior to its founding in 1987, the U.S. semiconductor industry was the largest provider of semiconductor chips in the world. However, this preeminence was being challenged by new firms in Japan, South Korea, and elsewhere; an early analysis (SEMATECH, 1992) suggested that U.S. market share would shrink from 85% in 1988 to 20% in 1993. Already the industry had begun to experience a "decay" in their supply and materials infrastructure, caused by a lack of large-scale investments in capital and research and development, proven drivers of success in the advanced electronics industry (Ferguson, 1988). Amidst concern about the decline in U.S. dominance, an opportunity tension arose within the top firms in the industry.

Opportunity Tension and Disequilibrium Organizing for SEMATECH

At its heart, the opportunity of SEMATECH was to revitalize the semiconductor industry through radical cooperation between its highly competitive member firms. Such a vision became possible through a recognition of the massive demand for sustained growth in the sector, along with the idea that an industry-wide co-operative could achieve results that no firm could do alone (Barron, 1990). With this opportunity came a rising tension, felt in the gap between U.S. semiconductor companies and their Japanese rivals, who were out-producing American firms by a factor of 3:2, leading to a doubling of their market share to 50%, compared to a 30% drop for the United States (Ferguson, 1988).

The mutual opportunity tension led to an agreement, a collaboration across the entire industry and by federal government, a proposed creation of a research consortium for technology development whose results would be disseminated to all participating firms. The initial disequilibrium organizing there was impressive: Virtually all of the largest semiconductor firms in the country signed onto the agreement, and each member company invested heavily into the consortium. Within a year, a financial commitment of $100,000,000 *annually* across all firms was initiated, an amount that was matched by the U.S. government. Thus the proposal was initiated with a five-year budget of $1,000,000,000 (Browning et al., 1995). Likewise, each company assigned up to 200 personnel into the consortium; by 1995 the total workforce had grown to 800.

These resources were directed into two incredibly challenging tasks: decrease the size of lines etched on chips by a factor of 7 (from ~1 micron to .35 micron) while increasing production efficiency. These aims led to continuously high levels of disequilibrium organizing, as Browning and colleagues (1995, p. 123) report:

> The level of effort was so high while Noyce was CEO that many interviewees reported they could not have kept it up much longer. People worked around the clock and on weekends. The parking lots were never empty.... These extraordinary levels of energy and effort kept the organization growing.

Stress and Experiments at SEMATECH

As expected for generative emergence, this dramatic infusion of resources and activity led to increases in stress and experiments. Browning and colleagues identify a number of stress points in the company. For example, the core objectives for the consortium were contested from the outset and for many years: "[D]ifferences over the goals at SEMATECH were highly visible at meetings we observed in the summer of 1992" (Browning et al., 1995, p. 124). An equally challenging conflict emerged between the top two leaders of the organization, resulting in "a rift [that] developed and grew between Noyce [the CEO] and Paul Castrucci, the COO the board of directors had selected.... Their difficulties in reaching agreement resulted in the COO's resignation."

Other stress was caused by a management-induced ambiguity about each individual's status. Many mid-level employees were not given a job title; even though Noyce told people that they could invent their own job titles, "employees felt a lack without them." More stress was induced in the attempt to merge so many different company cultures and perceptions of what the work of the consortium was to be. In summarizing these and other examples, Browning et al. (p. 125) conclude that "the mix of private agendas, new faces, and an equivocal structure made the early experience of SEMATECH chaotic."

This stress and chaos were met by a series of experiments, alternative ways of understanding the industry and its status quo. To begin, Noyce created a unique model of shared leadership—an Office of the Chief Executive that was co-created by himself and two senior colleagues. "The three confer frequently, attend important meetings together, and generally work closely together" (p. 117). Another key experiment was the challenge by the leaders, "If it's not competitive, change it." This aim for continuous innovation was a shift from the previous focus on efficiency. For example, the standard criterion for suppliers—low cost—was "shown to be inappropriate" in the new era. Likewise, companies initiated an experiment, to shift focus toward "total-cost-of-ownership," accounting for installation, servicing, reliability, and life cycle of the product (Browning et al. 1995, p. 126).

Other experiments reflected the degree of interdependence across the consortium that had never been seen in the industry, a new value that was amplified by a growing sense of reciprocity (Blau, 1964; Muthusamy & White, 2005). In particular, Intel "took the lead" in offering to contribute more high-level performers as a way of increasing their influence and catalyzing more outcomes overall. A different sort of experiment was driven by Ann Bowers Noyce, an HR executive at Apple and the wife of the CEO, who "induced Noyce to take women ... seriously and give them opportunities" (Browning et al. 1995, p. 132). Experiments were also generated to deal with challenges of communication, structuring, and standards.

Emphasizing the aggregate shift that was achieved as members experimented with new values and models, Browning et al. suggest (p. 140),

> Because of the instabilities and turbulence that led to the critical condition ... participants turned away from values associated with cutthroat competition, secrecy, and proprietary standards.... The semiconductor industry needed to operate qualitatively differently than it had in the past.

Amplification to a Critical Event

Given the fact that these data are not longitudinal, it is hard post-hoc to discern an amplification or to identify a particular critical event from their published analysis. At the same time, several aspects of the story reflect amplification. For example, after an initial period of uncertainty there were clear increases in engineering efforts to reduce the size of etched lines on semiconductor chips—success built on success to create a momentum in the organization. This momentum was further amplified by an increase in the numbers of personnel dedicated to the consortium.

As for a critical event, Browning et al. (1995) suggest there may have been several. For example, the sudden death of Bob Noyce, in 1990, initiated a round of change and newness in the organization. Another critical event was the conclusion of the initial five-year charter for SEMATECH, which led to an intense round of negotiations and agreements for a second five-year contract, which was confirmed by nearly all the original companies.

New Order through Recombinations

The dynamic state that ultimately emerged at SEMATECH involved a fundamental shift away from shared government support to a fully sustainable self-funding model whereby the value created by the consortium was more than sufficient to justify annual dues by member companies; these covered all operational costs. In formal terms (from SEMATECH, 2012),

> By 1994, it had become clear that the U.S. semiconductor industry—both device makers and suppliers—had regained strength and market share; at that time, the SEMATECH Board of Directors voted to seek an end to matching federal funding after 1996, reasoning that the industry had returned to health and should no longer receive government support.

This new order was imbued with recombinations from within and outside the industry. Many of the structures that informed the consortium were "borrowed from elsewhere in the industry" and adapted in unique ways to serve the new organization. More important was the reformulation of priorities. For example, whereas the original focus of the cooperative was to serve member companies, the new dynamic state emphasized the role of suppliers to the industry. In fact, nearly half of all the resources in the consortium were directed to help the suppliers in the industry, a strong example of building capacity throughout the entire system. A similar aspect of the new order was the allocation of approximately $5,000,000/year to the national laboratory system in the United States—money to support engineering programs and their students, ultimately increasing the scientific capacity nationwide and thus fuel the continued growth of the industry.

Stabilizing Feedback

A number of stabilizing feedbacks were evident at SEMATECH. Browning et al. describe these in some detail under the construct of "self-amplifying reciprocity" within the consortium (Browning et al., 2005, p. 131):

> Each firm's contribution to the efforts to found and operate SEMATECH built on and enlarged the contributions of others. Individual contributions had a multiplier effect because they established and reinforced norms that required all to join in. . . . The result of this reciprocity was a group-based trust [in] the norms of reciprocity and cooperation [that] persisted because participants could use data from past experiences to predict others' future actions.

Like the institutional norms of Bransonizing, which helped reinforce and stabilize the new order there, the norms of reciprocity and cooperation became stabilizing feedbacks that helped sustain and solidify the long-term value of the consortium. For example, one outcome of these emergent norms was that "free-riding behaviors became discredited as both counter-normative and inimical to gaining full benefits from membership" (Browning et al., 1995, p. 142). Instead, companies found multiple ways to use cooperation to their benefit and the benefit of the consortium, thus stabilizing the value of the endeavor.

Outcomes of Generative Emergence

Many of the important outcomes of the consortium have already been mentioned. Primarily, the new organizational form and dynamic state generated huge advances in the core technologies and their manufacture, bringing the United States back into parity with its Asian counterparts. Moreover, these advances continued long after the initial project had reached its conclusion; the dynamic state is now 25 years old and its member companies include some of the top names in the industry, plus an increasing number of international partners. The consortium has developed a strategic university partnership through the sponsorship of the College of Nanoscale Science and Engineering at SUNY Albany.[3] In addition, the infusion of capital and resources to the semiconductor supply network has significantly increased the capacity of the industry as a whole.

FURTHER EXAMPLES OF EMERGENCE CYCLES

These two examples—the generative emergence of Starbucks that culminated in their IPO (1988–1992), and the generative emergence of the SEMATECH consortium (1990–1995)—offer a view of emergence as a cycle. In these cases, the generality of the data makes it hard to identify specific shifts between stages. Even so, the cases do provide narrative confirmation of the cyclical nature of emergence. Two other studies have identified cycles of emergence that are somewhat less fuzzy, including our research on new venture creation at HealthInfo (Lichtenstein, Dooley, & Lumpkin, 2006), and an extension of our analysis of Republic of Tea (Lichtenstein & Kurjanowicz, 2010).

A Cycle of Emergence, from HealthInfo to HealthUSA

Using techniques that were similar to my dissertation, my colleagues and I (Lichtenstein et al., 2006) tracked the activities of a nascent entrepreneur just as she started pursuing her start-up of a health-based company focused on healthy eating—HealthInfo. Specifically, she wanted to create a website that would identify healthy restaurants in virtually every large city in the United States. Her vision was to set up a site that would allow for easy search of healthy restaurants. The main challenges were to finish an initial round of data capture (travel) to a few large cities she had not been to and in developing a system to sustain the accuracy of restaurant information.

Our analysis showed that she produced an increase in disequilibrium organizing, and in stress, leading to a punctuated shift in her overall vision, her organizing strategy, and her tactics (see Figure 15.3). In our paper we suggested that these represent an emergence event, which we defined as "a coordinated and punctuated shift in multiple modes of entrepreneurial organizing at virtually the same time, which generates a qualitatively different state—a new identity—within a nascent venture" (Lichtenstein et al., 2006, p. 167). These came together in her language

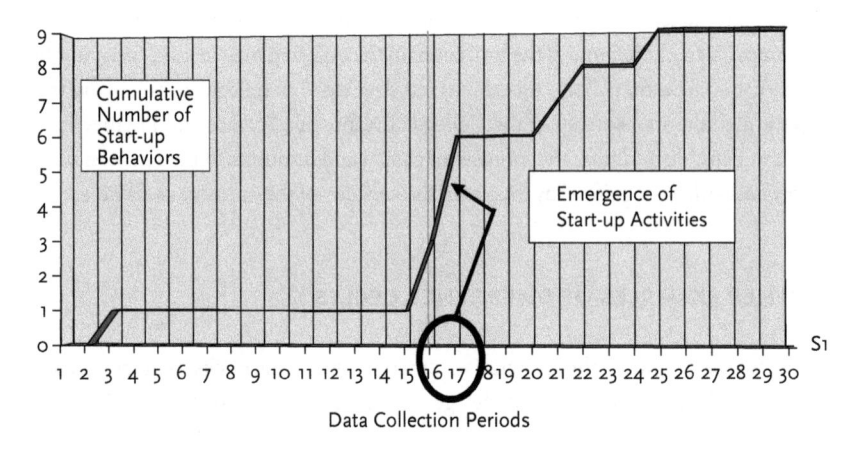

Figure 15.3: Punctuated Shift in Start-up Behaviors, in the Cycle of Emergence at HealthInfo

Generative Emergence

and organizing which now refocused on 10 coordinated health-based companies, "HealthUSA," of which HealthInfo was but one.

Once she started considering the broader vision for this combined "higher-level" entity, her entrepreneurial actions started to change as well. The shift expanded her market analysis, increased the range of possible innovations and cross-company synergies, and led her to become engaged in additional products. As a result, her time and energy for HealthInfo was reduced. In the months that followed, her focus shifted farther away from the venture, until she essentially stopped organizing around HealthInfo. Given the time-sensitive nature of restaurant information, this reduction rapidly reduced the viability of that effort. Within a couple of years, the entire endeavor was nonactive.

Here the cycle of emergence leads to an outcome that is not very adaptive (see Figure 15.4). Initially it appeared that having 10 co-evolving firms organized around similar principles and markets could dramatically increase the capacity of the system. However, the emergent dynamic state was not sustainable—it did not provide the entrepreneur with the necessary time (and motivation) to keep all of the requisite opportunity tensions alive. In sum, this case starts the cycle with the creation of HealthInfo, it has its greatest momentum in the emergence of HealthUSA, but peters out because of the lack of capacity that the emergent *actually* provides to the system and its entrepreneur.

Two Cycles of Emergence at Republic of Tea

A cycle of emergence perspective provides some helpful insight to the Republic of Tea case. As described in Chapter 12, the venture was initiated by a shared opportunity tension, a vision for a unique tea company that was amplified through a long series of follow-up ideas, plans, and even a few tangible actions to explore the viability of the concept. This cycle of emergence is short, however, and inconclusive.

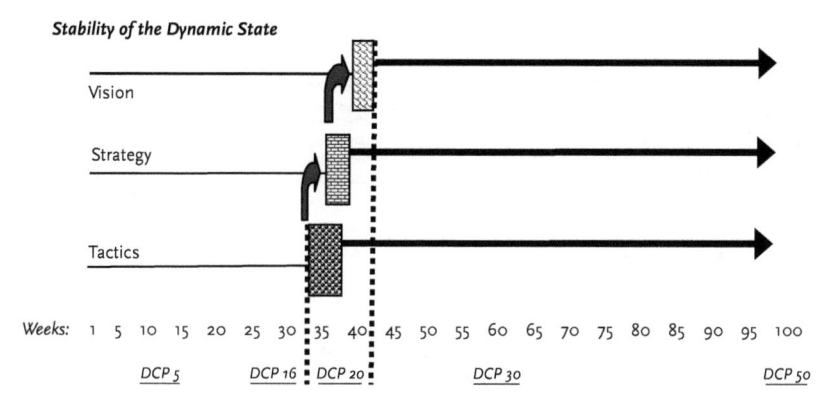

Figure 15.4: Punctuated Shift in All Areas—Single Cycle of Emergence at HealthInfo

After an initial surge of activity, mainly in ideas and plans, it became clear to the main entrepreneur that the opportunity itself was not well enough thought out, an issue that was paralleled by the unbalanced power dynamics between the young "doer" and the older "mentor." This first cycle does not yield emergence; instead, the organizing process just silently drops away. The main entrepreneur goes back to work, the venture is left "open"—no formal closure happened between the two founders—and 18 months pass.

Then, for reasons that are subtle and interesting (Lichtenstein & Kurjanowicz, 2010), the main entrepreneur found his way back to the venture, this time with a whole new set of experiences and interest. In a sense, the opportunity tension in this next cycle is much more promising: The entrepreneur has identified a precise business opportunity for a specific market, and his creative energy soars as he really sees how the business could take off. This clarity becomes enacted in his organizing: He identifies suppliers, distribution channels, a marketing plan with value-based pricing, and an entire organizing model that is projected to generate very high value to customers and to the owners. These two cycles of emergence are represented in Figure 15.5.

The outcome of cycle 2 is an incorporated start-up venture that was selling products to customers all over the world. First-year sales amounted to $660,000; by year 3 the company was selling over $4,000,000 annually in tea, with a net profit of over 15%. Thus cycle 2 represents a huge success, driven in part by the tangibility of organizing. Another aspect of the cycle 2 success may be that the actual amount

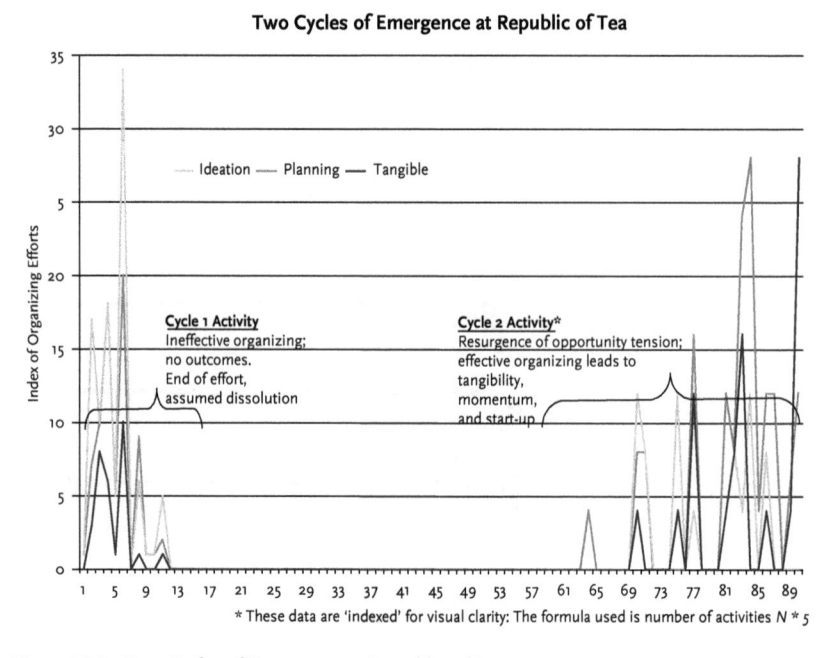

Figure 15.5: Two Cycles of Emergence at Republic of Tea

of organizing in cycle 2 is far less than that in cycle 1, a fact that is obscured in Figure 15.5. (There the number of activities on each week in cycle 2 is not equivalent to the number of activities in cycle 1; the latter takes the number of activities *multiplied by* 5 in order to show the pattern of momentum more clearly. Note that same data transformation was done in the previous chart of cycle 1 organizing at Republic of Tea—see Figure 12.1 in Chapter 12; there too the data are actual number of activities multiple of 5.) It is possible that the clearer opportunity tension in the second round, along with a stronger ability to resolve the dynamics between the founders, means that far less effort was needed to create a far more effective outcome.

Cycles of Emergence in My Dissertation Firms

The presence of cycles is altogether evident at DevelopNet, ApplySci, and, to a lesser extent, ServiceCo. What distinguishes these from the examples in this chapter is that each of those ventures had already started and reached a stable dynamic state. Then, some years after start-up, each one decided to "get to the next level"—to push the company toward a major leap in its success. To capture with integrity this difference, I describe these as cycles of re-emergence, and explore it in the next chapter.

NOTES

1. To be clear: The reinitiation may or may not occur, but either way, only after time has passed. Few systems are continuously reforming, although consider the growing literature on continuously transforming organizations (Rindova & Kotha, 2001; Tsoukas & Chia, 2002; Garud et al., 2006).
2. To my mind, the Starbucks of today—a global company with international interests, is quite different from the entrepreneurial organization started by Howard Schwartz in 1987.
3. http://cnse.albany.edu/Home.aspx.

REFERENCES

Anderson, P. 1999. Complexity theory and organization science. *Organization Science,* 10: 216–32.

Andrews, M. 1992. *Avenues for Growth.* Long Beach, CA: Speciality Coffee Association of America.

Bailey, K. 1987. Restoring order: Relating entropy to energy and information. *Systems Research,* 4(2): 83–92.

Baker, T., & Nelson, R. 2005. Creating something from nothing: Resource construction through entrepreneurial bricolage. *Administrative Science Quarterly,* 50: 239–366.

Barron, J. J. 1990. Consortia: High-tech co-ops. *Byte,* 15(June): 15:269.

Bhide, A. 1992. Bootstrap finance: The art of start-ups. *Harvard Business Review*, 70(6): 109–17.

Blau, P. M. 1964. *Exchange and Power in Social Life*. New York: John Wiley & Sons.

Browning, L., Beyer, J., & Shetler, J. 1995. Building cooperation in a competitive industry: Sematech and the semiconductor industry. *Academy of Management Journal*, 38: 113–51.

Chiles, T., Meyer, A., & Hench, T. 2004. Organizational emergence: The origin and transformation of Branson, Missouri's musical theaters. *Organization Science*, 15(5): 499–520.

Cilliers, P. 1998. *Complexity and Postmodernism: Understanding Complex Systems*. New York: Routledge.

Corning, P., & Kline, S. J. 1998. Thermodynamics, information and life revisited, part I: "To be or entropy." *Systems Research and Behavioral Science*, 15: 273–95.

Dyke, C. 1992. From entropy to economy: A thorny path. *Advances in Human Ecology*, 1: 149–76.

Ferguson, C. H. 1988. From the people who brought you voodoo economics. *Harvard Business Review*, 66(3): 55–63.

Garud, R., & Karnoe, P. 2001. *Path Dependence and Creation*. Mahwah, NJ: Lawrence Erlbaum & Associates.

Garud, R., Kumaraswamy, A., & Karnøe, P. 2010. Path dependence or path creation? *Journal of Management Studies*, 47(4): 760–74.

Garud, R., Kumaraswamy, A., & Sambamurthy, V. 2006. Emergent by design: Performance and transformation at Infosys Technologies. *Organization Science*, 17: 277–86.

Goldstein, J., Hazy, J., & Lichtenstein, B. 2010. *Complexity and the Nexus of Leadership: Leveraging Nonlinear Science to Create Ecologies of Innovation*. New York: Palgrave Macmillan.

Holland, J. 1995. *Hidden Order*. Redwood City, CA: Addison-Wesley.

Holland, J. 1998. *Emergence: From Chaos to Order*. Cambridge, MA: Perseus Books.

Johnson, S. 2001. *Emergence: The Connected Lives of Ants, Brains, Cities, and Software*. New York: Scribner

Katz, J. 1993. The dynamics of organizational emergence: A contemporary group formation perspective. *Entrepreneurship Theory and Practice*, 17(2–Winter): 97–101.

Koehn, N. 2001. *Howard Schultz and Starbucks Coffee Company*. Boston: Harvard Business School Press.

Leifer, R. 1989. Understanding organizational transformation using a dissipative structure model. *Human Relations*, 42: 899–916.

Levie, J., & Lichtenstein, B. 2010. A terminal assessment of stages theory: Introducing a dynamic states approach to entrepreneurship. *Entrepreneurship Theory and Practice*, 34(2–March): 314–54.

Lichtenstein, B. 1995. Evolution or transformation: A critique and alternative to punctuated equilibrium. *Best Papers Proceedings, National Academy to Management*. 1995: 291–95.

Lichtenstein, B. 2000. Self-organized transitions: A pattern amid the "chaos" of transformative change. *Academy of Management Executive*, 14(4): 128–41.

Lichtenstein, B., Dooley, K., & Lumpkin, T. 2006. Measuring emergence in the dynamics of new venture creation. *Journal of Business Venturing*, 21: 153–75.

Lichtenstein, B., & Jones, C. 2004. A self-organization theory of radical entrepreneurship. *Best Papers Proceedings, National Academy of Management*: OMT Division; CD format.

Lichtenstein, B., & Kurjanowicz, B. 2010. Tangibility, momentum, and the emergence of The Republic of Tea. *ENTER Journal*, 1: 125–48.

MacIntosh, R., & MacLean, D. 1999. Conditioned emergence: A dissipative structures approach to transformation. *Strategic Management Journal*, 20: 297–316.

Maguire, S., McKelvey, B., Mirabeau, L., & Oztas, N. 2006. Complexity science and organization studies. In S. Clegg, C. Hardy, W. Nord, & T. Lawrence (Eds.), *Handbook of Organization Studies* (2nd ed., 165–214. London: SAGE Publications.

Muthusamy, S. K., & White, M. 2005. Learning and knowledge transfer in strategic alliances. *Organization Studies*, 26(3): 415–41.

Nonaka, I. 1988. Creating organizational order out of chaos: Self-renewal in Japanese firms. *California Management Review*, 30(Spring): 57–73.

Plowman, D. A., Baker, L., Beck, T., Kulkarni, M., Solansky, S., & Travis, D. 2007. Radical change accidentally: The emergence and amplification of small change. *Academy of Management Journal*, 50: 515–43.

Rindova, V., & Fombrun, C. 2001. Entrepreneurial action in the creation of the specialty coffee niche. In C. B. Schoonhoven & E. Romanelli (Eds.), *The Entrepreneurship Dynamic* (236–61). Palo Alto, CA: Stanford University Press.

Rindova, V., & Kotha, S. 2001. Continuous "morphing": Competing through dynamic capabilities, form, and function. *Academy of Management Journal*, 44: 1263–80.

Rivkin, J., & Siggelkow, N. 2007. Patterned interactions in complex systems: Implications for exploration. *Management Science*, 53: 1068–85.

Salthe, S. 2010. Development (and evolution) of the universe. *Foundations of Science*, 15: 357–67.

SEMATECH. 2012. SEMATECH history—acceleration: SEMATECH achieves its first mission. Vol. 2012: SEMATECH.

Smith, C. 1986. Transformation and regeneration in social systems: A dissipative structure perspective. *Systems Research*, 3: 203–13.

Smith, C., & Gemmill, G. 1991. Self-organization in small groups: A study of group effectivenss within non-equilibrium conditions. *Human Relations*, 44: 697–716.

Tsoukas, H., & Chia, R. 2002. On organizational becoming: Rethinking organizational change. *Organization Science*, 13: 567–83.

Wilber, K. 1981. *Up From Eden*. Boulder, CO: Shambhala.

Wilber, K. 1982. *The Holographic Paradox*. Boston: Shambhala Press.

Wilber, K. 1983. *Eye to Eye*. Garden City, NY: Anchor Press/Doubleday.

Wilber, K. 1995. *Sex, Ecology, Spirituality*. Boston: Shambhalla Publications.

Wilber, K. 2001. *A Theory of Everything*. Boston: Shambhala.

CHAPTER 16

Re-Emergence: Cycles of Emergence over Time

EMERGENCE AND RE-EMERGENCE

As has been presented earlier, a cycle of emergence explains how any dynamic state—any intentionally produced endeavor or project or venture—emerges and continuously maintains itself. If so, then the five-phase model should be able to explain *re-emergence* as well, as the re-creation of an existing dynamic state into one wholly new. Re-emergence is the reformulation of an organization out of itself, leading to a recreation of the very *identity* of the organization—what the organization "is" and what its reason for being is, its identity, its presence and contribution in the social world.

Organizational re-emergence is more common than the dearth of research on the topic would suggest. One compelling approach is taken by Mullins and Komisar (2009), in their "Getting to Plan B." Similar instances of entrepreneurial remaking are provided in Baker and Nelson's (2005) study of bricolage. Formal academic research has treated re-emergence as a type of "transformation," a punctuated shift in the core structures or underlying values of an organization (Bartunek, 1984; Romanelli & Tushman, 1994; Bacharach, Bamberger, & Sonnenstuhl, 1996; Street & Gallupe, 2009). In this chapter I will explain why re-emergence is not the same as transformation, and suggest why this difference holds great value for management.

As a means of explaining the unique qualities of re-emergence, I start by suggesting several ways in which re-emergence builds on, but is different from, the initial emergence of a dynamic state. I pursue this analysis by working from the outside in, by exploring the differences in the substrate of emergence and that of re-emergence, in presenting the drivers of emergence vs. those of re-emergence, and in examining the scope of re-emergence. These three issues are presented next and illustrated through the case study examples that follow.

The Substrate of Re-emergence

As described in Chapter 8, all dynamic states emerge out of a substrate—the material, energetic, and informational ecosystem that contains all manner of components that get organized into an emergent entity. In generative emergence this substrate is an economic and social ecology, with myriad systems of relationships, opportunities, and resources that can be accessed by entrepreneurial individuals and organizations. For example, at Starbucks, the original substrate included Howard Schultz's social network, the slow changes happening in the coffee market, a surge in economic growth and upscale lifestyles, increased availability of high-quality coffee beans, and the particular culture of downtown Seattle. These were all incorporated into the organizing effort that ultimately resulted in the creation of Starbucks.

In re-emergence, the substrate is the same—the economic and social ecology of the organization. Even more salient, however, is the current dynamic state of the organization, out of which a new dynamic state might emerge. This, of course, includes its opportunity tension, core logic, and organizing model; it would incorporate the knowledge and learning in the venture, as well as further opportunities the entrepreneur has gained since the initial start-up. The dynamic state provides a strong base for re-emergence because many of the necessary elements of a newly created dynamic state are already present in the current state of the system. These "only" need to be reorganized or repurposed around a new opportunity tension and value creation for re-emergence to occur. This is not to say that re-emergence is easier than initial emergence. It is likely to be harder because of the routinization of systems and processes in a successful organization. In re-emergence, however, many of the components of a new dynamic state are already present; these and new ones can be garnered from the existing organization and supporting networks.

Thus, re-emergence is similar to emergence in that the substrate of each—a social ecology with material, relational, and energetic aspects—is the source for all the components and resources of the venture. Yet in re-emergence the basis for the firm is already established, and the entrepreneur can make very educated experiments toward leveraging these elements in high-potential ways. Re-emergence thus builds on emergence, offering a platform upon which to extend the capacity of the venture even further than it already is.

Triggers for Transformation vs. Aspiration for Re-Emergence

In each case of emergence I have presented, the entrepreneur begins with a powerful measure of opportunity tension—internal motivation and a clear business opportunity. These two interdependent qualities spur organizing activities toward an emerging goal. Entrepreneurial scholars have well describe this directed and inspired energy, in terms of vision (Baum, Locke, & Kirkpatrick, 1998; Lichtenstein & Jones, 2004; Osterwalder & Pigneur, 2010), intention (Bird, 1988, 1992; Krueger, Reilly, & Casrud, 2000; Boyatzis, 2006), and aspiration (March, 1988, 1991; Wiklund & Shepherd, 2003). In generative emergence the instigation of any round of organizing—whether emergence or re-emergence—is the aspiration and passion to generate more value.

Importantly, this main driver is quite different from the driver of organizational transformation proposed by management researchers. Long-held theories of "second-order" revolutionary change suggest that such transformations are mainly triggered by a crisis—a problem involving poor performance due to a lack of competitiveness (Greiner, 1972; Bartunek, 1984; Haveman, 1992; Romanelli & Tushman, 1994; Kotter, 1995). The theory underlying the claim that crises trigger transformation was first presented by Tushman and Romanelli (1985), in their framing of organizational evolution as incremental convergence punctuated by radical reorientations. They summarize the main forces that lead to reorientations (pp. 178, 204):

> To the extent that incremental modifications to [the organization] fail to maintain consistencies . . . the organization will fail to achieve a sustainable level of performance, and be forced to a fundamental reordering of activities. We . . . suggest two basic forces for change: (1) sustained low performance resulting from a lack of consistency among [organizational] activities . . . and (2) major changes in . . . the environment that render a prior strategic orientation . . . no longer effective. Given the pervasiveness of inertial forces, both perception and action are usually triggered only by sustained low performance, a major shift in the distribution of power, and/or organizational crises.

These underlying assumptions were more carefully explored by Sastry (1997), who put together a system dynamics model from the logics within the Tushman and Romanelli theory. Essentially, she found that the main trigger for transformation is a change in the competitive environment that decreases performance of the firm (p. 245):

> As a result of shifts in the external environment . . . the required strategic orientation . . . may change over time. Once the environment shifts, ever-increasing [commitment to] an inappropriate strategic orientation no longer benefits the organization. . . . When pressure for change has built up to a level high enough to overcome the effects of inertia, management relieves the pressure by changing the organization's strategic orientation.

In other words, transformation is triggered as a reaction to poor performance, which is caused when the company gets further and further out of step with its competitive environment. Only when this performance gap has hit a high enough threshold will senior managers make the move to reorientation.

A very similar story is told for executives who are attempting to produce major change. In a classic article in *Harvard Business Review*, Kotter (1995) describes "Why Transformation Efforts Fail." His main claim is clear (p. 59):

> But, in almost every case, the basic goal has been the same: To make fundamental changes in how business is conducted in order to help cope with a new, more challenging market environment.

The key word here is "cope"—to react, deal with, and attempt to overcome problems, which are caused by a more competitive market. Here again the trigger is an external shift that reduces the viability of the business; a transformation is then initiated to make the organization adaptive in its newly changed environment (Haveman, 1992). Researchers examining cognitive schema make similar arguments, that transformations are triggered by shifts in environmental conditions, which lead to a misalignment in "logics of action." Reframing those cognitive schema leads to significant organizational change (Bartunek, 1984; Bacharach et al., 1996).

Even in entrepreneurship, researchers have traditionally understood transformative change as being caused by significant problems or crises which, if they can be managed appropriately, can lead the way toward further developmental stages of growth (Greiner, 1972; Kazanjian, 1988; Terpstra & Olson, 1993). These models are similar to the ones for larger organizations in that they focus on a mismatch between the qualities of the venture and the needs it faces as it grows. This mismatch leads to a crisis that triggers a major overhaul of the business, hopefully positioning it for positive long-term growth (Greiner, 1972; Adizes, 1979; Kazanjian, 1988). Empirical study provides some evidence for this overall model (Tushman, Newman, & Romanelli, 1986).

In all these accounts of transformation, whether in larger organizations or in smaller entrepreneurial firms, external change leads to problems that build to a crisis, which triggers the need for a fundamental shift in how the organization operates. Managers or founders, *reacting* to negative or challenging circumstances, initiate a significant alteration of activities in an attempt to correct the problems and return the organization to positive functioning.

Note the difference between this crisis-driven transformation process and the proactive frame at the heart of generative emergence, namely an endogenous aspiration for new value creation. In contrast to the reactive model, re-emergence is sparked by an internally motivated vision for creating something new. Rather than sparked by crisis, generative emergence is initiated by a desire to create value that will make a distinct contribution to a specific market. This new value is enacted through an opportunity tension that leads to a (re)organizing of activities, resources, and operations.

In sum, transformation is driven by crisis, re-emergence by vision and positive action. How does this difference make a difference?[1]

REACTING TO CHANGE VS. INITIATING CREATIVE ACTION

The distinction between crises that trigger change and aspirations that initiate emergence has not been well explored in organization science. However, some insights from creativity research and elsewhere can guide our understanding of this difference.

Scholarship into organizational creativity has made important use of the distinction between proactive and reactive creativity (Heinzen, 1994; Kauffman, 2004), or between proactive and responsive creativity (Unsworth, 2001; Unsworth & Parker, 2003). These models present the proactive mode in ways that are quite similar to our notion of emergence: Proactive creativity is enacted through problem finding rather than problem solving per se; it envisions a possible future instead of reacting to a current problem. For example, Geir Kauffman (2004, p. 160) states:

> This process of first finding an interesting new problem, through envisioning a possible, desired future state of affairs as a step toward finding new solutions to problems may be called *proactive creativity* (see also Heinzen, 1999; Unsworth, 2001, for a similar argument, based on different conceptual frameworks). It is readily seen that this kind of creative problem solving, proceeding through the gates of new and smart problem finding, is at the very heart of the concept of creativity that was considered prototypical.

Unsworth and her colleagues (Unsworth, 2001; Unsworth & Parker, 2003) have also shown that proactive creativity is much more likely to spur useful new ideas in organizational settings (Axtell et al., 2000) than the other forms of creativity. In effect, having a clean slate for innovation produces far more opportunities for engaged innovation than occurs when someone is asked or told to use creativity to solve a particular problem (Unsworth, 2001). This distinction is made further by Heinzen (1994, 1999), who presents reactive creativity as a response to problems, frustrations, and thwarted goals (Heinzen, 1994, p. 140):

> Reactive creativity is the result of externally motivated demands and occurs in frustrating situations when an important goal is persistently thwarted. Reactive creativity can produce new and effective responses (as well as learned helplessness, depression, and displaced aggression), but is characterized by negative affect, often a sense of desperation as the organism searches for the one alternative response to escape pain.

In contrast, proactive creativity generates a positive and affirming mode of action:

> Proactive creativity is the process characterized by intrinsic motivation, positive affect, spreading activation, and focused self-discipline that produces new, effective products (broadly defined).... We look forward to being proactively creative—we stay up nights working on a favorite project and steal every hour to pursue our passion.

To my mind, he makes several allusions to entrepreneurial action, especially components of intrinsic motivation, spreading activation, and self-discipline, that has us stay up nights working on a favorite project or finishing a major endeavor.

Beyond these distinctions, there are only a few studies that explore the outcomes of proactive creativity (Heinzen, 1994). Kauffman explains (2004, p. 160):

> Surprisingly, very little is known about this aspect of creativity, which may be due to the constraints put on the concept of creative problem solving in the traditional theoretical paradigms. Also, this kind of process is more difficult to study, as Unsworth (2001) points out, than in the typical case of a controlled laboratory situation where the experimenter presents the task to be solved.

The challenges of measurement and outcome from proactive creativity have been slightly mitigated in organizational research. For example, the distinction between proactive and reactive leadership is at the heart of one of the classic typologies in strategic management, namely the Miles-Snow typology (Miles & Snow, 1978; Miles, Snow, Meyer, & Coleman, 1978). These researchers claimed that virtually all firms can be described as being either *prospector firms*, which rely on a proactive stance, *defender firms*, which use a more reactive stance, or *analyzer firms*, which take an information-rich approach to strategic decision-making. A host of research has confirmed the typology and found performance implications (as two examples, see Snow & Hambrick, 1980; Zahra & Pearce, 1990).

A somewhat more direct performance benefit to proactivity comes from research into "dynamic capabilities" of firms, and how they can lead to more "adaptive capacity." In particular, Newey and Zahra (2009) show that endogenous shifts are guided by "proactive entrepreneurial logic." This logic is separate from, but complements, reactive adaptations that are triggered by environmental shifts.

The connection between proactivity and success is embedded in most entrepreneurial research, mainly because founders are viewed as being proactive and self-directed. In complementary research, Baron and his colleagues identified self-efficacy—a more embodied concept—to be a key to successful start-up activity (Baron, 1998; Baron & Markman, 2003; Rauch & Frese, 2007). In another study, Yusuf (2012) explored the role of proactive thinking in "entrepreneurial exit." Specifically, she found that entrepreneurs who engaged in "intelligent exit" were proactive, applying learning to their analysis of long-term viability of the venture. In contrast those who pursued "reactive or uninformed exit" did so because of poor planning or an inability to solve problems. Here again, some evidence suggests that a proactive stance yields a more positive result.

In sum, whereas proactive initiative drives emergence, a reaction to crisis triggers transformation. Evidence shows that proactive creativity and action are more effective than reactive responses. The benefits of a proactive, aspirational driver of emergence include higher motivation, better solutions, more positive affect, and increased adaptive capacity.

From a systems perspective the outcomes of this shift are more direct. When reacting to crisis, the possible paths of action are highly constrained by the very conditions that gave rise to the crisis: The problem itself defines the dimensions within which a credible solution may be found (Goldstein, 2011). Even though, as Heinzen said (1994, p. 140), "reactive creativity can produce new and effective responses," the solution to a crisis-driven reaction can be based only in past action and current perception, limiting avenues of novelty. In the same way, path dependence limits the degrees of freedom in the system: The more reactive the organization is to its current crisis, the less openness it may have to unique solutions.

In contrast, proactive creation starts with essentially unlimited degrees of freedom, which are honed down on the basis of the extent and quality of existing resources, competencies, and operations. In path creation (Garud & Karnoe, 2001, 2003), new ideas can arise more spontaneously, through combinations others have not thought of before. Starting from an open slate an entrepreneur can envision anything she or he wants and can intentionally enact the most suitable and rewarding path to achieving it (Gartner, Bird, & Starr, 1992; Gartner, 1993; Sarasvathy, 2001a). As a result, the outcome becomes more integrated with the environment, partly because enacting the outcome does, in fact, effect tangible changes in the environment (Sarasvathy, 2001b; Sarasvathy & Venkataramen, 2011). In addition, this kind of entrepreneuring often yields enthusiasm and passion, as creativity scholars have shown (Heinzen, 1994; Unsworth, 2001; Unsworth & Parker, 2003; Kauffman, 2004).

Overall, my claim is that an impetus toward emergence is much more likely to generate positive and innovative outcomes than a reaction to crisis, with better entrepreneurial success, as numerous researchers have shown (Adler & Obstfeld, 2006; Baron, 2008; Cardon, Wincent, Singh, & Drnovsek, 2009). This is a second key difference between re-emergence and transformation. The third difference is in the operationalization of emergence vs. change, to which I now turn.

THE SCOPE OF RE-EMERGENCE VS. TRANSFORMATION

More insights can be gleaned by analyzing the differences tangibly: the structures and processes that actually shift in transformation, in contrast to emergence. This is essentially an extension of the research by Street and Gallupe (2009), who tested the operational differences between incremental change and radical transformation. In our case, we would push this comparison further, to examine the operational difference between transformation and the three degrees of emergence.

Studies that have carefully operationalized major change (including transformation and emergence) have been very careful in defining what constructs should be used for "measuring" what makes up an organization. For example, in the Romanelli and Tushman (1994) study, change was operationalized in terms of core "activity domains" of all organizations: *strategy, structure,* and *power distribution*;

they also noted the importance of *culture* and *control systems,* even though the latter two could not be measured in their data (Tushman & Romanelli, 1985). Together, these five domains reflect basic activity systems that are central to the organization's core competencies, and are necessary for long-term survival, a point that has been highlighted by Mintzberg (1979), McKelvey (1982), Hannan and Freeman (1984), and others. In Romanelli and Tushman's empirical study, a transformation was coded when changes were observed in the three domains.[2]

Street and Gallupe (2009) used the open systems model (Scott, 1981; Ashmos & Huber, 1987; from von Bertalanffy, 1968, 1972; Miller, 1978) to define organizations in terms of their inputs, process, and outputs. Using the same elements as Tushman and Romanelli, they consider *strategy, structure,* and *power* to be inputs, *practices* and *control systems* to reflect process, and *services* and *product market* as outputs. Changes in any one of these elements (e.g., strategy, or product markets) would be considered convergent change, whereas radical transformative change occurs when there is a shift in two or more elements within a short period of time.

An even stronger distinction can be made using the dynamic states framework, by coding possible changes over time in core logic, opportunity tension, organizing model, and value creation. Using similar methods, emergence would be coded as the creation or substantive innovation in *all four elements:* a new core logic and identity for "who we are" and "what we do" as a firm, an opportunity tension that motivates a new viable product-offering, a complete organizing model that sustainably generates that product offering, and a specific market or customer for whom the offering creates value. When all four have been enacted, a dynamic state has emerged. When all four are re-created, or start newly in a discernable way, the dynamic state will have re-emerged.

To rigorously deploy this framework, it is important to look more closely at the first element—core logic—and its connection to the notion of organizational identity (Dutton & Dukerich, 1991; Gioia, Schultz, & Corley, 2000) and deep structure (Drazin & Sandelands, 1992; MacIntosh & MacLean, 1999).

Deep Structure

A number of complexity researchers (Smith & Comer, 1994; Plowman et al., 2007) and others (Bartunek, 1984; Gersick, 1991) have used the autopoietic notion of "deep structure" to describe the most enduring quality of an organization—the "rules that generate and govern individual behavior and interactions" (Drazin & Sandelands 1992, p. 236). These rules are implicit but pervasive guidelines for action, embodied in the assumptions, habits, and routines of the organization (Arikan, 2010, p. 159). According to Heracleous and Barrett (2001, p. 758, cited in Arikan, 2010), deep structure describes the "set of relatively stable, largely implicit, and continually recurring processes and patterns that underlie and guide surface, observable events and actions."

These definitions are closely related to what I have been describing as the core logic for the firm—the underlying claim about what the organization *is*, what it should focus on, the basic guidelines for action. MacIntish and MacLean (1999, p. 305) also make clear this link between the two concepts. They support the claim that deep structure can be changed:

> The deep structure and rules are often barely articulated views on what the organization represents and how it operates, e.g., the kind of business which is taken on or the type of people recruited.... The organization can then formulate a new deep structure which may involve some, but not all, of the old rules alongside some new ones. Again these new rules may be process oriented (e.g., the way things are done) or content oriented, what kind of business is conducted; or both.

In a small entrepreneurial venture, core logic is closely aligned with opportunity tension, for both reflect the essential value that the members propose to create through the organizing project. Yet, of the two, core logic is deeper, more embedded, more implicit, for like a dominant logic it is a filter that determines what can be perceived and acted upon (Dubinskas, 1994), drawing the boundaries of possibility and action for the organization. These boundaries are the choices being made by the entrepreneur, as he or she begins to enact the organization. As Bettis and Prahalad (1995, p. 7) explain in their extension of the initial ideas (from Prahalad & Bettis, 1986),

> We have come to view the dominant logic as an information filter.... Organizational attention is focused only on data deemed relevant by the dominant logic. Other data are largely ignored.

Core Logic Is the Apex of the Firm

In my formulation of core logic, what's relevant to the organizing effort is based on a shared belief about the long-term aims of the organization, which guides each members' decisions and actions. Core logic thus reflects "core values and beliefs [that] set constraints as to where, how and why a firm competes" (Tushman & Romanelli, 1985, p. 175). Tushman and Romenelli were seminal in their recognition that core beliefs are at the top of an elemental hierarchy for the firm, for these core logics lay the premise and set the intention and direction for all the other elements, and thus for all action in the venture.

In their description of the "Hierarchy of Organizing Activities" (Tushman & Romanelli, 1985, Table 2, p. 179), Tushman and Romanelli show that a shift in these core values and beliefs will have *an irreversible effect in the other core domains* of strategy, power, structure, and controls. When all four shift—when there is a discernable transformation of core values, power, structure, and controls—the company is in an all-encompassing shift that they call a "re-creation." Here they reference the re-emergence of the organization.

Furthermore, in their model, a shift in more than one of the domains, without a corresponding shift in core values, is termed a "reorientation," involving "rapid and discontinuous changes in products and markets served, distribution of power and resources within the firm and fundamental changes in structure and controls" (p. 180). In generative emergence, these—without a shift in core logic—can produce up to second-degree emergence; more often they result in first-degree emergence.

In sum, re-emergence can be operationalized as an *expressed shift in the core logic of the venture*. Core logic underlies decisions and action, it helps determine the boundaries and constraints that determine what is relevant to pursue, it generates perceptions about what the organization "means." These shifts are likely to be revealed in tangible changes to the opportunity tension of the firm as a new value proposition and motivation to enact the new aspiration arise. Likewise, re-emergence would be clearly expressed in a venture's organizing model through revisions and re-creations of activities, resources, and collaborations, markets, customers, and product(s). These shifts would ultimately be revealed in the value creation of the organization: who is served and what value they receive.

To that proposition I add a claim about process. Namely, re-emergence will occur through cycles, using the same five phases of generative emergence. Empirically, a cycle of re-emergence would flow from a described opportunity tension, through the enactment of a new organizing model that yields positive outcomes which sustain the effort. However, unlike these tidy assumptions that come with the model, in practice, the re-emergence of a dynamic state is likely to be a much more iterative process. The results of this will be see in the interpretations of results.

This cyclical process, even in its iterated form, is exemplified in the four ventures from my dissertation. The rest of this chapter draws together data from the two cases that went through an entire cycle of re-emergence, namely DevelopNet and ApplySci.

RE-EMERGENCE AT DEVELOPNET

Five Phases of Re-Emergence

The substrate at DevelopNet was a successful company started by a professor of computer science at one of the top technology-based universities in the Boston region. Drawing on a unique simulation modeling program he had developed, he grew the company through a series of Small Business Innovation Research grants and by developing applications of the program for U.S. Department of Defense clients throughout the United States. Although his contracts were relatively small, his reputation was strong; over 6+ years he had built a small but successful company.

From that place of success he crafted a new business plan in March 1996, in which he reformulated every aspect of the company, aspiring to launch a nationwide network of offices that would sell his technology to numerous markets across the country. He started making those changes by altering the main productivity goals for his programmers, having them focus on completing a new website, rather than pursue billable client work. The website—a rare addition in 1996—was to house the newly applied technology and also provide marketing support by making advance demos available to potential customers. With this decision, almost immediately these "organization building" activities jumped, steadily increasing for nearly 30 weeks. Figure 16.1 shows this rise as it extends in the weeks before my arrival (i.e., from 13 weeks before my first interview; week "n" in the figure). Disequilibrium organizing (operationalized here as work activity) continues to peak at around data collection period (DCP) 6–10, moving to a final rise in DCP 13 and ending with a small uptick in DCP 15. At this point the CEO was able to see the "writing on the wall"—DevelopNet hit negative cash flow in DCP 14 and 15; therefore, he called a few long-standing DOD clients and was fortunate to secure some small consulting projects to tide the company over during the transition to come.

A similar rise-and-fall pattern occurred with stress and experiments; both show a rise parallel to disequilibrium organizing from March 1996 through DCP 25 and beyond. In this case fiscal stress is operationalized as the monthly difference (gap or excess) between the *projected revenues* from the new business plan versus the *actual*

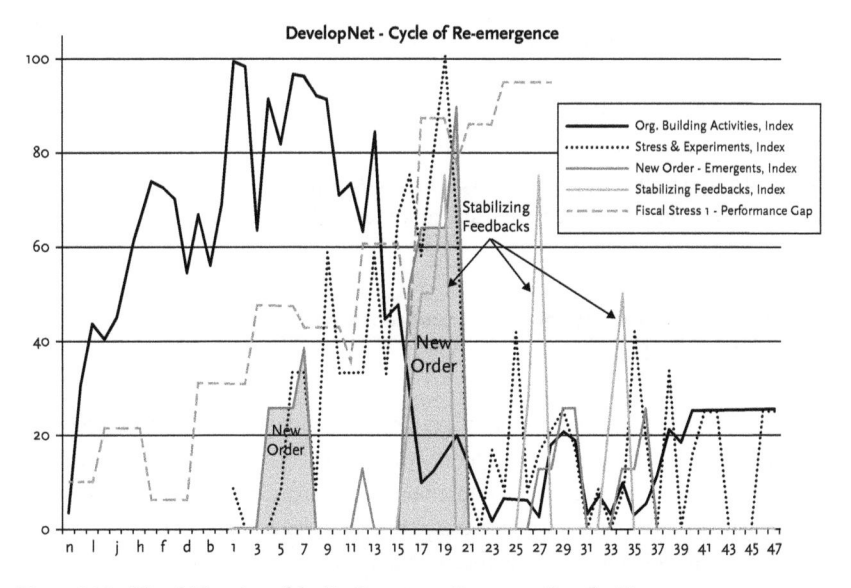

Figure 16.1: Visual Mapping of the Re-Emergence Process at DevelopNet

income in the firm. After a slow rise starting around week "c," this metric shows a relatively steady increase all the way through DCP 29, which was the farthest that the business plan projected (i.e., to the end of the year). Aside from the dips in DCP 11 and in DCP 16, which represent small, one-time increases in revenues, the rise in fiscal stress is nearly parallel with the rise in work activities. Similarly, stress and experiments go up sharply in DCP 9, then show three peaks at DCP 13, 16, and 20. However, after the critical event, once the new order had emerged, the internal stress in the company decreased dramatically.

The critical event—a decision by the final venture capital firm to drop DevelopNet from consideration—occurs at DCP 16: "When HT Ventures said they weren't going to fund this. That was the critical event." In that moment he exclaimed, "We've hit the trip wire ... Retrenching" (CEO, DevelopNet; DCP 16). This ultimately led to a total re-creation of the firm—a different core logic, a new opportunity tension, and multiple shifts in the organizing model. In his words:

> We've abandoned the charge-up-the-hill-to-the-$100-million-dollar-company . . . [Instead we'll] license the technology, and keep them busy with consulting. (CEO, DevelopNet; DCP 20).

As presented in Chapter 13, his decision generates multiple emergents, which are represented in Figure 16.1 as a cumulative re-creation from DCP 16 through DCP 20. These emergents include a new organizational design with 60% fewer employees, a new value proposition, a new service/offering, a new customer market, a new revenue model, and new internal systems. Finally, note several spikes of stabilizing feedback—one during the change itself, another that follows on DCP 27, and a third on DCP 34.

Note, too, a much smaller episode of new order from DCP 4 to DCP 8. In brief, this represents a cumulative series of first-order emergents: a new marketing structure, a new sales function, the receipt of a small amount of venture capital ($50,000), and the public launch of their website. Even though this is an internal reorganization rather than a re-emergence, it is intriguing to see how it occurs at the peak of disequilibrium organizing, and at initial peaks of stress and experiments.

Comparing an Ideal Model of Re-Emergence with the Actual Data at DevelopNet

In theory, the five-phase process has a "predictable" or ideal temporal flow. According to the logic of the theory, re-emergence would begin within a currently successful dynamic state, out of which the entrepreneur would express aspiration → disequilibrium organizing, leading to stress and experiments, which together peak at a critical threshold. Immediately following that would be the creation of emergents, followed by stabilizing feedback. This "ideal sequencing" is described in Figure 16.2 (left side).

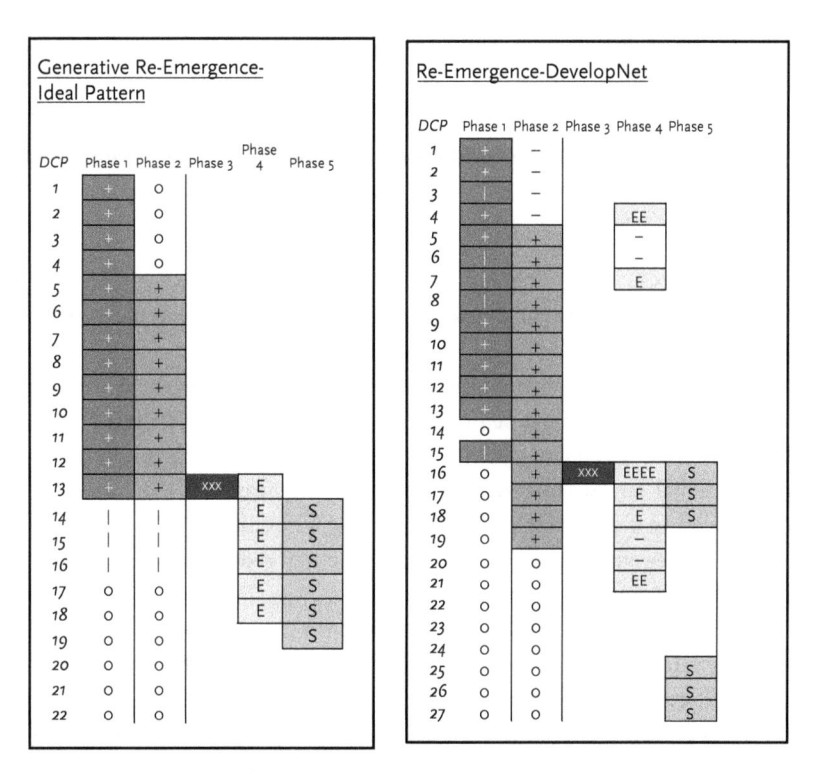

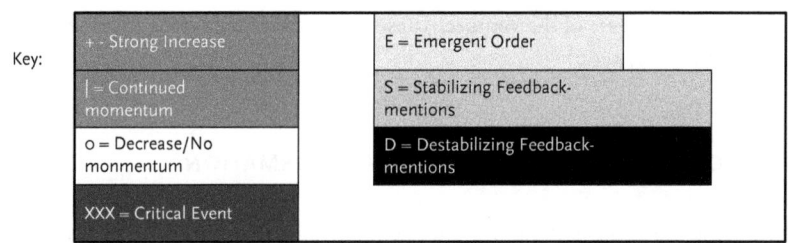

Figure 16.2: Phases in the Cycle of Re-Emergence—Ideal and Actual Pattern at DevelopNet

Key:
- + = Strong Increase
- | = Continued momentum
- o = Decrease/No momentum
- XXX = Critical Event
- E = Emergent Order
- S = Stabilizing Feedback-mentions
- D = Destabilizing Feedback-mentions

Operationally, each phase is a column in the table; increases in each of the variables are listed as "+" or "|" within the phase's color (darker grey for disequilibrium organizing).

For comparison, Figure 16.2 also presents the actual data at DevelopNet, in a parallel table (right side), coded in terms of "momentum" in each data series, with "+" meaning a positive increase compared to the week before and "|" meaning a continuation at a similar rate; a zero sign (0) indicates a decrease in the value and/or the momentum compared to the week before.

My comparison coding begins at DCP 1, continues through the critical event at DCP 16, and extends through DCP 29. These data conform well to the ideal model. Disequilibrium organizing maintains momentum from DCP 1 through

RE-EMERGENCE: CYCLES OF EMERGENCE OVER TIME [357]

DCP 15; stress and experiments are first coded in DCP 5 and continue increasing through DCP 19. The critical event occurs at DCP 16; this is followed by five weeks of cumulative order creation, which is buttressed by stabilizing feedback. According to this analysis, DevelopNet is a nearly perfect replication of the ideal model of dynamic states emergence.

Re-Emergence in Core Logic, Organizing Model, and Opportunity Tension

In my presentation of emergence, precedence has been given to third-degree emergence, the creation of a semi-autonomous dynamic state, an agent that has "a life of its own." This alone would "count" as generative emergence in my model. In operational terms, (re)emergence would be confirmed if there are data that reveal a shift in the core logic of the firm, along with shifts in opportunity tension (second-degree emergence), and the replacement or redefinition of the organizing model (first-degree emergence).

My analysis used the qualitative data from my cases; a sample of quotes from my 750+ interviews is presented in Table 16.1. Comments have been organized into the three degrees of emergence; these distinctions are supported by my on-site observation. As these comments show, all three orders of emergence occur at nearly the same time, between DCP 16 and DCP 20. These shifts are salient to the CEO and to most members of the venture. These data strongly suggest the presence of a cycle of re-emergence.

APPLYSCI—RE-EMERGENCE, THEN TRANSFORMATION

The story at ApplySci is somewhat more complicated than that of its smaller counterpart. Like DevelopNet, its substrate was the current form of the company; in this case there were 20+ members, most of whom were scientists and technicians, all hired to work with a new-to-the-world technology, which could be applied to solve problems in a number of different fields. A biomedical branch of the company had at one point spun out from the materials science group. Later the two ventures merged back together to gain economies of scale while the laboratory and scientific staff struggled to develop an application that would be technically viable and financially valuable.

Five Phases of Re-Emergence at ApplySci

ApplySci's disequilibrium organizing was well captured in the combined work activities of the scientists, as described in Chapter 10. The number of these

Table 16.1. CYCLE OF RE-EMERGENCE AT DEVELOPNET

DCP Week	Organizing Model, First Degree Emergence	Opportunity, Value Proposition Second Degree	Core Logic, Identity Third Degree	Qualitative Expression
DCP 16	Redesign			(CFO) will look for a new job. (Sales manger) as well.
DCP 17	Redesign new role			[Product manager let go. A second programmer leaves on his own]. [I'm the new] Director of Customer Support. Now everyone thinks they can bother me!
DCP 16		New value proposition		If a company is going to use our product we'll give them the software. The new track is, you buy our labor. That cuts down on some of the profit, but it makes the sale enormously easier. On a longer-term basis, it gives us credibility.
DCP 20		New value proposition		A couple of "game" things we're putting funding proposals in for. One is doing... a string of video games. The other is... an Internet game.
DCP 16			New core logic	So we've abandoned the attempt to do a nationwide sales thing, because we don't have the deep pockets.... So we're shifting to... a specialist consulting organization.
DCP 20			New identity	I feel better about what we're doing as far as, essentially focusing finally on just consulting.... Not trying to sell a product... in the visual market place... We're not that.
DCP 27			New core logic, follow-up	[B]uild up our local regional webserver activity, bundling webservers for medium-sized organizations.... It's a shift we've been aiming for for a while.

activities had been growing for some time; data include all activities in archived lab books from January of 1996 through DCP 39, when the replacement CEO essentially banned me from collecting further data. A close look at work activity shows a gradual overall increase from week "ze" (31 weeks before DCP 1) through DCP 15, then after a slow-down through the Christmas holidays, and a final major ramp-up that peaks on DCP 28. After that, it was "all downhill"—poor lab results and no customers led to the firing of the CTO, which reduced motivation and direction to pursue more tests. Finally, on DCP 36, all scientific staff were fired, essentially stopping all activity in the company. These data are presented in Figure 16.3.

Two measures of stress show a similar and parallel rise. Fiscal stress at ApplySci, like at DevelopNet, is represented by the gap between projected net income (i.e., projected revenues minus expenses) and actual monthly net income. This figure is relatively stable from January to July 1996, then the performance gap rises around DCP 8 and rises dramatically after DCP 23, peaking at DCP 25. At DCP 26, a new set of projections were calculated; however, already by DCP 30 the gap is high. Even with changed figures the losses kept piling up, since no consistent revenues were forthcoming from the technology.

Stress and experiments also rise quickly from DCP 3 through DCP 8, then continue with high variance from week to week. Figure 16.3 shows a decrease in stress and experiments following the emergence of new order on DCP 25. Although there are fewer mentions of stress, some of the expressions are far more intense—people felt there was a major problem and no direct avenue for fixing it. Note a final peak

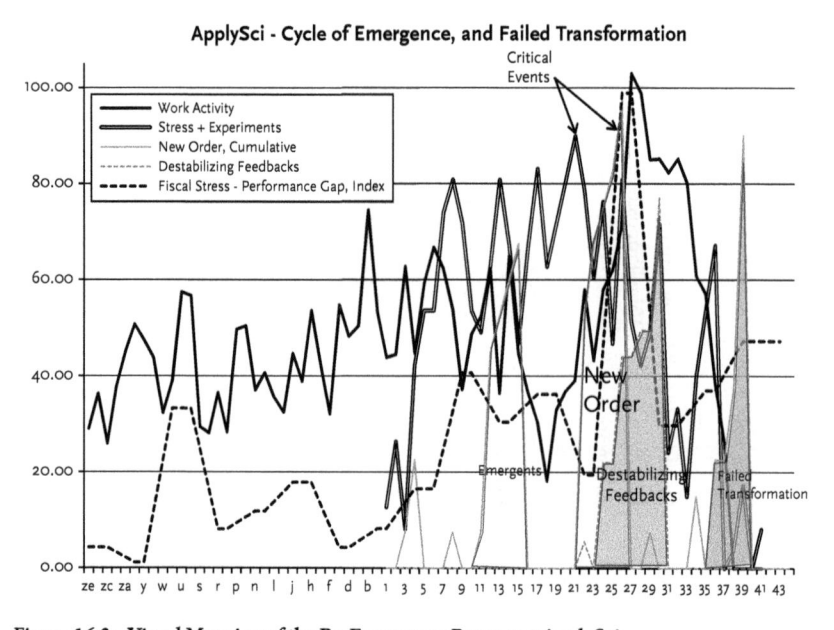

Figure 16.3: Visual Mapping of the Re-Emergence Process at ApplySci

in stress and experiments at DCP 35, followed by the firing of the CEO and the "take-over" of the firm by a board-appointed V.P. on DCP 36.

(Readers have complained that the time-series data in Figure 16.3 are overly complicated, which is true on first glance. A useful way to examine the figure is to focus on each metric one at a time, with an eye to the overall pattern—an increase in disequilibrium organizing through a peak at DCP 28, with a parallel increase in stress and experiments from DCP 8 through DCP 25.)

A critical event did occur near the peak of disequilibrium organizing and increasing stress, at DCP 22. Initially, this was the decision by a major medical products manufacturer, BigCo, to include ApplySci in its IPO, thus assuring long-term financial security for the small venture. Unfortunately, this commitment never came to fruition, BigCo decided to drop ApplySci from its portfolio before the offering, leaving ApplySci without any suitors and virtually no live clients. This setback led to an ultimatum by the board to the CEO, on DCP 27: "Sign a major contract within a month or we will close the firm." In the end, that's exactly what happened.

The new order that emerged—an attempted new dynamic state—was based on a fundamentally different core logic: to become the technology partner of BigCo and focus all their formulation efforts in that direction, toward the medical products field. The new core logic spurred tangible shifts in their organizing model, including the announcement of a new strategy, a structural redesign, new controls and accountability, a new market, with new marketing requirements, and a total physical rearrangement of the offices and labs. These shifts are represented in the new order that emerges in DCP 21–26. A precursor to that re-emergence is a smaller set of first-degree emergents that occur on DCP 11–16, which essentially set the stage for the major shift. In my estimation, these two episodes work together, the first priming the conditions for the second. Descriptions of these changes are presented in Tables 16.2 and 16.3, which organizes a sample of quotes according to the three degrees of emergence.

There were feedbacks to the emergence at ApplySci, but unfortunately these were mainly destabilizing. The primary issue was the unexpected loss of the partnership. This was very destabilizing because the entire new dynamic state was organized around BigCo's technical goals and strategic aims; without these, the new order could gain no stabilization. Equally problematic was the aforementioned decision on the very first week of the new design by the V.P. of Industrial Applications to "borrow" lab technicians who could help solve a critical client issue on the materials side (which hadn't yet been closed down). As described in Chapter 14 on feedbacks, this contradiction to the new design was highly disruptive, destabilizing the organization that the rest of the company was trying to form.

The cycle continues as these destabilizing feedbacks aggregated together to essentially wipe out the viability of the new dynamic state, leaving the company more vulnerable than it had been. After that, over the next six weeks, work activity dissipated to near zero, and although there was a concomitant decrease in stress, the perceptions of employees were increasingly negative, as these examples suggest:

Table 16.2. CYCLE 1, FIRST OSCILLATION TO PRESUMED SUCCESS

DCP Week	Organizing Model *First Degree Emergence*	Opportunity, Value Proposition *Second Degree*	Core Logic, Identity *Third Degree*	Qualitative Expression
DCP 12	Product focus			It's more on the product side now, which is good. Go on to a new challenge.
DCP 12	New activities			That will require going into the production mode; freezing the development process where it is.
DCP 12	New design			We're doing a shift dividing into industrial and medical sides; people will be moved one way or the other.
DCP 13	New customer			Yesterday we completed a materials transfer agreement with ConsumerCo.
DCP 12		Markets		Narrow down to 3 basic fields.... They are: health care, nasal, and still do ophthalmic.
DCP 14		Value proposition		We have much more confidence—we feel we have a product that we can make reproducible. Now we have something real.... That's a big psychological thing.... So I'm much more forceful with customers. It's a big psychological turn.
DCP 15		Target markets		There is a real market [in health care]—the big companies are involved. Sometimes you think it's just niche players. We met with people who were from a division of BigCo. BigCo2 is working on [similar issues]. I just though it was just little players. But no, its bigger than that. So, we think there's something.
DCP 12			Core logic	Our talk has moved from "do we have value" to "what is our value." The result goes from a quasi-negative to a very positive. Yesterday's meeting was a result from this change in mindset.
DCP 13			Core logic	If there's an abrupt change in thinking that's happening now, it will be in place by then (by Jan. 1). Now, where the ferment is happening—we're switching our orientation. It's based upon knowing we have a stable product, that appears to have tremendous capability.
DCP 13			Identity/logic	My vision is we've been making a huge transition.
DCP 14			identity	We're entering the next stage, hopefully. Keep your fingers crossed.

Table 16.3. CYCLE 1, SECOND OSCILLATION OF THE SAME CYCLE

DCP Week	Organizing Model First Degree Emergence	Opportunity, Value Proposition Second Degree	Core Logic, Identity Third Degree Emergence	Qualitative Expression
DCP 22	New design			We're growing up, just about time to get a firm budget. We started that process before, now we're ready to nail it down.... You can see the matrix. Business functions + Functional categories. Define them for real.
DCP 22	Design/meeting			Given the whole reorganization I think it's coming out pretty interesting.... You saw the meeting of the non-managers. We're cohering. Last week, we kind of all gelled: if we're going to do this, let's do this together. We all stepped out of individual roles.
DCP 23	Activities focus			One is a commitment to be working on some set things and a specific product over the next nine months. And implication that when working on that not taken away to do other things. So a focus. Before it was an ad hoc thing.
DCP 22		Single client/market		In theory "HealthCo" is taking a proposal to their Board of Directors today.... They're making a strategic decision, to become a full line ophthalmic player. We give them the capacity to do that.... And they're trying to go public. Partly what they want to do is put this into public document. So this in preparation for shift in next week or two.
DCP 23			Core logic	The whole company, except five people, is working together for one goal. Never happened here. This is two-thirds of company.... That's a major shift in the corporation, to concentrate on one thing.

- We seem to be more chaotic and more divided than we ever have been. (Senior Scientist, DCP 28)
- The state of the company is anxious. (Receptionist, DCP 29)
- Basically, we've been kind of at each other's throat. But we found that everyone feels the same way we do. The unfocused, uncertainty, unknowns are beginning to wear at us.... Very very destructive. (Senior Lab Technician, DCP 29)
- I don't know. It looks very shaky now that we will be able to pull through.... It's a very gloomy outlook. (V.P. Biomedical, DCP 30)
- But now I don't think the technology is strong enough. . . . So I'm fairly resigned. . . . I'm reaching conclusions—on the negative side. (Senior Operations Manager, DCP 30)
- It's started to come apart. (CTO, DCP 31)

Even the CEO was depressed, saying:

- Like most people I'm waiting for Gado. (CEO, DCP 32)

Perhaps unsurprisingly, within a month the CEO had been fired.

A Final Attempt: Transformation That Also Fails

Once the deal with BigCo fell apart, and the board-imposed deadline to close any major deal was approaching with no potentials at hand, the company made a final attempt, through a crisis-driven transformation. Facing significant financial losses and at risk of losing all investments, the board initiated a turnaround of the flailing organization. First they fired chief technology officer (CTO); in his place they installed the original inventor of the technology. Then, on DCP 36, the board installed a new Vice President of Development, a CFO for the company. Her ostensible aim was to help close new deals. However, it turned out that she was the board's pick to be the new CEO, and the board wasted no time in instigating the shift they wanted.

Within two weeks the board had fired the CEO and given the position to the newly hired CFO. Two weeks later (on DCP 39) she fired more than half of the employees as a cost-cutting move. Strategically, she followed her expertise into the drug delivery industry, and took control of all client negotiations. However, she ran up against the same problems that her predecessor faced, and she quickly realized that a quick deal with a major company was not forthcoming. At that point, she and the board decided to sell the company. This was accomplished in about a month, for stock options that were then valued at half the amount of investments made up to then by the board. The posted loss was $6,000,000.

This set of moves exemplified a transformation rather than generative emergence, for all the reasons mentioned earlier, and as shown in Table 16.4. It was triggered by a crisis, and its main goal was to become more adaptive—in this case, by

Table 16.4. CYCLE 2 AT APPLYSCI: TRANSFORMATION (FAILED EMERGENCE) AND DISSOLUTION

DCP Week	Organizing Model *First Degree Emergence*	Opportunity, Value Proposition *Second Degree*	Core Logic, Identity *Third Degree*	Qualitative Expression
DCP 39	Design leadership			I got a phone call a half-hour later; they had decided I was no longer being productive. (CEO)
DCP 40	Design			(Refers to the list of remaining employees). We have [names 10 people, including self]. (Down from 23)
DCP 41	Activities, Internal			So I think we're now switching to more normal structure. We decide where we're going. We decide the route from A to Z.
DCP 47	Culture			Well, when [new CEO] is here no one talks, and the minute she's gone no one does any work. It's not a productive environment, it's not friendly. It's totality the opposite of the way it used to be. Completely. Very strange.
DCP 39		Value creation		It was clear already, we are going to switch from industrial to drug delivery. A lot of people who were not involved in drug delivery, already were shifted into drug delivery. [Names four].
DCP 41		Value proposition: new product		We're going to work on our own internal product. It's a much more traditional pharmaceutical approach. You pick a project, a target and an audience. Then you preach what you have. If you've done your homework, people listen.
DCP 45		Opportunity: harvest new goal		We are trying to sell the company. That's what we're trying to do. Reduces internal activity, and emphasizes external activity. So internally quiet.
DCP 45		Goal, objective		The only thing they're concentrating on is selling the company. So. They're just holding out.
DCP 45		Goal, objective		The main objective for her [new CEO] is to make money back for the board. Trying to get (the most she can for the company). But … she doesn't know much it's worth.

dramatically reducing costs. Far from path creation, the approach taken by the new CEO was to choose a market that was determined by her industry experience, and a path that was dependent on potential partners rather than inventive of new possibilities. The entire process was not very successful. As one person described,

> The main objective for her is to make money back for the board.... But she's going back to the same thing that [the previous CEO] was doing.... She doesn't trust people; she wants to insulate herself from anything going on here.... So people are very discouraged. (Senior Operations Manager, DCP 47)

As is the case with many transformation efforts, this effort failed. Perhaps the main problem was the unexpected results of scaling-up the technology, to find that the formulation was not stable over time—a key requirement for biomedical products. More insights can be gained through a close analysis of their dynamics.

The Ideal Re-Emergence vs. the Real Pattern at ApplySci

Figures 16.4 and 16.5 show important differences between the ideal pattern of re-emergence and what actually happened at ApplySci. These examinations provide the basis for claiming that the data show two cycles: a cycle of emergence, and a cycle of transformation. Although neither instance is successful, comparing them offers insights into the process and reveals the differences between the two.

In the first instance, which I'm claiming is re-emergence, ApplySci scientists enact a significant rise in disequilibrium organizing (see Figure 16.4). This rise continues with just a couple of breaks from DCP *d* (four weeks before my first data collection period) all the way through DCP 29, where it levels off. As the theory predicts, this is followed by a rise in stress and experiments—the data represented are from fiscal stress, that is, performance gap. Here again stress rises with only a couple of very short breaks, and then resolves as soon as the new order emerges.

The significant emergence of new order occurs directly after the critical event on DCP 22, and cumulates for several weeks until the second critical event at DCP 27. However, it is clear that destabilizing feedbacks begin almost immediately, growing in importance throughout the new order emergence and beyond. These destabilizing feedbacks reflect the lack of coherence that the new dynamic state held and paved the way for the last-ditch effort by the board. In sum, this first instance is a cycle of re-emergence that is not successful, resulting in a dissolution of order, the beginning of the downfall of the company.

The second instance begins at DCP 31; several dynamics here suggest that this was a transformation, and a failed one as well. Most striking is the total lack of disequilibrium organizing—no activity is logged in the firm at all (see Figure 16.5). Instead, note the rapid and strong rise in stress (the performance gap measure).

ApplySci Rea-Emergence

DCP	Phase 1	Phase 2	Phase 3	Phase 4	Phase 5
d	+	o			
c	+	o			
b	++	o			
a	+	o			
1		o			
2	+	+			
3	++	+			
4		+			
5	+				
6	+				
7	+	+			
8	o	+			
9	o				
10	o	o			
11	+	o			
12	++	+	X	E	
13		++		E	
14	++			E	
15		o		E	
16	o	+		E	
17	o	+		E	
18	o				
19	+	+			
20	+	+			
21	+	+			
22	++		XXX	EEE	D
23		o		EE	
24	+	+		E	DDD
25	+	o		E	
26	+	++		E	DDDD
27	++	o	XX	EEE	
28	++	o			D
29		o			
30		+			DDDD
31		o			
32	+	+			
33		o			

Figure 16.4: Phases in the Pattern of Re-Emergence at ApplySci

This confirms my earlier assessment, that the change was triggered by crisis, which shows up in the qualitative data as well as the quantitative metrics. At the peak of the crisis is the critical event, the firing of the CEO and the installation of a new one. This is followed by layoffs, and all of the negative experiences expressed in previous quotes. After a couple of mentions of stabilizing feedback, most of the rest

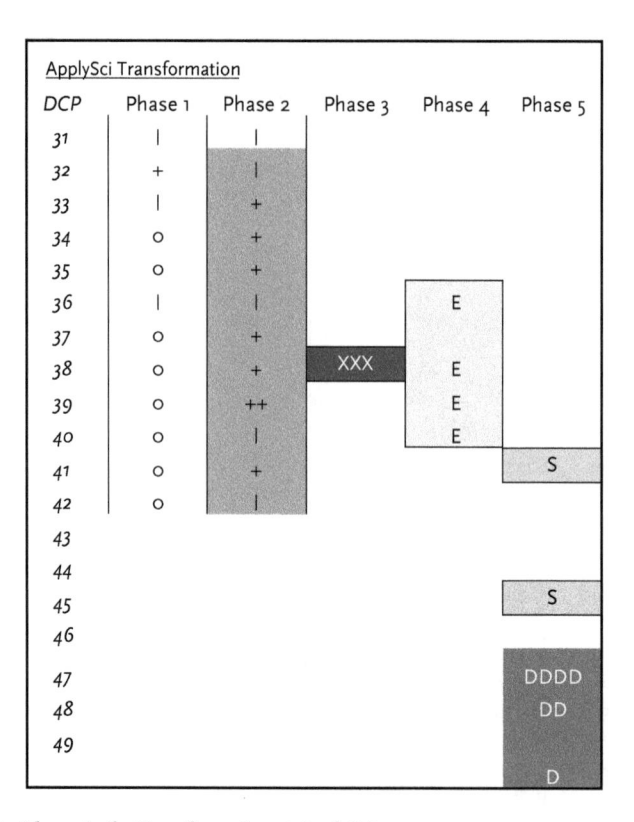

ApplySci Transformation					
DCP	Phase 1	Phase 2	Phase 3	Phase 4	Phase 5
31	I	I			
32	+	I			
33	I	+			
34	o	+			
35	o	+			
36	I	I		E	
37	o	+			
38	o	+	XXX	E	
39	o	++		E	
40	o	I		E	
41	o	+			S
42	o	I			
43					
44					
45					S
46					
47					DDDD
48					DD
49					D

Figure 16.5: Phases in the Transformation at ApplySci

of the case reveals destabilizing feedbacks, which ultimately led to the sale of the company.

Tables 16.2 and 16.3 give a range of quotes describing the emergents from two "oscillations" of the cycle of emergence. These are separated by two months or so, and both reflect the same core logic, as suggested by the similarity in descriptions of the core logic and identity across these two examples of re-emergence. Both show instances of third-degree emergence, as well as second-degree and first-degree emergence. Although ultimately unsuccessful—mainly because of the destabilizing feedback—the process and outcomes strongly suggest re-emergence.

In contrast, Table 16.4 provides data on the second instance, transformation. In this process, interviews with members reveal high levels of frustration and disappointment. In terms of degrees of emergence, my data from this era at ApplySci did not reveal any instances of core logic change, and only weak examples of second-degree and first-degree emergence. Thus, the latter instance appears to be a transformation.

In the end, ApplySci disbanded—the venture could not "make the leap" to commercializing its technology. Although this in and of itself is not so unusual, the dynamics revealed by generative emergence offer a very different view than an analysis from strategic management. While there were problems with the technology and how it was managed, and there were missteps by the entrepreneur and key employees, my analysis argues that the failure can be explained solely by the system-level dynamics. In the first instance, re-emergence was possible but was thwarted by a stream of dysfunctional destabilizing feedback, which negated the new order that had been organized in the venture. The second instance, an attempted transformation instigated by crisis, also failed, mainly due to the path-dependent tendency to define solutions in terms of the current (crisis-oriented) options, which severely limits creative options. In both instances the system itself reveals the dynamics that led to the venture's failure.

System-level dynamic explanations provide a great deal of leverage for organizational action and entrepreneurial leadership. For example, Sterman's system dynamics work shows how patterns of interaction lead to undiagnosable problems that managers can only understand through a system-level analysis (Sterman 1989; Repenning & Sterman, 2001). Likewise, Lichtenstein, Carter, Dooley, and Gartner (2007) show that new venture creation is far better explained through the system-level dynamics of entrepreneurial action than through an examination of the particular tasks each founder accomplishes. In the present case of re-emergence vs. transformation, understanding the dynamics of these two processes and how they are different provides numerous access points for shifting the system toward success rather than failure. They provide a theoretical tool for explaining new order, and leverage points for helping to create it.

NOTES

1. This phrase is derived from Bateson's definition of information: A difference that makes a difference. One of my early papers draws from this idea, to present systems thinking as a postmodern movement (Lichtenstein, 1991).
2. Specifically, a transformation was coded whenever all three domains changed, regardless of the time period. A revolutionary transformation occurred when the period of change lasted two years or less.

REFERENCES

Adizes, I. 1979. Organizational passages—Diagnosing and treating lifecycle problems of organizations. *Organizational Dynamics*, 8(1): 3–25.

Adler, P., & Obstfeld, D. 2006. The role of affect in creative projects and exploratory search. *Industrial and Corporate Change*, 16: 19–50.

Arikan, A. 2010. Regional entrepreneurial transformation: A complex systems perspective. *Journal of Small Business Management*, 48(2): 152–73.

Ashmos, D., & Huber, G. 1987. The system paradign in organization theory: Correcting the record and suggesting the future. *Academy of Management Review*, 12: 607–21.

Axtell, C., Holman, D., Unsworth, K., Wall, T., Waterson, P. E., & Harrington, E. 2000. Shopfloor innovation: Facilitating the suggestin and implementation of ideas. *Journal of Occupational and Organizational Psychology*, 73(3): 265–85.

Bacharach, S., Bamberger, P., & Sonnenstuhl, W. 1996. The organizational transformation process: The micropolitics of dissonance reduction and the alignment of logics of action. *Administrative Science Quarterly*, 41: 477–506.

Baker, T., & Nelson, R. 2005. Creating something from nothing: Resource construction through entrepreneurial bricolage. *Administrative Science Quarterly*, 50: 239–366.

Baron, R. 1998. Cognitive mechanisms in entrepreneurship: Why and when entrepreneurs think differently than other people. *Journal of Business Venturing*, 13: 275–94.

Baron, R. 2008. The role of affect in the entrepreneurial process. *Academy of Management Review*, 33: 328–40.

Baron, R., & Markman, G. 2003. Beyond social capital: The role of entrepreneurs' social competence in their financial success. *Journal of Business Venturing*, 18: 41–60.

Baum, R., Locke, E., & Kirkpatrick, S. 1998. A longitudinal study of the relation of vision and vision communication to venture growth in entrepreneurial firms. *Journal of Applied Psychology*, 83: 43–54.

Bartunek, J. 1984. Changing interpretive schemes and organizationl restructuring: The example of a religious order. *Administrative Science Quarterly*. 29: 224–41.

Bettis, R., & Prahalad, C. K. 1995. The dominant logic: Retrospective and extention. *Strategic Management Journal*, 16: 5–14.

Bird, B. 1988. Implementing entrepreneurial ideas: The case for intention. *Academy of Management Review*, 13: 442–53.

Bird, B. 1992. The operations of intentions in time: The emergence of new ventures. *Entrepreneurship Theory and Practice*, Fall: 11–20.

Boyatzis, R. 2006. An overview of intentional change from a complexity perspective. *Journal of Management Development*, 25: 607–23.

Cardon, M., Wincent, J., Singh, J., & Drnovsek, M. 2009. The nature and experience of entrepreneurial passion. *Academy of Management Review*, 34(3): 511–32.

Drazin, R., & Sandelands, L. 1992. Autogenesis: A perspective on the process of organizing. *Organization Science*, 3: 230–49.

Dubinskas, F. 1994. On the edge of chaos: A metaphor for transformative change. *Journal of Management Inquiry*, 3: 355–66.

Dutton, J., & Dukerich, J. 1991. Keeping an eye on the mirror: The role of image and identity in organizational adaptation. *Academy of Management Journal*, 34: 517–54.

Gartner, W. 1993. Words lead to deeds: Towards an organizational emergence vocabulary. *Journal of Business Venturing*, 8: 231–39.

Gartner, W., Bird, B., & Starr, J. 1992. Acting as if: Differentiating entrepreneurial from organizational behavior. *Entrepreneurship Theory and Practice*, 16(3): 13–30.

Garud, R., & Karnoe, P. 2001. *Path Dependence and Creation*. Mahwah, NJ: Lawrence Erlbaum & Associates.

Garud, R., & Karnøe, P. 2003. Bricolage versus breakthrough: Distributed and embedded agency in technology entrepreneurship. *Research Policy*, 32: 277–301.

Gersick, C. 1991. Revolutionary change theories: A multilevel exploration of the punctuated equilibrium paradigm. *Academy of Management Review*, 16: 10–36.

Gioia, D., Schultz, M., & Corley, K. 2000. Organizational identity, image, and adaptive instability. *Academy of Management Review*, 25: 63–81.

Goldstein, J. 2011. Probing the nature of complex systems: Parameters, modeling, interventions—part 1. *Emergence: Complexity and Organization*, 13(3): 94–121.

Greiner, L. 1972. Evolution and revolutions as organizations grow. *Harvard Business Review,* 50(4): 37–46.

Hannan, M., & Freeman, J. 1984. Structural inertia and organizational change. *American Sociological Review,* 49: 149–64.

Haveman, H. 1992. Between a rock and a hard place: Organizational change and performance under conditions of fundamental environmental transformation. *Administrative Science Quarterly,* 37: 48–75.

Heinzen, T. E. 1994. Situational affect: Proactive and reactive creativity. In M. Shaw & M. Runco (Eds.), *Creativity and Affect* (127–46). Westport, CT: Ablex Publishing.

Heinzen, T. E. 1999. Proactive creativity. In M. Runco & S. R. Pritzker (Eds.), *Encyclopedia of Creativity* (Vol. 1: 429–34). San Diego: Academic Press, Elsevier.

Heracleous, L., & Barrett, M. 2001. Organizational change as discourse: Communicative actions and deep structures in the context of information technology implementation. *Academy of Management Journal,* 44: 755–78.

Kauffman, G. 2004. Two kinds of creativity—But which ones? *Creativity and Innovation Management,* 13(3): 154–64.

Kazanjian, R. 1988. Relation of dominant problems to stages of growth in technology-based new ventures. *Academy of Management Journal,* 31: 257–79.

Kotter, J. 1995. Leading change: Why transformation efforts fail. *Harvard Business Review,* March-April: 59–67.

Krueger, N., Reilly, M., & Casrud, A. 2000. Competing models of entrepreneurial intentions. *Journal of Business Venturing,* 14: 411–32.

Lictenstein, B. 1991. A difference that makes a difference: Cybernetic inquiry and post-modern philosophy. In F. Geyer (Ed.) *Cybernetics of Complex Systems.* Salinas, CA: Intersystems Press.

Lichtenstein, B., & Jones, C. 2004. A self-organization theory of radical entrepreneurship. *Best Papers Proceedings, National Academy of Management*: OMT Division; CD format.

MacIntosh, R., & MacLean, D. 1999. Conditioned emergence: A dissipative structures approach to transformation. *Strategic Management Journal,* 20: 297–316.

March, J. 1988. Variable risk preferences and adaptive aspirations. *Journal of Economic Behavior and Organizatin,* 9: 5–24.

March, J. 1991. Exploration and exploitation in organization learning. *Organization Science,* 2: 71–87.

McKelvey, B. 1982. *Organizational Systematics.* Berkeley, CA: University of California Press.

Miles, R., & Snow, C. C. 1978. *Organizational Strategy, Structure, and Process.* New York: McGraw-Hill.

Miles, R., Snow, C. C., Meyer, A., & Coleman, H. J. 1978. Organizational strategy, structure and process. *Academy of Management Review,* 3(3): 546–62.

Miller, J. G. 1978. *Living Systems.* New York: McGraw-Hill Book Company.

Mintzberg, H. 1979. *The Structuring of Organizations.* Englewood Cliffs, NJ: Prentice-Hall.

Mullins, J., & Komisar, R. 2009. *Getting to Plan B: Breaking Through to a Better Business Model.* Boston, MA: Harvard Business Review Press.

Newey, L., & Zahra, S. 2009. The evolving firm: How dynamic and operating capabilities interact to enable entrepreneurship. *British Journal of Management,* 20(Supplement 1): S81-S100.

Osterwalder, A., & Pigneur, Y. 2010. *Business Model Generation: A Handbook for Visionaries, Game Changers, and Challengers.* Hoboken, NJ: John Wiley & Sons.

Plowman, D. A., Baker, L., Beck, T., Kulkarni, M., Solansky, S., & Travis, D. 2007. Radical change accidentally: The emergence and amplification of small change. *Academy of Management Journal,* 50: 515–43.

Prahalad, C. K., & Bettis, R. 1986. The dominant logic: A new lingage between diversity and performance. *Strategic Management Journal*, 7: 485–501.

Rauch, A., & Frese, M. 2007. Let's put the person back into entrepreneurship research: A meta-analysis on the relationship between business owners' personality traits, business creation, and success. *Eurpoean Journal of Work and Organizational Psychology*, 16(4): 353–85.

Repenning, N., & Sterman, J. 2001. Nobody ever gets credit for fixing problems that never happened: Creating and sustaining process improvement. *California Management Review*, 43(4): 64–88.

Romanelli, E., & Tushman, M. 1994. Organizational transformaton as punctuated equilibrium: An empirical test. *Academy of Management Journal*, 37: 1141–66.

Sarasvathy, S. 2001a. Causation and effectuation: Toward a theoretical shift from economic inevitability to entrepreneurial contingency. *Academy of Management Review*, 26: 243–63.

Sarasvathy, S. 2001b. Effectual rationality in entrepreneurial strategies: Existence and bounds. *Academy of Management Best Papers Proceedings*, Vol. 61: ENT, D1–D7.

Sarasvathy, S., & Venkataramen, S. 2011. Entrepreneurship as method: Open questions for an entrepreneurial future. *Entrepreneurship Theory and Practice*, 35(1): 113–35.

Sastry, A. 1997. Problems and paradoxes in a model of punctuated organizational change. *Administrative Science Quarterly*, 42(2): 237–75.

Scott, R. 1981. *Organizations: Rational, Natural, and Open Systems*. Englewood Cliffs, New Jersey: Prentice-Hall.

Smith, C., & Comer, D. 1994. Change in the small group: A dissipative structure perspective. *Human Relations*, 47: 553–81.

Snow, C. C., & Hambrick, D. 1980. Strategy, distinctive competence, and organizational performance. *Administrative Science Quarterly*, 25(2): 317–36.

Sterman, J. 1989. Misperceptions of feedback in dynamic decision making. *Organizational Behavior and Human Decision Processes*, 43(3): 301–44.

Street, C., & Gallupe, R. B. 2009. A proposal for operationalizing the pace and scope of organizational change in management studies. *Organizational Research Methods*, 12: 720–37.

Terpstra, D., & Olson, P. 1993. Entrepreneurial start-up and growth: A classification of problems. *Entrepreneurship Theory and Practice*, 17(3): 5–20.

Tushman, M., Newman, W. H., & Romanelli, E. 1986. Convergence and upheaval: Managing the unsteady pace of organizational evolution. *California Management Review*, 29(1): 29–44.

Tushman, M., & Romanelli, E. 1985. Organizational evolution: A metamorphosis model of convergence and reorientation. *Research in Organizational Behavior*, 7: 171–22.

Unsworth, K. 2001. Unpacking creativity. *Academy of Management Review*, 26(2): 289–97.

Unsworth, K., & Parker, S. 2003. Proactivity and innovation: Promoting a new workforce for the new workplace. In D. Holman, T. Wall, C. Clegg, P. Sparrow, & A. Howard (Eds.), *The New Workplace: A Guide to the Human Impact of Modern Working Practices* (175–96). New York: John Wiley & Sons.

von Bertalanffy, L. 1968. *General Systems Theory*. New York: Braziller Books.

Von Bertalanffy, L. 1972. The history and status of general systems theory. *Academy of Management Journal*, 15(4): 407–26.

Wiklund, J., & Shepherd, D. 2003. Aspiring for, and achieving growth: The moderating role of resources and opportunities. *Journal of Management Studies*, 40(8): 1919–41.

Yusuf, J.-E. 2012. A tale of two exits: Nascent entrepreneur learning activities and disengagement from start-up. *Small Business Economics*, 39(3): 783–99.

Zahra, S., & Pearce, J. 1990. Research evidence on the Miles-Snow typology. *Journal of Management*, 16(4): 751–68.

CHAPTER 17

Boundaries of Emergence and Re-Emergence

The past seven chapters have introduced the five phases of generative emergence and how those phases combine into cycles, of emergence and re-emergence. There is yet one important detail that remains for a complete description of generative emergence, namely the role of *boundaries* in the emergence process. According to recent scholarship (Goldstein, Hazy, & Lichtenstein, 2010; Goldstein, 2011), order creation is only viable within a strong container, whose boundaries provide the necessary constraints for the process (Juarrero, 1999). The first part of this chapter takes up this theme, identifying ways in which the "container" of generative emergence plays a substantive role in its accomplishment. In the second part of the chapter, I use these distinctions to formulate the theoretical boundary conditions (Whetten, 1989) that delineate the range of applications for the five-phase process model.

BOUNDARIES AS CONSTRUCTIVE CONSTRAINTS

As mentioned in the context of the Bénard experiment, moving a chemical or thermodynamic system into a far-from-equilibrium state is only possible when the system is fully contained, that is, in a physical container that is closed to material inputs, even if open to energy (heat) inputs. Earlier (in Chapter 9) I described this as a "nonporous vessel" within which the emergent phenomena—the hexagonal rotating "cells" of order—emerge. In most of these experiments the container is a squat cylinder, with a diameter of about 6 inches and short height, around 1 inch.

It turns out that the dimensions of the boundary are important, as Goldstein (2011, p. 107) noted in reviewing research on the impact of the container on "self-organization" in physical systems:

Not only did Berge, Pompeau, and Vidal (1984) find that in the Bénard convection the distance separating two neighboring currents depend on the vertical height of the container, Weiss (1987) discovered that the number of convection rolls, surely a key aspect of the emergent order observed in the Bénard system, could be curtailed by decreasing the ratio of the horizontal dimension to the vertical height of the container.

Goldstein summarizes several experiments by Swenson, then concludes:

> The presence of containers as constraints has been shown by Rod Swenson (1998) to be a necessary ingredient in resolving the apparent discrepancy between the emerging of novel order seen in self-organization and the manner by which the Second Law's entropy increase has been associated with a spontaneous degradation of order. It is the constraints brought about by the containment in self-organizing systems which channel the "ordered flow" of energy.

In all these ways, the container—the physical boundary of the experiment—is instrumental in the formation of order. Obviously, without a container of any kind the molecules would simply scatter all over the lab table and floor, with no probability of interacting. However, the container is more than a set of boundaries. Its spatial geometry (internal form, size, characteristics) presents a constraint on the forces across the molecules to interact in a certain way. In the experiments of dissipative structures theory, the container is a crucial determinant of the outcomes.

In contrast to the tangibility of a container for exo-organizing, the "container" for generative emergence—an agent's social ecology—is not nearly so well defined. As I suggested (in Chapter 7), this social ecology contains within it all of the networks, opportunities, resources, and knowledge that go into the creation of a new organization. Through these resources, entrepreneurs *create the boundaries* of their ventures (Katz & Gartner, 1988; Sarasvathy, 2001; Aldrich & Reuf, 2006), by focusing on a specific opportunity tension, by identifying a specific target market, and through leveraging the constraints of the organizing model, all of which enables the business to work.

The notion of constraint is helpful in defining the boundaries of generative emergence, by conscribing the qualities of the "container." Goldstein is convincing about this link; he shows that in both exemplars of dissipative structures—the emergence of laser light, and the emergence of order in the Bénard experiments—it is the constraints which serve to "channel the emergent phenomena" (Goldstein, 2011, p. 107).

This idea, of the value of constraints, is picked up even more strongly by Alicia Juarrero (1999), who initiates her argument by recognizing the relational nature of constraints (pp. 132–133):

> In physical mechanics, that is, constraints are said to "compel" and "force" behavior. The term suggests, however, not an external force that pushes, but a thing's connection

to something else. The point to be made ... is that by "constraints" Lindsay (1961) clearly means something other than Newtonian forces that is nevertheless causal. [It is] the orderly context ... which ... constrains them. Constraints are therefore relational properties that parts acquire in virtue of being unified—not just aggregated—into a systematic whole.

Then she suggests that constraints are not solely limitations of possible action, but are constructive; they open up new possibilities across the system (Juarrero 1999, p. 133):

> But if all constraints restricted a thing's degrees of freedom in this way, organisms ... would progressively do less and less. However, precisely the opposite is empirically observed. Some constraints must therefore not only reduce the number of alternatives; they must simultaneously create new possibilities.... [C]onstraints can simultaneously open up as well as close off options.

From this perspective, the application of constraints, judiciously limiting the range of possibilities, can increase the likelihood of generative emergence. For example, constraining entrepreneurial action may increase the likelihood that a new venture will emerge. Constraints focus the attention of an entrepreneur, limiting distractions and increasing perseverance, allowing for an emergence of order. It is intriguing to note a similarity to artistic creation. For example, the dimensions of a canvas have a positive influence on structuring the actions of the painter—the constraints (the physical limits of the surface) open up potentialities for creation. Likewise, the layout of a stage gives form and presence to a dancer's expression, just as the voicing of a chord drives the improvisation of the jazz musician. As Juarrero says, constraints are causes of emergence. Much more can be explored in this regard.

THEORETICAL BOUNDARY CONDITIONS OF THE MODEL
Exploring Emergence "within" Boundaries

At a different level altogether, acknowledging the role of the container in generative emergence yields some implications about the boundaries of the theory itself. Specifically, the need to define and thus incorporate the container into the five-phase process suggests that the theory should apply to social entities that can be perceived by others, due to their boundaries that can be seen and responded to. In formal terms, this yields specific boundary conditions of the model (Whetten, 1989), namely that the five-phase process should be observable in boundaried social ecologies. These include organizations, ventures, projects, and some initiatives and endeavors.

Thus far, all of the examples of a cycle of emergence in this book have operated at the level of organizations; in fact, almost all of the research applying dissipative structures to emergence has been based on studies at the organizational unit of analysis (including Smith, 1986; Nonaka, 1988; Smith & Gemmill, 1991; Smith & Comer, 1994; Lichtenstein, 1998, 2000; MacIntosh & MacLean, 1999; Lichtenstein & Jones, 2004; Lichtenstein, Dooley, & Lumpkin, 2006; Lichtenstein, Carter, Dooley, & Gartner, 2007; Lichtenstein & Kurjanowicz, 2010). This suggests a boundary condition for the five-phase model, namely emergence in and of organizations.

Emergence *in* organizations refers to research in which the substrate for emergence is an existing organization, *within which* something new (tangible) emerges. Examples include a new work group or department in a company, a new product or technology, or a new organizing model. In contrast, emergence *of* organizations refers to the creation of a new organization as a semi-autonomous unit, a new dynamic state, as is explored in entrepreneurship.

There is second dimension of emergence that also refers to the substrate but focuses on its temporality and primacy. Specifically, is this the *first time* that emergence has occurred in this substrate; in other words, is it the very first instance of this system as a social entity? In many cases it is not. Thus, re-emergence refers to a re-creation or remaking of an existing dynamic state—a third-degree radical emergence that remakes the core logic, opportunity tension, and organizing model of the firm. Taken together, these two dimensions identify four possible avenues for research in generative emergence, as shown in Figure 17.1.

Before exploring these four avenues for emergence research, a clarification about the meaning of these boundary conditions is in order. In brief, the boundary conditions reflect a claim that the five-phase sequence of generative emergence will be (most) visible in organizational-level instances of emergence, specifically, when examining emergence or re-emergence in and of organizations.

This is not to say that generative emergence is limited to organizational-level instances. As noted in Chapter 7, the five phases are operative across virtually all

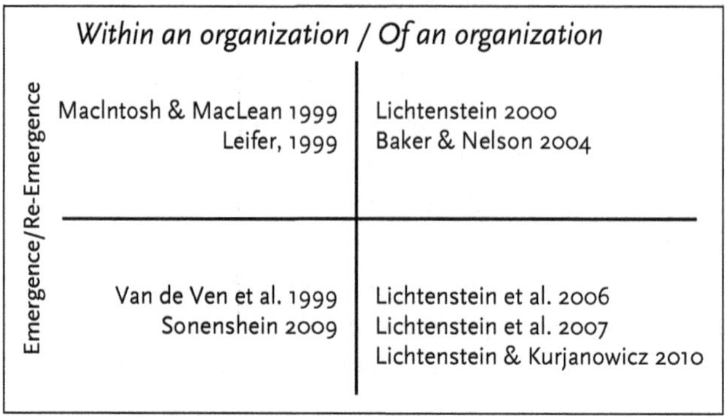

	Within an organization	*Of an organization*
Re-Emergence	MacIntosh & MacLean 1999 Leifer, 1999	Lichtenstein 2000 Baker & Nelson 2004
Emergence	Van de Ven et al. 1999 Sonenshein 2009	Lichtenstein et al. 2006 Lichtenstein et al. 2007 Lichtenstein & Kurjanowicz 2010

Figure 17.1: Typology of Generative Emergence Research at the Organizational Unit of Analysis

inductive studies of emergence, whether *within* organizations, *of* organizations (entrepreneurship), or *across* organizations.[1] Thus, the full range of applications includes emergences in groups, organizations, collaboratives (alliances), industries, and across multiple units of analysis.

However, most complexity studies have focused on the qualities and aspects of emergence, rather than on the *sequence* of those aspects. Many emergence studies use the term *conditions* to identify the key aspects of emergence in their study. For example, Plowman et al. (2007) identify four "conditions" of emergence; similarly, Chiles et al. (2004) identify four "conditions" that give rise to a cycle of emergence. Likewise, Lichtenstein and Plowman (2009) emphasized the "conditions for emergence" across the three papers they analyzed.

By avoiding a specific sequence, it is much easier to find links between these models, to apply generative emergence to many units of analysis. In contrast, the five phases that I have proposed are a *sequence* that leads to a cycle of emergence. This sequence is mostly likely to be expressed within or of organizations, as suggested by the boundary conditions.

Following this thinking, competent applications of generative emergence can be made across two dimensions of research design: whether one is examining (1) emergence or re-emergence, and whether this is happening (2) *in* organizations or *of* organizations. Placed as a 2 × 2 typology, these dimensions can be unpacked, as a way of emphasizing the research questions and opportunities that can be asked of generative emergence within a specific context.

What follows is a brief guide to the kinds of emergence research that has been done in each of the four quadrants of the 2 × 2 typology. Later in the chapter, more extensions will be made to applications of emergence or re-emergence that are beyond organizations themselves.

A Typology of Generative Emergence Research

Emergence of Organization

The most intuitive type (category) of organizational-level emergence is the emergence *of* an organization, what Gartner has described as "organizational emergence" (Gartner, 1985, 1988, 1993, 2001). Here, an opportunity or idea is pursued—organized—by a nascent entrepreneur (Gartner, Carter, & Reynolds, 2004). Given a strong enough motivation, the entrepreneur's idea will initiate a flurry of organizing activities to capitalize on the opportunity. If they're successful, a new organization will emerge, a distinct social entity or "agent" comes into being. Customers and stakeholders perceive and interact with this entity, which is perceived to be something more than simply the activities of its founder. This intangible shift into existence as a business or organization then distinguishes the organization as a new unit of social reality—a higher-order entity that influences its members and its society.

A good deal of research has explored this process of organizational emergence, from the early work of Paul Reynolds, Nancy Carter, Bill Gartner, and many more who have studied new-venture creation processes (Katz & Gartner, 1988; Reynolds & Miller, 1992; Carter, Gartner, & Reynolds, 1996; Gartner & Carter, 2003; Gartner, Shaver, Carter, & Reynolds, 2004; Lichtenstein et al., 2007; Brush, Manolova, & Edelman, 2008).

Avenues for further research in this category are rich. For example, the data collection in the second version of the Panel Study of Entrepreneurial Dynamics (PSED) (Reynolds, Carter, Gartner, Greene, & Cox, 2002) includes a set of entrepreneurial behaviors, yet adds a crucial component that was missing from PSED 1, namely the formal incorporation of the business. Such a legitimating action may help deepen our understanding of the timing and even the dynamics of organizational emergence. The PSED data have been very useful already in explaining the dynamics of opportunity tension and emergence in new ventures (Lichtenstein et al., 2007; Storm, 2012).

Re-Emergence of Organization

The re-emergence of existing organizations occurs when entrepreneurial ventures "reinvent" themselves, as did so many of the small firms studied by Baker and Nelson (2005). This reinvention process has been marvelously presented for entrepreneurs by Mullins and Romisar in their *Getting to Plan B* (Mullins & Komisar, 2009). Here the substrate of emergence is the current dynamic state of the organization. This sustained (sustaining) dynamic state is the starting point for a push by the entrepreneur to get the venture "to the next stage," to its next "level" of growth or performance (Levie & Lichtenstein, 2010). Generative emergence provides much more clarity on the process of getting to this next level or state of development and suggests some key dynamics that affect the outcomes, especially whether the organization survives or collapses.

A good deal of research has explored this category of emergence, and much more could be done. For example, the dynamics of this process can be explored using longitudinal data from the organization, a task made easier by the fact that some of these data can be collected archivally through activity and performance streams of the organization.[2] Given a large enough database, research could explore for a correspondence between the dynamics of the five phases and the outcomes of emergence in terms of performance and capacity. Likewise, researchers could apply these constructs in a prospective way, to seek "leverage points" (Meadows, 1982; see also Gunderson & Holling, 2001) that support and perhaps catalyze the process.

Theoretical research in this arena can help define the origin and mutability of a company's "identity" among others, extending the work of Gioia and his colleagues (Gioia & Thomas, 1996; Gioia, Schultz, & Corley, 2000). To the degree that re-emergence leads to a literal name-change of the organization—a phenomenon that happened in three of the four ventures I studied[3]—research into the re-emergence of organizations can broaden our understanding of "failure" as a mechanism for learning and experience (McGrath, 1999; Stam, Audretsch, & Meijaard, 2008).

Emergence within Organizations

Studies of emergence within the boundaries of an organization include a wide spectrum of phenomena, from the emergence of a client-relationship management system to the launch of new products or services, to the entrepreneurship of spin-out ventures. Perhaps most emergence research in management has been done in this category, originated in part by the remarkable research on major innovation projects led by Andy Van de Ven and colleagues (Van de Ven, Angel, & Poole, 1989; Van de Ven & Pooley, 1992; Van de Ven & Poole, 1995; Van de Ven, Pooley, Garud, & Venkataramen, 1999). It is no mistake that my methodology and analytic approach is taken almost directly from their work, especially from Van de Ven and Poole (1990). Complexity-inspired research into the creation of new products and platforms could explore how the emergence of each new "revenue stream" reflects the creation of another dynamic state within the organization as a whole. Such work could take advantage of the classic and ongoing studies in project management as well.

Far less common are studies on the emergence of new work units and departments. Another area rich in potential is application of the principles of generative emergence to initiatives and endeavors within organizations, whether these arise in the pursuit of strategic goals or are employee-led projects. As examples, emergences within organizations have been identified by Sonenshein (2009) in his study of emergent human resources issues, by Nicholls-Nixon (2005) in her study of emergent processes in high-potential entrepreneurial firms, and by others; see Lichtenstein (2011) for a complete set.

Re-Emergence within Organizations

One way to distinguish emergence from re-emergence within organizations is to consider the systems and qualities that have existed in some tangible form from the company's start-up. Re-emergence is the re-creation of (one of) those systems and qualities. Using this lens, a good deal of research already exists on re-emergence within organizations. In particular, this includes the strategy emergence studies by Mintzberg and his colleagues (Mintzberg, 1978; Mintzberg & Waters, 1982) and, in a different way, the new efforts in strategy process that are being pursued by scholars in the European Group for Organization Studies and the Academy of

Management. A similar contribution in this area are the insightful studies into the re-emergence of routines (Feldman, 2000, 2004; Feldman & Pentland, 2003).

An extension would be to explore whether those processes are related to the five-phase cycle. Further, what are the performance implications of re-emergences of key organizational aspects like "strategy," in contrast to the wholesale re-emergence of the organization as a whole? An even broader way of framing this would be to pursue a kind of return-on-investment analysis, examining the outcomes of first-degree emergences, second-degree emergences, and third-degree emergences.

In sum, these four categories—emergence within organizations, emergence of organizations, re-emergence within organizations, and re-emergence of organizations—provide one template for considering how to pursue relevant research in generative emergence. Another approach is presented next, namely by extending the five phases to situations beyond organizations as a unit of analysis.

BEYOND THE BOUNDARIES: EXTENDING APPLICATIONS OF THE FIVE-PHASE PROCESS

My claim is that the five-phase process model will provide the most accurate explanations when applied to bounded social entities like organizations. At the same time, there already appear to be correlations to the five phases in units of analysis that are more inclusive than this. In the broadest sense, then, looking beyond the boundaries of organizations, how might research into generative emergence be applied? As one might expect, a host of studies exist at a wide range of levels, from the micro (individual) level (Juarrero, 1999; Boyatzis, 2008) to studies into the creation of collaboratives (Browning et al., 1995) and industries (Chiles, Tuggle, McMullen, Bierman, & Greening, 2010; Dew, Reed, Sarasvathy, & Wiltbank, 2011) and in institutional entrepreneurship (Garud, Jain, & Kumaraswamy, 2002; Maguire, Hardy, & Lawrence, 2004).

Studies in different contexts can be compared to generative emergence in and of organizations. In the discussion that follows I will focus on two interrelated issues that are parallel to the claims of boundary conditions. First I explore the content: What *conditions* or *phases of activity* are revealed by studies of emergence in each of these arenas? How do they reflect the five phases? Second is a question of sequence: Do the phases of emergence in those contexts follow a specific sequence, and, if so, how similar is that sequence to the five-phase model? What follows is a summary of different contexts that are ripe for applying generative emergence.

Psychology and Cognitive Development

A number of researchers have applied dynamical systems thinking to explain phases of human development. One well-known example is the work of Thelan and Smith

(1995; Thelen, 1995; Smith & Thelen, 2003), whose study of infant motor skills led them to reframe development as a dynamic system combining multiple layers of activity, rather than the more common "nature vs. nurture" approach. By applying the principles from Prigogine, Haken, and others, they showed how cognition develops through a series of phase shifts that reflect a process of "self-organization."

Other scholars have used dynamic modeling to explain psychological states and leadership emergence. Guastello has been a key proponent of this work, through his analysis of motivation and leadership using the archetypes from catastrophe theory (Guastello, 1987, 1998). His studies have been far more effective at explaining individual behavior than their linear counterparts (Guastello, 1995), findings that have made a lasting contribution to psychology (Guastello, 2001).

Boyatzis's Leadership Development

Pushing this individual level context into the arena of training, Boyatzis has pursued a series of studies that examine the "conditions for emergence" in leadership (Boyatzis & Kolb, 2000; Boyatzis, 2006a, 2006b, 2008). Applying aspects of complexity theory to intentional change theory, he and his colleagues have identified several qualities of leadership development that resonate with the phases of generative emergence. For example, his claim that *desire* is the driver of intentional change shows much similarity to opportunity tension: "The first discontinuity ... for the process of intentional change is the discovery of *why* you want to be" (Boyatzis, 2006, p. 613). He shows that this desire is a projection that pushes oneself forward, driving change. "We can access and engage deep emotional commitment and psychic energy ... [which are] inherent in dreams of the future and new possibilities, as well as the emotional driver of hope" (pp. 613–614). Like opportunity tension, this idea draws from a vision of a future possibility, which creates the passion and motivation to initiate and proceed through often challenging issues.

In his model, the vision for positive change acts as a "positive emotional attractor [that] pulls the person toward their ideal self." The attractor can also become a "destabilizing force" which sometimes leads to activities that "are often made in the context of experimenting with new behavior" (Boyatzis, 2006, p. 616). In some ways, this is similar to the stress and experimentation phase of generative emergence. "[T]he person needs flexibility to experiment, possibly fail, and then succeed with the new behavior" (Boyatzis, 2008, p. 307).

Finally, success is more likely when individuals surrounds themselves with others who affirm their goals and new directions and "provide feedback on our behavior" (Boyatzis, 2006, p. 617). These positive reflections by others "create a context within which we can interpret our progress on desired changes" and become more confident about the direction of our efforts. To my mind, these relationships are parallel to the stabilizing feedback phase of generative emergence, helping to ensure the sustainability of the emergent outcomes.

Juarrero's Intentional Action

An even stronger parallel between individual-level behavior and generative emergence can be drawn from the work on intentional action, by Alicia Juarrero (1999). She begins by reviewing literature showing that the brain constructs "progressively ordered, complex regions in neural state space" (Juarrero, 1999, pp. 177–178). She continues: "In response to feedback loops . . . previously independent neuron firings . . . suddenly entrain, producing a global pattern of distributed, coherent neural activity." Her use of entrainment is resonant with new order through recombination.

Juarrero's analysis of intentional action incorporates concepts that have further parallels to the generative emergence process. This starts from what she calls "forming a prior intention" (pp. 179–180), an act similar to forming an opportunity tension:

> [T]he feedback between external circumstances and internal dynamics can likewise drive neurological dynamics describing a person's current state of mind, far from equilibrium. "She worked herself into a frenzy," we say. The disequilibrium and instability that precipitate the restructuring can occur at the cognitive and emotional levels. . . . [I]f taken far from equilibrium, a person's existing mental attractor regime embodying meaning, desire, and similar mental properties might reorganize and thereby recontour the landscape.

In addition to referencing the link between cognition and emotion that is foundational to opportunity tension, she also references other phases of generative emergence. For example, the initial intention can lead the individual into disequilibrium, like disequilibrium organizing, in which "she works herself into a frenzy." This activity links to "instability," a characteristic of stress and experiments. Together, disequilibrium and instability "precipitate" a restructuring, perhaps similar to a critical event. The result, which she calls "a phase change or bifurcation," restructures the existing regime. In terms of outcomes, she references an increase in capacity when the process

> reorganize(s) the earlier state space into a more differentiated and complex set of operations. . . . The semantic space self-organized by (in) a prior intention automatically reduces the number of . . . possible behaviors [such that] only those now-meaningful alternatives described by the new "collective variable" need be considered. (Jurarro 1999, p. 180)

In these ways, Jurarro's perspective appears to have many similarities to generative emergence, opening several avenues for integrating individual-level emergences into the dynamics that generate projects, products, and organizations.

Emergence of Alliances and Economic Clusters

Two studies suggest a strong correlation to the five phases in the emergence of macro-organizational entities. Whether the sequence of the five phases holds is less certain.

A Cycle of Emergence at SEMATECH

Chapter 15 presented my analysis of SEMATECH as an exemplar of generative emergence, drawing on the in-depth research of Browning, Beyer, and Shetler (1995). Although the opportunity tension there was based on a crisis, a recognition that the United States was rapidly losing its lead in semiconductor innovation and market share to Asian counterparts, this precipitated the more important aspiration for cooperation that had never been seen in that industry. This shared realization led to an unprecedented organizing initiative to bring together fierce competitors. In tangible terms, the disequilibrium organizing was expressed as the huge infusion of money and social capital: A $1,000,000,000 budget was raised by the participating companies and the U.S. Government for the first five years of the project. Likewise, every company paid for key scientists to join the project full-time.

These inputs were met with stress, seen in visible differences in goals, in conflicts between the leaders, and in a high degree of ambiguity and equivocality, which Browning et al. (2005, p. 125) described as "chaotic." Experiments were attempted, including new norms for leadership, different standards based on quality rather than cost, and new values of reciprocity that had never before been seen in the industry. Although the data are too granular to identify specific amplification, there does appear to be an increase in momentum that built up toward the end of the initial five-year commitment.

The new order that emerged was a recombination of skills, resources, and knowledge in ways that no one could have foreseen. It turned out that the focus for the consortium was not, as planned, the development of the individual firms within it; instead, a majority of the resources were used to build the supplier network for all companies in the industry. This, along with major financial allocations to national innovation laboratories, dramatically increased the capacity of the industry as a whole. Finally, these outcomes were stabilized through shared norms of reciprocity, trust, and cooperation that decreased free-riding and increased the sustainability of the alliance, which continues to this day.

Overall, the emergence of this multi-organizational alliance appears to incorporate all five phases of generative emergence. My telling of the story emphasizes a sequential process to the cycle; however, this sequencing is not formally confirmed by the data, especially since the granularity of their data makes it impossible to know for sure. At a minimum this analysis confirms the presence of four conditions that correspond to four of the five phases.

Emergence of Economic Clusters—the Case of Branson, MO

One of the strongest applications of dissipative structures theory across organizations is Chiles and colleagues' (2004) description of how Branson, MO emerged from a tiny retirement community in the 1900s to become the second-most visited tourist destination in the United States today. Using quantitative time series drawn from more than a dozen sources ranging over 100+ years, and augmented by in-depth archival and qualitative analysis, they revealed the presence of four "conditions" of emergence that operate across four successive "cycles," or eras. Specifically, they showed how each era was initiated by "fluctuation dynamics"—small but influential events that significantly increased inputs to the area. In many ways, these fluctuation dynamics are similar to disequilibrium organizing. For example, they say that

> at the turn of the century three simple elements—"a lake, a book, and a train" (*Branson Daily News*, 1986)—ended Branson's era of isolation and initiated its emergence as a tourist destination. Together they provided sufficient energy to usher in a qualitatively new regime of order. (Chiles et al., 2004, pp. 8, 10)

Following this theme, Chiles et al. describe how the book *The Shepherd of the Hills* became a national best seller that "served as a magnet, drawing many curious visitors." At the same time, these increased inputs were facilitated by the first passenger railroad access, and soon thereafter by the creation of a lake which played a "monumental role in shifting the towns emphasis to tourism."[4]

Similar reflections of disequilibrium organizing are found in the initiation of the three new eras that emerged. In the 1950s, for example, "pioneering entrepreneurs ignited a creative explosion" (Chiles et al., 2004, p. 10) of Ozark-style musical theaters. Again, in the 1980s a series of country music stars moved to the area, starting "a chain reaction that moved the system into a new order." Finally, the 1990s saw the arrival of pop music icons, "a continuing influx of starts into Branson," including Andy Williams, whose arrival "went against the norm . . . filling a big hole. . . . It changed the frame of reference, broke the mindset of Branson . . . and ushered in a new regime of order." In all of these ways fluctuation dynamics are similar to disequilibrium organizing: New energy and resources are brought into the system, pushing it away from its current norm and toward a new regime of activity.

These fluctuation dynamics also represent experiments in the system. In a sense, each new theater was an experiment, a test that explored the potentiality in the market. "These pioneering entrepreneurs act[ed] on their perceptions that tourists needed something to do at night [and] to fulfill a market that wasn't being fulfilled, as one pioneer put it" (Chiles et al., 2004, p. 10). Likewise, one key entrepreneur "wanted to create a market, so he encouraged stars to start their own theaters. Eventually entrepreneurs and performers began to change their approach once they recognized the unique set of opportunities Branson offered" (p. 11). In this way, the experiments became influxes of energy, which generated further experiments, generating a positive feedback loop of activity.

"Positive feedback dynamics" is the term they use to describe the combinations of events and situations that catalyze each other, leading to acceleration and momentum for growth. In their study, the effects of these feedback loops sound very close to the dynamics of amplification. For example, they "catalyzed" change through a "self-reinforcing cycle" of "mutual causation" that "built momentum" and ultimately "set off . . . a chain reaction" of growth (Chiles et al., 2004, pp. 12–14). The authors tested their numerous examples of positive feedback loops through Poisson regression analysis of their time series, and found extremely strong statistical confirmation of these correlations across all 12 models.

The third aspect of emergence they found is "recombination dynamics," in which "existing elements are often recombined to create new ones in self-organizing systems" (p. 15). In parallel to our notion of new order through recombination, Chiles et al. describe how "Branson's entrepreneurs were adept at recombining existing elements such as abandoned airfields, used folding chairs from area attractions, old skating rinks, available dance pavilions, and vacant theater buildings in their efforts to create new theaters" (Chiles et al., 2004, p. 15). In addition, the success of a theater show would often lead the company star to establish new facilities, which then "freed physical capital that was recycled, refurbished, and recombined with the human and reputational capital provided by another headliner to better satisfy patrons, and so on in a continuous process of systemwide innovation."

Finally, their study was one of the first to highlight "stabilization dynamics" as an important quality of emergence; it is from them that I developed the construct. Their analysis shows how local culture "provided a powerful, stabilizing mechanism that . . . guided participants' choices in a way consistent with the town's accumulated evolutionary learning" (Chiles et al., 2004, p. 14). Such "cultural policing" was rooted in governmental policies and in collective marketing organizations, all of which supported "a strategy of delivering customers to Branson" by focusing their "marketing efforts to tell a single story consistent with the local culture" (p. 15). In their analysis, integrating new ideas into the accepted institutional frames of the region led to greater community acceptance of new acts, while also providing a distinct theme for the area. Just as entrepreneurs are told that focusing on a small specific niche or market segment will increase business, so too the consistency of values across the entire region served to increase tourism and positive reputation.

In sum, the four conditions of emergence presented by Chiles and his colleagues are parallel to four of the five phases of generative emergence. At the same time, these are not inherently a sequence, but happen in an ongoing manner. For example, Chiles and his colleagues discuss "cycles of emergence," but they don't refer to these cycles or their sequences when presenting the four conditions. In this case, then, a "nonsequential" five-phase model is applicable to processes of emergence *across* organizations, such as collaborations or economic clusters.

Emergence of Institutions and Institutional Schema

An increasing number of studies on industry creation and institutional entrepreneurship are based on a dynamic, process-oriented approach (examples include Lawrence, Winn, & Jennings, 2001; Garud et al., 2002; Lawrence, Hardy, & Phillips, 2002; Garud, Hardy, & Maguire, 2004; Maguire et al., 2004; Chiles, Bluedorn, & Gupta, 2007; Tan, 2007; Chiles et al., 2010; Dew et al., 2011, among others). An examination of these studies shows some links to complexity science explanations of emergence. These can be easily found in Tan's (2007) analysis of phase transitions, in Chiles and colleagues' (2007, 2010) dynamic creation approach to industry emergence, and in Garud and colleagues' studies—the exploration of path creation (Garud & Karnoe, 2001) and the emergence of dominant designs (Garud et al., 2002; also Garud, Kumaraswamy, & Sambamurthy, 2006). Mainly this literature emphasizes the conditions and forces that constrain and enable the origin of markets and institutions.

An Emerging Institution of Dispute Resolution

A few recent process studies of institutional entrepreneurship emphasize distinct stages of change, thus allowing for a more detailed comparison of those dynamics with the five-phase model. For example, Purdy and Gray's (2009) analysis of the emerging institutional field of dispute resolution identifies three stages of the process. The "innovation stage" was driven by the initial funding for a statewide office of alternative dispute resolution in Massachusetts, which was advocated by the entrepreneurial efforts of MIT professor Lawrence Susskind. This move caused a series of conflicts as the field moved into a kind of "disequilibrium" state. In this first stage, Purdy and Gray also describe a series of issues that emerged within the field, all of which created an "openness" to find solutions to the growing challenges in the effort to institutionalize this form of dispute resolution. Disequilibrium organizing and the conditions for experiments are demonstrated at this stage.

These issues gave rise to a "mobilization stage," in which new practices are proposed and promoted through new organizations and collaborations. Like experiments, these are attempts to solve the conflicts and resolve the uncertainty within the field. At the same time, these new practices were furthered by gaining access to legitimacy (legislation) and new resources, suggesting an interplay between disequilibrium and experiments. This interplay served to increase conflicts, however: "These factors contributed to the fragmentation of the population, perpetuating conflicting logics and hindering coalescence around a single organizational form" (Purdy & Gray, 2009, p. 374). Further stress was caused by resistance from existing institutions and the lack of national legislation on the issue.

In the "structuration stage," there emerges a kind dynamic order in the field, albeit one that is unstable and lacking coalescence. Legislative efforts end up legitimizing multiple logics, each of which pursues its own strategies for gaining consistent access to various resource pools. Their analysis identified four "mechanisms" through which different offices sought legitimacy—transformation, grafting, bridging, and exit. In a loose way these may be seen as methods of recombination and of stabilization, approaches for developing sustainable integrations or connections of the practices to existing institutions.

My retelling of their analysis does not do justice to the nuances in the process, nor are my five phases fully coincident with their three stages. Still, there are intriguing hints of generative emergence in the formation of this institution, enough to warrant further exploration.

Schema Emergence in Institutions

A recent paper by Bingham and Kahl (2013) provides a three-stage model to explain the emergence of a new schema, that is, the process by which individuals were able to assimilate a new schema into their work, in this case, the introduction of the computer into the life insurance field. Although the study of schemas is often pursued by psychology (at the individual level of analysis), these authors argue that "schema emergence in organizations is likely more complicated and dynamic than psychology theory suggests" (p. 16). Further, their study explores the institutionalization of schema throughout an entire industry. Thus I include it in this more macro framework.

To begin, Bingham and Kahl (2013) show how the introduction of the computer in the 1950s was facilitated through "assimilation" to an existing schema, meaning that a simple analogy was made between the new invention and the common idea of a machine. In this case, the later concept provided sufficient overlap in "core categories and relations" to the computer and was far more established than the competing analogy of computer as "brain." In some sense the potential disequilibrating effects of the innovation were reduced, by thinking of the technology in incremental terms, as a faster or more powerful machine.

Within a decade, however, this assimilation stage shifted into a stage of "deconstruction," in which the existing notion of machine was deconstructed to reveal many more powerful ways to use the technology. The shift was driven initially by criticisms about the "lack of return" on these investments—a simple kind of fiscal stress, which spurred a series of experiments that hoped to move beyond using computers simply as "super accounting machines." These experiments were facilitated by technical improvements in storage capacity and processing power, and in the learning and capability that experts were able to accomplish with these advances. For example, companies experimented with programming, finding it "significantly more useful than anticipated" (Bingham and Kahl, 2013, p. 24). As in the generative emergence model, these experiments "boosted the invocation of novel categories and relations," creating openings for further expansion of the schema.

Bingham and Kahl (2013, p. 26) argue that "creation alone does not complete emergence until it is proven to persist." This points to their third stage of "unitization." They define unitization as "the process through which a group of categories and relations get connected ... as a stand-alone unit, and no longer exists solely as individual components" (p. 26). This view is resonant with the creation of new order through recombination. Further, they operationalize emergence through the ideas of concentration and interconnection of the component terms. "The increasing connectedness indicates a unit structure emerged around the categories and relations ... distinct from the schema originally assimilated in the 1950s" (p. 26).

In sum, they show how an initial analogy provides the entrée for an innovation; over time, experiments reveal a tension between the original schema and broader alternatives. These tensions are resolved through a recombination of elements, leading to an emergent structure that guides further applications in the industry. In this way, their three stages have a logic that is somewhat similar to the dynamics of generative emergence.

Summary

As a means of exploring the applicability of the five-phase model to other contexts, I found that the dynamics of generative emergence within and of organizations may also be found in the emergence of cognition and leadership development, emergent alliances and clusters, and the emergence of institutions and their underlying cognitive schema. In other words, my narrative analysis revealed plausible connections between the stages of emergence in those studies and the five phases of generative emergence.

These links suggest a potential generalizability to the five-phase model, to contexts ranging from individuals to groups to organizations to alliances to clusters to institutions. At the same time, this correspondence is almost exclusively limited to the conditions of emergence, but not to the sequence of emergence. Thus, I am confident that the five phases represent the dynamics of generative emergence *within* and *of* organizations. Further, I hope these explorations can lead to some new research integrations of entrepreneurial cognition and action within emergence in and of individuals, projects, new ventures, collaborations, clusters, markets, and institutions.

NOTES

1. Specifically, all of the constructs developed in Browning, Beyer, and Shelter (1995), Nonaka (1998), MacIntosh and MacLean (1999), Lichtenstein (2000), Chiles, Meyer, and Hench (2004), and Plowman et al. (2007), as well as recent studies by Purdy and Gray (2009) and Anand, Gardner, and Morris (2007) fall within the five phases presented in the generative emergence model. See Chapter 7, Table 7.1.
2. Although I have been presenting mainly mixed-method studies (involving large amounts of qualitative data collection and analysis), a strong subset of the data from the four ventures was simply copied or calculated from longitudinal *archival* sources, that is, sources that were already being produced and kept by the organization. To take an amalgam from my studies, consider how disequilibrium organizing was calculated from time cards at DevelopNet; how experiments were counted from lab books at ApplySci; how fiscal stress was calculated from income statements or weekly cash-flow reports at DevelopNet, ApplySci, and AgencyInc, as was amplification in the first two.
3. Literal name-changes occurred at DevelopNet, ServiceCo, and ApplySci; these data are hard to fully reproduce given the constraints of keeping the organizations anonymous. DevelopNet experienced a name change (with an update in the corporate charter) from RSID (Reaction-Sensitive Information Dynamics, to try to come up with an equivalent name) to DevelopNet. New signs and letterhead were produced around the first month of my data collection. ServiceCo enacted a name change (again, updating its original charter) that formalized about 9 months after their re-emergence to what I might call "CreativeInc." ApplySci had a less distinctive "name change" that commenced about a year before my data collection (i.e., near the origin of the data presented in this book), by integrating its bio-tech spin-out company into itself.
4. In the quotes that follow, for clarity, I have removed the internal quote marks they use in their text to identify quotes from local newspapers, magazines, and brochures.

REFERENCES

Aldrich, H., & Reuf, M. 2006. *Organizations Evolving* (2nd ed.). Thousand Oaks, CA: SAGE Publications.

Anonymous. 1986. Branson owes success to White River, Wright and railroad. *Branson Daily News*, Progress Edition. Branson, MO.

Baker, T., & Nelson, R. 2005. Creating something from nothing: Resource construction through entrepreneurial bricolage. *Administrative Science Quarterly*, 50: 239–366.

Berge, P., Pompeau, Y., & Vidal, C. 1984. *Order within Chaos: Towards a Deterministic Approach to Turbulence*: New York: Wiley-VCH.

Bingham, C., & Kahl, S. 2013. The process of schema emergence: Assimilation, deconstruction, unitization and the plurality of analogies. *Academy of Management Journal*, 56(1): 14–34.

Boyatzis, R. 2006a. An overview of intentional change from a complexity perspective. *Journal of Management Development*, 25: 607–23.

Boyatzis, R. 2006b. Using tipping points of emotional intelligence and cognitive competencies to predict financial performance of leaders. *Psicothema*, 18(Supplement): 124–31.

Boyatzis, R. 2008. Leadership development from a complexity perspective. *Consulting Psychology Journal: Practice and Research*, 60: 298–313.

Boyatzis, R., & Kolb, D. 2000. Performance, learning and development as modes of growth and adaptation throughout our lives and careers. In M. Peiperl, M. Arthur, R. Goffee, & T. Morris (Eds.), *Career Frontiers* (76–98). New York: Oxford University Press.

Browning, L., Beyer, J., & Shetler, J. 1995. Building cooperation in a competitive industry: SEMATECH and the semiconductor industry. *Academy of Management Journal*, 38: 113–51.

Brush, C., Manolova, T., & Edelman, L. 2008. Properties of emerging organizations: An empirical test. *Journal of Business Venturing*, 23: 547–66.

Carter, N., Gartner, B., & Reynolds, P. 1996. Exploring start-up event sequences. *Journal of Business Venturing*, 11: 151–66.

Chiles, T., Bluedorn, A., & Gupta, V. 2007. Beyond creative destruction and entrepreneurial discovery: A radical Austrian approach to entrepreneurship. *Organization Studies*, 28: 467–93.

Chiles, T., Tuggle, C. S., McMullen, J., Bierman, L., & Greening, D. 2010. Dynamic creation: Elaborating a radical Austrian approach to entrepreneurship. *Organization Studies*, 31: 7–46.

Dew, N., Reed, S., Sarasvathy, S., & Wiltbank, R. 2011. On the entrepreneurial genesis of new markets: Effectual transformations versus causal search and selection. *Journal of Evolutionary Economics*, 21: 231–53.

Feldman, M. 2000. Organizational routines as a source of continuous change. *Organization Science*, 11: 611–29.

Feldman, M. 2004. Resources in emerging structures and processes of change. *Organization Science*, 15: 295–309.

Feldman, M., & Pentland, B. 2003. Reconceptualizing organizational routines and a source of flexibility and change. *Administrative Science Quarterly*, 48: 94–118.

Gartner, B. 2001. Is there an elephant in entrepreneurship research? Blind assumptions in theory development. *Entrepreneurship Theory and Practice*, 25(4): 27–40.

Gartner, W. 1985. A conceptual framework for describing the phenomonon of new venture creation. *Academy of Management Review*, 10: 696–706.

Gartner, W. 1988. "Who is an entrepreneur" is the wrong question. *American Journal of Small Business*, 12(4): 11–32.

Gartner, W. 1993. Words lead to deeds: Towards an organizational emergence vocabulary. *Journal of Business Venturing*, 8: 231–39.

Gartner, W., & Carter, N. 2003. Entrepreneurial behavior and firm organizing processes. In Z. J. Acs & D. B. Audretsch (Eds.), *Handbook of Entrepreneurship Research* (195–221). Boston: Kluwer.

Gartner, W., Carter, N., & Reynolds, P. 2004. Business start-up activities. In W. Gartner, K. Shaver, N. Carter, & P. Reynolds (Eds.), *Handbook of Entrepreneurial Dynamics* (285–98). Thousand Oaks, CA: SAGE Publications.

Gartner, W., Shaver, K., Carter, N., & Reynolds, P. (Eds.). 2004. *Handbook of Entrepreneurial Dynamics*. Thousand Oaks, CA: SAGE Publications.

Garud, R., Hardy, C., & Maguire, S. 2004. Special Issue on "Institutional Entrepreneurship". *Organization Studies*, 25: 1471–73.

Garud, R., Jain, S., & Kumaraswamy, A. 2002. Institutional entrepreneurship in the sponsorship of comon technological standards: The case of Sun Microsystems and Java. *Academy of Management Journal*, 45: 196–214.

Garud, R., & Karnoe, P. 2001. *Path Dependence and Creation*. Mahwah, NJ: Lawrence Erlbaum & Associates.

Garud, R., Kumaraswamy, A., & Sambamurthy, V. 2006. Emergent by design: Performance and transformation at Infosys Technologies. *Organization Science*, 17: 277–86.

Gioia, D., Schultz, M., & Corley, K. 2000. Organizational identity, image, and adaptive instability. *Academy of Management Review*, 25: 63–81.

Gioia, D., & Thomas, J. 1996. Institutional identity, image, and issue interpretation: Sense-making during strategic change in academia. *Administrative Science Quarterly*, 41: 370–403.

Goldstein, J. 2011. Probing the nature of complex systems: Parameters, modeling, interventions—part 1. *Emergence: Complexity and Organization*, 13(3): 94–121.

Goldstein, J., Hazy, J., & Lichtenstein, B. 2010. *Complexity and the Nexus of Leadership: Leveraging Nonlinear Science to Create Ecologies of Innovation* New York: Palgrave Macmillan.

Guastello, S. 1987. A butterfuly catastrophe model of motivation in organizations. *Journal of Applied Psychology*, 72: 165–82.

Guastello, S. 1995. *Chaos, Catastrophe, and Human Affairs: Applications of Nonlinear Dynamics to Work, Organizations, and Social Evolution.* Mahway, NJ: Lawrence Erlbaum and Associates.

Guastello, S. 1998. Self-organization and leadership emergence. *Nonlinear Dynamics, Psychology, and Life Sciences*, 2: 301–15.

Guastello, S. 2001. Nonlinear dynamics in psychology. *Discrete Dynamics in Nature and Society*, 6: 11–29.

Gunderson, L., & Holling, C. S. (Eds.). 2001. *Panarchy: Understanding Transformations in Human and Natural Systems.* Washington, DC: Island Press.

Juarrero, A. 1999. *Dynamics in Action: Intentional Behavior as a Complex System.* Cambridge, MA: MIT Press.

Katz, J., & Gartner, W. 1988. Properties of emerging organizations. *Academy of Management Review*, 13: 429–41.

Lawrence, T., Hardy, C., & Phillips, N. 2002. Institutional effects of interorganizational collaboration: The emergence of proto-institutions. *Academy of Management Journal*, 45: 281–90.

Lawrence, T., Winn, M., & Jennings, P. D. 2001. The temporal dynamics of institutionalization. *Academy of Management Review*, 26: 624–44.

Levie, J., & Lichtenstein, B. 2010. A terminal assessment of stages theory: Introducing a dynamic states approach to entrepreneurship. *Entrepreneurship Theory and Practice*, 34(2–March): 314–54.

Lichtenstein, B. 2000. Self-organized transitions: A pattern amid the "chaos" of transformative change. *Academy of Management Executive*, 14(4): 128–41.

Lichtenstein, B. 2011. Complexity science contributions to the field of entrepreneurship. In P. Allen, S. Maguire, & B. McKelvey (Eds.), *The SAGE Handbook of Complexity and Management* (471–93). Thousand Oaks, CA: SAGE Publications.

Lichtenstein, B., Carter, N., Dooley, K., & Gartner, W. 2007. Complexity dynamics of nascent entrepreneurship. *Journal of Business Venturing*, 22: 236–61.

Lichtenstein, B., Dooley, K., & Lumpkin, T. 2006. Measuring emergence in the dynamics of new venture creation. *Journal of Business Venturing*, 21: 153–75.

Lichtenstein, B., & Jones, C. 2004. A self-organization theory of radical entrepreneurship. *Best Papers Proceedings, National Academy of Management*: OMT Division; CD format.

Lichtenstein, B., & Kurjanowicz, B. 2010. Tangibility, momentum, and the emergence of The Republic of Tea. *ENTER Journal*, 1: 125–48.

Lichtenstein, B., & Plowman, D. A. 2009. The leadership of emergence: A complex systems leadership theory of emergence at successive organizational levels. *The Leadership Quarterly*, 20: 617–30.

Lindsay, R. 1961. *Physical Mechanics.* Princeton, NJ: Van Nostrand.

MacIntosh, R., & MacLean, D. 1999. Conditioned emergence: A dissipative structures approach to transformation. *Strategic Management Journal*, 20: 297–316.

Maguire, S., Hardy, C., & Lawrence, T. 2004. Institutional entrepreneurship in emerging fields: HIV/AIDS treatment advocacy in Canada. *Academy of Management Journal*, 47: 657–80.

McGrath, R. 1999. Falling forward: Real options reasoning and entrepreneurial failure. *Academy of Management Review*, 24: 13–31.

Meadows, D. 1982. Whole earth models and systems. *Coevolution Quarterly*, Summer: 98–108.

Mintzberg, H. 1978. Patterns in strategy formation. *Management Science*, 29: 934–48.

Mintzberg, H., & Waters, J. 1982. Tracking strategy capacity decisions: The use of a hierarchical production-planning system. *Academy of Management Review*, 25: 465–99.

Mullins, J., & Komisar, R. 2009. *Getting to Plan B: Breaking Through to a Better Business Model*. Boston, MA: Harvard Business Review Press.

Nicholls-Nixon, C. 2005. Rapid growth and high performance: The entrepreneur's "impossible dream?" *Academy of Management Executive*, 19(1): 77–89.

Nonaka, I. 1988. Creating organizational order out of chaos: Self-renewal in Japanese firms. *California Management Review*, 30(Spring): 57–73.

Plowman, D. A., Baker, L., Beck, T., Kulkarni, M., Solansky, S., & Travis, D. 2007. Radical change accidentally: The emergence and amplification of small change. *Academy of Management Journal*, 50: 515–43.

Purdy, J., & Gray, B. 2009. Conflicting logics, mechanisms of diffusion, and multi-level dynamics of emergence in institutional fields. *Academy of Management Journal*, 52: 355–80.

Reynolds, P., Carter, N., Gartner, W., Greene, P., & Cox, L. 2002. The entrepreneur next door: Characteristics of individuals starting companies in America. 54: Kauffman Foundation.

Reynolds, P., & Miller, B. 1992. New firm gestation: Conception, birth, and implications for research. *Journal of Business Venturing*, 7: 405–71.

Sarasvathy, S. 2001. Causation and effectuation: Toward a theoretical shift from economic inevitability to entrepreneurial contingency. *Academy of Management Review*, 26: 243–63.

Smith, C. 1986. Transformation and regeneration in social systems: A dissipative structure perspective. *Systems Research*, 3: 203–13.

Smith, C., & Comer, D. 1994. Change in the small group: A dissipative structure perspective. *Human Relations*, 47: 553–81.

Smith, C., & Gemmill, G. 1991. Self-organization in small groups: A study of group effectivenss within non-equilibrium conditions. *Human Relations*, 44: 697–716.

Smith, L., & Thelen, E. 2003. Development as a dynamic system. *Trends in Cognitive Science*, 7(8): 343–48.

Sonenshein, S. 2009. Emergence of ethical issues during strategic change implementation. *Organization Science*, 20: 223–39.

Stam, E., Audretsch, D., & Meijaard, J. 2008. Re-nascent entrepreneurship. *Journal of Evolutionary Economics*, 18(3/4): 493–507.

Storm, G. 2012. *Intention, economic opportunity and their impact on venture creation*. Ph.D. Dissertation, University of Nebraska.

Swenson, R. 1998. Thermodynamics, evolution, and behavior. In G. Greenberg & M. Haraway (Eds.), *Encyclopedia of Comparative Psychology* (207–18). New York: Garland Publishers.

Tan, J. 2007. Phase transitions and emergence of entrepreneurship: The transformation of Chinese SOEs over time. *Journal of Business Venturing*, 22: 77–96.

Thelan, E., & Smith, L. 1995. *A Dynamic Systems Approach to the Development of Cognition and Action*. Cambridge, MA: Bradford/MIT Press.

Thelen, E. 1995. Motor development: A new synthesis. *American Psychologist*, 50(2).

Van de Ven, A., Angel, H., & Poole, M. S. 1989. *Research on the Management of Innovation.* New York: Ballanger Books.

Van de Ven, A., & Polley, D. 1992. Learning while innovating. *Organization Science,* 3: 91–116.

Van de Ven, A., & Poole, M. S. 1990. Methods for studying innovation development in the Minnesota Innovation Research Program. *Organization Science,* 1: 313–35.

Van de Ven, A., & Poole, M. S. 1995. Explaining development and change in organizations. *Academy of Management Review,* 20: 510–540.

Van de Ven, A., Pooley, D., Garud, R., & Venkataramen, S. 1999. *The Innovation Journey.* New York: Oxford University Press.

Weiss, N. 1987. *Dynamics of convection.* Paper presented at the Dynamical Chaos: Proceedings of the Royal Society of London.

Whetten, D. 1989. What constitutes a theoretical contribution? *Academy of Management Review,* 14: 490–95.

CHAPTER 18

Enacting Emergence

This final chapter proposes a kind of emergence praxis—an exploration into how emergence might be intentionally pursued or enacted. I attempt this in three ways. First, I summarize research on leadership behaviors that can set the conditions for emergence. Second, I propose a way to enact an entire cycle of emergence, by instigating each of the five phases of generative emergence. Third, I hypothesize how generative emergence can be applied to social change.

ENACTING THE CONDITIONS FOR EMERGENCE

One of the areas in organization science that has received the most attention from emergence scholars is the field of leadership, through studies that have explored "complex systems leadership theory" (Hazy, Goldstein, & Lichtenstein, 2007) and "complexity leadership" (Uhl-Bien & Marion, 2008). Here and elsewhere, a community of complexity management scholars have pursued theoretical, methodological, and empirical applications of complexity to the art and practice of leadership (including Marion & Uhl-Bien, 2001; Buckle-Hennings & Dugan, 2007; Goldstein. 2007; Lichtenstein, 2007; Lichtenstein, Uhl-Bien, et al., 2007; McKelvey, 2007; McKelvey & Lichtenstein, 2007; Osborn & Hunt, 2007; Surie & Hazy, 2007; Uhl-Bien, Marion, & McKelvey, 2007; Goldstein, Hazy, & Lichtenstein, 2010).

At the core of this work is the way that managers and leaders can create the conditions for emergent ideas and action to occur. A theoretically rich framework has been developed by Uhl-Bien et al. (2007), who identify three general categories of action that are necessary for effective change: administrative leadership, adaptive leadership, and enabling leadership. Their analysis suggests several specific qualities that leaders can encourage as part of adaptive leadership for emergence, including interaction across networks, interdependencies across groups, and fostering creative tension. In concert with managing the interface between adaptive and administrative structures, leaders can help support innovation and positive change throughout their organizations (Uhl-Bien et al., 2007).

A parallel approach is to identify specific behaviors that are correlated with emergence. This was the approach taken throughout the study by Goldstein et al. (2010), which drew on a host of cases and research on creating "ecologies of innovation." Complementary to these studies is the analysis Plowman and I pursued (Lichtenstein & Plowman, 2009), which re-examined three major studies of emergence, to see how emergence was enacted by entrepreneurs and executives themselves. We correlated these leadership behaviors to the five phases, to identify nine leadership behaviors for enacting the conditions of emergence. What follows is a brief summary of these behaviors for "generative leadership" (Goldstein et al., 2010), focusing on the cases from which they are drawn: Mission Church (Plowman, Baker, et al., 2007), entrepreneurs in Branson, MO (Chiles, Meyer, & Hench, 2004), and the founders of the four fast-growth ventures (Lichtenstein, 2000a, 2000b). The overarching claim is that enacting these behaviors will facilitate the expression of the five phases and thus can lead to generative emergence. Those links will be made within each write-up and in the model that follows.

GENERATIVE LEADERSHIP—BEHAVIORS FOR PRODUCING EMERGENCE

1. Disrupt Existing Patterns

Perhaps the fastest way to initiate disequilibrium organizing is to pursue a shift in the way things have been done in the system (organization). Certainly this is true for entrepreneurship that remakes a core aspect of the industry, technology, or business model (Schumpeter, 1934; Christensen, 1997; Ireland, Hitt, & Simon, 2003). This energy of breaking down old patterns and beliefs was at the center of the re-emergence at Mission Church (Plowman, Baker, et al., 2007; Plowman, Solansky, et al., 2007), which at one time was one of the largest congregations in the entire metro region. With the rapid decline in membership and unsuccessful turnaround efforts, something in these core beliefs and identity seemed ready to change. This was accomplished by the new co-pastors, who pursued "controversial actions" that up-ended the "silk-and-stockings" heritage of the church. For example, the pastors distributed a book to church members describing the characteristics of "unhealthy" churches; the authors encouraged members to "address the cause of their sickness." Open discussions of the book increased uncertainty and created discomfort among parishioners. According to a staff member, "The (leaders) turned this world upside down, in a good way" (Plowman, Solansky, et. al., 2007, p. 349).

A component of this disruption is the introduction of uncertainty into the system. Similar disruptions in existing patterns were evident in the high-potential new ventures I studied. For example, the opportunity identified by DevelopNet's founder required them to use their proprietary software in an unproven way, for an uncertain market, in the just-emerging Internet; each of these increased uncertainty about the venture. At the same time, the entrepreneur believed the system would transform the IT side of one entire industry, leading to a projected revenue increase of more than 4000%.

2. Encourage Experiments and Fluctuations

As mentioned in the previous chapter, experiments were central to the emergence of Branson, MO. Examples included the first pioneering theaters there, and the first entrepreneurial tourist attraction in the area in the 1960s. Then, in 1983, Roy Clark cofounded the town's first celebrity theater. More than a popular nightspot, Clark's theater acted as a kind of "incubator," encouraging performers from Nashville and elsewhere to experiment with their own theaters along the Branson Mall. One of these experiments was Clark's invitation to his friend and pop music icon, Andy Williams. This resulted in Williams' decision to relocate to Branson, MO, a move that "transformed Branson . . . into a nationally known, mainstream tourist destination" (Chiles et al 2004, p. 509).

At the core of the re-emergence at Mission Church was a seemingly innocuous experiment by a loosely affiliated group of young adults: to serve breakfast to the homeless people who lived in the downtown neighborhood. The pastors, who had little involvement in it, O.K.'d this "unorthodox" idea. Within a few weeks, "Café Corazon" was serving over 200 breakfasts a week and the initiative became the seed for greater and greater emergence at the church over the next 5+ years. The seed itself grew through a series of experiments: six months into the effort a volunteer physician spontaneously started free medical check-ups, and then recruited other doctors and services, eventually opening a medical clinic that served up to a thousand homeless people each year. Further experiments with funding and alternative programs continued to occur, resulting in unanticipated income and programs to be funded. Here again, encouraging these experiments is a key catalyst to emergence.

3. Surface Conflict and Create Controversy

This direction at Mission Church was actively pursued by the new co-pastors, who created constructive conflict by welcoming homosexuals, inviting controversial speakers, and, perhaps most symbolically, unlocking the front doors during the week, making the church accessible to the public for the first time in its history. Moreover, as the first changes at the church intensified, the pastors used public media to surface and draw attention to the issues that were redefining the church. For example, at a business community network breakfast that was scheduled to discuss the homelessness problem, one of the pastors unexpectedly arrived with twelve showered homeless people, some of the best known "customers" of Café Corazon, the emergent project that was the seed to the transformation at the church. This surprising move generated a series of newspaper articles and other press that amplified the issue of its marginalized citizens in the city government and beyond. As a result, these actions further destabilized the organization.

Surfacing conflict can often create more challenges, as it did during a key period at ApplySci (Lichtenstein, 2000b). In order to take the last steps to finally commercialize their unique technology, a group of lab scientists and managers agreed to finally analyze a vexing and remaining obstacle to full-scale commercial production. Within a few weeks of that directive, the technicians revealed the first negative results: scaled-up samples were continuously nonuniform and ineffective in ways that none of the eight researchers on the project could explain. The lab group then increased its attention on the situation, surfacing the controversy, discussing it openly throughout the organization. As a result, some of the scientific assumptions underlying the technology had to be updated, limiting key commercial options. In light of their urgent push to secure revenue through a commercialization process, this "conflict" pushed the entire venture further into disequilibrium.

4. Support Rich Interactions Through a Culture of "Relational Space"

In complex adaptive systems, reciprocal interactions between agents lead to results that are amplified and thus are impossible to predict. Plowman, Solansky, et al. (2007) described this as "nonlinear interactions"—rich and meaningful exchanges that lead to unexpected and mutually supportive outcomes. Sensing the importance of this context for their turnaround efforts, the co-pastors at Mission Church initiated and facilitated many small groups within the congregation, bringing people together around shared interests, values, or life circumstances. Many of these groups started to meet weekly; over time, the church was sponsoring reading groups, sports activities, dance classes, and a whole host of activities that brought members together and fostered conversations. In this way, the leaders used low-key events and programs to develop rich and meaningful connections among members throughout the organization. This generated a kind of "relational space" in which people got to know each other quite well in small groups (Bradbury, Lichtenstein, Carroll, & Senge, 2010). *Relational space* refers to a certain high quality of interactions, reflecting a shared context of mutual respect, trust, and psychological safety in the relationship (Bradbury & Lichtenstein, 2000; see also Edmondson, 1999; Baer & Frese, 2003). As predicted by complexity theory and by managerial psychology, these rich interactions strengthened interpersonal networks, which helped amplify the changes as they emerged.

Such rich interactions were also key to the re-emergence of ServiceCo. After deciding to disband their second project, they decided to not use layoffs and to instead find ways to incorporate the 20 employees into the core business. Their strategy was to identify any underutilized intellectual capital across the company, in order to amplify the possibilities for change. They accomplished this through unprecedented, and rich, interactions with every employee over nearly six weeks. The founding team spent up to two hours with every one of the members and managers in the firm (40+ people), engaging in-depth conversations about the possible future of the company and how each member could best contribute. These unique connections revealed competencies that had been hidden among the staff, leading to more novelty that helped support and amplify the changes at ServiceCo (Lichtenstein, 2000b).

5. Catalyze Collective Action

Collective action, the next aspect of generative leadership, played a significant role in the emergences at Branson, MO, primarily through a number of influential organizational collectives around the region. By the 1920s, two such collectives were already helping draw tourists to the Ozarks by promoting the "Land of A Million Smiles." Increasing tourism was one of the critical resources that fueled Branson's astounding growth. Moreover, Branson's first theater started as a collective organization, back in 1955. In more recent years the Ozark Marketing Council has attracted increasing waves of tourists to the area, "channeling and accelerating" the resources necessary for emergence. Even more broadly, the collective organizing of entrepreneurs, financers, and community leaders created a context for the ongoing transformations of the region (Chiles et al., 2004).

Collective action was also at the core of emergence at Mission Church. Although certain aspects of Café Corezon could be ascribed to specific individuals, it was the collective behaviors that were most influential. For example, after accomplishing their goal of putting on one breakfast for 70 homeless "customers" in the neighborhood, the informal group gained a sense of collective action, deciding to continue the event weekly. Moreover, they decided to self-fund the effort, an expression of their collective interest and commitment.

6. Create Correlation Through Language and Symbols

An intriguing leadership behavior for emergence entails the facilitation of "correlation" across the system, reflecting a common or shared understanding (Marion & Uhl-Bien, 2001). Generative leadership suggests this can be generated by specific and repeated language that helps give meaning to unfolding events, or through symbols that foster the development of a shared understanding (Plowman, Solansky, et al., 2007). Examples of this type of "conscious sensegiving" occurred at Mission Church. Soon after the emergence of the Sunday morning breakfasts the pastors began developing a new ministry of the marginalized, through Sunday sermons that focused on the many biblical examples of helping marginalized citizens. The co-pastors also initiated the creation of a new mission statement for the church, which gave more meaning to the outreach efforts, the mission describing the church as a place of "unconditional love and justice in action." In the process, the co-pastors' started using terms like *dignity, respect, justice,* and *love* in their everyday interactions with congregants, thus helping to shift members' collective cognitive scripts and accepted norms toward the marginalized people they were now serving.

Other highly symbolic actions further catalyzed the emergence at Mission Church; only a few of them are presented here, but see Plowman, Baker, et al., (2007). One was the pastor's arrest, which ensued after interfering with police who were attempting to arrest one of the clients of the church's homeless shelter. Another involved the congregation's decision to remove the chapel's nameplate, honoring a long-time leader from a century before who was a well-known KKK member. They melted the nameplate and then turned it into a communion chalice, which they presented to their sister church, an African-American congregation in town. Symbolic actions like these, and the stories that come from them, helped distinguish and legitimize the change inside and beyond the church.

7. Recombine Resources

Leaders' ability to recombine resources or capabilities provide important benefits to emerging entities. The examples in Chiles et al. (2004, p. 513) are worth repeating, for the unique recombinations of space, capital, and other key resources were a driving force for emergence of the Branson theater cluster:

> The recombination involved in trading up to bigger, better facilities allowed theater entrepreneurs to better satisfy their patrons with an experience that was new and improved, and it freed physical capital that was recycled, refurbished, and recombined with the human and reputational capital provided by [the next] headliner [to utilize that theater], and so on in a continuous process of system-wide innovation.

Like organizations designed to reconfigure themselves (Garud, Kumaraswamy, & Sambamurthy, 2006), recombination and emergence were embedded into the mental models of Branson entrepreneurs, who incorporated possible reconfigurations right into their initial building designs.

Another example occurred at Mission Church. When Café Corazon became too large for the existing building to handle, the organizers requested the use of a large but closed and dilapidated wing of the church. The church agreed, instigating a reorganization that allowed them to extend the ministry beyond Sunday mornings. The recombination led to a homeless shelter that was open every day, with space for more clinics, a large area for clothes give-aways, and the incorporation of showers and other facilities for the marginalized neighbors.

8. Leaders as Role Models Who Accept "Tags"

Marion and Uhl-Bien (2001) argue that leaders who enable emergence do so by becoming catalysts for actions, and by assuming the role of "tags" (Holland, 1995)—an identifier for a valued set of behaviors. For example, although the co-pastors at Mission Church did not initiate or help organize the seed idea of Café Corizon, they themselves became "tags" for the project by being the ones to focus the attention of the entire church community around the issues of homelessness. Later, one of the pastors decided to pursue these efforts more directly, and according to local accounts he eventually became recognized as the community's spokesman for the city's homeless. His willingness to be tagged as a role model in this effort helped give energy and direction to the recombination, supporting in the emergence of the project as the new core of the church.

Such behaviors also occurred in the other studies. For example, Roy Clark and later Andy Williams made efforts to model behavior, using their status in ways that would benefit the entire region. In particular, Clark hand-picked individuals he thought would benefit from and be a benefit to the region (Chiles et al 2004, p. 511):

> "By booking stars for limited engagements and continually rotating them, Clark's theater . . . introduced them to Branson's possibilities, encouraging many to set up local theaters"—a driver of the "Country Music Explosion."

9. Leverage Local Constraints

Chiles and his colleagues (2004) described the behavior of "Bransonizing" as a stabilizing effort that integrated local norms. In Bransonizing, "locals counseled newcomers on the importance of fully reflecting local cultural values in their performances and maintaining the cultural consistency that had become central to Branson's national image" (Chiles et al., 2004, p. 512). As such a new theater could only be accepted in Branson if it enacted the shared values of "wholesome community with traditional moral fiber and friendliness."

A similar dynamic was expressed by the Mission Church leaders, who encouraged self-organization while at the same time applying constraints to its rapid growth. For example, just after the church opened a daytime shelter for the homeless, local businesses complained about homeless people standing in line in the morning at the same time that nearby hotel and bank employees were arriving at work. In response to their complaints, the pastors adjusted the hours of the homeless shelter to minimize this conflict. On the other hand, when some congregational members wanted to push the ministry toward full-scale social services, the pastors limited the growth of services into areas that they considered appropriate "ministry," thus distinguishing Mission Church from government agencies that served the poor.

10. Integrating The Conditions For Emergence

Each of these behaviors links to one of the five phases or conditions for emergence. Figure 18.1 makes these connections, and the associated claim that the more of each behavior—and the more of all the behaviors—the more likely new order will emerge in organizations and other social systems. This idea is ripe for experimentation, using an action-research methodology.

In sum, these cases provide intriguing suggestions for how leaders can encourage emergence. More examples are given in Goldstein et al. (2010) and throughout Hazy et al. (2007) and Uhl-Bien and Marion (2008).

ENACTING THE FIVE PHASES OF EMERGENCE

Up to now, all of the examples for a cycle of emergence have been descriptive, showing how entrepreneurial action can be *explained and described* through the five phases of generative emergence. Here I present a more proactive approach, suggesting how an entrepreneurial leader could *design and enact* each of the phases in order to create a new organization, project, or other social "agent." Of course, entrepreneurs do this all the time—they initiate action and pursue strategies to

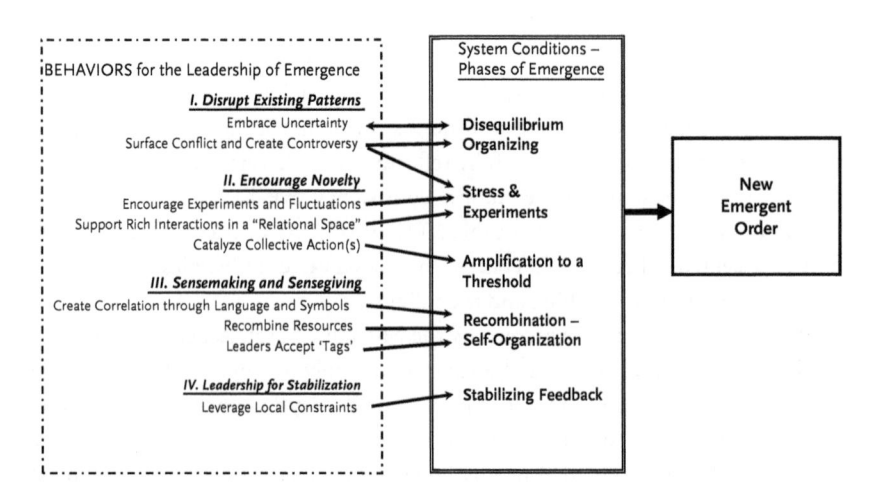

Figure 18.1: Behaviors that Co-generate the Conditions for New Emergent Order
Adopted from Lichtenstein and Plowman, (2009)

[402] *Generative Emergence*

create a new product, service, company, or event. In a similar way, what I am proposing here is that the five phases can be intentionally implemented, to generate emergence.

The inherent uncertainty, nonlinearity and lack of predictability in a cycle of emergence make this proposal risky at best. Still, the groundwork has been laid throughout the book for such a hypothesis, and it is worthy to sketch it out as a working proposition, and a guide to future research. To allow for the largest scope of generative emergence I will use entrepreneurship in the broadest terms, incorporating the literatures of strategic entrepreneurship and entrepreneurial orientation, in addition to applying the proposal to entrepreneurs.

Preparation: Assess the Social Ecology and Current Dynamic State

Emergence always occurs in reference to a "social ecology:" the communities and networks, resources and information, and institutional issues that inform and condition any organizing effort. As professionals we operate within a social ecology, made up of our colleagues, collective knowledge and skills we have gained; it also includes our neighborhood, city, economy, market structures, and physical and global environment. So to begin the creation of a social entity, one would put a renewed awareness on their social ecology. The more points of connection one can make at this phase, the more these can be leveraged within the organizational creation process.

Out of this social ecology, each individual has "constructed" (enacted) a kind of macro-dynamic state—the total personal ecology he or she actively maintains. In the language of organizing models (Chapter 8), individuals sustain themselves and their family through a composite of dynamic states. These include one's profession (revenue stream), which supports a set of living circumstances and activities that nourish oneself and one's family. In a tangible sense, one's personal dynamic state uses time—hours per week, as the key metric. At an individual level, then, an individual's current dynamic can be measured by the number of hours one places attention on each of the important aspects of one's life.[1]

For entrepreneurs, social innovators and all management professionals, assessing the current dynamic state is important for several reasons. Most "agentic" views of entrepreneurship show that the immediate environment often provides all that's necessary for the venture, so a close understanding of the current situation can provide insight into what might be a viable innovation in the ecology.[2] Further, since generative emergence culminates with a recombination of elements, taking time to consider a variety of options as the business ramps up can allow for more creative possibilities in their reorganization, sparking integrations that might further leverage resources. Finally, a competent assessment will likely turn up potential collaborators and colleagues to partner with in mutually supportive ways.

Phase 1: Initiate Disequilibrium Organizing

Generate Opportunity Tension

Ultimately the key to generative emergence is opportunity tension—a viable business opportunity matched by a passion, an internal motivation to enact it. Both elements of "opportunity tension" are crucial; economic potential and creative tension are interdependent.

First, the opportunity must be convincing enough that the entrepreneur and key stakeholders will commit themselves to the endeavor. "Convincing" in this sense means that the entrepreneur believes and has evidence that his or her value proposition is indeed valuable—valuable enough that its customers (any group of people being served) will purchase and use it. Further, there must be enough people with that need or desire, to make the entire endeavor worthwhile.[3] In formal terms, the founder or organizer needs to understand the market well enough to know that the product or service will satisfy a need, solve a problem, create delight in customers. That perception of opportunity has to link with a motivation to pursue it, to make the potentiality real.

Of course, no entrepreneur will know that their offering will be readily taken up—there is always a "leap of faith" in new venture creation (Kawasaki, 2004). Equally, there are no purely objective opportunities that can be captured with no risk. Every new venture has uncertainty and ambiguity that is resolved only through the action and skill of the entrepreneur. For example, in one study, a single technology (3D printing) was capitalized on in a disparate number of ways, emphasizing the inherent ambiguity in "opportunities" (Shane, 2000). Recent insights into entrepreneurial action show that opportunities unfold and become more clear through the process of experimentation and learning, such that the opportunity is co-created by the passion to enact it (Sarasvathy, 2001; Sarasvathy & Dew, 2005).

For all these reasons, it is impossible to know whether a particular opportunity tension will be strong enough or viable enough to generate an emergence. At the same time, a lack of clarity in the opportunity can perhaps be balanced by an extraordinarily strong passion to make something happen; high creative tension may partially substitute for a potential market. This balance is especially true in "necessity entrepreneurship," which is fully driven by the simple need to survive economically. On the other end of the spectrum, passion and motivation are especially necessary in some new-to-the-world innovations, whose feasibility cannot be discerned because they literally create an entire product-market. A good example is FedEx, which promised a service that no one believed was needed—until it was delivered, and then the market for next-day shipping exploded. Overall, anyone who wants to create a new endeavor has to begin with a very healthy dose of both: opportunity and creative tension.

Pursue Organizing that Creates Disequilibrium

As described in Chapters 6 and 7, an infusion of heat energy initiates the process of emergence in a dissipative structure. So too in the social sense: an infusion of "organizing energy" is what drives generative emergence. A major infusion of energy is the natural result of a strong opportunity tension, for the perception of possibility (profitability) and the passion to create it are *expressed in action*—tangible activities aimed at converting the potentiality into reality. In formal terms, organizing activities are the things an entrepreneur does to turn their nascent idea into a started venture (Gartner, 1993; Gartner & Carter, 2003; Gartner, Carter, & Reynolds, 2004; Lichtenstein, Dooley, & Lumpkin, 2006; Lichtenstein, Carter, Dooley, & Gartner, 2007).

Earlier, "disequilibrium organizing" was defined as pushing the system beyond its norm, outside its usual boundaries of activity. This idea is especially helpful in practice, as a guide for the kinds of actions that can lead to disequilibrium. For example, disequilibrium can be initiated by disrupting the normal functioning of a project group, a department, or an organization, as has been shown by Goldstein (1988, 1994; also Goldstein et al., 2010, p. 83). In fact, this is precisely how Anderson (1999, p. 222) described how entrepreneurial managers initiate innovation:

> Those with influence and/or authority turn the heat up [in] an organization by recruiting new sources of energy (e.g., members, suppliers, partners, and customers), by motivating stakeholders, by shaking up the organization, and by providing new sets of challenges that cannot be mastered by hewing to existing procedures.

In both cases, whether an entrepreneur enacts an opportunity through focused organizing activities or a manager creates disequilibrium by shaking up the current order of things, the system is pushed outside of its normal zone of operation, what might be called "outside the comfort zone" of the organization. This state of energy and imbalance, if it continues and increases, sets the stage for the shifts to come.

Phase 2: Stress and Experiments

Allow for Stress and Welcome Uncertainty

Anyone who has been involved in a start-up knows that the process is almost unbearably intense—frantic with urgency, filled with long hours, pushing forward even with the uncertainty and stress. These challenges are uncomfortable; they derive from the system as a whole, as it moves away from the norm and outside predictable patterns of behavior. In a truly entrepreneurial effort, the founder or organizer is asking other people and organizations to produce new behavior, take on a new mindset, and bring together resources in unusual ways. These new combinations may question long-held assumptions or require new skills or interdependencies that are challenging to produce. All of this leads to internal stress and even anxiety, which increase as the organizing effort grow more intense.

Just as individuals feel challenged in new and ambiguous situations, so too organizations in disequilibrium often experience a breakdown of expected patterns of interaction, leaving uncertainty and confusion in their place. Although this breakdown is the necessary precursor to opening new possibilities for action, it goes against directives to maintain the current dynamic state, as well as the innate organizational goal to remain intact with a stable identity (Pantzar & Csanyi, 1991; Drazin & Sandelands, 1992; Padgett, 2011). Thus, breaking apart these bonds of structure and inertia results in stress and discomfort for the individuals involved. All that is to say that stress should not by any means be avoided; it should even be welcomed because it signifies the successful movement toward disequilibrium, toward the direction of emergence. As Goldstein et al. (2010, p. 84) suggest,

> In response to all this uncertainty, an unfortunate but common knee-jerk reaction on the part of management is to run around trying to dampen experimental deviations—but this is generally a mistake.... The key to generative leadership is to live with—and even embrace—the discomfort of disequilibrium, encouraging experiments and amplifying successes in whatever form they may come.

Produce Experiments

At its heart, taking entrepreneurial action should mean developing a kind of internal experiment production system. In the face of disequilibrium, stress, and intensity, a generative leader tries new things again and again, countering uncertainty with possibility, meeting ambiguity with innovation. These experiments can be small or large, they can be directed at the immediate system or pursued throughout the ecology. Each one is a trial, a hypothesis that is examined in real time. If it works it is kept, if not, no harm lost. An experiment can be an innovation, a solution, a procedure—any tangible move that has the potential to shift the system into a new regime of order.

As the entrepreneurial stories have suggested, experiments can come from many different sources. Sometimes the entrepreneurs make a suggestion for a strategy that works; sometimes another member of the founding team tries something unexpected that improves the current situation. In other cases the idea can come from one of the line personnel, or from a customer or supplier. A successful organizer is not concerned with the origin of the move but with the outcome; she or he will highlight as many experiments as possible with the hope that more and more will stick. Ultimately, one of these will become the seed for a new dynamic state, the foundation for an emergent. Following up experiments from wherever they come increases momentum, leading to the next phase in the process.

Phase 3: Amplification to a Critical Threshold

According to the sciences of dissipative structures, autopoiesis, and complex adaptive systems, the only way to generate emergence is to push the system beyond its linear realm, into a nonlinear state where multiple streams of emergence can manifest. In practice this occurs when the organizing process gains momentum, where individual actions become linked into interdependent chains, and serendipitous connections are more and more common. The aim is to let the energy build, growing in intensity while continuing to produce experiments, with a focus on increased momentum and drive.

One marker for amplification is when outcomes become nonproportional to their inputs, that is, when a certain amount of effort does not produce an equivalent result. This can occur in both directions: when a system becomes nonlinear, "a great deal of effort may yield no change whatsoever while in some instances . . . a small input can become amplified within its container into a major system-wide emergence" (Goldstein et al., 2010, p. 84). In many was this shift in a dynamic state into nonlinearity is rather noticeable. In response, the key to success is to encourage this direction of reinforcing behaviors, even though it goes against every expectation of management, which in contrast strives for predictability and control.

At what point will the system shift into a new regime? Can such a moment be predicted, or planned? According to the cases presented up until now, the answer is no. However, *in retrospect* each entrepreneur knew that a specific meeting or decision point was critical to the long-term shaping of the venture. In each case, the critical decision initiated a major shift, a cascade of actions that had been being held back until the right moment. These choices, if they are organized into a short period of time, can impact the entire system, shifting it into a new regime. At the same time, they may point to the collapse of the effort, the end of the organizing process, or its transmutation into an entirely different state.

Note that the lack of predictability of when or how the critical event will ensue is a unique quality of any management theory. Since theory implies strict predictability, having a core quality of unpredictability presents an alternative approach to theorizing and enactment.[4]

Phase 4: New Order through Recombination

Iterate Emergence

In this linear description of a cycle of emergence, it appears that no new order emerges until the entire system shifts. In fact, this punctuated notion of order creation has been confirmed in a number of studies, including the four ventures in my study (Lichtenstein, 2000a, 2000b), as well as with the entrepreneur at HealthInfo that we tracked (Lichtenstein et al., 2006), and in other studies (Leifer, 1989; Romanelli & Tushman, 1994; Weick & Quinn, 1999; Chiles et al., 2004).

However, these studies don't argue that order is created all at once. There is an iterative nature of emergence—amidst the disequilibrium, stress, and experiments there arise new structures and innovations that, over time, shift the entire system into a new regime (Nonaka, 1988; Browning, Beyer, & Shetler, 1995; MacIntosh & MacLean, 1999; Plowman, Baker, et al., 2007). Thus, entrepreneurs identify and encourage as much new order as they can.

Drawing on the underlying science, any seed of "radical emergence" first becomes established in a local, limited regime within which it makes a clear improvement of some kind. If so, it can be extended into further regions, until it reaches throughout the system. For this reason, generative leaders should

> expect to see a new regime of order emerge first in one particular area or activity system of the organization, then by recognizing its potential, encourage and improve on that emergent structure as it spreads and expands throughout the organization as a whole. (Goldstein et al., 2010, p. 87).

In the same way that order is created in an interactive way, order doesn't stop being created after the critical event. Since emergent order is an outcome of the nonlinear dynamics in a system, the outcome itself pushes the system further into disequilibrium, thus sparking more order creation. Such self-reinforcing processes can, over time, increase the pace of each cycle of emergence, leading to a continuous emergence, a phenomenon shown by Brown and Eisenhardt (1997); Rindova and Kotha (2001); Garud and Van de Ven (2002); and Stebbins and Braganza (2009).

Encourage Recombination

The production of new order is an active process, a construction of patterns and structures from resources that are present in the ecology, as well as some that have been accessed through the organizing effort. Recombinations are often extensions of experiments; they involve a creative leap through which the entrepreneur makes unlikely connections between people, activities, ideas, or other elements—connections that allow the system to do more. The most effective emergence takes advantage of what's already there, by reordering and reforming it at its core. In this reformulation, new qualities and potentialities come into being, by leveraging resources and ideas that already exist. Recombinations "expand the pie" in a real way for all the agents in the ecology.

Overall, the main outcome of emergence is increased capacity; the newly formed dynamic state is better designed for its tasks and goals, and it is more effective in its use of energy and resources. As this occurs, the entire emerging system becomes more connected, requiring less and less direct intervention from the founders to retain its identity. In informal terms, generative emergence happens when the system "takes on a life of its own." This internal agency results from greater capacity and is the intangible expression of new creation.

Phase 5: Stabilizing Feedback

The early moments of creation are highly sensitive, as the new patterns and order are not yet tested within the social ecology. Thus, once the entrepreneur senses an emergence of the system, her task shifts to grounding or anchoring the emergent within the system. This can be done by instituting routines and habits of mind in the participants, affirming that the new order is "real" and should be maintained. Given that the new order may defy expectations and even go against the plans or desires of key people involved, providing this legitimacy can be a challenging task.

Ultimately the test is whether the new order sustainably increases capacity throughout the system. To the degree that it does, the system itself will seek its own stability.[5] Sustainability should be the keyword in this phase; how can the entrepreneur maintain the flow of resources and energy through the system in order to sustain the value creation it provides? This is as big an issue as the creation itself—whole books could be written about this kind of sustaining drive.

A Caveat

To be clear, this entire description—the hypothesis that emergence can be enacted—highlights only the process, without explaining the content of entrepreneurship, including the many types and sources of opportunities, necessary resources, strategies, environmental conditions, and market realities. These are well covered by the literature of entrepreneurship and strategic entrepreneurship. In contrast, this process-based version is my specific contribution to understanding entrepreneurship. If the five-phase process is viable, it adds a new dimension to entrepreneurial action that is worth exploring further.

ENACTING EMERGENCE FOR SOCIAL CHANGE

Can the generative emergence process be intentionally enacted in contexts beyond the organization? In other words, can the five-phase model be used to "produce" emergence at a social level, to create movements for social change? Given the caveats above, such a proposal seems somewhat unlikely. However, there are some hints that make it worthwhile to explore the prospect.

To begin, I have already described the work of Browning et al. (1995) and Chiles et al. (2004), which shows how the macro-emergence—the creation of an industry alliance or the emergence of a thriving economic cluster—can be explained as cycles of emergence. Likewise, I showed how the emergence of a new institution (Purdy & Gray, 2009) and the emergence of a new institutional schema (Bingham & Kahl, 2013) can also be explained using the five-phase model. These are not definitive, but are suggestive that the generative emergence process may be applicable at larger scales, bearing in mind all the constraints mentioned previously.

An additional hint is provided by the complexity science field of ecological resilience, developed by Gunderson and Holling (Holling, 1973, 2001; Gunderson & Holling, 2001). Their model of an "adaptive cycle" (see Figure 18.2) has an intriguing resonance to the process of generative emergence. This may offer insight into the praxis of social emergence.

Resilience and Ecosystem Transformation

As introduced in Chapter 3, resilience is a state of highly flexible adaptation that ecosystems can move into and enjoy for long periods of time. The dimensions and qualities of resonance were initially explored by Holling (1973), who engaged others in the research through the Resilience Alliance project.[6] One of the most important findings by Holling and his colleagues is the cyclic nature of ecosystems over time; this has become understood as an adaptive cycle with four phases. The cycle has been shown to operate in many natural-human ecosystems (see Holling 2001; Folke et al. 2004; Walker, Holling, Carpenter, & Kinzig 2004; Liu et al. 2007). Gunderson and Holling (2001, p. 27) present a definition for resilience, which, they explain,

> emphasizes conditions far from any equilibrium steady state, where instabilities can flip a system into another regime of behavior—i.e., to another stability domain (Holling 1973). In this case . . . the system changes its structure by changing the variables and processes that control behavior.

Their research has revealed four phases or functions in the adaptive cycle. Following traditional views of ecosystem succession, the first two phases include "exploitation, in which rapid colonization of recently disturbed areas is emphasized; and conservation, in which slow accumulation and storage of energy and material are emphasized" (Gunderson & Holling, 2001, p. 33). An ecosystem can remain in the conservation phase for quite some time.

However, Holling and his group noted a critical underlying issue that had been missed. Specifically, because of the increasing connectivity of the ecosystem, "the tightly bound accumulation of biomass and nutrients becomes increasingly fragile (overconnected, in systems terms)" (Gunderson & Holling, 2001, p. 34).

Essentially, the connections across species and biota in the ecosystem become increasingly tight, leading to an unexpected vulnerability to change. Note the similarity to "complexity catastrophe," the point in an NK computational model when the agents are so interconnected that the entire system grinds to a halt, being unable to adapt further.

Once this happens, the adaptive cycle shows that an ecosystem will move into "creative destruction," a release of accumulated resources triggered by some event which normally would be assimilated by the system. In Gunderson and Holling words (2001, p. 45):

> In the cases of extreme and growing rigidity, all systems become accidents waiting to happen. The trigger might be entirely random and external—a transient drying spell for the forest, a new critic appointed to the board of directors of the company, an election of a new minister of government responsible for the agency. We have seen all of these in earlier case examples (Gunderson, Holling, & Light, 1995). Such events previously would cause scarcely a ripple, but now the structural vulnerability provokes crisis and transformation.... In the shift from [one phase to the next], strong destabilizing positive feedbacks develop.

What happens next is called "reorganization"—a shift that "represents a sudden explosive increase in uncertainty" (Gunderson & Holling, 2001, p. 45). In this reorganization,

> the wide latitude and flexibility allowed [for] variables and actors means that unpredictable associations can form, some of which have the possibility of nucleating a novel reorganization and renewal.... [through] totally unexpected associations and recombinations." (p. 46)

Note the similarity between the reorganization phase and our recombination phase. In both models a buildup of energy and resources reaches a critical point; then a trigger dislodges the current dynamic state, initiating a substantive shift. This shift serves to unlock the rigidities, leading the system to new possibilities for reordering and reorganization. In this phase, novel associations and combinations can be generated. At that point the process continues as it started, through a rapid exploitation of the recently disturbed environment, based on the new organization. Gunderson and Holling (2000, p. 46) note how this new order is supported by hints of feedback:

> Where chance compatibility existed, sustaining relationships then could develop among key species to form and reinforce relationships that were mutually reinforcing. A self-organized system became possible.

This entire process is visualized in Figure 18.2.

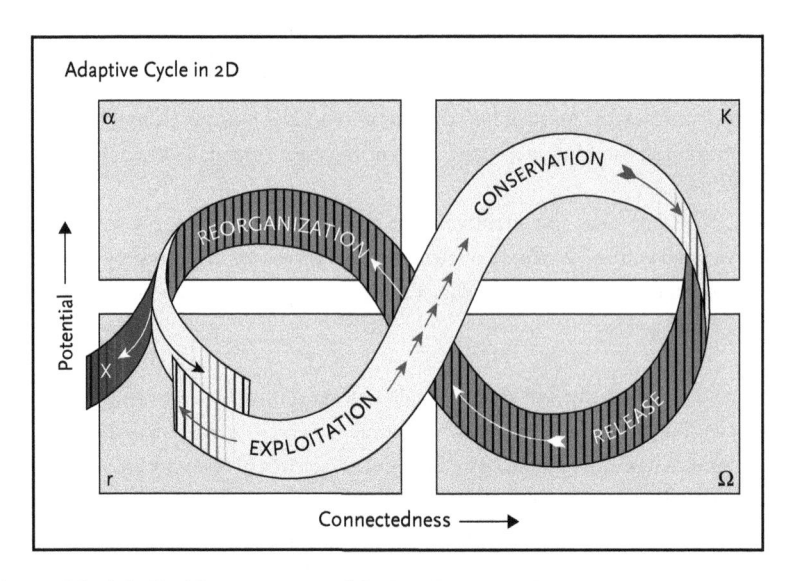

Figure 18.2: A Stylized Representation of the Four Ecosystem Functions
From Gunderson, L., & Holling, C. S. (Eds.). 2001. *Panarchy: Understanding Transformations in Human and Natural Systems* (p. 34). Washington, DC: Island Press. Reprinted with permission from Lance Gunderson and CS Holling.

Linking Resilience and Generative Emergence

The strong resonance between the four phases of resilience and the five phases of generative emergence is encouraging. The buildup of resources during ecosystem exploitation and conservation is parallel to the growth of a dynamic state, which is driven by the opportunity of the social ecosystem. However, in that dynamic state, as in many organizations and ecosystems, over time the pathways and structures that were adaptive can become increasingly rigid, revealing an implicit stress that builds in the system. Then a trigger occurs, releasing those patterns and initiating a rapid phase of reorganization. Amidst this "chaotic" shift, the available resources are recombined in new ways to take advantage of the new situation. Those innovations and new patterns which increase the capacity of the ecosystem will be selected and lead the next phase of growth—a new dynamic state.

This correspondence is somewhat surprising because the theory base for the two fields is completely different—dissipative structures versus ecological systems. Whereas dissipative structures are composed of homogeneous molecules in a container set far-from-equilibrium, ecological systems are composed of heterogeneous elements, each operating interdependently with its neighbors for survival. Yet, in both cases, when energy and resources are driven into the context for a long enough period of time, the entire system can shift, generating new order that increases the capacity and adaptability of the system.

To be clear, Gunderson and Holling (2001) are hesitant to apply their model to human organizations, even though they have dedicated attention to that goal.

"Hesitant" may be an understatement, given the following claim about the link between ecological and economic systems (pp. 55, 58):

> We start with a bias. Not that the adaptive cycle applies in all details to human organizations, but that it does not.... We have barely started this effort to rationalize such theoretical features of market economics with the adaptive cycle.... Both [attempts] encounter serious analytical problems when the natural parts of the linked economic/ecological system have nonlinearities and multistable states, and when there are interactions among nested sets of fast and slow variables. At a minimum we conclude that, in those circumstances, anticipating and creating useful surprises needs an actively adaptive approach, not a predictive, optimizing one.

With these challenges at the forefront, several analyses have explored the conditions under which an economy or ecosystem can "flip" into a new regime (Brock, Maler, & Perrings, 2001; Holling, 2001; Scheffer, Westley, Brock, & Holmgren, 2001; Carpenter & Brock, 2006). This attention on ecosystem flips has been necessary because of the empirical evidence that most ecosystem shifts are extremely negative, that is, most transformations in ecosystem functioning dramatically reduce the capacity of the ecosystem, in some cases reducing all productivity to near zero. This problem is exacerbated by hysteresis, namely that the pathway for getting the system back to positive functioning is extremely difficult, often impossible when institutional constraints are taken into account. In other words, the flip happens with a simple trigger, but reversing the process requires a much stronger force, which is not always possible to produce.

As such, the primary focus is on retaining the resilience of ecosystems and linked social-natural ecosystems. Insights into this process have improved efforts for social sustainability through the introduction of adaptive governance in local ecosystems and regions (Folke, Hahn, Olsson, & Norberg, 2005; Olsson et al., 2006; Folke et al., 2010) and through a series of propositions about sustained resilience in human and natural systems (Walker et al., 2006).

Generative Resilience?

At the same time, Gunderson and Holling's published focus does not preclude a complementary one, namely on the proactive creation of new social ecosystems. Integrating the cycle of emergence with the adaptive cycle yields an intriguing mix of dynamics, for both explore mutually beneficial states that create value for their participants (organisms and customers). In both cycles, these states may become too interconnected or rigid to adapt and thus become vulnerable to external change or entrepreneurial aspiration. A trigger, an event with nonproportional outcomes, dislodges the system; the system immediately seeks a reorganization. It does so by recombining elements into a new structure that takes advantage of new associations and opportunities. In a very general sense this new order becomes stabilized into the next adaptive cycle, starting with rapid growth and moving toward conservation again.

Of course, this is merely the sketch of an idea, hardly formalized into a proposal. But the notion is worth exploring. If economic ecosystems move through the same adaptive cycle—a claim that several of these scholars have made—then it is possible that human foresight and proactive design might be able to channel this cycle toward greater resilience and sustainability. It may be possible, working collaboratively across and within networks, to catalyze systemwide shifts and emergences. Likewise, applying these insights to sustainability may provide direction for how to increase the resilience of an economic and social system without catastrophic change. Further exploration is necessary to fill out any of these ideas.

SUMMARY

My hope is that the tools from generative emergence, and from complexity science more generally, can be brought to bear in the most important issues of our day. In the same way that resilience aims to preserve productive ecosystems and develop thriving social environments, so too the aspiration for generative emergence is to generate greater capacity—for individuals and societies—in a sustainable way. More broadly, my aspiration is that readers will be inspired by my call for a discipline of emergence, and find ways to further integrate this work in order to explore issues that are relevant to the sciences in general, and supportive of an equitable and creative society.

NOTES

1. "In daily life" means in all of the components of one's social ecology, including one's job, one's friends, one's communities—religious, school, social, athletic (yoga class, sports team), and so on.
2. Here I draw on entrepreneurial insights from the theories of effectuation (Sarasvathy, 2001), bricolage (Baker & Nelson, 2005; Garud & Karnoe, 2003), path creation (Garud, Kumaraswamy & Karnoe, 2010), and designed emergence (Garud, Kumaraswamy & Sambamurthy, 2006).
3. Of course, this is complex, since many entrepreneurs pursue ventures for non-monetary reasons; some keep up the venture for long periods of time, even when the company is losing money. In this way, and in reference to all forms of social innovation, a strict "accounting" of inputs and outcomes is not always realistic.
4. A wonderful explanation of this is presented in Matthews, White, and Long (1999).
5. This insight is at the core of autopoiesis and autogenesis, as found in Rosen (1971, 1973), Pantzar and Csanyi (1991), Drazin and Sandelands (1992), and Padgett (2011).
6. See http://www.resalliance.org/.

REFERENCES

Anderson, P. 1999. Complexity theory and organization science. *Organization Science*, 10: 216–32.

Baer, M., & Frese, M. 2003. Innovation is not enough: Climates for initiative and psychological safety, process innovations, and firm performance. *Journal of Organizational Behavior*, 24(1): 45–68.

Bingham, C., & Kahl, S. 2013. The process of schema emergence: Assimilation, deconstruction, unitization and the plurality of analogies. *Academy of Management Journal*, 56(1): 14–34.

Bradbury, H., & Lichtenstein, B. 2000. Relationality in organizational research: Exploring the "space between". *Organization Science*, 11: 551–64.

Bradbury, H., Lichtenstein, B., Carroll, J., & Senge, P. 2010. Relational space: Learning and innovation in a collaborative consortium for sustainability. *Research in Organizational Change and Development*, 18: 198–248.

Brock, W., Maler, K.-G., & Perrings, C. 2001. Resilience and sustainability: The economic anaysis of nonlinear dynamic systems. In L. Gunderson & C. S. Holling (Eds.), *Panarchy: Understanding Transformations in Human and Natural Systems* (261–92). Washington, DC: Island Press.

Brown, S., & Eisenhardt, K. 1997. The art of continuous change: Linking complexity theory and time-based evolution in relentlessly shifting organizations. *Administrative Science Quarterly*, 42: 1–34.

Browning, L., Beyer, J., & Shetler, J. 1995. Building cooperation in a competitive industry: SEMATECH and the semiconductor industry. *Academy of Management Journal*, 38: 113–51.

Buckle-Hennings, P., & Dugan, S. 2007. Leaders' detection of problematic self-organized patterns in the workplace. In J. Hazy, J. Goldstein, & B. Lichtenstein (Eds.), *Complex Systems Leadership Theory* (387–414). Mansfield, MA: ISCE Publishing.

Carpenter, S., & Brock, W. 2006. Rising variance: A leading indicator of ecological transition. *Ecology Letters*, 9(3): 311–18.

Chiles, T., Meyer, A., & Hench, T. 2004. Organizational emergence: The origin and transformation of Branson, Missouri's musical theaters. *Organization Science*, 15(5): 499–520.

Christensen, C. 1997. *The Innovator's Dilemma: When New Technologies Cause Great Firms to Fail*. Boston: Harvard Business School Press.

Drazin, R., & Sandelands, L. 1992. Autogenesis: A perspective on the process of organizing. *Organization Science*, 3: 230–49.

Edmondson, A. 1999. Psychological safety and learning behavior in work teams. *Administrative Science Quarterly*, 44: 350–83.

Folke, C., Carpenter, S., Walker, B., Scheffer, M., Chapin, T., & Rockstrom, J. 2010. Resilience thinking: Integrating resilience, adaptability and transformability. *Ecology and Society*, 15(4): 20–8.

Folke, C., Carpenter, S., Walker, B., Scheffer, M., Elmqvist, T., Gunderson, L., & Holling, C. S. 2004. Regime shifts, resilience, and biodiversity in ecosystem management. *Annual Review of Ecology, Evolution, and Systematics*, 35: 557–81.

Folke, C., Hahn, T., Olsson, P., & Norberg, J. 2005. Adaptive governance of social-ecological systems. *Annual Review of Environmental Resources*, 30: 441–73.

Gartner, W. 1993. Words lead to deeds: Towards an organizational emergence vocabulary. *Journal of Business Venturing*, 8: 231–39.

Gartner, W., & Carter, N. 2003. Entrepreneurial behavior and firm organizing processes. In Z. J. Acs & D. B. Audretsch (Eds.), *Handbook of Entrepreneurship Research* (195–221). Boston: Kluwer.

Gartner, W., Carter, N., & Reynolds, P. 2004. Business start-up activities. In W. Gartner, K. Shaver, N. Carter, & P. Reynolds (Eds.), *Handbook of Entrepreneurial Dynamics* (285–98). Thousand Oaks, CA: SAGE Publications.

Garud, R., Kumaraswamy, A., & Sambamurthy, V. 2006. Emergent by design: Performance and transformation at Infosys Technologies. *Organization Science*, 17: 277–86.

Garud, R., & Van de Ven, A. 2002. Strategic organizational change processes. In H. Pettigrew, H. Thomas, & R. Whittington (Eds.), *Handbook of Strategy and Management* (206–31). London: SAGE Publications.

Goldstein, J. 2007. A new model for emergence and its leadership implications. In J. Hazy, J. Goldstein, & B. Lichtenstein (Eds.), *Complex Systems Leadership Theory* (61–92). Mansfield, MA: ISCE Publishing.

Goldstein, J., Hazy, J., & Lichtenstein, B. 2010. *Complexity and the Nexus of Leadership: Leveraging Nonlinear Science to Create Ecologies of Innovation*. New York: Palgrave Macmillan.

Gunderson, L., & Holling, C. S. (Eds.). 2001. *Panarchy: Understanding Transformations in Human and Natural Systems*. Washington, DC: Island Press.

Gunderson, L., Holling, C. S., & Light, S. S. 1995. *Barriers and Bridges to the Renewal of Ecosystems and Institutions*. New York: Columbia University Press.

Hazy, J., Goldstein, J., & Lichtenstein, B. (Eds.). 2007. *Complex Systems Leadership Theory: New Perspectives from Complexity Science on Social and Organizational Effectiveness*. Mansfield, MA: ISCE Publishing.

Holland, J. 1995. *Hidden Order*. Redwood City, CA: Addison-Wesley.

Holling, C. S. 1973. Resilience and stability of ecological systems. *Annual Review of Ecology and Systematics*, 4: 1–23.

Holling, C. S. 2001. Understanding the complexity of economic, ecological, and social systems. *Ecosystems*, 4: 390–405.

Ireland, D., Hitt, M., & Simon, D. 2003. A model of strategic entrepreneurship: The construct and its dimensions. *Journal of Management*, 29(3): 963–89.

Kawasaki, G. 2004. *Art of the Start: The Time-Tested, Battle-Hardened Guide for Anyone Starting Anything*. New York: Penguin.

Leifer, R. 1989. Understanding organizational transformation using a dissipative structure model. *Human Relations*, 42: 899–916.

Lichtenstein, B. 2000a. Dynamics of rapid growth and change: A complexity theory of entrepreneurial transitions. In G. Liebcap (Ed.), *Advances in the Study of Entrepreneurship, Innovation, and Economic Growth*, Vol. 6: 161–92. Westport, CT: JAI Press.

Lichtenstein, B. 2000b. Self-organized transitions: A pattern amid the "chaos" of transformative change. *Academy of Management Executive*, 14(4): 128–41.

Lichtenstein, B. 2007. A matrix of complexity for leadership. In J. Hazy, J. Goldstein, & B. Lichtenstein (Eds.), *Complex Systems Leadership Theory* (285–304). Boston: ISCE Press.

Lichtenstein, B., Carter, N., Dooley, K., & Gartner, W. 2007. Complexity dynamics of nascent entrepreneurship. *Journal of Business Venturing*, 22: 236–61.

Lichtenstein, B., Dooley, K., & Lumpkin, T. 2006. Measuring emergence in the dynamics of new venture creation. *Journal of Business Venturing*, 21: 153–75.

Lichtenstein, B., & Plowman, D. A. 2009. The leadership of emergence: A complex systems leadership theory of emergence at successive organizational levels. *The Leadership Quarterly*, 20: 617–30.

Lichtenstein, B., Uhl-Bien, M., Marion, R., Seers, A., Orton, D., & Schreiber, C. 2007. Complexity leadership theory: Explaining the interactive process of leading in complex adaptive systems. *Emergence: Complexity and Organization*, 8(4): 2–12.

Liu, J., Dietz, T., Carpenter, S., Alberti, M., Folke, C., Moran, E., Pell, A. N., Deadman, P., Kratz, T., Lubchenco, J., Ostrom, E., Ouyang, Z., Provencher, W., Redman, C., Schneider, S., & Taylor, W. 2007. Complexity of coupled human and natural systems. *Science*, 317(Sept. 14): 1513–16.

MacIntosh, R., & MacLean, D. 1999. Conditioned emergence: A dissipative structures approach to transformation. *Strategic Management Journal*, 20: 297–316.

Marion, R., & Uhl-Bien, M. 2001. Leadership in complex organizations. *The Leadership Quarterly*, 12: 389–418.

McKelvey, B. 2007. Emergent strategy via complexity leadership: Using complexity science and adaptive tension to build distributed intelligence. In M. Uhl-Bien & R. Marion (Eds.), *Complexity and Leadership Volume I: Conceptual Foundations* (225–68). Charlotte, NC: Information Age Publishing.

McKelvey, B., & Lichtenstein, B. 2007. Leadership in the four stages of emergence. In J. Hazy, J. Goldstein, & B. Lichtenstein (Eds.), *Complex Systems Leadership Theory* (93–108). Boston: ISCE Publishing.

Nonaka, I. 1988. Creating organizational order out of chaos: Self-renewal in Japanese firms. *California Management Review*, 30(Spring): 57–73.

Olsson, P., Gunderson, L., Carpenter, S., Ryan, P., Lebel, L., Folke, C., & Holling, C. S. 2006. Shooting the rapids: Navigating transitions to adaptive governance of social-ecological systems. *Ecology and Society*, 11(1): Article 18.

Osborn, R., & Hunt, J. 2007. Leadership and the choice of order: Complexity and hierarchical perspectives near the edge of chaos. *Leadership Quarterly*, 18(4): 319–40.

Padgett, J. 2011. Autocatalysis in chemistry and the origin of life. In *The Emergence of Organizations and Markets* (33–70). Princeton, NJ: Princeton University Press.

Pantzar, M., & Csanyi, V. 1991. The replicative model of the evolution of the business organization. *Journal of Social and Biological Structures*, 14: 149–63.

Plowman, D. A., Baker, L., Beck, T., Kulkarni, M., Solansky, S., & Travis, D. 2007. Radical change accidentally: The emergence and amplification of small change. *Academy of Management Journal*, 50: 515–43.

Plowman, D. A., Solanksy, S., Beck, T., Baker, L., Kulkarni, M., & Travis, D. 2007. The role of leadership in emergent, self-organization. *The Leadership Quarterly*, 18(4): 341–56.

Purdy, J., & Gray, B. 2009. Conflicting logics, mechanisms of diffusion, and multi-level dynamics of emergence in institutional fields. *Academy of Management Journal*, 52: 355–80.

Rindova, V., & Kotha, S. 2001. Continuous "morphing": Competing through dynamic capabilities, form, and function. *Academy of Management Journal*, 44: 1263–80.

Romanelli, E., & Tushman, M. 1994. Organizational transformaton as punctuated equilibrium: An empirical test. *Academy of Management Journal*, 37: 1141–66.

Sarasvathy, S. 2001. Causation and effectuation: Toward a theoretical shift from economic inevitability to entrepreneurial contingency. *Academy of Management Review*, 26: 243–63.

Sarasvathy, S., & Dew, N. 2005. New market creation through transformation. *Journal of Evolutionary Economics*, 15: 533–65.

Scheffer, M., Westley, F., Brock, W., & Holmgren, M. 2001. Dynamic interaction of societies and ecosystems—Linking theories from ecology, economy, and sociology. In L. Gunderson & C. S. Holling (Eds.), *Panarchy: Understanding Transformations in Human and Natural Systems* (195–240). Washington, DC: Island Press.

Schumpeter, J. 1934. *The Theory of Economic Development*. Cambridge, MA: Harvard University Press.

Shane, S. 2000. Prior knowledge and the discovery of entrepreneurial opportunities. *Organization Science*, 11: 448–69.

Stebbins, H., & Braganza, A. 2009. Exploring continuous organizational transformation: Morphing through network interdependence. *Journal of Change Management*, 9: 27–48.

Surie, G., & Hazy, J. 2007. Generative leadership: Nuturing innovation in complex systems. In J. Hazy, J. Goldstein, & B. Lichtenstein (Eds.), *Complex Systems Leadership Theory* (349–67). Mansfield, MA: ISCE Publishing.

Uhl-Bien, M., & Marion, R. (Eds.). 2008. *Complexity Leadership. Part 1: Conceptual Foundations.* Charlotte, NC: Information Age Publishing.

Uhl-Bien, M., Marion, R., & McKelvey, B. 2007. Complexity leadership theory: Shifting leadership from the industrial age to the information era. *The Leadership Quarterly*, 18: 298–318.

Walker, B., Gunderson, L., Kinzig, A., Folke, C., Carpenter, S., & Schultz, L. 2006. A handful of hueristics and some propositions for understanding resilience in social-ecological systems. *Ecology and Society*, 11(1): 13–29.

Walker, B., Holling, C. S., Carpenter, S., & Kinzig, A. 2004. Resilience, adaptability and transformability in social-ecological systems. *Ecology and Society*, 9(2): 5.

Weick, K., & Quinn, R. 1999. Organizational change and development. *Annual Review of Psychology*, 50: 361–86.

BIBLIOGRAPHY

Abbott, A. 1988. Transcending general linear reality. *Sociological Theory*, 6(2): 169–86.
Abbott, A. 1992. From causes to events: Notes on narrative positivism. *Sociological Methods and Research*, 20: 428–55.
Abbott, A. 2001. *Time Matters*. Chicago: University of Chicago.
Adams, R. N. 1988. *The Eighth Day: Social Evolution as the Self-Organization of Energy*. Austin, TX: University of Texas.
Adizes, I. 1979. Organizational passages—Diagnosing and treating life cycle problems of organizations. *Organizational Dynamics*, 8(1): 3–25.
Adler, P., & Obstfeld, D. 2006. The role of affect in creative projects and exploratory search. *Industrial and Corporate Change*, 16: 19–50.
Afuah, A. 2004. *Business Models: A Strategic Management Approach*. Boston: McGraw Hill Irwin.
Aldrich, H. 1979. *Organizations and Environments*. Englewood Cliffs, NJ: Prentic-Hall.
Aldrich, H. 1999. *Organizations Evolving*. Newbury Park, CA: SAGE Publications.
Aldrich, H., & Fiol, M. 1994. Fools rush in? The institutional context of industry creation. *Academy of Management Review*, 14(1): 645–70.
Aldrich, H., & Kenworthy, A. 1999. The accidental entrepreneur: Campbellian antinomies and organizational foundings. In J. Baum & B. McKelvey (Eds.), *Variations in Organization Science* (19–24). Thousand Oaks, CA: SAGE Publications.
Aldrich, H., & Martinez, M. A. 2001. Many are called, but few are chosen: An evolutionary perspective for the study of entrepreneurship. *Entrepreneurship Theory and Practice*, 25(4, Summer): 41–56.
Aldrich, H., & Reuf, M. 2006. *Organizations Evolving* (2nd ed.). Thousand Oaks, CA: SAGE Publications.
Allen, P. 1982. Self-organization in the urban system. In W. Scheive & P. Allen (Eds.), *Self-Organization and Dissipative Structures: Applications in Physical and Social Sciences* (132–58). Austin, TX: University of Texas Press.
Allen, P., Maguire, S., & McKelvey, B. (Eds.). 2011. *The SAGE Handbook of Complexity and Management*. Thousand Oaks, CA: SAGE Publications.
Allen, P., & McGlade, J. 1987. Evolutionary drive: The effect of microscopic diversity, error making and noise. *Foundations of Physics*, 17: 723–8.
Allen, P., Strathern, M., & Baldwin, J. 2007. Complexity and the limits to learning. *Journal of Evolutionary Economics*, 17(4): 401–31.
Almandoz, J. 2012. Arriving at the starting line: The impat of community and financial logics on new banking ventures. *Academy of Management Journal*, 55(6): 1381–1406.
Alvarez, S., & Barney, J. 2007. Discovery and creation: Alternative theories of entrepreneurial action. *Strategic Entrepreneurship Journal*, 1: 11–27.

Alvarez, S., & Barney, J. 2013. Epistemology, opportunities, and entrepreneurship: Comments on Venkataraman et al. (2012) and Shane (2012). *Academy of Management Review*, 38(1): 154–6.

Amabile, T., Conti, R., Coon, H., Lazenby, J., & Herron, M. 1996. Assessing the work environment for creativity. *Academy of Management Journal*, 39: 1154–84.

Anand, N., Gardner, H., & Morris, T. 2007. Knowledge-based innovation: Emergence and embedding of new practice areas in management consulting firms. *Academy of Management Journal*, 50: 406–28.

Anderies, J., Walker, B., & Kinzig, A. 2006. Fifteen weddings and a funeral: Case studies and resilience-based management. *Ecology and Society*, 11(1): 21–32.

Anderson, P. 1972. More is different. *Science*, 177(4047): 393–6.

Anderson, P. 1999. Complexity theory and organization science. *Organization Science*, 10: 216–32.

Anderson, P., Meyer, A., Eisenhardt, K., Carley, K., & Pettigrew, A. 1999. Introduction to the special issue: Application of complexity theory to organization science. *Organization Science*, 10(3): 233–6.

Andrews, M. 1992. *Avenues for Growth*. Long Beach, CA: Speciality Coffee Association of America.

Andriani, P., & McKelvey, B. 2007. Beyond Gaussian averages: Redirecting organization science toward extreme events and power laws. *Journal of International Business Studies*, 38: 1212–30.

Andriani, P., & McKelvey, B. 2009. From Gaussian to Paretian thinking: Causes and implications of power laws in organizations. *Organization Science*, 20: 1053–71.

Ararwal, R., Sarkar, M., & Echambadi, R. 2002. The conditioning effect of time on firm survival: An industry life cycle approach. *Academy of Management Journal*, 45: 971–94.

Arbib, M. A. 1989. A view of brain theory. In E. F. Yates (Ed.) *Self-Organizing Systems: The Emergence of Order* (279–311). New York: Plenum Press.

Ardichvili, A., Cardozo, R., & Ray, S. 2003. A theory of entrepreneurial opportunity identification and development. *Journal of Business Venturing*, 18: 105–24.

Arikan, A. 2010. Regional entrepreneurial transformation: A complex systems perspective. *Journal of Small Business Management*, 48(2): 152–73.

Arrow, H., & Burns, K. L. 2004. Self-organizing culture: How norms emerge in small groups. In M. Schaller & C. Crandall (Eds.), *The Psychological Foundations of Culture* (171–99). Mahwah, NJ: Lawrence Erlbaum & Associates.

Arthur, B. 1988a. Competing technologies: An overiew. In G. Dosi, C. Freeman, R. Nelson, G. Silverberg, & L. Soete (Eds.), *Technical Change and Economic Theory* (590–607). London: Pinter Press.

Arthur, B. 1988b. Self-reinforcing mechanisms in economics. In P. Anderson, K. Arrow, & D. Pines (Eds.), *The Economy as an Evolving Complex System* (9–31). Reading, MA: Addison-Wesleuy.

Arthur, B. 1989. Competing technologies, increasing returns, and lock-in by historcial events. *Economic Journal*, 99: 116–31.

Arthur, B. 1990. Positive feedbacks in the economy. *Scientific American*, February: 92–9.

Arthur, B. 1994. *Increasing Returns and Path Dependence in the Economy*. Ann Arbor, MI: University of Michigan Press.

Artigiani, R. 1987. Revolution and evolution: Applying Prigogine's dissipative structures model. *Journal of Social and Psychological Structures*, 10: 249–64.

Ashby, R. 1956. *An Introduction to Cybernetics*. New York: John-Wiley & Sons.

Ashmos, D., & Huber, G. 1987. The system paradigm in organization theory: Correcting the record and suggesting the future. *Academy of Management Review*, 12: 607–21.

Augros, R., & Stanciu, G. 1987. *The New Biology: Discovering the Wisdom of Nature.* Boston: Shambhala Publications.

Axelrod, R. 1997. *The Complexity of Cooperation: Agent-Based Models of Competition and Cooperation.* Princeton, NJ: Princeton University Press.

Axelrod, R., & Bennett, D. S. 1993. A landscape theory of aggregation. *British Journal of Political Science,* 23: 211–33.

Axelrod, R., & Cohen, M. 2000. *Harnessing Complexity.* New York: Free Press.

Axelrod, R., Mitchell, W., Thomas, R., Bennett, D. S., & Bruderer, E. 1995. Coalition formation in standard-setting alliances. *Management Science,* 41: 1493–1508.

Axtell, C., Holman, D., Unsworth, K., Wall, T., Waterson, P. E., & Harrington, E. 2000. Shopfloor innovation: Facilitating the suggestion and implementation of ideas. *Journal of Occupational and Organizational Psychology,* 73(3): 265–85.

Ayto, J. 1991. *Dictionary of Word Origins: Histories of More than 8,000 English-Language Words.* New York: Arcade/Skyhorse Publishing.

Bacharach, S., Bamberger, P., & Sonnenstuhl, W. 1996. The organizational transformation process: The micropolitics of dissonance reduction and the alignment of logics of action. *Administrative Science Quarterly,* 41: 477–506.

Baer, M., & Frese, M. 2003. Innovation is not enough: Climates for initiative and psychological safety, process innovations, and firm performance. *Journal of Organizational Behavior,* 24(1): 45–68.

Bailey, K. 1987. Restoring order: Relating entropy to energy and information. *Systems Research,* 4(2): 83–92.

Bak, P. 1996. *How Nature Works: The Science of Self-Organized Criticality.* New York: Springer-Verlag.

Bak, P., & Chen, K. 1991. Self-organized criticality. *Scientific American,* January: 46–53.

Baker, G., & Gollub, J. 1996. *Chaotic Dynamics, An Introduction* (2nd ed.). Cambridge, UK: Cambridge University Press.

Baker, T., & Nelson, R. 2005. Creating something from nothing: Resource construction through entrepreneurial bricolage. *Administrative Science Quarterly,* 50: 329–66.

Baldwin, J., Murray, R., Winder, B., & Ridgway, K. 2004. A non-equilibrium thermodynamic model of industrial development: Analogy or homology. *Journal of Cleaner Production,* 12: 841–53.

Barabasi, A.-L., & Bonabeau, E. 2003. Scale-free networks. *Scientific American,* 288(May): 60–9.

Barley, S. 1986. Technology as an occasion for structuring. *Administrative Science Quarterly,* 31: 78–108.

Barley, S. 1990. Images of imaging: Notes on doing longitudinal field work. *Organization Science,* 1: 220–47.

Baron, J., Burton, D., & Hannan, M. 1996. The road taken: The origins and evolution of employment systems in emerging high-technology companies. *Industrial and Corporate Change,* 5: 239–76.

Baron, R. 1998. Cognitive mechanisms in entrepreneurship: Why and when entrepreneurs think differently than other people. *Journal of Business Venturing,* 13: 275–94.

Baron, R. 2004. The cognitive perspective: A valuable tool for answering entrepreneurship's basic "why?" questions. *Journal of Business Venturing,* 19: 221–40.

Baron, R. 2008. The role of affect in the entrepreneurial process. *Academy of Management Review,* 33: 328–40.

Baron, R., & Markman, G. 2003. Beyond social capital: The role of entrepreneurs' social competence in their financial success. *Journal of Business Venturing,* 18: 41–60.

Barron, J. J. 1990. Consortia: High-tech co-ops. *Byte,* 15(June): 15: 269.

Barton, S. 1994. Chaos, self-organization, and psychology. *American Psychologist,* 49: 5–14.

Bartunek, J. 1984. Changing interpretive schemes and organizationl restructuring: The example of a religious order. *Administrative Science Quarterly*, 29: 224–41.

Bartunek, J., & Moch, M. 1987. First order, second order and third order change and organization development interventions: A cognitive approach. *Journal of Applied Behavioral Science*, 23: 483–500.

Bar-Yam, Y. 1997. *Dynamics of Complex Systems*. Reading, MA: Addison-Wesley—Advanced Book Program.

Bar-Yam, Y. 2004. A mathematical theory of strong emergence using mutliscale variety. *Complexity*, 9(6): 15–24.

Bateson, G. 1980. *Mind and Nature—A Necessary Unity*. New York: Bantam Books.

Baum, J. 1999. Whole-part coevolutionary competition in organizations. In J. Baum & B. McKelvey (Eds.), *Variations in Organization Science* (113–36). Thousand Oaks, CA: SAGE Publications.

Baum, R., Locke, E., & Kirkpatrick, S. 1998. A longitudinal study of the relation of vision and vision communication to venture growth in entrepreneurial firms. *Journal of Applied Psychology*, 83: 43–54.

Bechtel, W., & Richardson, R. 1992. Emergent phenomena and complex systems. In A. Beckermann, H. Flohr, & J. Kim (Eds.), *Emergence or Reduction? Essays on the Prospects of Nonreductive Physicalism* (257–88). Berlin: Walter de Gruyter.

Bedau, M. 1997. Weak emergence. *Philosophical Perspectives*, 11(Mind, Causation, and World): 375–99.

Bedau, M. 2002. Downward causation and the autonomy of weak emergence. *Principia*, 6(1): 5–50.

Bedau, M., & Humphres, P. (Eds.). 2008. *Emergence: Contemporary Readings in Philosophy and Science*: Bradford Books—MIT Press.

Beer, S. 1981. *The Brain of the Firm: A Development in Management Cybernetics*. Chichester, UK: John Wiley & Sons.

Begun, J. 1994. Chaos and complexity: Frontiers of organization science. *Journal of Management Inquiry*, 3: 329–35.

Beinhocker, E. 1999. Robust adaptive strategies. *Sloan Management Review*, Spring: 95–106.

Bénard, H. 1901. Les tourbillons cellulaires dans une nappe liquide transportant de la chaleur par convection en régime permanent. *Annales de Chimie et de Physique*, 23: 62–114.

Berge, P., Pompeau, Y., & Vidal, C. 1984. *Order within Chaos: Towards a Deterministic Approach to Turbulence*: New York: Wiley-VCH.

Bergson, H. 1911. *Creative Evolution* [*L'evolution Creatrice*, 1907]. New York: Henry Holt.

Berkes, F., Colding, J., & Folke, C. 2000. Rediscovery of traditional ecological knowledge as adaptive management. *Ecological Applications*, 10: 1251–62.

Berkes, F., Colding, J., & Folke, C. (Eds.). 2003. *Navigating Social-Ecological Systems: Building Resilience for Complexity and Change*. Cambridge, UK: Cambridge University Press.

Berman, M. 1988. *The Reenchantment of the World*. New York: Bantam Books.

Bettis, R., & Prahalad, C. K. 1995. The dominant logic: Retrospective and extention. *Strategic Management Journal*, 16: 5–14.

Bhave, M. P. 1994. A process model of entrepreneurial venture creation. *Journal of Business Venturing*, 9: 223–42.

Bhide, A. 1992. Bootstrap finance: The art of start-ups. *Harvard Business Review*, 70(6): 109–17.

Bhide, A. 2000. *The Origin and Evolution of New Businesses*. New York: Oxford University Press.

Bigelow, J. 1982. A catastrophe model of organizational change. *Behavioral Science*, 27: 26–42.

Biggiero, L. 2001. Self-organizing processes in building entrepreneurial networks: A theoretical and empirical investigation. *Human Systems Management*, 20: 209–22.

Biggiero, L. 2002. The location of multinationals in industrial districts: Knowledge transfer in biomedical. *Journal of Technology Transfer*, 27(1): 111–22.

Bingham, C., & Kahl, S. 2013. The process of schema emergence: Assimilation, deconstruction, unitization and the plurality of analogies. *Academy of Management Journal*, 56(1): 14–34.

Binks, M., & Vale, P. 1990. *Entrepreneurship and Economic Change*. London: McGraw-Hill.

Bird, B. 1988. Implementing entrepreneurial ideas: The case for intention. *Academy of Management Review*, 13: 442–53.

Bird, B. 1992. The operations of intentions in time: The emergence of new ventures. *Entrepreneurship Theory and Practice*, Fall: 11–20.

Blank, S. 2012. Why the lean start-up changes everything. *Harvard Business Review*, 91(5): 63–72.

Blau, P. M. 1964. *Exchange and Power in Social Life*. New York: John Wiley & Sons.

Blitz, D. 1992. *Emergent Evolution: Qualitative Novelty and the Levels of Reality*. Boston: Kluwer Academic.

Boisot, M., & McKelvey, B. 2010. Integrating modernist and postmodernist perspectives on organizations: A complexity science bridge. *Academy of Management Review*, 35: 415–34.

Boisot, M., & McKelvey, B. 2011. Connectivity, extremes and adaptation: A power-law perspective on organizational effectiveness. *Journal of Management Inquiry*, 20(2): 119–33.

Bonner, J. T. 1959. Differentiation in social amoebae. *Scientific American*, 201: 152–62.

Boone, C., & Hendricks, W. 2009. Top management team diversity and firm performance: Moderators of functional-background and locus of control diversity. *Management Science*, 55(2): 165–80.

Boulding, K. 1961. *The Image: Knowledge in Life and Society*. Ann Arbor, MI: Ann Arbor Paperbooks.

Boulding, K. 1978. *Ecodynamics: A New Theory of Societal Evolution*. Newbury Park, CA: SAGE Publications.

Boulding, K. 1980. Equilibrium, entropy, development, and autopoiesis: Towards a disequilibrium economics. *Eastern Economic Journal*, 6(3–4): 179–88.

Boulding, K. 1981. *Evolutionary Economics*. Thousand Oaks, CA: SAGE Publications.

Boulding, K. 1988. *The World as a Total System*. Thousand Oaks, CA: SAGE Publications.

Boyatzis, R. 2006a. An overview of intentional change from a complexity perspective. *Journal of Management Development*, 25: 607–23.

Boyatzis, R. 2006b. Using tipping points of emotional intelligence and cognitive competencies to predict financial performance of leaders. *Psicothema*, 18(Supplement): 124–31.

Boyatzis, R. 2008. Leadership development from a complexity perspective. *Consulting Psychology Journal: Practice and Research*, 60: 298–313.

Boyatzis, R., & Kolb, D. 2000. Performance, learning and development as modes of growth and adaptation throughout our lives and careers. In M. Peiperl, M. Arthur, R. Goffee, & T. Morris (Eds.), *Career Frontiers* (76–98). New York: Oxford University Press.

Boyd, B., Henning, N., Reyna, E., Wang, D., & Welch, M. 2009. *Hybrid Organizations: New Business Models for Environmental Leadership*. Sheffield, UK: Greenleaf Publishing.

Bradbury, H., & Lichtenstein, B. 2000. Relationality in organizational research: Exploring the "space between". *Organization Science*, 11: 551–64.

Bradbury-Huang, H., Lichtenstein, B., Carroll, J., & Senge, P. 2010. Relational space: Learning and innovation in a collaborative consortium for sustainability. *Research in Organizational Change and Development*, 18: 109–48.

Branson Daily News. 1986. Branson owes success to White River, Wright and railroad. *Branson Daily News*, Progress Edition. Branson, MO.

Brewis, S. J., Papamichail, K. N., & Rajaram, V. 2011. Decision-making practices in commercial enterprises: A cybernetic intervention into a business model. *Journal of Organizational Transformation and Social Change*, 8(1): 35–49.

Broad, C. D. 1929. *Mind and Its Place in Nature*. New York: Harcourt, Brace.

Brock, W. A. 2000. Some Santa Fe scenery. In D. Colander (Ed.), *The Complexity Vision and the Teaching of Economics* (29–49). Chelternham, UK: Edward Elgar.

Brock, W. A., Maler, K.-G., & Perrings, C. 2001. Resilience and sustainability: The economic anaysis of nonlinear dynamic systems. In L. Gunderson & C. S. Holling (Eds.), *Panarchy: Understanding Transformations in Human and Natural Systems* (261–292). Washington, DC: Island Press.

Brooks, D., & Wiley, E. O. 1986. *Evolution as Entropy: Toward a Unified Theory of Biology*. Chicago: University of Chicago Press.

Brown, C. 1995. *Chaos and Catastrophe Theories*. Newbury Park, CA: SAGE Publications.

Brown, J. S., & Duguid, P. 1991. Organizational learning and communities-of-practice: Toward a unified view of working, learning, and innovation. *Organization Science*, 2: 40–57.

Brown, S., & Eisenhardt, K. 1997. The art of continuous change: Linking complexity theory and time-based evolution in relentlessly shifting organizations. *Administrative Science Quarterly*, 42: 1–34.

Brown, S., & Eisenhardt, K. 1998. *Competing on the Edge*. Boston: Harvard Business School Press.

Browning, L., Beyer, J., & Shetler, J. 1995. Building cooperation in a competitive industry: SEMATECH and the semiconductor industry. *Academy of Management Journal*, 38: 113–51.

Brush, C., & Greene, P. 1996. *Resources in the new venture creation process: Strategies for acquisition*. Paper presented at the National Academy of Management Meeting, Cincinnati, OH.

Brush, C., Manolova, T., & Edelman, L. 2008. Properties of emerging organizations: An empirical test. *Journal of Business Venturing*, 23: 547–66.

Bucherer, E., Eisert, U., & Gassmann, O. 2012. Towards systematic business model innovation: Lessons from product innovation management. *Creativity and Innovation Management*, 21(2): 183–98.

Buckle-Hennings, P., & Dugan, S. 2007. Leaders' detection of problematic self-organized patterns in the workplace. In J. Hazy, J. Goldstein, & B. Lichtenstein (Eds.), *Complex Systems Leadership Theory* (387–414). Mansfield, MA: ISCE Publishing.

Buenstorf, G. 2000. Self-organization and sustainability: Energetics of evolution and implications for ecological economics. *Ecological Economics*, 33: 119–34.

Burgelman, R. 1983. A process model of internal corporate venturing in the diversified major firm. *Administrative Science Quarterly*, 28: 223–44.

Busenitz, L., & Barney, J. 1997. Differences between entrepreneurs and managers in large organizations: Biases and hueristics in strategic decision-making. *Journal of Business Venturing*, 12(1): 9–30.

Bushev, M. 1994. *Synergetics: Chaos, Order, Self-Organization*. Singapore: World Scientific.

Butler, M. J. R., & Allen, P. M. 2008. Understanding policy implementation processes as self-organizing systems. *Public Management Review*, 10(3): 421–40.

Bygrave, W. 1989a. The entrepreneurship paradigm (I): A philosophical look at its research methodologies. *Entrepreneurship Theory and Practice*, 14(1): 7–26.

Bygrave, W. 1989b. The entrepreneurship paradigm (II): Chaos and catastrophes among quantum jumps. *Entrepreneurship Theory and Practice*, 14(2): 7–30.

Bygrave, W. 1993. Theory building in the entrepreneurship paradigm. *Journal of Business Venturing*, 8: 255–80.

Bygrave, W. 1997. The entrepreneurial process. In W. D. Bygrave (Ed.), *The Portable MBA in Entrepreneurship* (2nd ed., 1–26). New York: John Wiley & Sons.

Bygrave, W., & Hofer, C. 1991. Theorizing about entrepreneurship. *Entrepreneurship Theory and Practice*, 16(2): 13–23.

Capra, F. 1982. *The Turning Point*. New York: Bantam Books.

Capra, F. 1996. *The Web of Life*. New York: Anchor Books.

Cardon, M., Wincent, J., Singh, J., & Drnovsek, M. 2009. The nature and experience of entrepreneurial passion. *Academy of Management Review*, 34(3): 511–32.

Carland, J., Hoy, F., & Carland, J. A. 1988. "Who is an entrepreneur" is a question worth asking. *Amercian Journal of Small Business*, 12(4): 33–9.

Carley, K. 1990. Group stability: A socio-cognitive approach. *Advances in Group Processes*, 7: 1–44.

Carley, K. 1991. A theory of group stability. *American Journal of Sociology*, 56(3): 331–54.

Carley, K. 1992. Organizational learning and personnel turnover. *Organization Science*, 3: 20–46.

Carley, K. 1995. Computational and mathematical organization theory: Perspective and directions. *Computational and Mathematical Organization Theory*, 1: 39–56.

Carley, K. 1996. A comparison of artificial and human organizations. *Journal of Economic Behavior and Organization*, 31: 175–91.

Carley, K. 1998. Organizational adaptation. *Annuls of Operations Research*, 75: 25–47.

Carley, K. 1999a. Learning within and among organizations. *Advances in Strategic Management*, 16: 33–53.

Carley, K. 1999b. On the evolution of social and organizational networks. In S. Andrews & D. Knoke (Eds.), *Research in the Sociology of Organizations*, Vol. 16: 3–30. Stamford, CT: JAI Press.

Carley, K. 2000. Intra-organizational computation and complexity. *Working Paper*, Carnegie Mellon University.

Carley, K., & Hill, V. 2001. Structural change and learning within organizations. In A. Lomi & E. Larson (Eds.), *Dynamics of Organizations: Computational Modeling and Organizational Theories* (63–92). Cambridge, MA: MIT Press/AAAI Press.

Carley, K., & Lee, J.-S. 1998. Dynamic organizations: Organizational adaptation in a changing environment. *Advances in Strategic Management*, 15: 269–97.

Carley, K., & Prietula, M. 1994. *Computational Organization Theory*. Hillsdale, NJ: Lawrence Erlbaum & Associates.

Carley, K., & Svoboda, D. M. 1996. Modeling organization adaptation as a simulated annealing process. *Sociological Methods and Research*, 25: 138–68.

Carniero, R. 1970. A theory of the origin of the state. *Science*, 169: 733–8.

Carniero, R. 1987. The evolution of complexity in human societies and it mathematical expression. *International Journal of Comparative Sociology*, 28: 111–28.

Carnot, S. 1824. Reflections on the motive power of fire, and on machines fitted to develop that power. *The Second Law of Thermodynamics Benchmark Papers on Energy*, 5.

Carpenter, S., & Brock, W. 2006. Rising variance: A leading indicator of ecological transition. *Ecology Letters*, 9(3): 311–8.

Carroll, G. 1985. Concentration and specialization: The dynamics of niche width in organizational populations. *American Journal of Sociology*, 90: 1262–83.

Carroll, G. (Ed.). 1988. *Ecological Models of Organization*. Cambridge, MA: Ballinger.

Carter, N., Gartner, B., & Reynolds, P. 1996. Exploring start-up event sequences. *Journal of Business Venturing*, 11: 151–66.

Casrud, A., & Brannback, M. 2011. Entrepreneurial motivations: What do we still need to know? *Journal of Small Business Management*, 49(1): 9–26.

Casti, J. 1994. *Complexification*. New York: HarperPerennial.

Castelfranchi, C. 1998. Simulating with cognitive agents: The importance of cognitive emergence. In J. Sichman, R. Conte, & N. Gilbert (Eds.) *Multi-Agent Systems and Agent-Based Simulation* (26–44). Berlin: Springer.

Cauley, L. 1999. Losses in space—Iridium's downfall. *Wall Street Journal*. August 18, p. A1.
Chaisson, E. 2001. *Cosmic Evolution: The Rise of Complexity in Nature*. Cambridge, MA: Harvard University Press.
Chalmers, D. 2006. Strong and weak emergence. In P. Clayton & P. Davies (Eds.), *The Re-Emergence of Emergence: The Emergentist Hypothesis from Science to Religion* (244–56). New York: Oxford University Press.
Checkland, P. 1981. *Systems Thinking, Systems Practice*. Chichester, UK: John Wiley & Sons.
Cheng, Y., & Van de Ven, A. 1996. The innovation journey: Order out of chaos? *Organization Science*, 6: 593–614.
Chiasson, M., & Saunders, C. 2005. Reconciling diverse approaches to opportunity research using the structuration theory. *Journal of Business Venturing*, 20: 747–68.
Chiles, T., Bluedorn, A., & Gupta, V. 2007. Beyond creative destruction and entrepreneurial discovery: A radical Austrian approach to entrepreneurship. *Organization Studies*, 28: 467–93.
Chiles, T., & Meyer, A. 2001. Managing the emergence of clusters: An increasing returns approach to strategic change. *Emergence*, 3(3): 58–89.
Chiles, T., Meyer, A., & Hench, T. 2004. Organizational emergence: The origin and transformation of Branson, Missouri's musical theaters. *Organization Science*, 15(5): 499–520.
Chiles, T., Tuggle, C. S., McMullen, J., Bierman, L., & Greening, D. 2010. Dynamic creation: Elaborating a radical Austrian approach to entrepreneurship. *Organization Studies*, 31: 7–46.
Choi, T., Dooley, K., & Rungtusanatham, M. 2001. Supply networks and complex adaptive systems: Control vs. emergence. *Journal of Operations Management*, 19: 351–66.
Christensen, C. 1997. *The Innovator's Dilemma: When New Technologies Cause Great Firms to Fail*. Boston: Harvard Business School Press.
Cilliers, P. 1998. *Complexity and Postmodernism: Understanding Complex Systems*. New York: Routledge.
Clark, W., Holling, C. S., & Jones, D. D. 1995. Towards a structural view of resilience. International Institute of Applied Systems Analysis, WP-75-96.
Clayton, P., & Davies, P. 2006. *The Re-Emergence of Emergence: The Emergentist Hypothesis from Science to Religion*. New York: Oxford University Pres.
Clegg, S., Hardy, C., Nord, W., & Lawrence, T. (Eds.). 2006. *Handbook of Organization Studies*. London: SAGE Publications.
Clippinger, J. H. 1999. Order from the botton up: Complex adaptive systems and their management. In J. H. Clippinger (Ed.), *The Biology of Business* (1–30). San Francisco: Jossey-Bass.
Cohen, M., & Bacdayan, P. 1994. Organizational routines are stored as procedural memory: Evidence from a laboratory study. *Organization Science*, 5(4): 554–68.
Colbert, B. 2004. The complex resource-bbased view: Implications for theory and practice in strategic human resource management. *Academy of Management Review*, 29: 341–58.
Collins, C., Hanges, P., & Locke, E. 2004. The relationship of achievement motivation to entrepreneurial behavior: A meta-analysis. *Human Performance*, 17(1): 95–117.
Conte, R., Edmonds, B., Moss, S. & Sawyer, K. 1998. Sociology and social theory in agent based social simulation: A symposium. *Computational and Mathematical Organization Theory*, 7: 183–205.
Contractor, N., Whitbred, R., Fonti, F., Hyatt, A., O'Keefe, B., & Jones, P. 2000. Structuration theory and self-organizing networks. Presented at Organization Science Winter Conference, Keystone, CO.
Conway, J. 1970. The game of life. *Scientific American*, 223(4): 4.
Cook, T., & Campbell, D. 1979. *Quasi-Experimentation*. Boston: Houghton Mifflin.

Cooper, A., Gimeno-Gascon, F. J., & Woo, C. 1994. Initial human and financial capital as predictors of new venture performance. *Journal of Business Venturing*, 9: 371–96.

Corbett, A. 2005. Experiential learning within the process of opportunity identification and exploitation. *Entrepreneurship Theory and Practice*, 29(4): 473–92.

Coren, R. 1998. *The Evolutionary Trajectory: The Growth of Information in the History and Future of the Earth*. Amsterdam: Gordon and Breach Publishers.

Corning, P. 1983. *The Synergism Hypothesis: A Theory of Progressive Evolution*. New York: McGraw Hill.

Corning, P. 2002. The re-emergence of 'emergence': A vernerable concept in search of a theory. *Complexity*, 7(6): 18–30.

Corning, P. 2003. *Nature's Magic: Synergy in Evolution and the Fate of Humankind*. New York: Cambridge University Press.

Corning, P. 2005. *Holistic Darwinism: Synergy, Cybernetics, and the Bioeconomics of Evolution*. Chicago: Universtiy of Chicago Press.

Corning, P. 2012. The re-emergence of emergence, and the causal role of synergy in emergent evolution. *Synthese*, 185(2): 295–317.

Corning, P., & Kline, S. J. 1998a. Thermodynamics, information and life revisited, part I: 'To be or entropy'. *Systems Research and Behavioral Science*, 15: 273–95.

Corning, P., & Kline, S. J. 1998b. Thermodyamics, information and life revisited, part 2: 'Thermoeconomics' and 'control information'. *Systems Research and Behavioral Science*, 15: 453–82.

Cowan, G., Pines, D., & Meltzer, D. (Eds.). 1994. *Complexity: Metaphors, Models, and Reality*. (Vol. Proceedings #11). New York: Addison-Wesley.

Cramer, F. 1993. *Chaos and Order: The Complex Structure of Living Things* (D. L. Loewus, Trans.). New York: VCH.

Crowston, K. 1996. An approach to evolving novel organizational forms. *Computational and Mathematical Organization Theory*, 2: 29–47.

Crutchfield, J. 1994a. Is anything ever new? Considering emergence. In G. Cowan, D. Pines, & D. Meltzer (Eds.), *Complexity: Metaphors, Models, and Realty* (479–97). Reading, MA: Addison-Wesley.

Crutchfield, J. 1994b. The calculi of emergence: Computation, dynamics and induction. *Physica D: Nonlinear Phemonema*, 75(1): 11–54. Reprinted in SFI 94-03-016. Special Issue on the Proceedings of Complex Systems—From Complex Dynamics to Artificial Reality.

Csanyi, V., & Kampis, G. 1985. Autogenesis: Evolution of replicative systems. *Journal of Theoretical Biology*, 114: 303–21.

Csikszentmihalyi, M. 1990. *Flow: The Psychology of Optimal Experience*. New York: Harper & Row.

Csikszentmihalyi, M. 1996. *Creativity*. New York: HarperCollins.

Dacin, P., Dacin, M. T., & Matear, M. 2010. Social entrepreneurship: Why we don't need a new theory and how we move forward from here. *Academy of Management Perspectives*, 24(3): 37–57.

Dahl, M. 2011. Organizational change and employee stress. *Management Science*, 57(2): 240–56.

Daneke, G., & Dooley, K. 2007. The life-cycle revisited: Stage transitions and the failure of the Iridium project. In *Management of Engineering and Technology* (471–82). Portland, OR: IEEE Portland International Center for Management of Engineering and Technology.

Davidson, R. 1982. Economic dynamics. In W. C. Schieve & P. Allen (Eds.), *Self-Organization and Dissipative Structures: Applications in Physical and Social Sciences* (339–43). Austin, TX: University of Texas Press.

Davidsson, P. 2006. Nascent entrepreneurship: Empirical studies and developments. *Foundations and Trends in Entreprenuership*, 2(1): 1–76.

Davis, J., Eisenhardt, K., & Bingham, C. 2007. Developing theory through simulation methods. *Academy of Management Review*, 32: 480–99.

Deacon, T. 2003. The hierarchic logic of emergence: Untangling the interdependence of evolution and self-organization. In B. Weber & D. Depew (Eds.), *Evolution and Learning: The Baldwin Effect Reconsidered* (273–308). Cambridge, MA: MIT Press.

Deacon, T. 2006. Emergence: The hold at the wheel's hub. In P. Clayton & P. Davies (Eds.), *The Re-Emergence of Emergence: The Emergentist Hypothesis from Science to Religion* (111–50). New York: Oxford University Press.

De Bono, E. 2009. *Lateral Thinking: A Textbook of Creativity*. New York: Penguin.

Delmar, F., & Shane, S. 2003a. Does business planning facilitate the development of new ventures? *Strategic Management Journal*, 24: 1165–85.

Delmar, F., & Shane, S. 2003b. *Does the order of organizing activiites matter for new venture performance?* Paper presented at the Frontiers of Entrepreneurship, Babson College.

Delmar, F., & Shane, S. 2004. Legitimating first: Organizing activities and the survival of new ventures. *Journal of Business Venturing*, 19: 385–411.

Dennett, D. 1995. *Darwin's Dangerous Idea: Evolution and the Meanings of Life*. New York: Touchstone.

Denrell, J. 2003. Vicarious learning, understmpling of failure, and the myths of management. *Organization Science*, 14(3): 227–43.

Denzin, N. 1989. *The Research Act* (3rd ed.). Englewood Cliffs, NJ: Prentice Hall.

Depew, D., & Weber, B. (Eds.). 1985. *Evolution at a Crossroads: The New Biology and the New Philosophy of Science*. Cambridge, MA: MIT Press.

Depew, D., & Weber, B. 1994. *Darwinism Evolving*. New York: Oxford University Press.

DeTienne, D., Shepherd, D., & deCastro, J. O. 2008. The fallacy of 'only the strong survive": The effects of extrinsic motivation on the peristence decisions for underperforming firms. *Journal of Business Venturing*, 23(5): 528–46.

De Vany, A. 1996. Information, chance, and evolution: Alchian and the economics of self-organization. *Economic Inquiry*, 34: 427–42.

Dew, N., Read, S., Sarasvathy, S., & Wiltbank, R. 2008. Outlines of a behavioral theory of the entrepreneurial firm. *Journal of Economic Behavior and Organization*, 66(1): 37–59.

Dew, N., Read, S., Sarasvathy, S., & Wiltbank, R. 2009. Effectual versus predictive logics in entrepreneurial decision-making: Differences between experts and novices. *Journal of Business Venturing*, 24: 287–309.

Dew, N., Reed, S., Sarasvathy, S., & Wiltbank, R. 2011. On the entrepreneurial genesis of new markets: Effectual transformations versus causal search and selection. *Journal of Evolutionary Economics*, 21: 231–53.

De Wolf, T., & Holvoet, T. 2005. Emergence versus self-organization: Different concepts but promising when combined. *Lecture Notes in Computer Science*, 2464(Special Issue on Engineering Self-Organizing Systems): 77–91.

Dhillon, G., & Fabian, F. 2005. A fractal perspective on competencies necessary for managing information systems. *International Journal of Technology Management*, 31(1/2): 129–39.

DiMaggio, P., & Powell, W. 1983. The iron cage revisited: Institutional isomorphism and collective rationality in organizational fields. *American Sociological Review*, 48: 147–60.

Dimov, D. 2011. Grappling with the unbearable elusiveness of entrepreneurial opportunities. *Entrepreneurship Theory and Practice*, 35(1): 57–81.

DiRenzo, M., & Greenhaus, J. 2011. Job search and voluntary turnover in a boundaryless world: A control theroy perspective. *Academy of Management Review*, 36(3): 567–89.

Dooley, K. 1997. A complex adaptive systems model of organization change. *Nonlinear Dynamics, Psychology, and the Life Sciences*, 1: 69–97.

Dooley, K., Daneke, G., & Pathak, S. 2005. *Iridium's house of cards: The nature of entrepreneurial stages and stage transition*. Arizona State University.

Dooley, K., & Van de Ven, A. 1999. Explaining complex organizational dynamics. *Organization Science*, 10(3): 358–72.

Dosi, G., & Fagiolo, G. 1998. Exploring the unknown. On entrepreneurship, coordination and innovation-driven growth. In J. Lesourne & A. Orlean (Eds.), *Advances in Self-Organization and Evolutionary Economics* (308–52). London: Economica.

Douglas, A. E. 1994. *Symbiotic Interactions*. Oxford, UK: Oxford University Press.

Downey, A. 2009. *Think Complexity: Complexity Science and Computational Modeling*. Sebastopol, CA: O'Reilly Media.

Drazin, R., & Sandelands, L. 1992. Autogenesis: A perspective on the process of organizing. *Organization Science*, 3: 230–49.

Dubinskas, F. 1994. On the edge of chaos: A metaphor for transformative change. *Journal of Management Inquiry*, 3: 355–66.

Dutton, J., & Dukerich, J. 1991. Keeping an eye on the mirror: The role of image and identity in organizational adaptation. *Academy of Management Journal*, 34: 517–54.

Dyke, C. 1988. Cities as dissipative structures. In B. Weber, D. Depew, & J. Smith (Eds.), *Entropy, Information and Evolution: New Perspectives on Physical and Biological Evolution* (355–68). Cambridge, MA: MIT Press.

Dyke, C. 1992. From entropy to economy: A thorny path. *Advances in Human Ecology*, 1: 149–76.

Eckhardt, J. T., & Shane, S. 2006. Opportunities and entrepreneurship. *Journal of Management*, 29(3): 333–49.

Eckhardt, J. T., & Shane, S. 2013. Response to the commentaries: The individual-opportunity (IO) nexus integrates objective and subjective aspects of entrepreneurship. *Academy of Management Review*, 2013(1): 160–2.

Edmondson, A. 1999. Psychological safety and learning behavior in work teams. *Administrative Science Quarterly*, 44: 350–83.

Edmondson, A., & McManus, S. 2007. Methodological fit in management field research. *Academy of Management Review*, 32: 1155–79.

Eggers, J., Leahy, K., & Churchill, N. 1994. Stages of small business growth revisited. *Frontiers of Entreprenuerial Research*, 14: 131–44.

Ehrenfeld, J. 2007. Would industrial ecology exist without sustainability in the background? *Journal of Industrial Ecology*, 11: 73–84.

Eigen, M. 1971a. Molecular self-organization and the early stages of evolution. *Quarterly Reviews of Biophysics*, 4: 149–212.

Eigen, M. 1971b. Self-organization of matter and the evolution of biological macromolecules. *Naturwissenschaften*, 58: 465–523.

Eigen, M. 1992. *Steps Toward Life: A Perspective on Evolution* Oxford, UK: Oxford University Press.

Eigen, M., & Schuster, P. 1979. *The Hypercycle: A Principle of Natural Self-Organizing; In Three Parts*. New York: Springer.

Eisenhardt, K. 1989. Building theories from case study research. *Academy of Management Review*, 14: 532–50.

el-Hani, C., & Pereira, A. 2000. Higher level descriptions: Why should we preserve them? In P. Andersen, C. Emmeche, N. Finnemann, & P. V. Christiansen (Eds.), *Downward Causation: Minds, Bodies and Matter* (118–42). Aarhus, Denmark: Aarhus University Press.

Elliott, E., & Kiel, D. (Eds.). 1996. *Chaos Theory in the Social Sciences: Foundations and Applications*. Ann Arbor, MI: University of Michigan Press.

Ellis, G. 2006. On the nature of emergent reality. In P. Clayton & P. Davies (Eds.), *The Re-Emergence of Emergence: The Emergentist Hypothesis from Science to Religion* (79–110). New York: Oxford University Press.

Ellis, T. 2010. *The New Pioneers: Sustainable Business Success through Social Innovation and Social Entrepreneurship*. West Sussex, UK: John Wiley & Sons.

Emery, C. W., & Cooper, D. R. 1991. *Business Research Methods* (4th ed.). Homewood, IL: Irwin.

Eoyang, G. 1997. *Coping with Chaos*. Cheyanne, WY: Laguno Corporation.

Epstein, J. M., & Axtell, R. 1996. *Growing Artificial Societies: Social Science from the Bottom Up*. Cambridge, MA: MIT Press.

Erlandson, D., Harris, E., Skipper, B., & Allen, S. 1993. *Doing Naturalistic Inquiry*. Newbury Park, CA: SAGE Publications.

Espinosa, A., Harnden, R., & Walker, J. 2004. Cybernetics and participation: From theory to practice. *Systemic Practice and Action Research*, 17(6): 573–89.

Espinosa, A., Harnden, R., & Walker, J. 2008. A complexity approach to sustainability: Stafford Beer revisited. *European Journal of Operational Research*, 187: 636–51.

Ethiraj, S. K., & Levinthal, D. 2004. Modularity and innovation in complex systems. *Management Science*, 50: 159–73.

Eve, R., Horsfall, S., & Lee, M. 1997. *Chaos, Complexity, and Sociology*. Thousand Oaks, CA: SAGE Publications.

Farjoun, M., & Levin, M. 2011. A fractal approach to industry dynamism. *Organization Studies*, 32(6): 825–51.

Farmer, J. D., Kauffman, S., & Packard, N. 1986. Autocatalytic replication of polymers. *Physica D*, 22: 5–67.

Feldman, M. 2000. Organizational routines as a source of continuous change. *Organization Science*, 11: 611–29.

Feldman, M. 2004. Resources in emerging structures and processes of change. *Organization Science*, 15: 295–309.

Feldman, M., & Pentland, B. 2003. Reconceptualizing organizational routines and a source of flexibility and change. *Administrative Science Quarterly*, 48: 94–118.

Ferdig, M., & Ludema, J. 2005. Transformative interactions: Qualities of conversation that heighten the vitality of self-organizing change. In R. Woodman (Ed.), *Research in Organizational Change and Development*, Vol. 15: 171–207. New York: Elsevier Press.

Ferguson, C. H. 1988. From the people who brought you voodoo economics. *Harvard Business Review*, 66(3): 55–63.

Finke, R., & Bettle, J. 1996. *Chaotic Cognition: Principles and Applications*. Mahwah, NJ: Lawrence Erlbaum & Associates.

Finke, R., Ward, T., & Smith, S. (Eds.). 1995. *The Creative Cognition Approach*. Cambridge, MA: MIT Press.

Finkelstein, S., & Sanford, S. 2001. Learning from corporate mistakes: The rise and fall of Iridium. *Organizational Dynamics*, 29(2): 138–48.

Fisher, R. A. 1930. *The Genetical Theory of Natural Selection*. Oxford: Clarendon Press.

Fleming, L., & Sorenson, O. 2001. Technology as a complex adaptive system. *Research Policy*, 30: 1019–39.

Folke, C., Carpenter, S., Walker, B., Scheffer, M., Chapin, T., & Rockstrom, J. 2010. Resilience thinking: Integrating resilience, adaptability and transformability. *Ecology and Society*, 15(4): 20–8.

Folke, C., Carpenter, S., Walker, B., Scheffer, M., Elmqvist, T., Gunderson, L., & Holling, C. S. 2004. Regime shifts, resilience, and biodiversity in ecosystem management. *Annual Review of Ecology, Evolution, and Systematics*, 35: 557–81.

Folke, C., Hahn, T., Olsson, P., & Norberg, J. 2005. Adaptive governance of social-ecological systems. *Annual Review of Environmental Resources*, 30: 441–73.

Forrester, J. 1961. *Industrial Dynamics*. Cambridge, MA: MIT Press.

Foster, J. 2000. Competitive selection, self-organization and Joseph A. Schumpeter. *Journal of Evolutionary Economics*, 10: 311–28.

Foster, J. 2011. Energy, aesthetics and knowledge in complex economic systems. *Journal of Economic Behavior and Organization*, 80: 88–100.

Foster, J., & Metcalfe, J. S. 2012. Economic emergence: An evolutionary economic perspective. *Journal of Economic Behavior and Organization*, 82: 420–32.

Fritz, R. 1989. *The Path of Least Resistance*. New York: Fawcett Columbine.

Fritz, R. 1991. *Creating*. New York: Fawcett Columbine.

Fuller, R. B. 1969. *Operating Manual for Spaceship Earth*. New York: Simon and Schuster.

Fuller, T., & Moran, P. 2001. Small enterprises as complex adaptive systems: A methdological question? *Entrepreneurship and Regional Development*, 13: 47–63.

Fuller, T., Warren, L., & Argyle, P. 2008. Sustaining entrepreneurial business: A complexity perspective on processes that produce emergent practice. *International Entrepreneurship Management Journal*, 4: 1–17.

Ganco, M., & Agarwal, R. 2009. Performance differentials between diversifying entrants and entrepreneurial start-ups: A complexity approach. *Academy of Management Review*, 34: 228–53.

Gandhi, K. (Ed.). 1983. *The Evolution of Consciousness*. New York: Paragon House.

Garreau, J. 1992. *Edge City*. New York: Anchor Books.

Gartner, B. 2001. Is there an elephant in entrepreneurship research? Blind assumptions in theory development. *Entrepreneurship Theory and Practice*, 25(4): 27–40.

Gartner, B., & Starr, J. 1993. The nature of entrepreneruial work. In S. Birley & I. MacMillan (Eds.), *Entrepreneurship Research: Global Perspectives* (35–67). Amsterdam: North-Holland.

Gartner, W. 1985. A conceptual framework for describing the phenomonon of new venture creation. *Academy of Management Review*, 10: 696–706.

Gartner, W. 1988. "Who is an entrepreneur" is the wrong question. *American Journal of Small Business*, 12(4): 11–32.

Gartner, W. 1993. Words lead to deeds: Towards an organizational emergence vocabulary. *Journal of Business Venturing*, 8: 231–9.

Gartner, W. (Ed.). 2010. *ENTER—Entrepreneurial Narrative Theory Ethnomethodology and Reflexivity*. Clemson University: Spiro Institute for Entrepreneurial Leadership.

Gartner, W., Bird, B., & Starr, J. 1992. Acting as if: Differentiating entrepreneurial from organizational behavior. *Entrepreneurship Theory and Practice*, 16(3): 13–30.

Gartner, W., & Brush, C. 2007. Entrepreneurship as organizing: Emergence, newness and transformation. In T. H. M. Rice (Ed.), *Praeger Perspectives on Entrepreneurship*, Vol. 3: 1–20. Westport, CT: Prager Publishers.

Gartner, W., & Carter, N. 2003. Entrepreneurial behavior and firm organizing processes. In Z. J. Acs & D. B. Audretsch (Eds.), *Handbook of Entrepreneurship Research* (195–221). Boston: Kluwer.

Gartner, W., Carter, N., & Reynolds, P. 2004. Business start-up activities. In W. Gartner, K. Shaver, N. Carter, & P. Reynolds (Eds.), *Handbook of Entrepreneurial Dynamics* (285–98). Thousand Oaks, CA: SAGE Publications.

Gartner, W., Shaver, K., Carter, N., & Reynolds, P. (Eds.). 2004. *Handbook of Entrepreneurial Dynamics*. Thousand Oaks, CA: SAGE Publications.

Garud, R., & Guiliani, A. P. 2013. A narrative perspective on entrepreneurial opportunities. *Academy of Management Review*, 38(1): 157–60.

Garud, R., Hardy, C., & Maguire, S. 2004. Special issue on "Institutional Entrepreneurship". *Organization Studies*, 25: 1471–3.

Garud, R., Jain, S., & Kumaraswamy, A. 2002. Institutional entrepreneurship in the sponsorship of comon technological standards: The case of Sun Microsystems and Java. *Academy of Management Journal*, 45: 196–214.

Garud, R., & Karnøe, P. 2001. *Path Dependence and Creation*. Mahwah, NJ: Lawrence Erlbaum & Associates.

Garud, R., & Karnøe, P. 2003. Bricolage versus breakthrough: Distributed and embedded agency in technology entrepreneurship. *Research Policy*, 32: 277–301.

Garud, R., & Kotha, S. 1994. Using the brain as a metaphor to model flexible production systems. *Academy of Management Review*, 19(4): 671–98.

Garud, R., Kumaraswamy, A., & Karnøe, P. 2010. Path dependence or path creation? *Journal of Management Studies*, 47(4): 760–74.

Garud, R., Kumaraswamy, A., & Sambamurthy, V. 2006. Emergent by design: Performance and transformation at Infosys Technologies. *Organization Science*, 17: 277–86.

Garud, R., & Nayyar, P. 1994. Transformative capacity: Continual structuring by intertemporal technology transfer. *Strategic Management Journal*, 15: 365–85.

Garud, R., & Van de Ven, A. 1992. An empirical evaluation of the internal corporate venturing process. *Strategic Management Journal*, 13: 93–109.

Garud, R., & Van de Ven, A. 2002. Strategic organizational change processes. In H. Pettigrew, H. Thomas, & R. Whittington (Eds.), *Handbook of Strategy and Management* (206–31). London: SAGE Publications.

Gassmann, O., & Zeschky, M. 2008. Opening up the solution space: The role of analogical thinking for breakthrough product innovation. *Creativity and Innovation Management*, 17(2): 97–106.

Gavetti, G., & Levinthal, D. 2000. Looking forward and looking backward: Cognitive and experiential search. *Administrative Science Quarterly*, 45: 113–37.

Gavetti, G., Levinthal, D., & Rivkin, J. 2005. Strategy making in novel and complex worlds: The power of analogy. *Strategic Management Journal*, 26: 691–712.

Gell-Mann, M. 1994. *The Quark and the Jaguar*. New York: W. H. Freeman.

Gell-Mann, M. 2002. What is complexity? In A. Q. Curzio & M. Fortis (Eds.), *Complexity and Industrial Clusters* (13–24). Heidelberg, Germany: Physica-Verlag.

Gemmill, G., Boland, R., & Kolb, D. 2012. The socio-cognitive dynamics of entrepreneurial ideation. *Entrepreneurship Theory and Practice*, 36(5): 1053–73.

Gemmill, G., & Smith, C. 1985. A dissipative structure model of organization transformation. *Human Relations*, 38(8): 751–66.

Gentner, D. 1989. The mechanisms of analogical learning. In S. Vosnidou & A. Ortony (Eds.), *Similarity and Analogical Reasoning* (199–241). New York: Cambridge University Press.

George, G., & Bock, A. 2011. The business model in practice and its implications for entrepreneurship research. *Entrepreneurship Theory and Practice*, 35(1): 83–111.

Georgescu-Roegen, N. 1971. *The Entropy Law and the Economic Process*. Cambridge, MA: Harvard University Press.

Gersick, C. 1988. Time and transition in work teams. *Academy of Management Journal*, 29: 9–41.

Gersick, C. 1991. Revolutionary change theories: A multilevel exploration of the punctuated equilibrium paradigm. *Academy of Management Review*, 16: 10–36.

Gersick, C., & Hackman, R. 1990. Habitual routines in task-performing groups. *Organizational Behavior and Human Decision Processes*, 47: 65–97.

Gibbs, J. W. 1906. *The scientific papers of J. Willard Gibbs*. New York: Longmans, Green.

Giddens, A. 1984. *The Constitution of Society: Outline of the Theory of Structuration*. Cambridge, UK: Polity Press.

Gilbert, N., & Conte, R. (Eds.). 1995. *Artificial Societies: The Computer Simulation of Social Life.* London: Taylor & Francis.

Gilboa, S., Shirom, A., Fried, Y., & Cooper, C. 2008. A meta-analysis of work demand stressors and job performance: Examining main and moderating effects. *Personnel Psychology,* 61(2): 227–71.

Gilstrap, D. 2007. Dissipative structures in educational change: Prigogine and the academy. *International Journal of Leadership in Education,* 10: 49–69.

Gioia, D., Schultz, M., & Corley, K. 2000. Organizational identity, image, and adaptive instability. *Academy of Management Review,* 25: 63–81.

Gioia, D., & Thomas, J. 1996. Institutional identity, image, and issue interpretation: Sense-making during strategic change in academia. *Administrative Science Quarterly,* 41: 370–403.

Gleick, J. 1987. *Chaos: Making a New Science.* New York: Penguin.

Goerner, S. 1994. *Chaos and the Evolving Ecological Universe.* Langhorn, PA: Gordon & Breach.

Goldstein, J. 1988. A far-from-equilibrium systems approach to resistance to change. *Organizational Dynamics,* 15(1): 5–20.

Goldstein, J. 1994. *The Unshackled Organization.* Portland, OR: Productivity Press.

Goldstein, J. 1999. Emergence as a construct: History and issues. *Emergence,* 1(1): 49–72.

Goldstein, J. 2000. Emergence: A concept amid a thicket of conceptual snares. *Emergence,* 2(1): 5–22.

Goldstein, J. 2001. Emergence, radical novelty, and the philosophy of mathematics. In W. Sulis & I. Trofimova (Eds.), *Nonlinear Dynamics in the Life and Social Sciences* (133–52) NATO Science Series, Vol. 320. Amsterdam: IOS Press.

Goldstein, J. 2002. The singular nature of emergent levels: Suggestions for a theory of emergence. *Nonlinear Dynamics, Psychology and Life Sciences,* 6: 293–309.

Goldstein, J. 2003. The construction of emergent order, or, how to resist the temptation of hylozosim. *Nonlinear Dynamics, Psychology, and Life Sciences,* 7(4): 295–314.

Goldstein, J. 2007. A new model for emergence and its leadership implications. In J. Hazy, J. Goldstein, & B. Lichtenstein (Eds.), *Complex Systems Leadership Theory* (61–92). Mansfield, MA: ISCE Publishing.

Goldstein, J. 2011. Probing the nature of complex systems: Parameters, modeling, interventions—Part 1. *Emergence: Complexity and Organization,* 13(3): 94–121.

Goldstein, J., Hazy, J., & Lichtenstein, B. 2010. *Complexity and the Nexus of Leadership: Leveraging Nonlinear Science to Create Ecologies of Innovation.* New York: Palgrave Macmillan.

Granovetter, M. 1973. The strength of weak ties. *American Journal of Sociology,* 78: 1360–80.

Granovetter, M. 1978. Threshold models of collective behavior. *American Journal of Sociology,* 83: 1420–43.

Granovetter, M., & Soong, R. 1986. Threshold models of interpersonal effects in consumer demand. *Journal of Economic Behavior and Organization,* 7: 83–100.

Greenwood, R., & Hinings, C. R. 1993. Understanding strategic change: The contribution of archetypes. *Academy of Management Journal,* 36: 1052–81.

Greenwood, R., & Hinings, C. R. 1996. Understanding radical organizational change: Bringing together the old and the new institutionalism. *Academy of Management Review,* 21: 1022–54.

Grégoire, D., Barr, P., & Shepherd, D. 2010. Cognitive processes of opportunity recognition: The role of structural alignment. *Organization Science,* 21(2): 413.

Greiner, L. 1972. Evolution and revolutions as organizations grow. *Harvard Business Review,* 50(4): 37–46.

Gresov, C., Haveman, H., & Oliva, T. 1993. Organizational design, inertia and the dynamics of competetive response. *Organization Science,* 4: 181–208.

Groves, K., Vance, C., & Choi, T. 2011. Examining entrepreneurial cognition: An occupational analysis of balanced linear and nonlinear thinking and entrepreneurship success. *Journal of Small Business Management*, 49(3): 438–66.

Guastello, S. 1987. A butterfuly catastrophe model of motivation in organizations. *Journal of Applied Psychology*, 72: 165–82.

Guastello, S. 1995. *Chaos, Catastrophe, and Human Affairs: Applications of Nonlinear Dynamics to Work, Organizations, and Social Evolution*. Mahway, NJ: Lawrence Erlbaum & Associates.

Guastello, S. 1998. Self-organization and leadership emergence. *Nonlinear Dynamics, Psychology, and Life Sciences*, 2: 301–15.

Guastello, S. 2001. Nonlinear dynamics in psychology. *Discrete Dynamics in Nature and Society*, 6: 11–29.

Gunderson, L., & Holling, C. S. (Eds.). 2001. *Panarchy: Understanding Transformations in Human and Natural Systems*. Washington, DC: Island Press.

Gunderson, L., Holling, C. S., & Light, S. S. 1995. *Barriers and Bridges to the Renewal of Ecosystems and Institutions*. New York: Columbia University Press.

Gunz, H., Lichtenstein, B., & Long, R. 2002. Self-organization in career systems: A view from complexity science. *M@n@gement*, 5(1): 63–88.

Haken, H. 1977. *Synergetics*. Berlin: Springer-Verlag.

Haken, H. 2008. Self-organization. *Scholarpedia*, 3(8): 1401.

Hall, R. 1976. A system pathology of an organization: The rise and fall of the old *Saturday Evening Post*. *Administrative Science Quarterly*, 21: 185–211.

Hannan, M., & Freeman, J. 1984. Structural inertia and organizational change. *American Sociological Review*, 49: 149–64.

Harper, D., & Endres, A. 2012. The anatomy of emergence, with a focus on capital formation. *Journal of Economic Behavior and Organization*, 82: 352–67.

Harre, R., & Secord, P. F. 1979. *The Explanation of Social Behaviour*. Totowa, NJ: Littlefield, Adams & Company.

Haveman, H. 1992. Between a rock and a hard place: Organizational change and performance under conditions of fundamental environmental transformation. *Administrative Science Quarterly*, 37: 48–75.

Hayek, F. 1945. The use of knowledge in society. *American Economic Review*, 35: 519–30.

Hayek, F. 1967. *Studies in Philosophy, Politics and Economics*. Chicago: University of Chicago Press.

Hazy, J., Goldstein, J., & Lichtenstein, B. (Eds.). 2007. *Complex Systems Leadership Theory: New Perspectives from Complexity Science on Social and Organizational Effectiveness*. Mansfield, MA: ISCE Publishing.

Hechavarria, D., Renko, M., & Matthews, C. 2012. The nascent entrepreneurship hub: Goals, entrepreneurial self-efficacy and start-up outcomes. *Small Business Economics*, 39(3): 685–701.

Heinzen, T. E. 1994. Situational affect: Proactive and reactive creativity. In M. Shaw & M. Runco (Eds.), *Creativity and Affect* (127–46). Westport, CT: Ablex Publishing.

Heinzen, T. E. 1999. Proactive creativity. In M. Runco & S. R. Pritzker (Eds.), *Encyclopedia of Creativity*, Vol. 1: 429–34. San Diego: Academic Press, Elsevier.

Henderson, R., & Clark, K. 1990. Architectural innovation: The reconfiguration of existing product technologies and the failure of established firms. *Administrative Science Quarterly*, 35: 9–30.

Heracleous, L., & Barrett, M. 2001. Organizational change as discourse: Communicative actions and deep structures in the context of information technology implementation. *Academy of Management Journal*, 44: 755–78.

Herriott, S., Levinthal, D., & March, J. 1985. Learning from experience in organizations. *American Economic Review*, 75: 298–302.

Hills, G., & Singh, R. 2004. Opportunity recognition. In W. Gartner, K. Shaver, N. Carter, & P. Reynolds (Eds.), *Handbook of Entrepreneurial Dynamics* (259–72). Thousand Oaks, CA: SAGE Publications.

Hoffman, A. 1989. *Arguments on Evolution—A Paleontologist's Perspective*. New York: Oxford University Press.

Holland, J. 1975. *Adaptation in Natural and Artificial Systems*. Ann Arbor, MI: University of Michigan Press.

Holland, J. 1994. Echoing emergence: Objectives, rough definitions, and speculations of ECHO-class models. In G. Cowen, D. Pines, & D. Meltzer (Eds.), *Complexity: Metaphors, Models, and Reality* (309–43). Sante Fe, NM: Sante Fe Institute.

Holland, J. 1995. *Hidden Order*. Redwood City, CA: Addison-Wesley.

Holland, J. 1998. *Emergence: From Chaos to Order*. Cambridge, MA: Perseus Books.

Holling, C. S. 1973. Resilience and stability of ecological systems. *Annual Review of Ecology and Systematics*, 4: 1–23.

Holling, C. S. 2001. Understanding the complexity of economic, ecological, and social systems. *Ecosystems*, 4: 390–405.

Huber, G., & Glick, W. 1993. *Organizational Change and Redesign*. New York: Oxford University Press.

Hunter, L., & Thatcher, S. 2007. Feeling the heat: Effects of stress, commitment, and job experience on job performance. *Academy of Management Journal*, 50(4): 953–68.

Iannaccone, P. M., & Khokha, M. 1996. *Fractal Geometry in Biological Systems*. Boca Raton, FL: CRC Press.

Inkpen, A., Martin, M., & Fas-Pacheco, I. 2001. The rise and fall of Iridium. Glendale, AZ: Thunderbird, the American Graduate School of International Management.

Ireland, D., Hitt, M., & Simon, D. 2003. A model of strategic entrepreneurship: The construct and its dimensions. *Journal of Management*, 29(3): 963–89.

Jacquet, L. 2005. *March of the Penguins*. Warner Brothers.

Jansen, K. 2004. From persistence to pursuit: A longitudinal examination of momentum during the early stages of strategic change. *Organization Science*, 15: 276–95.

Jantsch, E. 1980. *The Self-Organizing Universe*. New York: Pergamon Press.

Johnson, N. 2009. *Simply Complexity: A Clear Guide to Complexity Theory*. Oxford, UK: Oneworld Publications.

Johnson, S. 2001. *Emergence: The Connected Lives of Ants, Brains, Cities, and Software*. New York: Scribner

Juarrero, A. 1999. *Dynamics in Action: Intentional Behavior as a Complex System*. Cambridge, MA: MIT Press.

Kahneman, D., Slovic, P., & Tversky, A. (Eds.). 1982. *Judgment under Uncertainty: Hueristics and Biases*. New York: Cambridge University Press.

Kahneman, D., & Tversky, A. 1979. Prospect theory: An analysis of decision under risk. *Econometrica*, 47(2): 263–92.

Kast, F., & Rosenzweig, J. 1972. General systems theory: Applications for organization and management. *Academy of Management Journal*, 15(4): 447–65.

Katz, J. 1993. The dynamics of organizational emergence: A contemporary group formation perspective. *Entrepreneurship Theory and Practice*, 17(2, Winter): 97–101.

Katz, J., & Gartner, W. 1988. Properties of emerging organizations. *Academy of Management Review*, 13: 429–41.

Katz, M. L., & Shapiro, C. 1985. Network externalities, competition and compatibility. *American Economic Review*, 75: 424–40.

Kauffman, G. 2004. Two kinds of creativity—But which ones? *Creativity and Innovation Management*, 13(3): 154–64.

Kauffman, S. 1993. *The Origins of Order*. New York: Oxford University Press.
Kauffman, S. 2000. *Investigations*. New York: Oxford University Press.
Kaufmann, H. 1991. *Time, Chance and Organizations*. Chatham, NJ: Chatham House.
Kawasaki, G. 2004. *Art of the Start: The Time-Tested, Battle-Hardened Guide for Anyone Starting Anything*. New York: Penguin.
Kazanjian, R. 1988. Relation of dominant problems to stages of growth in technology-based new ventures. *Academy of Management Journal*, 31: 257–79.
Kearney, E., Gebert, D., & Voelpel, S. 2009. When and how diversity benefits teams: The importance of team members' need for cognition. *Academy of Management Journal*, 52(3): 581–98.
Kegan, R., & Lahey, L. 2001. *How the Way We Talk Can Change the Way We Work: Seven Languages for Transformation*. San Francisco: Jossey-Bass.
Kelly, K. 1994. *Out of Control: The Rise of Neo-biological Civilization*. Reading, MA: Addison-Wesley.
Kickert, W. 1993. Autopoiesis and the science of (public) administration: Essence, sense and nonsense. *Organization Studies*, 14: 261–78.
Kim, D. 1993. The link between individual and organizational learning. *Slaon Management Review*, Fall: 37–50.
Kim, J. 1992. "Downward causation" in emergentism and nonreductive physicalism. In A. Beckermann, H. Flohr, & J. Kim (Eds.), *Emergence or Reduction? Essays on the Prospects of Nonreductive Physicalism* (119–38). Berlin: Walter de Gruyter.
Kim, J. 1999. Making sense of emergence. *Philosophical Studies*, 95: 3–36.
Kirzner, I. M. 1997. Entrepreneurial discovery and the competitive market process: An Austrian approach. *Journal of Economic Literature*, 35: 60–85.
Klee, R. 1984. Micro-determinism and concepts of emergence. *Philosophy of Science*, 51: 44–63.
Knott, A. M. 2003. Persistent heterogeneity and sustainable innovation. *Strategic Management Journal*, 24(8): 687–705.
Koehn, N. 2001. *Howard Schultz and Starbucks Coffee Company*. Boston: Harvard Business School.
Koestler, A. 1979. *Janis—A Summing Up*. New York: Random House.
Kotter, J. 1995. Leading change: Why transformation efforts fail. *Harvard Business Review*, March-April: 59–67.
Krueger, N., Reilly, M., & Casrud, A. 2000. Competing models of entrepreneurial intentions. *Journal of Business Venturing*, 14: 411–32.
Krugman, P. 1996. *The Self-Organizing Economy*. Cambridge, MA: Bradford Press.
Kuhn, T. S. 1970. *The Structure of Scientific Revolutions*. Chicago: University of Chicago Press.
Lang, K., & Lang, G. E. 1961. *Collective Dynamics*. New York: Thomas Crowell.
Langton, C. 1986. Studying artificial life with cellular automata. *Physica D: Nonlinear Phenomena*, 22(1): 120–49.
Langton, C. 1990. Computation to the edge of chaos: Phase transitions and emergent computation. *Physica D: Nonlinear Phenomena*, 42(1): 12–37.
Laporte, L. (Ed.). 1982. *The Fossil Record and Evolution*. San Francisco: W. H. Freeman
Laszlo, E. 1987. *Evolution—The Grand Synthesis*. Boston: Shambhala Publications.
Lawrence, T., Hardy, C., & Phillips, N. 2002. Institutional effects of interorganizational collaboration: The emergence of proto-institutions. *Academy of Management Journal*, 45: 281–90.
Lawrence, T., Winn, M., & Jennings, P. D. 2001. The temporal dynamics of institutionalization. *Academy of Management Review*, 26: 624–44.
Lee, Y., Amaral, L. A. N., Canning, D., Meyer, M., & Stanley, E. 1998. Universal features in the growth dynamics of complex organizations. *Physical Review (Amerian Physical Society)—Letters*, 81(15): 3275–82.

Leifer, R. 1989. Understanding organizational transformation using a dissipative structure model. *Human Relations*, 42: 899–916.
Le Maho, Y. 1977. The emperor penguin: A strategy to live and breed in the cold. *American Scientist*, 65: 680–93.
Lenox, M., Rockart, S., & Lewin, A. 2006. Interdependency, competition and the distribution of firm and industry profits. *Management Science*, 52: 757–72.
Leonard, D., & Sensiper, S. 1998. The role of tacit knowledge in group innovation. *California Management Review*, 40(3): 112–32.
Lesourne, J. 1993. Self-organization as a process in evolution of economic systems. In R. Day & P. Chen (Eds.), *Nonlinear Dynamics and Evolutionary Economics* (150–66). New York: Oxford University Press.
Lesourne, J., & Orlean, A. (Eds.). 1998. *Advances in Self-Organization and Evolutionary Economics*. London: Economica.
Levie, J., & Lichtenstein, B. 2010. A terminal assessment of stages theory: Introducing a dynamic states approach to entrepreneurship. *Entrepreneurship Theory and Practice*, 34(2, March): 314–54.
Levinthal, D. 1991. Organizational adaptation and environmental selection—Interrelated processes of change. *Organization Science*, 2: 140–4.
Levinthal, D. 1997. Adaptation on rugged landscapes. *Management Science*, 43: 934–50.
Levinthal, D., & March, J. 1993. The myopia of learning. *Strategic Management Journal*, 14(Special Winter Issue): 95–112.
Levinthal, D., & Myatt, J. 1994. Co-evolution of capabilities and industry: The evolution of mutual fund processing. *Strategic Management Journal*, 15(Special Issue): 45–62.
Levinthal, D., & Warglien, M. 1999. Landscape deisgn: Designing for local action in complex worlds. *Organization Science*, 10(3): 342–57.
Levi-Strauss, C. 1967. *The Savage Mind*. Chicago: University of Chicago Press.
Levy, D. 1994. Chaos theory and strategy. *Strategic Management Journal*, 15: 167–78.
Levy, D., & Lichtenstein, B. 2010. Non-linear meltdowns and the potential for emergence: Complex systems theory and social-environmental sustainability. In A. Hoffman & M. T. Dacin (Eds.), *Oxford Handbook on Business and the Environment* (591–610). New York: Oxford University Press.
Levy, M., & Solomon, S. 1997. New evidence for the power-law distribution of wealth. *Physica A: Statistical Mechanics and its Applications*, 242(1): 90–94.
Lewes, G. H. 1875. *Problems of Life and Mind, Volume 2*. London: Kegan Paul, Trench & Turbner.
Lewin, A. 1999. Application of complexity theory to organization science. *Organization Science*, 10(3): 215.
Lewin, R. 1992. *Complexity: Life on the Edge of Chaos*. New York: MacMillan.
Li, H., & Tesfatsion, L. 2012. Co-learning patterns as emegent market phenomena: An electricity market illustration *Journal of Economic Behavior and Organization* 82(2): 395–419.
Lichtenstein, B. 1995. Evolution or transformation: A critique and alternative to punctuated equilibrium. *Best Papers Proceedings, National Academy to Management*. 1995: 291–95.
Lichtenstein, B. 1998. *Self-organized change in entrepreneurial ventures: A dynamic, non-linear model*. Doctoral dissertation, Boston College/UMI.
Lichtenstein, B. 2000a. Dynamics of rapid growth and change: A complexity theory of entrepreneurial transitions. In G. Liebcap (Ed.), *Advances in the Study of Entrepreneurship, Innovation, and Economic Growth*, Vol. 6: 161–192. Westport, CT: JAI Press.
Lichtenstein, B. 2000b. Emergence as a process of self-organizing: New assumptions and insights from the study of nonlinear dynamic systems. *Journal of Organizational Change Management*, 13: 526–44.

Lichtenstein, B. 2000c. Generative knowledge and self-organized learning: Reflecting on Don Schon's research. *Journal of Management Inquiry*, 9(9): 47–54.

Lichtenstein, B. 2000d. Self-organized transitions: A pattern amid the "chaos" of transformative change. *Academy of Management Executive*, 14(4): 128–41.

Lichtenstein, B. 2002. Entrepreneurship as emergence: Insights and methods from philosophy and complexity science. Paper presented at the Lally-Darden Entrepreneurship Theory Retreat, Arlie, VA.

Lichtenstein, B. 2007. A matrix of complexity for leadership. In J. Hazy, J. Goldstein, & B. Lichtenstein (Eds.), *Complex Systems Leadership Theory* (285–304). Boston: ISCE Press.

Lichtenstein, B. 2009. Moving far from far-from-equliibrium: Opportunity tension as the catalyst of emergence. *Emergence: Complexity and Organization*, 11(4): 15–25.

Lichtenstein, B. 2011a. Complexity science contributions to the field of entrepreneurship. In P. Allen, S. Maguire, & B. McKelvey (Eds.), *The SAGE Handbook of Complexity and Management* (471–93). Thousand Oaks, CA: SAGE Publications.

Lichtenstein, B. 2011b. Levels and degrees of emergence: Toward a matrix of complexity in entrepreneurship. *International Journal of Complexity in Leadership and Management*, 1(3): 252–74.

Lichtenstein, B., & Brush, C. 2001. How do 'resource bundles' develop and change in new ventures? A dynamic model and longitudinal exploration. *Entrepreneurship Theory and Practice*, 25(3): 37–58.

Lichtenstein, B., Carter, N., Dooley, K., & Gartner, W. 2007. Complexity dynamics of nascent entrepreneurship. *Journal of Business Venturing*, 22: 236–61.

Lichtenstein, B., Dooley, K., & Lumpkin, T. 2006. Measuring emergence in the dynamics of new venture creation. *Journal of Business Venturing*, 21: 153–75.

Lichtenstein, B., & Jones, C. 2004. A self-organization theory of radical entrepreneurship. *Best Papers Proceedings, National Academy of Management*: OMT Division; CD format.

Lichtenstein, B., & Kurjanowicz, B. 2010. Tangibility, momentum, and the emergence of The Republic of Tea. *ENTER Journal*, 1: 125–48.

Lichtenstein, B., Lumpkin, T., & Schrader, R. 2003. Organizational learning by new ventures: Concepts, applications and opportunities. In J. Katz & D. Shepherd (Eds.), *Advances in Entrepreneurship, Firm Emergnece and Growth*, Vol. 6: 11–36. Westport, CT: JAI Press.

Lichtenstein, B., & McKelvey, B. 2011. Four types of emergence: A typology of complexity and its implications for a science of management. *International Journal of Complexity in Leadership and Management*, 1(4): 339–78.

Lichtenstein, B., & Plowman, D. A. 2009. The leadership of emergence: A complex systems leadership theory of emergence at successive organizational levels. *The Leadership Quarterly*, 20: 617–30.

Lichtenstein, B., Uhl-Bien, M., Marion, R., Seers, A., Orton, D., & Schreiber, C. 2007. Complexity leadership theory: Explaining the interactive process of leading in complex adaptive systems. *Emergence: Complexity and Organization*, 8(4): 2–12.

Lindberg, C., Herzog, A., Merry, M., & Goldstein, J. 1998. Life at the edge of chaos. *Physician Executive*, 24(1): 6–21.

Lindgren, P. 2012. Business model innovation leadership: How do SMEs strategically lead business model innovation? *Journal of Business and Management*, 7(14): 53–66.

Lindsay, R. 1961. *Physical Mechanics*. Princeton, NJ: Van Nostrand.

Link, A., & Siegel, D. 2007. *Innovation, Entrepreneurship and Technological Change*. New York: Oxford University Press.

Liu, J., Dietz, T., Carpenter, S., Alberti, M., Folke, C., Moran, E., Pell, A. N., Deadman, P., Kratz, T., Lubchenco, J., Ostrom, E., Ouyang, Z., Provencher, W., Redman, C., Schneider, S., &

Taylor, W. 2007. Complexity of coupled human and natural systems. *Science*, 317(Sept. 14): 1513–6.

Lomi, A., & Larsen, E. 1996. Interacting locally and evolving globally: A computational approach to the dynamics of organizational populations. *Academy of Management Journal*, 39(5): 1287–1321.

Lomi, A., & Larson, E. 1997. A computational approach to the evolution of competitive strategy. *Journal of Mathematical Sociology*, 22: 151–76.

Long, W., & McMullan, W. E. 1984. *Mapping the new venture opportunity identification process*. Paper presented at the Frontiers of Entrepreneurship Research, Wellesley, MA.

Loorbach, D. 2010. Transition management for sustainable development: A prescriptive, complexity-based governance framework. *Governancee*, 23: 161–83.

Lorenz, E. 1963. Deterministic nonperiodic flow. *Journal of the Atmospheric Sciences*, 20: 130–41.

Lotka, A. 1922. Contribution to the energetics of evolution. *Proceedings of the National Academy of Sciences U S A*, 6: 147–51.

Lotka, A. 1945. The law of evolution as a maximal principle. *Human Biology*, 17: 167–94.

Lounsbury, M., & Crumley, E. 2007. New practice creation: An institutional perspective on innovation. *Organization Studies*, 28: 993–1012.

Low, M., & Abrahamson, E. 1997. Movements, bandwagons, and clones: Industry evolution and the entrepreneurial process. *Journal of Business Venturing*, 12: 435–58.

Luhmann, N. 1986. The autopoiesis of social systems. In F. Geyer & J. van der Zouwen (Eds.), *Sociocybernetic Paradoxes: Observation, Control and Evolution of Self-Steering Systems* (172–92). Thousand Oaks, CA: SAGE Publications.

Luhmann, N. 1990. *Essays on Self-Reference*. New York: Columbia University Press.

Lumpkin, G. T., & Dess, G. 1996. Clarifying the entrepreneurial orientation construct and linking it to performance. *Academy of Management Review*, 21: 135–72.

Lumpkin, G. T., & Lichtenstein, B. 2005. The role of organizational learning in the opportunity recognition process. *Entrepreneurship Theory and Practice*, 29(4): 451–72.

MacCormack, A., & Herman, K. 2001. *The Rise and Fall of Iridium*. Boston: Harvard Business School.

MacIntosh, R., & MacLean, D. 1999. Conditioned emergence: A dissipative structures approach to transformation. *Strategic Management Journal*, 20: 297–316.

Macy, M. 1991. Chains of cooperation: Threshold effects in collective action. *American Sociological Review*, 56: 730–47.

Macy, M., & Skvoretz, J. 1998. The evolution of trust and cooperation between strangers: A computational model. *American Sociological Review*, 63: 638–60.

Maguire, S., & Hardy, C. 2009. Discourse and deinstitutionalization: The decline of DDT. *Academy of Management Review*, 52: 148–78.

Maguire, S., Hardy, C., & Lawrence, T. 2004. Institutional entrepreneurship in emerging fields: HIV/AIDS treatment advocacy in Canada. *Academy of Management Journal*, 47: 657–80.

Maguire, S., & McKelvey, B. 1999. Complexity and management: Moving from fad to firm foundations. *Emergence*, 1(2): 19–61.

Maguire, S., McKelvey, B., Mirabeau, L., & Oztas, N. 2006. Complexity science and organization studies. In S. Clegg, C. Hardy, W. Nord, & T. Lawrence (Eds.), *Handbook of Organization Studies* (2nd ed., 165–214). London, UK: SAGE Publications.

Malerba, F., Nelson, R., Orsenigo, L., & Winter, S. 1999. "History-friendly" models of industry evolution: The computer industry. *Industrial and Corporate Change*, 8: 3–40.

Mandelbrot, B. 1983. *The Fractal Geometry of Nature*. New York: Freeman Press.

March, J. 1981. Footnotes to organizational change. *Administrative Science Quarterly*, 26: 563–77.

March, J. 1988. Variable risk preferences and adaptive aspirations. *Journal of Economic Behavior and Organizatin*, 9: 5–24.

March, J. 1991. Exploration and exploitation in organization learning. *Organization Science*, 2: 71–87.

March, J. 1994. The evolution of evolution. In J. Baum & J. Singh (Eds.), *Evolutionary Dynamics of Organizations* (39–52). New York: Oxford University Press.

Margulis, L. 1967. On the origin of mitosing cells. *Journal of Theoretical Biology*, 14: 225–74.

Margulis, L. 1971. Symbiosis and evolution. *Scientific American*, 225(2): 49–57.

Margulis, L. 1981. *Symbiosis in Cell Evolution: Life and its Environment on the Early Earth*. New York: Freeman.

Margulis, L. 1992. Biodiversity: Molecular biological domains, symbiosis and kingdom origins. *Biosystems*, 27: 39–51.

Margulis, L. 1998. *Symbiotic Planet: A New View of Evolution*. New York: Basic Books.

Marion, R. 1999. *The Edge of Organization*. Thousand Oaks, CA: SAGE Publications.

Marion, R., & Uhl-Bien, M. 2001. Leadership in complex organizations. *The Leadership Quarterly*, 12: 389–418.

Maruyama, M. 1963. The second cybernetics. *American Scientist*, 51: 164–79.

Masterson, M. 2008. *Ready, Fire, Aim: Zero to $100 Million in No Time Flat*. New York: John Wiley & Sons.

Matilla-Garcia, M., & Marin, M. R. 2010. A new test for chaos and determinsm based on symbolic dynamicsk. *Journal of Economic Behavior and Organization*, 76(3): 600–14.

Maturana, H. R., & Varela, F. J. 1980. *Autopoiesis and Cognition*. Dordrecht, Holland: D. Reidel Publishing.

May, R. 1974. Biological populations with nonoverlapping generations: Stable points, stable cycles, and chaos. *Science*, 186: 645–7.

May, R. 1976. Simple mathematical models with very complicated dynamics. *Nature*, 26: 455–67.

Mayr, E. 1991. *One Long Argument: Charles Darwin and the Genesis of Modern Evolutionary Thought*. Cambridge, MA: Harvard University Press.

McClelland, J. L., Botvinick, M., Noelle, D., Plaut, D., Rogers, T., Seidenberg, M., & Smith, L. 2010. Letting structure emerge: Connectionist and dynamical systems approaches to cognition. *Trends in Cognitive Science*, 14(8): 348–56.

McClintock, M. 1971. Menstrual synchrony and suppression. *Nature*, 229(January 22): 244–5.

McClintock, M. 1984. Estrous synchrony: Modulation of ovarian cycle length by female pheromones. *Physiology & Behavior*, 32(5): 701–5.

McGrath, R. 1999. Falling forward: Real options reasoning and entrepreneurial failure. *Academy of Management Review*, 24: 13–31.

McKelvey, B. 1982. *Organizational Systematics*. Berkeley, CA: University of California Press.

McKelvey, B. 1997. Quasi-natural organization science. *Organization Science*, 8: 351–80.

McKelvey, B. 1999a. Avoiding complexity catastrophe in coevolutionary pockets: Strategies for rugged landscapes. *Organization Science*, 10(3): 294–321.

McKelvey, B. 1999b. Complexity theory in organization science: Seizing the promise or becoming a fad? *Emergence*, 1(1): 5–32.

McKelvey, B. 1999c. Self-organization, complexity catastrophe, and microstate models at the edge of chaos. In J. Baum & B. McKelvey (Eds.), *Variations in Organization Science* (279–310). Thousand Oaks, CA: SAGE Publications.

McKelvey, B. 1999d. Toward a Campbellian realist organization science. In J. Baum & B. McKelvey (Eds.), *Variations in Organization Science* (383–412). Thousand Oaks, CA: SAGE Publications.

McKelvey, B. 2001. What is complexity science? It is really order creation science? *Emergence*, 3(1): 137–57.

McKelvey, B. 2002. Model-centered organization science epistemology. In J. Baum (Ed.), *Companion to Organizations* (752–80). Thousand Oaks, CA: SAGE Publications.

McKelvey, B. 2004a. Toward a 0th law of thermodynamics: Order creation complexity dynamics from physics and biology to bioeconomics. *Bioeconomics*, 6: 65–96.

McKelvey, B. 2004b. Toward a complexity science of entrepreneurship. *Journal of Business Venturing*, 19: 313–42.

McKelvey, B. 2007. Emergent strategy via complexity leadership: Using complexity science and adaptive tension to build distributed intelligence. In M. Uhl-Bien & R. Marion (Eds.), *Complexity and Leadership Volume I: Conceptual Foundations* (225–68). Charlotte, NC: Information Age Publishing.

McKelvey, B., Li, M., Xu, H., & Vidgen, R. 2013. Re-thinking Kauffman's NK fitness landscape: From artifact and groupthink to weak-tie effects. *Human Systems Management*, 32(1): 17–42.

McKelvey, B., & Lichtenstein, B. 2007. Leadership in the four stages of emergence. In J. Hazy, J. Goldstein, & B. Lichtenstein (Eds.), *Complex Systems Leadership Theory* (93–108). Boston: ISCE Publishing.

McKelvey, B., Lichtenstein, B., & Andriani, P. 2012. When organizations and ecosystems interact: Toward a law of requisite fractality in firms. *International Journal of Complexity in Leadership and Management*, 2(1/2): 104–36.

McMullan, J., Plummer, L., & Acs, Z. 2007. What is an entrepreneurial opportunity? *Small Business Economics*, 28: 273–83.

McMullan, J., & Shepherd, D. 2006. Entrepreneurial action and the role of uncertainty in the theory of the entrepreneur. *Academy of Managment Review*, 31: 132–52.

Mead, H. 1938. *The Philosophy of the Act*. Chicago: University of Chicago Press.

Meadows, D. 1982. Whole earth models and systems. *Coevolution Quarterly*, Summer: 98–108.

Meadows, D., Meadows, D., Randers, J., & Behrens, W. 1972. *The Limits to Growth: A Report to the Club of Rome*. New York: Universe Press.

Meyer, A., Gaba, V., & Colwell, K. 2005. Organizing far from equilibrium: Nonlinear change in organizational fields. *Organization Science*, 16: 456–73.

Mihata, K. 1997. The persistence of emergence. In R. Eve, S. Horsfall, & M. Lee (Eds.), *Chaos, Complexity, and Sociology: Myths, Models and Theories* (30–8). Thousand Oaks, CA: SAGE Publications.

Miles, M. B., & Huberman, A. M. 1994. *Qualitative Data Analysis*. Thousand Oaks, CA: SAGE Publications.

Miles, R., & Snow, C. C. 1978. *Organizational Strategy, Structure, and Process*. New York: McGraw-Hill.

Miles, R., Snow, C. C., Meyer, A., & Coleman, H. J. 1978. Organizational strategy, structure and process. *Academy of Management Review*, 3(3): 546–62.

Miller, J. G. 1978. *Living Systems*. New York: McGraw-Hill.

Mintzberg, H. 1978. Patterns in strategy formation. *Management Science*, 29: 934–48.

Mintzberg, H. 1979. *The Structuring of Organizations*. Englewood Cliffs, NJ: Prentice-Hall.

Mintzberg, H., & Waters, J. 1985. Of strategies, deliberate and emergent. *Strategic Management Journal*, 6(3): 257–72.

Mitchell, J., & Shepherd, D. 2010. To thine own self be true: Images of self, images of opportunity, and entrepreneurial action. *Journal of Business Venturing*, 25(1): 138.

Mitchell, M. 2009. *Complexity: A Guided Tour*. New York: Oxford University Press.

Mitchell, R. 1992. You are relaxed. You are content. You are approaching 'Tea Mind.' *Business Week*, Issue 3295: 44–5.

Mitchell, R., Parker, V., & Giles, M. 2012. Open-mindedness in diverse team performance: Investigating a three-way interaction. *International Journal of Human Resource Management*, 23(17): 3652–72.

Monge, P. 1990. Theoretical and analytical issues in studying organizational processes. *Organization Science*, 1: 406–30.

Moore, G. 2002. *Crossing the Chasm: Marketing and Selling Disruptive Products to Mainstream Customers*. New York: HarperBusiness.

Morel, B., & Ramanujam, R. 1999. Through the looking glass of complexity: The dynamics of organizations as adaptive and evolving systems. *Organization Science*, 10(3): 278–93.

Morgan, C. L. 1923. *Emergent Evolution*. London: Williams & Norgate.

Morgan, C. L. 1926. *Life, Mind and Spirit*. London: Williams & Norgate

Morgan, C. L. 1933. *The Emergence of Novelty*. New York: Henry Holt & Co.

Morowitz, H. 1966. Physical background of cycles in biological systems. *Journal of Theoretical Biology*, 13: 60–2.

Morowitz, H. 1968. *Energy Flow in Biology: Biological Organization as a Problem in Thermal Physics*. New York: Academic Press.

Morowitz, H. 1992. *Beginnings of Cellular Life: Metabolism Recapitulates Biogenesis*. New Haven, CT: Yale University Press.

Morowitz, H. 2002. *The Emergence of Everything*. New York: Oxford University Press.

Morris, M., Schindette, M., & Allen, J. 2005. The entrepreneur's business model: Towards a unified perspective. *Journal of Business Research*, 58(6): 726–35.,

Mullins, J. 2006. *The New Business Road Test*. New York: Financial Times Press.

Mullins, J., & Komisar, R. 2009. *Getting to Plan B: Breaking Through to a Better Business Model*. Boston: Harvard Business Review Press.

Muthusamy, S. K., & White, M. 2005. Learning and knowledge transfer in strategic alliances. *Organization Studies*, 26(3): 415–41.

Nagel, E. 1961. *The Structure of Science*. New York: Harcourt Brace and World.

Nair, A., Narasimhan, R., & Choi, T. 2009. Supply networks as a complex adaptive system: Toward simulation-based theory building on evolutionary decision making. *Decision Sciences*, 40(4): 783–815.

Newey, L., & Zahra, S. 2009. The evolving firm: How dynamic and operating capabilities interact to enable entrepreneurship. *British Journal of Management*, 20(Supplement 1): S81-S100.

Newman, D. 1996. Emergence and strange attractors. *Philosophy of Science*, 63: 245–61.

Nicholls-Nixon, C. 2005. Rapid growth and high performance: The entrepreneur's "impossible dream?" *Academy of Management Executive*, 19(1): 77–89.

Nicolis, G. 1989. Physics of far-from-equilibrium systems and self-organization. In P. Davies (Ed.), *The New Physics*. New York: Cambridge University Press.

Nicolis, G., & Prigogine, I. 1989. *Exploring Complexity*. New York: W. H. Freeman.

Nonaka, I. 1988. Creating organizational order out of chaos: Self-renewal in Japanese firms. *California Management Review*, 30(Spring): 57–73.

Nystrom, H. 1979. *Creativity and Innovation*. New York: John Wiley & Sons.

Obloj, T., Obloj, K., & Pratt, M. 2010. Dominant logic and the entrepreneurial firms' performance in a transition economy. *Entrepreneurship Theory and Practice*, 34(1): 151–71.

Obstfeld, D. 2005. Social networks, the Tertius Lungens orientation, and involvement in innovation. *Administrative Science Quarterly*, 50: 100–30.

Odum, H. 1969. The strategy of ecosystem development. *Science*, 164: 262–70.

Odum, H. 1971. *Environment, Power & Society*. New York: Wiley Interscience.

Odum, H. 1988. Self-organization, transformity, and information. *Science*, 242: 1132–9.

Odum, H., & Odum, E. 1976. *Energy Basis for Man and Nture*. New York: McGraw Hill.

Odum, H., & Pinkerton, R. 1955. Time's speed regulator: The optimum efficiency for maximum power output in physical and biological systems. *American Scientist*, 43(2): 331–43.

Olson, E., & Eoyang, G. 2001. *Facilitating Organization Change*. San Francisco: Jossey-Bass.

Olsson, P., Gunderson, L., Carpenter, S., Ryan, P., Lebel, L., Folke, C., & Holling, C. S. 2006. Shooting the rapids: Navigating transitions to adaptive governance of social-ecological systems. *Ecology and Society*, 11(1): Article 18.

O'Mahony, S., & Ferraro, F. 2007. The emergence of governance in an open source community. *Academy of Management Journal*, 50: 1097–1106.

Osborn, R., & Hunt, J. 2007. Leadership and the choice of order: Complexity and hierarchical perspectives near the edge of chaos. *Leadership Quarterly*, 18(4): 319–40.

Osterwalder, A. 2009. How to systematically build business models beyond profit. SlideShare.com. http://www.slideshare.net/Alex.Osterwalder/business-models-beyond-profit-social-entrepreneurship-lecture-wise-etienne-eichenberger-iqbal-quadir-grameen-bank-grameen-phone

Osterwalder, A. 2010. What is a business model. SlideShare.com. http://www.slideshare.net/Alex.Osterwalder/what-is-a-business-model

Osterwalder, A., & Pigneur, Y. 2010. *Business Model Generation: A Handbook for Visionaries, Game Changers, and Challengers*. Hoboken, NJ: John Wiley & Sons.

Padgett, J. 2011. Autocatalysis in chemistry and the origin of life. In J. Padgett & W. Powell (Eds.), *The Emergence of Organizations and Markets* (33–70). Princeton, NJ: Princeton University Press.

Padgett, J., & Ansell, C. 1993. Robust action and the rise of the Medici, 1400–1434. *American Journal of Sociology*, 98(6): 1259–1319.

Padgett, J., Lee, D., & Collier, N. 2003. Economic production as chemistry. *Industrial and Corporate Change*, 12(4): 843–77.

Padgett, J., & Powell, W. 2011. *The Emergence of Organizations and Markets*. Princeton, NJ: Princeton University Press.

Page, S. 2007. *The Difference: How the Power of Diversity Creates Bettter Groups, Firms, Schools, and Societies*. Princeton, NJ: Princeton University Press.

Pantzar, M., & Csanyi, V. 1991. The replicative model of the evolution of the business organization. *Journal of Social and Biological Structures*, 14: 149–63.

Pareto, V. 1897. *Cours d'Economie Politique*. Paris: Rouge and Cie.

Pascale, R. 1999. Surfing the edge of chaos. *Sloan Management Review*, Spring: 83–94.

Pathak, S., Day, J., Nair, A., Sawaya, W., & Kristal, M. 2007. Complexity and adaptivity in supply networks: Building supply network theory using a complex adaptive systems perspective. *Decision Sciences*, 38: 547–80.

Paul, D. L., Butler, J. C., Pearlson, K. E., & Whinston, A. B. 1996. Computationally modeling organizational learning and adaptability as resource allocation. *Computational and Mathematical Organization Theory*, 2: 301–24.

Pegasus-Communications. 1999. *Organizational Learning at Work*. Waltham, MA: Pegasus Communications.

Pentland, B., & Rueter, H. 1994. Organizational routines as grammars of action. *Administrative Science Quarterly*, 39: 484–510.

Pietgen, H. O., Jurgens, H., & Saupe, D. 2004. *Chaos and Fractals: New Frontiers of Science* (2nd ed.). New York: Springer-Verlag.

Pihlström, S. 2002. The re-emergence of the emergence debate. *Principia*, 6: 133–81.

Plowman, D. A., Baker, L., Beck, T., Kulkarni, M., Solansky, S., & Travis, D. 2007. Radical change accidentally: The emergence and amplification of small change. *Academy of Management Journal*, 50: 515–43.

Plowman, D. A., Solanksy, S., Beck, T., Baker, L., Kulkarni, M., & Travis, D. 2007. The role of leadership in emergent, self-organization. *The Leadership Quarterly*, 18(4): 341–56.

Poirer, G., Amin, E., & Aggleton, J. 2008. Qualitatively different hippocampal subfield engagement emerges with mastery of a spatial memory task by rats. *Journal of Neuroscience*, 28(5): 1034-45.

Poole, M. S., Van de Ven, A., Dooley, K., & Holmes, M. 2000. *Organizational Change and Innovation Processes: Theory and Methods for Research*. New York: Oxford University Press.

Popper, S. 1926. Emergence. *Journal of Philosophy*, 23: 241–5.

Porter, M., & Siggelkow, N. 2008. Contextual interactions within activity systems and sustainability of competitive advantage. *Academy of Management Perspectives*, 22(2): 34–56.

Prahalad, C. K., & Bettis, R. 1986. The dominant logic: A new lingage between diversity and performance. *Strategic Management Journal*, 7: 485–501.

Prietula, M. 2011. Thoughts on complexity and computational models. In P. Allen, S. Maguire, & B. McKelvey (Eds.), *The SAGE Handbook of Complexity and Management* (93–110). Thousand Oaks, CA: SAGE Publications.

Prigogine, I. 1955. *Introduction to the Thermodynamics of Irreversible Processes*. New York: John Wiley & Sons.

Prigogine, I., & Glansdorff, P. 1971. *Thermodynamic Theory of Structure, Stability, and Fluctuations*. New York: John Wiley & Sons.

Prigogine, I., Nicolis, G., & Babloyantz, A. 1972. A thermodynamics of evolution. *Physics Today*, 23: 23–8.

Prigogine, I., & Stengers, I. 1984. *Order out of Chaos*. New York: Bantam Books.

Prottas, D. 2011. Person-environment fit and self-employment: Opportunities and needs for achievement, affiliation, autonomy and dominance. *North American Journal of Psychology*, 13(3): 403–26.

Purdy, J., & Gray, B. 2009. Conflicting logics, mechanisms of diffusion, and multi-level dynamics of emergence in institutional fields. *Academy of Management Journal*, 52: 355–80.

Quinn, J. B. 1989. Strategic change: Logical incrementalism. *Sloan Management Review*, Summer, 45–60.

Rauch, A., & Frese, M. 2007. Let's put the person back into entrepreneurship research: A meta-analysis on the relationship between business owners' personality traits, business creation, and success. *Eurpoean Journal of Work and Organizational Psychology*, 16(4): 353–85.

Reid, R. 2007. *Biological Emergences: Evolution by Natural Experiment*. Cambridge, MA: Bradford Books—MIT Press.

Repenning, N. 2002. A simulation-based approach to understanding the dynamics of innovation implementation. *Organization Science*, 13(2): 109–27.

Repenning, N., & Sterman, J. 2001. Nobody ever gets credit for fixing problems that never happened: Creating and sustaining process improvement. *California Management Review*, 43(4): 64–88.

Reuf, M. 2002. Strong ties, weak ties and islands: Structural and cultural predictors of organizational innovation. *Industrial and Corporate Change*, 11(3): 427–49.

Reuf, M., Aldrich, H., & Carter, N. 2003. The structure of founding teams: Homophily, strong ties and isolation among U.S. entrepreneurs. *American Sociological Review*, 68: 195–225.

Reynolds, P. 2000. National panal study of U.S. Business start-ups: Background and methodology. In J. K. R. Brockhaus (Ed.), *Advances in Entrepreneurship, Firm Emergence, and Growth*, Vol. 4: 153–227. Stamford, CT: JAI Press.

Reynolds, P., Carter, N., Gartner, W., Greene, P., & Cox, L. 2002. *The entrepreneur next door: Characteristics of individuals starting companies in AmericaEwing Marion Kauffman Foundation*, Kansas City, MO.

Reynolds, P., & Miller, B. 1992. New firm gestation: Conception, birth, and implications for research. *Journal of Business Venturing*, 7: 405–71.

Rindova, V., Barry, D., & Ketchen, D. 2009. Entrepreneuring as emancipation. *Academy of Management Review*, 34(3): 477–91.

Rindova, V., & Fombrun, C. 2001. Entrepreneurial action in the creation of the specialty coffee niche. In C. B. Schoonhoven & E. Romanelli (Eds.), *The Entrepreneurship Dynamic* (236–61). Palo Alto, CA: Stanford University Press.

Rindova, V., & Kotha, S. 2001. Continuous "morphing": Competing through dynamic capabilities, form, and function. *Academy of Management Journal*, 44: 1263–80.

Rivkin, J. 2000. Imitation of complex strategies. *Management Science*, 46: 824–44.

Rivkin, J., & Siggelkow, N. 2003. Balancing search and stability: Interdependencies among elements of organizational design. *Management Science*, 49: 290–311.

Rivkin, J., & Siggelkow, N. 2007. Patterned interactions in complex systems: Implications for exploration. *Management Science*, 53: 1068–85.

Robb, F. 1990. On the application of the theory of emergence and of the law of maximum entropy production to social processes. *Systems Practice*, 3: 389–99.

Robinson, O., & Griffiths, A. 2005. Coping with the stress of transformational change in a government department. *Journal of Applied Behavioral Science*, 41(2): 204–21.

Romanelli, E., & Tushman, M. 1994. Organizational transformaton as punctuated equilibrium: An empirical test. *Academy of Management Journal*, 37: 1141–66.

Romme, G., Zollo, M., & Berends, P. 2010. Dynamic capabilities, deliberate learning and environmental dynamism: A simulation model. *Industrial and Corporate Change*, 19(4): 1271–99.

Rosen, R. 1971. Some realizations of (M,R)-systems and their interpretation. *Bulletin of Mathematical Biophysics*, 33: 309–19.

Rosen, R. 1973. On the dynamical realization of (M,R)-systems. *Bulletin of Mathematical Biology*, 35: 1–9.

Rosser, J. B. 1992. The dialogue between the economic and the ecologic theories of evolution. *Journal of Economic Behavior and Organization*, 17: 195–215.

Rothschild, M. 1992. *Bionomics: Economy as Ecosystem*. New York: Holt & Company.

Rudolph, J., & Repenning, N. 2002. Disaster dynamics: Understanding the role of quantity in organizational collapse. *Administrative Science Quarterly*, 47: 1–30.

Ryan, A. 2007. Emergence is coupled to scope, not level. *Complexity*, 13(2): 66–77.

Salthe, S. 1985. *Evolving Hierarchical Systems: Their Structure and Representation*. New York: Columbia University Press.

Salthe, S. 1989. Self-organization of/in hierarchically structured systems. *Systems Research*, 6(3): 199–208.

Salthe, S. 1993. *Development and Evolution: Complexity and Change in Biology*. Cambridge, MA: Bradford—MIT Press.

Salthe, S. 2010. Development (and evolution) of the universe. *Foundations of Science*, 15: 357–67.

Santos, F., & Eisenhardt, K. 2009. Constructing markets and shaping boundaries: Entrepreneurial power in nascent fields. *Academy of Management Journal*, 52: 643–71.

Sarasson, Y., Dean, T., & Hilliard, B. 2006. Entrepreneurship as the nexus of individual and opportunity: A structuration view. *Journal of Business Venturing*, 21: 286–305.

Sarasvathy, S. 2001a. Causation and effectuation: Toward a theoretical shift from economic inevitability to entrepreneurial contingency. *Academy of Management Review*, 26: 243–63.

Sarasvathy, S. 2001b. Effectual rationality in entrepreneurial strategies: Existence and bounds. *Academy of Management Best Papers Proceedings*, Vol. 61: ENT, D1–D7.

Sarasvathy, S., & Dew, N. 2005. New market creation through transformation. *Journal of Evolutionary Economics*, 15: 533–65.

Sarasvathy, S., & Venkataramen, S. 2011. Entrepreneurship as method: Open questions for an entrepreneurial future. *Entrepreneurship Theory and Practice*, 35(1): 113–35.

Sastry, A. 1997. Problems and paradoxes in a model of punctuated organizational change. *Administrative Science Quarterly*, 42(2): 237–75.

Savage, D., & Torgler, B. 2012. Nerves of steel? Stress, work performance and elite athletes. *Applied Economics*, 44(19): 2423–35.

Saviotti, P. P., & Mani, G. S. 1998. Technological evolution, self-organization, and knowledge. *Journal of High Technology Management Research*, 9: 255–70.

Sawyer, K. 2001. Simulating emergence and downward causation in small groups. In S. Moss & P. Davidsson (Eds.), *Multi-Agent-Based Simulation* (49–67). Berlin: Springer.

Sawyer, K. 2002. Nonreductive individualsm, part 1: Supervenience and wild disjunction. *Philosophy of the Social Sciences*, 32: 537–59.

Sawyer, K. 2003a. *Improvised Dialogues: Emergence and Creativity in Conversation*. Westfield, CT: Greenwood Press.

Sawyer, K. 2003b. Nonreductive individualism, part 2: Social causation. *Philosophy of the Social Sciences*, 33: 203–24.

Sawyer, K. 2004. The mechanisms of emergence. *Philosophy of the Social Sciences*, 34: 260–82.

Sawyer, K. 2005. *Social Emergence: Societies as Complex Systems*. New York: Cambridge University Press.

Sawyer, K., & DeZutter, S. 2009. Distributed creativity: How collective creations emerge from collaboration. *Psychology of Aesthetics, Creativity, and the Arts*, 3(2): 81–92.

Saynisch, M. 2010. Beyond frontiers of traditional project management: An approach to evolutionary, self-organizational principles and the complexity theory—Results of the research program. *Project Management Journal*, 41(2): 21–37.

Scheffer, M., Westley, F., Brock, W., & Holmgren, M. 2001. Dynamic interaction of societies and ecosystems—Linking theories from ecology, economy, and sociology. In L. Gunderson & C. S. Holling (Eds.), *Panarchy: Understanding Transformations in Human and Natural Systems* (195–240). Washington, DC: Island Press.

Scheinkman, J., & Woodfordd, J. 1994. Self-organized criticality and economic fluctuations. *American Economic Review*, 84: 417–21.

Schelling, T. 1978. *Micromotives and Macrobehavior*. New York: W. W. Norton.

Schieve, W., & Allen, P. (Eds.). 1982. *Self-Organization and Dissipative Structures: Applications in the Physical and Social Sciences*. Austin, TX: University of Texas Press.

Schindehutte, M., & Morris, M. 2009. Advancing strategic entrepreneurship research: The role of complexity science in shifting the paradigm. *Entrepreneurship Theory and Practice*, 33(1): 241–76.

Schindehutte, M., Morris, M., & Allen, J. 2006. Beyond achievement: Entrepreneurship as extreme experience. *Small Business Economics*, 27(4/5): 349–68.

Schneider, E., & Sagan, D. 2005. *Into the Cool: Energy Flow, Thermodynamics, and Life*: Chicago: University of Chicago Press.

Schoonhoven, C. B., & Romanelli, E. (Eds.). 2001. *The Entrepreneurship Dynamic*. Stanford, CA: Stanford Business Books.

Schröder, J. 1998. Emergence: Non-deducibility or downwards causation? *Philosophical Quarterly*, 48(193): 433–52.

Schrödinger, E. 1944. *What Is Life?* Cambridge, UK: Cambridge University Press.

Schumpeter, J. 1934. *The Theory of Economic Development*. Boston: Harvard University Press.

Scott, R. 1981. *Organizations: Rational, Natural, and Open Systems*. Englewood Cliffs, NJ: Prentice-Hall.

Scully, M., & Segal, A. 2002. Passion with an umbrella: Grassroots activists in the workplace. In M. Lounsbury & M. Ventresca (Eds.), *Social Structure and Organizations Revisited* (Vol. 19: 125–69). Oxford, UK: JAI/Elsevier Science.

SEMATECH. 2012. SEMATECH history—Acceleration: SEMATECH achieves its first mission.

Senge, P., Roberts, C., Ross, R., Smith, B., & Kleiner, A. 1994. *The Fifth Discipline Fieldbook*. New York: Currency/Doubleday.

Senge, P. M. 2006. *The Fifth Discipline* (revised ed.). New York: Doubleday.

Servat, D., Perrier, E., Treuil, J. P., & Drogoul, A. 1998. When agents emerge from agents: Introducing multi-scale viewpoints in multi-agent simulations. In J. Sichman, R. Conte, & N. Gilbert (Eds.), *Multi-Agent Systems and Agent-Based Simulation* (183–98). Berlin: Springer-Verlag.

Shane, S. 2000. Prior knowledge and the discovery of entrepreneurial opportunities. *Organization Science*, 11: 448–69.

Shane, S. 2005. *Finding Fertile Ground: Identifying Extraordinary Opportunities for New Ventures*. Upper Saddle River, NJ: Wharton School/Pearson Education.

Shane, S., & Venkataraman, S. 2000. The promise of entrepreneurship as a field of research. *Academy of Management Review*, 25: 217–26.

Shaver, K., & Scott, L. 1991. Person, process, choice: The psychology of new venture creation. *Entrepreneurship Theory and Practice*, 16(2): 23–46.

Sheldrake, R. 1981. *A New Science of Life*. Los Angeles: J. P. Tarcher.

Sheldrake, R. 1988. *The Presence of the Past*. New York: Time Books.

Siggelkow, N., & Rivkin, J. 2005. Speed and search: Designing organizations for turbulence and complexity. *Organization Science*, 16: 101–22.

Siggelkow, N., & Rivkin, J. 2006. When exploration backfires: Unintended consequences of multilevel organizational search. *Academy of Management Journal*, 49: 779–96.

Simon, H. 1955. A behavioral model of rational choice. *Quarterly Journal of Economics*, 69(1): 99–118.

Simon, H. 2002. Near decomposability and the speed of evolution. *Industrial and Corporate Change*, 11: 587–99.

Simpson, G. G. 1944. *Tempo and Mode in Evolution*. New York: Columbia University Press.

Slevin, D., & Covin, J. 1997. Time, growth, complexity, and transitions: Entrepreneurial challenges for the future. *Entrepreneurship Theory and Practice*, 22(2, Winter): 53–68.

Smith, C. 1986. Transformation and regeneration in social systems: A dissipative structure perspective. *Systems Research*, 3: 203–13.

Smith, C., & Comer, D. 1994. Change in the small group: A dissipative structure perspective. *Human Relations*, 47: 553–81.

Smith, C., & Gemmill, G. 1991. Self-organization in small groups: A study of group effectivenss within non-equilibrium conditions. *Human Relations*, 44: 697–716.

Smith, D. M. 2011. *The Elephant in the Room: How Relationships Make or Break the Success of Leaders and Organizations*. San Francisco: Jossey-Bass.

Smith, L., & Thelen, E. 2003. Development as a dynamic system. *Trends in Cognitive Science*, 7(8): 343–8.

Snow, C. C., & Hambrick, D. 1980. Strategy, distinctive competence, and organizational performance. *Administrative Science Quarterly*, 25(2): 317–36.

Sommer, S., Loch, C., & Dong, J. 2009. Managing complexity and unforseeable uncertainty in startup companies: An empirical study. *Organization Science*, 20: 118–33.

Sonenshein, S. 2009. Emergence of ethical issues during strategic change implementation. *Organization Science*, 20: 223–39.

Sorenson, O. 1997. *The complexity catastrophe: Interdependence and adaptability in organizational evolution.* Ph.D. dissertation, Stanford University.

Sorenson, O. 2002. Interorganizational complexity and computation. In J. Baum (Ed.), *Companion to Organizations* (664–85). Malden, MA: Blackwell Publishers.

Sorenson, O., & Audia, P. 2000. The social structure of entrepreneurial activity: Geographic concentration of footwear production in the U.S., 1940–1989. *American Journal of Sociology*, 106: 424–61.

Sorenson, O., Rivkin, J., & Fleming, L. 2006. Complexity, networks and knowledge flow. *Research Policy*, 35: 994–1017.

Sperry, R. 1969. A modified concetp of consciousness. *Psychological Review*, 76: 532–6.

Sperry, R. 1986. Discussion: Macro- versus micro-determinism. *Philosophy of Science*, 53: 265–70.

Sperry, R. 1991. In defense of mentalism and emergent interaction. *Journal of Mind and Behavior*, 122: 221–46.

Stacey, R. 1995. The science of complexity: An alternative perspective for strategic choice processes. *Strategic Management Journal*, 16: 477–95.

Stake, R. 1994. Case studies. In N. Denzin & Y. Lincoln (Eds.), *Handbook of Qualitative Studies* (236–47). Newbury Park, CA: SAGE Publications.

Stam, E., Audretsch, D., & Meijaard, J. 2008. Re-nascent entrepreneurship. *Journal of Evolutionary Economics*, 18(3/4): 493–507.

Stanley, M., Amaral, L., Buldyrev, S., Havlin, S., Leschhorn, H., Maass, P., Salinger, M., & Stanley, E. 1996. Scaling behavior in the growth of companies. *Nature*, 379: 804–6.

Staudenmayer, N., Tyre, M., & Perlow, L. 2002. Time to change: Temporal shifts as enablers of organizational change. *Organization Science*, 13(5): 583–97.

Stauder, M., & Kirchhoff, B. 2004. Funding the first year of business. In W. Gartner, K. Shaver, N. Carter, & P. Reynolds (Eds.), *Handbook of Entrepreneurial Dynamics* (352–71). Thousand Oaks, CA: SAGE Publications.

Staw, B. 1981. The escalation of commitment to a course of action. *Academy of Management Review*, 6: 577–87.

Stebbins, H., & Braganza, A. 2009. Exploring continuous organizational transformation: Morphing through network interdependence. *Journal of Change Management*, 9: 27–48.

Sterman, J. 1989. Misperceptions of feedback in dynamic decision making. *Organizational Behavior and Human Decision Processes*, 43(3): 301–44.

Sterman, J. 2000. *Business Dynamics.* Chicago: Irwin-McGraw-Hill.

Sterman, J. 2002. All models are wrong: Reflections on becoming a systems scientist. *System Dynamics Review*, 18(4): 501–32.

Sterman, J., & Wittenberg, J. 1999. Path dependence, competition, and succession in the dynamics of scientific revolutions. *Organization Science*, 10: 322–41.

Stevenson, B. W. 2012. Developing an awareness and understanding of self-organization as it relates to organizational development and leadership issues. *Emergence: Complexity & Organization*, 14(2): 69–85.

Stevenson, H., & Harmeling, S. 1990. Entrepreneurial management's need for a more 'chaotic' theory. *Journal of Business Venturing*, 5: 1–14.

Steyaert, C. 2007. Entrepreneuring as a conceptual attractor? A review of process theories in 20 years of entrepreneurship studies. *Entrepreneurship and Regional Development*, 19(6): 453–77.

Storm, G. 2012. *Intention, economic opportunity and their impact on venture creation.* Ph.D. dissertation, University of Nebraska.

Street, C., & Gallupe, R. B. 2009. A proposal for operationalizing the pace and scope of organizational change in management studies. *Organizational Research Methods*, 12: 720–37.

Strogatz, S. 2003. *Sync: How Order Emerges from Chaos in the Universe, Nature, and Daily Life.* New York: Hyperion.
Sulis, W., & Combs, A. (Eds.). 1996. *Nonlinear Dynamics in Human Behavior.* Singapore: World Scientific Press.
Sullivan, S., & Bhagat, R. 1992. Organizational stress, job satisfaction and job performance: Where do we go from here? *Journal of Management,* 18(2): 353–75.
Surana, A., Kumara, S., Greaves, M., & Raghavan, U. N. 2005. Supply-chain networks: A complex adaptive systems perspective. *International Journal of Production Research,* 43(20): 4235–65.
Surie, G., & Hazy, J. 2007. Generative leadership: Nuturing innovation in complex systems. In J. Hazy, J. Goldstein, & B. Lichtenstein (Eds.), *Complex Systems Leadership Theory* (349–67). Mansfield, MA: ISCE Publishing.
Swenson, R. 1988. *Emergence and the principle of maximum entropy production: Multi-level system theory, evolution, and nonequilibrium thermodynamics.* Paper presented at the Proceedings of the 32nd Annual Meeting of the ISGSR.
Swenson, R. 1989. Emergent attractor and the law of maximum entropy production: Foundations to a theory of general evolution. *Systems Research,* 6(3): 187–97.
Swenson, R. 1991. End-directed physics and evolutionary ordering. In F. Geyr (Ed.), *Cybernetics of Complex Systems* (41–60). Salinas, CA: Intersystems Press.
Swenson, R. 1992a. Autocatakinetics, yes—autopoiesis, no: Steps toward a unified theory of evolutionary ordering. *International Journal of General Systems,* 21: 207–28.
Swenson, R. 1992b. Order, evolution, and natural law: Fundamental relations in complex system theory. In C. Negoita (Ed.), *Cybernetics and Applied Systems* (125–47). New York: Marcel Dekker.
Swenson, R. 1997. Autocatakinetics, evolution, and the law of maximum entropy production: A principled foundation towards the study of human ecology. *Advances in Human Ecology,* 6: 1–47.
Swenson, R. 1998. Thermodynamics, evolution, and behavior. In G. Greenberg & M. Haraway (Eds.), *Encyclopedia of Comparative Psychology* (207–18). New York: Garland Publishers.
Swenson, R. 2010. Selection is entailed by self-organization and natural selection is a special case. *Biological Theory,* 5(2): 167–81.
Tan, J. 2007. Phase transitions and emergence of entrepreneurship: The transformation of Chinese SOEs over time. *Journal of Business Venturing,* 22: 77–96.
Tapsell, P., & Woods, C. 2010. Social entrepreneurship and innovation: Self-organization in an indigenous context. *Entrepreneurship & Regional Development,* 22(6): 535–56.
Terpstra, D., & Olson, P. 1993. Entrepreneurial start-up and growth: A classification of problems. *Entrepreneurship Theory and Practice,* 17(3): 5–20.
Tesfatsion, L. 2011. Agent-based modeling and institutional design. *Eastern Economic Journal,* 37: 13–19.
Thelen, E. 1995. Motor development: A new synthesis. *American Psychologist,* 50(2): 79–95.
Thelen, E., & Smith, L. 1995. *A Dynamic Systems Approach to the Development of Cognition and Action.* Cambridge, MA: Bradford/MIT Press.
Thom, R. 1975. *Structural Stability and Morphogenesis.* Reading, MA: Addison-Wesley.
Thomas, I., Frankhauser, P., & Badariotti, D. 2012. Comparing the fractality of European urban neighborhoods: Do national contexts matter? *Journal of Geographic Systems,* 14(2): 189–208.
Thompson, J. 1967. *Organizations in Action.* New York: McGraw Hill.
Timmons, J. 1999. *New Venture Creation* (5th ed.). Homewood, IL: Richard D. Irwin.
Tsoukas, H. 1991. The missing link: A transformational view of metaphors in organizational science. *Academy of Management Review,* 16(3): 566–85.

Tsoukas, H., & Chia, R. 2002. On organizational becoming: Rethinking organizational change. *Organization Science*, 13: 567–83.

Tushman, M., Newman, W. H., & Romanelli, E. 1986. Convergence and upheaval: Managing the unsteady pace of organizational evolution. *California Management Review*, 29(1): 29–44.

Tushman, M., & Romanelli, E. 1985. Organizational evolution: A metamorphosis model of convergence and reorientation. *Research in Organizational Behavior*, 7: 171–222.

Tversky, A., & Kahneman, D. 1992. Advances in prospect theory: Cumulative representation of uncertainty. *Journal of Risk and Uncertainty*, 5(4): 297–323.

Uhl-Bien, M., & Marion, R. (Eds.). 2008. *Complexity Leadership. Part 1: Conceptual Foundations*. Charlotte, NC: Information Age Publishing.

Uhl-Bien, M., Marion, R., & McKelvey, B. 2007. Complexity leadership theory: Shifting leadership from the Industrial Age to the Information Era. *The Leadership Quarterly*, 18: 298–318.

Ulanowicz, R. 1980. An hypothesis on the development of natural communities. *Journal of Theoretical Biology*, 85: 225–45.

Ulanowicz, R. 1983. Identifying the structure of cycling in ecosystems. *Mathematical Biosciences*, 65: 219–37.

Ulanowicz, R. 1987. Growth and development: Variational principles reconsidered. *European Journal of Operational Research*, 30: 173–78.

Ulanowicz, R. 2002. Ecology, a dialog between the quick and the dead. *Emergence*, 4(1–2): 34–52.

Ulrich, H., & Probst, J. B. (Eds.). 1984. *Self-Organization and Management of Social Systems*. Berlin: Springer-Verlag.

Unsworth, K. 2001. Unpacking creativity. *Academy of Management Review*, 26(2): 289–97.

Unsworth, K., & Parker, S. 2003. Proactivity and innovation: Promoting a new workforce for the new workplace. In D. Holman, T. Wall, C. Clegg, P. Sparrow, & A. Howard (Eds.), *The New Workplace: A Guide to the Human Impact of Modern Working Practices* (175–96). New York: John Wiley & Sons.

Vakola, M., & Nikolaou, L. 2005. Attitudes towards organizational change: What is the role of employees' stress and commitment? *Employee Relations*, 27(2): 160–74.

Van de Ven, A. 1992. Longitudinal methods for studying the process of entrepreneurship. In D. L. Sexton, & J. D. Kasarda (Eds.), *The State of the Art of Entrepreneurship* (214–42). Boston: PWS-Kent Publishers.

Van de Ven, A., Angel, H., & Poole, M. S. 1989. *Research on the Management of Innovation*. New York: Ballanger Books.

Van de Ven, A., & Poole, M. S. 1990. Methods for studying innovation development in the Minnesota Innovation Research Program. *Organization Science*, 1: 313–35.

Van de Ven, A., & Poole, M. S. 1995. Explaining development and change in organizations. *Academy of Management Review*, 20: 510–40.

Van de Ven, A., & Pooley, D. 1992. Learning while innovating. *Organization Science*, 3: 91–116.

Van de Ven, A., Pooley, D., Garud, R., & Venkataramen, S. 1999. *The Innovation Journey*. New York: Oxford University Press.

Viega, L. B., & Magrini, A. 2009. Eco-industrial park development in Rio de Janeiro, Brazil: A tool for sustainable development. *Journal of Cleaner Production*, 145: 638–49.

von Bertalanffy, L. 1950. The theory of open systems in physics and biology. *Science*, 111(Jan. 13): 23–8.

von Bertalanffy, L. 1956. General systems theory. *General Systems*, 1: 1–10.

von Bertalanffy, L. 1968. *General Systems Theory*. New York: Braziller Books.

Von Bertalanffy, L. 1972. The history and status of general systems theory. *Academy of Management Journal*, 15(4): 407–26.

von Foerster, H. 1960. On self-organizing systems and their environments. In M. Yovitz & S. Cameron (Eds.), *Self-Organizing Systems* (31–50). New York: Pergamon Press.

von Neumann, J. 1966. *Theory of Self-Reproducing Automata*. Champaign, IL: University of Illinois Press.

Waldrop, M. 1992. *Complexity*. New York: Touchstone/Simon & Schuster.

Walker, B., Gunderson, L., Kinzig, A., Folke, C., Carpenter, S., & Schultz, L. 2006. A handful of hueristics and some propositions for understanding resilience in social-ecological systems. *Ecology and Society*, 11(1): 13–29.

Walker, B., Holling, C. S., Carpenter, S., & Kinzig, A. 2004. Resilience, adaptability and transformability in social-ecological systems. *Ecology and Society*, 9(2): 5.

Wallner, T., & Menrad, M. 2012. High performance work systems as an enabling structure for self-organized learning processes. *International Journal of Advanced Corporate Learning*, 5(4): 32–37.

Walsh, I., & Bartunek, J. 2011. Cheating the fates: Organizational founding in the wake of demise. *Academy of Management Journal*, 54(5): 1017–44.

Weber, B., Depew, B., Dyke, C., Salthe, S., Schneider, E., Ulanowicz, R., & Wicken, J. 1989. Evolution in thermodynamic perspective: An ecological approach. *Biology and Philosophy*, 4: 373–405.

Weber, B. H., Depew, D. J., & Smith, J. D. (Eds.). 1990. *Entropy, Information, and Evolution*. Cambridge, MA: MIT Press.

Webster's. 1996. *Merriam-Webster's Collegiate Dictionary* (10th ed.). Springfield, MA: Merriam-Webster.

Weick, K. 1977. Organization design: Organizations as self-designing systems. *Organizational Dynamics*, 6(2): 30–46.

Weick, K. 1995. *Sensemaking in Organizations*. Newbury Park, CA: SAGE Publications.

Weick, K., & Quinn, R. 1999. Organizational change and development. *Annual Review of Psychology*, 50: 361–86.

Weick, K., & Roberts, K. 1993. Collective mind in organizations: Heedful interrelating on flight decks. *Administrative Science Quarterly*, 38: 357–81.

Weick, K., Sutcliffe, K., & Obstfeld, D. 2005. Organizing and the process of sensemaking. *Organization Science*, 16: 409–21.

Weimerskirch, H., Martin, J., Clerquin, Y., Alexandre, P., & Jiraskova, S. 2001. Energy saving in flight formation. *Nature*, 413(6857): 697–8.

Weiner, N. 1948/1961. *Cybernetics*. Cambridge, MA: MIT Press.

Weisbuch, G., Kirman, A., & Herreiner, D. 1998. Market organization. In J. Lesourne & A. Orlean (Eds.), *Advances in Self-Organization and Evolutionary Economics* (160–82). London: Economica.

Weiss, N. 1987. *Dynamics of convection*. Paper presented at the Dynamical Chaos: Proceedings of the Royal Society of London.

West, B., Brown, J. H., & Enquist, B. J. 1997. A general model for the origin of allometric scaling laws in biology. *Science*, 274(4, 5309): 122–6.

Westley, F., Olsson, P., Folke, C., Homer-Dixon, T., Vredenburg, H., Loorbach, D., Thompson, J., Nilsson, M., Lambin, E., Sendzimir, J., Banerjee, B., Galaz, V., & van der Leeuw, S. 2011. Tipping toward sustainability: Emerging pathways of transformation. *Ambio*, 40: 762–80.

Whetten, D. 1989. What constitutes a theoretical contribution? *Academy of Management Review*, 14: 490–5.

Whitten, W., & McClintock, M. 1999. Pheromones and regulation of ovulation. *Nature*, 401(6750): 232–3.

Wicken, J. 1979. The generation of complexity in evolution: A thermodynamic and information-theoretical discussion. *Journal of Theoretical Biology*, 77(3): 349–65.

Wicken, J. 1980. A thermodynamic theory of evolution. *Journal of Theoretical Biology*, 87(1): 9–23.
Wicken, J. 1981. Evolutionary self-organization and the entropy principle: Teology and mechanism. *Nature and System*, 3: 129–41.
Wicken, J. 1985. Thermodynamics and the conceptual structure of evolutionary theory. *Journal of Theoretical Biology*, 117: 363–83.
Wicken, J. 1986. Evolutionary self-organization and entropic dissipation in biological and socioeconomic systems. *Journal of Social and Biological Structures*, 9: 261–73.
Wicken, J. 1988. Thermodynamics, evolution, and emergence: Ingredients for a new synthesis. In B. Weber, D. Depew, & J. D. Smith (Eds.), *Entropy, Information, and Evolution: New Perspectives on Physical and Biological Evolution* (139–72). Cambridge, MA: MIT Press.
Wicken, J. 1989. Evolution and thermodynamics: The new paradigm. *Systems Research and Behavioral Science*, 15: 365–72.
Wiklund, J., & Shepherd, D. 2003. Aspiring for and achieving growth: The moderating role of resources and opportunities. *Journal of Management Studies*, 40(8): 1919–41.
Wilber, K. 1995. *Sex, Ecology, Spirituality*. Boston: Shambhala Publications.
Wiley, E. O., & Brooks, D. 1983. Victims of history—A nonequilibrium approach to evolution. *Systemic Zoology*, 31: 1–24.
Wilson, E. O., & Holldobler, B. 1990. *The Ants*. Cambridge, MA: Harvard University Press.
Wimsatt, W. 1994. The ontology of complex systems: Levels of organization, perspectives, and causal thickets. *Canadian Journal of Philosophy*, 24(Supplement 1): 207–74.
Wimsatt, W. 1997. Aggregativity: Reductive hueristics for finding emergence. *Philosophy of Science*, 64(Supplement): S372–84.
Wolf, A., Swift, J. B., Swinney, H. L., & Vastano, J. A. 1985. Determining Lyapunov exponents from a time series. *Physica*, 16D: 285–317.
Wright, S. 1932. *The roles of mutations, inbreeding, cross-breeding and selection in evolution*. Paper presented at the 11th International Conference of Genetics.
Xu, Y. 2011. Entrepreneurial social capital and cognitive model of innovation. *Management Research Review*, 34(8): 910–26.
Yin, R. 1989. *Case Study Research*. Newbury Park, CA: SAGE Publications.
Yusuf, J.-E. 2012. A tale of two exits: Nascent entrepreneur learning activities and disengagement from start-up. *Small Business Economics*, 39(3): 783–99.
Zahra, S., & Pearce, J. 1990. Research evidence on the Miles-Snow typology. *Journal of Management*, 16(4): 751–68.
Zaror, G., & Guastello, S. 2000. Self-organization and leadership emergence: A cross-cultural replication. *Nonlinear Dynamics, Psychology, and Life Sciences*, 4: 113–20.
Zeeman, E. 1977. *Catastrophe Theory: Selected Papers*. Reading, MA: Addison-Wesley.
Zhabotinsky, A. M., & Zaikin, A. 1971. Spatial effects in a self-oscillating chemical system. In E. E. Sel'kov (Ed.), *Oscillatory Processes in Biological and Chemical Systems II*. Moscow: Science Publishers.
Ziegler, M., Ziegler, P., & Rosenzweig, B. 1994. *The Republic of Tea: The Story of the Creation of a Business, as Told Through the Personal Letters of Its Founders*. New York: Currency-Doubleday.
Zimmerman, B., & Hurst, D. 1993. Breaking the boundaries: The fractal organization. *Journal of Management Inquiry*, 2: 334–54.
Zimmerman, M., & Zeitz, G. 2002. Beyond survival: Achieving new venture growth by building legitimacy. *Academy of Management Review*, 27(3): 414–31.
Zipf, G. K. 1949. *Human Behavior and the Principle of Least Effort*. New York: Hafner.
Zohar, A., & Borkman, T. 1997. Emergent order and self-organization: A case study of alcoholics anonymous. *Nonprofit and Voluntary Sector Quarterly*, 26: 527–52.

Zott, C., & Amit, R. 2007. Business model design and the performance of entrepreneurial firms. *Organization Science*, 18(2): 181–99.

Zuijderhoudt, R. 1990. Chaos and the dynamics of self-organization. *Human Systems Management*, 9: 225–38.

Zurek, W. H., & Schieve, W. C. 1982. Nucleation paradigm: Survival threshold in population dynamics. In W. Schieve & P. Allen (Eds.), *Self-Organization and Dissipative Structures: Applications in the Physical and Social Sciences* (203–24). Austin, TX: University of Texas Press.

INDEX

Page numbers followed by the italicized letters *b, f, t,* or *n* indicate material found in boxes, figures, tables or notes.

Abrahamson, E., 226
Academy of Management, 379–380
Academy of Management Review, 7
action, intentional, 53, 235, 382
activity domains, 351–352
Adams, R. N., 185–186
adaptive cycle, 28, 90, 410–414
Agarwal, R., 140, 221
agency. *See also* intent/intentionality; intentional action
    in experiments, 213*n*13
    "facticity" and, 120
    in generative emergence, 54–55, 204, 225
    interdependence of, 117, 119
    internal, 409
    in opportunity tension, 204
    social entities and, 197, 199
    as structioning, 237
AgencyInc
    amplification at, 289
    characteristics of, 240–241*t*
    critical events in, 291*t*
    disequilibrium organizing at, 242*t*, 247–248
    emergents in, 312–313
    experiment examples, 272*t*
    organizational stress, 265–266*t*
    venture summary, 239
agent-based model/modeling (ABM)
    in complexity science, 8, 138
    in emergence studies, 20, 47
    examples of, 86–87
    in first-degree emergence, 122
    managerial insights from, 71*t*
    originating discipline, 19*t*
    potential for, 227*n*3
agents
    behavior of, 166, 194, 196–198
    in cellular automata, 82–83
    heterogeneity of, 145*n*1
    in social analysis, 65
    stabilizing feedback and, 323
Aldrich, H., 226
American school, of complexity, 131, 282
amplification
    at AgencyInc, 289
    at ApplySci, 287–289
    bifurcation points in, 282
    control parameter in, 282
    to critical threshold, 180, 231, 279, 282–283, 328*f*, 407
    at DevelopNet, 285–287, 317*f*
    in five-phase process model, 24–25, 180, 183*t*
    of fluctuations, 155
    at The Republic of Tea, 283–285
    at SEMATECH, 335–336
    at Starbucks, 331
    stress and, 280
    of system, 279–281
    at threshold point, 164–165
    through feedback, 304
analogy
    from dissipative structures theory, 149, 163, 166, 171, 259, 321, 325
    in innovation, 387–388
    from NK landscape theory, 11
    from science to social phenomena, 92, 173
    as term, 186*n*1

analogy (*Cont.*)
    from thermodynamics, 282
    in transformational metaphors, 172
    validity of, 182, 184
analyzer firms, 350
Anand, N., 316
Anderson, P., 46, 81
Andriani, P., 78, 79, 222
ApplySci
    amplification at, 287–289
    characteristics of, 240–241*t*
    critical events in, 291*t*
    destabilizing feedback at, 319–321
    disequilibrium organizing at, 242*t*, 244–246
    emergents in, 305*t*
    experiment examples, 272*t*
    innovation challenge, 271
    new dynamic state in, 310*t*
    organizational stress, 265–266*t*, 267*f*
    re-emergence at, 308–309, 358–364
    self-organization in, 220
    stabilizing feedback at, 317*f*
    transformation at, 364–369
    venture summary, 239
Arthur, B., 76
ascendency
    in complexity science, 87
    ecological, 90–92, 109, 150, 160
    of ecosystems, 50
    managerial insights from, 71*t*
    originating discipline, 19*t*
Ashmos, D., 177
aspiration
    in disequilibrium organizing, 178–179
    examples of, 236, 239, 246, 330, 363
    for initiating creative action, 349–350
    in opportunity tension, 204, 205, 210
    in organizational emergence, 5, 26, 177
    in re-emergence, 346–347
autocatalysis
    in complexity science, 87–89
    emergence drivers in, 56–57
    in generative emergence, 54
    managerial insights from, 71*t*
    originating discipline, 19*t*
    prototype summary, 17, 48–49
    stress and, 260
autogenesis
    in complexity science, 87–89
    managerial insights from, 71*t*

autopoiesis
    amplification and, 407
    in complexity science, 18, 67, 71*t*, 87–89
    in human systems, 260
    managerial insights from, 71*t*
    originating discipline, 19*t*
    stress and, 260
Axelrod, R., 83
Axtell, R., 87

Bak, P., 46, 77
Baker, T., 299, 300, 304, 345, 378
Baron, R., 350
Barrett, M., 352
Bar-Yam, Y., 111, 112, 121, 124*n*6, 298
BDS statistics, 136
Bechtel, W., 113
Bedau, M., 121, 123*n*5, 298
Beer, S., 76
Beinhocker, E., 11
Belousov-Zhabotinsky (B-Z) reaction. *See* B-Z reaction
Bennett, D. S., 83
Berge, P., 374
Bergson, H., 109
Bérnard, H., 151
Bérnard experiment
    containers/boundaries in, 237, 373–374
    description of, 151–154
    in equilibrium state, 173
    exo-organization and, 47
    fluctuations and, 164–165, 174
    processes/outcomes in, 163–165
    recombination and, 156, 175
Bertalanffy, L. von, 66
Beyer, J., 328
bifurcation points, 180, 282, 298, 382
Biggiero, L., 134
Bingham, C., 387–388
biological/energetic approaches, 87–92. *See also* autocatalysis; autogenesis; autopoiesis; directionality in evolution; dissipative structures; ecological ascendency; ecosystem resilience
Bird, B., 225
Blank, Steven, 206
Boisot, M., 79
Boulding, K., 45, 66, 170
boundaries/boundary conditions
    in Bérnard experiment, 237

as constructive constraints, 373–374
containers and, 194–196, 200
in dynamic states, 211t
of emergence, 26–27, 375–377
of new organizations, 198
theoretical conditions, 375–380
Boyatzis, R., 381
Branson, MO (study of emergence in)
collective action, role of, 399
cycle of emergence in, 327
description of, 142–144
disequilibrium organizing in, 235
experiments and, 397
five-phase process model application, 384–386
recombination of resources, 303, 400
stabilizing feedback and, 315–316, 337
bricolage, 117, 180, 299, 345
Broad, C. D., 109–110
Brock, W. A., 222
Brown, J. H., 222
Brown, S., 133–134, 144
Browning, L., 328, 336, 410
Brusselator, in systemwide oscillations, 162
business model. *See also* organizing model
core elements of, 206–209
value creation and, 54
Business Model Canvas (Osterwalder), 208f
business strategy experiments, 272t
business vision, 138
Butler, J. C., 85
Bygrave, Bill, 137
B-Z reaction
containers/boundaries in, 237
as dissipative structure experiment, 21–22, 160–162
in equilibrium state, 173
processes/outcomes in, 164–166
recombination and, 175
spiral waves in, 164f

capacity. *See also* increased capacity
in dissipative structures, 176–177
quality of emergence in, 118–119
Carley, K., 86, 87
Carnot, S., 150, 166n1
Carpenter, S., 90
Carter, N., 141, 369, 378
catastrophe theory
as complexity science, 74
in describing complexity, 137

managerial insights from, 69t
originating discipline, 19t
causal agency, 54–55
causal intricacy, 145n1
causality, 110, 132
cellular automata (CA)
in complexity science, 82–84
managerial insights from, 70t
originating discipline, 19t
centripetal vortex, 49
Chaisson, E., 91–92
change, vs. emergence/re-emergence, 4–6
channels
in *Business Model Canvas*, 208f
in organizing model, 207
Chaos: Making a New Sense (Gleick), 68
chaos theories, 68
chaotic attractors, 136
Checkland, P., 113
chemical clock experiment, 21–22
Chen, K., 46, 77
Cheng, Y., 136, 137, 224
Chiles, T. *See also* Branson, MO (study of emergence in)
Branson emergence study of, 142–144
on "Bransonizing," 401
on cyclical nature of emergence, 327, 377
on disequilibrium organizing, 235
on dissipative structures theory, 384–385
on increasing returns, 76
on macro-emergence, 410
on resource recombination, 303
church. *See* Mission Church
"Cities as Dissipative Structures" (Dyke), 170
Clausius, R., 150
Clippinger, J. H., 12
cognitive/emotional stress, 261, 265t
coherence, 115
coherent structures, 121
collaborative emergence
drivers of, 54, 56–57
prototype summary, 17, 45, 51–53
collective action
catalyzing of, 399
emergence drivers in, 56–57
prototype summary, 18, 55
complex adaptive systems (CAS)
as complexity science, 81–82
managerial insights from, 70t
originating discipline, 19t

complex interactions, 125n12
complexity. *See also* complexity science
　application types, 132
　discovering/describing, 136–138
　metaphors in, 20, 132, 133–135, 144
　models of, 20, 138–141
　schools of, 131
Complexity Applications in Management, 11
complexity models, 20, 138–141
complexity science. *See also specific sciences*
　assumptions in, 65
　biological/energetic approaches in, 87–92
　computational models of, 82–87
　emergence in, 2
　expanded potential for, 8–10
　fields of, 18, 19t, 69–71t
　foundations of, 67–68, 72
　generative emergence and, 57–58
　main texts of, 68
　mathematical/analytical sciences in, 72–82
　origins of, 65–67
　visual map of, 67f
complexity theory, cycle of emergence in, 328
computational agents, 12, 17, 54, 82, 142
computational models. *See also* agent-based model/modeling (ABM); cellular automata (CA); genetic algorithms (GA); NK landscape models/research
　agents in, 131, 138, 141
　complex adaptive systems (CAS) as, 81
　of complexity science, 82
　emergent patterns in, 227n3
　emergents, focus on, 6
　genetic algorithm use, 85
　in order creation studies, 13
　problems/limitations with, 8, 9, 59n6
　stabilizing feedback in, 315
computational order
　emergence drivers in, 56–57
　prototype summary, 17, 47–48
computational science/studies, 68, 221
condensation, linear/nonlinear states and, 155–156
conflict
　creation of, 397–398
　interpersonal, 263, 266t
constrained generating procedure (CGP), 85, 226–227n2

constraints, leverage of, 401–402
CONSTRUCT/CONSTRUCT-O models, 86
containers
　creation of, 237–238
　in dissipative structures, 165, 194–196
continuous change, 133
control parameters, 282
controversy creation, 397–398
convergence, in markets, 142
core logic
　for ApplySci, 310t
　for DevelopNet, 307–308t, 358
　opportunity tension and, 353–354
　in organizing efforts, 203
　for ServiceCo, 313t
　in third-degree emergence, 305t
Corning, P.
　on emergence, 113, 116–117
　on entropy, 171, 185, 186
　on increased capacity, 118
　on Schrödinger, 170
　on synergy, 46, 58n1, 58n2
cost structure, in *Business Model Canvas*, 208f
creative action, initiation of, 349–351
creative tension, 7, 179, 204, 234, 404
creativity
　in emergence, 5, 26, 174, 233, 236
　in proactive change, 349–351
creativity, in emergence, 5
crisis, organizational change and, 5
critical events
　dynamics of, 281–283, 407–408
　examples of, 290–293
　in five-phase process model, 24–25
　in re-emergence, 267, 357, 361
　at SEMATECH, 335–336
　at Starbucks, 331
critical threshold
　amplification to, 180, 231, 279, 282–283, 328f, 407
　in far-from-equilibrium regime, 162
Crowston, K., 85–86
Crutchfield, J., 132, 136, 142, 144, 220–221
cultural policing, 385
customer segments/relationships
　in *Business Model Canvas*, 208f
　in organizing model, 207
cybernetics
　managerial insights from, 69t
　originating discipline, 19t
　as positive feedback process, 75–76

[458]　Index

cycle of emergence
  empirical studies of, 327–328, 338–341
  examples of
    HealthUSA, 338–339
    Republic of Tea, 339–341
    SEMATECH, 333–337
    Starbucks, 329–333
  five-phase sequence of, 326f
  five-phases of change as, 325–326
  interdependence/interaction in, 326–327
  temporal feedback loop, 328f

data collection/sampling methods, 248–252
deep structure, 297, 352–353
defender firms, 350
Depew, B., 91
determinist chaos theory
  chaotic attractors in, 136
  as complexity science, 72–73
  managerial insights from, 69t
  originating discipline, 19t
  in system dynamics, 133
DevelopNet
  amplification at, 285–287
  characteristics of, 240–241t
  critical events in, 281, 290–291, 356
  destabilizing feedback at, 321t
  disequilibrium organizing at, 239, 242–243, 355
  emergents in, 305t
  experiment examples, 272t, 355
  ideal sequencing, 356–358
  new dynamic state in, 307t
  order creation in, 306
  organizational stress, 265–266t, 267f
  re-emergence at, 354–358
  stabilizing feedback at, 316–319
  venture summary, 239
deviation amplification, 180, 279
DeWolf, T., 125n12
"The Dialogue Between the Economic and the Ecologic Theories of Evolution" (Rosser), 170
directionality in evolution, 71t, 90–91, 109
DiRenzo, M., 76
disaster dynamics, 280
disequilibrium organizing. *See also* AgencyInc; ApplySci; DevelopNet; ServiceCo
  in five-phase process model, 178–179, 183t

initiation of, 404–405
organizing activities, 234–237
personal stress in, 260–263
at SEMATECH, 334
at Starbucks, 330
system stress in, 259–260
thermodynamics in, 24
dispute resolution, 386–387
dissipative structures
  analogy use in, 172
  Bérnard experiment, 21, 47, 151–154, 164–165
  B-Z reaction in, 161–162, 164–166
  chemical clock experiment, 21–22
  as complexity science, 89
  vs. computational modeling, 10
  containers/boundaries in, 194–196
  deterministic behavior in, 197
  as emergence model, 171–172
  energy input/outputs in, 198–200
  experimental conditions in, 165–166
  far-from equilibrium dynamics in, 154–155
  fluctuation and, 155
  homogeneity of, 153f
  increased coherence/capacity in, 160–161
  inputs/outputs in, 166
  managerial insights from, 71t
  mapping emergence process in, 173–178
  metaphor from, 193–194
  nucleation mechanism in, 156
  order-creation dynamics in, 21
  originating discipline, 19t
  origins of order in, 157f
  processes/outcomes in, 163–165
  stabilizing feedback in, 321–323
  stationary disequilibrium in, 157–158
  systemwide oscillations in, 162
  thermodynamics in, 149–151
  work examples in, 171–172
dissolution, as outcome, 219–220, 301
divergence, in markets, 142–143
Dooley, K., 137, 141, 180, 223, 280, 369
downward causation, 14t, 23, 51, 109, 123n4, 223, 224, 298
Dyke, C., 91, 170
dynamic states
  components/model of, 22–23
  conditions for, 211t
  degrees of emergence in, 298–301

Index [459]

dynamic states (*Cont.*)
  elements of, 202, 203f
  emergence of, 31n21
  feedback loops in, 209–210, 304
  generative emergence and, 200–202, 210–211
  opportunity tension in, 204–205
  social ecology and, 202–203
  value creation in, 209–210

ecological ascendency, 87, 90–91, 150, 160
ecosystem resilience
  characteristics of, 273n
  as complexity science, 89–90
  managerial insights from, 71t
  originating discipline, 19t
  systemic property of, 2
ecosystems
  as emergence example, 1–2
  function of, 412f
  transformation of, 410–411
edge-city simulations, 83–84
edge of chaos concept, 133, 134–135
effectuation, theory of, 261
Eien, M., 87–88, 91
Eisenhardt, K., 133–134, 144
elan vital, 109
Ellis, G., 44, 45, 121
emergence. *See also* cycle of emergence; re-emergence
  aspiration in, 5
  assumptions of, 115
  boundaries of, 26–27
  vs. change/transformation, 4–6
  characteristics of, 125n12
  complexity science and, 8–10
  as computational issue, 8
  constructional nature of, 116–117
  creativity and, 5
  cycles of, 25–26
  data capturing for, 248–252
  describing, 1–3
  in dynamic states, 298–301
  examples of, 1–2, 6
  experiments in, 268–269
  five-phase process model, 177–178. *See also* entrepreneurship
  general model of, 13–15
  hierarchies of, 121
  increased capacity through, 161f
  of institutions, 386–388

  iterative nature of, 407–408
  levels of, 14t, 44–45
  mapping process of, 173–178
  meanings of, 6
  methods for studying, 18–19
  as new level of order, 158
  opportunity tension in, 232
  problems/potentialities and, 4
  process/outcome debate, 6–8
  realness in, 113, 114
  as recombination, 156
  scholarship of, 2–3
  "self-organization" problems with, 10–13
  social ecology and, 202–203
  transformative metaphor in, 173f
  vocabulary for, 133
Emergence (journal), 11
emergence, defining
  in evolutionary studies, 108–110
  increased capacity, 118–119
  outcome continuum in, 121–122
  in philosophy, 110–111
  process/outcome distinction in, 120–121
  self-transcending construction, 116–118
  in social entities, 114–115
  strong emergence, 112–114, 119–120
  weak emergence, 111–112
emergence, prototypes of
  autocatalysis, 48–49
  collaborative emergence, 51–53
  collective action, 55
  computational order, 47–48
  drivers of, 56–57
  exo-organization, 46–47
  generative emergence, 53–55
  relational properties, 45–46
  summary of, 16–18
  symbiogenesis, 49–51
emergence outcomes
  dissolution, 219–220
  first-degree order emergence, 220–222
  second-degree systemic emergence, 223–224
  as substrate for new cycle, 328–329
  third-degree radical emergence, 224–226
emergence processes
  far-from equilibrium states, 173–174
  fluctuation, 174
  nonlinearity, 174–175

outcomes of, 176–177
  recombination in, 175–176
  stability in, 176
emergence studies, types of, 20–21
"emergentists," 108–110
emergents
  patterns of, 121
  range of, 43–45
  resultants distinction, 108
emergent systems, organizations as, 2
EMERGY, 184
enacting emergence
  conditions for, 395–396, 402
  five-phase process model and, 402–403
  praxis for, 28–29
  preparation for, 403
  for social change, 409–414
enacting emergence, behaviors for
  collective action in, 399
  controversy creation, 397–398
  correlation creation, 399–400
  disruption, 395–396
  experiments/fluctuation in, 397
  leadership in, 401
  local constraint leverage, 401–402
  recombination of resources, 400–401
  "relational space" interactions, 398–399
Endres, A., 115
energetically open system, 212n6
energy input/outputs, in dissipative structures, 198–200
entrepreneurial exit, 350
entrepreneurship
  amplification, 180
  business opportunities, 7
  in complexity studies, 183t
  disequilibrium organizing, 178–179
  emergence study, 2
  isomorphic mapping and, 182
  motivation in, 233–234
  nascent entrepreneurship, 140–141
  organizational emergence, 7–8
  organizing in, 234–237
  outcomes of, 181–182
  as recognized/created, 232–233
  recombinations, 180–181
  stabilizing feedback, 181
  stress and experiments, 179–180
  uncertainty and, 261
entropy, 150–151, 153, 160, 161f, 166n2, 170–171. See also negentropy

epistasis, 9
Epstein, J. M., 87
Equist, B. J., 222
European Group for Organization Studies, 379–380
European school, of complexity, 131, 282
evolution
  directionality in, 71t, 90–91, 109
  dissipative structures in, 184–186
evolutionary complexity, originating discipline, 19t
evolutionary studies, emergence and, 108–110
exo-organization
  emergence drivers in, 56–57
  generative emergence vs., 200
  prototype summary, 17, 46–47
experiments
  in five-phase process model, 24, 179–180, 183t
  new venture examples, 271–272
  origins of, 269–271
  production of, 406–407
  role of, 268–269
  at SEMATECH, 334–335
  at Starbucks, 330–331

far-from equilibrium dynamics. See also Bérnard experiment
  critical threshold in, 162
  in dissipative structures, 154–155, 163
  in emergence processes, 173–174
  in thermodynamics, 150
  as type 1 metaphor, 133
feedback loops, 209–210, 304. See also positive feedback; stabilizing feedback
financial stress, 262–263, 265t
first-degree order emergence
  in dynamic states, 298–299
  internal order and, 220–222
  in order creation, 297, 304
  in organizing model, 305t
  as outcome, 7, 23, 121–122, 220–222, 226, 354, 380
  power laws as, 222–223
  in re-emergence, 306, 361, 368
fiscal stress, 266t
fiscal tension, 263
fitness, model of, 139
five-phase emergence sequence, 326f

Index [461]

five-phase process model
  amplification in, 24–25, 180, 183t
  critical events in, 24–25
  disequilibrium organizing in, 178–179, 183t
  of emergence, 177–178. *See also* entrepreneurship
  experiments in, 24, 179–180, 183t
  of generative emergence, 24–25
  isomorphic mapping in, 182
  new order creation in, 25
  recombination in, 25, 180–181, 183t
  stabilizing feedback in, 25, 181, 183t
  stress in, 24, 179–180, 183t
five-phase process model, applications of. *See also* Branson, MO (study of emergence in); SEMATECH
  intentional action, 382
  leadership development, 381
  psychology/cognitive development, 380–381
Fleming, L., 84, 138, 139, 221
fluctuation
  amplification of, 155
  emergence processes and, 174
  near threshold point, 164
"flux," in ecosystems, 273n
Fodor, J., 124n7
Foerster, H. von, 66
"fold and cusp" model, 74
Forrester, J., 79
fractals
  as complexity science, 75
  managerial insights from, 69t
  originating discipline, 19t
Fritz, R., 204
"From Entropy to Economy: A Thorny Patch" (Dyke), 170
Fuller, B., 66, 93n1

Gallupe, R. B., 351–352
Ganco, M., 140, 221
Gardner, H., 316
Garreau, J., 83
Gartner, W., 29n2, 120, 133, 141, 224–225, 235, 283, 369, 377–378
Garud, R., 172, 322
Gaussian distribution, 78, 79
Gell-Mann, M., 81
General Electric, 236
general linear reality, 65, 78, 110, 154

general systems theory
  complexity science and, 66–67
  higher level of order in, 158–159
General System Theory (von Bertalanffy), 66
generative complexity, 20, 141–144
generative emergence. *See also* five-phase process model
  amplification dynamics in, 282
  application to organizations, 22
  complexity science and, 57–58
  conditions for, 211t
  defining, 19–20
  drivers of, 56–57
  dynamic states and, 210–211
  exo-organization vs., 200
  experiments in, 268–269
  five-phase process model of, 24–25
  outcomes of, 23–24
  prototype summary, 17–18, 53–55
  resilience and, 412–414
  self-organization problem in, 10–11
  at Starbucks, 329–330
  stress in, 260–263
  typology of, 375–380
generative emergence, outcomes of
  dissolution, 219–220
  first-degree order emergence, 220–222
  second-degree systemic emergence, 223–224
  third-degree radical emergence, 224–226
generative leadership, 28, 142, 396, 399, 406
genetic algorithms (GA)
  in complexity science, 85–86
  managerial insights from, 70t
  originating discipline, 19t
genuine novelty, 115
Georgescu-Roegen, N., 170
Getting to Plan B (Mullins and Komisar), 345, 378
Gibbs, J. W., 170
Gleick, J., 68
global-level structures, 121
Goldstein, J.
  on complexity science, 67
  on containers as constraints, 374
  on disequilibrium, 405, 406
  on emergence levels, 125n11
  on emergence outcomes, 220, 298
  on emergence prototypes, 45
  on innovation, 396

on processes/outcomes distinction, 120
on role of experiments, 269
on self-organization, 12, 13, 195
on self-transcending constructions (STCs), 116
on structioning, 117
on symbiogenesis, 49
Grameen Bank, 209
Gray, B., 386
Greenhaus, J., 76
Guastello, S., 73, 74, 282, 381
Gunderson, L., 28, 410, 411, 412–413
Gunz, H., 77–78

Hall, R., 80
Harper, D., 115
HealthInfo, 223, 338–339
HealthUSA, 223, 338–339
Heinzen, T. E., 349, 351
Heracleous, L., 352
"Hierarchy of Organizing Activities" (Tushman and Romanelli), 353–354
Holland, J., 81, 85
Holling, C. S., 28, 90, 410, 411, 412–413
Holvoet, T., 125n12
Huber, G., 177
human agency, 54–55

ideation, 293–294n2
identity
  for ApplySci, 310t
  for DevelopNet, 307–308t
  for ServiceCo, 313t
  in third-degree emergence, 305t
  in transformational metaphors, 172
incommensurability, example of, 108–109
increased capacity
  dissipative structures and, 176–177
  in dynamic states, 31n21
  as emergence outcome, 161f
  as emergence quality, 118–119, 120
  emergent order and, 165
increasing returns
  managerial insights from, 69t
  originating discipline, 19t
  as positive feedback process, 76–77
innovation
  challenges of, 261–262, 265t
  measurement of, 139
In Search of Strategy, 11
insects, behavior of, 52

insight, in transformational metaphors, 172
institutional schema, 386–388
intent/intentionality, 53–54, 204, 234
intentional action, 53, 235, 382
interaction, rules of, 48
interdependence
  of agency, 117
  in ecosystems, 1–2
  in emergence processes, 329
interpersonal conflict, 263, 266t
interpretivist vs. objectivist work, 131–132
intrinsic emergence, 132, 142, 144
Iridium, 301–303
irreducibility, 115
isomorphic mapping
  in emergence processes, 195f
  in five-phase process model, 182
isomorphism, 172, 173f

Juarrero, A., 26, 53, 374, 375, 382

Kahl, S., 387–388
Katz, J., 327
Kauffman, G., 349
Kauffman, S., 84, 88, 139, 140, 281
key activities
  in *Business Model Canvas*, 208f
  in organizing model, 207
Kinzig, A., 90
Kiva Foundation, 209
Kline, S. J., 170, 171, 185, 186
Komisar, R., 345, 378
Kotha, S., 172, 322
Kotter, J., 348
Krugman, P., 79, 83
Kuhn, T. S., 107

laser light, formation of, 46–47
leaders. *See also* enacting emergence, behaviors for; generative leadership
  development of, 381
  as role models, 401
Lean Business Canvas (Blank), 206
learning experiments, 272t
Leifer, R., 327
Levinthal, D., 221
Lewes, G. H., 108, 109
Lewin, R., 68, 262
Lichtenstein, B.
  on conditions for emergence, 377
  on dissipative structures, 171–172

Lichtenstein, B. (*Cont.*)
  on generative leadership, 396
  on hierarchy of value, 144
  on new-venture creation, 223, 369
  in typology of generative emergence research, 376f
  on vacancy chains (employee turnover), 77–78
limited structuring, 133–134
Lindsay, R., 375
linear reality. *See* general linear reality
Living Systems (Miller), 66
lock and key description (Bar-Yam), 124n6
Long, R., 77–78
Lotka, A., 91, 170
Low, M., 226
Lumpkin, G. T., 223
Lyapunov exponents, 136

MacIntosh, R., 353
MacLean, D., 353
macroeconomic systems, emergent, 115
Maguire, S., 11, 131–132
management, emergence applications in
  complexity metaphors, 133–135
  complexity models, 138–141
  discovering/describing complexity, 136–138, 144
  generative complexity, 141–144
Margulis, L., 49–50
market dynamics, order creating, 142
marketing/sales challenges, 265t
materially closed system, 212n6
material realization, 115
Maturana, H. R., 88
maximum entropy, 151, 160, 166n2. *See also* entropy
McClintock, M., 111–112
McKelvey, B.
  on complexity science, 58
  on complexity types, 131–132
  on disequilibrium organizing, 235, 236
  on far-from-equilibrium state, 174
  on hierarchy of value, 144
  on NK model, 9, 221
  on outcomes, 121
  on Paretian distributions, 78, 79
  on power laws, 222
  on schools of complexity science, 10, 282
  on self-organization, 11

metaphors
  of complexity, 20, 132, 133–134, 144
  transformative, 169, 172, 173f, 195f, 322
Meyer, A., 76, 282
Mihata, K., 120, 121
Miles-Snow typology, 350
Miller, J. G., 66
Mintzberg, H., 379
Mirabeau, L., 131–132
Mission Church
  amplification at, 280–281
  collective action at, 399
  constraint leverage at, 401–402
  correlation creation at, 399–400
  disruption of existing patterns, 396
  radical emergence at, 225
  recombination of resources, 303–304, 400–401
  re-emergence at, 397–398
MIT Sloan Management Review, 11
mobilization stage, 386
Morgan, Conrad Lloyd, 109
Morris, T., 316
Motorola, 301–302
Mullins, J., 345, 378
multi-agent learning models, 71t
mutual causality, 20, 23, 30n21, 117, 119, 120, 122, 224–226

nascent entrepreneurship (study of), 140–141
near-decomposability, 125n12
negative entropy, 151, 169. *See also* entropy
negentropy, 170, 184
Nelson, R., 299, 300, 304, 345, 378
new entry (study of), 140
Newey, L., 350
new order creation
  dissolution and, 304
  in five-phase process model, 25
  through recombination, 297–298, 303–304
Nicholls-Nixon, C., 379
Nicolis, G., 151, 155, 157, 166–167n3
NKC model, 140
NK landscape models/research
  Beinhocker's review of, 11
  in complexity science, 84–85, 139
  first-degree emergence in, 221
  managerial insights from, 70t
  methodology critique, 9

[464] Index

originating discipline, 19t
predictive power of, 8
nominal emergence, 121, 125n13
non-aggregativity, 125n12
non-deducibility, 110, 113
non-distributivity of systemic properties, 115
nonlinear change, 282
nonlinear dynamics, 133
nonlinear interactions, 398
nonlinearity, emergence processes and, 174–175
non-localization, 125n12
nonreducibility, 20, 23, 30n21, 119, 124n8
nonreductive individualism, 115
Noyce, B., 334–336
nucleation mechanism, 156

objectivist vs. interpretivist work, 131–132
Odum, E., 170
Odum, H., 91, 170, 184
Olson, P., 264
online bartering, 213n15
opportunity tension
   for ApplySci, 244, 310t
   aspiration in, 204, 205, 210
   cycles of, 326, 328f, 330–331, 340, 346
   definition of, 22, 179–204-5
   for DevelopNet, 307–308t, 356, 358
   in disequilibrium organizing, 179
   as dynamic state element, 202, 203f, 209, 211t
   entrepreneur's intention in, 234
   as origin of emergence, 204–205, 210, 232–237, 404–405
   in re-emergence, 348, 352–354, 358
   at Republic of Tea, 339–341
   in second/third degree emergence, 298–300, 305t
   at SEMATECH, 334, 383
   for ServiceCo, 313t
   similarity to 'adaptive tension,' 252n3
   stress caused by, 259–260
order creation. See new order creation
ORGAHEAD model, 87
organizational change, crisis and, 5
organizational scientists, emergence study by, 2
organizational stress
   examples of, 265–266t
   increase in, 259–260

literature analyses, 263–264
personal stress and, 260–263
organizations
   application of emergence to, 22
   complexity science and, 92
   as emergent systems, 2
   intentional creation of, 53
organizing model
   for ApplySci, 310t
   defined, 205–206
   for DevelopNet, 307–308t, 358
   as dynamic state element, 22, 203f, 205
   in first-degree emergence, 305t
   Osterwalder's nine building blocks, 206, 207f, 208
   for ServiceCo, 313t
   for value creation, 205–209
organizing moves, 293–294n2
Osterwalder, A., 206–209
outcome continuum, 121–122
Oztas, N., 131–132

Padgett, J., 49, 88
pain, as emergent property, 114
Panel Study of Entrepreneurial Dynamics (PSED), 7, 141, 233, 378
Pareto distributions, 77–79, 222
Pascale, R., 11
path creation, 329, 351, 366
Paul, D. L., 85
Pearlson, K. E., 85
personal stress, types of, 260–263
perturbations, in experiments, 268–269
philosophy, emergence and, 110–111
Pigneur, Y., 206–209
Pinkerton, R., 91
Plowman, D., 225, 303–304, 322, 377, 396, 398
political alliances (study on), 83
Pompeau, Y., 374
positive feedback. See also feedback loops; stabilizing feedback
   in complexity science, 75–77
   managerial insights from, 69t
   mechanisms, 135
   originating discipline, 19t
Powell, W., 88
power laws
   in complexity science, 77
   as first-degree emergence, 222–223
   managerial insights from, 69t
   originating discipline, 19t

Prigogine, I.
   on Bérnard experiment, 21, 162
   on B-Z reaction, 163
   on dissipative structures theory, 89
   on nonequilibrium systems, 166–167n3
   on nucleation mechanism, 156
   on role of experiments, 270
   on stationary disequilibrium, 157
   on thermodynamics, 149–151, 155
proactive creativity, 5, 349–350, 351
process experiments, 272t
process/outcome distinction, 120–121
prospector firms, 350
prototypes of emergence
   autocatalysis, 48–49
   collaborative emergence, 51–53
   collective action, 55
   computational order, 47–48
   exo-organization, 46–47
   generative emergence, 53–55
   relational properties, 45–46
   symbiogenesis, 49–51
psychological sciences, emergence study by, 2
psychology/cognitive development, 380–381
punctuated dis-equilibrium, 142
punctuated emergences, 142, 327
Purdy, J., 386

qualitative novelty, 19, 23, 30n21, 109, 119, 226–227n2

reactive creativity, 5, 349, 351
"Ready, Fire, Aim," 261
realness, emergence and, 113, 114
recombination
   dynamics of, 385
   emergence as, 156, 165
   in emergence processes, 175
   encouragement of, 408–409
   in five-phase process model, 25, 180–181, 183t
   new order creation through, 297–298, 407–408
   at SEMATECH, 336–337
   at Starbucks, 331–332
   of systems, 297, 303–304
re-emergence
   of ApplySci, 358–364
   vs. change/transformation, 4–6

   core logic in, 353–354
   creative action in, 349–351
   critical events in, 267, 357, 361
   cycles of, 26
   deep structure in, 352–353
   of DevelopNet, 354–358
   qualities of, 345
   substrate of, 346
   vs. transformation, 351–352
   triggers for, 346–348
Reid, R., 50
relational properties
   emergence drivers in, 56–57
   prototype summary, 17, 45–46
relational space, 398–399, 402f
reorganization, 411
Repenning, N., 280
The Republic of Tea, 283–285, 339–341
resilience. *See* ecosystem resilience
Resilience Alliance project, 90, 410
resultants/emergents distinction, 108
Reuf, M., 226
revenue streams
   in *Business Model Canvas*, 208f
   in organizing model, 207
Reynolds, P., 141, 378
Richardson, R., 113
Romanelli, E., 347, 351–352, 353
Rosen, R., 315
Rosser, J. B., 170
Rudolph, J., 280
rules of interaction, 48
Ryan, A., 113

SAGE Handbook of Organization Studies, 131–132, 135
Salthe, S., 91
"sandpile" paradigm experiment, 77
Santa Fe Institute, 132
Sastry, A., 347
Saturday Evening Post (study of), 80
Sawyer, K.
   on computational models/simulations, 8–9, 59n6, 221
   on downward causation, 123n4
   on emergence qualities, 125n12, 142
   on multiple realizability, 124n7
   on nonreducibility, 124n8
   on social emergence, 51–52
   on strong emergence, 114–115
Schelling, T., 82–83

schema emergence, 387–388
Schneider, E., 91
Schrödinger, Erwin, 151, 170, 184
Schultz, H., 330–332, 346
second-degree systemic emergence
  in dynamic states, 298–300
  in order creation, 223–224, 297, 304
  as outcome, 7, 23, 121–122, 223–224, 226
  in re-emergence, 306, 354, 368, 380
segregation in cities (study on), 82–83
self-organization
  constraints and, 195
  lack of rigor in, 11–12
  problems with, 10–11
  simplicity and, 12–13
  as type 1 metaphor, 133
self-organized criticality
  as complexity science, 77–78
  managerial insights from, 69t
  originating discipline, 19t
self-transcending construction, 116–118
SEMATECH
  amplification, 335–336
  collaboration with, 25, 329
  collective action, 55
  critical events, 335–336
  cycle of emergence at, 333–337, 383
  disequilibrium organizing at, 334
  opportunity tension at, 334
  recombination, 336–337
  stabilizing feedback at, 337
  stress and experiments at, 334–335
sensitivity to initial conditions, 135
ServiceCo
  characteristics of, 240–241t
  critical events in, 291t, 292–293
  disequilibrium organizing at, 242t, 246–247
  emergents in, 305t
  experiment examples, 272t
  organizational stress, 265–266t
  re-emergence at, 311–312, 398–399
  venture summary, 239
The Shepherd of the Hills (Wright), 384
Shetler, J., 328
Siggelkow, N., 221
Simon, H., 83
Smith, A., 2
Smith, C., 269
Smith, L., 380–381

social change, enacting emergence for, 409–414
social ecology
  in dynamic state model, 203f
  entrepreneurial action in, 260
  stabilizing feedback in, 322
social emergence
  vs. computational order, 48
  drivers of, 52b
  as prototype, 51–52, 54
  in range of emergents, 45
social entities
  containers/boundaries and, 194–196
  diversity and, 197
  emergence and, 114–115, 173–174
  nonlinear qualities and, 175
"Social Evolution as the Self-Organization of Energy" (Adams), 185–186
social innovation, emergence concept in, 4
social movements theory, 55
social science, emergence levels in, 14t
sociological studies, emergence dynamics in, 2
Sonenshein, S., 299, 379
Sorenson, O., 84, 138, 139, 221
Sperry, R., 109
spiral waves, in B-Z reaction, 164f
stability
  in emergence processes, 176
  or emergent order, 165
stabilization dynamics, 385
stabilizing feedback
  vs. destabilizing feedback, 319–321
  in dissipative structures theory, 321–323
  in emergence, 315–316, 409
  examples of, 316–319
  in five-phase process model, 25, 181, 183t
  at SEMATECH, 337
  at Starbucks, 332
Stanley, M., 78, 222
Starbucks
  amplification/critical event, 331
  disequilibrium organizing at, 330
  generative emergence substrate, 329–330
  outcomes of emergence, 333
  recombination, 331–332
  re-emergence of, 346
  stabilizing feedback, 332
  stress and experiments, 330–331

Starr, J., 225
stationary disequilibrium, 157–158, 163, 166–167n3
Stengers, I., 155, 156, 163, 270
Sterman, J., 79, 369
strange attractors, 135, 136–137
strategic organizing, 138
Street, C., 351–352
stress
    allowing for, 405–406
    amplification and, 280
    application/increase in, 259–260
    definition of, 259
    in five-phase process model, 24, 179–180, 183t
    in generative emergence, 260–263
    personal, 260–263
    at SEMATECH, 334–335
    at Starbucks, 330–331
strong emergence, 112–114, 119–120, 123n5, 125n13
structioning, 20, 23, 31n21, 117–118, 120, 237
structural coupling, 88
structuration stage, 387
structure dependence of systemic properties, 115
substrate
    at ApplySci, 358
    at DevelopNet, 354
    in dynamic states, 22, 327
    in emergence cycle, 326f, 376, 378
    in emergence outcomes, 328–329
    of re-emergence, 346
    social ecology as, 202–204, 212n1
    at Starbucks, 329–330
supervenience, 123n4, 124n7
surface catalysis, 163
surface conflict, 397–398
Susskind, L., 386
"swallowtail" equation, 74
Swenson, R., 89, 91, 150, 156, 160, 166n2, 374
symbiocosms, 50
symbiogenesis
    emergence drivers in, 56–57
    prototype summary, 17, 49–51
symbiosis, 55
symmetry-breaking, 46
synergism hypothesis, 118
synergy, 46, 58n1, 58n2

system components, recombination of, 303–304
system dynamics
    in complexity science, 79–81
    managerial insights from, 70t
    originating discipline, 19t
systemic resistance, 262
systemwide oscillations, 162–163

tactical organizing, 138
tangibility, 294n2
technological invention, study of, 84
technology innovation, 138–139
technology/product experiments, 272t
Terpstra, D., 264
Tesfatsion, L., 86
Thelan, E., 380–381
theoretical identity, in emergence processes, 173f
thermodynamics
    conduction/convection process in, 159
    of evolution, 185
    extension into ecology/economy, 169–170
    paradigm shift in, 149–151
third-degree radical emergence
    in dynamic states, 297, 298–301
    mutual causality and, 224–226
    in order creation, 23, 303, 304, 305t
    as outcome, 7, 121–122, 220, 224–226
    re-emergence and, 306, 358, 368, 376, 380
tourist areas (study of emergence in), 142–144. See also Branson, MO (study of emergence in)
transformation, vs. emergence/re-emergence, 4–6, 345, 346–348, 351–352
transformative metaphor, 169, 172, 173f, 195f, 322
Tsoukas, H., 172, 182, 322
Tushman, M., 347, 351–352, 353

Uhl-Bien, M., 12–13, 395
Ulanowicz, R., 49, 50, 91
uncertainty, in entrepreneurship, 261
unpredictability in principle, 115
Unsworth, K., 349

value creation
    defined, 22–23
    driver of, 53–54

dynamic states and, 203f, 209–210
organizing model in, 200–202, 205–209
in second/third degree emergence, 305t
as social innovation, 202
value proposition
in *Business Model Canvas*, 208f
in organizing model, 207
Van de Ven, A., 136, 137, 224, 379
Varela, F. J., 88
viable system model, 76
Vidal, C., 374
V-shape, of flying birds, 1, 5

Waldrop, M., 68
Walker, B., 90
water, vortex formation in, 158
weak emergence, 111–112, 125n13
Weber, B., 91

Weiss, N., 374
Welch, Jack, 236
West, B., 222
wetness, emergent property of, 108–109
Whinston, A. B., 85
"Why Transformation Efforts Fail" (Kotter), 348
Wicken, J., 91, 184–185
wild disjunction, 114, 124n8
Wimsatt, W., 110, 111
workload increase, 260–261, 265t

Yerkes-Dodson law, 293n1
Yusuf, J.-E., 350

Zahra, S., 350
zero-degree no emergence, 121–122
Zipf, G. K., 83, 222

Milton Keynes UK
Ingram Content Group UK Ltd.
UKHW020056020923
427950UK00005B/34